Spring Recipes

A Problem-Solution Approach

Gary Mak

Apress®

Spring Recipes: A Problem-Solution Approach

ISBN-13 (pbk): 978-1-59059-979-2

ISBN-10 (pbk): 1-59059-979-9

ISBN-13 (electronic): 978-1-4302-0624-8

ISBN-10 (electronic): 1-4302-0624-1

Printed and bound in the United States of America 9 8 7 6 5 4 3 2 1

Lead Editors: Steve Anglin, Tom Welsh
Technical Reviewers: Sam Brannen, Kris Lander
Editorial Board: Clay Andres, Steve Anglin, Ewan Buckingham, Tony Campbell, Gary Cornell, Jonathan Gennick, Matthew Moodie, Joseph Ottinger, Jeffrey Pepper, Frank Pohlmann, Ben Renow-Clarke, Dominic Shakeshaft, Matt Wade, Tom Welsh
Project Manager: Kylie Johnston
Copy Editor: Damon Larson
Associate Production Director: Kari Brooks-Copony
Production Editor: Laura Esterman
Compositor: Dina Quan
Proofreader: April Eddy
Indexer: Ron Strauss
Artist: April Milne
Cover Designer: Kurt Krames
Manufacturing Director: Tom Debolski

Distributed to the book trade worldwide by Springer-Verlag New York, Inc., 233 Spring Street, 6th Floor, New York, NY 10013. Phone 1-800-SPRINGER, fax 201-348-4505, e-mail `orders-ny@springer-sbm.com`, or visit `http://www.springeronline.com`.

For information on translations, please contact Apress directly at 2855 Telegraph Avenue, Suite 600, Berkeley, CA 94705. Phone 510-549-5930, fax 510-549-5939, e-mail `info@apress.com`, or visit `http://www.apress.com`.

Apress and friends of ED books may be purchased in bulk for academic, corporate, or promotional use. eBook versions and licenses are also available for most titles. For more information, reference our Special Bulk Sales–eBook Licensing web page at `http://www.apress.com/info/bulksales`.

The source code for this book is available to readers at `http://www.apress.com`.

Contents at a Glance

PART 3 ■ ■ ■ Advanced

Contents

About the Author

GARY MAK has been a technical architect and application developer on the enterprise Java platform for six years. In his career, Gary has developed a number of Java-based software projects, most of which are core application frameworks and software tools. He enjoys designing and implementing the complex parts of software projects.

Gary is a Sun-certified Java programmer and has a master's degree in computer science. His research interests include object-oriented technology, aspect-oriented technology, design patterns, and software reuse. Gary specializes in building enterprise applications on frameworks including Spring, Hibernate, JPA, Struts, JSF, and Tapestry. He has been using the Spring framework in his projects for four years, since Spring version 1.0. Gary is also an instructor of courses on enterprise Java, Spring, Hibernate, web services, and agile development. He has written a series of Spring and Hibernate tutorials as course materials, parts of which are open to the public, and they're gaining popularity in the Java community. In his spare time, he enjoys playing tennis and watching tennis competitions.

About the Technical Reviewers

SAM BRANNEN is a senior software engineer at SpringSource, where he serves as a core developer of the Spring framework. Sam is also a member of the SpringSource team for Spring and Tomcat Integrated Products. He has been developing Java applications since 1996 and enterprise applications since 1999. During this time, Sam has enjoyed designing complex software architectures and implementing custom solutions with a focus on scalable, testable, multitiered web and client-server applications using Java (J2EE/Java EE) and the Spring framework. Sam recently designed and implemented the new annotation-driven Spring TestContext framework included in Spring 2.5.

Prior to joining SpringSource, Sam gained experience building applications for customers in various business sectors ranging from e-commerce to banking, retail, automotive, and social communities. Sam has a degree in computer science from the Georgia Institute of Technology and currently resides in the United Kingdom with his wife, Vera.

From the moment his parents gave him a Spectrum 48K for his seventh birthday, it became clear that **KRIS LANDER** was always going to be an early adopter when it came to technology. Upon leaving school, with a computer addiction and a mild vitamin A deficiency, he decided to turn his childhood passion into a serious vocation, embarking on a degree in software engineering from the University of Wales.

Kris's constant thirst for emerging Java technologies has become a trademark throughout his professional career. He has been a Java web enterprise (J2EE) specialist from day one and a developer of applications using Spring since 2003, which has led him to work on many large-scale IT projects for corporate blue chip and successful new technology companies on both sides of the Atlantic. Based and brought up in London, in his spare time he enjoys good food and music production.

Acknowledgments

I'd like to thank my family, especially my wife, Ivy. She gave me mental support in writing this book and did a great job in taking care of our family. Without her love and support, I could never have finished this book.

Additionally, I'd like to thank the Apress team who worked for this book, in particular the following individuals:

> Steve Anglin, my acquisition editor, who recognized me and believed in me writing this book. He offered splendid ideas for this book's outline and organized a great team for the book.
>
> Tom Welsh, my development editor, who provided excellent support on both the literary and technical aspects of this book. He often encouraged me when I got into writing trouble, and offered solutions to me.
>
> Kylie Johnston, my project manager, who did a great job in managing the book schedule and responded to my requests very quickly. Her experience made the schedule very flexible so that I could do my job in a comfortable way.
>
> Kris Lander, who reviewed this book from a technical standpoint, pointed out my faults, and gave valuable suggestions based on his rich experience in Spring.
>
> Sam Brannen, my other technical reviewer, who gave a large number of professional comments that directly and immediately improved the book. His role as a core Spring developer made me very confident in his comments.
>
> Damon Larson, my copy editor, who did a nice job in correcting my grammatical mistakes, improving my words, and keeping the conventions consistent throughout the book.
>
> Laura Esterman, my production editor, who made this book look as nice as it does and handled my late modification requests.
>
> Dina Quan, Ron Strauss, and April Eddy, who were also instrumental in making this a great book.

Acknowledgments

Introduction

Since my first time using it in 2004, I have been a big fan of Spring and have used it in almost all my projects. I'm deeply attracted to Spring's simplicity and reasonableness. Spring is the simplest and most powerful Java/Java EE application framework I have ever used, and its ability to solve difficult problems in simple ways has made a strong impression on me. The solutions offered by Spring may not be the best all over the world, but they are the most reasonable ones that I can think of.

Spring addresses most aspects of Java/Java EE application development and offers simple solutions to them. By using Spring, you will be lead to use industry best practices to design and implement your applications. The releases of Spring 2.x have added many improvements and new features to the 1.x versions. This book focuses on the latest Spring 2.5 features for building enterprise Java applications.

As a course instructor on programming technologies, I always find that the biggest challenge my students face is how to get their experimental projects running. Many programming books include code examples, but most only include code fragments, not complete projects. Most of these books provide complete projects for you to download from their web sites, but they don't provide a chance for you to build the projects step by step on your own. I believe that you'll learn a lot from the project-building process, and that you'll gain confidence once you have gotten your projects running—this was my inspiration for writing this book.

As active Java developers, we often have to master a new technology or framework. Since we are only developers who use a technology, not students who have to take an exam, we don't need to keep everything in our mind. We only need an efficient way of making references when necessary. To benefit experienced readers, and beginner readers who have read this book from cover to cover, I've organized each chapter with multiple problem-solution–based recipes. This way, you'll be able to easily look up a solution for a particular problem.

The topics in this book are introduced by complete and real-world code examples that you can follow step by step. Instead of abstract descriptions on complex concepts, you will find live examples in this book. When you start a new project, you can consider copying the code and configuration files from this book, and then modifying them for your needs. This can save you a great deal of work over creating a project from scratch.

Who This Book Is For

This book is for Java developers who would like to gain hands-on experience rapidly on Java/Java EE development using the Spring framework. If you are already a developer using Spring in your projects, you can also use this book as a reference, and you'll find the code examples very useful.

You don't need much Java EE experience to read this book. However, it assumes that you know the basics of object-oriented programming with Java (e.g., creating a class/interface, implementing an interface, extending a base class, running a main class, setting up your classpath, and so on). It also assumes you have basic knowledge on web and database concepts and know how to create dynamic web pages and query databases with SQL statements.

How This Book Is Structured

This book covers Spring 2.5 from basic to advanced, and it introduces several common Spring projects that will bring significant value to your application development. It's divided into 19 chapters organized into 3 parts:

- *Part 1: Core*: This part focuses on the core concepts and mechanisms of the Spring framework. The chapters in this part aim to familiarize you with Spring's core so that you can learn about other topics and uses of Spring quickly.
    - *Chapter 1: Inversion of Control and Containers*: This chapter introduces the core concept of Spring—the IoC design principal—and the importance of containers. If you are already familiar with IoC, feel free to skip this chapter.
    - *Chapter 2: Introduction to Spring*: This chapter gives you an overview of Spring's architecture and related projects. It also demonstrates how to set up Spring in your development environment.
    - *Chapter 3: Bean Configuration in Spring*: This chapter introduces basic bean configuration in the Spring IoC container. Understanding the features in this chapter is required for reading the subsequent chapters.
    - *Chapter 4: Advanced Spring IoC Container*: This chapter covers the advanced features and internal mechanisms of the Spring IoC container. Although these features may not be used as frequently as those in Chapter 3, they are indispensable to a powerful container.
    - *Chapter 5: Dynamic Proxy and Classic Spring AOP*: This chapter explains why you need AOP and how you can modularize crosscutting concerns with dynamic proxies and classic Spring AOP. If you already understand AOP and want to use Spring AOP in Spring 2.x directly, feel free to skip to Chapter 6.
    - *Chapter 6: Spring 2.x AOP and AspectJ Support*: This chapter covers Spring 2.x AOP usage and some advanced AOP topics, including how to integrate the AspectJ framework into Spring applications.
- *Part 2: Fundamentals*: This part involves the fundamental topics of the Spring framework. The topics covered in this part are used frequently in developing enterprise applications.
    - *Chapter 7: Spring JDBC Support*: This chapter shows how Spring can simplify JDBC's uses through its JDBC accessing framework. It also serves as an introduction to Spring's data access module.
    - *Chapter 8: Transaction Management in Spring*: This chapter discusses Spring's different transaction management approaches and explains transaction attributes in detail.

- *Chapter 9: Spring ORM Support*. This chapter focuses on how to integrate popular ORM frameworks, including Hibernate and JPA, into Spring applications.
- *Chapter 10: Spring MVC Framework*: This chapter covers web-based application development using the Spring Web MVC framework, with both the traditional approach and the new annotation-based approach.
- *Chapter 11: Integrating Spring with Other Web Frameworks*: This chapter introduces how to integrate the Spring framework with several popular web application frameworks, including Struts, JSF, and DWR.
- *Chapter 12: Spring Testing Support*: This chapter covers basic testing techniques in Java applications and the testing support features offered by the Spring framework.

- *Part 3: Advanced*: This part covers advanced topics of the Spring framework and related projects. However, thoroughly covering each of these topics would require an entire book. The aim of these chapters is to provide you with the useful basics and usages specific to Spring.
    - *Chapter 13: Spring Security*: This chapter introduces how to secure applications using the Spring Security framework, formerly known as Acegi Security. This chapter focuses on securing web applications using Spring Security 2.0.
    - *Chapter 14: Spring Portlet MVC Framework*: This chapter covers portlet application development using the Spring Portlet MVC framework, and focuses on the portlet-specific features that are different from Web MVC.
    - *Chapter 15: Spring Web Flow*: This chapter introduces how to use Spring Web Flow to model and manage your web application's UI flows. This chapter focuses on using Spring Web Flow 2.0 in Spring MVC and JSF.
    - *Chapter 16: Spring Remoting and Web Services*: This chapter covers Spring's support for various remoting technologies, including RMI, Hessian, Burlap, HTTP Invoker, and Web Services. It also introduces developing contract-first web services using Spring Web Services.
    - *Chapter 17: Spring Support for EJB and JMS*: This chapter discusses how to develop EJB 2.x and 3.0 components with Spring's EJB support, and how to use Spring's JMS support to simplify sending, receiving, and listening for JMS messages.
    - *Chapter 18: Spring Support for JMX, E-mail, and Scheduling*: This chapter discusses how to export Spring beans as JMX MBeans and access remote MBeans. This chapter also introduces how to send e-mail and schedule tasks with Spring's e-mail and scheduling support.
    - *Chapter 19: Scripting in Spring*: This chapter discusses how to use popular scripting languages, including JRuby, Groovy, and BeanShell, in Spring applications.

Each chapter of this book discusses a Spring topic with multiple problem-solution recipes. You can look up a solution for a particular problem and see how the solution works in the "How It Works" section. Each chapter demonstrates a topic with a complete real-world example. The example within a chapter is coherent, but examples are independent between chapters.

Conventions

Sometimes when I want you to pay particular attention to a part within a code example, I will make this part's font bold. Please note that a bold part doesn't reflect a code change from the last version. In cases when a code line is too long to fit the page width, I will break it with a code continuation character (➥). Please note that when you try out the code, you have to concatenate the line by yourself without any space.

Prerequisites

Because the Java programming language is platform independent, you are free to choose any supported operating system. However, I should let you know that I am using Microsoft Windows because the file system paths I present in this book are Windows-based. You can simply convert these paths into your operating system's format before trying out the code.

To make the most of the book, you should install JDK version 1.5 or higher. You should also have a Java IDE installed to make development easier. For this book, I have been using Eclipse Web Tools Platform (WTP) to develop my projects, and I recommend you install it also.

Downloading the Code

The source code for this book is available from the Apress web site (`http://www.apress.com`), in the Source Code/Download section. The source code is organized by chapters, each of which includes one or more independent Eclipse projects. Please refer to `readme.txt`, located in the root, for setting up and running the source code.

Contacting the Author

I always welcome your questions and feedback regarding to the contents of this book. You can send your comments to `springrecipes@metaarchit.com` and access the book discussion and updates on `http://www.metaarchit.com`.

PART 1

Core

CHAPTER 1

Inversion of Control and Containers

In this chapter, you will learn the *Inversion of Control (IoC)* design principle, used by many modern containers to decouple dependencies between components. The Spring framework provides a powerful and extensible IoC container for you to manage your components. This container lies at the heart of the Spring framework and integrates closely with Spring's other modules. This chapter aims to give you the prerequisite knowledge you need to start using Spring quickly.

When talking about components in the Java EE platform, most developers will think of EJB (Enterprise JavaBeans). The EJB specification clearly defines the contract between EJB components and EJB containers. By running in an EJB container, EJB components can get the benefits of life cycle management, transaction management, and security services. However, in EJB versions prior to 3.0, a single EJB component requires a remote/local interface, a home interface, and a bean implementation class. These EJBs are called heavyweight components due to their complexity.

Moreover, in those EJB versions, an EJB component can only run within an EJB container and must look up other EJBs with JNDI (Java Naming and Directory Interface). So EJB components are technology dependent because they cannot be reused and tested outside the scope of an EJB container.

Many lightweight containers are designed to overcome the shortcomings of EJB. They are lightweight in that they can support simple Java objects as components. A challenge posed by lightweight containers is how to decouple dependencies between components. IoC has proved to be an effective solution to this problem.

While IoC is a general design principle, *Dependency Injection (DI)* is a concrete design pattern that embodies this principle. As DI is the most typical (if not the only) realization of IoC, the terms IoC and DI are often used interchangeably.

Upon finishing this chapter, you will be able to write a simple IoC container that is conceptually similar to the Spring IoC container. If you are already familiar with IoC, feel free to go directly to Chapter 2, which introduces the overall architecture and setup of the Spring framework.

1-1. Using a Container to Manage Your Components

Problem

The basic idea of object-oriented design is to break your system into a group of reusable objects. Without a central module to manage the objects, they have to create and manage their own dependencies. As a result, the objects are tightly coupled.

Solution

You need a *container* to manage the objects that make up your system. A container centralizes the creation of objects and acts as a registry to provide lookup services. A container is also responsible for managing the life cycle of objects and providing a platform for the objects to run on.

Objects running inside a container are called *components*. They must conform to the specification defined by the container.

How It Works

Separating Interface from Implementation

Suppose you are going to develop a system, one of whose functions is to generate different types of reports in either HTML or PDF format. According to the "separating interface from implementation" principle in object-oriented design, you should create a common interface for generating reports. Let's assume that the contents of the report are a table of records, appearing in the form of a two-dimensional string array.

```
package com.apress.springrecipes.report;

public interface ReportGenerator {

    public void generate(String[][] table);
}
```

Then you create two classes, `HtmlReportGenerator` and `PdfReportGenerator`, to implement this interface for HTML reports and PDF reports. For the purpose of this example, skeleton methods will suffice.

```
package com.apress.springrecipes.report;

public class HtmlReportGenerator implements ReportGenerator {

    public void generate(String[][] table) {
        System.out.println("Generating HTML report ...");
    }
}
```

```
package com.apress.springrecipes.report;

public class PdfReportGenerator implements ReportGenerator {
```

```
    public void generate(String[][] table) {
        System.out.println("Generating PDF report ...");
    }
}
```

The println statements in the method bodies will let you know when each method has been executed.

With the report generator classes ready, you can start creating the service class ReportService, which acts as a service provider for generating different types of reports. It provides methods such as generateAnnualReport(), generateMonthlyReport(), and generateDailyReport() for generating reports based on the statistics of different periods.

```
package com.apress.springrecipes.report;

public class ReportService {

    private ReportGenerator reportGenerator = new PdfReportGenerator();

    public void generateAnnualReport(int year) {
        String[][] statistics = null;
        //
        // Gather statistics for the year ...
        //
        reportGenerator.generate(statistics);
    }

    public void generateMonthlyReport(int year, int month) {
        String[][] statistics = null;
        //
        // Gather statistics for the month ...
        //
        reportGenerator.generate(statistics);
    }

    public void generateDailyReport(int year, int month, int day) {
        String[][] statistics = null;
        //
        // Gather statistics for the day ...
        //
        reportGenerator.generate(statistics);
    }
}
```

As the report generation logic has already been implemented in the report generator classes, you can create an instance of either class as a private field and make a call to it whenever you need to generate a report. The output format of the reports depends on which report generator class is instantiated.

Figure 1-1 shows the UML class diagram for the current dependencies between ReportService and different ReportGenerator implementations.

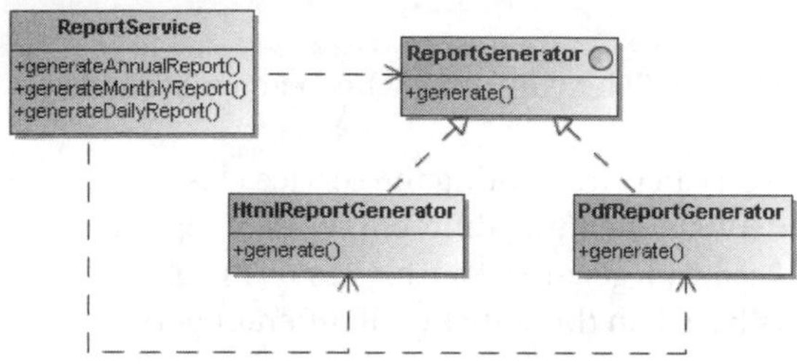

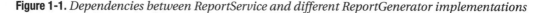

Figure 1-1. *Dependencies between ReportService and different ReportGenerator implementations*

For now, ReportService is creating the instance of ReportGenerator internally, so it has to be aware of which concrete class of ReportGenerator to use. This will cause a direct dependency from ReportService to either of the ReportGenerator implementations. Later you will be able to eliminate the dependency lines to the ReportGenerator implementations completely.

Employing a Container

Suppose that your report-generating system is designed for more than one organization to use. Some of the organizations may prefer HTML reports while the others may prefer PDF. You have to maintain two different versions of ReportService for different report formats. One creates an instance of HtmlReportGenerator while another creates an instance of PdfReportGenerator.

The cause of this inflexible design is that you have created the instance of ReportGenerator inside ReportService directly, so that it needs to know which ReportGenerator implementation to use. Do you remember the dependency lines from ReportService to HtmlReportGenerator and PdfReportGenerator in the class diagram (see Figure 1-1)? As a result, any switch of report generator implementation involves modification of ReportService.

To solve this problem, you need a container to manage the components that make up your system. A full-featured container would be extremely complex, but let's begin by having you create a very simple one:

```
package com.apress.springrecipes.report;
...
public class Container {

    // The global instance of this Container class for the components to locate.
    public static Container instance;

    // A map for storing the components with their IDs as the keys.
    private Map<String, Object> components;

    public Container() {
        components = new HashMap<String, Object>();
        instance = this;
```

```
        ReportGenerator reportGenerator = new PdfReportGenerator();
        components.put("reportGenerator", reportGenerator);

        ReportService reportService = new ReportService();
        components.put("reportService", reportService);
    }

    public Object getComponent(String id) {
        return components.get(id);
    }
}
```

In the preceding container example, a map is used to store the components with their IDs as the keys. The container initializes the components and puts them into the map in its constructor. At this moment, there are only two components, ReportGenerator and ReportService, working in your system. The getComponent() method is used to retrieve a component by its ID. Also note that the public static instance variable holds the global instance of this Container class. This is for the components to locate this container and look up other components.

With a container to manage your components, you can replace the ReportGenerator instance creation in ReportService with a component lookup statement.

```
package com.apress.springrecipes.report;

public class ReportService {

    private ReportGenerator reportGenerator =
        (ReportGenerator) Container.instance.getComponent("reportGenerator");

    public void generateAnnualReport(int year) {
        ...
    }

    public void generateMonthlyReport(int year, int month) {
        ...
    }

    public void generateDailyReport(int year, int month, int day) {
        ...
    }
}
```

This modification means that ReportService doesn't have to worry about which ReportGenerator implementation to use, so you don't have to modify ReportService any more when you want to switch report generator implementation.

Now by looking up a report generator through the container, your ReportService is more reusable than before, because it has no direct dependency on either ReportGenerator implementation. You can configure and deploy different containers for different organizations without modifying the ReportService itself.

Figure 1-2 shows the UML class diagram after employing a container to manage your components.

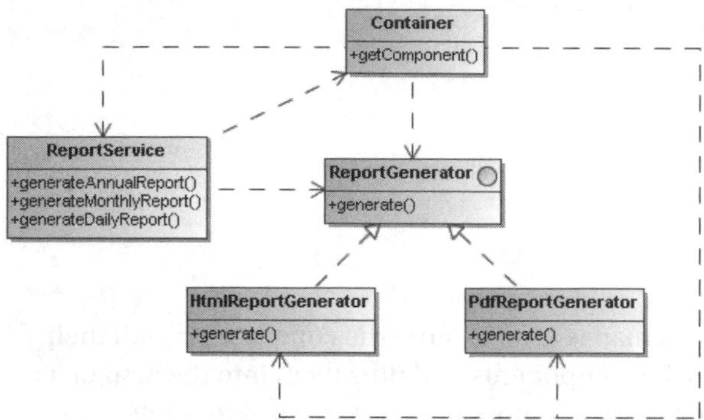

Figure 1-2. *Employing a container to manage your components*

The central class `Container` has dependencies on all the components under its management. Also note that the dependencies from `ReportService` to the two `ReportGenerator` implementations have been eliminated. Instead, a dependency line from `ReportService` to `Container` has been added, as it has to look up a report generator from `Container`.

Now you can write a `Main` class to test your container and components:

```
package com.apress.springrecipes.report;

public class Main {

    public static void main(String[] args) {
        Container container = new Container();
        ReportService reportService =
            (ReportService) container.getComponent("reportService");
        reportService.generateAnnualReport(2007);
    }
}
```

In the `main()` method, you first create a container instance and retrieve the `ReportService` component from it. Then when you call the `generateAnnualReport()` method on `ReportService`, `PdfReportGenerator` will handle the report generation request, as it has been specified by the container.

In conclusion, employing a container can help reduce coupling between different components within a system, and hence increase the independence and reusability of each component. In this way, you are actually separating configuration (e.g., which type of report generator to use) from programming logic (e.g., how to generate a report in PDF format) in order to promote overall system reusability. You can continue to enhance your container by reading a configuration file for component definition, which will be discussed later in this chapter.

1-2. Using a Service Locator to Reduce Lookup Complexity

Problem

Under a container's management, components depend on each other through their interfaces, not their implementations. However, they can only look up the container by using complex proprietary code.

Solution

To reduce the lookup complexity of your components, you can apply one of Sun's core Java EE design patterns, *Service Locator*. The idea behind this pattern is as simple as using a service locator to encapsulate the complex lookup logic, while exposing simple methods for lookup. Then, any component can delegate lookup requests to this service locator.

How It Works

Suppose you have to reuse the `ReportGenerator` and `ReportService` components in other containers with different lookup mechanisms, such as JNDI. For `ReportGenerator` there's no problem. But it would be trickier for `ReportService`, because you have embedded the lookup logic in the component itself. You will have to change the lookup logic before it can be reused.

```
package com.apress.springrecipes.report;

public class ReportService {

    private ReportGenerator reportGenerator =
        (ReportGenerator) Container.instance.getComponent("reportGenerator");
    ...
}
```

A service locator can be a simple class that encapsulates the lookup logic and exposes simple methods for component lookup.

```
package com.apress.springrecipes.report;

public class ServiceLocator {

    private static Container container = Container.instance;

    public static ReportGenerator getReportGenerator() {
        return (ReportGenerator) container.getComponent("reportGenerator");
    }
}
```

Then in `ReportService`, you make a call to `ServiceLocator` to look up a report generator, instead of performing the lookup directly.

```
package com.apress.springrecipes.report;

public class ReportService {

    private ReportGenerator reportGenerator =
        ServiceLocator.getReportGenerator();

    public void generateAnnualReport(int year) {
        ...
    }

    public void generateMonthlyReport(int year, int month) {
        ...
    }

    public void generateDailyReport(int year, int month, int day) {
        ...
    }
}
```

Figure 1-3 shows the UML class diagram after applying the Service Locator pattern. Note that the original dependency line from `ReportService` to `Container` now goes through `ServiceLocator`.

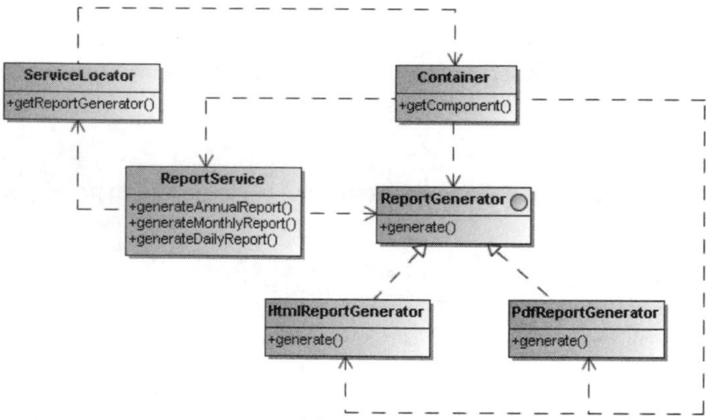

Figure 1-3. *Applying the Service Locator pattern to reduce lookup complexity*

Applying the Service Locator pattern can help to separate the lookup logic from your components, and hence reduce the lookup complexity of your components. This pattern can also increase the reusability of your components in different environments with different lookup mechanisms. Remember that it is a common design pattern used in resource (not only component) lookup.

1-3. Applying Inversion of Control and Dependency Injection

Problem

When your component needs an external resource, such as a data source or a reference to another component, the most direct and sensible approach is to perform a lookup. Let's consider this motion an *active* lookup. The shortcoming of this kind of lookup is that your component needs to know about resource retrieval, even though you have used a service locator to encapsulate the lookup logic.

Solution

A better solution to resource retrieval is to apply IoC. The idea of this principle is to invert the direction of resource retrieval. In a traditional lookup, components seek resources by making requests to a container, and the container duly returns the resources in question. With IoC, the container itself actively delivers resources to its managed components. A component has only to choose a way of accepting the resources. This could be described as a *passive* form of lookup.

IoC is a general principle, while DI is a concrete design pattern that embodies this principle. In the DI pattern, a container is responsible for injecting appropriate resources into each component in some predetermined way, such as via a setter method.

How It Works

To apply the DI pattern, your `ReportService` may expose a setter method to accept a property of the `ReportGenerator` type.

```
package com.apress.springrecipes.report;

public class ReportService {

    private ReportGenerator reportGenerator; // No need to look up actively

    public void setReportGenerator(ReportGenerator reportGenerator) {
        this.reportGenerator = reportGenerator;
    }

    public void generateAnnualReport(int year) {
        ...
    }

    public void generateMonthlyReport(int year, int month) {
        ...
    }

    public void generateDailyReport(int year, int month, int day) {
        ...
    }
}
```

The container is responsible for injecting the necessary resources into each component. As there's no active lookup any more, you can erase the static instance variable in Container and delete the ServiceLocator class as well.

```
package com.apress.springrecipes.report;
...
public class Container {

    // No need to expose itself for the components to locate
    // public static Container instance;

    private Map<String, Object> components;

    public Container() {
        components = new HashMap<String, Object>();

        // No need to expose the current instance of container
        // instance = this;

        ReportGenerator reportGenerator = new PdfReportGenerator();
        components.put("reportGenerator", reportGenerator);

        ReportService reportService = new ReportService();
        reportService.setReportGenerator(reportGenerator);
        components.put("reportService", reportService);
    }

    public Object getComponent(String id) {
        return components.get(id);
    }
}
```

Figure 1-4 shows the UML class diagram after applying IoC. Note that the dependency line from ReportService to Container (see Figure 1-2) can be eliminated even without the help of ServiceLocator.

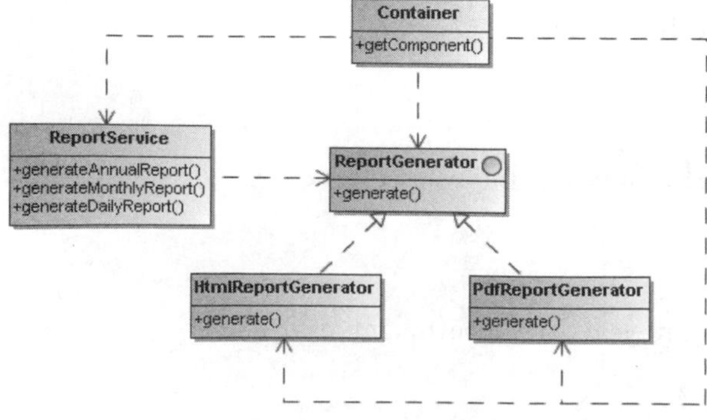

Figure 1-4. *Applying the IoC principle for resource retrieval*

The IoC principle resembles Hollywood's infamous catchphrase, "Don't call us, we'll call you," so it is sometimes called the "Hollywood principle." Moreover, as DI is the most typical implementation of IoC, the terms IoC and DI are often used interchangeably.

1-4. Understanding Different Types of Dependency Injection

Problem

Injecting a dependency via a setter method is not the only way of implementing DI. You will need different types of DI in different scenarios.

Solution

There are three main types of DI:

- Interface injection (Type 1 IoC)
- Setter injection (Type 2 IoC)
- Constructor injection (Type 3 IoC)

Of these, setter injection and constructor injection are widely accepted and supported by most IoC containers.

How It Works

For comparison, it's better to introduce the DI types in order of their popularity and efficiency, rather than by the type number.

Setter Injection (Type 2 IoC)

Setter injection is the most popular type of DI and is supported by most IoC containers. The container injects dependency via a setter method declared in a component. For example, `ReportService` can implement setter injection as follows:

```
package com.apress.springrecipes.report;

public class ReportService {

    private ReportGenerator reportGenerator;

    public void setReportGenerator(ReportGenerator reportGenerator) {
        this.reportGenerator = reportGenerator;
    }
    ...
}
```

The container has to inject dependencies by calling the setter methods after instantiating each component.

```
package com.apress.springrecipes.report;
...
public class Container {

    public Container() {
        ...
        ReportService reportService = new ReportService();
        reportService.setReportGenerator(reportGenerator);
        components.put("reportService", reportService);
    }
    ...
}
```

Setter injection is popular for its simplicity and ease of use since most Java IDEs support automatic generation of setter methods. However, there are some minor issues with this type. The first is that, as a component designer, you cannot be sure that a dependency will be injected via the setter method. If a component user forgets to inject a required dependency, the evil NullPointerException will be thrown and it will be hard to debug. But the good news is that some advanced IoC containers (e.g., the Spring IoC container) can help you to check for particular dependencies during component initialization.

Another shortcoming of setter injection has to do with code security. After the first injection, a dependency may still be modified by calling the setter method again, unless you have implemented your own security measures to prevent this. The careless modification of dependencies may cause unexpected results that can be very hard to debug.

Constructor Injection (Type 3 IoC)

Constructor injection differs from setter injection in that dependencies are injected via a constructor rather than setter methods. This type of injection, too, is supported by most IoC containers. For example, ReportService may accept a report generator as a constructor argument. But if you do it this way, the Java compiler will not add a default constructor for this class, because you have defined an explicit one. The common practice is to define a default constructor explicitly for code compatibility.

```
package com.apress.springrecipes.report;

public class ReportService {

    private ReportGenerator reportGenerator;

    public ReportService() {}

    public ReportService(ReportGenerator reportGenerator) {
        this.reportGenerator = reportGenerator;
    }
    ...
}
```

The container passes dependencies as constructor arguments during the instantiation of each component.

```
package com.apress.springrecipes.report;
...
public class Container {

    public Container() {
        ...
        ReportService reportService = new ReportService(reportGenerator);
        components.put("reportService", reportService);
    }
    ...
}
```

Constructor injection can avoid some of the problems posed by setter injection. You have to provide all dependencies declared in a constructor argument list, so it is not possible for a user to miss any. And once a dependency is injected, it cannot be modified any more, so the careless modification problem does not arise.

On the other hand, constructor injection has a restriction of its own. Unlike setter injection, there is no method with a meaningful name, such as `setSomething()`, that tells you which dependency you are injecting. When invoking a constructor, you can only specify the arguments by their positions. If you want to find out more about different overloaded versions of constructors and their required arguments, you have to consult the javadoc. Moreover, if you have a lot of dependencies to inject for a component, the constructor argument list will be very long, reducing code readability.

Interface Injection (Type 1 IoC)

Alone among the three types of injection, interface injection is seldom used. To apply it, components must implement a particular interface defined by the container, so that the container can inject dependencies via this interface. Note that there are no special requirements or characteristics for the interface. It's simply an interface defined by the container for communication purposes, and different containers may define different interfaces for their components to implement.

For your simple container, you can define your own interface as shown in the next code sample. There's only one method declared in this interface: `inject()`. The container will call this method on each component that has implemented this interface and pass in all the managed components as a map, with the component IDs as the keys.

```
package com.apress.springrecipes.report;
...
public interface Injectable {

    public void inject(Map<String, Object> components);
}
```

A component must implement this interface for the container to inject dependencies. It can get the required components from the map by their IDs. As a result, the components can refer to each other without looking up the container actively.

```
package com.apress.springrecipes.report;
...
public class ReportService implements Injectable {

    private ReportGenerator reportGenerator;

    public void inject(Map<String, Object> components) {
        reportGenerator = (ReportGenerator) components.get("reportGenerator");
    }
    ...
}
```

The container has to inject all of the components, as a map, into each component to build dependencies. Note that this action must be taken after all the components have been initialized.

```
package com.apress.springrecipes.report;
...
public class Container {

    public Container() {
        ...
        ReportGenerator reportGenerator = new PdfReportGenerator();
        components.put("reportGenerator", reportGenerator);

        ReportService reportService = new ReportService();
        components.put("reportService", reportService);

        reportService.inject(components);
    }
    ...
}
```

The shortcoming of interface injection is very obvious. It requires that all components must implement a particular interface for the container to inject dependencies. As this interface is container specific, your components have to rely on the container and cannot be reused outside its scope. This kind of injection is also called "intrusive," because the container-specific code has "intruded" on your components. For this reason, most IoC containers don't support this type of injection.

1-5. Configuring a Container with a Configuration File

Problem

For a container to manage components and their dependencies, it must be configured with the proper information beforehand. Configuring your container with Java code means that you have to recompile your source code each time after modification—hardly an efficient way of configuring a container!

Solution

A better way is to use a text-based, human-readable configuration file. Either a properties file or an XML file would be a good choice. Such files do not need to be recompiled, so they speed things up if you have to make frequent changes.

How It Works

Now you will create a container based on setter injection, the easiest type to configure. For other types of injection, the configuration is much the same. First of all, let's make sure the `ReportService` class has a setter method that accepts a report generator.

```
package com.apress.springrecipes.report;

public class ReportService {

    private ReportGenerator reportGenerator;

    public void setReportGenerator(ReportGenerator reportGenerator) {
        this.reportGenerator = reportGenerator;
    }
    ...
}
```

To configure a container from a file, you must first decide the file format. This time you will choose a properties file for simplicity's sake, although XML is more powerful and expressive. A properties file consists of a list of entries, each of which is a key/value pair of string type.

If you analyze the programming configuration in `Container`, you will find that there are only two kinds of configuration for your simple container. You can express them as properties in the following ways:

New component definition: You use the component name as the key and the fully qualified class name as the value.

Dependency injection: You join the component name with the property name to form the key, with a dot as a separator. Remember that a setter method for this property must be defined in the component class. Then the value is the reference name of another component to be injected.

To change the preceding programming configuration to properties-based configuration, you create the `components.properties` file with the following content:

```
# Define a new component "reportGenerator"
reportGenerator=com.apress.springrecipes.report.PdfReportGenerator

# Define a new component "reportService"
reportService=com.apress.springrecipes.report.ReportService
# Inject the component "reportGenerator" into property "reportGenerator"
reportService.reportGenerator=reportGenerator
```

Then your container has to read this configuration file and interpret its contents as component and dependency definitions. It also has to create component instances and inject dependencies as specified in the configuration file.

When implementing the container, you will have to manipulate component properties via reflection. To simplify matters, you can take advantage of a third-party library called Commons BeanUtils. This is part of the Apache Commons (`http://commons.apache.org/`) project that provides a set of tools for manipulating the properties of a class. The BeanUtils library requires another library from the same project, called Commons Logging.

■ **Note** You can download Commons BeanUtils and Commons Logging from the Apache Commons web site. Then include the downloaded JAR files `commons-beanutils.jar` and `commons-logging.jar` in your classpath.

Now you are ready to reimplement `Container` with this new idea. The first step is to load the properties file into a `java.util.Properties` object to get a list of properties. Then iterate over each property entry, which is made up of a key and a value. As mentioned before, there are two possible kinds of configuration:

- If there's no dot in the entry key, it is a new component definition. For this kind of configuration, you instantiate the specified class via reflection and then put the component into the map.
- Otherwise, the entry must be a dependency injection. You split its key into two parts, before and after the dot. The first part of the key is the component name and the second part is the property to set. With the help of the `PropertyUtils` class provided by Commons BeanUtils, you can refer that property to another component by the name specified in the entry value.

```
package com.apress.springrecipes.report;
...
import org.apache.commons.beanutils.PropertyUtils;

public class Container {

    private Map<String, Object> components;
```

```
    public Container() {
        components = new HashMap<String, Object>();

        try {
            Properties properties = new Properties();
            properties.load(new FileInputStream("components.properties"));
            for (Map.Entry entry : properties.entrySet()) {
                String key = (String) entry.getKey();
                String value = (String) entry.getValue();
                processEntry(key, value);
            }
        } catch (Exception e) {
           throw new RuntimeException(e);
        }
    }

    private void processEntry(String key, String value) throws Exception {
        String[] parts = key.split("\\.");

        if (parts.length == 1) {
            // New component definition
            Object component = Class.forName(value).newInstance();
            components.put(parts[0], component);
        } else {
            // Dependency injection
            Object component = components.get(parts[0]);
            Object reference = components.get(value);
            PropertyUtils.setProperty(component, parts[1], reference);
        }
    }

    public Object getComponent(String id) {
        return components.get(id);
    }
}
```

Note that in the processEntry() method, you have to split the entry key with a dot. In regular expressions, a single dot matches any character, so you have to quote it with a slash. Again, a slash has to be quoted in a Java string, which results in two slashes.

With these enhancements, your container has become highly reusable, as it reads a text-based configuration file for component definition. Now not even a single line of Java code has to be modified when you change your component definition. Although this container is not powerful enough for production use, it has fulfilled its purpose by demonstrating the core principle and mechanism of an IoC container.

1-6. Summary

In this chapter, you have learned to use a container to manage your components. This can help reduce coupling between different components. A component can look up other dependent components through the container. However, direct lookup will bind your components to the container with complex code. You can write a service locator to encapsulate the lookup logic and delegate the lookup requests to it.

Active lookup is a direct and sensible approach for resource retrieval. However, it requires your components to know about resource retrieval. When using the IoC principle, your component has only to choose a way of accepting resources and the container will deliver resources to your components. DI is a concrete design pattern that conforms to the principle of IoC. There are three main types of DI: setter injection, constructor injection, and interface injection.

You can configure your container using Java code or a text-based configuration file. The latter is more flexible because there's no need to recompile your source code each time you change it.

You have written a simple IoC container to read a properties file. This container is conceptually similar to the Spring IoC container.

In the next chapter, you will get an overview of the Spring framework's architecture and how to set it up.

CHAPTER 2

Introduction to Spring

In this chapter, you will have an overview of the Spring framework. Spring's architecture is divided into multiple modules in a hierarchical fashion. You will learn about the major functions of each module and see a summary of the highlights of Spring 2.0 and 2.5. Spring is not just an application framework but also a platform that hosts several related projects, which are called the Spring Portfolio projects. This chapter will give you an outline of their features.

Before you start with Spring, you have to install it on your local development machine. The Spring framework's installation is very simple. However, to get the most out of Spring, you have to understand the structure of its installation directory and what's contained in each subdirectory.

The Spring development team has created an Eclipse plug-in called Spring IDE to make developing Spring applications easier. You will learn about how to install this IDE and use its bean-supporting features.

Upon finishing this chapter, you will have a solid understanding of Spring's overall architecture and major features. You will also be able to install the Spring framework and Spring IDE on your machine.

2-1. Introducing the Spring Framework

The Spring framework (`http://www.springframework.org/`) is a comprehensive Java/Java EE application framework hosted by SpringSource (`http://www.springsource.com/`), which was formerly known as Interface21. Spring addresses many aspects of Java/Java EE application development, and it can help you to build high-quality, high-performance applications more quickly.

The heart of the Spring framework is a lightweight IoC container that is able to add enterprise services to simple Java objects declaratively. Spring makes extensive use of an excellent programming methodology—AOP (aspect-oriented programming)—to provide these services to its components. Within the Spring IoC container's scope, components are also called beans.

The Spring framework itself incorporates many design patterns, including the GoF (Gang of Four) object-oriented patterns and Sun's core Java EE patterns. By using the Spring framework, you will be lead to use industry best practices to design and implement your applications.

Spring is not designed to compete with existing technologies in particular areas. On the contrary, it integrates with many leading technologies to make them easier to use. That makes Spring an appropriate solution in many usage scenarios.

Introducing Spring's Modules

The architecture of the Spring framework is divided into modules, as shown in Figure 2-1. Spring's module assembling is so flexible that your applications can build on top of their different subsets in different usage scenarios.

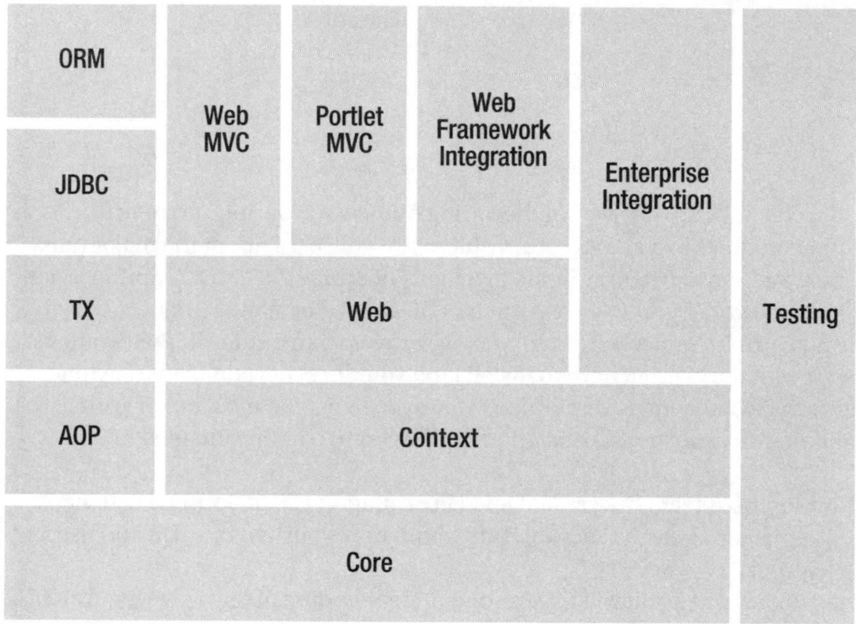

Figure 2-1. *An overview of the Spring framework's modules*

In Figure 2-1, the modules are organized in hierarchical fashion, with the upper modules depending on the lower ones. As you can see, the Core module lies at the very bottom since it's the foundation of the Spring framework.

Core: This module provides core functions of the Spring framework. It provides a basic Spring IoC container implementation called `BeanFactory`. The basic IoC container features will be introduced in Chapter 3.

Context: This module builds on top of the Core module. It extends the Core module's functions and provides an advanced Spring IoC container implementation called `ApplicationContext`, which adds features such as internationalization (I18N) support, event-based communication, and resource loading. These advanced IoC container features will be covered in Chapter 4.

AOP: This module establishes an aspect-oriented programming framework, which is referred to as Spring AOP. AOP is another of Spring's fundamental concepts besides IoC. Chapters 5 and 6 will cover both the classic and new Spring AOP approaches, and also integrating AspectJ with Spring.

JDBC: This module defines an abstract layer on top of the native JDBC API, which supports programming against JDBC in a template-based approach that dispenses with boilerplate code. It also parses database vendor–specific error codes into Spring's `DataAccessException` hierarchy. The details of Spring's JDBC support will be covered in Chapter 7.

TX: This module supports both programmatic and declarative approaches for you to manage transactions. These can be used to add transaction capability to your simple Java objects. Transaction management will be discussed thoroughly in Chapter 8.

ORM: This module integrates popular object/relational mapping frameworks such as Hibernate, JDO, TopLink, iBATIS, and JPA into Spring. The details of Spring's ORM integration will be covered in Chapter 9.

Web MVC: This module establishes a web application framework conforming to the model-view-controller (MVC) design pattern. This framework is built with the Spring framework's facilities so that you can use all Spring's features in web application development. The Spring MVC framework will be introduced in Chapter 10.

Web Framework Integration: This module makes it easier for you to use Spring as a back-end implementation for other popular web frameworks such as Struts, JSF, WebWork, and Tapestry. Chapter 11 will introduce integrating Spring with several popular web frameworks.

Testing: This module provides support for both unit testing and integration testing. It establishes the Spring TestContext framework, which abstracts underlying testing frameworks such as JUnit 3.8, JUnit 4.4, and TestNG. Testing Spring applications will be discussed in Chapter 12.

Portlet MVC: This module establishes a portlet framework, also conforming to the MVC design pattern. The Portlet MVC framework will be introduced in Chapter 14.

Enterprise Integration: This module integrates popular enterprise services, including several remoting technologies, EJB, JMS, JMX, e-mail, and scheduling, into Spring to make them easier to use. Spring's enterprise integration will be covered in Chapters 16, 17, and 18.

Introducing Spring's Releases

Two and a half years after the Spring framework 1.0 was released in March 2004, in October 2006, the first major upgrade—Spring 2.0—was released with the following major improvements and new features:

XML schema–based configuration: In Spring 1.x, XML bean configuration files only support DTDs, and everything you can define within them must be through the `<bean>` element. Spring 2.0 supports XML schema–based configuration, which allows you to use Spring's new tags. As a result, your bean configuration files can be much simpler and clearer. You will take advantage of Spring's XML schema–based configuration throughout this book. For a look at its basis, please see Chapter 3.

Annotation-driven configuration: As a complement to XML-based configuration, Spring 2.0 supports annotation-driven configuration in certain modules, such as `@Required`, `@Transactional`, `@PersistenceContext`, and `@PersistenceUnit`. For usage of these annotations, please refer to Chapters 3, 8, and 9.

New Spring AOP approach: The classic AOP usage in Spring 1.x is through a set of proprietary Spring AOP APIs. Spring 2.0 introduces a brand-new AOP approach through writing POJOs with either AspectJ annotations or XML schema–based configuration. Chapter 6 discusses this new AOP approach in detail.

Easier transaction declaration: Declaring transactions in Spring 2.0 is much easier. You can take advantage of the new Spring AOP approach to declare transaction advices, or apply the `@Transactional` annotations with the `<tx:annotation-driven>` tag. Chapter 8 discusses transaction management in detail.

JPA support: Spring 2.0 introduces support for the Java Persistence API in its ORM module. JPA support is covered in Chapter 9.

Form tag library: Spring 2.0 introduces a new form tag library to make developing forms in Spring MVC easier. Spring's form tag library usage will be introduced in Chapter 10.

Asynchronous JMS support: Spring 1.x only supports receiving JMS messages synchronously through `JmsTemplate`. Spring 2.0 adds support for asynchronous JMS reception through message-driven POJOs. This will be covered in Chapter 17.

Scripting language support: Spring 2.0 supports implementing beans with the scripting languages JRuby, Groovy, and BeanShell. Chapter 19 introduces Spring's scripting language support.

In November 2007, Spring 2.5 was released to enhance Spring 2.0 with the following new features. Spring 2.5 is the current release at the time of writing.

Annotation-driven configuration: Spring 2.0 added support for several annotations to simplify bean configuration. Spring 2.5 supports more, including `@Autowired` and the JSR-250 annotations `@Resource`, `@PostConstruct`, and `@PreDestroy`. For usage of these annotations, please refer to Chapters 3 and 4.

Component scanning: Spring 2.5 can automatically detect your components with particular stereotype annotations from the classpath without manual configuration. The component-scanning feature will be discussed in Chapter 3.

AspectJ load-time weaving support: Spring 2.5 supports weaving AspectJ aspects into the Spring IoC container at load time, letting you use AspectJ aspects beyond the reach of Spring AOP's support. AspectJ load-time weaving support will be discussed in Chapter 6.

Annotation-based web controllers: Spring 2.5 supports a new annotation-based approach to web controller development. It can auto-detect your controller classes with the `@Controller` annotation, and also the information you configure in the `@RequestMapping`, `@RequestParam`, and `@ModelAttribute` annotations. Chapter 10 will cover this feature in detail.

Enhanced testing support: Spring 2.5 establishes a new testing framework called Spring TestContext framework, which provides annotation-driven testing support and abstracts the underlying testing frameworks. This framework will be discussed in Chapter 12.

Finally, note that the Spring framework is designed to be backward compatible, so it is very easy for you to migrate your Spring 1.x applications to Spring 2.0, and also from 2.0 to 2.5.

Introducing Spring's Projects

Spring is not only an application framework. It also serves as a platform for several open source projects that are based on the core *Spring Framework* project. At the time of writing this book, there are the following Spring Portfolio projects:

Spring IDE: This project provides Eclipse plug-ins to increase your productivity in developing Spring's bean configuration files. Since version 2.0, Spring IDE also supports Spring AOP and Spring Web Flow. You will learn how to install Spring IDE in this chapter.

Spring Security: This project, previously known as Acegi Security, defines a security framework for enterprise applications, especially those developed with Spring. It provides security options for authentication, authorization, and access control for you to apply in your applications. This framework will be discussed in Chapter 13.

Spring Web Flow: This project allows you to model complex user actions within a web application as flows. You can develop and reuse these web flows easily with Spring Web Flow. This will be introduced in Chapter 15.

Spring Web Services: This project focuses on the development of contract-first and document-driven web services. It integrates many methods of manipulating XML. Spring Web Services will be introduced in Chapter 16.

Spring Rich Client: This project establishes a framework, constructed on top of the Spring framework, for rich GUI applications developed with Swing.

Spring Batch: This project offers a framework for batch processing in enterprise applications, focusing on processing large volumes of information.

Spring Modules: This project integrates other tools and projects as modules to extend the Spring framework, without expanding the core Spring module.

Spring Dynamic Modules: This project supports creating Spring applications to run on the OSGi (Open Services Gateway initiative) service platform, which allows application modules to be installed, updated, and removed dynamically.

Spring Integration: This project provides an extension to the Spring framework that supports enterprise integration with external systems via high-level adapters.

Spring LDAP: This project provides a library that simplifies LDAP operations and handles LDAP exceptions through a template-based approach.

Spring JavaConfig: This project provides a Java-based alternative to configuring components in the Spring IoC container.

Spring BeanDoc: This project helps you to generate documentation and diagrams based on Spring's bean configuration file.

Spring .NET: This project, as its name indicates, is a .NET version of the Spring framework that makes .NET application development easier.

2-2. Installing the Spring Framework

Problem

You would like to develop a Java/Java EE application using the Spring framework. First of all, you will have to install it on your local machine.

Solution

The Spring framework's installation is very simple. You can simply download the Spring framework 2.5 release in ZIP format and extract it to a directory of your choice to complete the installation.

How It Works

Installing JDK

Before you install the Spring framework, you should have JDK installed on your machine. Spring 2.5 requires JDK 1.4 or higher. For this book, I strongly recommend that you install JDK 1.5 or higher so that you can use features such as annotations, autoboxing/unboxing, varargs, type-safe collections, and for-each loops.

Installing a Java IDE

Although an IDE is not absolutely required for developing Java applications, you should probably install one to make development easier. As Spring's configuration is mostly based on XML, you should choose an IDE with features that support XML editing, such as XML validation and XML auto-completion. If you do not have a favorite Java IDE or would like to choose another one, I recommend installing Eclipse Web Tools Platform (WTP), which can be downloaded from `http://www.eclipse.org/webtools/`. Eclipse WTP is very easy to use and includes many powerful Java-, web-, and XML-supporting features. Also, Spring provides a plug-in for Eclipse called Spring IDE.

Downloading and Installing Spring

From Spring's web site, you can choose to download the Spring framework 2.5 release. Then you will be directed to `http://sourceforge.net/` to download a Spring distribution, as shown in Figure 2-2.

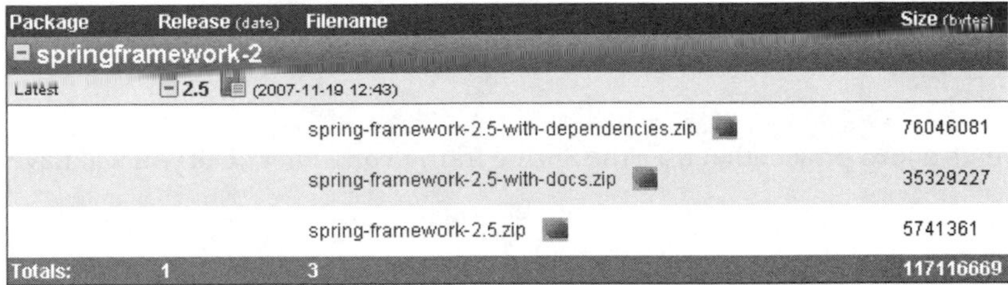

Package	Release (date)	Filename	Size (bytes)
springframework-2			
Latest	2.5 (2007-11-19 12:43)		
		spring-framework-2.5-with-dependencies.zip	76046081
		spring-framework-2.5-with-docs.zip	35329227
		spring-framework-2.5.zip	5741361
Totals:	1	3	117116669

Figure 2-2. *Downloading a Spring distribution*

As you can see from Figure 2-2, there are three distributions of the Spring framework 2.5 release that you can download. The first contains the entire Spring framework, including Spring's JAR files, dependent libraries, documentation, complete source code, and sample applications. The second only contains Spring's JAR files and documentation. The last only contains Spring's JAR files. Of them, I strongly recommend you download the distribution with all dependencies—that is, `spring-framework-2.5-with-dependencies.zip`. Although the size of this distribution is greater, it contains most of the libraries that you need for developing Spring applications.

After downloading the Spring distribution, extract it to a directory of your choice. In this book, I assume that you are using the Windows platform for development and have installed Spring into `c:\spring-framework-2.5`.

Exploring Spring's Installation Directory

If you have downloaded and installed the Spring distribution with dependencies, your Spring installation directory should have the subdirectories listed in Table 2-1.

Table 2-1. *Subdirectories in Spring's Installation Directory*

Directory	What It Contains
`aspectj`	Source code and test cases for Spring aspects used in AspectJ
`dist`	JAR files for Spring modules and weaving support, and resource files such as DTD and XSD
`docs`	Spring's API javadoc, reference documentation in PDF and HTML format, and a Spring MVC step-by-step tutorial
`lib`	JAR files for Spring's dependent libraries, organized by project
`mock`	Source code for Spring's mock objects and testing support
`samples`	Several sample applications for demonstrating how to use Spring
`src`	Source code for most parts of the Spring framework
`test`	Test cases for testing the Spring framework
`tiger`	Source code, test cases, and mock objects for Spring that are specific to JDK 1.5 and higher

2-3. Setting Up a Spring Project

Problem

You would like to create a Java project that uses the Spring framework. First of all you will have to set it up.

Solution

A Spring project's setup includes setting up the classpath and creating one or more bean configuration files to configure beans in the Spring IoC container. After that, you can instantiate the Spring IoC container with this bean configuration file and get your bean instances from it.

How It Works

Setting Up the Classpath

To start a Spring project, you have to include the JAR files that contain the Spring modules you are going to use and their dependent libraries in the classpath. For convenience's sake, you may include the single `spring.jar` file that contains all standard Spring modules, although its size is large (around 2.7 MB). It's located in the `dist` directory of the Spring installation. Or you may select the stand-alone modules that you are going to use from the `dist/modules` directory.

Another required JAR file for a Spring project is `commons-logging.jar`, which is located in the `lib/jakarta-commons` directory. The Spring framework uses this library to output its logging message, so you must include it in your classpath. The classpath configuration for a Java project varies between IDEs.

In this book, I always include `spring.jar` and `commons-logging.jar` in the classpath of my projects without any special mention.

Creating the Bean Configuration File

A typical Spring project requires one or more bean configuration files to configure beans in the Spring IoC container. You can place your bean configuration files in either the classpath or a file system path. For easier testing within an IDE, I recommend you place it in the classpath of your project. In this book, I assume that you create your bean configuration file in the root of the classpath, with the name `beans.xml`, unless specially mentioned.

To demonstrate a Spring project's creation, let's create the following `HelloWorld` class, which accepts a `message` property via setter injection. In its `hello()` method, you construct a hello message and print it to the console.

```
package com.apress.springrecipes.hello;

public class HelloWorld {

    private String message;

    public void setMessage(String message) {
        this.message = message;
    }
```

```
    public void hello() {
        System.out.println("Hello! " + message);
    }
}
```

To configure a bean of type HelloWorld with a message in the Spring IoC container, you create the following bean configuration file. According to this book's convention, let's create it in the root of the classpath with the name beans.xml.

```
<beans xmlns="http://www.springframework.org/schema/beans"
    xmlns:xsi="http://www.w3.org/2001/XMLSchema-instance"
    xsi:schemaLocation="http://www.springframework.org/schema/beans
        http://www.springframework.org/schema/beans/spring-beans-2.5.xsd">

    <bean id="helloWorld" class="com.apress.springrecipes.hello.HelloWorld">
        <property name="message" value="How are you?" />
    </bean>
</beans>
```

Using Beans from the Spring IoC Container

You can write the following Main class to instantiate the Spring IoC container with the bean configuration file beans.xml, located in the root of the classpath. Then you can get the helloWorld bean from it for your use.

```
package com.apress.springrecipes.hello;

import org.springframework.context.ApplicationContext;
import org.springframework.context.support.ClassPathXmlApplicationContext;

public class Main {

    public static void main(String[] args) {
        ApplicationContext context =
            new ClassPathXmlApplicationContext("beans.xml");

        HelloWorld helloWorld = (HelloWorld) context.getBean("helloWorld");
        helloWorld.hello();
    }
}
```

If everything is fine, you should see the following output in your console, preceded by several lines of Spring's logging messages:

```
Hello! How are you?
```

2-4. Installing Spring IDE

Problem

You would like to install an IDE that can assist you in developing Spring applications.

Solution

If you are an Eclipse user, you can install Spring's official Eclipse plug-ins, called Spring IDE (`http://springide.org/`). IntelliJ IDEA has similar Spring support features, but they are not as powerful or updated as Spring IDE. In this book, I will focus on Spring IDE only. There are three ways you can install Spring IDE:

- Add Spring IDE's update site (`http://springide.org/updatesite/`) in Eclipse's update manager and install it online.
- Download Spring IDE's archived update site and install it in Eclipse's update manager as a local site.
- Download Spring IDE's archive and extract it into Eclipse's installation directory.

Of these, I strongly recommend installing Spring IDE from its update site if your machine has an Internet connection available. Failing that, you should install it from an archived local site. These methods can help you to check if all Spring IDE's dependent plug-ins are installed already.

How It Works

From Eclipse's Help menu, choose Software Updates ➤ Find and Install. Eclipse will then ask you whether you would like to update currently installed features or install new features. For the first time installing Spring IDE, choose "Search for new features to install."

Next, you will see a list of existing update sites. If you can't see Spring IDE's update site here, add it by selecting Add Remote Site, and enter the name and URL of this site, as shown in Figure 2-3.

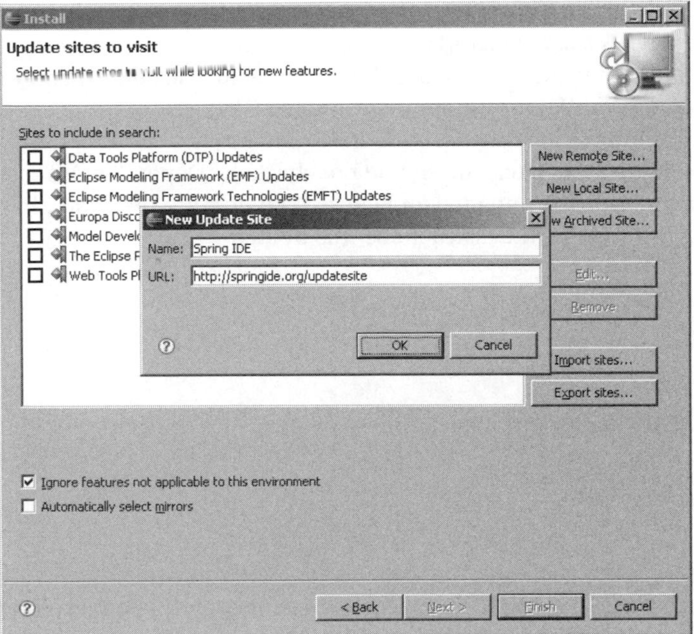

Figure 2-3. *Adding an update site for Spring IDE*

After selecting the mirror site for your update, you should see a list of Spring IDE's features and their dependencies, as shown in Figure 2-4.

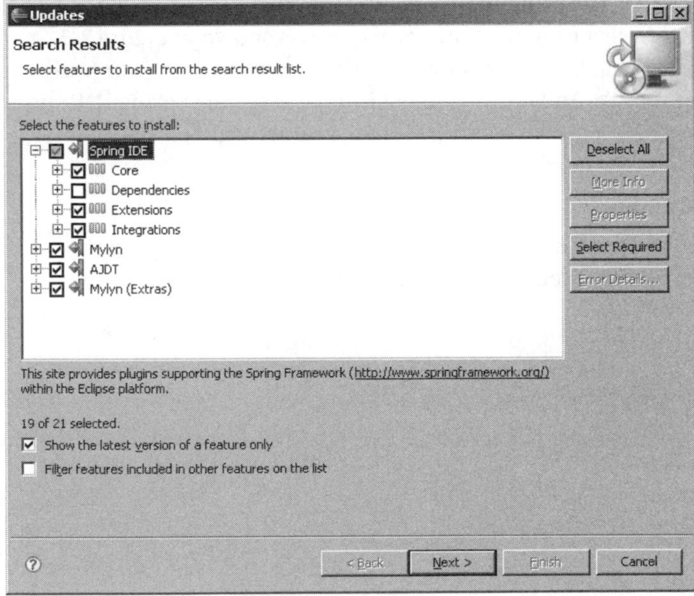

Figure 2-4. *Selecting Spring IDE features to install*

Spring IDE 2.0.2 integrates with two other Eclipse plug-ins: Eclipse Mylyn and AJDT (AspectJ Development Tools). Mylyn is a task-focused UI that can integrate multiple development tasks and reduce information overload. AJDT is an Eclipse plug-in focused on AspectJ development. Spring IDE integrates with AJDT to support Spring 2.0 AOP development. You can optionally install Spring IDE's integration features with these plug-ins.

Note that if you are using Eclipse 3.3 or later, you should not check the Dependencies category under the Spring IDE feature, which is intended for Eclipse 3.2 only. After that, you can easily complete the installation by following the instructions step by step.

2-5. Using Spring IDE's Bean-Supporting Features

Problem

You would like to use Spring IDE's bean-supporting features to help you develop Spring applications.

Solution

Spring IDE provides rich bean-supporting features that can increase your productivity in developing Spring applications. By using Spring IDE, you can view your beans in both explorer and graph mode. Moreover, Spring IDE can assist you in writing the contents of your bean configuration file and also validating its correctness.

How It Works

Creating a Spring Project

To create a Spring project in Eclipse with Spring IDE installed, from the File menu choose New ➤ Project, and select Spring Project from the Spring category, as shown in Figure 2-5.

If you would like to turn an existing Java project into a Spring project, select your project, right-click it, and choose Spring Tools ➤ Add Spring Project Nature to enable Spring IDE support for this project. A Spring project's icon has a small "S" in the upper-right corner.

Creating a Spring Bean Configuration File

To create a bean configuration file, from the File menu, choose New ➤ Other, and select Spring Bean Definition from the Spring category, as shown in Figure 2-6.

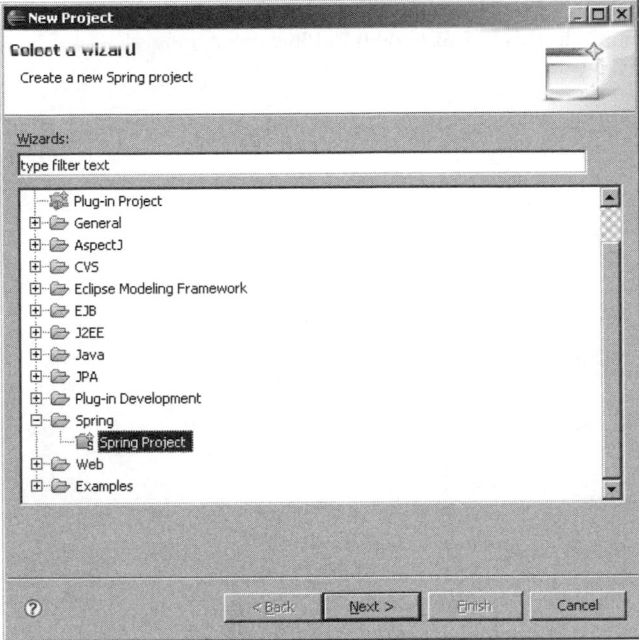

Figure 2-5. *Creating a Spring project*

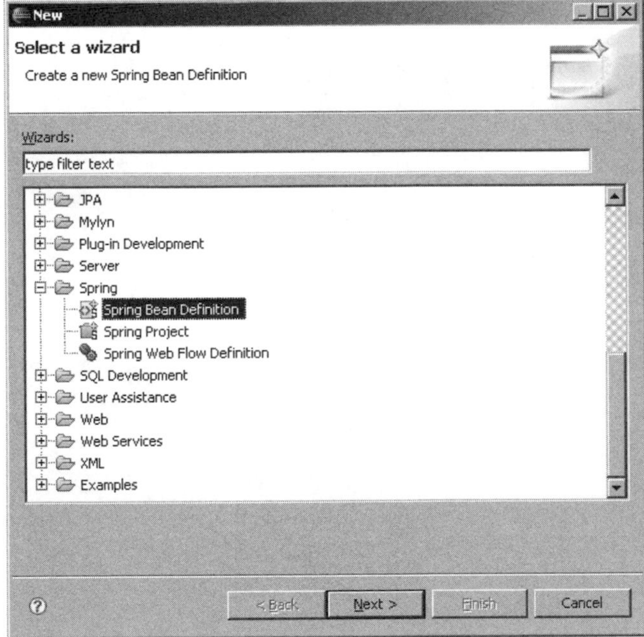

Figure 2-6. *Creating a Spring bean configuration file*

After choosing the location and name of this bean configuration file, you are asked to select which XSD namespaces to include in this file, as shown in Figure 2-7.

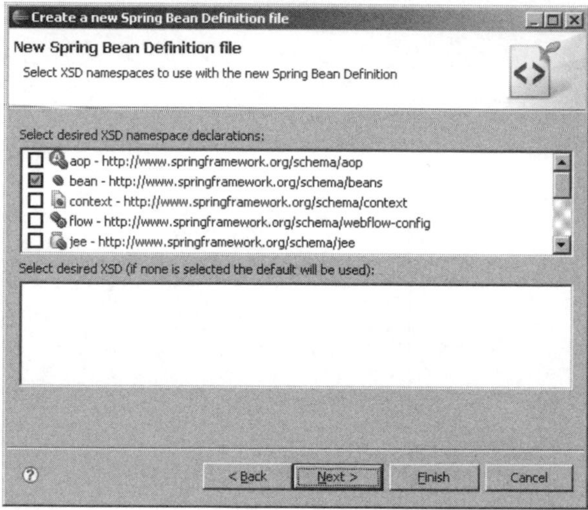

Figure 2-7. *Selecting the XSD namespaces to include in a bean configuration file*

If you would like to specify an existing XML file as a Spring bean configuration file, you can right-click your project and choose Properties. From Beans Support, located in the Spring category, you can add your XML files, as shown in Figure 2-8.

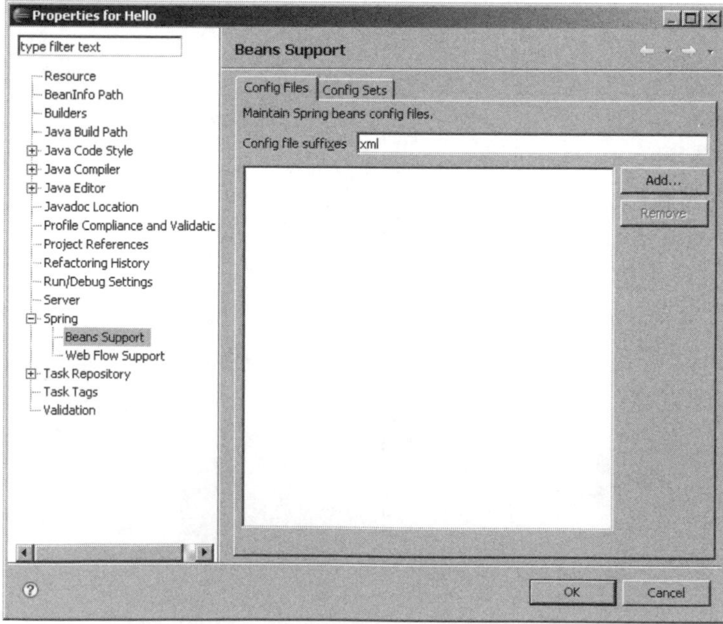

Figure 2-8. *Specifying bean configuration files in a Spring project*

Viewing Spring Beans in Spring Explorer

To better illustrate Spring IDE's exploring and graphic features, let's create the following Holiday class. For simplicity's sake, I'm omitting the getter and setter methods of this class. You can easily generate them by choosing Source ➤ Generate Getters and Setters.

```
package com.apress.springrecipes.hello;

public class Holiday {

    private int month;
    private int day;
    private String greeting;

    // Getters and Setters
    ...
}
```

Then modify your HelloWorld class to add a holidays property of the java.util.List type and also its setter method.

```
package com.apress.springrecipes.hello;

import java.util.List;

public class HelloWorld {
    ...
    private List<Holiday> holidays;

    public void setHolidays(List<Holiday> holidays) {
        this.holidays = holidays;
    }
}
```

In the bean configuration file, you declare a christmas and a newYear bean whose type is Holiday. Then you set the holidays property of the helloWorld bean to contain references to these two beans.

```
<beans ...>
    <bean id="helloWorld" class="com.apress.springrecipes.hello.HelloWorld">
        <property name="message" value="How are you?" />
        <property name="holidays">
            <list>
                <ref local="christmas" />
                <ref local="newYear" />
            </list>
        </property>
    </bean>
```

```
    <bean id="christmas" class="com.apress.springrecipes.hello.Holiday">
        <property name="month" value="12" />
        <property name="day" value="25" />
        <property name="greeting" value="Merry Christmas!" />
    </bean>

    <bean id="newYear" class="com.apress.springrecipes.hello.Holiday">
        <property name="month" value="1" />
        <property name="day" value="1" />
        <property name="greeting" value="Happy New Year!" />
    </bean>
</beans>
```

To view your beans in Spring Explorer, right-click your bean configuration file and choose Show In ➤ Spring Explorer, and then you can explore them, as shown in Figure 2-9.

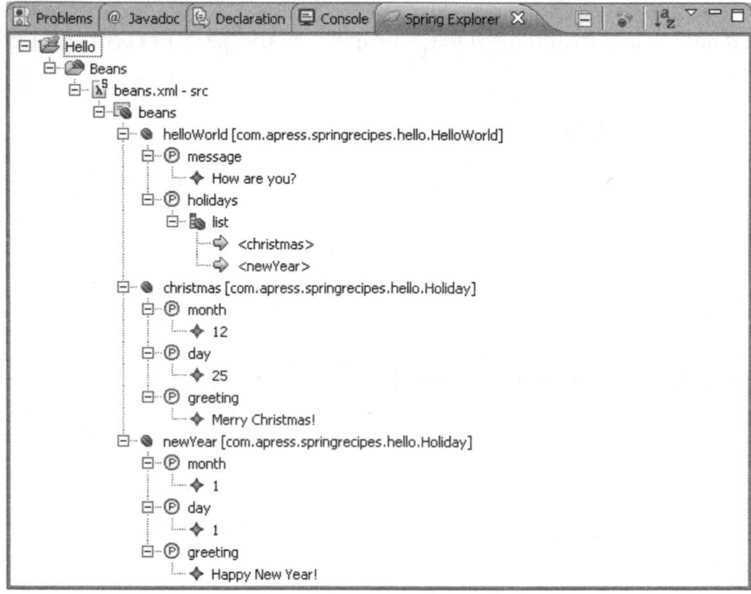

Figure 2-9. *Exploring Spring beans in Spring Explorer*

In Spring Explorer, you can double-click an element, and your cursor will jump to its corresponding declaration in the bean configuration file. So, you can begin editing this element very conveniently.

Viewing Spring Beans in Spring Beans Graph

You can right-click a bean element (or its root element) in Spring Explorer and then choose Open Graph to view your beans in a graph, as shown in Figure 2-10.

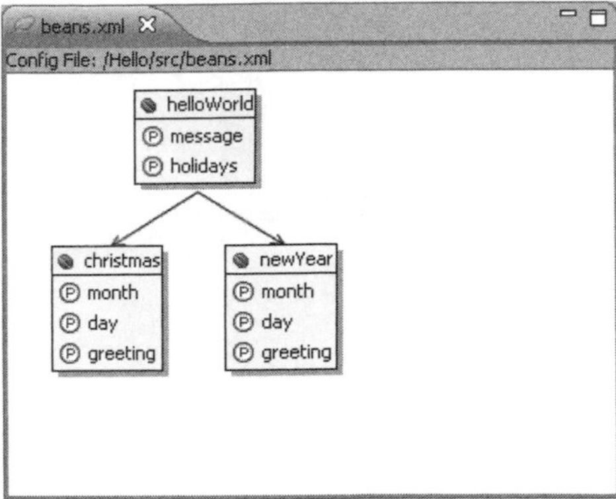
beans.xml
Config File: /Hello/src/beans.xml
helloWorld
message
holidays
christmas
month
day
greeting
newYear
month
day
greeting

Figure 2-10. *Viewing Spring beans in Spring Beans Graph*

Using Content Assist in Bean Configuration Files

Spring IDE supports using Eclipse's content assist feature to edit class names, property names, and bean name references. The default key combination to activate content assist in Eclipse is Ctrl+Space. For example, you can use content assist to complete a property name as shown in Figure 2-11.

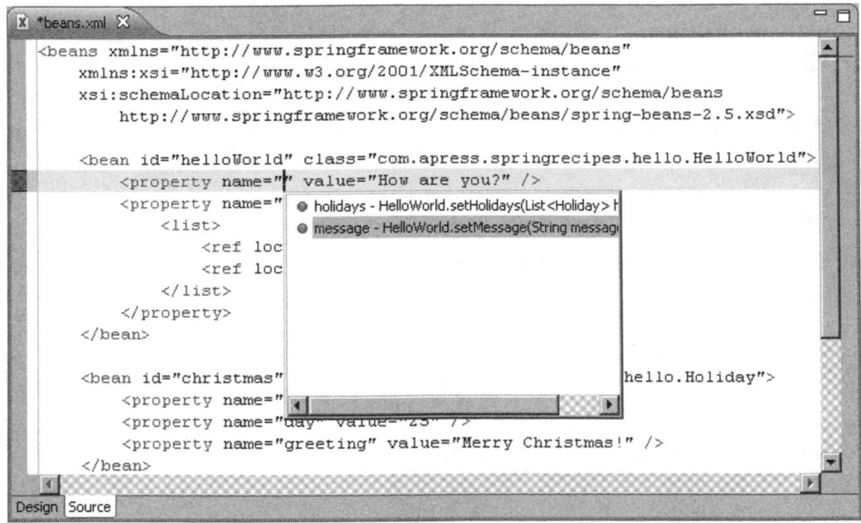
*beans.xml
<beans xmlns="http://www.springframework.org/schema/beans"
xmlns:xsi="http://www.w3.org/2001/XMLSchema-instance"
xsi:schemaLocation="http://www.springframework.org/schema/beans
http://www.springframework.org/schema/beans/spring-beans-2.5.xsd">
<bean id="helloWorld" class="com.apress.springrecipes.hello.HelloWorld">
<property name="" value="How are you?" />
holidays - HelloWorld.setHolidays(List<Holiday>
message - HelloWorld.setMessage(String messag
</list>
</property>
</bean>
hello.Holiday">
<property name="greeting" value="Merry Christmas!" />
</bean>
Design
Source

Figure 2-11. *Using content assist in bean configuration files*

Validating Bean Configuration Files

Each time you save your bean configuration file, Spring IDE automatically validates its correctness against bean classes, property names, bean name references, and so on. If there's any error in the file, Spring IDE will highlight this error, as shown in Figure 2-12.

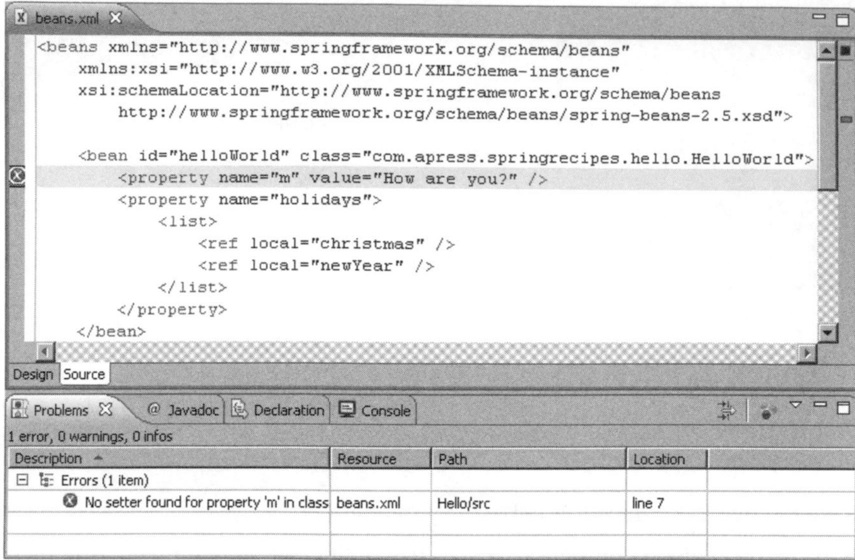
beans.xml
<beans xmlns="http://www.springframework.org/schema/beans"
xmlns:xsi="http://www.w3.org/2001/XMLSchema-instance"
xsi:schemaLocation="http://www.springframework.org/schema/beans
http://www.springframework.org/schema/beans/spring-beans-2.5.xsd">
<bean id="helloWorld" class="com.apress.springrecipes.hello.HelloWorld">
<property name="m" value="How are you?" />
<property name="holidays">
<list>
<ref local="christmas" />
<ref local="newYear" />
</list>
</property>
</bean>
Design Source
Problems Javadoc Declaration Console
1 error, 0 warnings, 0 infos
Description Resource Path Location
Errors (1 item)
No setter found for property 'm' in class beans.xml Hello/src line 7

Figure 2-12. *Validating bean configuration files with Spring IDE*

Searching Spring Beans

Spring IDE supports searching beans according to certain criteria. From the Search menu, choose Beans, and then you can search your beans, as shown in Figure 2-13.

Search
Spring Beans Search
Spring Pointcut Matches
Search string
helloWorld
Case sensitive
(* = any string, ? = any character, \ = escape for literals: * ? \)
Regular expression
Search For
Beans by name
Beans referencing this bean
Beans by class
Child beans of this bean
Beans by property name
Scope
Workspace
Selected resources
Enclosing projects
Working set:
Choose...
Customize...
Search
Cancel

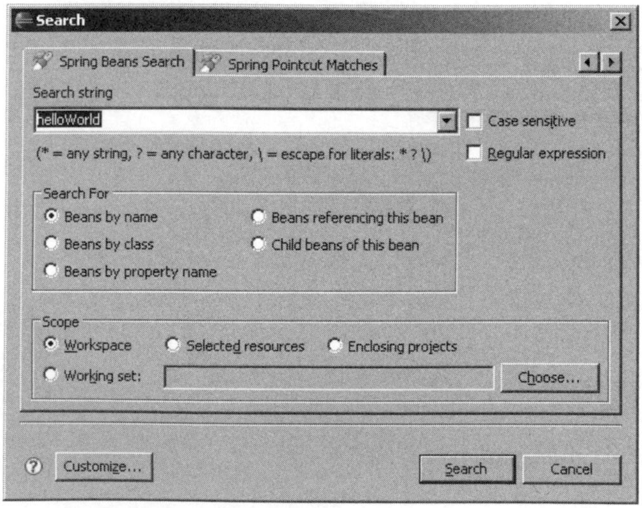

Figure 2-13. *Searching Spring Beans*

2-6. Summary

In this chapter, you have learned the Spring framework's overall architecture and major functions, as well as the general purpose of each subproject. The installation of the Spring framework is very simple. You just download it and extract it into a directory. You saw an overview of the contents in each subdirectory of Spring's installation directory. You also created a very simple Spring project, which demonstrated how a typical Spring project is set up. This project also defined some project conventions that I will use throughout this book.

The Spring team has created an Eclipse plug-in called Spring IDE to simplify Spring application development. In this chapter, you installed this IDE and learned how to use its basic bean-supporting features.

In the next chapter, you will learn about the basic bean configuration in the Spring IoC container.

2.6 Summary

CHAPTER 3

Bean Configuration in Spring

In this chapter, you will learn basic component configuration in the Spring IoC container. As the heart of the Spring framework, the IoC container is designed to be highly adaptive and configurable. It provides a set of facilities to make your component configuration as simple as possible. So, you can easily configure your components to run in the Spring IoC container.

In Spring, components are also called "beans." Note that this is a different concept from the JavaBeans specification defined by Sun. The beans declared in the Spring IoC container are not necessarily required to be JavaBeans. They can be any POJOs (Plain Old Java Objects). The term *POJO* means an ordinary Java object without any specific requirements, such as to implement a specific interface or to extend a specific base class. This term is used to distinguish lightweight Java components from heavyweight components in other complex component models (e.g., EJB components in versions prior to 3.0).

Upon finishing this chapter, you will be able to build a complete Java application using the Spring IoC container. Besides, if you review your old Java applications, you may find that you can significantly simplify and improve them by using the Spring IoC container.

3-1. Configuring Beans in the Spring IoC Container

Problem

Spring offers a powerful IoC container to manage the beans that make up an application. To utilize the container services, you have to configure your beans to run in the Spring IoC container.

Solution

You can configure your beans in the Spring IoC container through XML files, properties files, or even APIs. This book will concentrate on the XML-based configuration because of its simplicity and maturity. If you are interested in the other methods, you can consult the Spring documentation to find out more about bean configuration.

Spring allows you to configure your beans in one or more bean configuration files. For a simple application, you can simply centralize your beans in a single configuration file. But for a large application with a lot of beans, you should separate them in multiple configuration files according to their functionalities.

How It Works

Suppose you are going to develop an application for generating sequence numbers. In this application, there may be many series of sequence numbers to generate for different purposes. Each one of them will have its own prefix, suffix, and initial value. So, you have to create and maintain multiple generator instances in your application.

Creating the Bean Class

In accordance with the requirements, you create the `SequenceGenerator` class that has three properties, `prefix`, `suffix`, and `initial`, that can be injected via setter methods or a constructor. The private field `counter` is for storing the current numeric value of this generator. Each time you call the `getSequence()` method on a generator instance, you will get the last sequence number with the prefix and suffix joined. You declare this method as `synchronized` to make it thread-safe.

```
package com.apress.springrecipes.sequence;

public class SequenceGenerator {

    private String prefix;
    private String suffix;
    private int initial;
    private int counter;

    public SequenceGenerator() {}

    public SequenceGenerator(String prefix, String suffix, int initial) {
        this.prefix = prefix;
        this.suffix = suffix;
        this.initial = initial;
    }

    public void setPrefix(String prefix) {
        this.prefix = prefix;
    }

    public void setSuffix(String suffix) {
        this.suffix = suffix;
    }

    public void setInitial(int initial) {
        this.initial = initial;
    }

    public synchronized String getSequence() {
        StringBuffer buffer = new StringBuffer();
        buffer.append(prefix);
        buffer.append(initial + counter++);
```

```
        buffer.append(suffix);
        return buffer.toString();
    }
}
```

As you see, this SequenceGenerator class applies both constructor injection and setter injection for the properties prefix, suffix, and initial.

Creating the Bean Configuration File

To declare beans in the Spring IoC container via XML, you first have to create an XML bean configuration file with an appropriate name, such as beans.xml. You can put this file in the root of the classpath for easier testing within an IDE. At the beginning of this XML file, you can specify the Spring 2.0 DTD to import the valid structure of a bean configuration file for Spring 2.x. In this configuration file, you can define one or more beans under the root element <beans>.

```
<!DOCTYPE beans PUBLIC "-//SPRING//DTD BEAN 2.0//EN"
    "http://www.springframework.org/dtd/spring-beans-2.0.dtd">

<beans>
    ...
</beans>
```

The configuration of Spring is backward compatible, so you can continue to use your existing 1.0 configuration files (with the Spring 1.0 DTD) in Spring 2.x. But in this way, you will not be able to use the new configuration facilities introduced in Spring 2.x. The usage of the old configuration files is mainly for transitional purposes.

Spring 2.x also supports using XSD to define the valid structure of an XML bean configuration file. XSD has many advantages over the traditional DTD. The most significant advantage in Spring 2.x is that it allows you to use custom tags from different schemas to make the bean configuration simpler and clearer. So, I strongly recommend using Spring XSD instead of DTD whenever possible. Spring XSD is version specific but backward compatible. If you are using Spring 2.5, you should define the Spring 2.5 XSD to make use of the new 2.5 features.

```
<beans xmlns="http://www.springframework.org/schema/beans"
    xmlns:xsi="http://www.w3.org/2001/XMLSchema-instance"
    xsi:schemaLocation="http://www.springframework.org/schema/beans
        http://www.springframework.org/schema/beans/spring-beans-2.5.xsd">
    ...
</beans>
```

Declaring Beans in the Bean Configuration File

Each bean should provide a unique name and a fully qualified class name for the Spring IoC container to instantiate it. For each bean property of simple type (e.g., String and other primitive types), you can specify a <value> element for it. Spring will attempt to convert your value into the declaring type of this property. To configure a property via setter injection, you use the <property> element and specify the property name in its name attribute.

```
<bean name="sequenceGenerator"
    class="com.apress.springrecipes.sequence.SequenceGenerator">
    <property name="prefix">
        <value>30</value>
    </property>
    <property name="suffix">
        <value>A</value>
    </property>
    <property name="initial">
        <value>100000</value>
    </property>
</bean>
```

You can also configure bean properties via constructor injection by declaring them in the `<constructor-arg>` elements. There's not a `name` attribute in `<constructor-arg>` because constructor arguments are position-based.

```
<bean name="sequenceGenerator"
    class="com.apress.springrecipes.sequence.SequenceGenerator">
    <constructor-arg>
        <value>30</value>
    </constructor-arg>
    <constructor-arg>
        <value>A</value>
    </constructor-arg>
    <constructor-arg>
        <value>100000</value>
    </constructor-arg>
</bean>
```

In the Spring IoC container, each bean's name should be unique, although duplicate names are allowed for overriding bean declaration. A bean's name can be defined by the `name` attribute of the `<bean>` element. Actually, there's a preferred way of identifying a bean. It is through the standard XML `id` attribute, whose purpose is to identify an element within an XML document. In this way, if your text editor is XML aware, it can help to validate each bean's uniqueness at design time.

```
<bean id="sequenceGenerator"
    class="com.apress.springrecipes.sequence.SequenceGenerator">
    ...
</bean>
```

However, XML has restrictions on the characters that can appear in the XML `id` attribute, but usually you won't use those special characters in a bean name. Moreover, Spring allows you to specify multiple names, separated by commas, for a bean in the `name` attribute. But you can't do so in the `id` attribute, as commas are not allowed there.

In fact, neither the bean name nor the bean ID is required for a bean. A bean that has no name defined is called an *anonymous bean*.

Defining Bean Properties by Shortcut

Spring supports a shortcut for specifying the value of a simple type property. You can present a value attribute in the <property> element instead of enclosing a <value> element inside.

```
<bean id="sequenceGenerator"
    class="com.apress.springrecipes.sequence.SequenceGenerator">
    <property name="prefix" value="30" />
    <property name="suffix" value="A" />
    <property name="initial" value="100000" />
</bean>
```

This shortcut also works for constructor arguments.

```
<bean name="sequenceGenerator"
    class="com.apress.springrecipes.sequence.SequenceGenerator">
    <constructor-arg value="30" />
    <constructor-arg value="A" />
    <constructor-arg value="100000" />
</bean>
```

Spring 2.x provides another convenient shortcut for you to define properties. It's by using the p schema to define bean properties as attributes of the <bean> element. This can shorten the lines of XML configuration.

```
<beans xmlns="http://www.springframework.org/schema/beans"
    xmlns:xsi="http://www.w3.org/2001/XMLSchema-instance"
    xmlns:p="http://www.springframework.org/schema/p"
    xsi:schemaLocation="http://www.springframework.org/schema/beans
        http://www.springframework.org/schema/beans/spring-beans-2.5.xsd">

    <bean id="sequenceGenerator"
        class="com.apress.springrecipes.sequence.SequenceGenerator"
        p:prefix="30" p:suffix="A" p:initial="100000" />
</beans>
```

3-2. Instantiating the Spring IoC Container

Problem

You have to instantiate the Spring IoC container for it to create bean instances by reading their configurations. Then you can get the bean instances from the IoC container to use.

Solution

Spring provides two types of IoC container implementation. The basic one is called *bean factory*. The more advanced one is called *application context*, which is a compatible extension to the bean factory. Note that the bean configuration files for these two types of IoC container are identical.

The application context provides more advanced features than the bean factory while keeping the basic features compatible. So, I strongly recommend using the application context for every application unless the resources of this application are restricted, such as when running in an applet or a mobile device.

The interfaces for the bean factory and the application context are `BeanFactory` and `ApplicationContext`, respectively. The interface `ApplicationContext` is a subinterface of `BeanFactory` for maintaining compatibility.

How It Works

Instantiating a Bean Factory

To instantiate a bean factory, you have to load the bean configuration file into a `Resource` object first. For example, the following statement loads your configuration file from the root of the classpath:

```
Resource resource = new ClassPathResource("beans.xml");
```

`Resource` is only an interface, while `ClassPathResource` is one of its implementations for loading a resource from the classpath. Other implementations of the `Resource` interface, such as `FileSystemResource`, `InputStreamResource`, and `UrlResource`, are used to load a resource from other locations. Figure 3-1 shows the common implementations of the `Resource` interface in Spring.

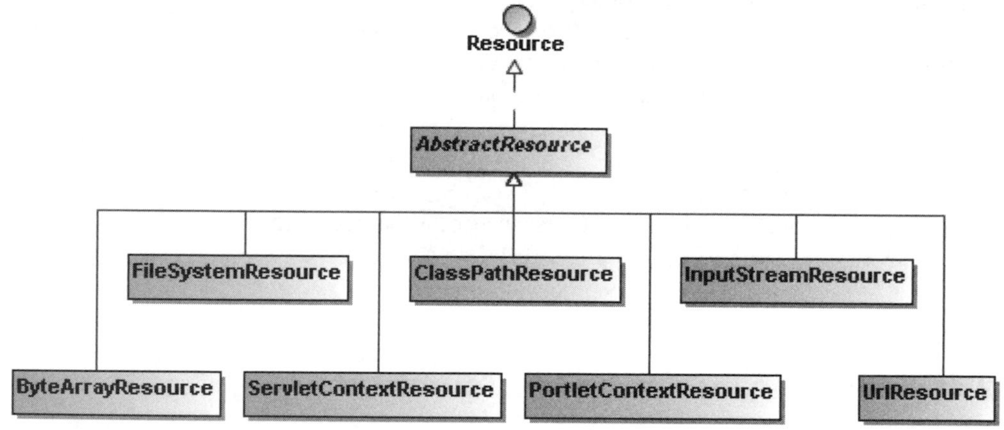

Figure 3-1. *Common implementations of the Resource interface*

Next, you can use the following statement to instantiate a bean factory by passing in a `Resource` object with the configuration file loaded:

```
BeanFactory factory = new XmlBeanFactory(resource);
```

As mentioned, `BeanFactory` is only an interface for abstracting the operations of a bean factory, while `XmlBeanFactory` is the implementation that builds a bean factory from an XML configuration file.

Instantiating an Application Context

Like BeanFactory, ApplicationContext is an interface only. You have to instantiate an implementation of it. The ClassPathXmlApplicationContext implementation builds an application context by loading an XML configuration file from the classpath. You can also specify multiple configuration files for it.

```
ApplicationContext context = new ClassPathXmlApplicationContext("beans.xml");
```

Besides ClassPathXmlApplicationContext, there are several other ApplicationContext implementations provided by Spring. FileSystemXmlApplicationContext is used to load XML configuration files from the file system, while XmlWebApplicationContext and XmlPortletApplicationContext can be used in web and portal applications only. Figure 3-2 shows the common implementations of the ApplicationContext interface in Spring.

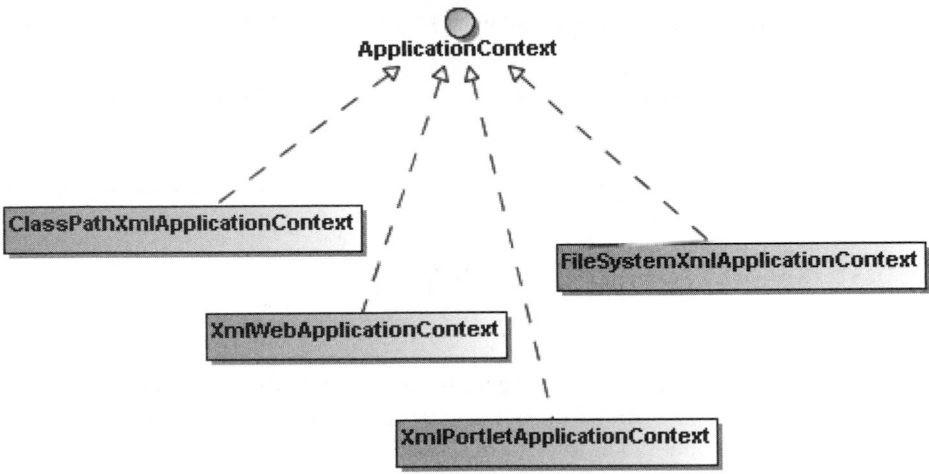

Figure 3-2. *Common implementations of the ApplicationContext interface*

Getting Beans from the IoC Container

To get a declared bean from a bean factory or an application context, you just make a call to the getBean() method and pass in the unique bean name. The return type of the getBean() method is java.lang.Object, so you have to cast it to its actual type before using it.

```
SequenceGenerator generator =
    (SequenceGenerator) context.getBean("sequenceGenerator");
```

Up to this step, you are free to use the bean just like any object you created using a constructor. The complete source code for running the sequence generator application is given in the following Main class:

```
package com.apress.springrecipes.sequence;

import org.springframework.context.ApplicationContext;
import org.springframework.context.support.ClassPathXmlApplicationContext;
```

```
public class Main {

    public static void main(String[] args) {
        ApplicationContext context =
            new ClassPathXmlApplicationContext("beans.xml");

        SequenceGenerator generator =
            (SequenceGenerator) context.getBean("sequenceGenerator");

        System.out.println(generator.getSequence());
        System.out.println(generator.getSequence());
    }
}
```

If everything is fine, you should see the following sequence numbers output, along with some logging messages that you may not be interested in:

```
30100000A
30100001A
```

3-3. Resolving Constructor Ambiguity

Problem

When you specify one or more constructor arguments for a bean, Spring will attempt to find an appropriate constructor in the bean class and pass in your arguments for bean instantiation. However, if your arguments can be applied to more than one constructor, it may cause ambiguity in constructor matching. In this case, Spring may not be able to invoke your expected constructor.

Solution

You can specify the attributes `type` and `index` for the `<constructor-arg>` element to assist Spring in finding your expected constructor.

How It Works

Now let's add a new constructor to the `SequenceGenerator` class with `prefix` and `suffix` as arguments.

```
package com.apress.springrecipes.sequence;

public class SequenceGenerator {
    ...
    public SequenceGenerator(String prefix, String suffix) {
        this.prefix = prefix;
        this.suffix = suffix;
```

```
    }
}
```

In its bean declaration, you can specify one or more constructor arguments through the <constructor-arg> elements. Spring will attempt to find an appropriate constructor for that class and pass in your arguments for bean instantiation. Recall that there's not a name attribute in <constructor-arg>, as constructor arguments are position-based.

```
<bean id="sequenceGenerator"
    class="com.apress.springrecipes.sequence.SequenceGenerator">
    <constructor-arg value="30" />
    <constructor-arg value="A" />
    <property name="initial" value="100000" />
</bean>
```

It's easy for Spring to find a constructor for these two arguments, as there is only one constructor that requires two arguments. Suppose you have to add another constructor to SequenceGenerator with prefix and initial as arguments.

```
package com.apress.springrecipes.sequence;

public class SequenceGenerator {
    ...
    public SequenceGenerator(String prefix, String suffix) {
        this.prefix = prefix;
        this.suffix = suffix;
    }

    public SequenceGenerator(String prefix, int initial) {
        this.prefix = prefix;
        this.initial = initial;
    }
}
```

To invoke this constructor, you make the following bean declaration to pass a prefix and an initial value. The remaining suffix is injected through the setter method.

```
<bean id="sequenceGenerator"
    class="com.apress.springrecipes.sequence.SequenceGenerator">
    <constructor-arg value="30" />
    <constructor-arg value="100000" />
    <property name="suffix" value="A" />
</bean>
```

However, if you run the application now, you will get the following result:

```
300A
301A
```

The cause of this unexpected result is that the first constructor, with prefix and suffix as arguments, has been invoked, but not the second. This is because Spring resolved both of your arguments as String type by default and considered that the first constructor was most suitable, as no type conversion was required. To specify the expected type of your arguments, you have to set it in the type attribute in <constructor-arg>.

```
<bean id="sequenceGenerator"
    class="com.apress.springrecipes.sequence.SequenceGenerator">
    <constructor-arg type="java.lang.String" value="30" />
    <constructor-arg type="int" value="100000" />
    <property name="suffix" value="A" />
</bean>
```

Now add one more constructor to SequenceGenerator with initial and suffix as arguments, and modify your bean declaration for it accordingly.

```
package com.apress.springrecipes.sequence;

public class SequenceGenerator {
    ...
    public SequenceGenerator(String prefix, String suffix) {
        this.prefix = prefix;
        this.suffix = suffix;
    }

    public SequenceGenerator(String prefix, int initial) {
        this.prefix = prefix;
        this.initial = initial;
    }

    public SequenceGenerator(int initial, String suffix) {
        this.initial = initial;
        this.suffix = suffix;
    }
}
```

```
<bean id="sequenceGenerator"
    class="com.apress.springrecipes.sequence.SequenceGenerator">
    <constructor-arg type="int" value="100000" />
    <constructor-arg type="java.lang.String" value="A" />
    <property name="prefix" value="30" />
</bean>
```

If you run the application again, you may get the right result or the following unexpected result:

```
30100000null
30100001null
```

The reason for this uncertainty is that Spring internally scores each constructor for compatibility with your arguments. But during the scoring process, the order in which your arguments appear in the XML is not considered. This means that from the view of Spring, the second and the third constructors will get the same score. Which one to pick depends on which one is matched first. According to the Java Reflection API, or more accurately the Class.getDeclaredConstructors() method, the constructors returned will be in an arbitrary order that may differ from the declaration order. All these factors, acting together, cause ambiguity in constructor matching.

To avoid this problem, you have to indicate the indexes of your arguments explicitly through the index attribute of <constructor-arg>. With both the type and index attributes set, Spring will be able to find the expected constructor for a bean accurately.

```
<bean id="sequenceGenerator"
    class="com.apress.springrecipes.sequence.SequenceGenerator">
    <constructor-arg type="int" index="0" value="100000" />
    <constructor-arg type="java.lang.String" index="1" value="A" />
    <property name="prefix" value="30" />
</bean>
```

However, if you are quite sure that your constructors won't cause ambiguity, you can skip the type and index attributes.

3-4. Specifying Bean References

Problem

The beans that make up your application often need to collaborate with each other to complete the application's functions. For beans to access each other, you have to specify bean references in the bean configuration file.

Solution

In the bean configuration file, you can specify a bean reference for a bean property or a constructor argument by the <ref> element. It's as easy as specifying a simple value by the <value> element. You can also enclose a bean declaration in a property or a constructor argument directly as an inner bean.

How It Works

Accepting a string value as the prefix of your sequence generator is not flexible enough to adapt to future requirements. It would be better if the prefix generation could be customized with some kind of programming logic. You can create the PrefixGenerator interface to define the prefix generation operation.

```
package com.apress.springrecipes.sequence;

public interface PrefixGenerator {

    public String getPrefix();
}
```

One prefix generation strategy is to use a particular pattern to format the current system date. Let's create the DatePrefixGenerator class that implements the PrefixGenerator interface.

```
package com.apress.springrecipes.sequence;
...
public class DatePrefixGenerator implements PrefixGenerator {

    private DateFormat formatter;

    public void setPattern(String pattern) {
        this.formatter = new SimpleDateFormat(pattern);
    }

    public String getPrefix() {
        return formatter.format(new Date());
    }
}
```

The pattern of this generator will be injected through the setter method setPattern() and then used to create a java.text.DateFormat object to format the date. As the pattern string will not be used any more once the DateFormat object is created, it's not necessary to store it in a private field.

Now you can declare a bean of type DatePrefixGenerator with an arbitrary pattern string for date formatting.

```
<bean id="datePrefixGenerator"
    class="com.apress.springrecipes.sequence.DatePrefixGenerator">
    <property name="pattern" value="yyyyMMdd" />
</bean>
```

Specifying Bean References for Setter Methods

To apply this prefix generator approach, the SequenceGenerator class should accept an object of type PrefixGenerator instead of a simple prefix string. You may choose setter injection to accept this prefix generator. You have to delete the prefix property and its setter methods and constructors that cause compile errors.

```
package com.apress.springrecipes.sequence;

public class SequenceGenerator {
    ...
    private PrefixGenerator prefixGenerator;

    public void setPrefixGenerator(PrefixGenerator prefixGenerator) {
        this.prefixGenerator = prefixGenerator;
    }

    public synchronized String getSequence() {
        StringBuffer buffer = new StringBuffer();
```

```
        buffer.append(prefixGenerator.getPrefix());
        buffer.append(initial + counter++);
        buffer.append(suffix);
        return buffer.toString();
    }
}
```

Then a SequenceGenerator bean can refer to the datePrefixGenerator bean as its prefixGenerator property by enclosing a <ref> element inside.

```
<bean id="sequenceGenerator"
    class="com.apress.springrecipes.sequence.SequenceGenerator">
    <property name="initial" value="100000" />
    <property name="suffix" value="A" />
    <property name="prefixGenerator">
        <ref bean="datePrefixGenerator" />
    </property>
</bean>
```

The bean name in the <ref> element's bean attribute can be a reference to any bean in the IoC container, even if it's not defined in the same XML configuration file. If you are referring to a bean in the same XML file, you should use the local attribute, as it is an XML ID reference. Your XML editor can help to validate whether a bean with that ID exists in the same XML file (i.e., the reference integrity).

```
<bean id="sequenceGenerator"
    class="com.apress.springrecipes.sequence.SequenceGenerator">
    ...
    <property name="prefixGenerator">
        <ref local="datePrefixGenerator" />
    </property>
</bean>
```

There is also a convenient shortcut to specify a bean reference in the ref attribute of the <property> element.

```
<bean id="sequenceGenerator"
    class="com.apress.springrecipes.sequence.SequenceGenerator">
    ...
    <property name="prefixGenerator" ref="datePrefixGenerator" />
</bean>
```

But in this way, your XML editor will not be able to validate the reference integrity. Actually, it has the same effect as specifying the <ref> element's bean attribute.

Spring 2.x provides another convenient shortcut for you to specify bean references. It's by using the p schema to specify bean references as attributes of the <bean> element. This can shorten the lines of XML configuration.

```
<beans xmlns="http://www.springframework.org/schema/beans"
    xmlns:xsi="http://www.w3.org/2001/XMLSchema-instance"
    xmlns:p="http://www.springframework.org/schema/p"
```

```
    xsi:schemaLocation="http://www.springframework.org/schema/beans
        http://www.springframework.org/schema/beans/spring-beans-2.5.xsd">

    <bean id="sequenceGenerator"
        class="com.apress.springrecipes.sequence.SequenceGenerator"
        p:suffix="A" p:initial="1000000"
        p:prefixGenerator-ref="datePrefixGenerator" />
</beans>
```

To distinguish a bean reference from a simple property value, you have to add the `-ref` suffix to the property name.

Specifying Bean References for Constructor Arguments

Bean references can also be applied to constructor injection. For example, you can add a constructor that accepts a `PrefixGenerator` object as an argument.

```
package com.apress.springrecipes.sequence;

public class SequenceGenerator {
    ...
    private PrefixGenerator prefixGenerator;

    public SequenceGenerator(PrefixGenerator prefixGenerator) {
        this.prefixGenerator = prefixGenerator;
    }
}
```

In the `<constructor-arg>` element, you can enclose a bean reference by `<ref>` just like in the `<property>` element.

```
<bean id="sequenceGenerator"
    class="com.apress.springrecipes.sequence.SequenceGenerator">
    <constructor-arg>
        <ref local="datePrefixGenerator" />
    </constructor-arg>
    <property name="initial" value="100000" />
    <property name="suffix" value="A" />
</bean>
```

The shortcut for specifying a bean reference also works for `<constructor-arg>`.

```
<bean id="sequenceGenerator"
    class="com.apress.springrecipes.sequence.SequenceGenerator">
    <constructor-arg ref="datePrefixGenerator" />
    ...
</bean>
```

Declaring Inner Beans

Whenever a bean instance is used for one particular property only, it can be declared as an inner bean. An inner bean declaration is enclosed in <property> or <constructor-arg> directly, without any id or name attribute set. In this way, the bean will be anonymous so that you can't use it anywhere else. In fact, even if you define an id or a name attribute for an inner bean, it will be ignored.

```
<bean id="sequenceGenerator"
    class="com.apress.springrecipes.sequence.SequenceGenerator">
    <property name="initial" value="100000" />
    <property name="suffix" value="A" />
    <property name="prefixGenerator">
        <bean class="com.apress.springrecipes.sequence.DatePrefixGenerator">
            <property name="pattern" value="yyyyMMdd" />
        </bean>
    </property>
</bean>
```

An inner bean can also be declared in a constructor argument.

```
<bean id="sequenceGenerator"
    class="com.apress.springrecipes.sequence.SequenceGenerator">
    <constructor-arg>
        <bean class="com.apress.springrecipes.sequence.DatePrefixGenerator">
            <property name="pattern" value="yyyyMMdd" />
        </bean>
    </constructor-arg>
    <property name="initial" value="100000" />
    <property name="suffix" value="A" />
</bean>
```

3-5. Checking Properties with Dependency Checking

Problem

In a production-scale application, there may be hundreds or thousands of beans declared in the IoC container, and the dependencies between them are often very complicated. One of the shortcomings of setter injection is that you cannot make sure a property will be injected. It's very hard for you to check if all required properties have been set.

Solution

Spring's dependency checking feature can help you to check if all properties of certain types have been set on a bean. You simply have to specify the dependency checking mode in the dependency-check attribute of <bean>. Note that the dependency checking feature can only check if the properties have been set, but can't check if their value is not null. Table 3-1 lists all the dependency checking modes supported by Spring.

Table 3-1. *Dependency Checking Modes Supported by Spring*

Mode	Description
none*	No dependency checking will be performed. Any properties can be left unset.
simple	If any properties of the simple types (the primitive and collection types) have not been set, an UnsatisfiedDependencyException will be thrown.
objects	If any properties of the object types (other than the simple types) have not been set, an UnsatisfiedDependencyException will be thrown.
all	If any properties of any type have not been set, an UnsatisfiedDependencyException will be thrown.

* *The default mode is* none, *but this can be changed by setting the* default-dependency-check *attribute of the* <beans> *root element. This default mode will be overridden by a bean's own mode if specified. You must set this attribute with great care as it will alter the default dependency checking mode for all the beans in the IoC container.*

How It Works

Checking Properties of the Simple Types

Suppose the suffix property was not set for the sequence generator. Then the generator would generate sequence numbers whose suffix was the string null. This kind of issue is often very hard to debug, especially in a complicated bean. Fortunately, Spring is able to check if all properties of certain types have been set. To ask Spring to check properties of the simple types (i.e., the primitive and collection types), set the dependency-check attribute of <bean> to simple.

```
<bean id="sequenceGenerator"
    class="com.apress.springrecipes.sequence.SequenceGenerator"
    dependency-check="simple">
    <property name="initial" value="100000" />
    <property name="prefixGenerator" ref="datePrefixGenerator" />
</bean>
```

If any properties of such types have not been set, an UnsatisfiedDependencyException will be thrown, indicating the unset property.

```
Exception in thread "main"
org.springframework.beans.factory.UnsatisfiedDependencyException: Error creating
bean with name 'sequenceGenerator' defined in class path resource [beans.xml]:
Unsatisfied dependency expressed through bean property 'suffix': Set this property
value or disable dependency checking for this bean.
```

Checking Properties of the Object Types

If the prefix generator is not set, then the evil `NullPointerException` will be thrown when prefix generation is requested. To enable dependency checking for bean properties of object types, (i.e., other than simple types), change the `dependency-check` attribute to `objects`.

```
<bean id="sequenceGenerator"
    class="com.apress.springrecipes.sequence.SequenceGenerator"
    dependency-check="objects">
    <property name="initial" value="100000" />
    <property name="suffix" value="A" />
</bean>
```

Then when you run the application, Spring will notify you that the `prefixGenerator` property has not been set.

```
Exception in thread "main"
org.springframework.beans.factory.UnsatisfiedDependencyException: Error creating
bean with name 'sequenceGenerator' defined in class path resource [beans.xml]:
Unsatisfied dependency expressed through bean property 'prefixGenerator': Set this
property value or disable dependency checking for this bean.
```

Checking Properties of All Types

If you would like to check all bean properties whatever the type is, you can change the `dependency-check` attribute to `all`.

```
<bean id="sequenceGenerator"
    class="com.apress.springrecipes.sequence.SequenceGenerator"
    dependency-check="all">
    <property name="initial" value="100000" />
</bean>
```

Dependency Checking and Constructor Injection

Spring's dependency checking feature will only check if a property has been injected via the setter method. So, even if you have injected the prefix generator via a constructor, an `UnsatisfiedDependencyException` will still be thrown.

```
<bean id="sequenceGenerator"
    class="com.apress.springrecipes.sequence.SequenceGenerator"
    dependency-check="all">
    <constructor-arg ref="datePrefixGenerator" />
    <property name="initial" value="100000" />
    <property name="suffix" value="A" />
</bean>
```

3-6. Checking Properties with the @Required Annotation

Problem

Spring's dependency checking feature can only check for all properties of certain types. It's not flexible enough to check for particular properties only. In most cases, you would like to check if particular properties have been set, but not all properties of certain types.

Solution

`RequiredAnnotationBeanPostProcessor` is a Spring bean post processor that checks if all the bean properties with the `@Required` annotation have been set. A *bean post processor* is a special kind of Spring bean that is able to perform additional tasks on each bean before its initialization. To enable this bean post processor for property checking, you must register it in the Spring IoC container. Note that this processor can only check if the properties have been set, but can't check if their value is not null.

How It Works

Suppose that both the `prefixGenerator` and `suffix` properties are required for a sequence generator. You can annotate their setter methods with `@Required`.

```
package com.apress.springrecipes.sequence;

import org.springframework.beans.factory.annotation.Required;

public class SequenceGenerator {

    private PrefixGenerator prefixGenerator;
    private String suffix;
    ...
    @Required
    public void setPrefixGenerator(PrefixGenerator prefixGenerator) {
        this.prefixGenerator = prefixGenerator;
    }

    @Required
    public void setSuffix(String suffix) {
        this.suffix = suffix;
    }
    ...
}
```

To ask Spring to check if these properties have been set on all sequence generator instances, you have to register a `RequiredAnnotationBeanPostProcessor` instance in the IoC container. If you are using a bean factory, you have to register this bean post processor through the API. Otherwise, you can just declare an instance of this bean post processor in your application context.

```
<bean class="org.springframework.beans.factory.annotation.➥
    RequiredAnnotationBeanPostProcessor" />
```

If you are using Spring 2.5, you can simply include the `<context:annotation-config>` element in your bean configuration file, and a `RequiredAnnotationBeanPostProcessor` instance will automatically get registered.

```
<beans xmlns="http://www.springframework.org/schema/beans"
    xmlns:xsi="http://www.w3.org/2001/XMLSchema-instance"
    xmlns:context="http://www.springframework.org/schema/context"
    xsi:schemaLocation="http://www.springframework.org/schema/beans
        http://www.springframework.org/schema/beans/spring-beans-2.5.xsd
        http://www.springframework.org/schema/context
        http://www.springframework.org/schema/context/spring-context-2.5.xsd">

    <context:annotation-config />
    ...
</beans>
```

If any properties with `@Required` have not been set, a `BeanInitializationException` will be thrown by this bean post processor.

```
Exception in thread "main" org.springframework.beans.factory.BeanCreationException:
Error creating bean with name 'sequenceGenerator' defined in class path resource
[beans.xml]: Initialization of bean failed; nested exception is
org.springframework.beans.factory.BeanInitializationException: Property
'prefixGenerator' is required for bean 'sequenceGenerator'
```

In addition to the `@Required` annotation, `RequiredAnnotationBeanPostProcessor` can also check the properties with your custom annotation. For example, you can create the following annotation type:

```
package com.apress.springrecipes.sequence;
...
@Retention(RetentionPolicy.RUNTIME)
@Target(ElementType.METHOD)
public @interface Mandatory {
}
```

And then you can apply this annotation to the setter methods of the required properties.

```
package com.apress.springrecipes.sequence;

public class SequenceGenerator {

    private PrefixGenerator prefixGenerator;
    private String suffix;
    ...
    @Mandatory
```

```
    public void setPrefixGenerator(PrefixGenerator prefixGenerator) {
        this.prefixGenerator = prefixGenerator;
    }

    @Mandatory
    public void setSuffix(String suffix) {
        this.suffix = suffix;
    }
    ...
}
```

To check for the properties with this annotation type, you have to specify it in the `requiredAnnotationType` property of `RequiredAnnotationBeanPostProcessor`.

```
<bean class="org.springframework.beans.factory.annotation.➥
    RequiredAnnotationBeanPostProcessor">
    <property name="requiredAnnotationType">
        <value>com.apress.springrecipes.sequence.Mandatory</value>
    </property>
</bean>
```

3-7. Auto-Wiring Beans with XML Configuration

Problem

When a bean requires access to another bean, you can wire it by specifying the reference explicitly. However, if your container can wire your beans automatically, it can save you the trouble of configuring the wirings manually.

Solution

The Spring IoC container can help you to wire your beans automatically. You only have to specify the auto-wiring mode in the `autowire` attribute of `<bean>`. Table 3-2 lists the auto-wiring modes supported by Spring.

Table 3-2. *Auto-Wiring Modes Supported by Spring*

Mode	Description
no*	No auto-wiring will be performed. You must wire the dependencies explicitly.
byName	For each bean property, wire a bean whose name is the same as the property's.
byType	For each bean property, wire a bean whose type is compatible with the property's. If more than one bean is found, an `UnsatisfiedDependencyException` will be thrown.
constructor	For each argument of each constructor, first find a bean whose type is compatible with the argument's. Then pick the constructor with the most matching arguments. In case of any ambiguity, an `UnsatisfiedDependencyException` will be thrown.

Mode	Description
autodetect	If a default constructor with no argument is found, the dependencies will be auto-wired by type. Otherwise, they will be auto-wired by constructor.

* *The default mode is* no, *but this can be changed by setting the* default-autowire *attribute of the* <beans> *root element. This default mode will be overridden by a bean's own mode if specified.*

Although the auto-wiring feature is very powerful, the cost is that it will reduce the readability of your bean configurations. As auto-wiring is performed by Spring at runtime, you cannot derive how your beans are wired from the bean configuration file. In practice, I recommend applying auto-wiring only in applications whose component dependencies are not complicated.

How It Works

Auto-Wiring by Type

You can set the autowire attribute of the sequenceGenerator bean to byType and leave the prefixGenerator property unset. Then Spring will attempt to wire a bean whose type is compatible with PrefixGenerator. In this case, the datePrefixGenerator bean will be wired automatically.

```
<beans ...>
    <bean id="sequenceGenerator"
        class="com.apress.springrecipes.sequence.SequenceGenerator"
        autowire="byType">
        <property name="initial" value="100000" />
        <property name="suffix" value="A" />
    </bean>

    <bean id="datePrefixGenerator"
        class="com.apress.springrecipes.sequence.DatePrefixGenerator">
        <property name="pattern" value="yyyyMMdd" />
    </bean>
</beans>
```

The main problem of auto-wiring by type is that sometimes there will be more than one bean in the IoC container compatible with the target type. In this case, Spring will not be able to decide which bean is most suitable for the property, and hence cannot perform auto-wiring. For example, if you have another prefix generator generating the current year as the prefix, auto-wiring by type will be broken immediately.

```
<beans ...>
    <bean id="sequenceGenerator"
        class="com.apress.springrecipes.sequence.SequenceGenerator"
        autowire="byType">
        <property name="initial" value="100000" />
        <property name="suffix" value="A" />
    </bean>
```

```
    <bean id="datePrefixGenerator"
        class="com.apress.springrecipes.sequence.DatePrefixGenerator">
        <property name="pattern" value="yyyyMMdd" />
    </bean>

    <bean id="yearPrefixGenerator"
        class="com.apress.springrecipes.sequence.DatePrefixGenerator">
        <property name="pattern" value="yyyy" />
    </bean>
</beans>
```

Spring will throw an UnsatisfiedDependencyException if more than one bean is found for auto-wiring.

```
Exception in thread "main"
org.springframework.beans.factory.UnsatisfiedDependencyException: Error creating
bean with name 'sequenceGenerator' defined in class path resource [beans.xml]:
Unsatisfied dependency expressed through bean property 'prefixGenerator': No unique
bean of type [com.apress.springrecipes.sequence.PrefixGenerator] is defined:
expected single matching bean but found 2: [datePrefixGenerator,
yearPrefixGenerator]
```

Auto-Wiring by Name

Another mode of auto-wiring is byName, which can sometimes resolve the problems of auto-wiring by type. It works very similarly to byType, but in this case, Spring will attempt to wire a bean with the same name, rather than with the compatible type. As the bean name is unique within a container, auto-wiring by name will not cause ambiguity.

```
<beans ...>
    <bean id="sequenceGenerator"
        class="com.apress.springrecipes.sequence.SequenceGenerator"
        autowire="byName">
        <property name="initial" value="100000" />
        <property name="suffix" value="A" />
    </bean>

    <bean id="prefixGenerator"
        class="com.apress.springrecipes.sequence.DatePrefixGenerator">
        <property name="pattern" value="yyyyMMdd" />
    </bean>
</beans>
```

However, auto-wiring by name will not work in all cases. Sometimes it's not possible for you to make the name of the target bean the same as your property. In practice, you often need to specify ambiguous dependencies explicitly, while keeping others auto-wired. That means you employ a mixture of explicit wiring and auto-wiring.

Auto-Wiring by Constructor

The auto-wiring mode constructor works like byType, but it's rather more complicated. For a bean with a single constructor, Spring will attempt to wire a bean with a compatible type for each constructor argument. But for a bean with multiple constructors, the process is more complicated. Spring will first attempt to find a bean with a compatible type for each argument of each constructor. Then it will pick the constructor with the most matching arguments.

Suppose that SequenceGenerator has one default constructor and one constructor with an argument PrefixGenerator.

```
package com.apress.springrecipes.sequence;

public class SequenceGenerator {

    public SequenceGenerator() {}

    public SequenceGenerator(PrefixGenerator prefixGenerator) {
        this.prefixGenerator = prefixGenerator;
    }
    ...
}
```

In this case, the second constructor will be matched and picked because Spring can find a bean whose type is compatible with PrefixGenerator.

```
<beans ...>
    <bean id="sequenceGenerator"
        class="com.apress.springrecipes.sequence.SequenceGenerator"
        autowire="constructor">
        <property name="initial" value="100000" />
        <property name="suffix" value="A" />
    </bean>

    <bean id="datePrefixGenerator"
        class="com.apress.springrecipes.sequence.DatePrefixGenerator">
        <property name="pattern" value="yyyyMMdd" />
    </bean>
</beans>
```

However, multiple constructors in a class may cause ambiguity in constructor argument matching. The situation may be further complicated if you ask Spring to determine a constructor for you. So, if you use this auto-wiring mode, take great care to avoid ambiguity.

Auto-Wiring by Auto-Detection

The auto-wiring mode autodetect asks Spring to decide the auto-wiring mode between byType and constructor. If a default constructor with no argument is found for that bean, byType will be chosen. Otherwise, constructor will be chosen. As the SequenceGenerator class has a default constructor defined, byType will be chosen. That means the prefix generator will be injected via the setter method.

```
<beans ...>
    <bean id="sequenceGenerator"
        class="com.apress.springrecipes.sequence.SequenceGenerator"
        autowire="autodetect">
        <property name="initial" value="100000" />
        <property name="suffix" value="A" />
    </bean>

    <bean id="datePrefixGenerator"
        class="com.apress.springrecipes.sequence.DatePrefixGenerator">
        <property name="pattern" value="yyyyMMdd" />
    </bean>
</beans>
```

Auto-Wiring and Dependency Checking

As you have seen, if Spring finds more than one candidate bean for auto-wiring, it will throw an `UnsatisfiedDependencyException`. On the other hand, if the auto-wiring mode is set to `byName` or `byType`, and Spring cannot find a matching bean to wire, it will leave the property unset, which may cause a `NullPointerException` or a value that has not been initialized. However, if you would like to be notified when auto-wiring cannot wire your beans, you should set the `dependency-check` attribute to `objects` or `all`. In that case, an `UnsatisfiedDependencyException` will be thrown whenever auto-wiring doesn't work.

```
<bean id="sequenceGenerator"
    class="com.apress.springrecipes.sequence.SequenceGenerator"
    autowire="byName" dependency-check="objects">
    <property name="initial" value="100000" />
    <property name="suffix" value="A" />
</bean>
```

3-8. Auto-Wiring Beans with @Autowired and @Resource

Problem

Auto-wiring by setting the `autowire` attribute in the bean configuration file will wire all properties of a bean. It's not flexible enough to wire particular properties only. Moreover, you can only auto-wire beans either by type or by name. If neither strategy satisfies your requirements, you must wire your beans explicitly.

Solution

Spring 2.5 makes extensive enhancements to the auto-wiring feature. You can auto-wire a particular property by annotating a setter method, a constructor, a field, or even an arbitrary method with the `@Autowired` annotation, or the `@Resource` annotation defined in JSR-250: Common Annotations for the Java Platform. That means you have one more option besides setting the `autowire` attribute to satisfy your requirements. However, this annotation-based option requires you to be using Java 1.5 or higher.

How It Works

To ask Spring to auto-wire the bean properties with @Autowired or @Resource, you have to register an AutowiredAnnotationBeanPostProcessor instance in the IoC container. If you are using a bean factory, you have to register this bean post processor through the API. Otherwise, you can just declare an instance of it in your application context.

```
<bean class="org.springframework.beans.factory.annotation.➥
    AutowiredAnnotationBeanPostProcessor" />
```

Or you can simply include the <context:annotation-config> element in your bean configuration file and an AutowiredAnnotationBeanPostProcessor instance will automatically get registered.

```
<beans xmlns="http://www.springframework.org/schema/beans"
    xmlns:xsi="http://www.w3.org/2001/XMLSchema-instance"
    xmlns:context="http://www.springframework.org/schema/context"
    xsi:schemaLocation="http://www.springframework.org/schema/beans
        http://www.springframework.org/schema/beans/spring-beans-2.5.xsd
        http://www.springframework.org/schema/context
        http://www.springframework.org/schema/context/spring-context-2.5.xsd">

    <context:annotation-config />
    ...
</beans>
```

Auto-Wiring a Single Bean of Compatible Type

The @Autowired annotation can be applied to a particular property for Spring to auto-wire it. As an example, you can annotate the setter method of the prefixGenerator property with @Autowired. Then Spring will attempt to wire a bean whose type is compatible with PrefixGenerator.

```
package com.apress.springrecipes.sequence;

import org.springframework.beans.factory.annotation.Autowired;

public class SequenceGenerator {
    ...
    @Autowired
    public void setPrefixGenerator(PrefixGenerator prefixGenerator) {
        this.prefixGenerator = prefixGenerator;
    }
}
```

If you have a bean whose type is compatible with PrefixGenerator defined in the IoC container, it will be set to the prefixGenerator property automatically.

```
<beans ...>
    ...
    <bean id="sequenceGenerator"
        class="com.apress.springrecipes.sequence.SequenceGenerator">
        <property name="initial" value="100000" />
        <property name="suffix" value="A" />
    </bean>

    <bean id="datePrefixGenerator"
        class="com.apress.springrecipes.sequence.DatePrefixGenerator">
        <property name="pattern" value="yyyyMMdd" />
    </bean>
</beans>
```

By default, all the properties with @Autowired are required. When Spring can't find a matching bean to wire, it will throw an exception. If you would like a certain property to be optional, set the required attribute of @Autowired to false. Then when Spring can't find a matching bean, it will leave this property unset.

```
package com.apress.springrecipes.sequence;

import org.springframework.beans.factory.annotation.Autowired;

public class SequenceGenerator {
    ...
    @Autowired(required = false)
    public void setPrefixGenerator(PrefixGenerator prefixGenerator) {
        this.prefixGenerator = prefixGenerator;
    }
}
```

In addition to the setter method, the @Autowired annotation can also be applied to a constructor. Then Spring will attempt to find a bean with the compatible type for each of the constructor arguments.

```
package com.apress.springrecipes.sequence;

import org.springframework.beans.factory.annotation.Autowired;

public class SequenceGenerator {
    ...
    @Autowired
    public SequenceGenerator(PrefixGenerator prefixGenerator) {
        this.prefixGenerator = prefixGenerator;
    }
}
```

The @Autowired annotation can also be applied to a field, even if it is not declared as public. In this way, you can omit the need of declaring a setter method or a constructor for this field. Spring will inject the matched bean into this field via reflection. However, annotating a non-public field with @Autowired will reduce code testability since the code will be difficult to unit test.

```
package com.apress.springrecipes.sequence;

import org.springframework.beans.factory.annotation.Autowired;

public class SequenceGenerator {

    @Autowired
    private PrefixGenerator prefixGenerator;
    ...
}
```

You may even apply the @Autowired annotation to a method with an arbitrary name and an arbitrary number of arguments. Then Spring will attempt to wire a bean with the compatible type for each of the method arguments.

```
package com.apress.springrecipes.sequence;

import org.springframework.beans.factory.annotation.Autowired;

public class SequenceGenerator {
    ...
    @Autowired
    public void inject(PrefixGenerator prefixGenerator) {
        this.prefixGenerator = prefixGenerator;
    }
}
```

Auto-Wiring All Beans of Compatible Type

The @Autowired annotation can also be applied to a property of array type to have Spring auto-wire all the matching beans. For example, you can annotate a PrefixGenerator[] property with @Autowired. Then Spring will auto-wire all the beans whose type is compatible with PrefixGenerator at one time.

```
package com.apress.springrecipes.sequence;

import org.springframework.beans.factory.annotation.Autowired;

public class SequenceGenerator {

    @Autowired
    private PrefixGenerator[] prefixGenerators;
    ...
}
```

If you have multiple beans whose type is compatible with the PrefixGenerator defined in the IoC container, they will be added to the prefixGenerators array automatically.

```
<beans ...>
    ...
    <bean id="datePrefixGenerator"
        class="com.apress.springrecipes.sequence.DatePrefixGenerator">
        <property name="pattern" value="yyyyMMdd" />
    </bean>

    <bean id="yearPrefixGenerator"
        class="com.apress.springrecipes.sequence.DatePrefixGenerator">
        <property name="pattern" value="yyyy" />
    </bean>
</beans>
```

In a similar way, you can apply the @Autowired annotation to a type-safe collection. Spring is able to read the type information of this collection and auto-wire all the beans whose type is compatible.

```
package com.apress.springrecipes.sequence;

import org.springframework.beans.factory.annotation.Autowired;

public class SequenceGenerator {

    @Autowired
    private List<PrefixGenerator> prefixGenerators;
    ...
}
```

If Spring notices that the @Autowired annotation is applied to a type-safe java.util.Map with strings as the keys, it will add all the beans of the compatible type, with the bean names as the keys, to this map.

```
package com.apress.springrecipes.sequence;

import org.springframework.beans.factory.annotation.Autowired;

public class SequenceGenerator {

    @Autowired
    private Map<String, PrefixGenerator> prefixGenerators;
    ...
}
```

Auto-Wiring by Type with Qualifiers

By default, auto-wiring by type will not work when there is more than one bean with the compatible type in the IoC container. However, Spring allows you to specify a candidate bean by providing its name in the @Qualifier annotation.

```
package com.apress.springrecipes.sequence;

import org.springframework.beans.factory.annotation.Autowired;
import org.springframework.beans.factory.annotation.Qualifier;

public class SequenceGenerator {

    @Autowired
    @Qualifier("datePrefixGenerator")
    private PrefixGenerator prefixGenerator;
    ...
}
```

Then Spring will attempt to find a bean with that name in the IoC container and wire it into the property.

```
<bean id="datePrefixGenerator"
    class="com.apress.springrecipes.sequence.DatePrefixGenerator">
    <property name="pattern" value="yyyyMMdd" />
</bean>
```

The @Qualifier annotation can also be applied to a method argument for auto-wiring.

```
package com.apress.springrecipes.sequence;

import org.springframework.beans.factory.annotation.Autowired;
import org.springframework.beans.factory.annotation.Qualifier;

public class SequenceGenerator {
    ...
    @Autowired
    public void inject(
            @Qualifier("datePrefixGenerator") PrefixGenerator prefixGenerator) {
        this.prefixGenerator = prefixGenerator;
    }
}
```

You can further create a custom qualifier annotation type for the auto-wiring purpose. This annotation type must be annotated with @Qualifier itself.

```
package com.apress.springrecipes.sequence;
...
import org.springframework.beans.factory.annotation.Qualifier;
```

```
@Retention(RetentionPolicy.RUNTIME)
@Target({ElementType.FIELD, ElementType.PARAMETER })
@Qualifier
public @interface Generator {

    String value();
}
```

Then you can apply this annotation to an @Autowired bean property. It will ask Spring to auto-wire the bean with this qualifier annotation and the specified value.

```
package com.apress.springrecipes.sequence;

import org.springframework.beans.factory.annotation.Autowired;

public class SequenceGenerator {

    @Autowired
    @Generator("prefix")
    private PrefixGenerator prefixGenerator;
    ...
}
```

You have to provide this qualifier to the target bean that you want to be auto-wired into the preceding property. The qualifier is added by the <qualifier> element with the type attribute. The qualifier value is specified in the value attribute.

```
<bean id="datePrefixGenerator"
    class="com.apress.springrecipes.sequence.DatePrefixGenerator">
    <qualifier type="Generator" value="prefix" />
    <property name="pattern" value="yyyyMMdd" />
</bean>
```

Auto-Wiring by Name

If you would like to auto-wire bean properties by name, you can annotate a setter method, a constructor, or a field with the JSR-250 @Resource annotation. By default, Spring will attempt to find a bean with the same name as this property. But you can specify the bean name explicitly in its name attribute.

Note To use the JSR-250 annotations, you have to include common-annotations.jar (located in the lib/j2ee directory of the Spring installation) in your classpath. However, if your application is running on Java SE 6 or Java EE 5, you needn't include this JAR file.

```
package com.apress.springrecipes.sequence;

import javax.annotation.Resource;

public class SequenceGenerator {

    @Resource(name = "datePrefixGenerator")
    private PrefixGenerator prefixGenerator;
    ...
}
```

3-9. Inheriting Bean Configuration

Problem

When configuring beans in the Spring IoC container, you may have more than one bean sharing some common configurations, such as bean properties and attributes in the <bean> element. You often have to repeat these configurations for multiple beans.

Solution

Spring allows you to extract the common bean configurations to form a *parent bean*. The beans that inherit from this parent bean are called *child beans*. The child beans will inherit the bean configurations, including bean properties and attributes in the <bean> element, from the parent bean to avoid duplicate configurations. The child beans can also override the inherited configurations when necessary.

The parent bean can act as a configuration template and also as a bean instance at the same time. However, if you want the parent bean to act only as a template that cannot be retrieved, you must set the abstract attribute to true, asking Spring not to instantiate this bean.

You must note that not all attributes defined in the parent <bean> element will be inherited. For example, the autowire and dependency-check attributes will not be inherited from the parent. To find out more about which attributes will be inherited from the parent and which won't, please refer to the Spring documentation about bean inheritance.

How It Works

Suppose you need to add a new sequence generator instance whose initial value and suffix are the same as the existing ones.

```
<beans ...>
    <bean id="sequenceGenerator"
        class="com.apress.springrecipes.sequence.SequenceGenerator">
        <property name="initial" value="100000" />
        <property name="suffix" value="A" />
        <property name="prefixGenerator" ref="datePrefixGenerator" />
    </bean>
```

```
    <bean id="sequenceGenerator1"
        class="com.apress.springrecipes.sequence.SequenceGenerator">
        <property name="initial" value="100000" />
        <property name="suffix" value="A" />
        <property name="prefixGenerator" ref="datePrefixGenerator" />
    </bean>

    <bean id="datePrefixGenerator"
        class="com.apress.springrecipes.sequence.DatePrefixGenerator">
        <property name="pattern" value="yyyyMMdd" />
    </bean>
</beans>
```

To avoid duplicating the same properties, you can declare a base sequence generator bean with those properties set. Then the two sequence generators can inherit this base generator so that they also have those properties set automatically. You needn't specify the `class` attributes of the child beans if they are the same as the parent's.

```
<beans ...>
    <bean id="baseSequenceGenerator"
        class="com.apress.springrecipes.sequence.SequenceGenerator">
        <property name="initial" value="100000" />
        <property name="suffix" value="A" />
        <property name="prefixGenerator" ref="datePrefixGenerator" />
    </bean>

    <bean id="sequenceGenerator" parent="baseSequenceGenerator" />

    <bean id="sequenceGenerator1" parent="baseSequenceGenerator" />
    ...
</beans>
```

The inherited properties can be overridden by the child beans. For example, you can add a child sequence generator with a different initial value.

```
<beans ...>
    <bean id="baseSequenceGenerator"
        class="com.apress.springrecipes.sequence.SequenceGenerator">
        <property name="initial" value="100000" />
        <property name="suffix" value="A" />
        <property name="prefixGenerator" ref="datePrefixGenerator" />
    </bean>

    <bean id="sequenceGenerator2" parent="baseSequenceGenerator">
        <property name="initial" value="200000" />
    </bean>
    ...
</beans>
```

The base sequence generator bean can now be retrieved as a bean instance to use. If you want it to act as a template only, you have to set the `abstract` attribute to `true`. Then Spring will not instantiate this bean.

```
<bean id="baseSequenceGenerator" abstract="true"
    class="com.apress.springrecipes.sequence.SequenceGenerator">
    ...
</bean>
```

You can also omit the class of the parent bean and let the child beans specify their own, especially when the parent bean and child beans are not in the same class hierarchy, but share some properties of the same name. In this case, the parent bean's `abstract` attribute must be set to `true`, as the parent bean can't be instantiated. For example, let's add another `ReverseGenerator` class that has an `initial` property also.

```
package com.apress.springrecipes.sequence;

public class ReverseGenerator {

    private int initial;

    public void setInitial(int initial) {
        this.initial = initial;
    }
}
```

Now `SequenceGenerator` and `ReverseGenerator` don't extend the same base class—that is, they're not in the same class hierarchy, but they have a property of the same name: `initial`. To extract this common `initial` property, you need a `baseGenerator` parent bean with no `class` attribute defined.

```
<beans ...>
    <bean id="baseGenerator" abstract="true">
        <property name="initial" value="100000" />
    </bean>

    <bean id="baseSequenceGenerator" abstract="true" parent="baseGenerator"
        class="com.apress.springrecipes.sequence.SequenceGenerator">
        <property name="suffix" value="A" />
        <property name="prefixGenerator" ref="datePrefixGenerator" />
    </bean>

    <bean id="reverseGenerator" parent="baseGenerator"
        class="com.apress.springrecipes.sequence.ReverseGenerator" />

    <bean id="sequenceGenerator" parent="baseSequenceGenerator" />

    <bean id="sequenceGenerator1" parent="baseSequenceGenerator" />
```

```
    <bean id="sequenceGenerator2" parent="baseSequenceGenerator">
        ...
    </bean>
    ...
</beans>
```

Figure 3-3 shows the object diagram for this generator bean hierarchy.

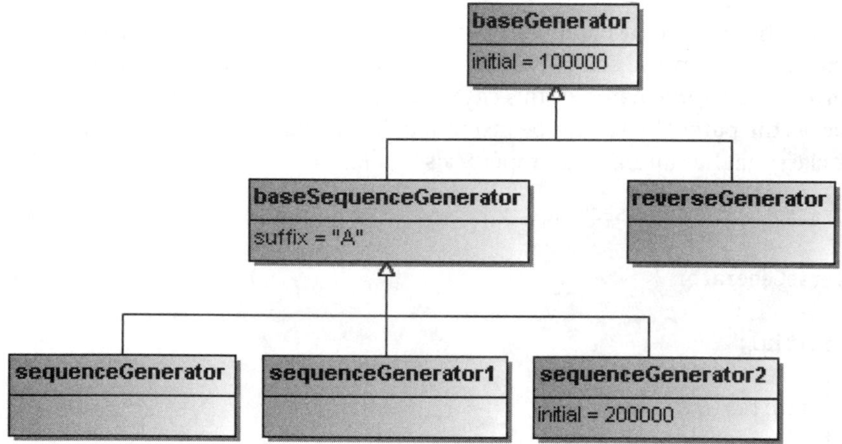

Figure 3-3. *Object diagram for the generator bean hierarchy*

3-10. Defining Collections for Bean Properties

Problem

Sometimes your bean properties may be of a collection type that contains multiple elements. You would like to configure these collection properties in Spring's bean configuration file rather than by coding.

Solution

The Java Collections framework defines a set of interfaces, implementations, and algorithms for different types of collections, such as lists, sets, and maps. Figure 3-4 shows a simplified UML class diagram that may help you to understand the Java Collections framework better.

`List`, `Set`, and `Map` are the core interfaces representing three main types of collections. For each collection type, Java provides several implementations with different functions and characteristics from which you can choose. In Spring, these types of collections can be easily configured with a group of built-in XML tags, such as `<list>`, `<set>`, and `<map>`.

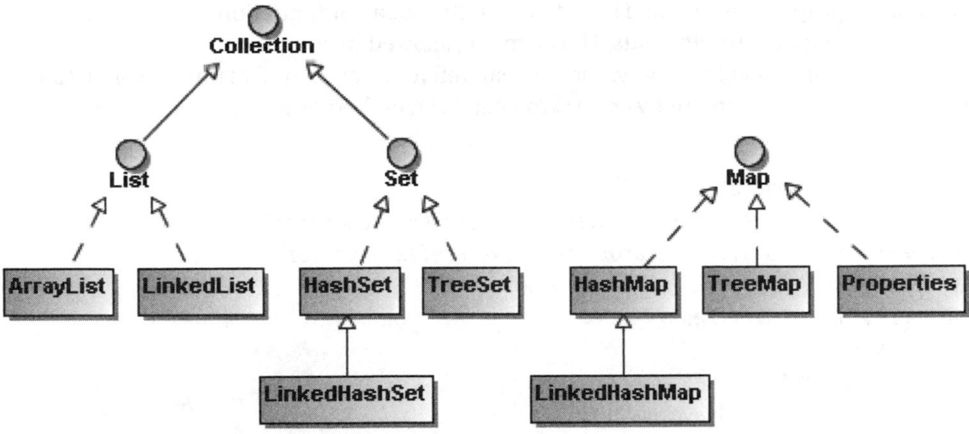

Figure 3-4. *Simplified class diagram for the Java Collections framework*

How It Works

Suppose you are going to allow more than one suffix for your sequence generator. The suffixes will be appended to the sequence numbers with hyphens as the separators. You may consider accepting suffixes of arbitrary data types and converting them into strings when appending to the sequence numbers.

Lists, Arrays, and Sets

First, let's use a `java.util.List` collection to contain your suffixes. A *list* is an ordered and indexed collection whose elements can be accessed either by index or with a for-each loop.

```
package com.apress.springrecipes.sequence;
...
public class SequenceGenerator {
    ...
    private List<Object> suffixes;

    public void setSuffixes(List<Object> suffixes) {
        this.suffixes = suffixes;
    }

    public synchronized String getSequence() {
        StringBuffer buffer = new StringBuffer();
        ...
        for (Object suffix : suffixes) {
            buffer.append("-");
            buffer.append(suffix);
        }
        return buffer.toString();
    }
}
```

To define a property of java.util.List type in the bean configuration, you specify a <list> tag that contains the elements. The elements allowed inside the <list> tag can be a simple constant value specified by <value>, a bean reference by <ref>, an inner bean definition by <bean>, or a null element by <null>. You can even embed other collections in a collection.

```
<bean id="sequenceGenerator"
    class="com.apress.springrecipes.sequence.SequenceGenerator">
    <property name="prefixGenerator" ref="datePrefixGenerator" />
    <property name="initial" value="100000" />
    <property name="suffixes">
        <list>
            <value>A</value>
            <bean class="java.net.URL">
                <constructor-arg value="http" />
                <constructor-arg value="www.apress.com" />
                <constructor-arg value="/" />
            </bean>
            <null />
        </list>
    </property>
</bean>
```

Conceptually, an *array* is very similar to a list in that it's also an ordered and indexed collection that can be accessed by index. The main difference is that the length of an array is fixed and cannot be extended dynamically. In the Java Collections framework, an array and a list can be converted to each other through the Arrays.asList() and List.toArray() methods. For your sequence generator, you can use an Object[] array to contain the suffixes and access them either by index or with a for-each loop.

```
package com.apress.springrecipes.sequence;
...
public class SequenceGenerator {
    ...
    private Object[] suffixes;

    public void setSuffixes(Object[] suffixes) {
        this.suffixes = suffixes;
    }
    ...
}
```

The definition of an array in the bean configuration file is identical to a list denoted by the <list> tag.

```
<bean id="sequenceGenerator"
    class="com.apress.springrecipes.sequence.SequenceGenerator">
    ...
    <property name="suffixes">
```

```
        <list>
            <value>A</value>
            <bean class="java.net.URL">
                <constructor-arg value="http" />
                <constructor-arg value="www.apress.com" />
                <constructor-arg value="/" />
            </bean>
            <null />
        </list>
    </property>
</bean>
```

Another common collection type is a *set*. As you see in Figure 3-4, both `java.util.List` and `java.util.Set` extend the same interface, `java.util.Collection`. A set differs from a list in that it is neither ordered nor indexed, and it can store unique objects only. That means no duplicate element can be contained in a set. When the same element is added to a set for the second time, it will replace the old one. The equality of elements is determined by the `equals()` method.

```
package com.apress.springrecipes.sequence;
...
public class SequenceGenerator {
    ...
    private Set<Object> suffixes;

    public void setSuffixes(Set<Object> suffixes) {
        this.suffixes = suffixes;
    }
    ...
}
```

To define a property of `java.util.Set` type, use the `<set>` tag to define the elements in the same way as a list.

```
<bean id="sequenceGenerator"
    class="com.apress.springrecipes.sequence.SequenceGenerator">
    ...
    <property name="suffixes">
        <set>
            <value>A</value>
            <bean class="java.net.URL">
                <constructor-arg value="http" />
                <constructor-arg value="www.apress.com" />
                <constructor-arg value="/" />
            </bean>
            <null />
        </set>
    </property>
</bean>
```

Although there's not an order concept in the original set semantics, Spring preserves the order of your elements by using java.util.LinkedHashSet, an implementation of the java.util.Set interface that does preserve element order.

Maps and Properties

A *map* is a table that stores its entries in key/value pairs. You can get a particular value from a map by its key, and also iterate the map entries with a for-each loop. Both the keys and values of a map can be of arbitrary type. Equality between keys is also determined by the equals() method. For example, you can modify your sequence generator to accept a java.util.Map collection that contains suffixes with keys.

```
package com.apress.springrecipes.sequence;
...
public class SequenceGenerator {
    ...
    private Map<Object, Object> suffixes;

    public void setSuffixes(Map<Object, Object> suffixes) {
        this.suffixes = suffixes;
    }

    public synchronized String getSequence() {
        StringBuffer buffer = new StringBuffer();
        ...
        for (Map.Entry entry : suffixes.entrySet()) {
            buffer.append("-");
            buffer.append(entry.getKey());
            buffer.append("@");
            buffer.append(entry.getValue());
        }
        return buffer.toString();
    }
}
```

In Spring, a map is defined by the <map> tag, with multiple <entry> tags as children. Each entry contains a key and a value. The key must be defined inside the <key> tag. There is no restriction on the type of the key and value, so you are free to specify a <value>, <ref>, <bean>, or <null> element for them. Spring will also preserve the order of the map entries by using java.util.LinkedHashMap.

```
<bean id="sequenceGenerator"
    class="com.apress.springrecipes.sequence.SequenceGenerator">
    ...
    <property name="suffixes">
        <map>
            <entry>
                <key>
                    <value>type</value>
```

```
                </key>
                <value>A</value>
            </entry>
            <entry>
                <key>
                    <value>url</value>
                </key>
                <bean class="java.net.URL">
                    <constructor-arg value="http" />
                    <constructor-arg value="www.apress.com" />
                    <constructor-arg value="/" />
                </bean>
            </entry>
        </map>
    </property>
</bean>
```

There are shortcuts to defining map keys and values as attributes of the <entry> tag. If they are simple constant values, you can define them by key and value. If they are bean references, you can define them by key-ref and value-ref.

```
<bean id="sequenceGenerator"
    class="com.apress.springrecipes.sequence.SequenceGenerator">
    ...
    <property name="suffixes">
        <map>
            <entry key="type" value="A" />
            <entry key="url">
                <bean class="java.net.URL">
                    <constructor-arg value="http" />
                    <constructor-arg value="www.apress.com" />
                    <constructor-arg value="/" />
                </bean>
            </entry>
        </map>
    </property>
</bean>
```

A java.util.Properties collection is very similar to a map. It also implements the java.util.Map interface and stores entries in key/value pairs. The only difference is that the keys and values of a Properties collection are always strings.

```
package com.apress.springrecipes.sequence;
...
public class SequenceGenerator {
    ...
    private Properties suffixes;
```

```
    public void setSuffixes(Properties suffixes) {
        this.suffixes = suffixes;
    }
    ...
}
```

To define a java.util.Properties collection in Spring, use the <props> tag with multiple <prop> tags as children. Each <prop> tag must have a key attribute defined and the corresponding value enclosed.

```
<bean id="sequenceGenerator"
    class="com.apress.springrecipes.sequence.SequenceGenerator">
    ...
    <property name="suffixes">
        <props>
            <prop key="type">A</prop>
            <prop key="url">http://www.apress.com/</prop>
        </props>
    </property>
</bean>
```

Merging the Collection of the Parent Bean

If you define your beans with inheritance, a child bean's collection can be merged with that of its parent by setting the merge attribute to true. For a <list> collection, the child elements will be appended after the parent's to preserve the order. So, the following sequence generator will have four suffixes: A, B, A, and C.

```
<beans ...>
    <bean id="baseSequenceGenerator"
        class="com.apress.springrecipes.sequence.SequenceGenerator">
        <property name="prefixGenerator" ref="datePrefixGenerator" />
        <property name="initial" value="100000" />
        <property name="suffixes">
            <list>
                <value>A</value>
                <value>B</value>
            </list>
        </property>
    </bean>

    <bean id="sequenceGenerator" parent="baseSequenceGenerator">
        <property name="suffixes">
            <list merge="true">
                <value>A</value>
                <value>C</value>
            </list>
        </property>
```

```
    </bean>
    ...
</beans>
```

For a <set> or <map> collection, the child elements will overwrite the parent's if they have the same value. So, the following sequence generator will have three suffixes: A, B, and C.

```
<beans ...>
    <bean id="baseSequenceGenerator"
        class="com.apress.springrecipes.sequence.SequenceGenerator">
        <property name="prefixGenerator" ref="datePrefixGenerator" />
        <property name="initial" value="100000" />
        <property name="suffixes">
            <set>
                <value>A</value>
                <value>B</value>
            </set>
        </property>
    </bean>

    <bean id="sequenceGenerator" parent="baseSequenceGenerator">
        <property name="suffixes">
            <set merge="true">
                <value>A</value>
                <value>C</value>
            </set>
        </property>
    </bean>
    ...
</beans>
```

3-11. Specifying the Data Type for Collection Elements

Problem

By default, Spring treats every element in a collection as a string. You have to specify the data type for your collection elements if you are not going to use them as strings.

Solution

You can either specify the data type for each collection element by the type attribute of the <value> tag, or specify the data type for all elements by the value-type attribute of the collection tag. If you are using Java 1.5 or higher, you can define a type-safe collection so that Spring will read your collection's type information.

How It Works

Now suppose you are going to accept a list of integer numbers as the suffixes of your sequence generator. Each number will be formatted into four digits by an instance of `java.text.DecimalFormat`.

```
package com.apress.springrecipes.sequence;
...
public class SequenceGenerator {
    ...
    private List<Object> suffixes;

    public void setSuffixes(List<Object> suffixes) {
        this.suffixes = suffixes;
    }

    public synchronized String getSequence() {
        StringBuffer buffer = new StringBuffer();
        ...
        DecimalFormat formatter = new DecimalFormat("0000");
        for (Object suffix : suffixes) {
            buffer.append("-");
            buffer.append(formatter.format((Integer) suffix));
        }
        return buffer.toString();
    }
}
```

Then define several suffixes for your sequence generator in the bean configuration file as usual.

```
<bean id="sequenceGenerator"
    class="com.apress.springrecipes.sequence.SequenceGenerator">
    <property name="prefixGenerator" ref="datePrefixGenerator" />
    <property name="initial" value="100000" />
    <property name="suffixes">
        <list>
            <value>5</value>
            <value>10</value>
            <value>20</value>
        </list>
    </property>
</bean>
```

However, when you run this application, you will encounter a `ClassCastException`, indicating that the suffixes cannot be cast into integers because their type is `String`. Spring treats every element in a collection as a string by default. You have to set the `type` attribute of the `<value>` tag to specify the element type.

```
<bean id="sequenceGenerator"
    class="com.apress.springrecipes.sequence.SequenceGenerator">
    ...
    <property name="suffixes">
        <list>
            <value type="int">5</value>
            <value type="int">10</value>
            <value type="int">20</value>
        </list>
    </property>
</bean>
```

Or you may set the value-type attribute of the collection tag to specify the type for all elements in this collection.

```
<bean id="sequenceGenerator"
    class="com.apress.springrecipes.sequence.SequenceGenerator">
    ...
    <property name="suffixes">
        <list value-type="int">
            <value>5</value>
            <value>10</value>
            <value>20</value>
        </list>
    </property>
</bean>
```

In Java 1.5 or higher, you can define your suffixes list with a type-safe collection that stores integers.

```
package com.apress.springrecipes.sequence;
...
public class SequenceGenerator {
    ...
    private List<Integer> suffixes;

    public void setSuffixes(List<Integer> suffixes) {
        this.suffixes = suffixes;
    }

    public synchronized String getSequence() {
        StringBuffer buffer = new StringBuffer();
        ...
        DecimalFormat formatter = new DecimalFormat("0000");
        for (int suffix : suffixes) {
            buffer.append("-");
            buffer.append(formatter.format(suffix));
        }
```

```
        return buffer.toString();
    }
}
```

Once you have defined your collections in a type-safe way, Spring will be able to read the collection's type information through reflection. In this way, you no longer need to specify the value-type attribute of <list>.

```
<bean id="sequenceGenerator"
    class="com.apress.springrecipes.sequence.SequenceGenerator">
    ...
    <property name="suffixes">
        <list>
            <value>5</value>
            <value>10</value>
            <value>20</value>
        </list>
    </property>
</bean>
```

3-12. Defining Collections Using Factory Beans and the Utility Schema

Problem

When using the basic collection tags to define collections, you can't specify the concrete class of a collection, such as LinkedList, TreeSet, or TreeMap. Moreover, you cannot share a collection among different beans by defining it as a stand-alone bean for other beans to refer to.

Solution

Spring provides a couple of options to overcome the shortcomings of the basic collection tags. One option is to use corresponding collection factory beans like ListFactoryBean, SetFactoryBean, and MapFactoryBean. A *factory bean* is a special kind of Spring bean that is used for creating another bean. The second option is to use collection tags such as <util:list>, <util:set>, and <util:map> in the util schema introduced in Spring 2.x.

How It Works

Specifying the Concrete Class for Collections

You can use a collection factory bean to define a collection and specify its target class. For example, you can specify the targetSetClass property for SetFactoryBean. Then Spring will instantiate the specified class for this collection.

```
<bean id="sequenceGenerator"
    class="com.apress.springrecipes.sequence.SequenceGenerator">
    <property name="prefixGenerator" ref="datePrefixGenerator" />
    <property name="initial" value="100000" />
```

```
    <property name="suffixes">
        <bean class="org.springframework.beans.factory.config.SetFactoryBean">
            <property name="targetSetClass">
                <value>java.util.TreeSet</value>
            </property>
            <property name="sourceSet">
                <set>
                    <value>5</value>
                    <value>10</value>
                    <value>20</value>
                </set>
            </property>
        </bean>
    </property>
</bean>
```

Or you can use a collection tag in the `util` schema to define a collection and set its target class (e.g., by the `set-class` attribute of `<util:set>`). But you must remember to add the `util` schema definition to your `<beans>` root element.

```
<beans xmlns="http://www.springframework.org/schema/beans"
    xmlns:xsi="http://www.w3.org/2001/XMLSchema-instance"
    xmlns:util="http://www.springframework.org/schema/util"
    xsi:schemaLocation="http://www.springframework.org/schema/beans
        http://www.springframework.org/schema/beans/spring-beans-2.5.xsd
        http://www.springframework.org/schema/util
        http://www.springframework.org/schema/util/spring-util-2.5.xsd">

    <bean id="sequenceGenerator"
        class="com.apress.springrecipes.sequence.SequenceGenerator">
        ...
        <property name="suffixes">
            <util:set set-class="java.util.TreeSet">
                <value>5</value>
                <value>10</value>
                <value>20</value>
            </util:set>
        </property>
    </bean>
    ...
</beans>
```

Defining Stand-Alone Collections

Another advantage of collection factory beans is that you can define a collection as a stand-alone bean for other beans to refer to. For example, you can define a stand-alone set by using `SetFactoryBean`.

```
<beans ...>
    <bean id="sequenceGenerator"
        class="com.apress.springrecipes.sequence.SequenceGenerator">
        ...
        <property name="suffixes">
            <ref local="suffixes" />
        </property>
    </bean>

    <bean id="suffixes"
        class="org.springframework.beans.factory.config.SetFactoryBean">
        <property name="sourceSet">
            <set>
                <value>5</value>
                <value>10</value>
                <value>20</value>
            </set>
        </property>
    </bean>
    ...
</beans>
```

Or you can define a stand-alone set by using the `<util:set>` tag in the `util` schema.

```
<beans ...>
    <bean id="sequenceGenerator"
        class="com.apress.springrecipes.sequence.SequenceGenerator">
        ...
        <property name="suffixes">
            <ref local="suffixes" />
        </property>
    </bean>

    <util:set id="suffixes">
        <value>5</value>
        <value>10</value>
        <value>20</value>
    </util:set>
    ...
</beans>
```

3-13. Scanning Components from the Classpath

Problem

In order for the Spring IoC container to manage your components, you declare them one by one in the bean configuration file. However, it can save you a lot of work if Spring can automatically detect your components without manual configuration.

Solution

Spring 2.5 provides a powerful feature called *component scanning*. It can automatically scan, detect, and instantiate your components with particular stereotype annotations from the classpath. The basic annotation denoting a Spring-managed component is `@Component`. Other more particular stereotypes include `@Repository`, `@Service`, and `@Controller`. They denote components in the persistence, service, and presentation layers, respectively.

How It Works

Suppose you are asked to develop your sequence generator application using database sequences, and store the prefix and suffix of each sequence in a table. First, you create the domain class `Sequence` containing the `id`, `prefix`, and `suffix` properties.

```
package com.apress.springrecipes.sequence;

public class Sequence {

    private String id;
    private String prefix;
    private String suffix;

    // Constructors, Getters, and Setters
    ...
}
```

Then you create an interface for the Data Access Object (DAO), which is responsible for accessing data from the database. The `getSequence()` method loads a `Sequence` object from the table by its ID, while the `getNextValue()` method retrieves the next value of a particular database sequence.

```
package com.apress.springrecipes.sequence;

public interface SequenceDao {

    public Sequence getSequence(String sequenceId);
    public int getNextValue(String sequenceId);
}
```

In a production application, you should implement this DAO interface using a data access technology such as JDBC or object/relational mapping. But for testing purposes, let's use maps to store the sequence instances and values.

```
package com.apress.springrecipes.sequence;
...
public class SequenceDaoImpl implements SequenceDao {

    private Map<String, Sequence> sequences;
    private Map<String, Integer> values;
```

```
    public SequenceDaoImpl() {
        sequences = new HashMap<String, Sequence>();
        sequences.put("IT", new Sequence("IT", "30", "A"));
        values = new HashMap<String, Integer>();
        values.put("IT", 100000);
    }

    public Sequence getSequence(String sequenceId) {
        return sequences.get(sequenceId);
    }

    public synchronized int getNextValue(String sequenceId) {
        int value = values.get(sequenceId);
        values.put(sequenceId, value + 1);
        return value;
    }
}
```

You also need a service object, acting as a façade, to provide the sequence generation service. Internally, this service object will interact with the DAO to handle the sequence generation requests. So, it requires a reference to the DAO.

```
package com.apress.springrecipes.sequence;

public class SequenceService {

    private SequenceDao sequenceDao;

    public void setSequenceDao(SequenceDao sequenceDao) {
        this.sequenceDao = sequenceDao;
    }

    public String generate(String sequenceId) {
        Sequence sequence = sequenceDao.getSequence(sequenceId);
        int value = sequenceDao.getNextValue(sequenceId);
        return sequence.getPrefix() + value + sequence.getSuffix();
    }
}
```

Finally, you have to configure these components in the bean configuration file to make the sequence generator application work. You can auto-wire your components to reduce the amount of configurations.

```
<beans ...>
    <bean id="sequenceService"
        class="com.apress.springrecipes.sequence.SequenceService"
        autowire="byType" />
```

```
    <bean id="sequenceDao"
        class="com.apress.springrecipes.sequence.SequenceDaoImpl" />
</beans>
```

Then you can test the preceding components with the following `Main` class:

```
package com.apress.springrecipes.sequence;

import org.springframework.context.ApplicationContext;
import org.springframework.context.support.ClassPathXmlApplicationContext;

public class Main {

    public static void main(String[] args) {
        ApplicationContext context =
            new ClassPathXmlApplicationContext("beans.xml");

        SequenceService sequenceService =
            (SequenceService) context.getBean("sequenceService");

        System.out.println(sequenceService.generate("IT"));
        System.out.println(sequenceService.generate("IT"));
    }
}
```

Scanning Components Automatically

The component scanning feature provided by Spring 2.5 can automatically scan, detect, and instantiate your components from the classpath. By default, Spring is able to detect all components with a stereotype annotation. The basic annotation type that denotes a Spring-managed component is `@Component`. You can apply it to your `SequenceDaoImpl` class.

```
package com.apress.springrecipes.sequence;

import org.springframework.stereotype.Component;

@Component
public class SequenceDaoImpl implements SequenceDao {
    ...
}
```

Also, you apply this stereotype annotation to the `SequenceService` class for Spring to detect it. In addition, you apply the `@Autowired` annotation to the DAO field for Spring to auto-wire it by type.

```
package com.apress.springrecipes.sequence;

import org.springframework.beans.factory.annotation.Autowired;
import org.springframework.stereotype.Component;
```

```
@Component
public class SequenceService {

    @Autowired
    private SequenceDao sequenceDao;
    ...
}
```

With the stereotype annotations applied to your component classes, you can ask Spring to scan them by declaring a single XML element, `<context:component-scan>`. In this element, you need to specify the package for scanning your components. Then the specified package and all its subpackages will be scanned. You can use commas to separate multiple packages for scanning.

Note that this element will also register an `AutowiredAnnotationBeanPostProcessor` instance, which is able to auto-wire properties with the `@Autowired` annotation.

```
<beans xmlns="http://www.springframework.org/schema/beans"
    xmlns:xsi="http://www.w3.org/2001/XMLSchema-instance"
    xmlns:context="http://www.springframework.org/schema/context"
    xsi:schemaLocation="http://www.springframework.org/schema/beans
        http://www.springframework.org/schema/beans/spring-beans-2.5.xsd
        http://www.springframework.org/schema/context
        http://www.springframework.org/schema/context/spring-context-2.5.xsd">

    <context:component-scan base-package="com.apress.springrecipes.sequence" />
</beans>
```

The `@Component` annotation is the basic stereotype for denoting components of general purposes. Actually, there are other specific stereotypes denoting components in different layers. First, the `@Repository` stereotype denotes a DAO component in the persistence layer.

```
package com.apress.springrecipes.sequence;

import org.springframework.stereotype.Repository;

@Repository
public class SequenceDaoImpl implements SequenceDao {
    ...
}
```

Then, the `@Service` stereotype denotes a service component in the service layer.

```
package com.apress.springrecipes.sequence;

import org.springframework.beans.factory.annotation.Autowired;
import org.springframework.stereotype.Service;

@Service
public class SequenceService {
```

```
    @Autowired
    private SequenceDao sequenceDao;
    ...
}
```

There's another component stereotype, @Controller, denoting a controller component in the presentation layer. It will be introduced in Chapter 10.

Filtering Components to Scan

By default, Spring will detect all classes annotated with @Component, @Repository, @Service, @Controller, or your custom annotation type that is itself annotated with @Component. You can customize the scan by applying one or more include/exclude filters.

Spring supports four types of filter expressions. The annotation and assignable types are for you to specify an annotation type and a class/interface for filtering. The regex and aspectj types allow you to specify a regular expression and an AspectJ pointcut expression for matching the classes.

For example, the following component scan includes all classes whose name contains the word Dao or Service, and excludes the classes with the @Controller annotation:

```
<beans ...>
    <context:component-scan base-package="com.apress.springrecipes.sequence">
        <context:include-filter type="regex"
            expression="com\.apress\.springrecipes\.sequence\..*Dao.*" />
        <context:include-filter type="regex"
            expression="com\.apress\.springrecipes\.sequence\..*Service.*" />
        <context:exclude-filter type="annotation"
            expression="org.springframework.stereotype.Controller" />
    </context:component-scan>
</beans>
```

As you have applied include filters to detect all classes whose name contains the word Dao or Service, the SequenceDaoImpl and SequenceService components can be auto-detected even without a stereotype annotation.

Naming Detected Components

By default, Spring will name the detected components by lowercasing the first character of the non-qualified class name. For example, the SequenceService class will be named as sequenceService. You can define the name for a component explicitly by specifying it in the stereotype annotation's value.

```
package com.apress.springrecipes.sequence;
...
import org.springframework.stereotype.Service;

@Service("sequenceService")
public class SequenceService {
    ...
}
```

```
package com.apress.springrecipes.sequence;

import org.springframework.stereotype.Repository;

@Repository("sequenceDao")
public class SequenceDaoImpl implements SequenceDao {
    ...
}
```

You can develop your own naming strategy by implementing the BeanNameGenerator interface and specifying it in the name-generator attribute of the <context:component-scan> element.

3-14. Summary

In this chapter, you have learned the basic bean configuration in the Spring IoC container. Spring supports several types of bean configuration. Among them, XML is simplest and most mature. Spring provides two types of IoC container implementation. The basic one is the bean factory, while the advanced one is the application context. If possible, you should use the application context unless resources are restricted. Spring supports both setter injection and constructor injection for defining bean properties, which can be simple values, collections, or bean references.

Dependency checking and auto-wiring are two valuable container features provided by Spring. Dependency checking helps to check if all required properties are set, while auto-wiring can wire your beans automatically either by type, name, or annotation. The old style of configuring these two features is by XML attributes, while the new style is by annotations and bean post processors, which allow greater flexibility.

Spring provides support for bean inheritance by extracting the common bean configurations to form a parent bean. The parent bean can act as a configuration template, a bean instance, or both at the same time.

As collections are essential programming elements of Java, Spring provides various collection tags for you to configure collections in the bean configuration file easily. You can use the collection factory beans or the collection tags in the utility schema to specify more details for a collection, and also define collections as stand-alone beans to share between multiple beans.

Finally, Spring can auto-detect your components from the classpath. By default, it can detect all components with particular stereotype annotations. But you can further include or exclude your components with filters. Component scanning is a powerful feature that can reduce the amount of configurations.

In the next chapter, you will learn the advanced Spring IoC container features that have not been introduced in this chapter.

CHAPTER 4

Advanced Spring IoC Container

In this chapter, you will learn the advanced features and internal mechanisms of the Spring IoC container, which can help you to increase your efficiency when developing Spring applications. Although these features may not be used frequently, they are indispensable to a comprehensive and powerful container. They are also the foundation of other modules of the Spring framework.

The Spring IoC container itself is designed to be easily customizable and extensible. It allows you to customize the default container behaviors through configuration, and also extend the container's features by registering your container plug-ins that conform to the container specification.

Upon finishing this chapter, you will be very familiar with most features of the Spring IoC container. This will give you a useful basis for learning about different topics of Spring in the subsequent chapters.

4-1. Creating Beans by Invoking a Constructor

Problem

You would like to create a bean in the Spring IoC container by invoking its constructor, which is the most common and direct way of creating beans. It is equivalent to using the `new` operator to create objects in Java.

Solution

Normally, when you specify the `class` attribute for a bean, you are asking the Spring IoC container to create the bean instance by invoking its constructor.

How It Works

Suppose you are going to develop a shop application to sell products online. First of all, you create the `Product` class, which has several properties, such as the product name and price. As there are many types of products in your shop, you make the `Product` class abstract for different product subclasses to extend.

```
package com.apress.springrecipes.shop;

public abstract class Product {

    private String name;
    private double price;

    public Product() {}

    public Product(String name, double price) {
        this.name = name;
        this.price = price;
    }

    // Getters and Setters
    ...

    public String toString() {
        return name + " " + price;
    }
}
```

Then you create two product subclasses, Battery and Disc. Each of them has its own properties.

```
package com.apress.springrecipes.shop;

public class Battery extends Product {

    private boolean rechargeable;

    public Battery() {
        super();
    }

    public Battery(String name, double price) {
        super(name, price);
    }

    // Getters and Setters
    ...
}
```

```
package com.apress.springrecipes.shop;

public class Disc extends Product {
```

```
    private int capacity;

    public Disc() {
        super();
    }

    public Disc(String name, double price) {
        super(name, price);
    }

    // Getters and Setters
    ...
}
```

To define some products in the Spring IoC container, you create the following bean configuration file:

```
<beans xmlns="http://www.springframework.org/schema/beans"
    xmlns:xsi="http://www.w3.org/2001/XMLSchema-instance"
    xsi:schemaLocation="http://www.springframework.org/schema/beans
        http://www.springframework.org/schema/beans/spring-beans-2.5.xsd">

    <bean id="aaa" class="com.apress.springrecipes.shop.Battery">
        <property name="name" value="AAA" />
        <property name="price" value="2.5" />
        <property name="rechargeable" value="true" />
    </bean>

    <bean id="cdrw" class="com.apress.springrecipes.shop.Disc">
        <property name="name" value="CD-RW" />
        <property name="price" value="1.5" />
        <property name="capacity" value="700" />
    </bean>
</beans>
```

If there's no `<constructor-arg>` element specified, the default constructor with no argument will be invoked. Then for each `<property>` element, Spring will inject the value through the setter method. The preceding bean configuration is equivalent to the following code snippet:

```
Product aaa = new Battery();
aaa.setName("AAA");
aaa.setPrice(2.5);
aaa.setRechargeable(true);

Product cdrw = new Disc();
cdrw.setName("CD-RW");
cdrw.setPrice(1.5);
cdrw.setCapacity(700);
```

Otherwise, if there are one or more <constructor-arg> elements specified, Spring will invoke the most appropriate constructor that matches your arguments.

```
<beans ...>
    <bean id="aaa" class="com.apress.springrecipes.shop.Battery">
        <constructor-arg value="AAA" />
        <constructor-arg value="2.5" />
        <property name="rechargeable" value="true" />
    </bean>

    <bean id="cdrw" class="com.apress.springrecipes.shop.Disc">
        <constructor-arg value="CD-RW" />
        <constructor-arg value="1.5" />
        <property name="capacity" value="700" />
    </bean>
</beans>
```

As there is no constructor ambiguity for the Product class and subclasses, the preceding bean configuration is equivalent to the following code snippet:

```
Product aaa = new Battery("AAA", 2.5);
aaa.setRechargeable(true);

Product cdrw = new Disc("CD-RW", 1.5);
cdrw.setCapacity(700);
```

You can write the following Main class to test your products by retrieving them from the Spring IoC container:

```
package com.apress.springrecipes.shop;

import org.springframework.context.ApplicationContext;
import org.springframework.context.support.ClassPathXmlApplicationContext;

public class Main {

    public static void main(String[] args) throws Exception {
        ApplicationContext context =
            new ClassPathXmlApplicationContext("beans.xml");

        Product aaa = (Product) context.getBean("aaa");
        Product cdrw = (Product) context.getBean("cdrw");
        System.out.println(aaa);
        System.out.println(cdrw);
    }
}
```

4-2. Creating Beans by Invoking a Static Factory Method

Problem

You would like to create a bean in the Spring IoC container by invoking a *static factory method*, whose purpose is to encapsulate the object-creation process in a static method. The client who requests an object can simply make a call to this method without knowing about the creation detail.

Solution

Spring supports creating a bean by invoking a static factory method, which should be specified in the `factory-method` attribute.

How It Works

For example, you can write the following `createProduct()` static factory method to create a product from a predefined product ID. According to the product ID, this method will decide which concrete product class to instantiate. If there is no product matching this ID, it will throw an `IllegalArgumentException`.

```
package com.apress.springrecipes.shop;

public class ProductCreator {

    public static Product createProduct(String productId) {
        if ("aaa".equals(productId)) {
            return new Battery("AAA", 2.5);
        } else if ("cdrw".equals(productId)) {
            return new Disc("CD-RW", 1.5);
        }
        throw new IllegalArgumentException("Unknown product");
    }
}
```

To declare a bean created by a static factory method, you specify the class hosting the factory method in the `class` attribute and the factory method's name in the `factory-method` attribute. Finally, you pass the method arguments by using the `<constructor-arg>` elements.

```
<beans ...>
    <bean id="aaa" class="com.apress.springrecipes.shop.ProductCreator"
        factory-method="createProduct">
        <constructor-arg value="aaa" />
    </bean>

    <bean id="cdrw" class="com.apress.springrecipes.shop.ProductCreator"
        factory-method="createProduct">
        <constructor-arg value="cdrw" />
    </bean>
</beans>
```

In case of any exception thrown by the factory method, Spring will wrap it with a `BeanCreationException`. The equivalent code snippet for the preceding bean configuration is shown following:

```
Product aaa = ProductCreator.createProduct("aaa");
Product cdrw = ProductCreator.createProduct("cdrw");
```

4-3. Creating Beans by Invoking an Instance Factory Method

Problem

You would like to create a bean in the Spring IoC container by invoking an *instance factory method,* whose purpose is to encapsulate the object-creation process in a method of another object instance. The client who requests an object can simply make a call to this method without knowing about the creation detail.

Solution

Spring supports creating a bean by invoking an instance factory method. The bean instance should be specified in the `factory-bean` attribute, while the factory method should be specified in the `factory-method` attribute.

How It Works

For example, you can write the following `ProductCreator` class by using a configurable map to store the predefined products. The `createProduct()` instance factory method finds a product by looking up the supplied `productId` in the map. If there is no product matching this ID, it will throw an `IllegalArgumentException`.

```
package com.apress.springrecipes.shop;
...
public class ProductCreator {

    private Map<String, Product> products;

    public void setProducts(Map<String, Product> products) {
        this.products = products;
    }

    public Product createProduct(String productId) {
        Product product = products.get(productId);
        if (product != null) {
            return product;
        }
        throw new IllegalArgumentException("Unknown product");
    }
}
```

To create products from this ProductCreator class, you first have to declare an instance of it in the IoC container and configure its product map. You may declare the products in the map as inner beans. To declare a bean created by an instance factory method, you specify the bean hosting the factory method in the factory-bean attribute, and the factory method's name in the factory-method attribute. Finally, you pass the method arguments by using the <constructor-arg> elements.

```
<beans ...>
    <bean id="productCreator"
        class="com.apress.springrecipes.shop.ProductCreator">
        <property name="products">
            <map>
                <entry key="aaa">
                    <bean class="com.apress.springrecipes.shop.Battery">
                        <property name="name" value="AAA" />
                        <property name="price" value="2.5" />
                    </bean>
                </entry>
                <entry key="cdrw">
                    <bean class="com.apress.springrecipes.shop.Disc">
                        <property name="name" value="CD-RW" />
                        <property name="price" value="1.5" />
                    </bean>
                </entry>
            </map>
        </property>
    </bean>

    <bean id="aaa" factory-bean="productCreator"
        factory-method="createProduct">
        <constructor-arg value="aaa" />
    </bean>

    <bean id="cdrw" factory-bean="productCreator"
        factory-method="createProduct">
        <constructor-arg value="cdrw" />
    </bean>
</beans>
```

In case of any exception thrown by the factory method, Spring will wrap it with a BeanCreationException. The equivalent code snippet for the preceding bean configuration is shown following:

```
ProductCreator productCreator = new ProductCreator();
productCreator.setProducts(...);

Product aaa = productCreator.createProduct("aaa");
Product cdrw = productCreator.createProduct("cdrw");
```

4-4. Creating Beans Using Spring's Factory Bean

Problem

You would like to create a bean in the Spring IoC container using Spring's factory bean. A *factory bean* is a bean that serves as a factory for creating other beans within the IoC container. Conceptually, a factory bean is very similar to a factory method, but it is a Spring-specific bean that can be identified by the Spring IoC container during bean construction.

Solution

The basic requirement of a factory bean is to implement the `FactoryBean` interface. For your convenience, Spring provides an abstract template class, `AbstractFactoryBean`, for you to extend. Factory beans are mostly used to implement framework facilities. Here are some examples:

- When looking up an object (such as a data source) from JNDI, you can use `JndiObjectFactoryBean`.
- When using classic Spring AOP to create a proxy for a bean, you can use `ProxyFactoryBean`.
- When creating a Hibernate session factory in the IoC container, you can use `LocalSessionFactoryBean`.

However, as a framework user, you seldom have to write custom factory beans, because they are framework-specific and cannot be used outside the scope of the Spring IoC container. Actually, you are always able to implement an equivalent factory method for a factory bean.

How It Works

Although you'll seldom have to write custom factory beans, you may better understand their internal mechanisms through an example. For example, you can write a factory bean for creating a product with a discount applied to the price. It accepts a `product` property and a `discount` property to apply the discount to the product and return it as a new bean.

```
package com.apress.springrecipes.shop;

import org.springframework.beans.factory.config.AbstractFactoryBean;

public class DiscountFactoryBean extends AbstractFactoryBean {

    private Product product;
    private double discount;

    public void setProduct(Product product) {
        this.product = product;
    }
```

```
    public void setDiscount(double discount) {
        this.discount = discount;
    }

    public Class getObjectType() {
        return product.getClass();
    }

    protected Object createInstance() throws Exception {
        product.setPrice(product.getPrice() * (1 - discount));
        return product;
    }
}
```

By extending the `AbstractFactoryBean` class, your factory bean can simply override the `createInstance()` method to create the target bean instance. In addition, you have to return the target bean's type in the `getObjectType()` method for the auto-wiring feature to work properly.

Next, you can declare your product instances with `DiscountFactoryBean`. Each time you request a bean that implements the `FactoryBean` interface, the Spring IoC container will use this factory bean to create the target bean and return it to you. If you are sure that you want to get the factory bean instance itself, you can use the bean name preceded by &.

```
<beans ...>
    <bean id="aaa"
        class="com.apress.springrecipes.shop.DiscountFactoryBean">
        <property name="product">
            <bean class="com.apress.springrecipes.shop.Battery">
                <constructor-arg value="AAA" />
                <constructor-arg value="2.5" />
            </bean>
        </property>
        <property name="discount" value="0.2" />
    </bean>

    <bean id="cdrw"
        class="com.apress.springrecipes.shop.DiscountFactoryBean">
        <property name="product">
            <bean class="com.apress.springrecipes.shop.Disc">
                <constructor-arg value="CD-RW" />
                <constructor-arg value="1.5" />
            </bean>
        </property>
        <property name="discount" value="0.1" />
    </bean>
</beans>
```

The preceding factory bean configuration works in a similar way to the following code snippet:

```
DiscountFactoryBean &aaa = new DiscountFactoryBean();
&aaa.setProduct(new Battery("AAA", 2.5));
&aaa.setDiscount(0.2);
Product aaa = (Product) &aaa.createInstance();

DiscountFactoryBean &cdrw = new DiscountFactoryBean();
&cdrw.setProduct(new Disc("CD-RW", 1.5));
&cdrw.setDiscount(0.1);
Product cdrw = (Product) &cdrw.createInstance();
```

4-5. Declaring Beans from Static Fields

Problem

You would like to declare a bean in the Spring IoC container from a static field. In Java, constant values are often declared as static fields.

Solution

To declare a bean from a static field, you can make use of either the built-in factory bean `FieldRetrievingFactoryBean`, or the `<util:contant>` tag in Spring 2.x.

How It Works

First, let's define two product constants in the `Product` class.

```
package com.apress.springrecipes.shop;

public abstract class Product {

    public static final Product AAA = new Battery("AAA", 2.5);
    public static final Product CDRW = new Disc("CD-RW", 1.5);
    ...
}
```

To declare a bean from a static field, you can make use of the built-in factory bean `FieldRetrievingFactoryBean` and specify the fully qualified field name in the `staticField` property.

```
<beans ...>
    <bean id="aaa" class="org.springframework.beans.factory.config.➥
        FieldRetrievingFactoryBean">
        <property name="staticField">
            <value>com.apress.springrecipes.shop.Product.AAA</value>
        </property>
    </bean>
```

```
    <bean id="cdrw" class="org.springframework.beans.factory.config.➥
        FieldRetrievingFactoryBean">
        <property name="staticField">
            <value>com.apress.springrecipes.shop.Product.CDRW</value>
        </property>
    </bean>
</beans>
```

The preceding bean configuration is equivalent to the following code snippet:

```
Product aaa = com.apress.springrecipes.shop.Product.AAA;
Product cdrw = com.apress.springrecipes.shop.Product.CDRW;
```

As an alternative to specifying the field name in the `staticField` property explicitly, you can set it as the bean name of `FieldRetrievingFactoryBean`. The downside is that your bean name may get rather long and verbose.

```
<beans ...>
    <bean id="com.apress.springrecipes.shop.Product.AAA"
        class="org.springframework.beans.factory.config.➥
            FieldRetrievingFactoryBean" />

    <bean id="com.apress.springrecipes.shop.Product.CDRW"
        class="org.springframework.beans.factory.config.➥
            FieldRetrievingFactoryBean" />
</beans>
```

Spring 2.x allows you to declare a bean from a static field by using the `<util:constant>` tag. Compared to using `FieldRetrievingFactoryBean`, it is a simpler way of declaring beans from static fields. But before this tag can work, you must add the `util` schema definition to your `<beans>` root element.

```
<beans xmlns="http://www.springframework.org/schema/beans"
    xmlns:xsi="http://www.w3.org/2001/XMLSchema-instance"
    xmlns:util="http://www.springframework.org/schema/util"
    xsi:schemaLocation="http://www.springframework.org/schema/beans
        http://www.springframework.org/schema/beans/spring-beans-2.5.xsd
        http://www.springframework.org/schema/util
        http://www.springframework.org/schema/util/spring-util-2.5.xsd">

    <util:constant id="aaa"
        static-field="com.apress.springrecipes.shop.Product.AAA" />

    <util:constant id="cdrw"
        static-field="com.apress.springrecipes.shop.Product.CDRW" />
</beans>
```

4-6. Declaring Beans from Object Properties

Problem

You would like to declare a bean in the Spring IoC container from an object property or a nested property (i.e., a property path).

Solution

To declare a bean from an object property or a property path, you can make use of either the built-in factory bean PropertyPathFactoryBean or the <util:property-path> tag in Spring 2.x.

How It Works

As an example, let's create a ProductRanking class with a bestSeller property whose type is Product.

```
package com.apress.springrecipes.shop;

public class ProductRanking {

    private Product bestSeller;

    public Product getBestSeller() {
        return bestSeller;
    }

    public void setBestSeller(Product bestSeller) {
        this.bestSeller = bestSeller;
    }
}
```

In the following bean declaration, the bestSeller property is declared by an inner bean. By definition, you cannot retrieve an inner bean by its name. However, you can retrieve it as a property of the productRanking bean. The factory bean PropertyPathFactoryBean can be used to declare a bean from an object property or a property path.

```
<beans ...>
    <bean id="productRanking"
        class="com.apress.springrecipes.shop.ProductRanking">
        <property name="bestSeller">
            <bean class="com.apress.springrecipes.shop.Disc">
                <property name="name" value="CD-RW" />
                <property name="price" value="1.5" />
            </bean>
        </property>
    </bean>
```

```
    <bean id="bestSeller"
        class="org.springframework.beans.factory.config.PropertyPathFactoryBean">
        <property name="targetObject" ref="productRanking" />
        <property name="propertyPath" value="bestSeller" />
    </bean>
</beans>
```

Note that the `propertyPath` property of `PropertyPathFactoryBean` can accept not only a single property name, but also a property path with dots as the separators. The preceding bean configuration is equivalent to the following code snippet:

```
Product bestSeller = productRanking.getBestSeller();
```

In addition to specifying the `targetObject` and `propertyPath` properties explicitly, you can combine them as the bean name of `PropertyPathFactoryBean`. The downside is that your bean name may get rather long and verbose.

```
<bean id="productRanking.bestSeller"
    class="org.springframework.beans.factory.config.PropertyPathFactoryBean" />
```

Spring 2.x allows you to declare a bean from an object property or a property path by using the `<util:property-path>` tag. Compared to using `PropertyPathFactoryBean`, it is a simpler way of declaring beans from properties. But before this tag can work, you must add the `util` schema definition to your `<beans>` root element.

```
<beans xmlns="http://www.springframework.org/schema/beans"
    xmlns:xsi="http://www.w3.org/2001/XMLSchema-instance"
    xmlns:util="http://www.springframework.org/schema/util"
    xsi:schemaLocation="http://www.springframework.org/schema/beans
        http://www.springframework.org/schema/beans/spring-beans-2.5.xsd
        http://www.springframework.org/schema/util
        http://www.springframework.org/schema/util/spring-util-2.5.xsd">
    ...
    <util:property-path id="bestSeller" path="productRanking.bestSeller" />
</beans>
```

You can test this property path by retrieving it from the IoC container and printing it to the console.

```
package com.apress.springrecipes.shop;
...
public class Main {

    public static void main(String[] args) throws Exception {
        ...
        Product bestSeller = (Product) context.getBean("bestSeller");
        System.out.println(bestSeller);
    }
}
```

4-7. Setting Bean Scopes

Problem

When you declare a bean in the configuration file, you are actually defining a template for bean creation, not an actual bean instance. When a bean is requested by the getBean() method or a reference from other beans, Spring will decide which bean instance should be returned according to the bean scope. Sometimes you have to set an appropriate scope for a bean other than the default scope.

Solution

In Spring 2.x, a bean's scope is set in the scope attribute of the <bean> element. By default, Spring creates exactly one instance for each bean declared in the IoC container, and this instance will be shared in the scope of the entire IoC container. This unique bean instance will be returned for all subsequent getBean() calls and bean references. This scope is called singleton, which is the default scope of all beans. Table 4-1 lists all valid bean scopes in Spring.

Table 4-1. *Valid Bean Scopes in Spring*

Scope	Description
singleton	Creates a single bean instance per Spring IoC container
prototype	Creates a new bean instance each time when requested
request	Creates a single bean instance per HTTP request; only valid in the context of a web application
session	Creates a single bean instance per HTTP session; only valid in the context of a web application
globalSession	Creates a single bean instance per global HTTP session; only valid in the context of a portal application

In Spring 1.x, singleton and prototype are the only two valid bean scopes, and they are specified by the singleton attribute (i.e., singleton="true" or singleton="false"), not the scope attribute.

How It Works

To demonstrate the concept of bean scope, let's consider a shopping cart example in your shop application. First, you create the ShoppingCart class as follows:

```
package com.apress.springrecipes.shop;
...
public class ShoppingCart {

    private List<Product> items = new ArrayList<Product>();

    public void addItem(Product item) {
        items.add(item);
    }
```

```
    public List<Product> getItems() {
        return items;
    }
}
```

Then you declare some product beans and a shopping cart bean in the IoC container as usual:

```
<beans ...>
    <bean id="aaa" class="com.apress.springrecipes.shop.Battery">
        <property name="name" value="AAA" />
        <property name="price" value="2.5" />
    </bean>

    <bean id="cdrw" class="com.apress.springrecipes.shop.Disc">
        <property name="name" value="CD-RW" />
        <property name="price" value="1.5" />
    </bean>

    <bean id="dvdrw" class="com.apress.springrecipes.shop.Disc">
        <property name="name" value="DVD-RW" />
        <property name="price" value="3.0" />
    </bean>

    <bean id="shoppingCart" class="com.apress.springrecipes.shop.ShoppingCart" />
</beans>
```

In the following Main class, you can test your shopping cart by adding some products to it. Suppose that there are two customers navigating in your shop at the same time. The first one gets a shopping cart by the getBean() method and adds two products to it. Then, the second customer also gets a shopping cart by the getBean() method and adds another product to it.

```
package com.apress.springrecipes.shop;

import org.springframework.context.ApplicationContext;
import org.springframework.context.support.ClassPathXmlApplicationContext;

public class Main {

    public static void main(String[] args) {
        ApplicationContext context =
            new ClassPathXmlApplicationContext("beans.xml");

        Product aaa = (Product) context.getBean("aaa");
        Product cdrw = (Product) context.getBean("cdrw");
        Product dvdrw = (Product) context.getBean("dvdrw");

        ShoppingCart cart1 = (ShoppingCart) context.getBean("shoppingCart");
        cart1.addItem(aaa);
```

```
        cart1.addItem(cdrw);
        System.out.println("Shopping cart 1 contains " + cart1.getItems());

        ShoppingCart cart2 = (ShoppingCart) context.getBean("shoppingCart");
        cart2.addItem(dvdrw);
        System.out.println("Shopping cart 2 contains " + cart2.getItems());
    }
}
```

As a result of the preceding bean declaration, you can see that the two customers get the same shopping cart instance.

```
Shopping cart 1 contains [AAA 2.5, CD-RW 1.5]
Shopping cart 2 contains [AAA 2.5, CD-RW 1.5, DVD-RW 3.0]
```

This is because Spring's default bean scope is `singleton`, which means Spring creates exactly one shopping cart instance per IoC container.

```
<bean id="shoppingCart"
    class="com.apress.springrecipes.shop.ShoppingCart"
    scope="singleton" />
```

In your shop application, you expect each customer to get a different shopping cart instance when the `getBean()` method is called. To ensure this behavior, you should change the scope of the `shoppingCart` bean to `prototype`. Then Spring will create a new bean instance for each `getBean()` method call and reference from the other bean.

```
<bean id="shoppingCart"
    class="com.apress.springrecipes.shop.ShoppingCart"
    scope="prototype" />
```

Now if you run the `Main` class again, you can see that the two customers get a different shopping cart instance.

```
Shopping cart 1 contains [AAA 2.5, CD-RW 1.5]
Shopping cart 2 contains [DVD-RW 3.0]
```

4-8. Customizing Bean Initialization and Destruction

Problem

Many real-world components have to perform certain types of initialization tasks before they are ready to be used. Such tasks include opening a file, opening a network/database connection, allocating memory, and so on. Also, they have to perform the corresponding destruction tasks at the end of their life cycle. So, you have a need to customize bean initialization and destruction in the Spring IoC container.

Solution

In addition to bean registration, the Spring IoC container is also responsible for managing the life cycle of your beans, and it allows you to perform custom tasks at particular points of their life cycle. Your tasks should be encapsulated in callback methods for the Spring IoC container to call at a suitable time.

The following list shows the steps through which the Spring IoC container manages the life cycle of a bean. This list will be expanded as more features of the IoC container are introduced.

1. Create the bean instance either by a constructor or by a factory method.
2. Set the values and bean references to the bean properties.
3. **Call the initialization callback methods.**
4. The bean is ready to be used.
5. **When the container is shut down, call the destruction callback methods.**

There are three ways that Spring can recognize your initialization and destruction callback methods. First, your bean can implement the `InitializingBean` and `DisposableBean` life cycle interfaces and implement the `afterPropertiesSet()` and `destroy()` methods for initialization and destruction. Second, you can set the `init-method` and `destroy-method` attributes in the bean declaration and specify the callback method names. In Spring 2.5, you can also annotate the initialization and destruction callback methods with the life cycle annotations `@PostConstruct` and `@PreDestroy`, which are defined in JSR-250: Common Annotations for the Java Platform. Then you can register a `CommonAnnotationBeanPostProcessor` instance in the IoC container to call these callback methods.

How It Works

To understand how the Spring IoC container manages the life cycle of your beans, let's consider an example involving the checkout function. The following `Cashier` class can be used to check out the products in a shopping cart. It records the time and the amount of each checkout in a text file.

```
package com.apress.springrecipes.shop;
...
public class Cashier {

    private String name;
    private String path;
    private BufferedWriter writer;

    public void setName(String name) {
        this.name = name;
    }
```

```
    public void setPath(String path) {
        this.path = path;
    }

    public void openFile() throws IOException {
        File logFile = new File(path, name + ".txt");
        writer = new BufferedWriter(new OutputStreamWriter(
                new FileOutputStream(logFile, true)));
    }

    public void checkout(ShoppingCart cart) throws IOException {
        double total = 0;
        for (Product product : cart.getItems()) {
            total += product.getPrice();
        }
        writer.write(new Date() + "\t" + total + "\r\n");
        writer.flush();
    }

    public void closeFile() throws IOException {
        writer.close();
    }
}
```

In the Cashier class, the openFile() method opens the text file with the cashier name as the file name in the specified system path. Each time you call the checkout() method, a checkout record will be appended to the text file. Finally, the closeFile() method closes the file to release its system resources.

Then you declare a cashier bean with the name cashier1 in the IoC container. This cashier's checkout records will be recorded in the file c:/cashier/cashier1.txt. You should create this directory in advance or specify another existing directory.

```
<beans ...>
    ...
    <bean id="cashier1" class="com.apress.springrecipes.shop.Cashier">
        <property name="name" value="cashier1" />
        <property name="path" value="c:/cashier" />
    </bean>
</beans>
```

However, in the Main class, if you try to check out a shopping cart with this cashier, it will result in a NullPointerException. The reason for this exception is that no one has called the openFile() method for initialization beforehand.

```
package com.apress.springrecipes.shop;

import org.springframework.context.ApplicationContext;
import org.springframework.context.support.FileSystemXmlApplicationContext;
```

```
public class Main {

    public static void main(String[] args) throws Exception {
        ApplicationContext context =
            new FileSystemXmlApplicationContext("beans.xml");
        ...
        Cashier cashier1 = (Cashier) context.getBean("cashier1");
        cashier1.checkout(cart1);
    }
}
```

Where should you make a call to the openFile() method for initialization? In Java, the initialization tasks should be performed in the constructor. But would it work here if you call the openFile() method in the default constructor of the Cashier class? No, because the openFile() method requires both the name and path properties to be set before it can determine which file to open.

```
package com.apress.springrecipes.shop;
...
public class Cashier {
    ...
    public void openFile() throws IOException {
        File logFile = new File(path, name + ".txt");
        writer = new BufferedWriter(new OutputStreamWriter(
                new FileOutputStream(logFile, true)));
    }
}
```

When the default constructor is invoked, these properties have not been set yet. So you may add a constructor that accepts the two properties as arguments, and call the openFile() method at the end of this constructor. However, sometimes you may not be allowed to do so, or you might prefer to inject your properties via setter injection. Actually, the best time to call the openFile() method is after all properties have been set by the Spring IoC container.

Implementing the InitializingBean and DisposableBean Interfaces

Spring allows your bean to perform initialization and destruction tasks in the callback methods afterPropertiesSet() and destroy() by implementing the InitializingBean and DisposableBean interfaces. During bean construction, Spring will notice that your bean implements these interfaces and call the callback methods at a suitable time.

```
package com.apress.springrecipes.shop;
...
import org.springframework.beans.factory.DisposableBean;
import org.springframework.beans.factory.InitializingBean;

public class Cashier implements InitializingBean, DisposableBean {
    ...
    public void afterPropertiesSet() throws Exception {
```

```
        openFile();
    }

    public void destroy() throws Exception {
        closeFile();
    }
}
```

Now if you run your Main class again, you will see that a checkout record is appended to the text file c:/cashier/cashier1.txt. However, implementing such proprietary interfaces will make your beans Spring-specific and thus unable to be reused outside the Spring IoC container.

Setting the init-method and destroy-method Attributes

A better approach of specifying the initialization and destruction callback methods is by setting the init-method and destroy-method attributes in your bean declaration.

```
<bean id="cashier1" class="com.apress.springrecipes.shop.Cashier"
    init-method="openFile" destroy-method="closeFile">
    <property name="name" value="cashier1" />
    <property name="path" value="c:/cashier" />
</bean>
```

With these two attributes set in the bean declaration, your Cashier class no longer needs to implement the InitializingBean and DisposableBean interfaces. You can also delete the afterPropertiesSet() and destroy() methods as well.

Annotating the @PostConstruct and @PreDestroy Annotations

In Spring 2.5, you can annotate the initialization and destruction callback methods with the JSR-250 life cycle annotations @PostConstruct and @PreDestroy.

Note To use the JSR-250 annotations, you have to include common-annotations.jar (located in the lib/j2ee directory of the Spring installation) in your classpath. However, if your application is running on Java SE 6 or Java EE 5, you needn't include this JAR file.

```
package com.apress.springrecipes.shop;
...
import javax.annotation.PostConstruct;
import javax.annotation.PreDestroy;

public class Cashier {
    ...
    @PostConstruct
    public void openFile() throws IOException {
```

```
        File logFile = new File(path, name + ".txt");
        writer = new BufferedWriter(new OutputStreamWriter(
                new FileOutputStream(logFile, true)));
    }

    @PreDestroy
    public void closeFile() throws IOException {
        writer.close();
    }
}
```

Then you register a CommonAnnotationBeanPostProcessor instance in the IoC container to call the initialization and destruction callback methods with the life cycle annotations. In this way, you no longer need to specify the init-method and destroy-method attributes for your bean.

```
<beans ...>
    ...
    <bean class="org.springframework.context.annotation.➥
        CommonAnnotationBeanPostProcessor" />

    <bean id="cashier1" class="com.apress.springrecipes.shop.Cashier">
        <property name="name" value="cashier1" />
        <property name="path" value="c:/cashier" />
    </bean>
</beans>
```

Or you can simply include the <context:annotation-config> element in your bean configuration file and a CommonAnnotationBeanPostProcessor instance will automatically get registered. But before this tag can work, you must add the context schema definition to your <beans> root element.

```
<beans xmlns="http://www.springframework.org/schema/beans"
    xmlns:xsi="http://www.w3.org/2001/XMLSchema-instance"
    xmlns:context="http://www.springframework.org/schema/context"
    xsi:schemaLocation="http://www.springframework.org/schema/beans
        http://www.springframework.org/schema/beans/spring-beans-2.5.xsd
        http://www.springframework.org/schema/context
        http://www.springframework.org/schema/context/spring-context-2.5.xsd">

    <context:annotation-config />
    ...
</beans>
```

4-9. Making Beans Aware of the Container

Problem

A well-designed component should not have direct dependencies on its container. However, sometimes it's necessary for your beans to be aware of the container's resources.

Solution

Your beans can be aware of the Spring IoC container's resources by implementing certain "aware" interfaces, as shown in Table 4-2. Spring will inject the corresponding resources to your beans via the setter methods defined in these interfaces.

Table 4-2. *Common Aware Interfaces in Spring*

Aware Interface	Target Resource
`BeanNameAware`	The bean name of its instances configured in the IoC container
`BeanFactoryAware`	The current bean factory, through which you can invoke the container's services
`ApplicationContextAware*`	The current application context, through which you can invoke the container's services
`MessageSourceAware`	A message source, through which you can resolve text messages
`ApplicationEventPublisherAware`	An application event publisher, through which you can publish application events
`ResourceLoaderAware`	A resource loader, through which you can load external resources

* *In fact, the* `ApplicationContext` *interface extends the* `MessageSource`, `ApplicationEventPublisher`, *and* `ResourceLoader` *interfaces, so you only need to be aware of the application context to access all these services. However, the best practice is to choose an aware interface with minimum scope that can satisfy your requirement.*

The setter methods in the aware interfaces will be called by Spring after the bean properties have been set, but before the initialization callback methods are called, as illustrated in the following list:

1. Create the bean instance either by a constructor or by a factory method.
2. Set the values and bean references to the bean properties.
3. **Call the setter methods defined in the aware interfaces.**
4. Call the initialization callback methods.
5. The bean is ready to be used.
6. When the container is shut down, call the destruction callback methods.

Keep in mind that once your beans implement the aware interfaces, they are bound to Spring and may not work properly outside the Spring IoC container. You must consider carefully whether it's necessary to implement such proprietary interfaces.

How It Works

For example, you can make your cashier bean aware of its bean name in the IoC container by implementing the `BeanNameAware` interface. When this bean name is injected, you can save it as the cashier name. This can save you the trouble of setting another `name` property for the cashier.

```
package com.apress.springrecipes.shop;
...
import org.springframework.beans.factory.BeanNameAware;

public class Cashier implements BeanNameAware {
    ...
    public void setBeanName(String beanName) {
        this.name = beanName;
    }
}
```

You can simplify your cashier bean declaration by using the bean name as the cashier name. In this way, you can erase the configuration of the `name` property and perhaps the `setName()` method as well.

```
<bean id="cashier1" class="com.apress.springrecipes.shop.Cashier">
    <property name="path" value="c:/cashier" />
</bean>
```

Note Do you remember that you can specify the field name and the property path as the bean names of `FieldRetrievingFactoryBean` and `PropertyPathFactoryBean` directly? In fact, both factory beans implement the `BeanNameAware` interface.

4-10. Creating Bean Post Processors

Problem

You would like to register your own plug-ins in the Spring IoC container to process the bean instances during construction.

Solution

A *bean post processor* allows additional bean processing before and after the initialization callback method. The main characteristic of a bean post processor is that it will process all the bean instances in the IoC container one by one, not just a single bean instance. Typically, bean post processors are used for checking the validity of bean properties or altering bean properties according to particular criteria.

The basic requirement of a bean post processor is to implement the `BeanPostProcessor` interface. You can process every bean before and after the initialization callback method by implementing the `postProcessBeforeInitialization()` and `postProcessAfterInitialization()` methods. Then Spring will pass each bean instance to these two methods before and after calling the initialization callback method, as illustrated in the following list:

1. Create the bean instance either by a constructor or by a factory method.
2. Set the values and bean references to the bean properties.
3. Call the setter methods defined in the aware interfaces.
4. **Pass the bean instance to the** `postProcessBeforeInitialization()` **method of each bean post processor.**
5. Call the initialization callback methods.
6. **Pass the bean instance to the** `postProcessAfterInitialization()` **method of each bean post processor.**
7. The bean is ready to be used.
8. When the container is shut down, call the destruction callback methods.

When using a bean factory as your IoC container, bean post processors can only be registered programmatically, or more accurately, via the `addBeanPostProcessor()` method. However, if you are using an application context, the registration will be as simple as declaring an instance of the processor in the bean configuration file, and then it will get registered automatically.

How It Works

Suppose you would like to ensure that the logging path of `Cashier` exists before the logging file is open. This is to avoid `FileNotFoundException`. As this is a common requirement for all components that require storage in the file system, you had better implement it in a general and reusable manner. A bean post processor is an ideal choice to implement such a feature in Spring.

First of all, for the bean post processor to distinguish which beans should be checked, you create a marker interface, `StorageConfig`, for your target beans to implement. Moreover, for your bean post processor to check for path existence, it must be able to access the `path` property. This can be done by adding the `getPath()` method to this interface.

```
package com.apress.springrecipes.shop;

public interface StorageConfig {

    public String getPath();
}
```

Then you should make the Cashier class implement this marker interface. Your bean post processor will only check the beans that implement this interface.

```
package com.apress.springrecipes.shop;
...
public class Cashier implements BeanNameAware, StorageConfig {
    ...
    public String getPath() {
        return path;
    }
}
```

Now you are ready to write a bean post processor for path checking. As the best time to perform path checking is before the file is opened in the initialization method, you implement the postProcessBeforeInitialization() method to perform the checking.

```
package com.apress.springrecipes.shop;
...
import org.springframework.beans.BeansException;
import org.springframework.beans.factory.config.BeanPostProcessor;

public class PathCheckingBeanPostProcessor implements BeanPostProcessor {

    public Object postProcessBeforeInitialization(Object bean, String beanName)
            throws BeansException {
        if (bean instanceof StorageConfig) {
            String path = ((StorageConfig) bean).getPath();
            File file = new File(path);
            if (!file.exists()) {
                file.mkdirs();
            }
        }
        return bean;
    }

    public Object postProcessAfterInitialization(Object bean, String beanName)
            throws BeansException {
        return bean;
    }
}
```

During bean construction, the Spring IoC container will pass all the bean instances to your bean post processor one by one, so you must filter the beans by checking the marker interface StoreConfig. If a bean implements this interface, you can access its path property by the getPath() method and check for its existence in the file system. If that path doesn't exist, just create it with the File.mkdirs() method.

Both the postProcessBeforeInitialization() and postProcessAfterInitialization() methods must return an instance for the bean being processed. That means you may even replace the original bean instance with a brand-new instance in your bean post processor.

Remember that you must return the original bean instance even though you do nothing in the method.

To register a bean post processor in an application context, just declare an instance of it in the bean configuration file. The application context will be able to detect which bean implements the BeanPostProcessor interface and register it to process all other bean instances in the container.

```
<beans ...>
    ...
    <bean class="com.apress.springrecipes.shop.PathCheckingBeanPostProcessor" />

    <bean id="cashier1" class="com.apress.springrecipes.shop.Cashier"
        init-method="openFile" destroy-method="closeFile">
        ...
    </bean>
</beans>
```

Note that if you specify the initialization callback method in the init-method attribute, or if you implement the InitializingBean interface, your PathCheckingBeanPostProcessor will work fine because it will process the cashier bean before the initialization method is called.

However, if the cashier bean relies on the JSR-250 annotations @PostConstruct and @PreDestroy, and also a CommonAnnotationBeanPostProcessor instance to call the initialization method, your PathCheckingBeanPostProcessor will not work properly. This is because your bean post processor has a lower priority than CommonAnnotationBeanPostProcessor by default. As a result, the initialization method will be called before your path checking.

```
<beans ...>
    ...
    <bean class="org.springframework.context.annotation.➥
        CommonAnnotationBeanPostProcessor" />

    <bean class="com.apress.springrecipes.shop.PathCheckingBeanPostProcessor" />

    <bean id="cashier1" class="com.apress.springrecipes.shop.Cashier">
        ...
    </bean>
</beans>
```

To define the processing order of bean post processors, you can have them implement the Ordered or PriorityOrdered interface, and return their order in the getOrder() method. Lower value returned by this method represents higher priority, and the order value returned by the PriorityOrdered interface will always precede that returned by the Ordered interface.

As CommonAnnotationBeanPostProcessor implements the PriorityOrdered interface, your PathCheckingBeanPostProcessor must also implement this interface to have a chance to precede it.

```
package com.apress.springrecipes.shop;
...
import org.springframework.beans.factory.config.BeanPostProcessor;
import org.springframework.core.PriorityOrdered;
```

```
public class PathCheckingBeanPostProcessor implements BeanPostProcessor,
        PriorityOrdered {

    private int order;

    public int getOrder() {
        return order;
    }

    public void setOrder(int order) {
        this.order = order;
    }
    ...
}
```

Now in the bean configuration file, you should assign a lower order value to your PathCheckingBeanPostProcessor for it to check and create the path of the cashier bean before its initialization method is called by CommonAnnotationBeanPostProcessor. As the default order of CommonAnnotationBeanPostProcessor is Ordered.LOWEST_PRECEDENCE, you can simply assign a zero order value to your PathCheckingBeanPostProcessor.

```
<beans ...>
    ...
    <bean class="org.springframework.context.annotation.➥
        CommonAnnotationBeanPostProcessor" />

    <bean class="com.apress.springrecipes.shop.PathCheckingBeanPostProcessor">
        <property name="order" value="0" />
    </bean>

    <bean id="cashier1" class="com.apress.springrecipes.shop.Cashier">
        <property name="path" value="c:/cashier" />
    </bean>
</beans>
```

As zero is the default order value of your PathCheckingBeanPostProcessor, you can simply omit this setting. Moreover, you can continue to use <context:annotation-config> to get CommonAnnotationBeanPostProcessor registered automatically.

```
<beans ...>
    ...
    <context:annotation-config />

    <bean class="com.apress.springrecipes.shop.PathCheckingBeanPostProcessor" />
</beans>
```

4-11. Externalizing Bean Configurations

Problem

When configuring beans in the configuration file, you must remember that it's not a good practice to mix deployment details, such as the file path, server address, username, and password, with your bean configurations. Usually, the bean configurations are written by application developers while the deployment details are matters for the deployers or system administrators.

Solution

Spring comes with a bean factory post processor called `PropertyPlaceholderConfigurer` for you to externalize part of the bean configurations into a properties file. You can use variables of the form `${var}` in your bean configuration file and `PropertyPlaceholderConfigurer` will load the properties from a properties file and use them to replace the variables.

A *bean factory post processor* differs from a bean post processor in that its target is the IoC container—either the bean factory or the application context—not the bean instances. It will take effect on the IoC container after it loads the bean configurations but before any of the bean instances are created. The typical usage of a bean factory post processor is to alter the bean configurations before the beans are instantiated. Spring comes with several bean factory post processors for you to use. In practice, you seldom need to write your own bean factory post processors.

How It Works

Previously, you specified the logging path for a cashier in the bean configuration file. It is not a good practice to mix such deployment details with your bean configurations. A better approach is to extract the deployment details into a properties file, such as `config.properties`, in the root of the classpath. Then define the logging path in this file.

```
cashier.path=c:/cashier
```

Now you can use variables of the form `${var}` in your bean configuration file. To load the external properties from a properties file and use them to replace the variables, you have to register the bean factory post processor `PropertyPlaceholderConfigurer` in your application context. You can specify either one properties file in the `location` property or multiple properties files in the `locations` property.

```
<beans ...>
    ...
    <bean class="org.springframework.beans.factory.config.➥
        PropertyPlaceholderConfigurer">
        <property name="location">
            <value>config.properties</value>
        </property>
    </bean>
```

```
    <bean id="cashier1" class="com.apress.springrecipes.shop.Cashier">
        <property name="path" value="${cashier.path}" />
    </bean>
</beans>
```

Implemented as a bean factory post processor, PropertyPlaceholderConfigurer will replace the variables in your bean configuration file with the external properties before your beans get instantiated.

In Spring 2.5, the registration of PropertyPlaceholderConfigurer can be simply through the <context:property-placeholder> element.

```
<beans xmlns="http://www.springframework.org/schema/beans"
    xmlns:xsi="http://www.w3.org/2001/XMLSchema-instance"
    xmlns:context="http://www.springframework.org/schema/context"
    xsi:schemaLocation="http://www.springframework.org/schema/beans
        http://www.springframework.org/schema/beans/spring-beans-2.5.xsd
        http://www.springframework.org/schema/context
        http://www.springframework.org/schema/context/spring-context-2.5.xsd">

    <context:property-placeholder location="config.properties" />
    ...
</beans>
```

4-12. Resolving Text Messages

Problem

For an application to support internationalization (I18N for short, as there are 18 characters between the first character, *i*, and the last character, *n*), it requires the capability of resolving text messages for different locales.

Solution

Spring's application context is able to resolve text messages for a target locale by their keys. Typically, the messages for one locale should be stored in one separate properties file. This properties file is called a *resource bundle*.

MessageSource is an interface that defines several methods for resolving messages. The ApplicationContext interface extends this interface so that all application contexts are able to resolve text messages. An application context delegates the message resolution to a bean with the exact name messageSource. ResourceBundleMessageSource is the most common MessageSource implementation that resolves messages from resource bundles for different locales.

How It Works

As an example, you can create the following resource bundle, messages_en_US.properties, for the English language in the United States. Resource bundles will be loaded from the root of the classpath.

```
alert.checkout=A shopping cart has been checked out.
```

To resolve messages from resource bundles, you use ResourceBundleMessageSource as your MessageSource implementation. This bean's name must be set to messageSource for the application context to detect it. You have to specify the base name of the resource bundles for ResourceBundleMessageSource.

```
<beans ...>
    ...
    <bean id="messageSource"
        class="org.springframework.context.support.ResourceBundleMessageSource">
        <property name="basename">
            <value>messages</value>
        </property>
    </bean>
</beans>
```

For this MessageSource definition, if you look up a text message for the United States locale, whose preferred language is English, the resource bundle messages_en_US.properties, which matches both the language and country, will be considered first. If there's no such resource bundle or the message can't be found, the one messages_en.properties that matches the language only will be considered. If this resource bundle still can't be found, the default messages.properties for all locales will be chosen finally. For more information on resource bundle loading, you can refer to the javadoc of the java.util.ResourceBundle class.

Now you can ask the application context to resolve a message by the getMessage() method. The first argument is the key corresponding to the message and the third is the target locale.

```
package com.apress.springrecipes.shop;

import org.springframework.context.ApplicationContext;
import org.springframework.context.support.FileSystemXmlApplicationContext;

public class Main {

    public static void main(String[] args) throws Exception {
        ApplicationContext context =
            new FileSystemXmlApplicationContext("beans.xml");
        ...
        String alert = context.getMessage("alert.checkout", null, Locale.US);
        System.out.println(alert);
    }
}
```

The second argument of the getMessage() method is an array of message parameters. In the text message, you can define multiple parameters by index:

```
alert.checkout=A shopping cart costing {0} dollars has been checked out at {1}.
```

You have to pass in an object array to fill in the message parameters. The elements in this array will be converted into strings before filling in the parameters.

```
package com.apress.springrecipes.shop;
...
public class Main {

    public static void main(String[] args) throws Exception {
        ...
        String alert = context.getMessage("alert.checkout",
                new Object[] { 4, new Date() }, Locale.US);
        System.out.println(alert);
    }
}
```

In the `Main` class, you can resolve text messages because you can access the application context directly. But for a bean to resolve text messages, it has to implement either the `ApplicationContextAware` interface or the `MessageSourceAware` interface. Now you can delete the message resolution from the `Main` class.

```
package com.apress.springrecipes.shop;
...
import org.springframework.context.MessageSource;
import org.springframework.context.MessageSourceAware;

public class Cashier implements BeanNameAware, MessageSourceAware,
        StorageConfig {
    ...
    private MessageSource messageSource;

    public void setMessageSource(MessageSource messageSource) {
        this.messageSource = messageSource;
    }

    public void checkout(ShoppingCart cart) throws IOException {
        ...
        String alert = messageSource.getMessage("alert.checkout",
                new Object[] { total, new Date() }, Locale.US);
        System.out.println(alert);
    }
}
```

4-13. Communicating with Application Events

Problem

In the typical communication model between components, the sender has to locate the receiver to call a method on it. In this case, the sender component must be aware of the receiver component. This kind of communication is direct and simple, but the sender and receiver components are tightly coupled.

When using an IoC container, your components can communicate by interface rather than by implementation. This communication model can help reduce coupling. However, it is only efficient when a sender component has to communicate with one receiver. When a sender needs to communicate with multiple receivers, it has to call the receivers one by one.

Solution

Spring's application context supports event-based communication between its beans. In the event-based communication model, the sender component just publishes an event without knowing who the receiver will be. Actually, there may be more than one receiver component. Also, the receiver needn't know who is publishing the event. It can listen to multiple events from different senders at the same time. In this way, the sender and receiver components are loosely coupled.

In Spring, all event classes must extend the `ApplicationEvent` class. Then any bean can publish an event by calling an application event publisher's `publishEvent()` method. For a bean to listen to certain events, it must implement the `ApplicationListener` interface and handle the events in the `onApplicationEvent()` method. Actually, Spring will notify a listener of all events, so you must filter the events by yourself.

How It Works

Defining Events

The first step of enabling event-based communication is to define the event. Suppose you would like your cashier bean to publish a `CheckoutEvent` after the shopping cart has been checked out. This event includes two properties: the payment amount and the checkout time. In Spring, all events must extend the abstract class `ApplicationEvent` and pass the event source as a constructor argument.

```
package com.apress.springrecipes.shop;
...
import org.springframework.context.ApplicationEvent;

public class CheckoutEvent extends ApplicationEvent {

    private double amount;
    private Date time;

    public CheckoutEvent(Object source, double amount, Date time) {
        super(source);
        this.amount = amount;
        this.time = time;
    }

    public double getAmount() {
        return amount;
    }
```

```
    public Date getTime() {
        return time;
    }
}
```

Publishing Events

To publish an event, you just create an event instance and make a call to the publishEvent() method of an application event publisher, which can be accessed by implementing the ApplicationEventPublisherAware interface.

```
package com.apress.springrecipes.shop;
...
import org.springframework.context.ApplicationEventPublisher;
import org.springframework.context.ApplicationEventPublisherAware;

public class Cashier implements BeanNameAware, MessageSourceAware,
        ApplicationEventPublisherAware, StorageConfig {
    ...
    private ApplicationEventPublisher applicationEventPublisher;

    public void setApplicationEventPublisher(
            ApplicationEventPublisher applicationEventPublisher) {
        this.applicationEventPublisher = applicationEventPublisher;
    }

    public void checkout(ShoppingCart cart) throws IOException {
        ...
        CheckoutEvent event = new CheckoutEvent(this, total, new Date());
        applicationEventPublisher.publishEvent(event);
    }
}
```

Listening to Events

Any bean defined in the application context that implements the ApplicationListener interface will be notified of all events. So in the onApplicationEvent() method, you have to filter the events that your listener wants to handle. In the following listener, suppose you would like to send an e-mail to the customer notifying them about the checkout.

```
package com.apress.springrecipes.shop;
...
import org.springframework.context.ApplicationEvent;
import org.springframework.context.ApplicationListener;

public class CheckoutListener implements ApplicationListener {
```

```
    public void onApplicationEvent(ApplicationEvent event) {
        if (event instanceof CheckoutEvent) {
            double amount = ((CheckoutEvent) event).getAmount();
            Date time = ((CheckoutEvent) event).getTime();

            // Do anything you like with the checkout amount and time
            System.out.println("Checkout event [" + amount + ", " + time + "]");
        }
    }
}
```

Next, you have to register this listener in the application context to listen for all events. The registration is as simple as declaring a bean instance of this listener. The application context will recognize the beans that implement the `ApplicationListener` interface and notify them of each event.

```
<beans ...>
    ...
    <bean class="com.apress.springrecipes.shop.CheckoutListener" />
</beans>
```

Finally, notice that the application context itself will also publish container events such as `ContextClosedEvent`, `ContextRefreshedEvent`, and `RequestHandledEvent`. If any of your beans want to be notified of these events, they can implement the `ApplicationListener` interface.

4-14. Registering Property Editors in Spring

Problem

A property editor is a feature of the JavaBeans API for converting property values to and from text values. Each property editor is designed for a certain type of property only. You may wish to employ property editors to simplify your bean configurations.

Solution

The Spring IoC container supports using property editors to help with bean configurations. For example, with a property editor for the `java.net.URL` type, you can specify a URL string for a property of the `URL` type. Spring will automatically convert the URL string into a URL object and inject it into your property. Spring comes with several property editors for converting bean properties of common types.

Typically, you should register a property editor in the Spring IoC container before it can be used. The `CustomEditorConfigurer` is implemented as a bean factory post processor for you to register your custom property editors before any of the beans get instantiated.

How It Works

As an example, suppose you would like your product ranking to be based on sales for a particular period. For this change, you add the `fromDate` and `toDate` properties to your `ProductRanking` class.

```
package com.apress.springrecipes.shop;
...
public class ProductRanking {

    private Product bestSeller;
    private Date fromDate;
    private Date toDate;

    // Getters and Setters
    ...
}
```

To specify the value for a java.util.Date property in a Java program, you can convert it from a date string of particular pattern with the help of the DateFormat.parse() method.

```
DateFormat dateFormat = new SimpleDateFormat("yyyy-MM-dd");
productRanking.setFromDate(dateFormat.parse("2007-09-01"));
productRanking.setToDate(dateFormat.parse("2007-09-30"));
```

To write the equivalent bean configuration in Spring, you first declare a dateFormat bean with the pattern configured. As the parse() method is called for converting the date strings into date objects, you can consider it as an instance factory method to create the date beans.

```
<beans ...>
    ...
    <bean id="dateFormat" class="java.text.SimpleDateFormat">
        <constructor-arg value="yyyy-MM-dd" />
    </bean>

    <bean id="productRanking"
        class="com.apress.springrecipes.shop.ProductRanking">
        <property name="bestSeller">
            <bean class="com.apress.springrecipes.shop.Disc">
                <property name="name" value="CD-RW" />
                <property name="price" value="1.5" />
            </bean>
        </property>
        <property name="fromDate">
            <bean factory-bean="dateFormat" factory-method="parse">
                <constructor-arg value="2007-09-01" />
            </bean>
        </property>
        <property name="toDate">
            <bean factory-bean="dateFormat" factory-method="parse">
                <constructor-arg value="2007-09-30" />
            </bean>
        </property>
    </bean>
</beans>
```

As you can see, the preceding configuration is too complicated for setting date properties. Actually, the Spring IoC container is able to convert the text values for your properties by using property editors. The `CustomDateEditor` class that comes with Spring is for converting date strings into `java.util.Date` properties. First, you have to declare an instance of it in the bean configuration file.

```
<beans ...>
    ...
    <bean id="dateEditor"
        class="org.springframework.beans.propertyeditors.CustomDateEditor">
        <constructor-arg>
            <bean class="java.text.SimpleDateFormat">
                <constructor-arg value="yyyy-MM-dd" />
            </bean>
        </constructor-arg>
        <constructor-arg value="true" />
    </bean>
</beans>
```

This editor requires a `DateFormat` object as the first constructor argument. The second argument indicates whether this editor allows empty values.

Next you have to register this property editor in a `CustomEditorConfigurer` instance so that Spring can convert properties whose type is `java.util.Date`. Now you can specify a date value in text format for any `java.util.Date` properties:

```
<beans ...>
    ...
    <bean class="org.springframework.beans.factory.config.CustomEditorConfigurer">
        <property name="customEditors">
            <map>
                <entry key="java.util.Date">
                    <ref local="dateEditor" />
                </entry>
            </map>
        </property>
    </bean>

    <bean id="productRanking"
        class="com.apress.springrecipes.shop.ProductRanking">
        <property name="bestSeller">
            <bean class="com.apress.springrecipes.shop.Disc">
                <property name="name" value="CD-RW" />
                <property name="price" value="1.5" />
            </bean>
        </property>
        <property name="fromDate" value="2007-09-01" />
        <property name="toDate" value="2007-09-30" />
    </bean>
</beans>
```

You can test whether your CustomDateEditor configuration works with the following Main class:

```
package com.apress.springrecipes.shop;

import org.springframework.context.ApplicationContext;
import org.springframework.context.support.ClassPathXmlApplicationContext;

public class Main {

    public static void main(String[] args) throws Exception {
        ApplicationContext context =
            new ClassPathXmlApplicationContext("beans.xml");
        ...
        ProductRanking productRanking =
            (ProductRanking) context.getBean("productRanking");
        System.out.println(
                "Product ranking from " + productRanking.getFromDate() +
                " to " + productRanking.getToDate());
    }
}
```

In addition to CustomDateEditor, Spring comes with several property editors for converting common data types, such as CustomNumberEditor, ClassEditor, FileEditor, LocaleEditor, StringArrayPropertyEditor, and URLEditor. Among them, ClassEditor, FileEditor, LocaleEditor, and URLEditor are preregistered by Spring, so you don't need to register them again. For more information on using these editors, you can consult the javadoc of these classes in the org.springframework.beans.propertyeditors package.

4-15. Creating Custom Property Editors

Problem

In addition to registering the built-in property editors, you may want to write your own custom property editors for converting your custom data types.

Solution

You can write custom property editors by implementing the java.beans.PropertyEditor interface or extending the convenient support class java.beans.PropertyEditorSupport.

How It Works

For example, let's write a property editor for the Product class. You can design the string representation of a product as three parts, which are the concrete class name, the product name, and the price. Each part is separated by a comma. Then you can write the following ProductEditor class for converting them:

```
package com.apress.springrecipes.shop;

import java.beans.PropertyEditorSupport;

public class ProductEditor extends PropertyEditorSupport {

    public String getAsText() {
        Product product = (Product) getValue();
        return product.getClass().getName() + "," + product.getName() + ","
                + product.getPrice();
    }

    public void setAsText(String text) throws IllegalArgumentException {
        String[] parts = text.split(",");
        try {
            Product product = (Product) Class.forName(parts[0]).newInstance();
            product.setName(parts[1]);
            product.setPrice(Double.parseDouble(parts[2]));
            setValue(product);
        } catch (Exception e) {
            throw new IllegalArgumentException(e);
        }
    }
}
```

The getAsText() method converts a property into a string value, while the setAsText() method converts a string back into a property. The property value is retrieved and set by calling the getValue() and setValue() methods.

Next you have to register your custom editor in a CustomEditorConfigurer instance before it can be used. Registration is the same as for the built-in editors. Now you can specify a product in text format for any property whose type is Product.

```
<beans ...>
    ...
    <bean class="org.springframework.beans.factory.config.CustomEditorConfigurer">
        <property name="customEditors">
            <map>
                ...
                <entry key="com.apress.springrecipes.shop.Product">
                    <bean class="com.apress.springrecipes.shop.ProductEditor" />
                </entry>
            </map>
        </property>
    </bean>

    <bean id="productRanking"
        class="com.apress.springrecipes.shop.ProductRanking">
        <property name="bestSeller">
```

```
            <value>com.apress.springrecipes.shop.Disc,CD-RW,1.5</value>
        </property>
        ...
    </bean>
</beans>
```

In fact, the JavaBeans API will automatically search a property editor for a class. For a property editor to be searched correctly, it must be located in the same package as the target class, and the name must be the target class name with `Editor` as its suffix. If your property editor is provided in this convention, such as in the preceding `ProductEditor`, there's no need to register it again in the Spring IoC container.

4-16. Loading External Resources

Problem

Sometimes your application may need to read external resources (e.g., text files, XML files, properties file, or image files) from different locations (e.g., a file system, classpath, or URL). Usually, you have to deal with different APIs for loading resources from different locations.

Solution

Spring's resource loader provides a unified `getResource()` method for you to retrieve an external resource by a resource path. You can specify different prefixes for this path to load resources from different locations. To load a resource from a file system, you use the `file` prefix. To load a resource from the classpath, you use the `classpath` prefix. You may also specify a URL in this resource path.

`Resource` is a general interface in Spring for representing an external resource. Spring provides several implementations for the `Resource` interface, as shown in Figure 4-1. The resource loader's `getResource()` method will decide which `Resource` implementation to instantiate according to the resource path.

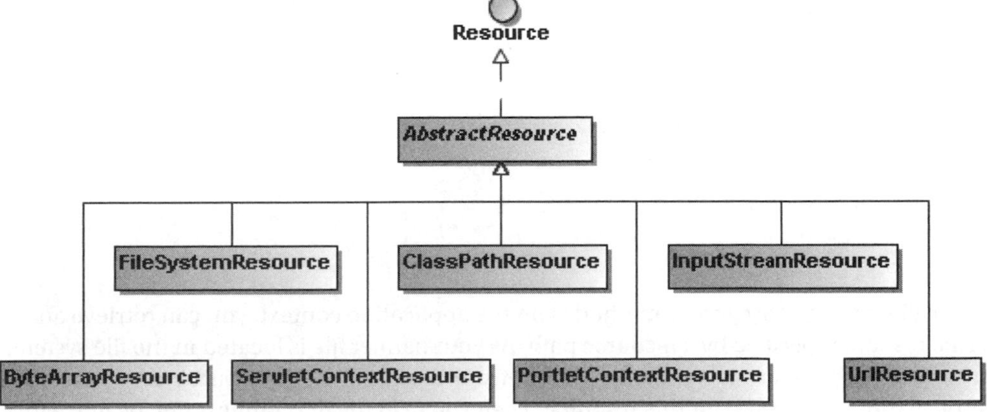

Figure 4-1. *Common implementations of the Resource interface*

How It Works

Suppose you would like to display a banner at the startup of your shop application. The banner is made up of the following characters and stored in a text file called `banner.txt`. This file can be put in the current path of your application.

```
***********************
* Welcome to My Shop! *
***********************
```

Next you have to write the `BannerLoader` class to load the banner and output it to the console. As it requires access to a resource loader for loading the resource, it has to implement either the `ApplicationContextAware` interface or the `ResourceLoaderAware` interface.

```
package com.apress.springrecipes.shop;
...
import org.springframework.context.ResourceLoaderAware;
import org.springframework.core.io.Resource;
import org.springframework.core.io.ResourceLoader;

public class BannerLoader implements ResourceLoaderAware {

    private ResourceLoader resourceLoader;

    public void setResourceLoader(ResourceLoader resourceLoader) {
        this.resourceLoader = resourceLoader;
    }

    public void showBanner() throws IOException {
        Resource banner = resourceLoader.getResource("file:banner.txt");
        InputStream in = banner.getInputStream();

        BufferedReader reader = new BufferedReader(new InputStreamReader(in));
        while (true) {
            String line = reader.readLine();
            if (line == null)
                break;
            System.out.println(line);
        }
        reader.close();
    }
}
```

By calling the `getResource()` method from the application context, you can retrieve an external resource specified by a resource path. As your banner file is located in the file system, the resource path should start with the `file` prefix. You can call the `getInputStream()` method to retrieve the input stream for this resource. Then you read the file contents line by line with `BufferedReader` and output them to the console.

Finally, you declare a BannerLoader instance in the bean configuration file to display the banner. As you would like to show the banner at startup, you specify the showBanner() method as the initialization method.

```
<bean id="bannerLoader"
    class="com.apress.springrecipes.shop.BannerLoader"
    init-method="showBanner" />
```

Resource Prefixes

The previous resource path specifies a resource in the relative path of the file system. You can specify an absolute path as well.

```
file:c:/shop/banner.txt
```

When your resource is located in the classpath, you have to use the classpath prefix. If there's no path information presented, it will be loaded from the root of the classpath.

```
classpath:banner.txt
```

If the resource is located in a particular package, you can specify the absolute path from the classpath root.

```
classpath:com/apress/springrecipes/shop/banner.txt
```

Besides a file system path or the classpath, a resource can also be loaded by specifying a URL.

```
http://springrecipes.apress.com/shop/banner.txt
```

If there's no prefix presented in the resource path, the resource will be loaded from a location according to the application context. For FileSystemXmlApplicationContext, the resource will be loaded from the file system. For ClassPathXmlApplicationContext, it will be loaded from the classpath.

Injecting Resources

In addition to calling the getResource() method to load a resource explicitly, you can inject it by using a setter method:

```
package com.apress.springrecipes.shop;
...
import org.springframework.core.io.Resource;

public class BannerLoader {

    private Resource banner;

    public void setBanner(Resource banner) {
        this.banner = banner;
    }
```

```
    public void showBanner() throws IOException {
        InputStream in = banner.getInputStream();
        ...
    }
}
```

In the bean configuration, you can simply specify the resource path for this Resource property. Spring will use the preregistered property editor ResourceEditor to convert it into a Resource object before injecting it into your bean.

```
<bean id="bannerLoader"
    class="com.apress.springrecipes.shop.BannerLoader"
    init-method="showBanner">
    <property name="banner">
        <value>classpath:com/apress/springrecipes/shop/banner.txt</value>
    </property>
</bean>
```

4-17. Summary

In this chapter, you have learned various ways of creating a bean, which include invoking a constructor, invoking a static/instance factory method, using a factory bean, and retrieving it from a static field/object property. The Spring IoC container makes it easy to create beans in these ways.

In Spring 2.x, you can specify the bean scope to control which bean instance should be returned when requested. The default bean scope is singleton—Spring creates a single and shared bean instance per Spring IoC container. Another common scope is prototype—Spring creates a new bean instance each time when requested.

You can customize the initialization and destruction of your beans by specifying the corresponding callback methods. In addition, your beans can implement certain aware interfaces to be made aware of the container's configurations and infrastructures. The Spring IoC container will call these methods at particular points of a bean's life cycle.

Spring supports registering bean post processors in the IoC container to perform additional bean processing before and after the initialization callback methods. Bean post processors can process all the beans in the IoC container. Typically, bean post processors are used for checking the validity of bean properties or altering the bean properties according to particular criteria.

You have also learned about certain advanced IoC container features, such as externalizing bean configuration into properties files, resolving text messages from resource bundles, publishing and listening to application events, using property editors to convert property values from text values, and loading external resources. You will find these features very useful when developing applications with Spring.

In the next chapter, you will learn about another core feature of the Spring framework: aspect-oriented programming.

CHAPTER 5

Dynamic Proxy and Classic Spring AOP

In this chapter, you will first learn the nature of crosscutting concerns and how they can be modularized with dynamic proxies. Then you will focus on the AOP usage in Spring version 1.x, which is referred to as classic Spring AOP. The usage of Spring AOP has changed significantly from version 1.x to 2.x. Classic Spring AOP is introduced mainly for compatibility purposes. Each time you start a new project with Spring 2.x, you should choose the new Spring AOP approach, which will be introduced thoroughly in the next chapter.

Aspect-oriented programming (AOP) is a new methodology to complement traditional *object-oriented programming (OOP)*. The motivation of AOP is not to substitute for OOP. In fact, AOP is often used together with OOP. In the world of OOP, applications are organized with classes and interfaces. These elements are good for implementing the core business requirements, but not the crosscutting concerns (i.e., the functions or requirements that span multiple modules of an application). Crosscutting concerns are very common in enterprise applications. The typical examples include logging, validation, and transaction management.

AOP provides another way for developers to organize their application structures. Instead of the classes and interfaces of OOP, the main programming elements of AOP are *aspects*. You may imagine that an aspect modularizes crosscutting concerns like a class modularizes states and behaviors in OOP.

Besides the IoC container, another core module of the Spring framework is its AOP framework. Currently, there are many AOP frameworks on the market implemented for different purposes and based on different technologies, but only the following three open source AOP frameworks have entered the mainstream:

- AspectJ, merged with AspectWerkz since version 5 (`http://www.eclipse.org/aspectj/`)
- JBoss AOP, as a subproject of the JBoss application server (`http://labs.jboss.com/jbossaop/`)
- Spring AOP, as part of the Spring framework (`http://www.springframework.org/`)

Among them, AspectJ is the most complete and popular AOP framework in the Java community. By comparison, Spring AOP is not a competitor of AspectJ to provide another complete AOP implementation. Its purpose is only to provide an AOP solution that can consistently integrate with its IoC container. In fact, Spring AOP will only handle crosscutting concerns for the beans declared in its IoC container.

The core implementation technology of Spring AOP is dynamic proxy. Although the usage of Spring AOP has changed significantly from version 1.x to 2.x, the implementation technology remains the same. Moreover, Spring AOP is backward compatible, so you can continue to use your Spring 1.x AOP elements in Spring 2.x.

- In Spring version 1.x, the AOP usage is through a set of proprietary Spring AOP APIs.
- In Spring version 2.0, the AOP usage is through writing POJOs with either AspectJ annotations or XML-based configurations in the bean configuration file.

Upon finishing this chapter, you will be able to identify the crosscutting concerns in an application and modularize them with classic Spring AOP. You will also gain basic knowledge on the core implementation technology for Spring AOP: dynamic proxy. It can help you to better understand the mechanism of Spring AOP.

5-1. Problems with Non-Modularized Crosscutting Concerns

By definition, a crosscutting concern is a functionality that spans multiple modules of an application. This kind of concern is often hard to modularize with the traditional object-oriented approach. To understand crosscutting concerns, let's start with a simple calculator example. First, you create two interfaces, `ArithmeticCalculator` and `UnitCalculator`, for arithmetic calculation and measurement unit conversion.

```
package com.apress.springrecipes.calculator;

public interface ArithmeticCalculator {

    public double add(double a, double b);
    public double sub(double a, double b);
    public double mul(double a, double b);
    public double div(double a, double b);
}
```

```
package com.apress.springrecipes.calculator;

public interface UnitCalculator {

    public double kilogramToPound(double kilogram);
    public double kilometerToMile(double kilometer);
}
```

Then you provide a simple implementation for each calculator interface. The `println` statements notify you of when these methods are executed.

```
package com.apress.springrecipes.calculator;

public class ArithmeticCalculatorImpl implements ArithmeticCalculator {

    public double add(double a, double b) {
        double result = a + b;
```

```
        System.out.println(a + " + " + b + " = " + result);
        return result;
    }

    public double sub(double a, double b) {
        double result = a - b;
        System.out.println(a + " - " + b + " = " + result);
        return result;
    }

    public double mul(double a, double b) {
        double result = a * b;
        System.out.println(a + " * " + b + " = " + result);
        return result;
    }

    public double div(double a, double b) {
        double result = a / b;
        System.out.println(a + " / " + b + " = " + result);
        return result;
    }
}
```

```
package com.apress.springrecipes.calculator;

public class UnitCalculatorImpl implements UnitCalculator {

    public double kilogramToPound(double kilogram) {
        double pound = kilogram * 2.2;
        System.out.println(kilogram + " kilogram = " + pound + " pound");
        return pound;
    }

    public double kilometerToMile(double kilometer) {
        double mile = kilometer * 0.62;
        System.out.println(kilometer + " kilometer = " + mile + " mile");
        return mile;
    }
}
```

Tracing the Methods

A common requirement of most applications is to trace the activities that take place during program execution. For the Java platform, there are several logging implementations available for you to choose. However, if you would like your application to be independent of the logging implementation, you can make use of the Apache Commons Logging library. It provides abstract APIs that are implementation independent and allows you to switch between different implementations without modifying your code.

Note To use the Apache Commons Logging library, you have to include `commons-logging.jar` (located in the `lib/jakarta-commons` directory of the Spring installation) in your classpath.

For your calculators, you can log the beginning and ending of each method, as well as the method arguments and return values.

```
package com.apress.springrecipes.calculator;

import org.apache.commons.logging.Log;
import org.apache.commons.logging.LogFactory;

public class ArithmeticCalculatorImpl implements ArithmeticCalculator {

    private Log log = LogFactory.getLog(this.getClass());

    public double add(double a, double b) {
        log.info("The method add() begins with " + a + ", " + b);
        double result = a + b;
        System.out.println(a + " + " + b + " = " + result);
        log.info("The method add() ends with " + result);
        return result;
    }

    public double sub(double a, double b) {
        log.info("The method sub() begins with " + a + ", " + b);
        double result = a - b;
        System.out.println(a + " - " + b + " = " + result);
        log.info("The method sub() ends with " + result);
        return result;
    }

    public double mul(double a, double b) {
        log.info("The method mul() begins with " + a + ", " + b);
        double result = a * b;
        System.out.println(a + " * " + b + " = " + result);
        log.info("The method mul() ends with " + result);
        return result;
    }

    public double div(double a, double b) {
        log.info("The method div() begins with " + a + ", " + b);
        double result = a / b;
```

```
        System.out.println(a + " / " + b + " = " + result);
        log.info("The method div() ends with " + result);
        return result;
    }
}

package com.apress.springrecipes.calculator;

import org.apache.commons.logging.Log;
import org.apache.commons.logging.LogFactory;

public class UnitCalculatorImpl implements UnitCalculator {

    private Log log = LogFactory.getLog(this.getClass());

    public double kilogramToPound(double kilogram) {
        log.info("The method kilogramToPound() begins with " + kilogram);
        double pound = kilogram * 2.2;
        System.out.println(kilogram + " kilogram = " + pound + " pound");
        log.info("The method kilogramToPound() ends with " + pound);
        return pound;
    }

    public double kilometerToMile(double kilometer) {
        log.info("The method kilometerToMile() begins with " + kilometer);
        double mile = kilometer * 0.62;
        System.out.println(kilometer + " kilometer = " + mile + " mile");
        log.info("The method kilometerToMile() ends with " + mile);
        return mile;
    }
}
```

Now you are free to pick up a logging implementation supported by the Commons Logging library. Currently it mainly supports the Log4J library from Apache and the JDK Logging API (available for JDK 1.4 and higher versions). Of these, Log4J is the better choice, as it is more powerful and easier to configure.

■Note To use the Log4J library, you have to include `log4j-1.2.14.jar` (located in the `lib/log4j` directory of the Spring installation) in your classpath. Once the Log4J library is detected in the classpath, Commons Logging will use it as the underlying logging implementation.

You can configure the Log4J library through a properties file named `log4j.properties` in the root of the classpath. The following Log4J configuration file defines a log appender called `stdout` that will output log messages to the console in a format controlled by the specified pattern. For more information about logging patterns of Log4J, you can refer to the Log4J documentation.

```
### direct log messages to stdout ###
log4j.appender.stdout=org.apache.log4j.ConsoleAppender
log4j.appender.stdout.layout=org.apache.log4j.PatternLayout
log4j.appender.stdout.layout.ConversionPattern=➥
%d{yyyy-MM-dd HH:mm:ss} %5p %c{1}:%L - %m%n

### set root logger level ###
log4j.rootLogger=error, stdout

### set application logger level ###
log4j.logger.com.apress.springrecipes.calculator=info
```

Log4J supports six logging levels for you to set the urgency of your logging messages. Listed from highest to lowest, they are `fatal`, `error`, `warn`, `info`, `debug`, and `trace`. As specified in the preceding Log4J configuration file, the root (default) logging level for this application is `error`, which means that only logs for the `error` and `fatal` levels will be output by default. But for the `com.apress.springrecipes.calculator` package and its subpackages, the logs for levels higher than `info` will also be output.

To test the basic functionalities and the logging configuration of these two calculators, you can write the `Main` class as follows:

```
package com.apress.springrecipes.calculator;

public class Main {

    public static void main(String[] args) {
        ArithmeticCalculator arithmeticCalculator = new ArithmeticCalculatorImpl();
        arithmeticCalculator.add(1, 2);
        arithmeticCalculator.sub(4, 3);
        arithmeticCalculator.mul(2, 3);
        arithmeticCalculator.div(4, 2);

        UnitCalculator unitCalculator = new UnitCalculatorImpl();
        unitCalculator.kilogramToPound(10);
        unitCalculator.kilometerToMile(5);
    }
}
```

Validating the Arguments

Now let's consider adding a restriction to your calculators. Suppose you would like your calculators to support positive numbers only. At the beginning of each method, you make calls to the `validate()` method to check if all the arguments are positive numbers. For any negative numbers, you throw an `IllegalArgumentException`.

```
package com.apress.springrecipes.calculator;
...
public class ArithmeticCalculatorImpl implements ArithmeticCalculator {
    ...
    public double add(double a, double b) {
        validate(a);
        validate(b);
        ...
    }

    public double sub(double a, double b) {
        validate(a);
        validate(b);
        ...
    }

    public double mul(double a, double b) {
        validate(a);
        validate(b);
        ...
    }

    public double div(double a, double b) {
        validate(a);
        validate(b);
        ...
    }

    private void validate(double a) {
        if (a < 0) {
            throw new IllegalArgumentException("Positive numbers only");
        }
    }
}
```

```
package com.apress.springrecipes.calculator;
...
public class UnitCalculatorImpl implements UnitCalculator {
    ...
    public double kilogramToPound(double kilogram) {
        validate(kilogram);
        ...
    }

    public double kilometerToMile(double kilometer) {
        validate(kilometer);
```

```
        ...
    }

    private void validate(double a) {
        if (a < 0) {
            throw new IllegalArgumentException("Positive numbers only");
        }
    }
}
```

Identifying the Problems

As you can see, the original calculator methods expand as you add more and more non-business requirements, such as logging and validation. These systemwide requirements usually have to crosscut multiple modules, so they are called *crosscutting concerns* to distinguish them from the core business requirements, which are called the *core concerns* of a system. Typical crosscutting concerns within an enterprise application include logging, validation, pooling, caching, authentication, and transaction. Figure 5-1 shows the crosscutting concerns in your calculator application.

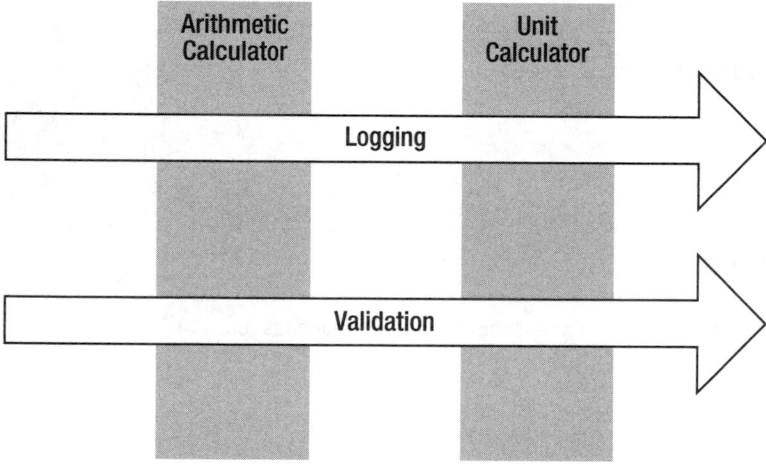

Figure 5-1. *Crosscutting concerns in the calculator application*

However, with only classes and interfaces as programming elements, the traditional object-oriented approach cannot modularize crosscutting concerns well. Developers often have to mix them with core concerns in the same modules. As a result, these crosscutting concerns are spread out in different modules of an application and are thus not modularized.

There are two main problems caused by non-modularized crosscutting concerns. The first is *code tangling*. Like the preceding calculator methods, each of them has to handle multiple concerns as well as the core calculation logic at the same time. This will lead to poor code maintainability and reusability. For instance, the preceding calculator implementations would be hard to reuse in another application that has no logging requirement and can accept negative numbers as operands.

Another problem caused by non-modularized crosscutting concerns is *code scattering*. For the logging requirement, you have to repeat the logging statements multiple times in multiple modules to fulfill a single requirement. Later, if the logging criteria change, you would have to modify all of the modules. Moreover, it is also hard to ensure that the logging requirement will be implemented consistently. If you have missed a logging statement somewhere, the overall system logging will be inconsistent.

For all these reasons, the calculators should concentrate on the core calculation logic only. Let's separate the logging and validation concerns from them.

```
package com.apress.springrecipes.calculator;

public class ArithmeticCalculatorImpl implements ArithmeticCalculator {

    public double add(double a, double b) {
        double result = a + b;
        System.out.println(a + " + " + b + " = " + result);
        return result;
    }

    public double sub(double a, double b) {
        double result = a - b;
        System.out.println(a + " - " + b + " = " + result);
        return result;
    }

    public double mul(double a, double b) {
        double result = a * b;
        System.out.println(a + " * " + b + " = " + result);
        return result;
    }

    public double div(double a, double b) {
        double result = a / b;
        System.out.println(a + " / " + b + " = " + result);
        return result;
    }
}
```

```
package com.apress.springrecipes.calculator;

public class UnitCalculatorImpl implements UnitCalculator {

    public double kilogramToPound(double kilogram) {
        double pound = kilogram * 2.2;
        System.out.println(kilogram + " kilogram = " + pound + " pound");
        return pound;
    }
```

```
    public double kilometerToMile(double kilometer) {
        double mile = kilometer * 0.62;
        System.out.println(kilometer + " kilometer = " + mile + " mile");
        return mile;
    }
}
```

5-2. Modularizing Crosscutting Concerns with Dynamic Proxy

Problem

As non-modularized crosscutting concerns will cause the code tangling and code scattering problems, you would like to seek a method to modularize them. However, they are often hard to modularize with the traditional object-oriented approach, as they span multiple modules of an application.

Solution

You can apply a design pattern called *proxy* to separate crosscutting concerns from core concerns. Proxy is one of the 23 GoF (Gang of Four) object-oriented design patterns, which belong to the "structural pattern" category.

The principle of the proxy design pattern is to wrap an object with a proxy and use this proxy to substitute for the original object. Any calls that were made to the original object will go through the proxy first. Figure 5-2 illustrates the general idea of the proxy design pattern.

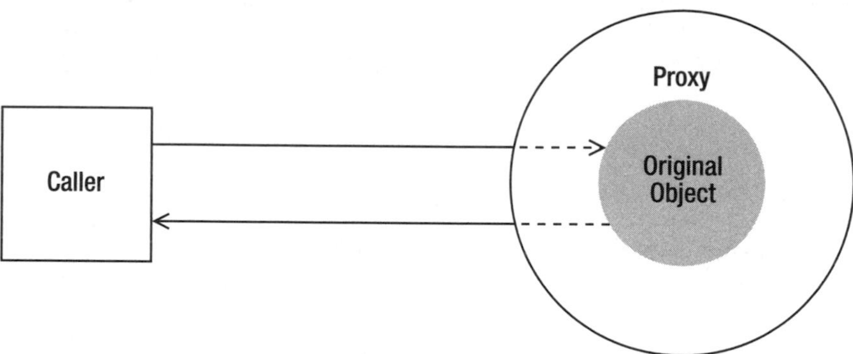

Figure 5-2. *General idea of the proxy design pattern*

The proxy object is responsible for deciding when and whether to forward method calls to the original object. In the meanwhile, the proxy can also perform additional tasks around each method call. So, the proxy would be a good place to implement the crosscutting concerns.

In Java, there are two ways to implement the proxy design pattern. The traditional one is to write a static proxy in pure object-oriented style. Static proxy works by wrapping an object with a dedicated proxy to perform additional tasks around each method call. The dedication means you have to write a proxy class for each interface to be able to substitute for the original implementation, which is very inefficient in a large application with hundreds or thousands of components.

Another method is through the dynamic proxy support offered by JDK version 1.3 or higher. It supports creating a proxy dynamically for any object. The only restriction is that the object must implement at least one interface, and only the calls to the methods declared in the interfaces will go through the proxy. However, there's another kind of proxy, CGLIB proxy, that doesn't have this restriction. It can handle all the methods declared in a class even if it doesn't implement any interface.

Dynamic proxies are implemented with the Java Reflection API, so they can be used in a more general way than static proxies. For this reason, dynamic proxy is one of the core technologies used by Spring for its AOP implementation.

How It Works

A JDK dynamic proxy requires an invocation handler to handle method invocations. An invocation handler is simply a class that implements the following `InvocationHandler` interface:

```
package java.lang.reflect;

public interface InvocationHandler {

    public Object invoke(Object proxy, Method method, Object[] args)
        throws Throwable;
}
```

The only method declared in this interface is `invoke()`. It allows you to control the overall invocation process yourself. The first argument of the `invoke()` method is the proxy instance whose method was being invoked. The second argument is the method object whose type is `java.lang.reflect.Method`. It represents the current method being invoked. The last argument is an array of arguments for invoking the target method. Finally, you have to return a value as the current method invocation's result.

Creating the Logging Proxy

By implementing the `InvocationHandler` interface, you can write an invocation handler that logs the method beginning and ending. You require a target calculator object to perform the actual calculation, which is passed in as a constructor argument.

```
package com.apress.springrecipes.calculator;

import java.lang.reflect.InvocationHandler;
import java.lang.reflect.Method;
import java.util.Arrays;

import org.apache.commons.logging.Log;
import org.apache.commons.logging.LogFactory;

public class CalculatorLoggingHandler implements InvocationHandler {
```

```
    private Log log = LogFactory.getLog(this.getClass());

    private Object target;

    public CalculatorLoggingHandler(Object target) {
        this.target = target;
    }

    public Object invoke(Object proxy, Method method, Object[] args)
            throws Throwable {
        // Log the method beginning with the method name and arguments.
        log.info("The method " + method.getName() + "() begins with "
                + Arrays.toString(args));

        // Perform the actual calculation on the target calculator object by calling
        // Method.invoke() and passing in the target object and method arguments.
        Object result = method.invoke(target, args);

        // Log the method ending with the returning result.
        log.info("The method " + method.getName() + "() ends with " + result);
        return result;
    }
}
```

By using reflection, the invoke() method is general enough to handle all method calls of the two calculators. You can access the method name by calling Method.getName(), and you can access the arguments in an object array. To perform the actual calculation, you make a call to invoke() on the method object and pass in the target calculator object and method arguments.

To create a JDK dynamic proxy instance with an invocation handler, you just make a call to the static method Proxy.newProxyInstance().

```
package com.apress.springrecipes.calculator;

import java.lang.reflect.Proxy;

public class Main {

    public static void main(String[] args) {
        ArithmeticCalculator arithmeticCalculatorImpl =
            new ArithmeticCalculatorImpl();

        ArithmeticCalculator arithmeticCalculator =
            (ArithmeticCalculator) Proxy.newProxyInstance(
                    arithmeticCalculatorImpl.getClass().getClassLoader(),
                    arithmeticCalculatorImpl.getClass().getInterfaces(),
                    new CalculatorLoggingHandler(arithmeticCalculatorImpl));
```

```
        ...
    }
}
```

The first argument of this method is the class loader to register this proxy. In most cases, you should define a proxy in the same class loader as the original class. The second argument consists of the interfaces for this proxy to implement. Only the calls to the methods declared in these interfaces will go through the proxy. Usually, you will proxy for all interfaces of the target class. The last argument is your invocation handler to handle the method invocation. By calling this method, you will get a proxy instance that was created by JDK dynamically. You can use it for calculation to have all method calls pass through the logging handler.

For reuse purpose, you can encapsulate the proxy creation code in a static method of the handler class.

```
package com.apress.springrecipes.calculator;
...
import java.lang.reflect.Proxy;

public class CalculatorLoggingHandler implements InvocationHandler {
    ...
    public static Object createProxy(Object target) {
        return Proxy.newProxyInstance(
                target.getClass().getClassLoader(),
                target.getClass().getInterfaces(),
                new CalculatorLoggingHandler(target));
    }
}
```

Now, the proxy creation code in the `Main` class is as simple as calling the static method.

```
package com.apress.springrecipes.calculator;

public class Main {

    public static void main(String[] args) {
        ArithmeticCalculator arithmeticCalculatorImpl =
            new ArithmeticCalculatorImpl();

        ArithmeticCalculator arithmeticCalculator =
            (ArithmeticCalculator) CalculatorLoggingHandler.createProxy(
                    arithmeticCalculatorImpl);
        ...
    }
}
```

With this general logging invocation handler, you can also create a proxy for `UnitCalculator` dynamically.

```
package com.apress.springrecipes.calculator;

public class Main {

    public static void main(String[] args) {
        ...
        UnitCalculator unitCalculatorImpl = new UnitCalculatorImpl();

        UnitCalculator unitCalculator =
            (UnitCalculator) CalculatorLoggingHandler.createProxy(
                    unitCalculatorImpl);
        ...
    }
}
```

Figure 5-3 illustrates the implementation of the logging concern with the proxy design pattern.

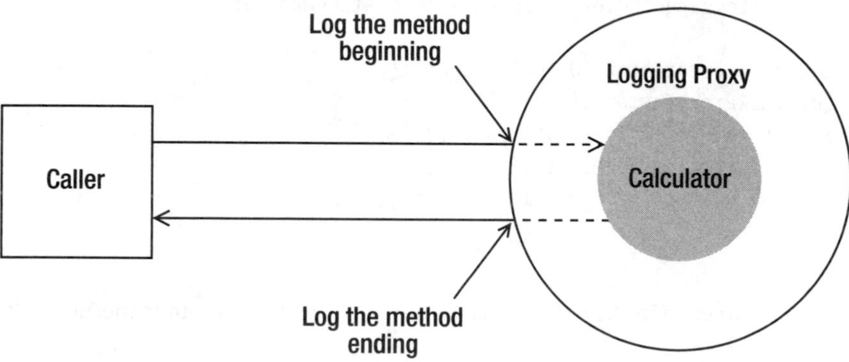

Figure 5-3. *Implementation of the logging concern with proxy*

Creating the Validation Proxy

Similarly, you can write a validation handler as shown following. As a different method may have a different number of arguments, you have to loop the argument array to validate each method argument.

```
package com.apress.springrecipes.calculator;

import java.lang.reflect.InvocationHandler;
import java.lang.reflect.Method;
import java.lang.reflect.Proxy;

public class CalculatorValidationHandler implements InvocationHandler {
```

```
    public static Object createProxy(Object target) {
        return Proxy.newProxyInstance(
                target.getClass().getClassLoader(),
                target.getClass().getInterfaces(),
                new CalculatorValidationHandler(target));
    }

    private Object target;

    public CalculatorValidationHandler(Object target) {
        this.target = target;
    }

    public Object invoke(Object proxy, Method method, Object[] args)
            throws Throwable {
        for (Object arg : args) {
            validate((Double) arg);
        }
        Object result = method.invoke(target, args);
        return result;
    }

    private void validate(double a) {
        if (a < 0) {
            throw new IllegalArgumentException("Positive numbers only");
        }
    }
}
```

In the Main class, you can wrap the logging proxy by a validation proxy to form a proxy chain. Any calculator method calls will go through the validation proxy first and then the logging proxy. That means validation will be performed prior to logging. If you prefer the reverse order, you should use the logging proxy to wrap the validation proxy instead.

```
package com.apress.springrecipes.calculator;

public class Main {

    public static void main(String[] args) {
        ArithmeticCalculator arithmeticCalculatorImpl =
            new ArithmeticCalculatorImpl();

        ArithmeticCalculator arithmeticCalculator =
            (ArithmeticCalculator) CalculatorValidationHandler.createProxy(
                    CalculatorLoggingHandler.createProxy(
                    arithmeticCalculatorImpl));
        ...
```

```
        UnitCalculator unitCalculatorImpl = new UnitCalculatorImpl();

        UnitCalculator unitCalculator =
            (UnitCalculator) CalculatorValidationHandler.createProxy(
                    CalculatorLoggingHandler.createProxy(
                    unitCalculatorImpl));
        ...
    }
}
```

Figure 5-4 illustrates the implementation of both the validation and logging concerns with the proxy design pattern.

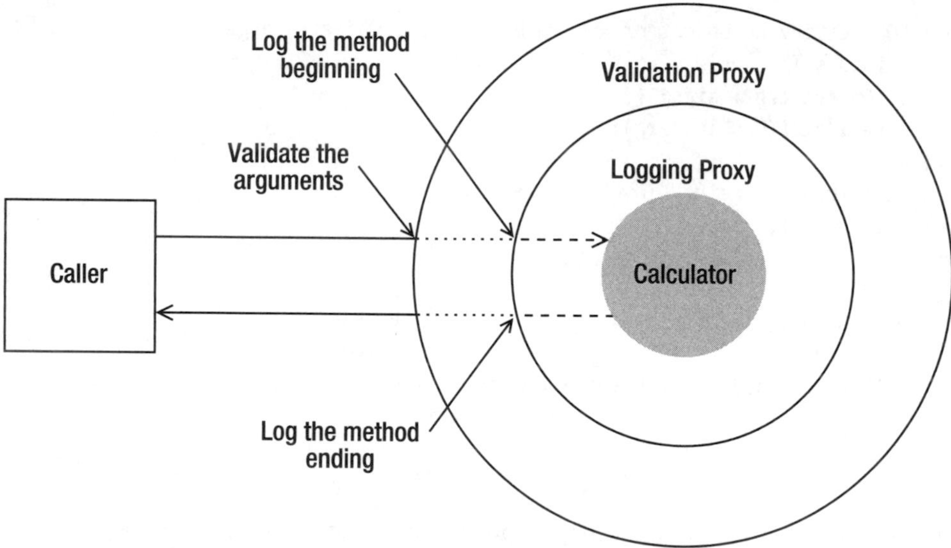

Figure 5-4. *Implementation of both the validation and logging concerns with proxy*

5-3. Modularizing Crosscutting Concerns with Classic Spring Advices

Problem

As crosscutting concerns are often hard to modularize with the traditional object-oriented approach, you would like to seek another approach to modularize them. Dynamic proxy is helpful in modularizing crosscutting concerns, but it's too demanding for an application developer to write such low-level proxy code.

Solution

AOP defines a group of high-level concepts for application developers to express their crosscutting concerns. First, the crosscutting action to take at a particular execution point is encapsulated in an *advice*. For example, you can encapsulate the logging and validation actions in one or more advices.

Classic Spring AOP supports four types of advices, each of which takes effect at different times of an execution point. In the formal AOP definition, there are many types of execution points, including method executions, constructor executions, and field accesses. However, Spring AOP only supports method executions. So, the definition of the four classic advice types can be narrowed down to the following:

- *Before advice*: Before the method execution
- *After returning advice*: After the method returns a result
- *After throwing advice*: After the method throws an exception
- *Around advice*: Around the method execution

When using the classic Spring AOP approach, advices are written by implementing one of the proprietary advice interfaces.

How It Works

The aim of Spring AOP is only to handle crosscutting concerns for the beans declared in its IoC container. So, before using Spring AOP to modularize crosscutting concerns, you have to migrate your calculator application to run within the Spring IoC container. You just declare the two calculators in Spring's bean configuration file.

```
<beans xmlns="http://www.springframework.org/schema/beans"
    xmlns:xsi="http://www.w3.org/2001/XMLSchema-instance"
    xsi:schemaLocation="http://www.springframework.org/schema/beans
        http://www.springframework.org/schema/beans/spring-beans-2.5.xsd">

    <bean id="arithmeticCalculator"
        class="com.apress.springrecipes.calculator.ArithmeticCalculatorImpl" />

    <bean id="unitCalculator"
        class="com.apress.springrecipes.calculator.UnitCalculatorImpl" />
</beans>
```

Then modify the `Main` class to get the calculator instances from the IoC container instead.

```
package com.apress.springrecipes.calculator;

import org.springframework.context.ApplicationContext;
import org.springframework.context.support.ClassPathXmlApplicationContext;

public class Main {
```

```
    public static void main(String[] args) {
        ApplicationContext context =
            new ClassPathXmlApplicationContext("beans.xml");

        ArithmeticCalculator arithmeticCalculator =
            (ArithmeticCalculator) context.getBean("arithmeticCalculator");
        ...

        UnitCalculator unitCalculator =
            (UnitCalculator) context.getBean("unitCalculator");
        ...
    }
}
```

Before Advices

A *before* advice takes effect before the method execution. It is created by implementing the `MethodBeforeAdvice` interface. In the `before()` method, you can get access to the method detail as well as the arguments.

```
package com.apress.springrecipes.calculator;

import java.lang.reflect.Method;
import java.util.Arrays;

import org.apache.commons.logging.Log;
import org.apache.commons.logging.LogFactory;
import org.springframework.aop.MethodBeforeAdvice;

public class LoggingBeforeAdvice implements MethodBeforeAdvice {

    private Log log = LogFactory.getLog(this.getClass());

    public void before(Method method, Object[] args, Object target)
            throws Throwable {
        log.info("The method " + method.getName() + "() begins with "
                + Arrays.toString(args));
    }
}
```

■ **Tip** The advice concept is similar to an invocation handler when using dynamic proxy.

With this advice ready, the next step is to apply it to your calculator beans. First, you have to declare an instance of this advice in the IoC container. Then, the most important step is to create a proxy for each of your calculator beans to apply this advice. Proxy creation in Spring AOP is accomplished by a factory bean called `ProxyFactoryBean`.

```
<beans ...>
    ...
    <bean id="loggingBeforeAdvice"
        class="com.apress.springrecipes.calculator.LoggingBeforeAdvice" />

    <bean id="arithmeticCalculatorProxy"
        class="org.springframework.aop.framework.ProxyFactoryBean">
        <property name="proxyInterfaces">
            <list>
                <value>
                    com.apress.springrecipes.calculator.ArithmeticCalculator
                </value>
            </list>
        </property>
        <property name="target" ref="arithmeticCalculator" />
        <property name="interceptorNames">
            <list>
                <value>loggingBeforeAdvice</value>
            </list>
        </property>
    </bean>

    <bean id="unitCalculatorProxy"
        class="org.springframework.aop.framework.ProxyFactoryBean">
        <property name="proxyInterfaces">
            <list>
                <value>
                    com.apress.springrecipes.calculator.UnitCalculator
                </value>
            </list>
        </property>
        <property name="target" ref="unitCalculator" />
        <property name="interceptorNames">
            <list>
                <value>loggingBeforeAdvice</value>
            </list>
        </property>
    </bean>
</beans>
```

Tip Creating a proxy with `ProxyFactoryBean` is similar to writing the proxy creation code when using dynamic proxy.

In the preceding bean configuration, you provided the proxies with the interfaces for them to implement. Only the calls to the methods declared in these interfaces will go through the proxy. The target object is the one that actually handles the method calls. In the interceptorNames property, you can specify a list of advice names for this proxy. The advices will be assigned the priority as their defining order. With all this information, ProxyFactoryBean will be able to create a proxy for the target object and register it in the IoC container.

By default, ProxyFactoryBean can automatically detect the interfaces that the target bean implements and proxy all of them. So, if you want to proxy all the interfaces of a bean, you needn't specify them explicitly.

```
<beans ...>
    ...
    <bean id="arithmeticCalculatorProxy"
        class="org.springframework.aop.framework.ProxyFactoryBean">
        <property name="target" ref="arithmeticCalculator" />
        <property name="interceptorNames">
            <list>
                <value>loggingBeforeAdvice</value>
            </list>
        </property>
    </bean>

    <bean id="unitCalculatorProxy"
        class="org.springframework.aop.framework.ProxyFactoryBean">
        <property name="target" ref="unitCalculator" />
        <property name="interceptorNames">
            <list>
                <value>loggingBeforeAdvice</value>
            </list>
        </property>
    </bean>
</beans>
```

ProxyFactoryBean will create a JDK proxy if your target bean implements any interface. If it doesn't, ProxyFactoryBean will create a CGLIB proxy instead, which can proxy all the methods declared in its class.

In the Main class, you should get the proxy beans from the IoC container instead to have your logging advice applied.

```
package com.apress.springrecipes.calculator;

import org.springframework.context.ApplicationContext;
import org.springframework.context.support.ClassPathXmlApplicationContext;

public class Main {
```

```
    public static void main(String[] args) {
        ApplicationContext context =
            new ClassPathXmlApplicationContext("beans.xml");

        ArithmeticCalculator arithmeticCalculator =
            (ArithmeticCalculator) context.getBean("arithmeticCalculatorProxy");
        ...

        UnitCalculator unitCalculator =
            (UnitCalculator) context.getBean("unitCalculatorProxy");
        ...
    }
}
```

After Returning Advices

In addition to a before advice, you can also write an *after returning* advice to log the method ending with the returning result.

```
package com.apress.springrecipes.calculator;

import java.lang.reflect.Method;

import org.apache.commons.logging.Log;
import org.apache.commons.logging.LogFactory;
import org.springframework.aop.AfterReturningAdvice;

public class LoggingAfterAdvice implements AfterReturningAdvice {

    private Log log = LogFactory.getLog(this.getClass());

    public void afterReturning(Object returnValue, Method method,
            Object[] args, Object target) throws Throwable {
        log.info("The method " + method.getName() + "() ends with "
                + returnValue);
    }
}
```

To make this advice effective, you declare an instance of it in the IoC container and add an entry to the `interceptorNames` properties:

```
<beans ...>
    ...
    <bean id="loggingAfterAdvice"
        class="com.apress.springrecipes.calculator.LoggingAfterAdvice" />

    <bean id="arithmeticCalculatorProxy"
        class="org.springframework.aop.framework.ProxyFactoryBean">
```

```
        <property name="target" ref="arithmeticCalculator" />
        <property name="interceptorNames">
            <list>
                <value>loggingBeforeAdvice</value>
                <value>loggingAfterAdvice</value>
            </list>
        </property>
    </bean>

    <bean id="unitCalculatorProxy"
        class="org.springframework.aop.framework.ProxyFactoryBean">
        <property name="target" ref="unitCalculator" />
        <property name="interceptorNames">
            <list>
                <value>loggingBeforeAdvice</value>
                <value>loggingAfterAdvice</value>
            </list>
        </property>
    </bean>
</beans>
```

After Throwing Advices

The third type of advice is an *after throwing* advice. First, to be able to produce an exception, you add a check to the `div()` method of the arithmetic calculator. If the divisor is zero, you throw an `IllegalArgumentException`.

```
package com.apress.springrecipes.calculator;

public class ArithmeticCalculatorImpl implements ArithmeticCalculator {
    ...
    public double div(double a, double b) {
        if (b == 0) {
            throw new IllegalArgumentException("Division by zero");
        }
        ...
    }
}
```

For the after throwing advice type, you have to implement the `ThrowsAdvice` interface. Note that this interface doesn't declare any methods. This is to let you handle different types of exceptions in different methods. However, each of the methods must have the name `afterThrowing` to handle a particular type of exceptions. The exception type is specified by the method argument type. For example, to handle `IllegalArgumentException`, you write the method as shown following. At runtime, the exception that is compatible with this type (i.e., this type and its subtypes) will be handled by this method.

```
package com.apress.springrecipes.calculator;

import org.apache.commons.logging.Log;
import org.apache.commons.logging.LogFactory;
import org.springframework.aop.ThrowsAdvice;

public class LoggingThrowsAdvice implements ThrowsAdvice {

    private Log log = LogFactory.getLog(this.getClass());

    public void afterThrowing(IllegalArgumentException e) throws Throwable {
        log.error("Illegal argument");
    }
}
```

You also have to declare an instance of this advice in the IoC container and add an entry to the interceptorNames properties:

```
<beans ...>
    ...
    <bean id="loggingThrowsAdvice"
        class="com.apress.springrecipes.calculator.LoggingThrowsAdvice" />

    <bean id="arithmeticCalculatorProxy"
        class="org.springframework.aop.framework.ProxyFactoryBean">
        <property name="target" ref="arithmeticCalculator" />
        <property name="interceptorNames">
            <list>
                <value>loggingBeforeAdvice</value>
                <value>loggingAfterAdvice</value>
                <value>loggingThrowsAdvice</value>
            </list>
        </property>
    </bean>

    <bean id="unitCalculatorProxy"
        class="org.springframework.aop.framework.ProxyFactoryBean">
        <property name="target" ref="unitCalculator" />
        <property name="interceptorNames">
            <list>
                <value>loggingBeforeAdvice</value>
                <value>loggingAfterAdvice</value>
                <value>loggingThrowsAdvice</value>
            </list>
        </property>
    </bean>
</beans>
```

If you need access to the method detail and the argument values, you can expand the argument list of the afterThrowing() method signature, as follows:

```
package com.apress.springrecipes.calculator;

import java.lang.reflect.Method;
import java.util.Arrays;
...
public class LoggingThrowsAdvice implements ThrowsAdvice {
    ...
    public void afterThrowing(Method method, Object[] args, Object target,
            IllegalArgumentException e) throws Throwable {
        log.error("Illegal argument " + Arrays.toString(args) + " for method "
                + method.getName() + "()");
    }
}
```

The method signatures in an after throwing advice must be of the following form. The first three arguments are optional, but you must declare either all or none of them.

```
afterThrowing([Method, args, target], Throwable subclass)
```

Around Advices

The last type of advice is an *around* advice. It is the most powerful of all the advice types. It gains full control of the method execution, so you can combine all the actions of the preceding advices into one single advice. You can even control when, and whether, to proceed with the original method execution.

In classic Spring AOP, an around advice has to implement the MethodInterceptor interface. This interface is defined by the AOP Alliance for compatibility between different AOP frameworks. The most important thing you must remember when writing an around advice is to call methodInvocation.proceed() to proceed with the original method execution. If you forget to perform this step, the original method will not be invoked. The following around advice is the combination of the before, after returning, and after throwing advices you created before:

```
package com.apress.springrecipes.calculator;

import java.util.Arrays;

import org.aopalliance.intercept.MethodInterceptor;
import org.aopalliance.intercept.MethodInvocation;
import org.apache.commons.logging.Log;
import org.apache.commons.logging.LogFactory;

public class LoggingAroundAdvice implements MethodInterceptor {

    private Log log = LogFactory.getLog(this.getClass());
```

```
    public Object invoke(MethodInvocation methodInvocation) throws Throwable {
        log.info("The method " + methodInvocation.getMethod().getName()
                + "() begins with "
                + Arrays.toString(methodInvocation.getArguments()));
        try {
            Object result = methodInvocation.proceed();
            log.info("The method " + methodInvocation.getMethod().getName()
                    + "() ends with " + result);
            return result;
        } catch (IllegalArgumentException e) {
            log.error("Illegal argument "
                    + Arrays.toString(methodInvocation.getArguments())
                    + " for method " + methodInvocation.getMethod().getName()
                    + "()");
            throw e;
        }
    }
}
```

The around advice type is very powerful and flexible in that you may even alter the original argument values and change the final return value. You must use this type of advice with great care, as the call to proceed with the original method execution may easily be forgotten.

Tip A common rule for choosing an advice type is to use the least powerful one that can satisfy your requirements.

As this advice is the combination of all the previous advices, you should specify only this advice for the proxies.

```
<beans ...>
    ...
    <bean id="loggingAroundAdvice"
        class="com.apress.springrecipes.calculator.LoggingAroundAdvice" />

    <bean id="arithmeticCalculatorProxy"
        class="org.springframework.aop.framework.ProxyFactoryBean">
        <property name="target" ref="arithmeticCalculator" />
        <property name="interceptorNames">
            <list>
                <value>loggingAroundAdvice</value>
            </list>
        </property>
    </bean>
```

```
    <bean id="unitCalculatorProxy"
        class="org.springframework.aop.framework.ProxyFactoryBean">
        <property name="target" ref="unitCalculator" />
        <property name="interceptorNames">
            <list>
                <value>loggingAroundAdvice</value>
            </list>
        </property>
    </bean>
</beans>
```

5-4. Matching Methods with Classic Spring Pointcuts

Problem

When you specify an advice for an AOP proxy, all of the methods declared in the target class/proxy interfaces will be advised. But in most situations, you only want some of them to be advised.

Solution

Pointcut is another core AOP concept, usually appearing as an expression, and allowing you to match certain program execution points to apply an advice. In classic Spring AOP, pointcuts are also declared as Spring beans by using pointcut classes.

Spring provides a family of pointcut classes for you to match program execution points. You can simply declare beans of these types in your bean configuration file to define pointcuts. However, if you find that the built-in pointcut classes cannot satisfy your needs, you can write your own by extending `StaticMethodMatcherPointcut` or `DynamicMethodMatcherPointcut`. The former matches execution points by the static class and method information only, while the latter matches them by the dynamic argument values as well.

How It Works

Method Name Pointcuts

To advise a single method only, you can make use of `NameMatchMethodPointcut` to match the method statically by its name. You can specify a particular method name or method name expression with wildcards in the `mappedName` property.

```
<bean id="methodNamePointcut"
    class="org.springframework.aop.support.NameMatchMethodPointcut">
    <property name="mappedName" value="add" />
</bean>
```

A pointcut must be associated with an advice to indicate where the advice should be applied. Such an association is called an *advisor* in classic Spring AOP. The class `DefaultPointcutAdvisor` is simply for associating a pointcut and an advice. An advisor is applied to a proxy in the same way as an advice.

```
<beans ...>
    ...
    <bean id="methodNameAdvisor"
        class="org.springframework.aop.support.DefaultPointcutAdvisor">
        <property name="pointcut" ref="methodNamePointcut" />
        <property name="advice" ref="loggingAroundAdvice" />
    </bean>

    <bean id="arithmeticCalculatorProxy"
        class="org.springframework.aop.framework.ProxyFactoryBean">
        <property name="target" ref="arithmeticCalculator" />
        <property name="interceptorNames">
            <list>
                <value>methodNameAdvisor</value>
            </list>
        </property>
    </bean>
</beans>
```

If you would like to match more than one method in a method name pointcut, you should set these methods in the `mappedNames` property instead, whose type is `java.util.List`.

```
<bean id="methodNamePointcut"
    class="org.springframework.aop.support.NameMatchMethodPointcut">
    <property name="mappedNames">
        <list>
            <value>add</value>
            <value>sub</value>
        </list>
    </property>
</bean>
```

For each of the common pointcut types, Spring also provides a convenient advisor class for you to declare an advisor in one shot. For `NameMatchMethodPointcut`, the advisor class is `NameMatchMethodPointcutAdvisor`.

```
<bean id="methodNameAdvisor"
    class="org.springframework.aop.support.NameMatchMethodPointcutAdvisor">
    <property name="mappedNames">
        <list>
            <value>add</value>
            <value>sub</value>
        </list>
    </property>
    <property name="advice" ref="loggingAroundAdvice" />
</bean>
```

Regular Expression Pointcuts

In addition to matching methods by name, you can also match them using a regular expression. You can make use of RegexpMethodPointcutAdvisor to specify one or more regular expressions. For example, the following regular expressions match the methods with the keyword mul or div in the method name:

```
<beans ...>
    ...
    <bean id="regexpAdvisor"
        class="org.springframework.aop.support.RegexpMethodPointcutAdvisor">
        <property name="patterns">
            <list>
                <value>.*mul.*</value>
                <value>.*div.*</value>
            </list>
        </property>
        <property name="advice" ref="loggingAroundAdvice" />
    </bean>

    <bean id="arithmeticCalculatorProxy"
        class="org.springframework.aop.framework.ProxyFactoryBean">
        <property name="target" ref="arithmeticCalculator" />
        <property name="interceptorNames">
            <list>
                <value>methodNameAdvisor</value>
                <value>regexpAdvisor</value>
            </list>
        </property>
    </bean>
</beans>
```

AspectJ Expression Pointcuts

The AspectJ framework defines a powerful pointcut expression language. You can make use of AspectJExpressionPointcutAdvisor to match your methods using an AspectJ pointcut expression. For example, the following AspectJ pointcut expression matches all the methods with the keyword To in the method name. The AspectJ pointcut language will be introduced in Chapter 6, which is on Spring 2.x AOP. For a more detailed explanation of the AspectJ pointcut language, please refer to the AspectJ documentation.

■ **Note** To use AspectJ expressions to define your pointcuts, you have to include aspectjweaver.jar (located in the lib/aspectj directory of the Spring installation) in your classpath.

```
<beans ...>
    ...
    <bean id="aspectjAdvisor"
        class="org.springframework.aop.aspectj.AspectJExpressionPointcutAdvisor">
        <property name="expression">
            <value>execution(* *.*To*(..))</value>
        </property>
        <property name="advice">
            <ref bean="loggingAroundAdvice" />
        </property>
    </bean>

    <bean id="unitCalculatorProxy"
        class="org.springframework.aop.framework.ProxyFactoryBean">
        <property name="target" ref="unitCalculator" />
        <property name="interceptorNames">
            <list>
                <value>aspectjAdvisor</value>
            </list>
        </property>
    </bean>
</beans>
```

5-5. Creating Proxies for Your Beans Automatically

Problem

When using classic Spring AOP, you need to create a proxy for each bean to be advised and link it with the target bean. As a result, there will be a large number of proxy beans declared in your bean configuration file.

Solution

Spring provides a facility called *auto proxy creator* to create proxies for your beans automatically. It is implemented as a bean post processor that will replace the target beans with the newly created proxies. With an auto proxy creator, you no longer need to create proxies manually with ProxyFactoryBean.

How It Works

Spring has two built-in auto proxy creator implementations for you to choose from. The first is BeanNameAutoProxyCreator, which requires a list of bean name expressions to be configured. In each bean name expression, you can use wildcards to match a group of beans. For example, the following auto proxy creator will create proxies for the beans whose names end with Calculator. Each of the proxies created will be advised by the advisors specified in the auto proxy creator.

```
<beans ...>
    ...
    <bean id="arithmeticCalculator"
        class="com.apress.springrecipes.calculator.ArithmeticCalculatorImpl" />

    <bean id="unitCalculator"
        class="com.apress.springrecipes.calculator.UnitCalculatorImpl" />

    <bean class="org.springframework.aop.framework.autoproxy.➥
        BeanNameAutoProxyCreator">
        <property name="beanNames">
            <list>
                <value>*Calculator</value>
            </list>
        </property>
        <property name="interceptorNames">
            <list>
                <value>methodNameAdvisor</value>
                <value>regexpAdvisor</value>
                <value>aspectjAdvisor</value>
            </list>
        </property>
    </bean>
</beans>
```

In the `Main` class, you can simply get the beans by their original names even without knowing that they have been proxied.

```
package com.apress.springrecipes.calculator;

import org.springframework.context.ApplicationContext;
import org.springframework.context.support.ClassPathXmlApplicationContext;

public class Main {

    public static void main(String[] args) {
        ApplicationContext context =
            new ClassPathXmlApplicationContext("beans.xml");

        ArithmeticCalculator calculator1 =
            (ArithmeticCalculator) context.getBean("arithmeticCalculator");
        ...

        UnitCalculator calculator2 =
            (UnitCalculator) context.getBean("unitCalculator");
        ...
    }
}
```

Another auto proxy creator implementation is `DefaultAdvisorAutoProxyCreator`. Note that there's nothing you have to configure for this auto proxy creator. It will automatically check for each bean with each advisor declared in the IoC container. If any of the beans is matched by an advisor's pointcut, `DefaultAdvisorAutoProxyCreator` will automatically create a proxy for it.

```
<bean class="org.springframework.aop.framework.autoproxy.➥
    DefaultAdvisorAutoProxyCreator" />
```

However, you must use this auto proxy creator with great care, as it may advise beans that you don't expect to be advised.

5-6. Summary

In this chapter, you have learned the importance of modularizing crosscutting concerns in an application. This kind of concern is often hard to modularize with the traditional object-oriented approach. Non-modularized crosscutting concerns will cause code tangling and code scattering problems.

Dynamic proxy can help to modularize crosscutting concerns, but it's too demanding for an application developer to use directly. However, it is one of the core implementation technologies for Spring AOP.

AOP is a complement to OOP that specializes in modularizing crosscutting concerns. It defines a set of high-level concepts such as advice and pointcut for application developers to express their crosscutting concerns.

An advice encapsulates the action to take at a particular program execution point. Classic Spring AOP supports four types of advice: before, after returning, after throwing, and around. To apply your advices to a bean in the Spring IoC container, you have to create a proxy by using `ProxyFactoryBean`.

A pointcut usually appears as an expression that matches certain program execution points to apply advices. In classic Spring AOP, a pointcut is declared as a Spring bean and associated with an advice by an advisor.

When using classic Spring AOP, you need to create a proxy for each bean to be advised. Spring provides auto proxy creators to create proxies for your beans automatically. With auto proxy creators, you no longer need to create proxies with `ProxyFactoryBean` manually.

In the next chapter, you will learn the new Spring 2.x AOP approach and its support for the AspectJ framework.

CHAPTER 6

Spring 2.x AOP and AspectJ Support

In this chapter, you will learn Spring 2.x AOP usage and some advanced AOP topics, such as advice precedence and introduction. The usage of the Spring AOP framework has changed significantly from version 1.x to 2.x. This chapter focuses on the new Spring AOP approach, which enables you to write more powerful and compatible aspects. Moreover, you will learn how to use the AspectJ framework in Spring applications.

In the last chapter, you learned how classic Spring AOP works through a set of proprietary Spring AOP APIs. In Spring version 2.x, you can write your aspects as POJOs with either AspectJ annotations or XML-based configurations in the bean configuration file. As these two types of configurations have the same effect indeed, most of this chapter will focus on AspectJ annotations while describing XML-based configurations for comparison's sake.

Notice that although the usage of Spring AOP has changed, the core implementation technology remains the same: dynamic proxy. Moreover, Spring AOP is backward compatible, so you can continue to use classic Spring advices, pointcuts, and auto proxy creators in Spring 2.x AOP.

As AspectJ is growing into a complete and popular AOP framework, Spring 2.x supports the use of POJO aspects written with AspectJ annotations in its AOP framework. Since AspectJ annotations will be supported by more and more AOP frameworks in the future, your AspectJ-style aspects are more likely to be reused in other AOP frameworks that support AspectJ.

Keep in mind that although you can apply AspectJ aspects in Spring 2.x AOP, this is not the same as using the AspectJ framework. In fact, there are some limitations on the use of AspectJ aspects in Spring AOP, as Spring only allows aspects to apply to beans declared in the IoC container. If you want to apply aspects outside this scope, you have to use the AspectJ framework, which will be introduced at the end of this chapter.

Upon finishing this chapter, you will be able to write POJO aspects to use in the Spring 2.x AOP framework. You should also be able to make use of the AspectJ framework in your Spring applications.

6-1. Enabling AspectJ Annotation Support in Spring

Problem

Spring version 2.x supports the use of POJO aspects written with AspectJ annotations in its AOP framework. But first you have to enable AspectJ annotation support in the Spring IoC container.

Solution

To enable AspectJ annotation support in the Spring IoC container, you only have to define an empty XML element `<aop:aspectj-autoproxy>` in your bean configuration file. Then Spring will automatically create proxies for any of your beans that are matched by your AspectJ aspects.

How It Works

For the sake of a clearer comparison with classic Spring AOP, the calculator sample used in the last chapter will continue to be used. Recall that you defined the following interfaces for your calculator application:

```
package com.apress.springrecipes.calculator;

public interface ArithmeticCalculator {

    public double add(double a, double b);
    public double sub(double a, double b);
    public double mul(double a, double b);
    public double div(double a, double b);
}
```

```
package com.apress.springrecipes.calculator;

public interface UnitCalculator {

    public double kilogramToPound(double kilogram);
    public double kilometerToMile(double kilometer);
}
```

Then you provided an implementation for each interface with `println` statements to let you know when the methods are executed.

```
package com.apress.springrecipes.calculator;

public class ArithmeticCalculatorImpl implements ArithmeticCalculator {

    public double add(double a, double b) {
        double result = a + b;
        System.out.println(a + " + " + b + " = " + result);
```

```
        return result;
    }

    public double sub(double a, double b) {
        double result = a - b;
        System.out.println(a + " - " + b + " = " + result);
        return result;
    }

    public double mul(double a, double b) {
        double result = a * b;
        System.out.println(a + " * " + b + " = " + result);
        return result;
    }

    public double div(double a, double b) {
        if (b == 0) {
            throw new IllegalArgumentException("Division by zero");
        }
        double result = a / b;
        System.out.println(a + " / " + b + " = " + result);
        return result;
    }
}

package com.apress.springrecipes.calculator;

public class UnitCalculatorImpl implements UnitCalculator {

    public double kilogramToPound(double kilogram) {
        double pound = kilogram * 2.2;
        System.out.println(kilogram + " kilogram = " + pound + " pound");
        return pound;
    }

    public double kilometerToMile(double kilometer) {
        double mile = kilometer * 0.62;
        System.out.println(kilometer + " kilometer = " + mile + " mile");
        return mile;
    }
}
```

To enable AspectJ annotation support for this application, you just define an empty XML element, `<aop:aspectj-autoproxy>`, in your bean configuration file. Moreover, you must add the aop schema definition to your `<beans>` root element. When the Spring IoC container notices the `<aop:aspectj-autoproxy>` element in your bean configuration file, it will automatically create proxies for your beans that are matched by your AspectJ aspects.

■ **Note** To use AspectJ annotations in your Spring application, you have to include the AspectJ libraries (aspectjrt.jar and aspectjweaver.jar, located in the lib/aspectj directory of the Spring installation) and their dependencies (asm-2.2.3.jar, asm-commons-2.2.3.jar, and asm-util-2.2.3.jar, located in the lib/asm directory) in your classpath.

```
<beans xmlns="http://www.springframework.org/schema/beans"
    xmlns:xsi="http://www.w3.org/2001/XMLSchema-instance"
    xmlns:aop="http://www.springframework.org/schema/aop"
    xsi:schemaLocation="http://www.springframework.org/schema/beans
        http://www.springframework.org/schema/beans/spring-beans-2.5.xsd
        http://www.springframework.org/schema/aop
        http://www.springframework.org/schema/aop/spring-aop-2.5.xsd">

    <aop:aspectj-autoproxy />

    <bean id="arithmeticCalculator"
        class="com.apress.springrecipes.calculator.ArithmeticCalculatorImpl" />

    <bean id="unitCalculator"
        class="com.apress.springrecipes.calculator.UnitCalculatorImpl" />
</beans>
```

Actually, this element will register AnnotationAwareAspectJAutoProxyCreator behind the scenes, which works in a similar way to the auto proxy creators introduced in Chapter 5, such as BeanNameAutoProxyCreator and DefaultAdvisorAutoProxyCreator.

6-2. Declaring Aspects with AspectJ Annotations

Problem

Since merging with AspectWerkz in version 5, AspectJ supports its aspects to be written as POJOs annotated with a set of AspectJ annotations. Aspects of this kind are also supported by the Spring 2.x AOP framework. But they must be registered in the Spring IoC container to take effect.

Solution

You register AspectJ aspects in Spring simply by declaring them as bean instances in the IoC container. With AspectJ enabled in the Spring IoC container, it will create proxies for your beans that are matched by your AspectJ aspects.

Written with AspectJ annotations, an aspect is simply a Java class with the @Aspect annotation. An advice is a simple Java method with one of the advice annotations. AspectJ supports five types of advice annotations: @Before, @After, @AfterReturning, @AfterThrowing, and @Around.

How It Works

Before Advices

To create a *before* advice to handle crosscutting concerns before particular program execution points, you use the @Before annotation and include the pointcut expression as the annotation value.

```
package com.apress.springrecipes.calculator;

import org.apache.commons.logging.Log;
import org.apache.commons.logging.LogFactory;
import org.aspectj.lang.annotation.Aspect;
import org.aspectj.lang.annotation.Before;

@Aspect
public class CalculatorLoggingAspect {

    private Log log = LogFactory.getLog(this.getClass());

    @Before("execution(* ArithmeticCalculator.add(..))")
    public void logBefore() {
        log.info("The method add() begins");
    }
}
```

This pointcut expression means the add() method execution of the ArithmeticCalculator interface. The preceding wildcard in this expression matches any modifier (public, protected, and private) and any return type. The two dots in the argument list match any number of arguments.

To register this aspect, you just declare a bean instance of it in the IoC container. The aspect bean may even be anonymous if there's no reference from other beans.

```
<beans ...>
    ...
    <bean class="com.apress.springrecipes.calculator.CalculatorLoggingAspect" />
</beans>
```

You can test your aspect with the following Main class:

```
package com.apress.springrecipes.calculator;

import org.springframework.context.ApplicationContext;
import org.springframework.context.support.ClassPathXmlApplicationContext;

public class Main {

    public static void main(String[] args) {
        ApplicationContext context =
            new ClassPathXmlApplicationContext("beans.xml");
```

```
        ArithmeticCalculator arithmeticCalculator =
            (ArithmeticCalculator) context.getBean("arithmeticCalculator");
        arithmeticCalculator.add(1, 2);
        arithmeticCalculator.sub(4, 3);
        arithmeticCalculator.mul(2, 3);
        arithmeticCalculator.div(4, 2);

        UnitCalculator unitCalculator =
            (UnitCalculator) context.getBean("unitCalculator");
        unitCalculator.kilogramToPound(10);
        unitCalculator.kilometerToMile(5);
    }
}
```

The execution points matched by a pointcut are called *join points*. In this term, a pointcut is an expression to match a set of join points, while an advice is the action to take at a particular join point.

For your advice to access the detail of the current join point, you can declare an argument of type `JoinPoint` in your advice method. Then you can get access to join point details such as the method name and argument values. Now you can expand your pointcut to match all methods by changing the class name and method name to wildcards.

```
package com.apress.springrecipes.calculator;
...
import java.util.Arrays;

import org.aspectj.lang.JoinPoint;
import org.aspectj.lang.annotation.Aspect;
import org.aspectj.lang.annotation.Before;

@Aspect
public class CalculatorLoggingAspect {
    ...
    @Before("execution(* *.*(..))")
    public void logBefore(JoinPoint joinPoint) {
        log.info("The method " + joinPoint.getSignature().getName()
                + "() begins with " + Arrays.toString(joinPoint.getArgs()));
    }
}
```

After Advices

An *after* advice is executed after a join point finishes, whenever it returns a result or throws an exception abnormally. The following after advice logs the calculator method ending. An aspect may include one or more advices.

```
package com.apress.springrecipes.calculator;
...
import org.aspectj.lang.JoinPoint;
```

```
import org.aspectj.lang.annotation.After;
import org.aspectj.lang.annotation.Aspect;

@Aspect
public class CalculatorLoggingAspect {
    ...
    @After("execution(* *.*(..))")
    public void logAfter(JoinPoint joinPoint) {
        log.info("The method " + joinPoint.getSignature().getName()
                + "() ends");
    }
}
```

After Returning Advices

An after advice is executed regardless of whether a join point returns normally or throws an exception. If you would like to perform logging only when a join point returns, you should replace the after advice with an *after returning* advice.

```
package com.apress.springrecipes.calculator;
...
import org.aspectj.lang.JoinPoint;
import org.aspectj.lang.annotation.AfterReturning;
import org.aspectj.lang.annotation.Aspect;

@Aspect
public class CalculatorLoggingAspect {
    ...
    @AfterReturning("execution(* *.*(..))")
    public void logAfterReturning(JoinPoint joinPoint) {
        log.info("The method " + joinPoint.getSignature().getName()
                + "() ends");
    }
}
```

In an after returning advice, you can get access to the return value of a join point by adding a `returning` attribute to the `@AfterReturning` annotation. The value of this attribute should be the argument name of this advice method for the return value to pass in. Then you have to add an argument to the advice method signature with this name. At runtime, Spring AOP will pass in the return value through this argument. Also note that the original pointcut expression needs to be presented in the `pointcut` attribute instead.

```
package com.apress.springrecipes.calculator;
...
import org.aspectj.lang.JoinPoint;
import org.aspectj.lang.annotation.AfterReturning;
import org.aspectj.lang.annotation.Aspect;
```

```
@Aspect
public class CalculatorLoggingAspect {
    ...
    @AfterReturning(
        pointcut = "execution(* *.*(..))",
        returning = "result")
    public void logAfterReturning(JoinPoint joinPoint, Object result) {
        log.info("The method " + joinPoint.getSignature().getName()
                + "() ends with " + result);
    }
}
```

After Throwing Advices

An *after throwing* advice is executed only when an exception is thrown by a join point.

```
package com.apress.springrecipes.calculator;
...
import org.aspectj.lang.JoinPoint;
import org.aspectj.lang.annotation.AfterThrowing;
import org.aspectj.lang.annotation.Aspect;

@Aspect
public class CalculatorLoggingAspect {
    ...
    @AfterThrowing("execution(* *.*(..))")
    public void logAfterThrowing(JoinPoint joinPoint) {
        log.error("An exception has been thrown in "
                + joinPoint.getSignature().getName() + "()");
    }
}
```

Similarly, the exception thrown by the join point can be accessed by adding a `throwing` attribute to the `@AfterThrowing` annotation. The type `Throwable` is the superclass of all errors and exceptions in the Java language. So, the following advice will catch any of the errors and exceptions thrown by the join points:

```
package com.apress.springrecipes.calculator;
...
import org.aspectj.lang.JoinPoint;
import org.aspectj.lang.annotation.AfterThrowing;
import org.aspectj.lang.annotation.Aspect;

@Aspect
public class CalculatorLoggingAspect {
    ...
    @AfterThrowing(
        pointcut = "execution(* *.*(..))",
```

```
        throwing = "e")
    public void logAfterThrowing(JoinPoint joinPoint, Throwable e) {
        log.error("An exception " + e + " has been thrown in "
                + joinPoint.getSignature().getName() + "()");
    }
}
```

However, if you are interested in one particular type of exception only, you can declare it as the argument type of the exception. Then your advice will be executed only when exceptions of compatible type (i.e., this type and its subtypes) are thrown.

```
package com.apress.springrecipes.calculator;
...
import java.util.Arrays;

import org.aspectj.lang.JoinPoint;
import org.aspectj.lang.annotation.AfterThrowing;
import org.aspectj.lang.annotation.Aspect;

@Aspect
public class CalculatorLoggingAspect {
    ...
    @AfterThrowing(
        pointcut = "execution(* *.*(..))",
        throwing = "e")
    public void logAfterThrowing(JoinPoint joinPoint,
            IllegalArgumentException e) {
        log.error("Illegal argument " + Arrays.toString(joinPoint.getArgs())
                + " in " + joinPoint.getSignature().getName() + "()");
    }
}
```

Around Advices

The last type of advice is an *around* advice. It is the most powerful of all the advice types. It gains full control of a join point, so you can combine all the actions of the preceding advices into one single advice. You can even control when, and whether, to proceed with the original join point execution.

The following around advice is the combination of the before, after returning, and after throwing advices you created before. Note that for an around advice, the argument type of the join point must be `ProceedingJoinPoint`. It's a subinterface of `JoinPoint` that allows you to control when to proceed with the original join point.

```
package com.apress.springrecipes.calculator;
...
import java.util.Arrays;
```

```
import org.aspectj.lang.ProceedingJoinPoint;
import org.aspectj.lang.annotation.Around;
import org.aspectj.lang.annotation.Aspect;

@Aspect
public class CalculatorLoggingAspect {
    ...
    @Around("execution(* *.*(..))")
    public Object logAround(ProceedingJoinPoint joinPoint) throws Throwable {
        log.info("The method " + joinPoint.getSignature().getName()
                + "() begins with " + Arrays.toString(joinPoint.getArgs()));
        try {
            Object result = joinPoint.proceed();
            log.info("The method " + joinPoint.getSignature().getName()
                    + "() ends with " + result);
            return result;
        } catch (IllegalArgumentException e) {
            log.error("Illegal argument "
                    + Arrays.toString(joinPoint.getArgs()) + " in "
                    + joinPoint.getSignature().getName() + "()");
            throw e;
        }
    }
}
```

The around advice type is very powerful and flexible in that you can even alter the original argument values and change the final return value. You must use this type of advice with great care, as the call to proceed with the original join point may easily be forgotten.

■ **Tip** A common rule for choosing an advice type is to use the least powerful one that can satisfy your requirements.

6-3. Accessing the Join Point Information

Problem

In AOP, an advice is applied to different program execution points, which are called join points. For an advice to take the correct action, it often requires detailed information about join points.

Solution

An advice can access the current join point information by declaring an argument of type `org.aspectj.lang.JoinPoint` in the advice method signature.

How It Works

For example, you can access the join point information through the following advice. The information includes the join point kind (only `method-execution` in Spring AOP), the method signature (declaring type and method name), and the argument values, as well as the target object and proxy object.

```
package com.apress.springrecipes.calculator;
...
import java.util.Arrays;

import org.aspectj.lang.JoinPoint;
import org.aspectj.lang.annotation.Aspect;
import org.aspectj.lang.annotation.Before;

@Aspect
public class CalculatorLoggingAspect {
    ...
    @Before("execution(* *.*(..))")
    public void logJoinPoint(JoinPoint joinPoint) {
        log.info("Join point kind : "
                + joinPoint.getKind());
        log.info("Signature declaring type : "
                + joinPoint.getSignature().getDeclaringTypeName());
        log.info("Signature name : "
                + joinPoint.getSignature().getName());
        log.info("Arguments : "
                + Arrays.toString(joinPoint.getArgs()));
        log.info("Target class : "
                + joinPoint.getTarget().getClass().getName());
        log.info("This class : "
                + joinPoint.getThis().getClass().getName());
    }
}
```

The original bean that was wrapped by a proxy is called the *target* object, while the proxy object is called the *this* object. They can be accessed by the join point's `getTarget()` and `getThis()` methods. From the following outputs, you can see that the classes of these two objects are not the same:

```
Join point kind : method-execution
Signature declaring type : com.apress.springrecipes.calculator.ArithmeticCalculator
Signature name : add
Arguments : [1.0, 2.0]
Target class : com.apress.springrecipes.calculator.ArithmeticCalculatorImpl
This class : $Proxy6
```

6-4. Specifying Aspect Precedence

Problem

When there's more than one aspect applied to the same join point, the precedence of the aspects is undefined unless you have explicitly specified it.

Solution

The precedence of aspects can be specified either by implementing the `Ordered` interface or by using the `@Order` annotation.

How It Works

Suppose you have written another aspect to validate the calculator arguments. There's only one before advice in this aspect.

```
package com.apress.springrecipes.calculator;

import org.aspectj.lang.JoinPoint;
import org.aspectj.lang.annotation.Aspect;
import org.aspectj.lang.annotation.Before;

@Aspect
public class CalculatorValidationAspect {

    @Before("execution(* *.*(double, double))")
    public void validateBefore(JoinPoint joinPoint) {
        for (Object arg : joinPoint.getArgs()) {
            validate((Double) arg);
        }
    }

    private void validate(double a) {
        if (a < 0) {
            throw new IllegalArgumentException("Positive numbers only");
        }
    }
}
```

To register this aspect in Spring, you simply declare a bean instance of this aspect in the bean configuration file.

```
<beans ...>
    ...
    <bean class="com.apress.springrecipes.calculator.CalculatorLoggingAspect" />

    <bean class="com.apress.springrecipes.calculator.➥
        CalculatorValidationAspect" />
</beans>
```

However, the precedence of the aspects will be undefined now. Be cautious that the precedence does not depend on the order of bean declaration. So, in order to specify the precedence, you have to make both of the aspects implement the Ordered interface. The lower value returned by the getOrder() method represents higher priority. So, if you prefer the validation aspect to be applied first, it should return a value lower than the logging aspect.

```
package com.apress.springrecipes.calculator;
...
import org.springframework.core.Ordered;

@Aspect
public class CalculatorValidationAspect implements Ordered {
    ...
    public int getOrder() {
        return 0;
    }
}
```

```
package com.apress.springrecipes.calculator;
...
import org.springframework.core.Ordered;

@Aspect
public class CalculatorLoggingAspect implements Ordered {
    ...
    public int getOrder() {
        return 1;
    }
}
```

Another way to specify precedence is through the @Order annotation. The order number should be presented in the annotation value.

```
package com.apress.springrecipes.calculator;
...
import org.springframework.core.annotation.Order;

@Aspect
@Order(0)
public class CalculatorValidationAspect {
    ...
}
```

```
package com.apress.springrecipes.calculator;
...
import org.springframework.core.annotation.Order;

@Aspect
@Order(1)
```

```
public class CalculatorLoggingAspect {
    ...
}
```

6-5. Reusing Pointcut Definitions

Problem

When writing AspectJ aspects, you can directly embed a pointcut expression in an advice annotation. However, the same pointcut expression may be repeated in multiple advices.

Solution

Like many other AOP implementations, AspectJ also allows you to define a pointcut independently to be reused in multiple advices.

How It Works

In an AspectJ aspect, a pointcut can be declared as a simple method with the `@Pointcut` annotation. The method body of a pointcut is usually empty, as it is unreasonable to mix a pointcut definition with application logic. The access modifier of a pointcut method controls the visibility of this pointcut as well. Other advices can refer to this pointcut by the method name.

```
package com.apress.springrecipes.calculator;
...
import org.aspectj.lang.annotation.Pointcut;

@Aspect
public class CalculatorLoggingAspect {
    ...
    @Pointcut("execution(* *.*(..))")
    private void loggingOperation() {}

    @Before("loggingOperation()")
    public void logBefore(JoinPoint joinPoint) {
        ...
    }

    @AfterReturning(
        pointcut = "loggingOperation()",
        returning = "result")
    public void logAfterReturning(JoinPoint joinPoint, Object result) {
        ...
    }

    @AfterThrowing(
        pointcut = "loggingOperation()",
        throwing = "e")
```

```
    public void logAfterThrowing(JoinPoint joinPoint, IllegalArgumentException e) {
        ...
    }

    @Around("loggingOperation()")
    public Object logAround(ProceedingJoinPoint joinPoint) throws Throwable {
        ...
    }
}
```

Usually, if your pointcuts are shared between multiple aspects, it is better to centralize them in a common class. In this case, they must be declared as `public`.

```
package com.apress.springrecipes.calculator;

import org.aspectj.lang.annotation.Aspect;
import org.aspectj.lang.annotation.Pointcut;

@Aspect
public class CalculatorPointcuts {

    @Pointcut("execution(* *.*(..))")
    public void loggingOperation() {}
}
```

When you refer to this pointcut, you have to include the class name as well. If the class is not located in the same package as the aspect, you have to include the package name also.

```
package com.apress.springrecipes.calculator;
...
@Aspect
public class CalculatorLoggingAspect {
    ...
    @Before("CalculatorPointcuts.loggingOperation()")
    public void logBefore(JoinPoint joinPoint) {
        ...
    }

    @AfterReturning(
        pointcut = "CalculatorPointcuts.loggingOperation()",
        returning = "result")
    public void logAfterReturning(JoinPoint joinPoint, Object result) {
        ...
    }

    @AfterThrowing(
        pointcut = "CalculatorPointcuts.loggingOperation()",
        throwing = "e")
    public void logAfterThrowing(JoinPoint joinPoint, IllegalArgumentException e) {
```

```
        ...
    }

    @Around("CalculatorPointcuts.loggingOperation()")
    public Object logAround(ProceedingJoinPoint joinPoint) throws Throwable {
        ...
    }
}
```

6-6. Writing AspectJ Pointcut Expressions

Problem

Crosscutting concerns may happen at different program execution points, which are called join points. Because of the variety of join points, you need a powerful expression language that can help in matching them.

Solution

The AspectJ pointcut language is a powerful expression language that can match various kinds of join points. However, Spring AOP only supports method execution join points for beans declared in its IoC container. For this reason, only those pointcut expressions supported by Spring AOP will be introduced here. For a full description of the AspectJ pointcut language, please refer to the AspectJ programming guide available on AspectJ's web site (http://www.eclipse.org/aspectj/).

Spring 2.x AOP makes use of the AspectJ pointcut language for its pointcut definition. Actually, Spring AOP interprets the pointcut expressions at runtime by using a library provided by AspectJ.

When writing AspectJ pointcut expressions for Spring AOP, you must keep in mind that Spring AOP only supports method execution join points for the beans in its IoC container. If you use a pointcut expression out of this scope, an IllegalArgumentException will be thrown.

How It Works

Method Signature Patterns

The most typical pointcut expressions are used to match a number of methods by their signatures. For example, the following pointcut expression matches all of the methods declared in the ArithmeticCalculator interface. The preceding wildcard matches methods with any modifier (public, protected, and private) and any return type. The two dots in the argument list match any number of arguments.

```
execution(* com.apress.springrecipes.calculator.ArithmeticCalculator.*(..))
```

You can omit the package name if the target class or interface is located in the same package as this aspect.

```
execution(* ArithmeticCalculator.*(..))
```

The following pointcut expression matches all the public methods declared in the ArithmeticCalculator interface:

```
execution(public * ArithmeticCalculator.*(..))
```

You can also restrict the method return type. For example, the following pointcut matches the methods that return a double number:

```
execution(public double ArithmeticCalculator.*(..))
```

The argument list of the methods can also be restricted. For example, the following pointcut matches the methods whose first argument is of primitive double type. The two dots then match any number of followed arguments.

```
execution(public double ArithmeticCalculator.*(double, ..))
```

Or, you can specify all the argument types in the method signature for the pointcut to match.

```
execution(public double ArithmeticCalculator.*(double, double))
```

Although the AspectJ pointcut language is powerful in matching various join points, sometimes you may not be able to find any common characteristics (e.g., modifiers, return types, method name patterns, or arguments) for the methods you would like to match. In such cases, you can consider providing a custom annotation for them. For instance, you can define the following annotation type. This annotation can be applied to both method level and type level.

```
package com.apress.springrecipes.calculator;

import java.lang.annotation.Documented;
import java.lang.annotation.ElementType;
import java.lang.annotation.Retention;
import java.lang.annotation.RetentionPolicy;
import java.lang.annotation.Target;

@Target( { ElementType.METHOD, ElementType.TYPE })
@Retention(RetentionPolicy.RUNTIME)
@Documented
public @interface LoggingRequired {
}
```

Then you can annotate all methods that require logging with this annotation. Note that the annotations must be added to the implementation class but not the interface, as they will not be inherited.

```
package com.apress.springrecipes.calculator;

public class ArithmeticCalculatorImpl implements ArithmeticCalculator {

    @LoggingRequired
    public double add(double a, double b) {
```

```
        ...
    }

    @LoggingRequired
    public double sub(double a, double b) {
        ...
    }

    @LoggingRequired
    public double mul(double a, double b) {
        ...
    }

    @LoggingRequired
    public double div(double a, double b) {
        ...
    }
}
```

Now you are able to write a pointcut expression to match all methods with this @LoggingRequired annotation.

```
@annotation(com.apress.springrecipes.calculator.LoggingRequired)
```

Type Signature Patterns

Another kind of pointcut expressions matches all join points within certain types. When applied to Spring AOP, the scope of these pointcuts will be narrowed to matching all method executions within the types. For example, the following pointcut matches all the method execution join points within the com.apress.springrecipes.calculator package:

```
within(com.apress.springrecipes.calculator.*)
```

To match the join points within a package and its subpackage, you have to add one more dot before the wildcard.

```
within(com.apress.springrecipes.calculator..*)
```

The following pointcut expression matches the method execution join points within a particular class:

```
within(com.apress.springrecipes.calculator.ArithmeticCalculatorImpl)
```

Again, if the target class is located in the same package as this aspect, the package name can be omitted.

```
within(ArithmeticCalculatorImpl)
```

You can match the method execution join points within all classes that implement the ArithmeticCalculator interface by adding a plus symbol.

```
within(ArithmeticCalculator+)
```

Your custom annotation @LoggingRequired can be applied to the class level instead of the method level.

```
package com.apress.springrecipes.calculator;

@LoggingRequired
public class ArithmeticCalculatorImpl implements ArithmeticCalculator {
    ...
}
```

Then you can match the join points within the classes that have been annotated with @LoggingRequired.

```
@within(com.apress.springrecipes.calculator.LoggingRequired)
```

Bean Name Patterns

Spring 2.5 supports a new pointcut type that is used to match bean names. For example, the following pointcut expression matches beans whose name ends with Calculator:

```
bean(*Calculator)
```

■ **Caution** This pointcut type is only supported in XML-based Spring AOP configurations, not in AspectJ annotations.

Combining Pointcut Expressions

In AspectJ, pointcut expressions can be combined with the operators && (and), || (or), and ! (not). For example, the following pointcut matches the join points within classes that implement either the ArithmeticCalculator or UnitCalculator interface:

```
within(ArithmeticCalculator+) || within(UnitCalculator+)
```

The operands of these operators can be any pointcut expressions or references to other pointcuts.

```
package com.apress.springrecipes.calculator;

import org.aspectj.lang.annotation.Aspect;
import org.aspectj.lang.annotation.Pointcut;

@Aspect
public class CalculatorPointcuts {

    @Pointcut("within(ArithmeticCalculator+)")
    public void arithmeticOperation() {}
```

```
    @Pointcut("within(UnitCalculator+)")
    public void unitOperation() {}

    @Pointcut("arithmeticOperation() || unitOperation()")
    public void loggingOperation() {}
}
```

Declaring Pointcut Parameters

One way to access join point information is by reflection (i.e., via an argument of type `org.aspectj.lang.JoinPoint` in the advice method). Besides, you can access join point information in a declarative way by using some kinds of special pointcut expressions. For example, the expressions `target()` and `args()` capture the target object and argument values of the current join point and expose them as pointcut parameters. These parameters will be passed to your advice method via arguments of the same name.

```
package com.apress.springrecipes.calculator;
...
import org.aspectj.lang.annotation.Aspect;
import org.aspectj.lang.annotation.Before;

@Aspect
public class CalculatorLoggingAspect {
    ...
    @Before("execution(* *.*(..)) && target(target) && args(a,b)")
    public void logParameter(Object target, double a, double b) {
        log.info("Target class : " + target.getClass().getName());
        log.info("Arguments : " + a + ", " + b);
    }
}
```

When declaring an independent pointcut that exposes parameters, you have to include them in the argument list of the pointcut method as well.

```
package com.apress.springrecipes.calculator;

import org.aspectj.lang.annotation.Aspect;
import org.aspectj.lang.annotation.Pointcut;

@Aspect
public class CalculatorPointcuts {
    ...
    @Pointcut("execution(* *.*(..)) && target(target) && args(a,b)")
    public void parameterPointcut(Object target, double a, double b) {}
}
```

Any advice that refers to this parameterized pointcut can access the pointcut parameters via method arguments of the same name.

```
package com.apress.springrecipes.calculator;
...
import org.aspectj.lang.annotation.Aspect;
import org.aspectj.lang.annotation.Before;

@Aspect
public class CalculatorLoggingAspect {
    ...
    @Before("CalculatorPointcuts.parameterPointcut(target, a, b)")
    public void logParameter(Object target, double a, double b) {
        log.info("Target class : " + target.getClass().getName());
        log.info("Arguments : " + a + ", " + b);
    }
}
```

6-7. Introducing Behaviors to Your Beans

Problem

Sometimes you may have a group of classes that share a common behavior. In OOP, they must extend the same base class or implement the same interface. This issue is actually a crosscutting concern that can be modularized with AOP.

In addition, the single inheritance mechanism of Java only allows a class to extend one base class at most. So, you cannot inherit behaviors from multiple implementation classes at the same time.

Solution

Introduction is a special type of advice in AOP. It allows your objects to implement an interface dynamically by providing an implementation class for that interface. It seems as if your objects had extended the implementation class at runtime.

Moreover, you are able to introduce multiple interfaces with multiple implementation classes to your objects at the same time. This can achieve the same effect as multiple inheritance.

How It Works

Suppose you have two interfaces, `MaxCalculator` and `MinCalculator`, to define the `max()` and `min()` operations.

```
package com.apress.springrecipes.calculator;

public interface MaxCalculator {

    public double max(double a, double b);
}
```

```
package com.apress.springrecipes.calculator;

public interface MinCalculator {

    public double min(double a, double b);
}
```

Then you have an implementation for each interface with `println` statements to let you know when the methods are executed.

```
package com.apress.springrecipes.calculator;

public class MaxCalculatorImpl implements MaxCalculator {

    public double max(double a, double b) {
        double result = (a >= b) ? a : b;
        System.out.println("max(" + a + ", " + b + ") = " + result);
        return result;
    }
}
```

```
package com.apress.springrecipes.calculator;

public class MinCalculatorImpl implements MinCalculator {

    public double min(double a, double b) {
        double result = (a <= b) ? a : b;
        System.out.println("min(" + a + ", " + b + ") = " + result);
        return result;
    }
}
```

Now suppose you would like `ArithmeticCalculatorImpl` to perform the `max()` and `min()` calculation also. As the Java language supports single inheritance only, it is not possible for the `ArithmeticCalculatorImpl` class to extend both the `MaxCalculatorImpl` and `MinCalculatorImpl` classes at the same time. The only possible way is to extend either class (e.g., `MaxCalculatorImpl`) and implement another interface (e.g., `MinCalculator`), either by copying the implementation code or delegating the handling to the actual implementation class. In either case, you have to repeat the method declarations.

With introduction, you can make `ArithmeticCalculatorImpl` dynamically implement both the `MaxCalculator` and `MinCalculator` interfaces by using the implementation classes `MaxCalculatorImpl` and `MinCalculatorImpl`. It has the same effect as multiple inheritance from `MaxCalculatorImpl` and `MinCalculatorImpl`. The brilliant idea behind introduction is that you needn't modify the `ArithmeticCalculatorImpl` class to introduce new methods. That means you can introduce methods to your existing classes even without source code available.

■ **Tip** You may wonder how an introduction can do that in Spring AOP. The answer is a *dynamic proxy*. As you may recall, you can specify a group of interfaces for a dynamic proxy to implement. Introduction works by adding an interface (e.g., `MaxCalculator`) to the dynamic proxy. When the methods declared in this interface are called on the proxy object, the proxy will delegate the calls to the back-end implementation class (e.g., `MaxCalculatorImpl`).

Introductions, like advices, must be declared within an aspect. You may create a new aspect or reuse an existing aspect for this purpose. In this aspect, you can declare an introduction by annotating an arbitrary field with the `@DeclareParents` annotation.

```
package com.apress.springrecipes.calculator;

import org.aspectj.lang.annotation.Aspect;
import org.aspectj.lang.annotation.DeclareParents;

@Aspect
public class CalculatorIntroduction {

    @DeclareParents(
        value = "com.apress.springrecipes.calculator.ArithmeticCalculatorImpl",
        defaultImpl = MaxCalculatorImpl.class)
    public MaxCalculator maxCalculator;

    @DeclareParents(
        value = "com.apress.springrecipes.calculator.ArithmeticCalculatorImpl",
        defaultImpl = MinCalculatorImpl.class)
    public MinCalculator minCalculator;
}
```

The `value` attribute of the `@DeclareParents` annotation type indicates which classes are the targets for this introduction. The interface to introduce is determined by the type of the annotated field. Finally, the implementation class used for this new interface is specified in the `defaultImpl` attribute.

Through these two introductions, you can dynamically introduce a couple of interfaces to the `ArithmeticCalculatorImpl` class. Actually, you can specify an AspectJ type-matching expression in the `value` attribute of the `@DeclareParents` annotation to introduce an interface to multiple classes. For the last step, don't forget to declare an instance of this aspect in the application context.

```
<beans ...>
    ...
    <bean class="com.apress.springrecipes.calculator.CalculatorIntroduction" />
</beans>
```

As you have introduced both the `MaxCalculator` and `MinCalculator` interfaces to your arithmetic calculator, you can cast it to the corresponding interface to perform the `max()` and `min()` calculations.

```
package com.apress.springrecipes.calculator;

public class Main {

    public static void main(String[] args) {
        ...
        ArithmeticCalculator arithmeticCalculator =
            (ArithmeticCalculator) context.getBean("arithmeticCalculator");
        ...
        MaxCalculator maxCalculator = (MaxCalculator) arithmeticCalculator;
        maxCalculator.max(1, 2);

        MinCalculator minCalculator = (MinCalculator) arithmeticCalculator;
        minCalculator.min(1, 2);
    }
}
```

6-8. Introducing States to Your Beans

Problem

Sometimes you may want to add new states to a group of existing objects to keep track of their usage, such as the calling count, the last modified date, and so on. It should not be a problem if all the objects have the same base class. However, it's difficult for you to add such states to different classes if they are not in the same class hierarchy.

Solution

You can introduce a new interface to your objects with an implementation class that holds the state field. Then you can write another advice to change the state according to a particular condition.

How It Works

Suppose you would like to keep track of the calling count of each calculator object. Since there is no field for storing the counter value in the original calculator classes, you need to introduce one with Spring AOP. First, let's create an interface for the operations of a counter.

```
package com.apress.springrecipes.calculator;

public interface Counter {

    public void increase();
    public int getCount();
}
```

Then just write a simple implementation class for this interface. This class has a count field for storing the counter value.

```
package com.apress.springrecipes.calculator;

public class CounterImpl implements Counter {

    private int count;

    public void increase() {
        count++;
    }

    public int getCount() {
        return count;
    }
}
```

To introduce the Counter interface to all your calculator objects with CounterImpl as the implementation, you can write the following introduction with a type-matching expression that matches all the calculator implementations:

```
package com.apress.springrecipes.calculator;
...
import org.aspectj.lang.annotation.Aspect;
import org.aspectj.lang.annotation.DeclareParents;

@Aspect
public class CalculatorIntroduction {
    ...
    @DeclareParents(
        value = "com.apress.springrecipes.calculator.*CalculatorImpl",
        defaultImpl = CounterImpl.class)
    public Counter counter;
}
```

This introduction introduces CounterImpl to each of your calculator objects. However, it's still not enough to keep track of the calling count. You have to increase the counter value each time a calculator method is called. You can write an after advice for this purpose. Note that you must get the *this* object but not the *target* object, as only the proxy object implements the Counter interface.

```
package com.apress.springrecipes.calculator;
...
import org.aspectj.lang.annotation.After;
import org.aspectj.lang.annotation.Aspect;

@Aspect
public class CalculatorIntroduction {
```

```
    ...
    @After("execution(* com.apress.springrecipes.calculator.*Calculator.*(..))"
            + " && this(counter)")
    public void increaseCount(Counter counter) {
        counter.increase();
    }
}
```

In the `Main` class, you can output the counter value for each of the calculator objects by casting them into the `Counter` type.

```
package com.apress.springrecipes.calculator;

public class Main {

    public static void main(String[] args) {
        ...
        ArithmeticCalculator arithmeticCalculator =
            (ArithmeticCalculator) context.getBean("arithmeticCalculator");
        ...

        UnitCalculator unitCalculator =
            (UnitCalculator) context.getBean("unitCalculator");
        ...

        Counter arithmeticCounter = (Counter) arithmeticCalculator;
        System.out.println(arithmeticCounter.getCount());

        Counter unitCounter = (Counter) unitCalculator;
        System.out.println(unitCounter.getCount());
    }
}
```

6-9. Declaring Aspects with XML-Based Configurations

Problem

Declaring aspects with AspectJ annotations is fine for most cases. However, if your JVM version is 1.4 or below (and hence doesn't support annotation), or you don't want your application to have a dependency on AspectJ, you shouldn't use AspectJ annotations to declare your aspects.

Solution

In addition to declaring aspects with AspectJ annotations, Spring supports declaring aspects in the bean configuration file. This type of declaration is done by using the XML elements in the `aop` schema.

In normal cases, annotation-based declaration is preferable to XML-based declaration. By using AspectJ annotations, your aspects will be compatible with AspectJ, whereas XML-based configurations are proprietary to Spring. As AspectJ is supported by more and more AOP frameworks, aspects written in annotation style will have a better chance of being reused.

How It Works

To enable AspectJ annotation support in Spring, you have already defined an empty XML element, <aop:aspectj-autoproxy>, in your bean configuration file. When declaring aspects with XML, this element is not necessary and should be deleted so that Spring AOP will ignore the AspectJ annotations. However, the aop schema definition must be retained in your <beans> root element because all the XML elements for AOP configuration are defined in this schema.

```
<beans xmlns="http://www.springframework.org/schema/beans"
    xmlns:xsi="http://www.w3.org/2001/XMLSchema-instance"
    xmlns:aop="http://www.springframework.org/schema/aop"
    xsi:schemaLocation="http://www.springframework.org/schema/beans
        http://www.springframework.org/schema/beans/spring-beans-2.5.xsd
        http://www.springframework.org/schema/aop
        http://www.springframework.org/schema/aop/spring-aop-2.5.xsd">

    <!--
    <aop:aspectj-autoproxy />
    -->
    ...
</beans>
```

Declaring Aspects

In the bean configuration file, all the Spring AOP configurations must be defined inside the <aop:config> element. For each aspect, you create an <aop:aspect> element to refer to a backing bean instance for the concrete aspect implementation. So, your aspect beans must have an identifier for the <aop:aspect> elements to refer to.

```
<beans ...>
    <aop:config>
        <aop:aspect id="loggingAspect" ref="calculatorLoggingAspect">
        </aop:aspect>

        <aop:aspect id="validationAspect" ref="calculatorValidationAspect">
        </aop:aspect>

        <aop:aspect id="introduction" ref="calculatorIntroduction">
        </aop:aspect>
    </aop:config>

    <bean id="calculatorLoggingAspect"
        class="com.apress.springrecipes.calculator.CalculatorLoggingAspect" />
```

```
    <bean id="calculatorValidationAspect"
        class="com.apress.springrecipes.calculator.CalculatorValidationAspect" />

    <bean id="calculatorIntroduction"
        class="com.apress.springrecipes.calculator.CalculatorIntroduction" />
    ...
</beans>
```

Declaring Pointcuts

A pointcut may be defined either under the `<aop:aspect>` element or directly under the `<aop:config>` element. In the former case, the pointcut will be visible to the declaring aspect only. In the latter case, it will be a global pointcut definition, which is visible to all the aspects.

You must remember that unlike AspectJ annotations, XML-based AOP configurations don't allow you to refer to other pointcuts by name within a pointcut expression. That means you must copy the referred pointcut expression and embed it directly.

```
<aop:config>
    <aop:pointcut id="loggingOperation" expression=
        "within(com.apress.springrecipes.calculator.ArithmeticCalculator+) || ➥
        within(com.apress.springrecipes.calculator.UnitCalculator+)" />

    <aop:pointcut id="validationOperation" expression=
        "within(com.apress.springrecipes.calculator.ArithmeticCalculator+) || ➥
        within(com.apress.springrecipes.calculator.UnitCalculator+)" />
    ...
</aop:config>
```

When using AspectJ annotations, you can join two pointcut expressions with the operator &&. However, the character & stands for "entity reference" in XML, so the pointcut operator && isn't valid in an XML document. You have to use the keyword and instead.

Declaring Advices

In the `aop` schema, there is a particular XML element corresponding to each type of advice. An advice element requires either a `pointcut-ref` attribute to refer to a pointcut or a `pointcut` attribute to embed a pointcut expression directly. The `method` attribute specifies the name of the advice method in the aspect class.

```
<aop:config>
    ...
    <aop:aspect id="loggingAspect" ref="calculatorLoggingAspect">
        <aop:before pointcut-ref="loggingOperation"
            method="logBefore" />

        <aop:after-returning pointcut-ref="loggingOperation"
            returning="result" method="logAfterReturning" />
```

```
        <aop:after-throwing pointcut-ref="loggingOperation"
            throwing="e" method="logAfterThrowing" />

        <aop:around pointcut-ref="loggingOperation"
            method="logAround" />
    </aop:aspect>

    <aop:aspect id="validationAspect" ref="calculatorValidationAspect">
        <aop:before pointcut-ref="validationOperation"
            method="validateBefore" />
    </aop:aspect>
</aop:config>
```

Declaring Introductions

Finally, an introduction can be declared inside an aspect using the <aop:declare-parents> element.

```
<aop:config>
    ...
    <aop:aspect id="introduction" ref="calculatorIntroduction">
        <aop:declare-parents
            types-matching=
                "com.apress.springrecipes.calculator.ArithmeticCalculatorImpl"
            implement-interface=
                "com.apress.springrecipes.calculator.MaxCalculator"
            default-impl=
                "com.apress.springrecipes.calculator.MaxCalculatorImpl" />

        <aop:declare-parents
            types-matching=
                "com.apress.springrecipes.calculator.ArithmeticCalculatorImpl"
            implement-interface=
                "com.apress.springrecipes.calculator.MinCalculator"
            default-impl=
                "com.apress.springrecipes.calculator.MinCalculatorImpl" />

        <aop:declare-parents
            types-matching=
                "com.apress.springrecipes.calculator.*CalculatorImpl"
            implement-interface=
                "com.apress.springrecipes.calculator.Counter"
            default-impl=
                "com.apress.springrecipes.calculator.CounterImpl" />

        <aop:after pointcut=
            "execution(* com.apress.springrecipes.calculator.*Calculator.*(..)) ➥
            and this(counter)"
```

```
            method="increaseCount" />
    </aop:aspect>
</aop:config>
```

6-10. Load-Time Weaving AspectJ Aspects in Spring

Problem

The Spring AOP framework only supports limited types of AspectJ pointcuts, and allows aspects to apply to beans declared in the IoC container. If you want to use additional pointcut types or apply your aspects to objects created outside the Spring IoC container, you have to use the AspectJ framework in your Spring application.

Solution

Weaving is the process of applying aspects to your target objects. With Spring AOP, weaving happens at runtime through dynamic proxies. In contrast, the AspectJ framework supports both compile-time and load-time weaving.

AspectJ *compile-time* weaving is done through a special AspectJ compiler called `ajc`. It can weave aspects into your Java source files and output woven binary class files. It can also weave aspects into your compiled class files or JAR files. This process is known as post-compile-time weaving. You can perform compile-time and post-compile-time weaving for your classes before declaring them in the Spring IoC container. Spring is not involved in the weaving process at all. For more information on compile-time and post-compile-time weaving, please refer to the AspectJ documentation.

AspectJ *load-time* weaving (also knows as LTW) happens when the target classes are loaded into JVM by a class loader. For a class to be woven, a special class loader is required to enhance the bytecode of the target class. Both AspectJ and Spring provide load-time weavers to add load-time weaving capability to the class loader. You only need simple configurations to enable these load-time weavers.

How It Works

To understand the AspectJ load-time weaving process in a Spring application, let's consider a calculator for complex numbers. First, you create the `Complex` class to represent complex numbers. You define the `toString()` method for this class to convert a complex number into the string representation `(a + bi)`.

```
package com.apress.springrecipes.calculator;

public class Complex {

    private int real;
    private int imaginary;

    public Complex(int real, int imaginary) {
        this.real = real;
```

```
        this.imaginary = imaginary;
    }

    // Getters and Setters
    ...

    public String toString() {
        return "(" + real + " + " + imaginary + "i)";
    }
}
```

Then you define an interface for the operations on complex numbers. For simplicity's sake, only add() and sub() are supported.

```
package com.apress.springrecipes.calculator;

public interface ComplexCalculator {

    public Complex add(Complex a, Complex b);
    public Complex sub(Complex a, Complex b);
}
```

The implementation code for this interface is as follows. Each time, you return a new complex object as the result.

```
package com.apress.springrecipes.calculator;

public class ComplexCalculatorImpl implements ComplexCalculator {

    public Complex add(Complex a, Complex b) {
        Complex result = new Complex(a.getReal() + b.getReal(),
                a.getImaginary() + b.getImaginary());
        System.out.println(a + " + " + b + " = " + result);
        return result;
    }

    public Complex sub(Complex a, Complex b) {
        Complex result = new Complex(a.getReal() - b.getReal(),
                a.getImaginary() - b.getImaginary());
        System.out.println(a + " - " + b + " = " + result);
        return result;
    }
}
```

Before this calculator can be used, it must be declared as a bean in the Spring IoC container.

```
<bean id="complexCalculator"
    class="com.apress.springrecipes.calculator.ComplexCalculatorImpl" />
```

Now you can test this complex number calculator with the following code in the `Main` class:

```
package com.apress.springrecipes.calculator;
...
public class Main {

    public static void main(String[] args) {
        ...
        ComplexCalculator complexCalculator =
            (ComplexCalculator) context.getBean("complexCalculator");
        complexCalculator.add(new Complex(1, 2), new Complex(2, 3));
        complexCalculator.sub(new Complex(5, 8), new Complex(2, 3));
    }
}
```

So far, the complex calculator is working fine. However, you may want to improve the performance of the calculator by caching complex number objects. As caching is a well-known crosscutting concern, you can modularize it with an aspect.

```
package com.apress.springrecipes.calculator;

import java.util.Collections;
import java.util.HashMap;
import java.util.Map;

import org.aspectj.lang.ProceedingJoinPoint;
import org.aspectj.lang.annotation.Around;
import org.aspectj.lang.annotation.Aspect;

@Aspect
public class ComplexCachingAspect {

    private Map<String, Complex> cache;

    public ComplexCachingAspect() {
        cache = Collections.synchronizedMap(new HashMap<String, Complex>());
    }

    @Around("call(public Complex.new(int, int)) && args(a,b)")
    public Object cacheAround(ProceedingJoinPoint joinPoint, int a, int b)
            throws Throwable {
        String key = a + "," + b;
        Complex complex = cache.get(key);
        if (complex == null) {
            System.out.println("Cache MISS for (" + key + ")");
            complex = (Complex) joinPoint.proceed();
            cache.put(key, complex);
        }
```

```
        else {
            System.out.println("Cache HIT for (" + key + ")");
        }
        return complex;
    }
}
```

In this aspect, you cache the complex objects in a map with their real and imaginary values as keys. For this map to be thread-safe, you should wrap it with a synchronized map. Then the most suitable time to look up the cache is when a complex object is created by invoking the constructor. You use the AspectJ pointcut expression `call` to capture the join points of calling the `Complex(int, int)` constructor. This pointcut is not supported by Spring AOP, so you haven't seen it in this chapter before.

Then you need an around advice to alter the return value. If a complex object of the same value is found in the cache, you return it to the caller directly. Otherwise, you proceed with the original constructor invocation to create a new complex object. Before you return it to the caller, you cache it in the map for subsequent usages.

Because this type of pointcut is not supported by Spring AOP, you have to use the AspectJ framework to apply this aspect. The configuration of the AspectJ framework is done through a file named `aop.xml` in the `META-INF` directory in the classpath root.

```
<!DOCTYPE aspectj PUBLIC "-//AspectJ//DTD//EN"
    "http://www.eclipse.org/aspectj/dtd/aspectj.dtd">

<aspectj>
    <weaver>
        <include within="com.apress.springrecipes.calculator.*" />
    </weaver>

    <aspects>
        <aspect
            name="com.apress.springrecipes.calculator.ComplexCachingAspect" />
    </aspects>
</aspectj>
```

In this AspectJ configuration file, you have to specify the aspects and which classes you want your aspects to weave in. Here you specify weaving `ComplexCachingAspect` into all the classes in the `com.apress.springrecipes.calculator` package.

Load-Time Weaving by the AspectJ Weaver

AspectJ provides a load-time weaving agent to enable load-time weaving. You only need to add a VM argument to the command that runs your application. Then your classes will get woven when they are loaded into the JVM.

```
java -javaagent:c:/spring-framework-2.5/lib/aspectj/aspectjweaver.jar➥
com.apress.springrecipes.calculator.Main
```

If you run your application with the preceding argument, you will get the following output and cache status. The AspectJ agent advises all calls to the `Complex(int, int)` constructor.

```
Cache MISS for (1,2)
Cache MISS for (2,3)
Cache MISS for (3,5)
(1 + 2i) + (2 + 3i) = (3 + 5i)
Cache MISS for (5,8)
Cache HIT for (2,3)
Cache HIT for (3,5)
(5 + 8i) - (2 + 3i) = (3 + 5i)
```

Load-Time Weaving by Spring 2.5 Load-Time Weaver

Spring 2.5 bundles several load-time weavers for different runtime environments. To turn on a suitable load-time weaver for your Spring application, you only need to declare the empty XML element `<context:load-time-weaver>`. This element is defined in the `context` schema, and it's only available for Spring 2.5 and higher.

```
<beans xmlns="http://www.springframework.org/schema/beans"
    xmlns:xsi="http://www.w3.org/2001/XMLSchema-instance"
    xmlns:aop="http://www.springframework.org/schema/aop"
    xmlns:context="http://www.springframework.org/schema/context"
    xsi:schemaLocation="http://www.springframework.org/schema/beans
        http://www.springframework.org/schema/beans/spring-beans-2.5.xsd
        http://www.springframework.org/schema/aop
        http://www.springframework.org/schema/aop/spring-aop-2.5.xsd
        http://www.springframework.org/schema/context
        http://www.springframework.org/schema/context/spring-context-2.5.xsd">

    <context:load-time-weaver />
    ...
</beans>
```

Spring will be able to detect the most suitable load-time weaver for your runtime environment. Some Java EE application servers have class loaders that support the Spring load-time weaver mechanism, so there's no need to specify a Java agent in their startup commands.

However, for a simple Java application, you still require a weaving agent provided by Spring to enable load-time weaving. You have to specify the Spring agent in the VM argument of the startup command.

```
java -javaagent:c:/spring-framework-2.5/dist/weaving/spring-agent.jar➥
com.apress.springrecipes.calculator.Main
```

However, if you run your application, you will get the following output and cache status. This is because the Spring agent only advises the `Complex(int, int)` constructor calls made by beans declared in the Spring IoC container. As the complex operands are created in the `Main` class, the Spring agent will not advise their constructor calls.

```
Cache MISS for (3,5)
(1 + 2i) + (2 + 3i) = (3 + 5i)
Cache HIT for (3,5)
(5 + 8i) - (2 + 3i) = (3 + 5i)
```

6-11. Configuring AspectJ Aspects in Spring

Problem

Spring AOP aspects are declared in the bean configuration file so that you can easily configure them. However, aspects to be used in the AspectJ framework are instantiated by the AspectJ framework itself. You have to retrieve the aspect instances from the AspectJ framework to configure them.

Solution

Each AspectJ aspect provides a static factory method called `aspectOf()`, which allows you to access the current aspect instance. In the Spring IoC container, you can declare a bean created by a factory method by specifying the `factory-method` attribute.

How It Works

For instance, you can allow the cache map of `ComplexCachingAspect` to be configured via a setter method and delete its instantiation from the constructor.

```
package com.apress.springrecipes.calculator;
...
import java.util.Collections;
import java.util.Map;

import org.aspectj.lang.annotation.Aspect;

@Aspect
public class ComplexCachingAspect {

    private Map<String, Complex> cache;

    public void setCache(Map<String, Complex> cache) {
        this.cache = Collections.synchronizedMap(cache);
    }
    ...
}
```

To configure this property in the Spring IoC container, you can declare a bean created by the factory method `aspectOf()`.

```
<bean class="com.apress.springrecipes.calculator.ComplexCachingAspect"
    factory-method="aspectOf">
    <property name="cache">
        <map>
            <entry key="2,3">
                <bean class="com.apress.springrecipes.calculator.Complex">
                    <constructor-arg value="2" />
                    <constructor-arg value="3" />
                </bean>
            </entry>
            <entry key="3,5">
                <bean class="com.apress.springrecipes.calculator.Complex">
                    <constructor-arg value="3" />
                    <constructor-arg value="5" />
                </bean>
            </entry>
        </map>
    </property>
</bean>
```

■ **Tip** You may wonder why your `ComplexCachingAspect` has a static factory method `aspectOf()` that you have not declared. This method is woven by AspectJ at load time to allow you to access the current aspect instance. So, if you are using Spring IDE, it may give you a warning because it cannot find this method in your class.

6-12. Injecting Spring Beans into Domain Objects

Problem

Beans declared in the Spring IoC container can wire themselves to one another through Spring's dependency injection capability. However, objects created outside the Spring IoC container cannot wire themselves to Spring beans via configuration. You have to perform the wiring manually with programming code.

Solution

Objects created outside the Spring IoC container are usually domain objects. They are often created using the `new` operator or from the results of database queries.

To inject a Spring bean into domain objects created outside Spring, you need the help of AOP. Actually, the injection of Spring beans is also a kind of crosscutting concern. As the domain objects are not created by Spring, you cannot use Spring AOP for injection. Spring supplies an AspectJ aspect specialized for this purpose. You can enable this aspect in the AspectJ framework.

How It Works

Suppose you have a global formatter to format complex numbers. This formatter accepts a pattern for formatting.

```
package com.apress.springrecipes.calculator;

public class ComplexFormatter {

    private String pattern;

    public void setPattern(String pattern) {
        this.pattern = pattern;
    }

    public String format(Complex complex) {
        return pattern.replaceAll("a", Integer.toString(complex.getReal()))
                .replaceAll("b", Integer.toString(complex.getImaginary()));
    }
}
```

Then you configure this formatter in the Spring IoC container and specify a pattern for it.

```
<bean id="complexFormatter"
    class="com.apress.springrecipes.calculator.ComplexFormatter">
    <property name="pattern" value="(a + bi)" />
</bean>
```

In the `Complex` class, you want to use this formatter in the `toString()` method to convert a complex number into string. It exposes a setter method for the `ComplexFormatter`.

```
package com.apress.springrecipes.calculator;

public class Complex {

    private int real;
    private int imaginary;
    ...
    private ComplexFormatter formatter;

    public void setFormatter(ComplexFormatter formatter) {
        this.formatter = formatter;
    }

    public String toString() {
        return formatter.format(this);
    }
}
```

However, as complex objects were not created within the Spring IoC container, they cannot be configured for dependency injection. You have to write code to inject a ComplexFormatter instance into each complex object.

The good news is that Spring includes AnnotationBeanConfigurerAspect in its aspect library for configuring the dependencies of any objects, even if they were not created by the Spring IoC container. First of all, you have to annotate your object type with the @Configurable annotation to declare that this type of object is configurable.

```
package com.apress.springrecipes.calculator;

import org.springframework.beans.factory.annotation.Configurable;

@Configurable
public class Complex {
    ...
}
```

Spring defines a convenient XML element, <context:spring-configured>, for you to enable the mentioned aspect. In Spring 2.0, this element is located in the aop schema. It has been moved to the context schema since Spring 2.5.

■Note To use the Spring aspect library for AspectJ, you have to include spring-aspects.jar (located in the dist/weaving directory of the Spring installation) in your classpath.

```
<beans ...>
    ...
    <context:load-time-weaver />

    <context:spring-configured />

    <bean class="com.apress.springrecipes.calculator.Complex"
        scope="prototype">
        <property name="formatter" ref="complexFormatter" />
    </bean>
</beans>
```

When a class with the @Configurable annotation is instantiated, the aspect will look for a prototype-scoped bean definition whose type is the same as this class. Then it will configure the new instances according to this bean definition. If there are properties declared in the bean definition, the new instances will also have the same properties set by the aspect.

Finally, the aspect needs to be enabled by the AspectJ framework to take effect. You can weave it into your classes at load time with the Spring agent.

```
java -javaagent:c:/spring-framework-2.5/dist/weaving/spring-agent.jar➥
com.apress.springrecipes.calculator.Main
```

Another way of linking up a configurable class with a bean definition is by the bean ID. You can present a bean ID as the @Configurable annotation value.

```
package com.apress.springrecipes.calculator;

import org.springframework.beans.factory.annotation.Configurable;

@Configurable("complex")
public class Complex {
    ...
}
```

Then you must add the id attribute to the corresponding bean definition to link with a configurable class.

```
<bean id="complex" class="com.apress.springrecipes.calculator.Complex"
    scope="prototype">
    <property name="formatter" ref="complexFormatter" />
</bean>
```

Similar to normal Spring beans, configurable beans can also support auto-wiring and dependency checking.

```
package com.apress.springrecipes.calculator;

import org.springframework.beans.factory.annotation.Autowire;
import org.springframework.beans.factory.annotation.Configurable;

@Configurable(
    value = "complex",
    autowire = Autowire.BY_TYPE,
    dependencyCheck = true)
public class Complex {
    ...
}
```

Note that the dependencyCheck attribute is of Boolean type but not enumeration type. When it's set to true, it has the same effect as dependency-check="objects"—that is, to check for non-primitive and non-collection types. With auto-wiring enabled, you no longer need to set the formatter property explicitly.

```
<bean id="complex" class="com.apress.springrecipes.calculator.Complex"
    scope="prototype" />
```

In Spring 2.5, you no longer need to configure auto-wiring and dependency checking at the class level for @Configurable. Instead, you can annotate the formatter's setter method with the @Autowired annotation.

```
package com.apress.springrecipes.calculator;

import org.springframework.beans.factory.annotation.Autowired;
import org.springframework.beans.factory.annotation.Configurable;

@Configurable("complex")
public class Complex {
    ...
    private ComplexFormatter formatter;

    @Autowired
    public void setFormatter(ComplexFormatter formatter) {
        this.formatter = formatter;
    }
}
```

Then enable the `<context:annotation-config>` element in the bean configuration file to process the methods with these annotations.

```
<beans ...>
    <context:annotation-config />
    ...
</beans>
```

6-13. Summary

In this chapter, you have learned how to write aspects with either AspectJ annotations or XML-based configurations in the bean configuration file, and how they are registered in the Spring IoC container. Spring 2.x AOP supports five types of advices: before, after, after returning, after throwing, and around.

You have also learned various types of pointcuts to match join points by method signature, type signature, and bean name. However, Spring AOP only supports method execution join points for beans declared in its IoC container. If you use a pointcut expression out of this scope, an exception will be thrown.

Introduction is a special type of AOP advice. It allows your objects to implement an interface dynamically by providing an implementation class. It can achieve the same effect as multiple inheritance. Introductions are often used to add behaviors and states to a group of existing objects.

If you want to use pointcut types that are not supported by Spring AOP, or apply your aspects to objects created outside the Spring IoC container, you have to use the AspectJ framework in your Spring application. Aspects can be woven into your classes by a load-time weaver. Spring also supplies several useful AspectJ aspects in its aspect library. One of them injects Spring beans into domain objects created outside of Spring.

In the next chapter, you will learn how the Spring JDBC framework can reduce the effort of accessing a relational database.

PART 2

Fundamentals

CHAPTER 7

■ ■ ■

Spring JDBC Support

In this chapter, you will learn how Spring can simplify your database access tasks. Data access is a common requirement for most enterprise applications, which usually require accessing data stored in relational databases. As an essential part of Java SE, JDBC (Java Database Connectivity) defines a set of standard APIs for you to access relational databases in a vendor-independent fashion.

The purpose of JDBC is to provide APIs through which you can execute SQL statements against a database. However, when using JDBC, you have to manage database-related resources by yourself and handle database exceptions explicitly. To make JDBC easier to use, Spring establishes a JDBC accessing framework by defining an abstract layer on top of the JDBC APIs.

As the heart of the Spring JDBC framework, JDBC templates are designed to provide template methods for different types of JDBC operations. Each template method is responsible for controlling the overall process and allows you to override particular tasks of the process. In this way, you can minimize your database access effort while retaining as much flexibility as possible.

Besides the JDBC template approach, the Spring JDBC framework supplies another more object-oriented approach for you to organize your data access logic. It enables you to model each database operation as a fine-grained operation object. Compared to the JDBC template approach, the JDBC operation object approach is just an alternative approach to organizing your data access logic. Some developers may prefer the former, while others like the latter better.

Upon finishing this chapter, you will be able to use the Spring JDBC framework to access relational databases. As part of the Spring data access module, the Spring JDBC framework is consistent with other parts of the module. So, learning about the JDBC framework is an ideal introduction to the entire data access module.

7-1. Problems with Direct JDBC

Suppose you are going to develop an application for vehicle registration, whose major functions are the basic CRUD (create, read, update, and delete) operations on vehicle records. These records will be stored in a relational database and accessed with JDBC. First, you design the following `Vehicle` class, which represents a vehicle in Java:

```
package com.apress.springrecipes.vehicle;

public class Vehicle {

    private String vehicleNo;
    private String color;
    private int wheel;
    private int seat;

    // Constructors, Getters and Setters
    ...
}
```

Setting Up the Application Database

Before developing your vehicle registration application, you have to set up the database for it. For the sake of low memory consumption and easy configuration, I have chosen Apache Derby (`http://db.apache.org/derby/`) as my database engine. Derby is an open source relational database engine provided under the Apache License and implemented in pure Java.

■ **Note** You can download the Apache Derby binary distribution (e.g., v10.3) from the Apache Derby web site and extract it to a directory of your choice to complete the installation.

Derby can run in either the embedded mode or the client/server mode. For testing purposes, the client/server mode is more appropriate because it allows you to inspect and edit data with any visual database tools that support JDBC—for example, the Eclipse Data Tools Platform (DTP).

■ **Note** To start the Derby server in the client/server mode, just execute the `startNetworkServer` script for your platform (located in the `bin` directory of the Derby installation).

After starting up the Derby network server on localhost, you can connect to it with the JDBC properties shown in Table 7-1.

■ **Note** You require Derby's client JDBC driver `derbyclient.jar` (located in the `lib` directory of the Derby installation) to connect to the Derby server.

Table 7-1. *JDBC Properties for Connecting to the Application Database*

Property	Value
Driver class	`org.apache.derby.jdbc.ClientDriver`
URL	`jdbc:derby://localhost:1527/vehicle;create=true`
Username	`app`
Password	`app`

The first time you connect to this database, the database instance `vehicle` will be created if it did not exist before, because you specified `create=true` in the URL. You can provide any values for the username and password, as Derby disables authentication by default. Next, you have to create the `VEHICLE` table for storing vehicle records with the following SQL statement. By default, this table will be created in the `APP` database schema.

```
CREATE TABLE VEHICLE (
    VEHICLE_NO     VARCHAR(10)     NOT NULL,
    COLOR          VARCHAR(10),
    WHEEL          INT,
    SEAT           INT,
    PRIMARY KEY (VEHICLE_NO)
);
```

Understanding the Data Access Object Design Pattern

A typical design mistake made by inexperienced developers is to mix different types of logic (e.g., presentation logic, business logic, and data access logic) in a single large module. This reduces the module's reusability and maintainability because of the tight coupling it introduces. The general purpose of the *Data Access Object (DAO)* pattern is to avoid these problems by separating data access logic from business logic and presentation logic. This pattern recommends that data access logic be encapsulated in independent modules called data access objects.

For your vehicle registration application, you can abstract the data access operations to insert, update, delete, and query a vehicle. These operations should be declared in a DAO interface to allow for different DAO implementation technologies.

```
package com.apress.springrecipes.vehicle;

public interface VehicleDao {

    public void insert(Vehicle vehicle);
    public void update(Vehicle vehicle);
    public void delete(Vehicle vehicle);
    public Vehicle findByVehicleNo(String vehicleNo);
}
```

Most parts of the JDBC APIs declare throwing `java.sql.SQLException`. But since this interface aims to abstract the data access operations only, it should not depend on the implementation technology. So, it's unwise for this general interface to declare throwing the JDBC-specific SQLException. A common practice when implementing a DAO interface is to wrap this kind of exception with a runtime exception.

Implementing the DAO with JDBC

To access the database with JDBC, you create an implementation for this DAO interface (e.g., JdbcVehicleDao). Because your DAO implementation has to connect to the database to execute SQL statements, you may establish database connections by specifying the driver class name, database URL, username, and password. However, in JDBC 2.0 or higher, you can obtain database connections from a preconfigured javax.sql.DataSource object without knowing about the connection details.

```
package com.apress.springrecipes.vehicle;

import java.sql.Connection;
import java.sql.PreparedStatement;
import java.sql.ResultSet;
import java.sql.SQLException;

import javax.sql.DataSource;

public class JdbcVehicleDao implements VehicleDao {

    private DataSource dataSource;

    public void setDataSource(DataSource dataSource) {
        this.dataSource = dataSource;
    }

    public void insert(Vehicle vehicle) {
        String sql = "INSERT INTO VEHICLE (VEHICLE_NO, COLOR, WHEEL, SEAT) "
                + "VALUES (?, ?, ?, ?)";
        Connection conn = null;
        try {
            conn = dataSource.getConnection();
            PreparedStatement ps = conn.prepareStatement(sql);
            ps.setString(1, vehicle.getVehicleNo());
            ps.setString(2, vehicle.getColor());
            ps.setInt(3, vehicle.getWheel());
            ps.setInt(4, vehicle.getSeat());
            ps.executeUpdate();
            ps.close();
        } catch (SQLException e) {
            throw new RuntimeException(e);
        } finally {
            if (conn != null) {
                try {
```

```
                    conn.close();
                } catch (SQLException e) {}
            }
        }
    }

    public Vehicle findByVehicleNo(String vehicleNo) {
        String sql = "SELECT * FROM VEHICLE WHERE VEHICLE_NO = ?";
        Connection conn = null;
        try {
            conn = dataSource.getConnection();
            PreparedStatement ps = conn.prepareStatement(sql);
            ps.setString(1, vehicleNo);

            Vehicle vehicle = null;
            ResultSet rs = ps.executeQuery();
            if (rs.next()) {
                vehicle = new Vehicle(rs.getString("VEHICLE_NO"),
                        rs.getString("COLOR"), rs.getInt("WHEEL"),
                        rs.getInt("SEAT"));
            }
            rs.close();
            ps.close();
            return vehicle;
        } catch (SQLException e) {
            throw new RuntimeException(e);
        } finally {
            if (conn != null) {
                try {
                    conn.close();
                } catch (SQLException e) {}
            }
        }
    }

    public void update(Vehicle vehicle) {}

    public void delete(Vehicle vehicle) {}
}
```

The vehicle insert operation is a typical JDBC update scenario. Each time this method is called, you obtain a connection from the data source and execute the SQL statement on this connection. Your DAO interface doesn't declare throwing any checked exceptions, so if a `SQLException` occurs, you have to wrap it with an unchecked `RuntimeException`. Finally, don't forget to release the connection in the `finally` block. Failing to do so may cause your application to run out of connections.

Here, the update and delete operations will be skipped because they are much the same as the insert operation from a technical point of view. For the query operation, you have to extract the data from the returned result set to build a vehicle object in addition to executing the SQL statement.

Configuring a Data Source in Spring

The `javax.sql.DataSource` interface is a standard interface defined by the JDBC specification. There are many data source implementations provided by different vendors and projects. It is very easy to switch between different data source implementations because they implement the common `DataSource` interface. As a Java application framework, Spring also provides several convenient but less powerful data source implementations. The simplest one is `DriverManagerDataSource`, which opens a new connection every time it's requested.

■ **Note** To access a database instance running on the Derby server, you have to include `derbyclient.jar` (located in the `lib` directory of the Derby installation) in your classpath.

```
<beans xmlns="http://www.springframework.org/schema/beans"
    xmlns:xsi="http://www.w3.org/2001/XMLSchema-instance"
    xsi:schemaLocation="http://www.springframework.org/schema/beans
        http://www.springframework.org/schema/beans/spring-beans-2.5.xsd">

    <bean id="dataSource"
        class="org.springframework.jdbc.datasource.DriverManagerDataSource">
        <property name="driverClassName"
            value="org.apache.derby.jdbc.ClientDriver" />
        <property name="url"
            value="jdbc:derby://localhost:1527/vehicle;create=true" />
        <property name="username" value="app" />
        <property name="password" value="app" />
    </bean>

    <bean id="vehicleDao"
        class="com.apress.springrecipes.vehicle.JdbcVehicleDao">
        <property name="dataSource" ref="dataSource" />
    </bean>
</beans>
```

`DriverManagerDataSource` is not an efficient data source implementation, as it opens a new connection for the client every time it's requested. Another data source implementation provided by Spring is `SingleConnectionDataSource`. As its name indicates, this maintains only a single connection that's reused all the time and never closed. Obviously, it is not suitable in a multithreaded environment.

Spring's own data source implementations are mainly used for testing purposes. However, many production data source implementations support connection pooling. For example, the DBCP (Database Connection Pooling Services) module of the Apache Commons Library has several data source implementations that support connection pooling. Of these, `BasicDataSource` accepts the same connection properties as `DriverManagerDataSource` and allows you to specify the initial connection size and maximum active connections for the connection pool.

Note To use the data source implementations provided by DBCP, you have to include `commons-dbcp.jar` and `commons-pool.jar` (located in the `lib/jakarta-commons` directory of the Spring installation) in your classpath.

```
<bean id="dataSource"
    class="org.apache.commons.dbcp.BasicDataSource">
    <property name="driverClassName"
        value="org.apache.derby.jdbc.ClientDriver" />
    <property name="url"
        value="jdbc:derby://localhost:1527/vehicle;create=true" />
    <property name="username" value="app" />
    <property name="password" value="app" />
    <property name="initialSize" value="2" />
    <property name="maxActive" value="5" />
</bean>
```

Many Java EE application servers build in data source implementations that you can configure from the server console. If you have a data source configured in an application server and exposed for JNDI lookup, you can use `JndiObjectFactoryBean` to look it up.

```
<bean id="dataSource"
    class="org.springframework.jndi.JndiObjectFactoryBean">
    <property name="jndiName" value="jdbc/VehicleDS" />
</bean>
```

In Spring 2.x, a JNDI lookup can be simplified by the `jndi-lookup` element defined in the `jee` schema.

```
<beans xmlns="http://www.springframework.org/schema/beans"
    xmlns:xsi="http://www.w3.org/2001/XMLSchema-instance"
    xmlns:jee="http://www.springframework.org/schema/jee"
    xsi:schemaLocation="http://www.springframework.org/schema/beans
        http://www.springframework.org/schema/beans/spring-beans-2.0.xsd
        http://www.springframework.org/schema/jee
        http://www.springframework.org/schema/jee/spring-jee-2.0.xsd">

    <jee:jndi-lookup id="dataSource" jndi-name="jdbc/VehicleDS" />
    ...
</beans>
```

Running the DAO

The following `Main` class tests your DAO by using it to insert a new vehicle to the database. If it succeeds, you can query the vehicle from the database immediately.

```
package com.apress.springrecipes.vehicle;

import org.springframework.context.ApplicationContext;
import org.springframework.context.support.ClassPathXmlApplicationContext;

public class Main {

    public static void main(String[] args) {
        ApplicationContext context =
            new ClassPathXmlApplicationContext("beans.xml");

        VehicleDao vehicleDao = (VehicleDao) context.getBean("vehicleDao");
        Vehicle vehicle = new Vehicle("TEM0001", "Red", 4, 4);
        vehicleDao.insert(vehicle);

        vehicle = vehicleDao.findByVehicleNo("TEM0001");
        System.out.println("Vehicle No: " + vehicle.getVehicleNo());
        System.out.println("Color: " + vehicle.getColor());
        System.out.println("Wheel: " + vehicle.getWheel());
        System.out.println("Seat: " + vehicle.getSeat());
    }
}
```

Now you are able to implement a DAO using JDBC directly. However, as you can see from the preceding DAO implementation, most of the JDBC code is similar and needs to be repeated for each database operation. Such redundant code will make your DAO methods much longer and less readable.

7-2. Using a JDBC Template to Update a Database

Problem

To implement a JDBC update operation, you have to perform the following tasks, most of which are redundant:

1. Obtain a database connection from the data source.
2. Create a `PreparedStatement` object from the connection.
3. Bind the parameters to the `PreparedStatement` object.
4. Execute the `PreparedStatement` object.
5. Handle `SQLException`.
6. Clean up the statement object and connection.

Solution

The JdbcTemplate class declares a number of overloaded update() template methods to control the overall update process. Different versions of the update() method allow you to override different task subsets of the default process. The Spring JDBC framework predefines several callback interfaces to encapsulate different task subsets. You can implement one of these callback interfaces and pass its instance to the corresponding update() method to complete the process.

How It Works

Updating a Database with a Statement Creator

The first callback interface to introduce is PreparedStatementCreator. You implement this interface to override the statement creation task (task 2) and the parameter binding task (task 3) of the overall update process. To insert a vehicle into the database, you implement the PreparedStatementCreator interface as follows:

```
package com.apress.springrecipes.vehicle;

import java.sql.Connection;
import java.sql.PreparedStatement;
import java.sql.SQLException;

import org.springframework.jdbc.core.PreparedStatementCreator;

public class InsertVehicleStatementCreator implements PreparedStatementCreator {

    private Vehicle vehicle;

    public InsertVehicleStatementCreator(Vehicle vehicle) {
        this.vehicle = vehicle;
    }

    public PreparedStatement createPreparedStatement(Connection conn)
            throws SQLException {
        String sql = "INSERT INTO VEHICLE (VEHICLE_NO, COLOR, WHEEL, SEAT) "
                + "VALUES (?, ?, ?, ?)";
        PreparedStatement ps = conn.prepareStatement(sql);
        ps.setString(1, vehicle.getVehicleNo());
        ps.setString(2, vehicle.getColor());
        ps.setInt(3, vehicle.getWheel());
        ps.setInt(4, vehicle.getSeat());
        return ps;
    }
}
```

When implementing the PreparedStatementCreator interface, you will get the database connection as the createPreparedStatement() method's argument. All you have to do in this method is to create a PreparedStatement object on this connection and bind your parameters to this object. Finally, you have to return the PreparedStatement object as the method's return value. Notice that the method signature declares throwing SQLException, which means that you don't need to handle this kind of exception yourself.

Now you can use this statement creator to simplify the vehicle insert operation. First of all, you have to create an instance of the JdbcTemplate class and pass in the data source for this template to obtain a connection from it. Then you just make a call to the update() method and pass in your statement creator for the template to complete the update process.

```
package com.apress.springrecipes.vehicle;
...
import org.springframework.jdbc.core.JdbcTemplate;

public class JdbcVehicleDao implements VehicleDao {
    ...
    public void insert(Vehicle vehicle) {
        JdbcTemplate jdbcTemplate = new JdbcTemplate(dataSource);
        jdbcTemplate.update(new InsertVehicleStatementCreator(vehicle));
    }
}
```

Typically, it is better to implement the PreparedStatementCreator interface and other callback interfaces as inner classes if they are used within one method only. This is because you can get access to the local variables and method arguments directly from the inner class, instead of passing them as constructor arguments. The only constraint on such variables and arguments is that they must be declared as final.

```
package com.apress.springrecipes.vehicle;
...
import org.springframework.jdbc.core.JdbcTemplate;
import org.springframework.jdbc.core.PreparedStatementCreator;

public class JdbcVehicleDao implements VehicleDao {
    ...
    public void insert(final Vehicle vehicle) {
        JdbcTemplate jdbcTemplate = new JdbcTemplate(dataSource);

        jdbcTemplate.update(new PreparedStatementCreator() {

            public PreparedStatement createPreparedStatement(Connection conn)
                    throws SQLException {
                String sql = "INSERT INTO VEHICLE "
                        + "(VEHICLE_NO, COLOR, WHEEL, SEAT) "
                        + "VALUES (?, ?, ?, ?)";
                PreparedStatement ps = conn.prepareStatement(sql);
                ps.setString(1, vehicle.getVehicleNo());
                ps.setString(2, vehicle.getColor());
                ps.setInt(3, vehicle.getWheel());
                ps.setInt(4, vehicle.getSeat());
```

```
                return ps;
            }
        });
    }
}
```

Now you can delete the preceding InsertVehicleStatementCreator class, as it will not be used anymore.

Updating a Database with a Statement Setter

The second callback interface, PreparedStatementSetter, as its name indicates, performs only the parameter binding task (task 3) of the overall update process.

```
package com.apress.springrecipes.vehicle;
...
import org.springframework.jdbc.core.JdbcTemplate;
import org.springframework.jdbc.core.PreparedStatementSetter;

public class JdbcVehicleDao implements VehicleDao {
    ...
    public void insert(final Vehicle vehicle) {
        String sql = "INSERT INTO VEHICLE (VEHICLE_NO, COLOR, WHEEL, SEAT) "
                + "VALUES (?, ?, ?, ?)";
        JdbcTemplate jdbcTemplate = new JdbcTemplate(dataSource);

        jdbcTemplate.update(sql, new PreparedStatementSetter() {

                    public void setValues(PreparedStatement ps)
                            throws SQLException {
                        ps.setString(1, vehicle.getVehicleNo());
                        ps.setString(2, vehicle.getColor());
                        ps.setInt(3, vehicle.getWheel());
                        ps.setInt(4, vehicle.getSeat());
                    }
                });
    }
}
```

Another version of the update() template method accepts a SQL statement and a PreparedStatementSetter object as arguments. This method will create a PreparedStatement object for you from your SQL statement. All you have to do with this interface is to bind your parameters to the PreparedStatement object.

Updating a Database with a SQL Statement and Parameter Values

Finally, the simplest version of the update() method accepts a SQL statement and an object array as statement parameters. It will create a PreparedStatement object from your SQL statement and bind the parameters for you. Therefore, you don't have to override any of the tasks in the update process.

```
package com.apress.springrecipes.vehicle;
...
import org.springframework.jdbc.core.JdbcTemplate;

public class JdbcVehicleDao implements VehicleDao {
    ...
    public void insert(final Vehicle vehicle) {
        String sql = "INSERT INTO VEHICLE (VEHICLE_NO, COLOR, WHEEL, SEAT) "
                + "VALUES (?, ?, ?, ?)";
        JdbcTemplate jdbcTemplate = new JdbcTemplate(dataSource);

        jdbcTemplate.update(sql, new Object[] { vehicle.getVehicleNo(),
                vehicle.getColor(),vehicle.getWheel(), vehicle.getSeat() });
    }
}
```

Of the three different versions of the `update()` method introduced, the last is the simplest, as you don't have to implement any callback interfaces. In contrast, the first is the most flexible because you can do any preprocessing of the `PreparedStatement` object before its execution. In practice, you should always choose the simplest version that meets all your needs.

There are also other overloaded `update()` methods provided by the `JdbcTemplate` class. Please refer to its javadoc for details.

Batch Updating a Database

Suppose you would like to insert a batch of vehicles into the database. If you call the `insert()` method multiple times, it will be very slow as the SQL statement will be compiled repeatedly. So, it would be better to add a new method to the DAO interface for inserting a batch of vehicles.

```
package com.apress.springrecipes.vehicle;
...
public interface VehicleDao {
    ...
    public void insertBatch(List<Vehicle> vehicles);
}
```

The `JdbcTemplate` class also offers the `batchUpdate()` template method for batch update operations. It requires a SQL statement and a `BatchPreparedStatementSetter` object as arguments. In this method, the statement is compiled only once and executed multiple times. If your database driver supports JDBC 2.0, this method automatically makes use of the batch update features to increase performance.

```
package com.apress.springrecipes.vehicle;
...
import org.springframework.jdbc.core.BatchPreparedStatementSetter;
import org.springframework.jdbc.core.JdbcTemplate;
```

```
public class JdbcVehicleDao implements VehicleDao {
    ...
    public void insertBatch(final List<Vehicle> vehicles) {
        String sql = "INSERT INTO VEHICLE (VEHICLE_NO, COLOR, WHEEL, SEAT) "
                + "VALUES (?, ?, ?, ?)";
        JdbcTemplate jdbcTemplate = new JdbcTemplate(dataSource);

        jdbcTemplate.batchUpdate(sql, new BatchPreparedStatementSetter() {

                    public int getBatchSize() {
                        return vehicles.size();
                    }

                    public void setValues(PreparedStatement ps, int i)
                            throws SQLException {
                        Vehicle vehicle = vehicles.get(i);
                        ps.setString(1, vehicle.getVehicleNo());
                        ps.setString(2, vehicle.getColor());
                        ps.setInt(3, vehicle.getWheel());
                        ps.setInt(4, vehicle.getSeat());
                    }
                });
    }
}
```

You can test your batch insert operation with the following code snippet in the `Main` class:

```
package com.apress.springrecipes.vehicle;
...
public class Main {

    public static void main(String[] args) {
        ...
        VehicleDao vehicleDao = (VehicleDao) context.getBean("vehicleDao");
        Vehicle vehicle1 = new Vehicle("TEM0002", "Blue", 4, 4);
        Vehicle vehicle2 = new Vehicle("TEM0003", "Black", 4, 6);
        vehicleDao.insertBatch(
                Arrays.asList(new Vehicle[] { vehicle1, vehicle2 }));
    }
}
```

7-3. Using a JDBC Template to Query a Database

Problem

To implement a JDBC query operation, you have to perform the following tasks, two of which (task 5 and task 6) are additional as compared to an update operation:

1. Obtain a database connection from the data source.
2. Create a PreparedStatement object from the connection.
3. Bind the parameters to the PreparedStatement object.
4. Execute the PreparedStatement object.
5. Iterate the returned result set.
6. Extract data from the result set.
7. Handle SQLException.
8. Clean up the statement object and connection.

Solution

The JdbcTemplate class declares a number of overloaded query() template methods to control the overall query process. You can override the statement creation task (task 2) and the parameter binding task (task 3) by implementing the PreparedStatementCreator and PreparedStatementSetter interfaces, just as you did for the update operations. Moreover, the Spring JDBC framework supports multiple ways for you to override the data extraction task (task 6).

How It Works

Extracting Data with a Row Callback Handler

RowCallbackHandler is the primary interface that allows you to process the current row of the result set. One of the query() methods iterates the result set for you and calls your RowCallbackHandler for each row. So, the processRow() method will be called once for each row of the returned result set.

```
package com.apress.springrecipes.vehicle;
...
import org.springframework.jdbc.core.JdbcTemplate;
import org.springframework.jdbc.core.RowCallbackHandler;

public class JdbcVehicleDao implements VehicleDao {
    ...
    public Vehicle findByVehicleNo(String vehicleNo) {
        String sql = "SELECT * FROM VEHICLE WHERE VEHICLE_NO = ?";
        JdbcTemplate jdbcTemplate = new JdbcTemplate(dataSource);

        final Vehicle vehicle = new Vehicle();
        jdbcTemplate.query(sql, new Object[] { vehicleNo },
                new RowCallbackHandler() {
                    public void processRow(ResultSet rs) throws SQLException {
                        vehicle.setVehicleNo(rs.getString("VEHICLE_NO"));
```

```
                    vehicle.setColor(rs.getString("COLOR"));
                    vehicle.setWheel(rs.getInt("WHEEL"));
                    vehicle.setSeat(rs.getInt("SEAT"));
                }
            });
        return vehicle;
    }
}
```

As there will be one row returned for the SQL query at maximum, you can create a vehicle object as a local variable and set its properties by extracting data from the result set. For a result set with more than one row, you should collect the objects as a list.

Extracting Data with a Row Mapper

The RowMapper interface is more general than RowCallbackHandler. Its purpose is to map a single row of the result set to a customized object, so it can be applied to a single-row result set as well as a multiple-row result set. From the viewpoint of reuse, it's better to implement the RowMapper interface as a normal class than as an inner class. In the mapRow() method of this interface, you have to construct the object that represents a row and return it as the method's return value.

```
package com.apress.springrecipes.vehicle;

import java.sql.ResultSet;
import java.sql.SQLException;

import org.springframework.jdbc.core.RowMapper;

public class VehicleRowMapper implements RowMapper {

    public Object mapRow(ResultSet rs, int rowNum) throws SQLException {
        Vehicle vehicle = new Vehicle();
        vehicle.setVehicleNo(rs.getString("VEHICLE_NO"));
        vehicle.setColor(rs.getString("COLOR"));
        vehicle.setWheel(rs.getInt("WHEEL"));
        vehicle.setSeat(rs.getInt("SEAT"));
        return vehicle;
    }
}
```

As mentioned, RowMapper can be used for either a single-row or multiple-row result set. When querying for a unique object like in findByVehicleNo(), you have to make a call to the queryForObject() method of JdbcTemplate.

```
package com.apress.springrecipes.vehicle;
...
import org.springframework.jdbc.core.JdbcTemplate;
```

```
public class JdbcVehicleDao implements VehicleDao {
    ...
    public Vehicle findByVehicleNo(String vehicleNo) {
        String sql = "SELECT * FROM VEHICLE WHERE VEHICLE_NO = ?";
        JdbcTemplate jdbcTemplate = new JdbcTemplate(dataSource);

        Vehicle vehicle = (Vehicle) jdbcTemplate.queryForObject(sql,
                new Object[] { vehicleNo }, new VehicleRowMapper());
        return vehicle;
    }
}
```

Spring 2.5 comes with a convenient `RowMapper` implementation, `BeanPropertyRowMapper`, which can automatically map a row to a new instance of the specified class. It first instantiates this class, and then maps each column value to a property by matching their names. It supports matching a property name (e.g., `vehicleNo`) to the same column name or the column name with underscores (e.g., `VEHICLE_NO`).

```
package com.apress.springrecipes.vehicle;
...
import org.springframework.jdbc.core.BeanPropertyRowMapper;
import org.springframework.jdbc.core.JdbcTemplate;

public class JdbcVehicleDao implements VehicleDao {
    ...
    public Vehicle findByVehicleNo(String vehicleNo) {
        String sql = "SELECT * FROM VEHICLE WHERE VEHICLE_NO = ?";
        JdbcTemplate jdbcTemplate = new JdbcTemplate(dataSource);

        Vehicle vehicle = (Vehicle) jdbcTemplate.queryForObject(sql,
                new Object[] { vehicleNo } ,
                BeanPropertyRowMapper.newInstance(Vehicle.class));
        return vehicle;
    }
}
```

Querying for Multiple Rows

Now let's see how to query for a result set with multiple rows. For example, suppose you need a `findAll()` method in the DAO interface to get all vehicles.

```
package com.apress.springrecipes.vehicle;
...
public interface VehicleDao {
    ...
    public List<Vehicle> findAll();
}
```

Without the help of RowMapper, you can still call the queryForList() method and pass in a SQL statement. The returned result will be a list of maps. Each map stores a row of the result set with the column names as the keys.

```
package com.apress.springrecipes.vehicle;
...
import org.springframework.jdbc.core.JdbcTemplate;

public class JdbcVehicleDao implements VehicleDao {
    ...
    public List<Vehicle> findAll() {
        String sql = "SELECT * FROM VEHICLE";
        JdbcTemplate jdbcTemplate = new JdbcTemplate(dataSource);

        List<Vehicle> vehicles = new ArrayList<Vehicle>();
        List<Map> rows = jdbcTemplate.queryForList(sql);
        for (Map row : rows) {
            Vehicle vehicle = new Vehicle();
            vehicle.setVehicleNo((String) row.get("VEHICLE_NO"));
            vehicle.setColor((String) row.get("COLOR"));
            vehicle.setWheel((Integer) row.get("WHEEL"));
            vehicle.setSeat((Integer) row.get("SEAT"));
            vehicles.add(vehicle);
        }
        return vehicles;
    }
}
```

You can test your findAll() method with the following code snippet in the Main class:

```
package com.apress.springrecipes.vehicle;
...
public class Main {

    public static void main(String[] args) {
        ...
        VehicleDao vehicleDao = (VehicleDao) context.getBean("vehicleDao");
        List<Vehicle> vehicles = vehicleDao.findAll();
        for (Vehicle vehicle : vehicles) {
            System.out.println("Vehicle No: " + vehicle.getVehicleNo());
            System.out.println("Color: " + vehicle.getColor());
            System.out.println("Wheel: " + vehicle.getWheel());
            System.out.println("Seat: " + vehicle.getSeat());
        }
    }
}
```

If you use a RowMapper object to map the rows in a result set, you will get a list of mapped objects from the query() method.

```
package com.apress.springrecipes.vehicle;
...
import org.springframework.jdbc.core.BeanPropertyRowMapper;
import org.springframework.jdbc.core.JdbcTemplate;

public class JdbcVehicleDao implements VehicleDao {
    ...
    public List<Vehicle> findAll() {
        String sql = "SELECT * FROM VEHICLE";
        JdbcTemplate jdbcTemplate = new JdbcTemplate(dataSource);

        List<Vehicle> vehicles = jdbcTemplate.query(sql,
                BeanPropertyRowMapper.newInstance(Vehicle.class));
        return vehicles;
    }
}
```

Querying for a Single Value

Finally, let's see how to query for a single-row and single-column result set. As an example, add the following operations to the DAO interface:

```
package com.apress.springrecipes.vehicle;
...
public interface VehicleDao {
    ...
    public String getColor(String vehicleNo);
    public int countAll();
}
```

To query for a single string value, you can call the overloaded queryForObject() method, which requires an argument of java.lang.Class type. This method will help you to map the result value to the type you specified. For integer values, you can call the convenient method queryForInt().

```
package com.apress.springrecipes.vehicle;
...
import org.springframework.jdbc.core.JdbcTemplate;

public class JdbcVehicleDao implements VehicleDao {
    ...
    public String getColor(String vehicleNo) {
        String sql = "SELECT COLOR FROM VEHICLE WHERE VEHICLE_NO = ?";
        JdbcTemplate jdbcTemplate = new JdbcTemplate(dataSource);
```

```
        String color = (String) jdbcTemplate.queryForObject(sql,
                new Object[] { vehicleNo }, String.class);
        return color;
    }

    public int countAll() {
        String sql = "SELECT COUNT(*) FROM VEHICLE";
        JdbcTemplate jdbcTemplate = new JdbcTemplate(dataSource);

        int count = jdbcTemplate.queryForInt(sql);
        return count;
    }
}
```

You can test these two methods with the following code snippet in the Main class:

```
package com.apress.springrecipes.vehicle;
...
public class Main {

    public static void main(String[] args) {
        ...
        VehicleDao vehicleDao = (VehicleDao) context.getBean("vehicleDao");
        int count = vehicleDao.countAll();
        System.out.println("Vehicle Count: " + count);
        String color = vehicleDao.getColor("TEM0001");
        System.out.println("Color for [TEM0001]: " + color);
    }
}
```

7-4. Simplifying JDBC Template Creation

Problem

It's not efficient to create a new instance of JdbcTemplate every time you use it, as you have to repeat the creation statement and spend the cost of creating a new object.

Solution

The JdbcTemplate class is designed to be thread-safe, so you can declare a single instance of it in the IoC container and inject this instance into all your DAO instances. Furthermore, the Spring JDBC framework offers a convenient class, JdbcDaoSupport, to simplify your DAO implementation. This class declares a jdbcTemplate property, which can be injected from the IoC container or created automatically from a data source. Your DAO can extend this class to have this property inherited.

How It Works

Injecting a JDBC Template

Until now, you have created a new instance of `JdbcTemplate` in each DAO method. Actually, you can have it injected at the class level and use this injected instance in all DAO methods. For simplicity's sake, the following code only shows the change to the `insert()` method.

```
package com.apress.springrecipes.vehicle;
...
import org.springframework.jdbc.core.JdbcTemplate;

public class JdbcVehicleDao implements VehicleDao {

    private JdbcTemplate jdbcTemplate;

    public void setJdbcTemplate(JdbcTemplate jdbcTemplate) {
        this.jdbcTemplate = jdbcTemplate;
    }

    public void insert(final Vehicle vehicle) {
        String sql = "INSERT INTO VEHICLE (VEHICLE_NO, COLOR, WHEEL, SEAT) "
                + "VALUES (?, ?, ?, ?)";

        jdbcTemplate.update(sql, new Object[] { vehicle.getVehicleNo(),
                vehicle.getColor(), vehicle.getWheel(), vehicle.getSeat() });

    }
    ...
}
```

A JDBC template requires a data source to be set. You can inject this property by either a setter method or a constructor argument. Then, you can inject this JDBC template into your DAO.

```
<beans ...>
    ...
    <bean id="jdbcTemplate"
        class="org.springframework.jdbc.core.JdbcTemplate">
        <property name="dataSource" ref="dataSource" />
    </bean>

    <bean id="vehicleDao"
        class="com.apress.springrecipes.vehicle.JdbcVehicleDao">
        <property name="jdbcTemplate" ref="jdbcTemplate" />
    </bean>
</beans>
```

Extending the JdbcDaoSupport Class

The JdbcDaoSupport class has a setDataSource() method and a setJdbcTemplate() method. Your DAO class can extend this class to have these methods inherited. Then you can either inject a JDBC template directly or inject a data source for it to create a JDBC template. The following code fragment is taken from Spring's JdbcDaoSupport class:

```
package org.springframework.jdbc.core.support;
...
public abstract class JdbcDaoSupport extends DaoSupport {

    private JdbcTemplate jdbcTemplate;

    public final void setDataSource(DataSource dataSource) {
        this.jdbcTemplate = createJdbcTemplate(dataSource);
        initTemplateConfig();
    }

    public final void setJdbcTemplate(JdbcTemplate jdbcTemplate) {
        this.jdbcTemplate = jdbcTemplate;
        initTemplateConfig();
    }

    public final JdbcTemplate getJdbcTemplate() {
        return jdbcTemplate;
    }
    ...
}
```

In your DAO methods, you can simply call the getJdbcTemplate() method to retrieve the JDBC template. You also have to delete the dataSource and jdbcTemplate properties, as well as their setter methods, from your DAO class, as they have already been inherited. Again, for simplicity's sake, only the change to the insert() method is shown.

```
package com.apress.springrecipes.vehicle;
...
import org.springframework.jdbc.core.support.JdbcDaoSupport;

public class JdbcVehicleDao extends JdbcDaoSupport implements VehicleDao {

    public void insert(final Vehicle vehicle) {
        String sql = "INSERT INTO VEHICLE (VEHICLE_NO, COLOR, WHEEL, SEAT) "
                + "VALUES (?, ?, ?, ?)";

        getJdbcTemplate().update(sql, new Object[] { vehicle.getVehicleNo(),
                vehicle.getColor(), vehicle.getWheel(), vehicle.getSeat() });
    }
    ...
}
```

By extending `JdbcDaoSupport`, your DAO class inherits the `setDataSource()` method. You can inject a data source into your DAO instance for it to create a JDBC template.

```
<beans ...>
    ...
    <bean id="vehicleDao"
        class="com.apress.springrecipes.vehicle.JdbcVehicleDao">
        <property name="dataSource" ref="dataSource" />
    </bean>
</beans>
```

7-5. Using the Simple JDBC Template with Java 1.5

Problem

The `JdbcTemplate` class works fine in most circumstances, but it can be further improved to take advantage of the Java 1.5 features.

Solution

`SimpleJdbcTemplate` is an evolution of `JdbcTemplate` that takes advantage of Java 1.5 features such as autoboxing, generics, and variable-length arguments to simplify its usage.

How It Works

Using a Simple JDBC Template to Update a Database

Many of the methods in the classic `JdbcTemplate` require statement parameters to be passed as an object array. In `SimpleJdbcTemplate`, they can be passed as variable-length arguments, which saves you the trouble of wrapping them in an array. To use `SimpleJdbcTemplate`, you can either instantiate it directly or retrieve its instance by extending the `SimpleJdbcDaoSupport` class.

```
package com.apress.springrecipes.vehicle;
...
import org.springframework.jdbc.core.simple.SimpleJdbcDaoSupport;

public class JdbcVehicleDao extends SimpleJdbcDaoSupport implements
        VehicleDao {

    public void insert(Vehicle vehicle) {
        String sql = "INSERT INTO VEHICLE (VEHICLE_NO, COLOR, WHEEL, SEAT) "
                + "VALUES (?, ?, ?, ?)";

        getSimpleJdbcTemplate().update(sql, vehicle.getVehicleNo(),
                vehicle.getColor(), vehicle.getWheel(), vehicle.getSeat());
    }
    ...
}
```

SimpleJdbcTemplate offers a convenient batch update method for you to specify a SQL statement and a batch of parameters in the form of List<Object[]> so that you don't need to implement the BatchPreparedStatementSetter interface.

```
package com.apress.springrecipes.vehicle;
...
import org.springframework.jdbc.core.simple.SimpleJdbcDaoSupport;

public class JdbcVehicleDao extends SimpleJdbcDaoSupport implements VehicleDao {
    ...
    public void insertBatch(List<Vehicle> vehicles) {
        String sql = "INSERT INTO VEHICLE (VEHICLE_NO, COLOR, WHEEL, SEAT) "
                + "VALUES (?, ?, ?, ?)";

        List<Object[]> parameters = new ArrayList<Object[]>();
        for (Vehicle vehicle : vehicles) {
            parameters.add(new Object[] { vehicle.getVehicleNo(),
                    vehicle.getColor(), vehicle.getWheel(), vehicle.getSeat() });
        }
        getSimpleJdbcTemplate().batchUpdate(sql, parameters);
    }
}
```

Using a Simple JDBC Template to Query a Database

When implementing the RowMapper interface, the return type of the mapRow() method is java.lang.Object. ParameterizedRowMapper is a subinterface that takes a type parameter as the return type of the mapRow() method.

```
package com.apress.springrecipes.vehicle;
...
import org.springframework.jdbc.core.simple.ParameterizedRowMapper;

public class VehicleRowMapper implements ParameterizedRowMapper<Vehicle> {

    public Vehicle mapRow(ResultSet rs, int rowNum) throws SQLException {
        Vehicle vehicle = new Vehicle();
        vehicle.setVehicleNo(rs.getString("VEHICLE_NO"));
        vehicle.setColor(rs.getString("COLOR"));
        vehicle.setWheel(rs.getInt("WHEEL"));
        vehicle.setSeat(rs.getInt("SEAT"));
        return vehicle;
    }
}
```

Using SimpleJdbcTemplate with ParameterizedRowMapper can save you the trouble of casting the type of the returned result. For the queryForObject() method, the return type is determined by the ParameterizedRowMapper object's type parameter, which is Vehicle in this case. Note that the statement parameters must be supplied at the end of the argument list since they are of variable length.

```
package com.apress.springrecipes.vehicle;
...
import org.springframework.jdbc.core.simple.SimpleJdbcDaoSupport;

public class JdbcVehicleDao extends SimpleJdbcDaoSupport implements
        VehicleDao {
    ...
    public Vehicle findByVehicleNo(String vehicleNo) {
        String sql = "SELECT * FROM VEHICLE WHERE VEHICLE_NO = ?";

        // No need to cast into Vehicle anymore.
        Vehicle vehicle = getSimpleJdbcTemplate().queryForObject(sql,
                new VehicleRowMapper(), vehicleNo);
        return vehicle;
    }
}
```

Spring 2.5 also comes with a convenient `ParameterizedRowMapper` implementation, `ParameterizedBeanPropertyRowMapper`, which can automatically map a row to a new instance of the specified class.

```
package com.apress.springrecipes.vehicle;
...
import org.springframework.jdbc.core.simple.ParameterizedBeanPropertyRowMapper;
import org.springframework.jdbc.core.simple.SimpleJdbcDaoSupport;

public class JdbcVehicleDao extends SimpleJdbcDaoSupport implements
        VehicleDao {
    ...
    public Vehicle findByVehicleNo(String vehicleNo) {
        String sql = "SELECT * FROM VEHICLE WHERE VEHICLE_NO = ?";

        Vehicle vehicle = getSimpleJdbcTemplate().queryForObject(sql,
                ParameterizedBeanPropertyRowMapper.newInstance(Vehicle.class),
                vehicleNo);
        return vehicle;
    }
}
```

When using the classic `JdbcTemplate`, the `findAll()` method has a warning from the Java compiler because of an unchecked conversion from `List` to `List<Vehicle>`. This is because the return type of the `query()` method is `List` rather than the type-safe `List<Vehicle>`. After switching to `SimpleJdbcTemplate` and `ParameterizedBeanPropertyRowMapper`, the warning will be eliminated immediately, as the returned `List` is parameterized with the same type as the `ParameterizedRowMapper` argument.

```
package com.apress.springrecipes.vehicle;
...
import org.springframework.jdbc.core.simple.ParameterizedBeanPropertyRowMapper;
import org.springframework.jdbc.core.simple.SimpleJdbcDaoSupport;

public class JdbcVehicleDao extends SimpleJdbcDaoSupport implements
        VehicleDao {
    ...
    public List<Vehicle> findAll() {
        String sql = "SELECT * FROM VEHICLE";

        List<Vehicle> vehicles = getSimpleJdbcTemplate().query(sql,
                ParameterizedBeanPropertyRowMapper.newInstance(Vehicle.class));
        return vehicles;
    }
}
```

When querying for a single value with `SimpleJdbcTemplate`, the return type of the `queryForObject()` method will be determined by the `class` argument (e.g., `String.class`). So, there's no need for you to perform type casting manually. Note that the statement parameters of variable length must also be supplied at the end of the argument list.

```
package com.apress.springrecipes.vehicle;
...
import org.springframework.jdbc.core.simple.SimpleJdbcDaoSupport;

public class JdbcVehicleDao extends SimpleJdbcDaoSupport implements
        VehicleDao {
    ...
    public String getColor(String vehicleNo) {
        String sql = "SELECT COLOR FROM VEHICLE WHERE VEHICLE_NO = ?";

        // No need to cast into String anymore.
        String color = getSimpleJdbcTemplate().queryForObject(sql,
                String.class, vehicleNo);
        return color;
    }
}
```

7-6. Using Named Parameters in a JDBC Template

Problem

In classic JDBC usages, SQL parameters are represented by the placeholder ? and bound by position. The trouble with positional parameters is that whenever the parameter order is changed, you have to change the parameter bindings as well. For a SQL statement with many parameters, it is very cumbersome to match the parameters by position.

Solution

Another option when binding SQL parameters in the Spring JDBC framework is to use named parameters. As the term implies, named SQL parameters are specified by name (starting with a colon) rather than by position. Named parameters are easier to maintain and also improve readability. Named parameters will be replaced by placeholders by the framework classes at runtime. Named parameters are only supported in `SimpleJdbcTemplate` and `NamedParameterJdbcTemplate`.

How It Works

When using named parameters in your SQL statement, you can provide the parameter values in a map with the parameter names as the keys.

```
package com.apress.springrecipes.vehicle;
...
import org.springframework.jdbc.core.simple.SimpleJdbcDaoSupport;

public class JdbcVehicleDao extends SimpleJdbcDaoSupport implements
        VehicleDao {

    public void insert(Vehicle vehicle) {
        String sql = "INSERT INTO VEHICLE (VEHICLE_NO, COLOR, WHEEL, SEAT) "
                + "VALUES (:vehicleNo, :color, :wheel, :seat)";

        Map<String, Object> parameters = new HashMap<String, Object>();
        parameters.put("vehicleNo", vehicle.getVehicleNo());
        parameters.put("color", vehicle.getColor());
        parameters.put("wheel", vehicle.getWheel());
        parameters.put("seat", vehicle.getSeat());

        getSimpleJdbcTemplate().update(sql, parameters);
    }
    ...
}
```

You can also provide a SQL parameter source, whose responsibility is to offer SQL parameter values for named parameters. There are two implementations of the `SqlParameterSource` interface. The basic one is `MapSqlParameterSource`, which wraps a map as its parameter source.

```
package com.apress.springrecipes.vehicle;
...
import org.springframework.jdbc.core.namedparam.MapSqlParameterSource;
import org.springframework.jdbc.core.namedparam.SqlParameterSource;
import org.springframework.jdbc.core.simple.SimpleJdbcDaoSupport;

public class JdbcVehicleDao extends SimpleJdbcDaoSupport implements
        VehicleDao {
```

```
    public void insert(Vehicle vehicle) {
        String sql = "INSERT INTO VEHICLE (VEHICLE_NO, COLOR, WHEEL, SEAT) "
                + "VALUES (:vehicleNo, :color, :wheel, :seat)";

        Map<String, Object> parameters = new HashMap<String, Object>();
        ...
        SqlParameterSource parameterSource =
            new MapSqlParameterSource(parameters);

        getSimpleJdbcTemplate().update(sql, parameterSource);
    }
    ...
}
```

Another implementation of `SqlParameterSource` is `BeanPropertySqlParameterSource`, which wraps a normal Java object as a SQL parameter source. For each of the named parameters, the property with the same name will be used as the parameter value.

```
package com.apress.springrecipes.vehicle;
...
import org.springframework.jdbc.core.namedparam.BeanPropertySqlParameterSource;
import org.springframework.jdbc.core.namedparam.SqlParameterSource;
import org.springframework.jdbc.core.simple.SimpleJdbcDaoSupport;

public class JdbcVehicleDao extends SimpleJdbcDaoSupport implements
        VehicleDao {

    public void insert(Vehicle vehicle) {
        String sql = "INSERT INTO VEHICLE (VEHICLE_NO, COLOR, WHEEL, SEAT) "
                + "VALUES (:vehicleNo, :color, :wheel, :seat)";

        SqlParameterSource parameterSource =
            new BeanPropertySqlParameterSource(vehicle);

        getSimpleJdbcTemplate().update(sql, parameterSource);
    }
    ...
}
```

Named parameters can also be used in batch update. You can provide either a `Map` array or a `SqlParameterSource` array for the parameter values.

```
package com.apress.springrecipes.vehicle;
...
import org.springframework.jdbc.core.namedparam.BeanPropertySqlParameterSource;
import org.springframework.jdbc.core.namedparam.SqlParameterSource;
import org.springframework.jdbc.core.simple.SimpleJdbcDaoSupport;
```

```
public class JdbcVehicleDao extends SimpleJdbcDaoSupport implements VehicleDao {
    ...
    public void insertBatch(List<Vehicle> vehicles) {
        String sql = "INSERT INTO VEHICLE (VEHICLE_NO, COLOR, WHEEL, SEAT) "
                + "VALUES (:vehicleNo, :color, :wheel, :seat)";

        List<SqlParameterSource> parameters = new ArrayList<SqlParameterSource>();
        for (Vehicle vehicle : vehicles) {
            parameters.add(new BeanPropertySqlParameterSource(vehicle));
        }

        getSimpleJdbcTemplate().batchUpdate(sql,
                parameters.toArray(new SqlParameterSource[0]));
    }
}
```

7-7. Modeling JDBC Operations As Fine-Grained Objects

Problem

You would like to organize your data access logic in a more object-oriented way by modeling each database operation as a fine-grained operation object.

Solution

Besides the JDBC template approach, the Spring JDBC framework supports modeling each database operation as a fine-grained operation object by extending one of the predefined JDBC operation classes (e.g., `SqlUpdate`, `MappingSqlQuery`, or `SqlFunction`). Before an operation object can be used, you have to perform the following tasks:

- Set the data source for this operation object.
- Set the SQL statement for this operation object.
- Declare the parameter types in correct order for this operation object.
- Call the `compile()` method on this operation object to compile the SQL statement.

The best place to perform these tasks is in an operation object's constructor. An operation object is thread-safe once it has been initialized with these tasks, so you can declare a single instance of it in the Spring IoC container for later use.

How It Works

Update Operation Objects

First, let's consider how to model the vehicle insert operation as an operation object. You can create the `VehicleInsertOperation` class by extending `SqlUpdate` for an update operation.

```
package com.apress.springrecipes.vehicle;

import java.sql.Types;

import javax.sql.DataSource;

import org.springframework.jdbc.core.SqlParameter;
import org.springframework.jdbc.object.SqlUpdate;

public class VehicleInsertOperation extends SqlUpdate {

    public VehicleInsertOperation(DataSource dataSource) {
        setDataSource(dataSource);
        setSql("INSERT INTO VEHICLE (VEHICLE_NO, COLOR, WHEEL, SEAT) "
                + "VALUES (?, ?, ?, ?)");
        declareParameter(new SqlParameter(Types.VARCHAR));
        declareParameter(new SqlParameter(Types.VARCHAR));
        declareParameter(new SqlParameter(Types.INTEGER));
        declareParameter(new SqlParameter(Types.INTEGER));
        compile();
    }

    public void perform(Vehicle vehicle) {
        update(new Object[] { vehicle.getVehicleNo(), vehicle.getColor(),
                vehicle.getWheel(), vehicle.getSeat() });
    }
}
```

Once an update operation object is properly initialized, you can make a call to its `update()` method and pass the parameter values in an object array. For better encapsulation, and to avoid invalid parameters, you can provide a custom `perform()` method to extract the parameters from a `Vehicle` object. Then you can declare its instance in the IoC container.

```
<bean id="vehicleInsertOperation"
    class="com.apress.springrecipes.vehicle.VehicleInsertOperation">
    <constructor-arg ref="dataSource" />
</bean>
```

The following code in the `Main` class shows how to use this operation object to insert a new vehicle:

```
package com.apress.springrecipes.vehicle;
...
public class Main {

    public static void main(String[] args) {
        ...
        VehicleInsertOperation operation =
            (VehicleInsertOperation) context.getBean("vehicleInsertOperation");
```

```
        Vehicle vehicle = new Vehicle("OBJ0001", "Red", 4, 4);
        operation.perform(vehicle);
    }
}
```

Query Operation Objects

For a query operation object, you can extend the `MappingSqlQuery` class to have the query and mapping logic centralized in a single class. For better encapsulation, you should also write a custom `perform()` method to pack the query parameters in an object array and cast the return type.

```
package com.apress.springrecipes.vehicle;

import java.sql.ResultSet;
import java.sql.SQLException;
import java.sql.Types;

import javax.sql.DataSource;

import org.springframework.jdbc.core.SqlParameter;
import org.springframework.jdbc.object.MappingSqlQuery;

public class VehicleQueryOperation extends MappingSqlQuery {

    public VehicleQueryOperation(DataSource dataSource) {
        setDataSource(dataSource);
        setSql("SELECT * FROM VEHICLE WHERE VEHICLE_NO = ?");
        declareParameter(new SqlParameter(Types.VARCHAR));
        compile();
    }

    protected Object mapRow(ResultSet rs, int rowNum) throws SQLException {
        Vehicle vehicle = new Vehicle();
        vehicle.setVehicleNo(rs.getString("VEHICLE_NO"));
        vehicle.setColor(rs.getString("COLOR"));
        vehicle.setWheel(rs.getInt("WHEEL"));
        vehicle.setSeat(rs.getInt("SEAT"));
        return vehicle;
    }

    public Vehicle perform(String vehicleNo) {
        return (Vehicle) findObject(new Object[] { vehicleNo });
    }
}
```

Then declare an instance of this operation object in the Spring IoC container.

```
<bean id="vehicleQueryOperation"
    class="com.apress.springrecipes.vehicle.VehicleQueryOperation">
    <constructor-arg ref="dataSource" />
</bean>
```

In the Main class, you can use this operation object to query for a vehicle by vehicle number.

```
package com.apress.springrecipes.vehicle;
...
public class Main {

    public static void main(String[] args) {
        ...
        VehicleQueryOperation operation =
            (VehicleQueryOperation) context.getBean("vehicleQueryOperation");
        Vehicle vehicle = operation.perform("OBJ0001");
        System.out.println("Vehicle No: " + vehicle.getVehicleNo());
        System.out.println("Color: " + vehicle.getColor());
        System.out.println("Wheel: " + vehicle.getWheel());
        System.out.println("Seat: " + vehicle.getSeat());
    }
}
```

Function Operation Objects

The SqlFunction operation object type is for querying a single value. For example, the vehicle count operation can be modeled with SqlFunction. Its run() method returns the result as an integer, which is appropriate in this case. If you want to return a result of some other type, you have to call the runGeneric() method.

```
package com.apress.springrecipes.vehicle;

import javax.sql.DataSource;

import org.springframework.jdbc.object.SqlFunction;

public class VehicleCountOperation extends SqlFunction {

    public VehicleCountOperation(DataSource dataSource) {
        setDataSource(dataSource);
        setSql("SELECT COUNT(*) FROM VEHICLE");
        compile();
    }

    public int perform() {
        return run();
    }
}
```

Then declare an instance of this operation object in the Spring IoC container.

```
<bean id="vehicleCountOperation"
    class="com.apress.springrecipes.vehicle.VehicleCountOperation">
    <constructor-arg ref="dataSource" />
</bean>
```

The following code in the `Main` class tests the operation object that queries for the total vehicle count:

```
package com.apress.springrecipes.vehicle;
...
public class Main {

    public static void main(String[] args) {
        ...
        VehicleCountOperation operation =
            (VehicleCountOperation) context.getBean("vehicleCountOperation");
        int count = operation.perform();
        System.out.println("Vehicle Count: " + count);
    }
}
```

7-8. Handling Exceptions in the Spring JDBC Framework

Problem

Many of the JDBC APIs declare throwing `java.sql.SQLException`, a checked exception that must be caught. It's very troublesome to handle this kind of exception every time you perform a database operation. You often have to define your own policy to handle this kind of exception. Failing to do so may lead to inconsistent exception handling.

Solution

The Spring framework offers a consistent data access exception-handling mechanism for its data access module, including the JDBC framework. In general, all exceptions thrown by the Spring JDBC framework are subclasses of `DataAccessException`, a type of `RuntimeException` that you are not forced to catch. It's the root exception class for all exceptions in Spring's data access module.

Figure 7-1 shows only part of the `DataAccessException` hierarchy in Spring's data access module. In total, there are more than 30 exception classes defined for different categories of data access exceptions.

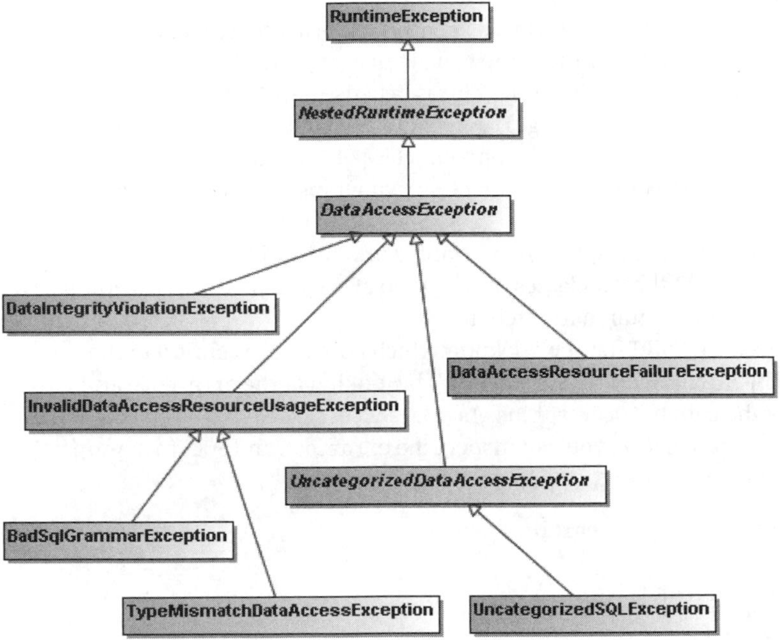

Figure 7-1. *Common exception classes in the DataAccessException hierarchy*

How It Works

Understanding Exception Handling in the Spring JDBC Framework

Until now, you haven't handled JDBC exceptions explicitly when using a JDBC template or JDBC operation objects. To help you understand the Spring JDBC framework's exception-handling mechanism, let's consider the following code fragment in the `Main` class, which inserts a vehicle. What happens if you insert a vehicle with a duplicate vehicle number?

```
package com.apress.springrecipes.vehicle;
...
public class Main {

    public static void main(String[] args) {
        ...
        VehicleDao vehicleDao = (VehicleDao) context.getBean("vehicleDao");
        Vehicle vehicle = new Vehicle("EX0001", "Green", 4, 4);
        vehicleDao.insert(vehicle);
    }
}
```

If you run the method twice, or the vehicle has already been inserted into the database, it will throw a DataIntegrityViolationException, a subclass of DataAccessException. In your DAO methods, you neither need to surround the code with a try/catch block nor declare throwing an exception in the method signature. This is because DataAccessException (and therefore its subclasses, including DataIntegrityViolationException) is an unchecked exception that you are not forced to catch. The direct parent class of DataAccessException is NestedRuntimeException, a core Spring exception class that wraps another exception in a RuntimeException.

When you use the classes of the Spring JDBC framework, they will catch SQLException for you and wrap it with one of the subclasses of DataAccessException. As this exception is a RuntimeException, you are not required to catch it.

But how does the Spring JDBC framework know which concrete exception in the DataAccessException hierarchy should be thrown? It's by looking at the errorCode and SQLState properties of the caught SQLException. As a DataAccessException wraps the underlying SQLException as the root cause, you can inspect the errorCode and SQLState properties with the following catch block:

```
package com.apress.springrecipes.vehicle;
...
import java.sql.SQLException;

import org.springframework.dao.DataAccessException;

public class Main {

    public static void main(String[] args) {
        ...
        VehicleDao vehicleDao = (VehicleDao) context.getBean("vehicleDao");
        Vehicle vehicle = new Vehicle("EX0001", "Green", 4, 4);
        try {
            vehicleDao.insert(vehicle);
        } catch (DataAccessException e) {
            SQLException sqle = (SQLException) e.getCause();
            System.out.println("Error code: " + sqle.getErrorCode());
            System.out.println("SQL state: " + sqle.getSQLState());
        }
    }
}
```

When you insert the duplicate vehicle again, notice that Apache Derby returns the following error code and SQL state:

```
Error code : -1
SQL state : 23505
```

If you refer to the Apache Derby reference manual, you will find the error code description shown in Table 7-2.

Table 7-2. *Apache Derby's Error Code Description*

SQL State	Message Text
23505	The statement was aborted because it would have caused a duplicate key value in a unique or primary key constraint or unique index identified by '*<value>*' defined on '*<value>*'.

Then how does the Spring JDBC framework know that state 23505 should be mapped to DataIntegrityViolationException? The error code and SQL state are database specific, which means different database products may return different codes for the same kind of error. Moreover, some database products will specify the error in the errorCode property, while others (like Derby) will do so in the SQLState property.

As an open Java application framework, Spring understands the error codes of most popular database products. Because of the large number of error codes, however, it can only maintain mappings for the most frequently encountered errors. The mapping is defined in the sql-error-codes.xml file, located in the org.springframework.jdbc.support package. The following snippet for Apache Derby is taken from this file:

```
<?xml version="1.0" encoding="UTF-8"?>
<!DOCTYPE beans PUBLIC "-//SPRING//DTD BEAN 2.0//EN"
    "http://www.springframework.org/dtd/spring-beans-2.0.dtd">

<beans>
    ...
    <bean id="Derby"
        class="org.springframework.jdbc.support.SQLErrorCodes">
        <property name="databaseProductName">
            <value>Apache Derby</value>
        </property>
        <property name="useSqlStateForTranslation">
            <value>true</value>
        </property>
        <property name="badSqlGrammarCodes">
            <value>
                42802,42821,42X01,42X02,42X03,42X04,42X05,42X06,42X07,42X08
            </value>
        </property>
        <property name="dataAccessResourceFailureCodes">
            <value>04501,08004,42Y07</value>
        </property>
        <property name="dataIntegrityViolationCodes">
            <value>22001,22005,23502,23503,23505,23513,X0Y32</value>
        </property>
        <property name="cannotAcquireLockCodes">
            <value>40XL1</value>
        </property>
        <property name="deadlockLoserCodes">
            <value>40001</value>
```

```
        </property>
    </bean>
</beans>
```

Note that the databaseProductName property is used to match the database product name returned by Connection.getMetaData().getDatabaseProductName(). This enables Spring to know which type of database is currently connecting. The useSqlStateForTranslation property means that the SQLState property, rather than the errorCode property, should be used to match the error code. Finally, the SQLErrorCodes class defines several categories for you to map database error codes. The code 23505 lies in the dataIntegrityViolationCodes category.

Customizing Data Access Exception Handling

The Spring JDBC framework only maps well-known error codes. Sometimes you may wish to customize the mapping yourself. For example, you might decide to add more codes to an existing category or define a custom exception for particular error codes.

In Table 7-2, the error code 23505 indicates a duplicate key error in Apache Derby. It is mapped by default to DataIntegrityViolationException. Suppose you would like to create a custom exception type, DuplicateKeyException, for this kind of error. It should extend DataIntegrityViolationException, as it is also a kind of data integrity violation error. Remember that for an exception to be thrown by the Spring JDBC framework, it must be compatible with the root exception class DataAccessException.

```
package com.apress.springrecipes.vehicle;

import org.springframework.dao.DataIntegrityViolationException;

public class DuplicateKeyException extends DataIntegrityViolationException {

    public DuplicateKeyException(String msg) {
        super(msg);
    }

    public DuplicateKeyException(String msg, Throwable cause) {
        super(msg, cause);
    }
}
```

By default, Spring will look up an exception from the sql-error-codes.xml file located in the org.springframework.jdbc.support package. However, you can override some of the mappings by providing a file with the same name in the root of the classpath. If Spring is able to find your custom file, it will look up an exception from your mapping first. However, if it does not find a suitable exception there, Spring will look up the default mapping.

For example, suppose you would like to map your custom DuplicateKeyException type to error code 23505. You have to add the binding via a CustomSQLErrorCodesTranslation bean, and then add this bean to the customTranslations category.

```
<?xml version="1.0" encoding="UTF-8"?>
<!DOCTYPE beans PUBLIC "-//SPRING//DTD BEAN 2.0//EN"
    "http://www.springframework.org/dtd/spring-beans-2.0.dtd">

<beans>
    <bean id="Derby"
        class="org.springframework.jdbc.support.SQLErrorCodes">
        <property name="databaseProductName">
            <value>Apache Derby</value>
        </property>
        <property name="useSqlStateForTranslation">
            <value>true</value>
        </property>
        <property name="customTranslations">
            <list>
                <ref local="duplicateKeyTranslation" />
            </list>
        </property>
    </bean>

    <bean id="duplicateKeyTranslation"
        class="org.springframework.jdbc.support.CustomSQLErrorCodesTranslation">
        <property name="errorCodes">
            <value>23505</value>
        </property>
        <property name="exceptionClass">
            <value>
                com.apress.springrecipes.vehicle.DuplicateKeyException
            </value>
        </property>
    </bean>
</beans>
```

Now if you remove the try/catch block surrounding the vehicle insert operation and insert a duplicate vehicle, the Spring JDBC framework will throw a DuplicateKeyException instead.

However, if you are not satisfied with the basic code-to-exception mapping strategy used by the SQLErrorCodes class, you may further implement the SQLExceptionTranslator interface and inject its instance into a JDBC template via the setExceptionTranslator() method.

7-9. Summary

In this chapter, you have learned how to use the Spring JDBC framework to simplify your database access tasks. When using JDBC directly without Spring's support, most of the JDBC code is similar and needs to be repeated for each database operation. Such redundant code will make your DAO methods much longer and less readable.

As the heart of the Spring JDBC framework, the JDBC template provides template methods for different types of JDBC operations. Each template method is responsible for controlling the overall process, and allows you to override particular tasks of the process by implementing a predefined callback interface.

The `JdbcTemplate` class is the classic Spring JDBC template. In order to take advantage of the Java 1.5 features, Spring provides `SimpleJdbcTemplate`, which makes use of features such as autoboxing, generics, and variable-length arguments to simplify its usage. Also, this class supports the usage of named parameters in SQL statements.

Besides the JDBC template approach, the Spring JDBC framework supports a more object-oriented approach by modeling each database operation as a fine-grained operation object. You can choose either approach according to your preferences and needs.

Spring offers a consistent data access exception-handling mechanism for its data access module, including the JDBC framework. If a `SQLException` is thrown, Spring will wrap it with an appropriate exception in the `DataAccessException` hierarchy. `DataAccessException` is an unchecked exception, so you are not forced to catch and handle every instance of it.

In the next chapter, you will learn about using the powerful transaction management features to manage transactions for your Spring applications.

CHAPTER 8

Transaction Management in Spring

In this chapter, you will learn about the basic concept of transactions and Spring's capabilities in the area of transaction management. Transaction management is an essential technique in enterprise applications to ensure data integrity and consistency. Spring, as an enterprise application framework, defines an abstract layer on top of different transaction management APIs. As an application developer, you can utilize Spring's transaction management facilities without having to know much about the underlying transaction management APIs.

Like the *bean-managed transaction (BMT)* and *container-managed transaction (CMT)* approaches in EJB, Spring supports both programmatic and declarative transaction management. The aim of Spring's transaction support is to provide an alternative to EJB transactions by adding transaction capabilities to POJOs.

Programmatic transaction management is achieved by embedding transaction management code in your business methods to control the commit and rollback of transactions. You usually commit a transaction if a method completes normally, and roll back a transaction if a method throws certain types of exceptions. With programmatic transaction management, you can further define your own rules to commit and roll back transactions.

However, when managing transactions programmatically, you have to include additional transaction management code in each transactional operation. As a result, the boilerplate transaction code is repeated in each of these operations. Moreover, it's hard for you to enable and disable transaction management for different applications. If you have a solid understanding of AOP, you should already have noticed that transaction management is a kind of crosscutting concern.

Declarative transaction management is preferable to programmatic transaction management in most cases. It's achieved by separating transaction management code from your business methods via declarations. Transaction management, as a kind of crosscutting concern, can be modularized with the AOP approach. Spring supports declarative transaction management through the Spring AOP framework. This can help you to enable transactions for your applications more easily and define a consistent transaction policy. However, declarative transaction management is less flexible, as you can't precisely control transactions through your code.

You can specify a set of transaction attributes to define your transactions at a fine level of granularity. The transaction attributes supported by Spring include the propagation behavior, isolation level, rollback rules, transaction timeout, and read-only. These attributes allow you to further customize the behavior of your transactions.

Upon finishing this chapter, you will be able to apply different transaction management strategies in your application. Moreover, you will be familiar with different transaction attributes to finely define your transactions.

8-1. Problems with Transaction Management

Transaction management is an essential technique in enterprise application development to ensure data integrity and consistency. Without transaction management, your data and resources may be corrupted and left in an inconsistent state. Transaction management is significantly important in a concurrent and distributed environment for recovering from unexpected errors.

In simple words, a transaction is a series of actions that are treated as a single unit of work. These actions should either complete entirely or take no effect at all. If all of the actions go well, the transaction should be committed permanently. In contrast, if any of them goes wrong, the transaction should be rolled back to the initial state as if nothing had happened.

The concept of transactions can be described with four key properties: *atomicity, consistency, isolation, and durability (ACID)*. These are described following:

Atomicity: A transaction is an atomic operation that consists of a series of actions. The atomicity of a transaction ensures that the actions either complete entirely or take no effect at all.

Consistency: Once all actions of a transaction have completed, the transaction is committed. Then your data and resources will be in a consistent state that conforms to business rules.

Isolation: As there may be many transactions processing with the same data set at the same time, each transaction should be isolated from others to prevent data corruption.

Durability: Once a transaction has completed, its result should be durable to survive any system failure. Usually, the result of a transaction is written to persistent storage.

To understand the importance of transaction management, let's begin with an example about purchasing books from an online book shop. First, you have to create a new schema for this application in your database. If you are choosing Apache Derby as your database engine, you can connect to it with the JDBC properties shown in Table 8-1.

Table 8-1. *JDBC Properties for Connecting to the Application Database*

Property	Value
Driver class	`org.apache.derby.jdbc.ClientDriver`
URL	`jdbc:derby://localhost:1527/bookshop;create=true`
Username	`app`
Password	`app`

For your book shop application, you have to create the following tables to store the application data:

```
CREATE TABLE BOOK (
    ISBN          VARCHAR(50)    NOT NULL,
    BOOK_NAME     VARCHAR(100)   NOT NULL,
    PRICE         INT,
    PRIMARY KEY (ISBN)
);

CREATE TABLE BOOK_STOCK (
    ISBN     VARCHAR(50)    NOT NULL,
    STOCK    INT            NOT NULL,
    PRIMARY KEY (ISBN),
    CHECK (STOCK >= 0)
);

CREATE TABLE ACCOUNT (
    USERNAME    VARCHAR(50)    NOT NULL,
    BALANCE     INT            NOT NULL,
    PRIMARY KEY (USERNAME),
    CHECK (BALANCE >= 0)
);
```

The BOOK table stores basic book information such as the name and price, with the book ISBN as the primary key. The BOOK_STOCK table keeps track of each book's stock. The stock value is restricted by a CHECK constraint to be a positive number. Although the CHECK constraint type is defined in SQL-99, not all database engines support it. If your database engine doesn't support CHECK constraints, please consult its documentation for similar constraint support. Finally, the ACCOUNT table stores customer accounts and their balances. Again, the balance is restricted to be positive.

The operations of your book shop are defined in the following BookShop interface. For now, there is only one operation: purchase().

```
package com.apress.springrecipes.bookshop;

public interface BookShop {

    public void purchase(String isbn, String username);
}
```

As you are going to implement this interface with JDBC, you create the following JdbcBookShop class. To better understand the nature of transactions, let's implement this class without the help of Spring's JDBC support.

```
package com.apress.springrecipes.bookshop;

import java.sql.Connection;
import java.sql.PreparedStatement;
import java.sql.ResultSet;
import java.sql.SQLException;
```

```
import javax.sql.DataSource;

public class JdbcBookShop implements BookShop {

    private DataSource dataSource;

    public void setDataSource(DataSource dataSource) {
        this.dataSource = dataSource;
    }

    public void purchase(String isbn, String username) {
        Connection conn = null;
        try {
            conn = dataSource.getConnection();

            PreparedStatement stmt1 = conn.prepareStatement(
                    "SELECT PRICE FROM BOOK WHERE ISBN = ?");
            stmt1.setString(1, isbn);
            ResultSet rs = stmt1.executeQuery();
            rs.next();
            int price = rs.getInt("PRICE");
            stmt1.close();

            PreparedStatement stmt2 = conn.prepareStatement(
                    "UPDATE BOOK_STOCK SET STOCK = STOCK - 1 " +
                    "WHERE ISBN = ?");
            stmt2.setString(1, isbn);
            stmt2.executeUpdate();
            stmt2.close();

            PreparedStatement stmt3 = conn.prepareStatement(
                    "UPDATE ACCOUNT SET BALANCE = BALANCE - ? " +
                    "WHERE USERNAME = ?");
            stmt3.setInt(1, price);
            stmt3.setString(2, username);
            stmt3.executeUpdate();
            stmt3.close();
        } catch (SQLException e) {
            throw new RuntimeException(e);
        } finally {
            if (conn != null) {
                try {
                    conn.close();
                } catch (SQLException e) {}
            }
        }
    }
}
```

For the purchase() operation, you have to execute three SQL statements in total. The first is to query the book price. The second and third update the book stock and account balance accordingly.

Then you can declare a book shop instance in the Spring IoC container to provide purchasing services. For simplicity's sake, you can use DriverManagerDataSource, which opens a new connection to the database for every request.

Note To access a database running on the Derby server, you have to include derbyclient.jar (located in the lib directory of the Derby installation) in your classpath.

```
<beans xmlns="http://www.springframework.org/schema/beans"
    xmlns:xsi="http://www.w3.org/2001/XMLSchema-instance"
    xsi:schemaLocation="http://www.springframework.org/schema/beans
        http://www.springframework.org/schema/beans/spring-beans-2.5.xsd">

    <bean id="dataSource"
        class="org.springframework.jdbc.datasource.DriverManagerDataSource">
        <property name="driverClassName"
            value="org.apache.derby.jdbc.ClientDriver" />
        <property name="url"
            value="jdbc:derby://localhost:1527/bookshop;create=true" />
        <property name="username" value="app" />
        <property name="password" value="app" />
    </bean>

    <bean id="bookShop" class="com.apress.springrecipes.bookshop.JdbcBookShop">
        <property name="dataSource" ref="dataSource" />
    </bean>
</beans>
```

To demonstrate the problems that can arise without transaction management, suppose you have the data shown in Tables 8-2, 8-3, and 8-4 entered in your bookshop database.

Table 8-2. *Sample Data in the BOOK Table for Testing Transactions*

ISBN	BOOK_NAME	PRICE
0001	The First Book	30

Table 8-3. *Sample Data in the BOOK_STOCK Table for Testing Transactions*

ISBN	STOCK
0001	10

Table 8-4. *Sample Data in the ACCOUNT Table for Testing Transactions*

USERNAME	BALANCE
user1	20

Then write the following Main class for purchasing the book with ISBN 0001 by the user user1. Since that user's account has only $20, it is not sufficient to purchase the book.

```
package com.apress.springrecipes.bookshop;

import org.springframework.context.ApplicationContext;
import org.springframework.context.support.ClassPathXmlApplicationContext;

public class Main {

    public static void main(String[] args) {
        ApplicationContext context =
            new ClassPathXmlApplicationContext("beans.xml");

        BookShop bookShop = (BookShop) context.getBean("bookShop");
        bookShop.purchase("0001", "user1");
    }
}
```

When you run this application, you will encounter a SQLException because the CHECK constraint of the ACCOUNT table has been violated. This is an expected result, as you were trying to debit more than the account balance. However, if you check the stock for this book in the BOOK_STOCK table, you will find that it was accidentally deducted by this unsuccessful operation! The reason is that you executed the second SQL statement to deduct the stock before you got an exception in the third statement.

As you can see, the lack of transaction management causes your data to be left in an inconsistent state. To avoid this inconsistency, your three SQL statements for the purchase() operation should be executed within a single transaction. Once any of the actions in a transaction fail, the entire transaction should be rolled back to undo all changes made by the executed actions.

Managing Transactions with JDBC Commit and Rollback

When using JDBC to update a database, by default each SQL statement will be committed immediately after its execution. This behavior is known as *auto-commit*. However, it does not allow you to manage transactions for your operations.

JDBC supports the primitive transaction management strategy of explicitly calling the commit() and rollback() methods on a connection. But before you can do that, you must turn off auto-commit, which is turned on by default.

```
package com.apress.springrecipes.bookshop;
...
public class JdbcBookShop implements BookShop {
    ...
```

```
    public void purchase(String isbn, String username) {
        Connection conn = null;
        try {
            conn = dataSource.getConnection();
            conn.setAutoCommit(false);
            ...
            conn.commit();
        } catch (SQLException e) {
            if (conn != null) {
                try {
                    conn.rollback();
                } catch (SQLException e1) {}
            }
            throw new RuntimeException(e);
        } finally {
            if (conn != null) {
                try {
                    conn.close();
                } catch (SQLException e) {}
            }
        }
    }
}
```

The auto-commit behavior of a database connection can be altered by calling the setAutoCommit() method. By default, auto-commit is turned on to commit each SQL statement immediately after its execution. To enable transaction management, you must turn off this default behavior and commit the connection only when all the SQL statements have been executed successfully. If any of the statements go wrong, you must roll back all changes made by this connection.

Now, if you run your application again, the book stock will not be deducted when the user's balance is insufficient to purchase the book.

Although you can manage transactions by explicitly committing and rolling back JDBC connections, the code required for this purpose is boilerplate code that you have to repeat for different methods. Moreover, this code is JDBC specific, so once you have chosen another data access technology, it needs to be changed also. Spring's transaction support offers a set of technology-independent facilities, including transaction managers, a transaction template, and transaction declaration support to simplify your transaction management tasks.

8-2. Choosing a Transaction Manager Implementation

Problem

Typically, if your application involves only a single data source, you can simply manage transactions by calling the commit() and rollback() methods on a database connection. However, if your transactions extend across multiple data sources or you prefer to make use of the transaction management capabilities provided by your Java EE application server, you may choose the Java Transaction API (JTA). Besides, you may have to call different proprietary transaction APIs for different object/relational mapping frameworks such as Hibernate and JPA.

As a result, you have to deal with different transaction APIs for different technologies. It would be hard for you to switch from one set of APIs to another.

Solution

Spring abstracts a general set of transaction facilities from different transaction management APIs. As an application developer, you can simply utilize the transaction facilities without having to know much about the underlying transaction APIs. With these facilities, your transaction management code will be independent of the specific transaction technology.

Spring's core transaction management abstraction is `PlatformTransactionManager`. It encapsulates a set of technology-independent methods for transaction management. Remember that a transaction manager is basically needed no matter which transaction management strategy (either programmatic or declarative) you choose in Spring.

How It Works

`PlatformTransactionManager` is a general interface for all Spring's transaction managers. Spring has several built-in implementations of this interface for use with different transaction management APIs:

- If you have to deal with only a single data source in your application and access it with JDBC, `DataSourceTransactionManager` should meet your needs.
- If you are using JTA for transaction management on a Java EE application server, you should use `JtaTransactionManager` to look up a transaction from the application server.
- If you are using an object/relational mapping framework to access a database, you should choose a corresponding transaction manager for this framework, such as `HibernateTransactionManager` and `JpaTransactionManager`.

Figure 8-1 shows the common implementations of the `PlatformTransactionManager` interface in Spring.

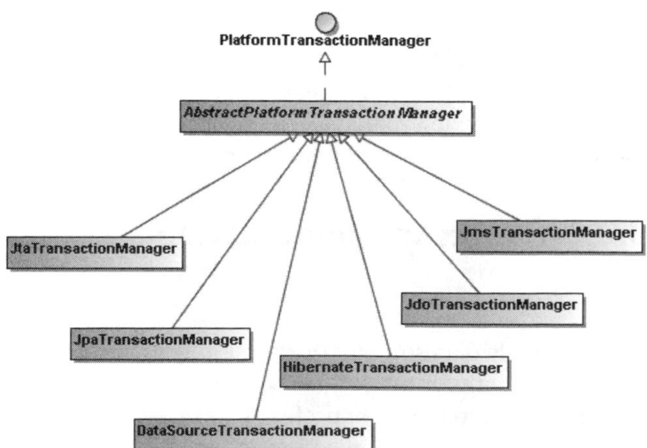

Figure 8-1. *Common implementations of the PlatformTransactionManager interface*

A transaction manager is declared in the Spring IoC container as a normal bean. For example, the following bean configuration declares a DataSourceTransactionManager instance. It requires the dataSource property to be set so that it can manage transactions for connections made by this data source.

```
<bean id="transactionManager"
    class="org.springframework.jdbc.datasource.DataSourceTransactionManager">
    <property name="dataSource" ref="dataSource" />
</bean>
```

8-3. Managing Transactions Programmatically with the Transaction Manager API

Problem

You have a need to precisely control when to commit and roll back transactions in your business methods, but you don't want to deal with the underlying transaction API directly.

Solution

Spring's transaction manager provides a technology-independent API that allows you to start a new transaction by calling the getTransaction() method, and manage it by calling the commit() and rollback() methods. As PlatformTransactionManager is an abstract unit for transaction management, the methods you called for transaction management are guaranteed to be technology independent.

How It Works

To demonstrate how to use the transaction manager API, let's create a new class, TransactionalJdbcBookShop, that will make use of the Spring JDBC template. As it has to deal with a transaction manager, you add a property of type PlatformTransactionManager and allow it to be injected via a setter method.

```
package com.apress.springrecipes.bookshop;

import org.springframework.dao.DataAccessException;
import org.springframework.jdbc.core.support.JdbcDaoSupport;
import org.springframework.transaction.PlatformTransactionManager;
import org.springframework.transaction.TransactionDefinition;
import org.springframework.transaction.TransactionStatus;
import org.springframework.transaction.support.DefaultTransactionDefinition;

public class TransactionalJdbcBookShop extends JdbcDaoSupport implements
        BookShop {

    private PlatformTransactionManager transactionManager;
```

```
    public void setTransactionManager(
            PlatformTransactionManager transactionManager) {
        this.transactionManager = transactionManager;
    }

    public void purchase(String isbn, String username) {
        TransactionDefinition def = new DefaultTransactionDefinition();
        TransactionStatus status = transactionManager.getTransaction(def);

        try {
            int price = getJdbcTemplate().queryForInt(
                    "SELECT PRICE FROM BOOK WHERE ISBN = ?",
                    new Object[] { isbn });

            getJdbcTemplate().update(
                    "UPDATE BOOK_STOCK SET STOCK = STOCK - 1 " +
                    "WHERE ISBN = ?", new Object[] { isbn });

            getJdbcTemplate().update(
                    "UPDATE ACCOUNT SET BALANCE = BALANCE - ? " +
                    "WHERE USERNAME = ?",
                    new Object[] { price, username });

            transactionManager.commit(status);
        } catch (DataAccessException e) {
            transactionManager.rollback(status);
            throw e;
        }
    }
}
```

Before you start a new transaction, you have to specify the transaction attributes in a transaction definition object of type TransactionDefinition. For this example, you can simply create an instance of DefaultTransactionDefinition to use the default transaction attributes.

Once you have a transaction definition, you can ask the transaction manager to start a new transaction with that definition by calling the getTransaction() method. Then it will return a TransactionStatus object to keep track of the transaction status. If all the statements execute successfully, you ask the transaction manager to commit this transaction by passing in the transaction status. As all exceptions thrown by the Spring JDBC template are subclasses of DataAccessException, you ask the transaction manager to roll back the transaction when this kind of exception is caught.

In this class, you have declared the transaction manager property of the general type PlatformTransactionManager. Now you have to inject an appropriate transaction manager implementation. As you are dealing with only a single data source and accessing it with JDBC, you should choose DataSourceTransactionManager.

```
<beans ...>
    ...
    <bean id="transactionManager"
        class="org.springframework.jdbc.datasource.DataSourceTransactionManager">
        <property name="dataSource" ref="dataSource" />
    </bean>

    <bean id="bookShop"
        class="com.apress.springrecipes.bookshop.TransactionalJdbcBookShop">
        <property name="dataSource" ref="dataSource" />
        <property name="transactionManager" ref="transactionManager" />
    </bean>
</beans>
```

8-4. Managing Transactions Programmatically with a Transaction Template

Problem

Suppose you have a code block, but not the entire body, of a business method that has the following transaction requirements:

- Start a new transaction at the beginning of the block.
- Commit the transaction after the block completes successfully.
- Roll back the transaction if an exception is thrown in the block.

If you call Spring's transaction manager API directly, the transaction management code can be generalized in a technology-independent manner. However, you may not want to repeat the boilerplate code for each similar code block.

Solution

As with the JDBC template, Spring also provides a transaction template to help you control the overall transaction management process. You just have to encapsulate your code block in a callback class that implements the `TransactionCallback` interface and pass it to the transaction template for execution. In this way, you don't need to repeat the boilerplate transaction management code for this block.

How It Works

A transaction template is created on a transaction manager just as a JDBC template is created on a data source. A transaction template executes a transaction callback object that encapsulates a transactional code block. You can implement the callback interface either as a separate class or as an inner class. If it's implemented as an inner class, you have to make the method arguments `final` for it to access.

```
package com.apress.springrecipes.bookshop;
...
import org.springframework.transaction.PlatformTransactionManager;
import org.springframework.transaction.TransactionStatus;
import org.springframework.transaction.support.TransactionCallbackWithoutResult;
import org.springframework.transaction.support.TransactionTemplate;

public class TransactionalJdbcBookShop extends JdbcDaoSupport implements
        BookShop {

    private PlatformTransactionManager transactionManager;

    public void setTransactionManager(
            PlatformTransactionManager transactionManager) {
        this.transactionManager = transactionManager;
    }

    public void purchase(final String isbn, final String username) {
        TransactionTemplate transactionTemplate =
            new TransactionTemplate(transactionManager);

        transactionTemplate.execute(new TransactionCallbackWithoutResult() {

            protected void doInTransactionWithoutResult(
                    TransactionStatus status) {

                int price = getJdbcTemplate().queryForInt(
                        "SELECT PRICE FROM BOOK WHERE ISBN = ?",
                        new Object[] { isbn });

                getJdbcTemplate().update(
                        "UPDATE BOOK_STOCK SET STOCK = STOCK - 1 " +
                        "WHERE ISBN = ?", new Object[] { isbn });

                getJdbcTemplate().update(
                        "UPDATE ACCOUNT SET BALANCE = BALANCE - ? " +
                        "WHERE USERNAME = ?",
                        new Object[] { price, username });
            }
        });
    }
}
```

A transaction template can accept a transaction callback object that implements either the `TransactionCallback` or `TransactionCallbackWithoutResult` interface. For the code block in the `purchase()` method for deducting the book stock and account balance, there's no result to be returned, so `TransactionCallbackWithoutResult` is fine. For any code blocks with return values, you should implement the TransactionCallback interface instead. The return value of the callback object will finally be returned by the template's execute() method.

During the execution of the callback object, if it throws an unchecked exception (e.g., RuntimeException and DataAccessException fall into this category), or if you explicitly called setRollbackOnly() on the TransactionStatus argument, the transaction will be rolled back. Otherwise, it will be committed after the callback object completes.

In the bean configuration file, the book shop bean still requires a transaction manager to create a transaction template.

```
<beans ...>
    ...
    <bean id="transactionManager"
        class="org.springframework.jdbc.datasource.DataSourceTransactionManager">
        <property name="dataSource" ref="dataSource" />
    </bean>

    <bean id="bookShop"
        class="com.apress.springrecipes.bookshop.TransactionalJdbcBookShop">
        <property name="dataSource" ref="dataSource" />
        <property name="transactionManager" ref="transactionManager" />
    </bean>
</beans>
```

You can also have the IoC container inject a transaction template instead of creating it directly. As a transaction template suffices for transaction management, there's no need for your class to refer to the transaction manager any more.

```
package com.apress.springrecipes.bookshop;
...
import org.springframework.transaction.support.TransactionTemplate;

public class TransactionalJdbcBookShop extends JdbcDaoSupport implements
        BookShop {

    private TransactionTemplate transactionTemplate;

    public void setTransactionTemplate(
            TransactionTemplate transactionTemplate) {
        this.transactionTemplate = transactionTemplate;
    }

    public void purchase(final String isbn, final String username) {
        transactionTemplate.execute(new TransactionCallbackWithoutResult() {
            protected void doInTransactionWithoutResult(TransactionStatus status) {
                ...
            }
        });
    }
}
```

Then you define a transaction template in the bean configuration file and inject it, instead of the transaction manager, into your book shop bean. Notice that the transaction template instance can be used for more than one transactional bean, as it is a thread-safe object. Finally, don't forget to set the transaction manager property for your transaction template.

```
<beans ...>
    ...
    <bean id="transactionManager"
        class="org.springframework.jdbc.datasource.DataSourceTransactionManager">
        <property name="dataSource" ref="dataSource" />
    </bean>

    <bean id="transactionTemplate"
        class="org.springframework.transaction.support.TransactionTemplate">
        <property name="transactionManager" ref="transactionManager" />
    </bean>

    <bean id="bookShop"
        class="com.apress.springrecipes.bookshop.TransactionalJdbcBookShop">
        <property name="dataSource" ref="dataSource" />
        <property name="transactionTemplate" ref="transactionTemplate" />
    </bean>
</beans>
```

8-5. Managing Transactions Declaratively with Classic Spring AOP

Problem

As transaction management is a kind of crosscutting concern, AOP is an ideal way of implementing it. However, if you would like to manage transactions declaratively in Spring 1.x, you have to use the classic Spring AOP approach.

Solution

Spring provides a classic around advice called `TransactionInterceptor` for transaction management. This advice controls the transaction management process like a transaction template, but it applies to the entire method body, not an arbitrary code block. By default, before the method begins, this advice starts a new transaction. If this method throws an unchecked exception, the transaction will be rolled back. Otherwise, it will be committed after the method completes.

In classic Spring AOP, you have to create a proxy for a bean using `ProxyFactoryBean` to apply the `TransactionInterceptor` advice. As transaction management is very common in enterprise applications, Spring provides a convenient class, `TransactionProxyFactoryBean`, which specializes in creating transaction proxies.

How It Works

First of all, let's consider implementing your book shop with Spring's JDBC support, but without any of the transaction management code.

```
package com.apress.springrecipes.bookshop;

import org.springframework.jdbc.core.support.JdbcDaoSupport;

public class JdbcBookShop extends JdbcDaoSupport implements BookShop {

    public void purchase(String isbn, String username) {
        int price = getJdbcTemplate().queryForInt(
                "SELECT PRICE FROM BOOK WHERE ISBN = ?", new Object[] { isbn });

        getJdbcTemplate().update(
                "UPDATE BOOK_STOCK SET STOCK = STOCK - 1 " +
                "WHERE ISBN = ?",
                new Object[] { isbn });

        getJdbcTemplate().update(
                "UPDATE ACCOUNT SET BALANCE = BALANCE - ? " +
                "WHERE USERNAME = ?",
                new Object[] { price, username });
    }
}
```

In your bean configuration file, you can declare a TransactionInterceptor advice that refers to the transaction manager. Then you can create a proxy with ProxyFactoryBean that applies this advice to the target bookShop bean.

```
<beans ...>
    ...
    <bean id="transactionManager"
        class="org.springframework.jdbc.datasource.DataSourceTransactionManager">
        <property name="dataSource" ref="dataSource" />
    </bean>

    <bean id="bookShop"
        class="com.apress.springrecipes.bookshop.JdbcBookShop">
        <property name="dataSource" ref="dataSource" />
    </bean>

    <bean id="transactionInterceptor" class="org.springframework.transaction.➥
        interceptor.TransactionInterceptor">
        <property name="transactionManager" ref="transactionManager" />
        <property name="transactionAttributes">
            <props>
                <prop key="purchase">PROPAGATION_REQUIRED</prop>
```

```
            </props>
        </property>
    </bean>

    <bean id="bookShopProxy"
        class="org.springframework.aop.framework.ProxyFactoryBean">
        <property name="target" ref="bookShop" />
        <property name="interceptorNames">
            <list>
                <value>transactionInterceptor</value>
            </list>
        </property>
    </bean>
</beans>
```

The methods that require transaction management can be specified in the TransactionInterceptor advice's transactionAttributes property. This property's type is Properties, where you have to specify the names of the transactional methods as the keys, and their transaction attributes as the values. It supports using wildcards in the keys so that you can specify the same set of transaction attributes for multiple methods. For each transactional method, you must specify at least the propagation transaction attribute. Here, you can choose the default value PROPAGATION_REQUIRED for simplicity's sake.

Your methods must be called on the proxy object to have transaction management support. So, in the Main class, you have to retrieve the bookShopProxy bean instead of the bookShop bean.

```
package com.apress.springrecipes.bookshop;
...
public class Main {

    public static void main(String[] args) {
        ...
        BookShop bookShop = (BookShop) context.getBean("bookShopProxy");
        bookShop.purchase("0001", "user1");
    }
}
```

Another option is to make use of the convenient class TransactionProxyFactoryBean, which specializes in creating transaction proxies. The information required for the TransactionInterceptor advice and the ProxyFactoryBean declaration can now be combined into a single TransactionProxyFactoryBean declaration.

```
<bean id="bookShopProxy" class="org.springframework.transaction.➥
    interceptor.TransactionProxyFactoryBean">
    <property name="target" ref="bookShop" />
    <property name="transactionManager" ref="transactionManager" />
    <property name="transactionAttributes">
        <props>
            <prop key="purchase">PROPAGATION_REQUIRED</prop>
```

```
        </props>
    </property>
</bean>
```

8-6. Managing Transactions Declaratively with Transaction Advices

Problem

As transaction management is a kind of crosscutting concern, you would like to manage transactions declaratively with the new AOP approach in Spring 2.x.

Solution

Spring 2.x offers a transaction advice that can be easily configured via the `<tx:advice>` element defined in the `tx` schema. This advice can be enabled with the AOP configuration facilities defined in the `aop` schema.

How It Works

To enable declarative transaction management in Spring 2.x, you can declare a transaction advice via the `<tx:advice>` element defined in the `tx` schema, so you have to add this schema definition to the `<beans>` root element beforehand. Once you have declared this advice, you need to associate it with a pointcut. Since a transaction advice is declared outside the `<aop:config>` element, it cannot link with a pointcut directly. You have to declare an advisor in the `<aop:config>` element to associate an advice with a pointcut.

■Note As Spring 2.x AOP uses AspectJ pointcut expressions to define pointcuts, you have to include `aspectjweaver.jar` (located in the `lib/aspectj` directory of the Spring installation) in your classpath.

```
<beans xmlns="http://www.springframework.org/schema/beans"
    xmlns:xsi="http://www.w3.org/2001/XMLSchema-instance"
    xmlns:tx="http://www.springframework.org/schema/tx"
    xmlns:aop="http://www.springframework.org/schema/aop"
    xsi:schemaLocation="http://www.springframework.org/schema/beans
        http://www.springframework.org/schema/beans/spring-beans-2.5.xsd
        http://www.springframework.org/schema/tx
        http://www.springframework.org/schema/tx/spring-tx-2.5.xsd
        http://www.springframework.org/schema/aop
        http://www.springframework.org/schema/aop/spring-aop-2.5.xsd">

    <tx:advice id="bookShopTxAdvice"
        transaction-manager="transactionManager">
        <tx:attributes>
```

```
            <tx:method name="purchase" />
        </tx:attributes>
    </tx:advice>

    <aop:config>
        <aop:pointcut id="bookShopOperation" expression=
            "execution(* com.apress.springrecipes.bookshop.BookShop.*(..))" />
        <aop:advisor advice-ref="bookShopTxAdvice"
            pointcut-ref="bookShopOperation" />
    </aop:config>
    ...
    <bean id="transactionManager"
        class="org.springframework.jdbc.datasource.DataSourceTransactionManager">
        <property name="dataSource" ref="dataSource" />
    </bean>

    <bean id="bookShop"
        class="com.apress.springrecipes.bookshop.JdbcBookShop">
        <property name="dataSource" ref="dataSource" />
    </bean>
</beans>
```

The preceding AspectJ pointcut expression matches all the methods declared in the BookShop interface. However, Spring AOP only supports public methods to be advised due to its proxy-based approach. So, only public methods can be made transactional with Spring AOP.

Each transaction advice requires an identifier and a reference to a transaction manager in the IoC container. The methods that require transaction management are specified with multiple <tx:method> elements inside the <tx:attributes> element. The method name supports wildcards for you to match a group of methods. You can also define transaction attributes for each group of methods, but here let's use the default attributes for simplicity's sake.

Now you can retrieve the bookShop bean from the Spring IoC container to use. As this bean's methods are matched by the pointcut, Spring will return a proxy that has transaction management enabled for this bean.

```
package com.apress.springrecipes.bookshop;
...
public class Main {

    public static void main(String[] args) {
        ...
        BookShop bookShop = (BookShop) context.getBean("bookShop");
        bookShop.purchase("0001", "user1");
    }
}
```

8-7. Managing Transactions Declaratively with the @Transactional Annotation

Problem

Declaring transactions in the bean configuration file requires knowledge of AOP concepts such as pointcuts, advices, and advisors. Developers who lack this knowledge might find it hard to enable declarative transaction management.

Solution

In addition to declaring transactions in the bean configuration file with pointcuts, advices, and advisors, Spring allows you to declare transactions simply by annotating your transactional methods with @Transactional and enabling the <tx:annotation-driven> element. However, Java 1.5 or higher is required to use this approach.

How It Works

To define a method as transactional, you can simply annotate it with @Transactional. Note that you should only annotate public methods due to the proxy-based limitations of Spring AOP.

```
package com.apress.springrecipes.bookshop;
...
import org.springframework.transaction.annotation.Transactional;

public class JdbcBookShop extends JdbcDaoSupport implements BookShop {

    @Transactional
    public void purchase(String isbn, String username) {
        ...
    }
}
```

You may apply the @Transactional annotation at the method level or the class level. When applying this annotation to a class, all of the public methods within this class will be defined as transactional. Although you can apply @Transactional to interfaces or method declarations in an interface, it's not recommended, as it may not work properly with class-based proxies (i.e., CGLIB proxies).

In the bean configuration file, you only have to enable the <tx:annotation-driven> element and specify a transaction manager for it. That's all you need to make it work. Spring will advise methods with @Transactional, or methods in a class with @Transactional, from beans declared in the IoC container. As a result, Spring can manage transactions for these methods.

```
<beans ...>
    <tx:annotation-driven transaction-manager="transactionManager" />
    ...
    <bean id="transactionManager"
        class="org.springframework.jdbc.datasource.DataSourceTransactionManager">
```

```
        <property name="dataSource" ref="dataSource" />
    </bean>

    <bean id="bookShop"
        class="com.apress.springrecipes.bookshop.JdbcBookShop">
        <property name="dataSource" ref="dataSource" />
    </bean>
</beans>
```

In fact, you can omit the transaction-manager attribute in the <tx:annotation-driven> element if your transaction manager has the name transactionManager. This element will automatically detect a transaction manager with this name. You only have to specify a transaction manager when it has a different name.

```
<beans ...>
    <tx:annotation-driven />
    ...
</beans>
```

8-8. Setting the Propagation Transaction Attribute

Problem

When a transactional method is called by another method, it is necessary to specify how the transaction should be propagated. For example, the method may continue to run within the existing transaction, or it may start a new transaction and run within its own transaction.

Solution

A transaction's propagation behavior can be specified by the *propagation* transaction attribute. Spring defines seven propagation behaviors, as shown in Table 8-5. These behaviors are defined in the org.springframework.transaction.TransactionDefinition interface. Note that not all types of transaction managers support all of these propagation behaviors.

Table 8-5. *Propagation Behaviors Supported by Spring*

Propagation	Description
REQUIRED	If there's an existing transaction in progress, the current method should run within this transaction. Otherwise, it should start a new transaction and run within its own transaction.
REQUIRES_NEW	The current method must start a new transaction and run within its own transaction. If there's an existing transaction in progress, it should be suspended.
SUPPORTS	If there's an existing transaction in progress, the current method can run within this transaction. Otherwise, it is not necessary to run within a transaction.
NOT_SUPPORTED	The current method should not run within a transaction. If there's an existing transaction in progress, it should be suspended.
MANDATORY	The current method must run within a transaction. If there's no existing transaction in progress, an exception will be thrown.

Propagation	Description
NEVER	The current method should not run within a transaction. If there's an existing transaction in progress, an exception will be thrown.
NESTED	If there's an existing transaction in progress, the current method should run within the nested transaction (supported by the JDBC 3.0 save point feature) of this transaction. Otherwise, it should start a new transaction and run within its own transaction.

How It Works

Transaction propagation happens when a transactional method is called by another method. For example, suppose a customer would like to check out all books to purchase at the book shop cashier. To support this operation, you define the Cashier interface as follows:

```
package com.apress.springrecipes.bookshop;
...
public interface Cashier {

    public void checkout(List<String> isbns, String username);
}
```

You can implement this interface by delegating the purchases to a book shop bean by calling its purchase() method multiple times. Note that the checkout() method is made transactional by applying the @Transactional annotation.

```
package com.apress.springrecipes.bookshop;
...
import org.springframework.transaction.annotation.Transactional;

public class BookShopCashier implements Cashier {

    private BookShop bookShop;

    public void setBookShop(BookShop bookShop) {
        this.bookShop = bookShop;
    }

    @Transactional
    public void checkout(List<String> isbns, String username) {
        for (String isbn : isbns) {
            bookShop.purchase(isbn, username);
        }
    }
}
```

Then define a cashier bean in your bean configuration file and refer to the book shop bean for purchasing books.

```
<bean id="cashier"
    class="com.apress.springrecipes.bookshop.BookShopCashier">
    <property name="bookShop" ref="bookShop" />
</bean>
```

To illustrate the propagation behavior of a transaction, enter the data shown in Tables 8-6, 8-7, and 8-8 in your bookshop database.

Table 8-6. *Sample Data in the BOOK Table for Testing Propagation Behaviors*

ISBN	BOOK_NAME	PRICE
0001	The First Book	30
0002	The Second Book	50

Table 8-7. *Sample Data in the BOOK_STOCK Table for Testing Propagation Behaviors*

ISBN	STOCK
0001	10
0002	10

Table 8-8. *Sample Data in the ACCOUNT Table for Testing Propagation Behaviors*

USERNAME	BALANCE
user1	40

The REQUIRED Propagation Behavior

When the user user1 checks out the two books from the cashier, the balance is sufficient to purchase the first book, but not the second.

```
package com.apress.springrecipes.bookshop;
...
public class Main {

    public static void main(String[] args) {
        ...
        Cashier cashier = (Cashier) context.getBean("cashier");
        List<String> isbnList =
                Arrays.asList(new String[] { "0001", "0002" });
        cashier.checkout(isbnList, "user1");
    }
}
```

When the book shop's purchase() method is called by another transactional method, such as checkout(), it will run within the existing transaction by default. This default propagation behavior is called REQUIRED. That means there will be only one transaction whose boundary is the beginning and ending of the checkout() method. This transaction will only be committed at the end of the checkout() method. As a result, the user can purchase none of the books. Figure 8-2 illustrates the REQUIRED propagation behavior.

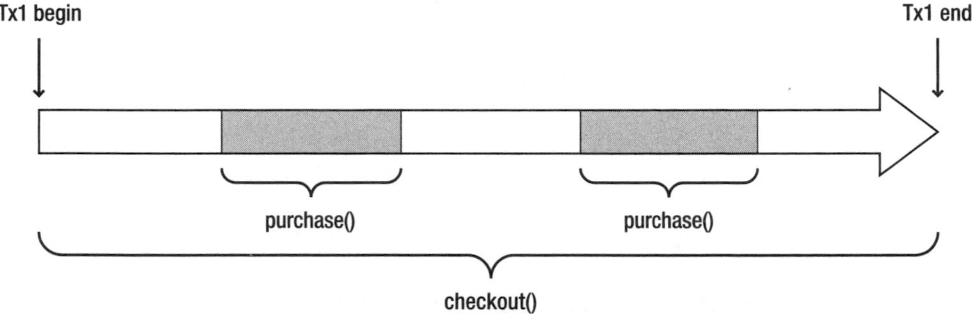

Figure 8-2. *The REQUIRED transaction propagation behavior*

However, if the purchase() method is called by a non-transactional method and there's no existing transaction in progress, it will start a new transaction and run within its own transaction.

The propagation transaction attribute can be defined in the @Transactional annotation. For example, you can set the REQUIRED behavior for this attribute as follows. In fact, this is unnecessary, as it's the default behavior.

```
package com.apress.springrecipes.bookshop;
...
import org.springframework.transaction.annotation.Propagation;
import org.springframework.transaction.annotation.Transactional;

public class JdbcBookShop extends JdbcDaoSupport implements BookShop {
    ...
    @Transactional(propagation = Propagation.REQUIRED)
    public void purchase(String isbn, String username) {
        ...
    }
}

package com.apress.springrecipes.bookshop;
...
import org.springframework.transaction.annotation.Propagation;
import org.springframework.transaction.annotation.Transactional;

public class BookShopCashier implements Cashier {
    ...
    @Transactional(propagation = Propagation.REQUIRED)
    public void checkout(List<String> isbns, String username) {
        ...
    }
}
```

The REQUIRES_NEW Propagation Behavior

Another common propagation behavior is `REQUIRES_NEW`. It indicates that the method must start a new transaction and run within its new transaction. If there's an existing transaction in progress, it should be suspended first.

```
package com.apress.springrecipes.bookshop;
...
import org.springframework.transaction.annotation.Propagation;
import org.springframework.transaction.annotation.Transactional;

public class JdbcBookShop extends JdbcDaoSupport implements BookShop {
    ...
    @Transactional(propagation = Propagation.REQUIRES_NEW)
    public void purchase(String isbn, String username) {
        ...
    }
}
```

In this case, there will be three transactions started in total. The first transaction is started by the `checkout()` method, but when the first `purchase()` method is called, the first transaction will be suspended and a new transaction will be started. At the end of the first `purchase()` method, the new transaction completes and commits. When the second `purchase()` method is called, another new transaction will be started. However, this transaction will fail and roll back. As a result, the first book will be purchased successfully while the second will not. Figure 8-3 illustrates the `REQUIRES_NEW` propagation behavior.

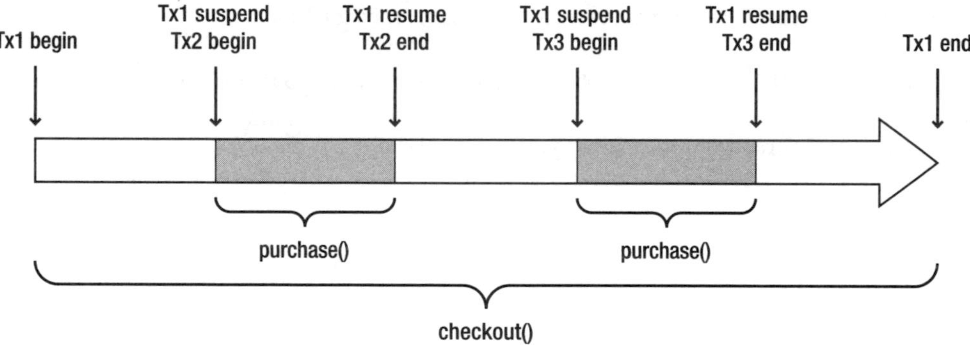

Figure 8-3. *The REQUIRES_NEW transaction propagation behavior*

Setting the Propagation Attribute in Transaction Advices, Proxies, and APIs

In a Spring 2.x transaction advice, the propagation transaction attribute can be specified in the `<tx:method>` element as follows:

```
<tx:advice ...>
    <tx:attributes>
        <tx:method name="..."
```

```
            propagation="REQUIRES_NEW" />
    </tx:attributes>
</tx:advice>
```

In classic Spring AOP, the propagation transaction attribute can be specified in the transaction attributes of `TransactionInterceptor` and `TransactionProxyFactoryBean` as follows:

```
<property name="transactionAttributes">
    <props>
        <prop key="...">PROPAGATION_REQUIRES_NEW</prop>
    </props>
</property>
```

In Spring's transaction management API, the propagation transaction attribute can be specified in a `DefaultTransactionDefinition` object and then passed to a transaction manager's `getTransaction()` method or a transaction template's constructor.

```
DefaultTransactionDefinition def = new DefaultTransactionDefinition();
def.setPropagationBehavior(TransactionDefinition.PROPAGATION_REQUIRES_NEW);
```

8-9. Setting the Isolation Transaction Attribute

Problem

When multiple transactions of the same application or different applications are operating concurrently on the same dataset, many unexpected problems may arise. You must specify how you expect your transactions to be isolated from one another.

Solution

The problems caused by concurrent transactions can be categorized into three types:

Dirty read: For two transactions T1 and T2, T1 reads a field that has been updated by T2 but not yet committed. Later, if T2 rolls back, the field read by T1 will be temporary and invalid.

Non-repeatable read: For two transactions T1 and T2, T1 reads a field and then T2 updates the field. Later, if T1 reads the same field again, the value will be different.

Phantom read: For two transactions T1 and T2, T1 reads some rows from a table and then T2 inserts new rows into the table. Later, if T1 reads the same table again, there will be additional rows.

In theory, transactions should be completely isolated from each other (i.e., serializable) to avoid all the mentioned problems. However, this isolation level will have great impact on performance because transactions have to run in serial order. In practice, transactions can run in lower isolation levels in order to improve performance.

A transaction's isolation level can be specified by the *isolation* transaction attribute. Spring supports five isolation levels, as shown in Table 8-9. These levels are defined in the `org.springframework.transaction.TransactionDefinition` interface.

Table 8-9. *Isolation Levels Supported by Spring*

Isolation	Description
DEFAULT	Uses the default isolation level of the underlying database. For most databases, the default isolation level is READ_COMMITTED.
READ_UNCOMMITTED	Allows a transaction to read uncommitted changes by other transactions. The dirty read, non-repeatable read, and phantom read problems may occur.
READ_COMMITTED	Allows a transaction to read only those changes that have been committed by other transactions. The dirty read problem can be avoided, but the non-repeatable read and phantom read problems may still occur.
REPEATABLE_READ	Ensures that a transaction can read identical values from a field multiple times. For the duration of this transaction, updates made by other transactions to this field are prohibited. The dirty read and non-repeatable read problems can be avoided, but the phantom read problem may still occur.
SERIALIZABLE	Ensures that a transaction can read identical rows from a table multiple times. For the duration of this transaction, inserts, updates, and deletes made by other transactions to this table are prohibited. All the concurrency problems can be avoided, but the performance will be low.

Note that transaction isolation is supported by the underlying database engine but not an application or a framework. However, not all database engines support all these isolation levels. You can change the isolation level of a JDBC connection by calling the setTransactionIsolation() method.

How It Works

To illustrate the problems caused by concurrent transactions, let's add two new operations to your book shop for increasing and checking the book stock.

```
package com.apress.springrecipes.bookshop;

public interface BookShop {
    ...
    public void increaseStock(String isbn, int stock);
    public int checkStock(String isbn);
}
```

Then you implement these operations as follows. Note that these two operations should also be declared as transactional.

```
package com.apress.springrecipes.bookshop;
...
import org.springframework.transaction.annotation.Transactional;

public class JdbcBookShop extends JdbcDaoSupport implements BookShop {
    ...
    @Transactional
    public void increaseStock(String isbn, int stock) {
```

```
        String threadName = Thread.currentThread().getName();
        System.out.println(threadName + " - Prepare to increase book stock");

        getJdbcTemplate().update(
                "UPDATE BOOK_STOCK SET STOCK = STOCK + ? " +
                "WHERE ISBN = ?",
                new Object[] { stock, isbn });

        System.out.println(threadName + " - Book stock increased by " + stock);
        sleep(threadName);

        System.out.println(threadName + " - Book stock rolled back");
        throw new RuntimeException("Increased by mistake");
    }

    @Transactional
    public int checkStock(String isbn) {
        String threadName = Thread.currentThread().getName();
        System.out.println(threadName + " - Prepare to check book stock");

        int stock = getJdbcTemplate().queryForInt(
                "SELECT STOCK FROM BOOK_STOCK WHERE ISBN = ?",
                new Object[] { isbn });

        System.out.println(threadName + " - Book stock is " + stock);
        sleep(threadName);

        return stock;
    }

    private void sleep(String threadName) {
        System.out.println(threadName + " - Sleeping");
        try {
            Thread.sleep(10000);
        } catch (InterruptedException e) {}
        System.out.println(threadName + " - Wake up");
    }
}
```

To simulate concurrency, your operations need to be executed by multiple threads. You can know the current status of the operations through the `println` statements. For each operation, you print a couple of messages to the console around the SQL statement's execution. The messages should include the thread name for you to know which thread is currently executing the operation.

After each operation executes the SQL statement, you ask the thread to sleep for 10 seconds. As you know, the transaction will be committed or rolled back immediately once the operation completes. Inserting a sleep statement can help to postpone the commit or rollback.

For the `increase()` operation, you eventually throw a `RuntimeException` to cause the transaction to roll back.

Before you start with the isolation level examples, enter the data from Tables 8-10 and 8-11 into your `bookshop` database.

Table 8-10. *Sample Data in the BOOK Table for Testing Isolation Levels*

ISBN	BOOK_NAME	PRICE
0001	The First Book	30

Table 8-11. *Sample Data in the BOOK_STOCK Table for Testing Isolation Levels*

ISBN	STOCK
0001	10

The READ_UNCOMMITTED and READ_COMMITTED Isolation Levels

`READ_UNCOMMITTED` is the lowest isolation level that allows a transaction to read uncommitted changes made by other transactions. You can set this isolation level in the `@Transaction` annotation of your `checkStock()` method.

```
package com.apress.springrecipes.bookshop;
...
import org.springframework.transaction.annotation.Isolation;
import org.springframework.transaction.annotation.Transactional;

public class JdbcBookShop extends JdbcDaoSupport implements BookShop {
    ...
    @Transactional(isolation = Isolation.READ_UNCOMMITTED)
    public int checkStock(String isbn) {
        ...
    }
}
```

You can create some threads to experiment on this transaction isolation level. In the following `Main` class, there are two threads you are going to create. Thread 1 increases the book stock while thread 2 checks the book stock. Thread 1 starts 5 seconds before thread 2.

```
package com.apress.springrecipes.bookshop;
...
public class Main {

    public static void main(String[] args) {
        ...
        final BookShop bookShop = (BookShop) context.getBean("bookShop");

        Thread thread1 = new Thread(new Runnable() {
            public void run() {
```

```
                try {
                    bookShop.increaseStock("0001", 5);
                } catch (RuntimeException e) {}
            }
        }, "Thread 1");

        Thread thread2 = new Thread(new Runnable() {
            public void run() {
                bookShop.checkStock("0001");
            }
        }, "Thread 2");

        thread1.start();
        try {
            Thread.sleep(5000);
        } catch (InterruptedException e) {}
        thread2.start();
    }
}
```

If you run the application, you will get the following result:

```
Thread 1 - Prepare to increase book stock
Thread 1 - Book stock increased by 5
Thread 1 - Sleeping
Thread 2 - Prepare to check book stock
Thread 2 - Book stock is 15
Thread 2 - Sleeping
Thread 1 - Wake up
Thread 1 - Book stock rolled back
Thread 2 - Wake up
```

First, thread 1 increased the book stock and then went to sleep. At that time, thread 1's transaction had not yet been rolled back. While thread 1 was sleeping, thread 2 started and attempted to read the book stock. With the READ_UNCOMMITTED isolation level, thread 2 would be able to read the stock value that had been updated by an uncommitted transaction.

However, when thread 1 wakes up, its transaction will be rolled back due to a RuntimeException, so the value read by thread 2 is temporary and invalid. This problem is known as *dirty read*, as a transaction may read values that are "dirty."

To avoid the dirty read problem, you should raise the isolation level of checkStock() to READ_COMMITTED.

```
package com.apress.springrecipes.bookshop;
...
import org.springframework.transaction.annotation.Isolation;
import org.springframework.transaction.annotation.Transactional;
```

```
public class JdbcBookShop extends JdbcDaoSupport implements BookShop {
    ...
    @Transactional(isolation = Isolation.READ_COMMITTED)
    public int checkStock(String isbn) {
        ...
    }
}
```

If you run the application again, thread 2 won't be able to read the book stock until thread 1 has rolled back the transaction. In this way, the dirty read problem can be avoided by preventing a transaction from reading a field that has been updated by another uncommitted transaction.

```
Thread 1 - Prepare to increase book stock
Thread 1 - Book stock increased by 5
Thread 1 - Sleeping
Thread 2 - Prepare to check book stock
Thread 1 - Wake up
Thread 1 - Book stock rolled back
Thread 2 - Book stock is 10
Thread 2 - Sleeping
Thread 2 - Wake up
```

In order that the underlying database can support the READ_COMMITTED isolation level, it may acquire an *update lock* on a row that was updated but not yet committed. Then other transactions must wait to read that row until the update lock is released, which happens when the locking transaction commits or rolls back.

The REPEATABLE_READ Isolation Level

Now let's restructure the threads to demonstrate another concurrency problem. Swap the tasks of the two threads so that thread 1 checks the book stock before thread 2 increases the book stock.

```
package com.apress.springrecipes.bookshop;
...
public class Main {

    public static void main(String[] args) {
        ...
        final BookShop bookShop = (BookShop) context.getBean("bookShop");

        Thread thread1 = new Thread(new Runnable() {
            public void run() {
                bookShop.checkStock("0001");
            }
        }, "Thread 1");
```

```
        Thread thread2 = new Thread(new Runnable() {
            public void run() {
                try {
                    bookShop.increaseStock("0001", 5);
                } catch (RuntimeException e) {}
            }
        }, "Thread 2");

        thread1.start();
        try {
            Thread.sleep(5000);
        } catch (InterruptedException e) {}
        thread2.start();
    }
}
```

If you run the application, you will get the following result:

```
Thread 1 - Prepare to check book stock
Thread 1 - Book stock is 10
Thread 1 - Sleeping
Thread 2 - Prepare to increase book stock
Thread 2 - Book stock increased by 5
Thread 2 - Sleeping
Thread 1 - Wake up
Thread 2 - Wake up
Thread 2 - Book stock rolled back
```

First, thread 1 read the book stock and then went to sleep. At that time, thread 1's transaction had not yet been committed. While thread 1 was sleeping, thread 2 started and attempted to increase the book stock. With the READ_COMMITTED isolation level, thread 2 would be able to update the stock value that was read by an uncommitted transaction.

However, if thread 1 reads the book stock again, the value will be different from its first read. This problem is known as *non-repeatable read* because a transaction may read different values for the same field.

To avoid the non-repeatable read problem, you should raise the isolation level of checkStock() to REPEATABLE_READ.

```
package com.apress.springrecipes.bookshop;
...
import org.springframework.transaction.annotation.Isolation;
import org.springframework.transaction.annotation.Transactional;

public class JdbcBookShop extends JdbcDaoSupport implements BookShop {
    ...
    @Transactional(isolation = Isolation.REPEATABLE_READ)
    public int checkStock(String isbn) {
```

```
        ...
    }
}
```

If you run the application again, thread 2 won't be able to update the book stock until thread 1 has committed the transaction. In this way, the non-repeatable read problem can be avoided by preventing a transaction from updating a value that has been read by another uncommitted transaction.

```
Thread 1 - Prepare to check book stock
Thread 1 - Book stock is 10
Thread 1 - Sleeping
Thread 2 - Prepare to increase book stock
Thread 1 - Wake up
Thread 2 - Book stock increased by 5
Thread 2 - Sleeping
Thread 2 - Wake up
Thread 2 - Book stock rolled back
```

In order that the underlying database can support the REPEATABLE_READ isolation level, it may acquire a *read lock* on a row that was read but not yet committed. Then other transactions must wait to update the row until the read lock is released, which happens when the locking transaction commits or rolls back.

The SERIALIZABLE Isolation Level

After a transaction has read several rows from a table, another transaction inserts new rows into the same table. If the first transaction reads the same table again, it will find additional rows that are different from the first read. This problem is known as *phantom read*. Actually, phantom read is very similar to non-repeatable read, but involves multiple rows.

To avoid the phantom read problem, you should raise the isolation level to the highest: SERIALIZABLE. Notice that this isolation level is the slowest, as it may acquire a read lock on the full table. In practice, you should always choose the lowest isolation level that can satisfy your requirements.

Setting the Isolation Level Attribute in Transaction Advices, Proxies, and APIs

In a Spring 2.x transaction advice, the isolation level can be specified in the <tx:method> element as follows:

```
<tx:advice ...>
    <tx:attributes>
        <tx:method name="..."
            isolation="REPEATABLE_READ" />
    </tx:attributes>
</tx:advice>
```

In classic Spring AOP, the isolation level can be specified in the transaction attributes of TransactionInterceptor and TransactionProxyFactoryBean as follows:

```
<property name="transactionAttributes">
    <props>
        <prop key="...">
            PROPAGATION_REQUIRED, ISOLATION_REPEATABLE_READ
        </prop>
    </props>
</property>
```

In Spring's transaction management API, the isolation level can be specified in a `DefaultTransactionDefinition` object and then passed to a transaction manager's `getTransaction()` method or a transaction template's constructor.

```
DefaultTransactionDefinition def = new DefaultTransactionDefinition();
def.setIsolationLevel(TransactionDefinition.ISOLATION_REPEATABLE_READ);
```

8-10. Setting the Rollback Transaction Attribute

Problem

By default, only unchecked exceptions (i.e., of type `RuntimeException` and `Error`) will cause a transaction to roll back, while checked exceptions will not. Sometimes you may wish to break this rule and set your own exceptions for rolling back.

Solution

The exceptions that cause a transaction to roll back or not can be specified by the *rollback* transaction attribute. Any exceptions not explicitly specified in this attribute will be handled by the default rollback rule (i.e., rolling back for unchecked exceptions and not rolling back for checked exceptions).

How It Works

A transaction's rollback rule can be defined in the `@Transactional` annotation via the `rollbackFor` and `noRollbackFor` attributes. These two attributes are declared as `Class[]`, so you can specify more than one exception for each attribute.

```
package com.apress.springrecipes.bookshop;
...
import org.springframework.transaction.annotation.Propagation;
import org.springframework.transaction.annotation.Transactional;

public class JdbcBookShop extends JdbcDaoSupport implements BookShop {
    ...
    @Transactional(
            propagation = Propagation.REQUIRES_NEW,
            rollbackFor = IOException.class,
            noRollbackFor = ArithmeticException.class)
    public void purchase(String isbn, String username) {
```

```
        ...
    }
}
```

In a Spring 2.x transaction advice, the rollback rule can be specified in the `<tx:method>` element. You can separate the exceptions with commas if there's more than one exception.

```
<tx:advice ...>
    <tx:attributes>
        <tx:method name="..."
            rollback-for="java.io.IOException"
            no-rollback-for="java.lang.ArithmeticException" />
        ...
    </tx:attributes>
</tx:advice>
```

In classic Spring AOP, the rollback rule can be specified in the transaction attributes of `TransactionInterceptor` and `TransactionProxyFactoryBean`. The minus sign indicates an exception to cause a transaction to roll back, while the plus sign indicates an exception to cause a transaction to commit.

```
<property name="transactionAttributes">
    <props>
        <prop key="...">
            PROPAGATION_REQUIRED, -java.io.IOException,
            +java.lang.ArithmeticException
        </prop>
    </props>
</property>
```

In Spring's transaction management API, the rollback rule can be specified in a `RuleBasedTransactionAttribute` object. As it implements the `TransactionDefinition` interface, it can be passed to a transaction manager's `getTransaction()` method or a transaction template's constructor.

```
RuleBasedTransactionAttribute attr = new RuleBasedTransactionAttribute();
attr.getRollbackRules().add(
    new RollbackRuleAttribute(IOException.class));
attr.getRollbackRules().add(
    new NoRollbackRuleAttribute(SendFailedException.class));
```

8-11. Setting the Timeout and Read-Only Transaction Attributes

Problem

As a transaction may acquire locks on rows and tables, a long transaction will tie up resources and have an impact on overall performance. Besides, if a transaction only reads but does not update data, the database engine could optimize this transaction. You can specify these attributes to increase the performance of your application.

Solution

The *timeout* transaction attribute indicates how long your transaction can survive before it is forced to roll back. This can prevent a long transaction from tying up resources. The *read-only* attribute indicates that this transaction will only read but not update data. That can help the database engine optimize the transaction.

How It Works

The timeout and read-only transaction attributes can be defined in the `@Transactional` annotation. Note that timeout is measured in seconds.

```
package com.apress.springrecipes.bookshop;
...
import org.springframework.transaction.annotation.Isolation;
import org.springframework.transaction.annotation.Transactional;

public class JdbcBookShop extends JdbcDaoSupport implements BookShop {
    ...
    @Transactional(
            isolation = Isolation.REPEATABLE_READ,
            timeout = 30,
            readOnly = true)
    public int checkStock(String isbn) {
        ...
    }
}
```

In a Spring 2.x transaction advice, the timeout and read-only transaction attributes can be specified in the `<tx:method>` element.

```
<tx:advice ...>
    <tx:attributes>
        <tx:method name="..."
            timeout="30"
            read-only="true" />
    </tx:attributes>
</tx:advice>
```

In classic Spring AOP, the timeout and read-only transaction attributes can be specified in the transaction attributes of `TransactionInterceptor` and `TransactionProxyFactoryBean`.

```
<property name="transactionAttributes">
    <props>
        <prop key="...">
            PROPAGATION_REQUIRED, timeout_30, readOnly
        </prop>
    </props>
</property>
```

In Spring's transaction management API, the timeout and read-only transaction attributes can be specified in a DefaultTransactionDefinition object and then passed to a transaction manager's getTransaction() method or a transaction template's constructor.

```
DefaultTransactionDefinition def = new DefaultTransactionDefinition();
def.setTimeout(30);
def.setReadOnly(true);
```

8-12. Managing Transactions with Load-Time Weaving

Problem

By default, Spring's declarative transaction management is enabled via its AOP framework. However, as Spring AOP can only advise public methods of beans declared in the IoC container, you are restricted to manage transactions within this scope using Spring AOP. Sometimes you may wish to manage transactions for non-public methods, or methods of objects created outside the Spring IoC container (e.g., domain objects).

Solution

Spring 2.5 also provides an AspectJ aspect named AnnotationTransactionAspect that can manage transactions for any methods of any objects, even if the methods are non-public or the objects are created outside the Spring IoC container. This aspect will manage transactions for any methods with the @Transactional annotation. You can choose either AspectJ's compile-time weaving or load-time weaving to enable this aspect.

How It Works

First of all, let's create a domain class Book, whose instances (i.e., domain objects) may be created outside the Spring IoC container.

```
package com.apress.springrecipes.bookshop;

import org.springframework.beans.factory.annotation.Autowired;
import org.springframework.beans.factory.annotation.Configurable;
import org.springframework.jdbc.core.JdbcTemplate;

@Configurable
public class Book {

    private String isbn;
    private String name;
    private int price;

    // Constructors, Getters and Setters
    ...

    private JdbcTemplate jdbcTemplate;
```

```
    @Autowired
    public void setJdbcTemplate(JdbcTemplate jdbcTemplate) {
        this.jdbcTemplate = jdbcTemplate;
    }

    public void purchase(String username) {
        jdbcTemplate.update(
                "UPDATE BOOK_STOCK SET STOCK = STOCK - 1 " +
                "WHERE ISBN = ?",
                new Object[] { isbn });

        jdbcTemplate.update(
                "UPDATE ACCOUNT SET BALANCE = BALANCE - ? " +
                "WHERE USERNAME = ?",
                new Object[] { price, username });
    }
}
```

This domain class has a `purchase()`method that will deduct the current book instance's stock and the user account's balance from the database. To utilize Spring's powerful JDBC support features, you can inject the JDBC template via setter injection.

You can use Spring's load-time weaving support to inject a JDBC template into book domain objects. You have to annotate this class with `@Configurable` to declare that this type of object is configurable in the Spring IoC container. Moreover, you can annotate the JDBC template's setter method with `@Autowired` to have it auto-wired.

Spring includes an AspectJ aspect, `AnnotationBeanConfigurerAspect`, in its aspect library for configuring object dependencies even if these objects are created outside the IoC container. To enable this aspect, you just define the `<context:spring-configured>` element in your bean configuration file. To weave this aspect into your domain classes at load time, you also have to define `<context:load-time-weaver>`. Finally, to auto-wire the JDBC template into book domain objects via `@Autowired`, you need `<context:annotation-config>` also.

Note To use the Spring aspect library for AspectJ, you have to include `spring-aspects.jar` (located in the `dist/weaving` directory of the Spring installation) in your classpath.

```
<beans xmlns="http://www.springframework.org/schema/beans"
    xmlns:xsi="http://www.w3.org/2001/XMLSchema-instance"
    xmlns:context="http://www.springframework.org/schema/context"
    xsi:schemaLocation="http://www.springframework.org/schema/beans
        http://www.springframework.org/schema/beans/spring-beans-2.5.xsd
        http://www.springframework.org/schema/context
        http://www.springframework.org/schema/context/spring-context-2.5.xsd">

    <context:load-time-weaver />
```

```
    <context:annotation-config />

    <context:spring-configured />

    <bean id="dataSource"
        class="org.springframework.jdbc.datasource.DriverManagerDataSource">
        <property name="driverClassName"
            value="org.apache.derby.jdbc.ClientDriver" />
        <property name="url"
            value="jdbc:derby://localhost:1527/bookshop;create=true" />
        <property name="username" value="app" />
        <property name="password" value="app" />
    </bean>

    <bean id="jdbcTemplate"
        class="org.springframework.jdbc.core.JdbcTemplate">
        <property name="dataSource" ref="dataSource" />
    </bean>
</beans>
```

In this bean configuration file, you can define a JDBC template on a data source, and then it will be auto-wired into book domain objects for them to access the database.

Now you can create the following `Main` class to test this domain class. Of course, there's no transaction support at this moment.

```
package com.apress.springrecipes.bookshop;

import org.springframework.context.ApplicationContext;
import org.springframework.context.support.ClassPathXmlApplicationContext;

public class Main {

    public static void main(String[] args) {
        ApplicationContext context =
            new ClassPathXmlApplicationContext("beans.xml");

        Book book = new Book("0001", "My First Book", 30);
        book.purchase("user1");
    }
}
```

For a simple Java application, you can weave this aspect into your classes at load time with the Spring agent specified as a VM argument.

```
java -javaagent:c:/spring-framework-2.5/dist/weaving/spring-agent.jar➥
com.apress.springrecipes.bookshop.Main
```

To enable transaction management for a domain object's method, you can simply annotate it with `@Transactional`, just as you did for methods of Spring beans.

```
package com.apress.springrecipes.bookshop;
...
import org.springframework.beans.factory.annotation.Configurable;
import org.springframework.transaction.annotation.Transactional;

@Configurable
public class Book {
    ...
    @Transactional
    public void purchase(String username) {
        ...
    }
}
```

Finally, to enable Spring's `AnnotationTransactionAspect` for transaction management, you just define the `<tx:annotation-driven>` element and set its mode to `aspectj`. Then the transaction aspect will automatically get enabled. You also have to provide a transaction manager for this aspect. By default, it will look for a transaction manager whose name is `transactionManager`.

```
<beans xmlns="http://www.springframework.org/schema/beans"
    xmlns:xsi="http://www.w3.org/2001/XMLSchema-instance"
    xmlns:context="http://www.springframework.org/schema/context"
    xmlns:tx="http://www.springframework.org/schema/tx"
    xsi:schemaLocation="http://www.springframework.org/schema/beans
        http://www.springframework.org/schema/beans/spring-beans-2.5.xsd
        http://www.springframework.org/schema/context
        http://www.springframework.org/schema/context/spring-context-2.5.xsd
        http://www.springframework.org/schema/tx
        http://www.springframework.org/schema/tx/spring-tx-2.5.xsd">
    ...
    <tx:annotation-driven mode="aspectj" />

    <bean id="transactionManager"
        class="org.springframework.jdbc.datasource.DataSourceTransactionManager">
        <property name="dataSource" ref="dataSource" />
    </bean>
</beans>
```

8-13. Summary

In this chapter, you have learned the importance of transaction management for ensuring data integrity and consistency. Without transaction management, your data and resources may be corrupted and left in an inconsistent state.

Spring's core transaction management abstraction is `PlatformTransactionManager`. This encapsulates a set of technology-independent methods that allow you to manage transactions without having to know much about the underlying transaction APIs. Spring has several built-in transaction manager implementations for different transaction management APIs.

Spring supports programmatic transaction management by calling the `commit()` and `rollback()` methods on a transaction manager. Conceptually, it is much like calling the same methods on a JDBC connection, but the methods declared in Spring's transaction manager are technology independent.

Another option for programmatic transaction management is to use a transaction template. You only need to encapsulate your operation in a callback object and pass it to a transaction template for execution. In this way, your operations needn't take account of low-level transaction details.

Spring supports declarative transaction management through its AOP framework. As Spring's AOP usage has changed significantly from version 1.x to 2.x, transactions can also be declared in different ways through AOP. In Spring 2.x, you can simply declare a transaction advice and apply it to your beans by defining a pointcut and an advisor. In classic Spring AOP, you have to create a transaction proxy using `TransactionInterceptor` or `TransactionProxyFactoryBean`.

In addition to declaring transactions with the AOP facilities, there's a more convenient way for declarative transaction management. You only have to apply the `@Transactional` annotation to the methods that require transaction management, and then enable the `<tx:annotation-driven>` element in your bean configuration file. Spring 2.5 provides an AspectJ aspect that can manage transactions for any methods with `@Transactional`, even if they are non-public or of objects that are created outside Spring. You can choose AspectJ's compile-time or load-time weaving to enable it.

Finally, you can define transaction attributes for your transactions. Spring supports five categories of transaction attributes in all. The propagation behavior specifies how a transaction should be propagated when a transactional method is called by another method. The isolation level specifies how a transaction should be isolated from others when multiple transactions are operating concurrently. The rollback rule specifies which kinds of exceptions should cause a rollback and which kinds shouldn't. The transaction timeout specifies how long a transaction can survive before it is forced to roll back. The read-only attribute specifies that a transaction will only read but not update data.

In the next chapter, you will learn how Spring supports using different object/relational mapping frameworks to implement data access services.

CHAPTER 9

Spring ORM Support

In this chapter, you will learn how to integrate *object/relational mapping (ORM)* frameworks into your Spring applications. Spring supports most of the popular ORM frameworks, including Hibernate, JDO, TopLink, iBATIS, and JPA. The focus of this chapter will be on Hibernate and the Java Persistence API (JPA). However, Spring's support for these ORM frameworks is consistent, so you can easily apply the techniques in this chapter to other ORM frameworks as well.

ORM is a modern technology for persisting objects into a relational database. An ORM framework persists your objects according to the mapping metadata you provide, such as the mappings between classes and tables, properties and columns, and so on. It generates SQL statements for object persistence at runtime, so you needn't write database-specific SQL statements unless you want to take advantage of database-specific features or provide optimized SQL statements of your own. As a result, your application will be database independent, and it can be easily migrated to another database in the future. Compared to the direct use of JDBC, an ORM framework can significantly reduce the data access effort of your applications.

Hibernate is a popular open source and high-performance ORM framework in the Java community. Hibernate supports most JDBC-compliant databases and can use specific dialects to access particular databases. Beyond the basic ORM features, Hibernate supports more advanced features like caching, cascading, and lazy loading. It also defines a querying language called *HQL (Hibernate Query Language)* for you to write simple but powerful object queries.

JPA defines a set of standard annotations and APIs for object persistence in both the Java SE and Java EE platforms. JPA is defined as part of the EJB 3.0 specification in JSR-220. JPA is just a set of standard APIs that require a JPA-compliant engine to provide persistence services. You can compare JPA to the JDBC API and a JPA engine to a JDBC driver. Hibernate can be configured as a JPA-compliant engine through an extension module called *Hibernate EntityManager*. This chapter will mainly demonstrate JPA with Hibernate as the underlying engine.

At the time of writing, the latest version of Hibernate is 3.2. Spring 2.0 supports both Hibernate 2.x and 3.x. The support for Hibernate 2.x is provided by the classes and interfaces in the `org.springframework.orm.hibernate` package, while the support for 3.x is in the `org.springframework.orm.hibernate3` package. You must be careful when importing the classes and interfaces to your application. Spring 2.5 supports only Hibernate 3.1 or higher. That means Hibernate 2.1 and Hibernate 3.0 won't be supported any more.

Upon finishing this chapter, you will be able to take advantage of Hibernate and JPA for data access in your Spring applications. You will also have a thorough understanding of Spring's data access module.

9-1. Problems with Using ORM Frameworks Directly

Suppose you are going to develop a course management system for a training center. The first class you create for this system is Course. This class is called an *entity class* or a *persistent class*, as it represents a real-world entity and its instances will be persisted to a database. Remember that for each entity class to be persisted by an ORM framework, a default constructor with no argument is required.

```
package com.apress.springrecipes.course;
...
public class Course {

    private Long id;
    private String title;
    private Date beginDate;
    private Date endDate;
    private int fee;

    // Constructors, Getters and Setters
    ...
}
```

For each entity class, you must define an identifier property to uniquely identify an entity. It's a best practice to define an auto-generated identifier, as this has no business meaning and thus won't be changed under any circumstances. Moreover, this identifier will be used by the ORM framework to determine an entity's state. If the identifier value is null, this entity will be treated as a new and unsaved entity. When this entity is persisted, an insert SQL statement will be issued; otherwise an update statement will. To allow the identifier to be null, you should choose a primitive wrapper type like java.lang.Integer and java.lang.Long for the identifier.

In your course management system, you need a DAO interface to encapsulate the data access logic. Let's define the following operations in the CourseDao interface:

```
package com.apress.springrecipes.course;
...
public interface CourseDao {

    public void store(Course course);
    public void delete(Long courseId);
    public Course findById(Long courseId);
    public List<Course> findAll();
}
```

Usually, when using ORM for persisting objects, the insert and update operations are combined into a single operation (e.g., store). This is to let the ORM framework (not you) decide whether an object should be inserted or updated.

In order for an ORM framework to persist your objects to a database, it must know the mapping metadata for the entity classes. You have to provide mapping metadata to it in its supported format. The native format for Hibernate is XML. However, as each ORM framework may have its own format for defining mapping metadata, JPA defines a set of persistent annotations for you to define mapping metadata in a standard format that has greater possibilities to be reused in other ORM frameworks.

Hibernate itself also supports the use of JPA annotations to define mapping metadata, so there are essentially three different strategies for mapping and persisting your objects with Hibernate and JPA:

- Using the Hibernate API to persist objects with Hibernate XML mappings
- Using the Hibernate API to persist objects with JPA annotations
- Using JPA to persist objects with JPA annotations

The core programming elements of Hibernate, JPA, and other ORM frameworks resemble those of JDBC. They are summarized in Table 9-1.

Table 9-1. *Core Programming Elements for Different Data Access Strategies*

Concept	JDBC	Hibernate	JPA
Resource	`Connection`	`Session`	`EntityManager`
Resource factory	`DataSource`	`SessionFactory`	`EntityManagerFactory`
Exception	`SQLException`	`HibernateException`	`PersistenceException`

In Hibernate, the core interface for object persistence is `Session`, whose instances can be obtained from a `SessionFactory` instance. In JPA, the corresponding interface is `EntityManager`, whose instances can be obtained from an `EntityManagerFactory` instance. The exceptions thrown by Hibernate are of type `HibernateException`, while those thrown by JPA may be of type `PersistenceException` or other Java SE exceptions like `IllegalArgumentException` and `IllegalStateException`. Note that all these exceptions are subclasses of `RuntimeException`, which you are not forced to catch and handle.

Persisting Objects Using the Hibernate API with Hibernate XML Mappings

To map entity classes with Hibernate XML mappings, you can provide a single mapping file for each class or a large file for several classes. Practically, you should define one for each class by joining the class name with `.hbm.xml` as the file extension for ease of maintenance. The middle extension `hbm` stands for Hibernate metadata.

The mapping file for the `Course` class should be named `Course.hbm.xml` and put in the same package as the entity class.

```
<!DOCTYPE hibernate-mapping
    PUBLIC "-//Hibernate/Hibernate Mapping DTD 3.0//EN"
    "http://hibernate.sourceforge.net/hibernate-mapping-3.0.dtd">

<hibernate-mapping package="com.apress.springrecipes.course">
    <class name="Course" table="COURSE">
        <id name="id" type="long" column="ID">
            <generator class="identity" />
        </id>
        <property name="title" type="string">
```

```
            <column name="TITLE" length="100" not-null="true" />
        </property>
        <property name="beginDate" type="date" column="BEGIN_DATE" />
        <property name="endDate" type="date" column="END_DATE" />
        <property name="fee" type="int" column="FEE" />
    </class>
</hibernate-mapping>
```

In the mapping file, you can specify a table name for this entity class and a table column for each simple property. You can also specify the column details such as column length, not-null constraints, and unique constraints. In addition, each entity must have an identifier defined, which can be generated automatically or assigned manually. In this example, the identifier will be generated using a table identity column.

Each application that uses Hibernate requires a global configuration file to configure properties such as the database settings (either JDBC connection properties or a data source's JNDI name), the database dialect, the mapping metadata's locations, and so on. When using XML mapping files to define mapping metadata, you have to specify the locations of the XML files. By default, Hibernate will read the `hibernate.cfg.xml` file from the root of the classpath. The middle extension `cfg` stands for configuration.

```
<!DOCTYPE hibernate-configuration PUBLIC
    "-//Hibernate/Hibernate Configuration DTD 3.0//EN"
    "http://hibernate.sourceforge.net/hibernate-configuration-3.0.dtd">

<hibernate-configuration>
    <session-factory>
        <property name="connection.driver_class">
            org.apache.derby.jdbc.ClientDriver
        </property>
        <property name="connection.url">
            jdbc:derby://localhost:1527/course;create=true
        </property>
        <property name="connection.username">app</property>
        <property name="connection.password">app</property>
        <property name="dialect">org.hibernate.dialect.DerbyDialect</property>
        <property name="show_sql">true</property>
        <property name="hbm2ddl.auto">update</property>

        <mapping resource="com/apress/springrecipes/course/Course.hbm.xml" />
    </session-factory>
</hibernate-configuration>
```

Before you can persist your objects, you have to create tables in a database schema to store the object data. When using an ORM framework like Hibernate, you usually needn't design the tables by yourself. If you set the `hbm2ddl.auto` property to `update`, Hibernate can help you to update the database schema and create the tables when necessary.

Now let's implement the DAO interface in the hibernate subpackage using the plain Hibernate API. Before you call the Hibernate API for object persistence, you have to initialize a Hibernate session factory (e.g., in the constructor).

■ **Note** To use Hibernate for object persistence, you have to include hibernate3.jar (located in the lib/hibernate directory of the Spring installation), antlr-2.7.6.jar (located in lib/antlr), asm-2.2.3.jar (located in lib/asm), cglib-nodep-2.1_3.jar (located in lib/cglib), dom4j-1.6.1.jar (located in lib/dom4j), ehcache-1.2.4.jar (located in lib/ehcache), jta.jar (located in lib/j2ee), commons-collections.jar and commons-logging.jar (located in lib/jakarta-commons), and log4j-1.2.14.jar (located in lib/log4j) in your classpath. To use Apache Derby as the database engine, you also have to include derbyclient.jar (located in the lib directory of the Derby installation).

```
package com.apress.springrecipes.course.hibernate;
...
import org.hibernate.Query;
import org.hibernate.Session;
import org.hibernate.SessionFactory;
import org.hibernate.Transaction;
import org.hibernate.cfg.Configuration;

public class HibernateCourseDao implements CourseDao {

    private SessionFactory sessionFactory;

    public HibernateCourseDao() {
        Configuration configuration = new Configuration().configure();
        sessionFactory = configuration.buildSessionFactory();
    }

    public void store(Course course) {
        Session session = sessionFactory.openSession();
        Transaction tx = session.getTransaction();
        try {
            tx.begin();
            session.saveOrUpdate(course);
            tx.commit();
        } catch (RuntimeException e) {
            tx.rollback();
            throw e;
        } finally {
            session.close();
        }
    }
```

```
    public void delete(Long courseId) {
        Session session = sessionFactory.openSession();
        Transaction tx = session.getTransaction();
        try {
            tx.begin();
            Course course = (Course) session.get(Course.class, courseId);
            session.delete(course);
            tx.commit();
        } catch (RuntimeException e) {
            tx.rollback();
            throw e;
        } finally {
            session.close();
        }
    }

    public Course findById(Long courseId) {
        Session session = sessionFactory.openSession();
        try {
            return (Course) session.get(Course.class, courseId);
        } finally {
            session.close();
        }
    }

    public List<Course> findAll() {
        Session session = sessionFactory.openSession();
        try {
            Query query = session.createQuery("from Course");
            return query.list();
        } finally {
            session.close();
        }
    }
}
```

The first step in using Hibernate is to create a `Configuration` object and ask it to load the Hibernate configuration file. By default, it loads `hibernate.cfg.xml` from the classpath root when you call the `configure()` method. Then you build a Hibernate session factory from this `Configuration` object. The purpose of a session factory is to produce sessions for you to persist your objects.

In the preceding DAO methods, you first open a session from the session factory. For any operation that involves database update, such as `saveOrUpdate()` and `delete()`, you must start a Hibernate transaction on that session. If the operation completes successfully, you commit the transaction. Otherwise, you roll it back if any `RuntimeException` happens. For read-only operations such as `get()` and HQL queries, there's no need to start a transaction. Finally, you must remember to close a session to release the resources held by this session.

You can create the following Main class to test run all the DAO methods. It also demonstrates an entity's typical life cycle.

```
package com.apress.springrecipes.course;
...
public class Main {

    public static void main(String[] args) {
        CourseDao courseDao = new HibernateCourseDao();

        Course course = new Course();
        course.setTitle("Core Spring");
        course.setBeginDate(new GregorianCalendar(2007, 8, 1).getTime());
        course.setEndDate(new GregorianCalendar(2007, 9, 1).getTime());
        course.setFee(1000);
        courseDao.store(course);

        List<Course> courses = courseDao.findAll();
        Long courseId = courses.get(0).getId();

        course = courseDao.findById(courseId);
        System.out.println("Course Title: " + course.getTitle());
        System.out.println("Begin Date: " + course.getBeginDate());
        System.out.println("End Date: " + course.getEndDate());
        System.out.println("Fee: " + course.getFee());

        courseDao.delete(courseId);
    }
}
```

Persisting Objects Using the Hibernate API with JPA Annotations

JPA annotations are standardized in the JSR-220 specification, so they're supported by all JPA-compliant ORM frameworks, including Hibernate. Moreover, the use of annotations will be more convenient for you to edit mapping metadata in the same source file.

The following Course class illustrates the use of JPA annotations to define mapping metadata.

■ **Note** To use JPA annotations in Hibernate, you have to include persistence.jar (located in the lib/j2ee directory of the Spring installation), hibernate-annotations.jar, and hibernate-commons-annotations.jar (located in lib/hibernate) in your classpath.

```
package com.apress.springrecipes.course;
...
import javax.persistence.Column;
import javax.persistence.Entity;
import javax.persistence.GeneratedValue;
import javax.persistence.GenerationType;
import javax.persistence.Id;
import javax.persistence.Table;

@Entity
@Table(name = "COURSE")
public class Course {

    @Id
    @GeneratedValue(strategy = GenerationType.IDENTITY)
    @Column(name = "ID")
    private Long id;

    @Column(name = "TITLE", length = 100, nullable = false)
    private String title;

    @Column(name = "BEGIN_DATE")
    private Date beginDate;

    @Column(name = "END_DATE")
    private Date endDate;

    @Column(name = "FEE")
    private int fee;

    // Constructors, Getters and Setters
    ...
}
```

Each entity class must be annotated with the `@Entity` annotation. You can assign a table name for an entity class in this annotation. For each property, you can specify a column name and column details using the `@Column` annotation. Each entity class must have an identifier defined by the `@Id` annotation. You can choose a strategy for identifier generation using the `@GeneratedValue` annotation. Here, the identifier will be generated by a table identity column.

Hibernate supports both native XML mapping files and JPA annotations as ways of defining mapping metadata. For JPA annotations, you have to specify the fully qualified names of the entity classes in `hibernate.cfg.xml` for Hibernate to read the annotations.

```
<hibernate-configuration>
    <session-factory>
        ...
        <!-- For Hibernate XML mappings -->
        <!--
```

```
        <mapping resource="com/apress/springrecipes/course/Course.hbm.xml" />
        -->

        <!-- For JPA annotations -->
        <mapping class="com.apress.springrecipes.course.Course" />
    </session-factory>
</hibernate-configuration>
```

In the Hibernate DAO implementation, the `Configuration` class you used is for reading XML mappings. If you use JPA annotations to define mapping metadata for Hibernate, you have to use its subclass, `AnnotationConfiguration`, instead.

```
package com.apress.springrecipes.course.hibernate;
...
import org.hibernate.SessionFactory;
import org.hibernate.cfg.AnnotationConfiguration;

public class HibernateCourseDao implements CourseDao {

    private SessionFactory sessionFactory;

    public HibernateCourseDao() {
        // For Hibernate XML mapping
        // Configuration configuration = new Configuration().configure();

        // For JPA annotation
        Configuration configuration = new AnnotationConfiguration().configure();

        sessionFactory = configuration.buildSessionFactory();
    }
    ...
}
```

Persisting Objects Using JPA with Hibernate As the Engine

In addition to persistent annotations, JPA defines a set of programming interfaces for object persistence. However, JPA is not a persistence implementation itself. You have to pick up a JPA-compliant engine to provide persistence services. Hibernate can be JPA-compliant through the Hibernate EntityManager extension module. With this extension, Hibernate can work as an underlying JPA engine to persist objects.

In a Java EE environment, you can configure the JPA engine in a Java EE container. But in a Java SE application, you have to set up the engine locally. The configuration of JPA is through the central XML file `persistence.xml`, located in the `META-INF` directory of the classpath root. In this file, you can set any vendor-specific properties for the underlying engine configuration.

Now let's create the JPA configuration file `persistence.xml` in the `META-INF` directory of the classpath root. Each JPA configuration file contains one or more `<persistence-unit>` elements. A *persistence unit* defines a set of persistent classes and how they should be persisted. Each persistence unit requires a name for identification. Here, you assign the name course to this persistence unit.

```
<persistence xmlns="http://java.sun.com/xml/ns/persistence"
    xmlns:xsi="http://www.w3.org/2001/XMLSchema-instance"
    xsi:schemaLocation="http://java.sun.com/xml/ns/persistence
        http://java.sun.com/xml/ns/persistence/persistence_1_0.xsd"
    version="1.0">

    <persistence-unit name="course">
        <properties>
            <property name="hibernate.ejb.cfgfile" value="/hibernate.cfg.xml" />
        </properties>
    </persistence-unit>
</persistence>
```

In this JPA configuration file, you configure Hibernate as your underlying JPA engine by referring to the Hibernate configuration file located in the classpath root. However, as Hibernate EntityManager will automatically detect XML mapping files and JPA annotations as mapping metadata, you have no need to specify them explicitly. Otherwise, you will encounter an org.hibernate.DuplicateMappingException.

```
<hibernate-configuration>
    <session-factory>
        ...
        <!-- Don't need to specify mapping files and annotated classes -->
        <!--
        <mapping resource="com/apress/springrecipes/course/Course.hbm.xml" />
        <mapping class="com.apress.springrecipes.course.Course" />
        -->
    </session-factory>
</hibernate-configuration>
```

As an alternative to referring to the Hibernate configuration file, you can also centralize all the Hibernate configurations in persistence.xml.

```
<persistence ...>
    <persistence-unit name="course">
        <properties>
            <property name="hibernate.connection.driver_class"
                value="org.apache.derby.jdbc.ClientDriver" />
            <property name="hibernate.connection.url"
                value="jdbc:derby://localhost:1527/course;create=true" />
            <property name="hibernate.connection.username" value="app" />
            <property name="hibernate.connection.password" value="app" />
            <property name="hibernate.dialect"
                value="org.hibernate.dialect.DerbyDialect" />
            <property name="hibernate.show_sql" value="true" />
            <property name="hibernate.hbm2ddl.auto" value="update" />
```

```
        </properties>
    </persistence-unit>
</persistence>'
```

In a Java EE environment, a Java EE container is able to manage the entity manager for you and inject it into your EJB components directly. But when you use JPA outside of a Java EE container (e.g., in a Java SE application), you have to create and maintain the entity manager by yourself.

Now let's implement the CourseDao interface in the jpa subpackage using JPA in a Java SE application. Before you call JPA for object persistence, you have to initialize an entity manager factory. The purpose of an entity manager factory is to produce entity managers for you to persist your objects.

■ **Note** To use Hibernate as the underlying JPA engine, you have to include hibernate-entitymanager.jar and jboss-archive-browsing.jar (located in the lib/hibernate directory of the Spring installation) in your classpath. As Hibernate EntityManager depends on Javassist (http://www.jboss.org/javassist/), you also have to include javassist.jar in your classpath. If you have Hibernate installed, you should find it in the lib directory of the Hibernate installation. Otherwise, you have to download it from its web site.

```
package com.apress.springrecipes.course.jpa;
...
import javax.persistence.EntityManager;
import javax.persistence.EntityManagerFactory;
import javax.persistence.EntityTransaction;
import javax.persistence.Persistence;
import javax.persistence.Query;

public class JpaCourseDao implements CourseDao {

    private EntityManagerFactory entityManagerFactory;

    public JpaCourseDao() {
        entityManagerFactory = Persistence.createEntityManagerFactory("course");
    }

    public void store(Course course) {
        EntityManager manager = entityManagerFactory.createEntityManager();
        EntityTransaction tx = manager.getTransaction();
        try {
            tx.begin();
            manager.merge(course);
            tx.commit();
        } catch (RuntimeException e) {
```

```
            tx.rollback();
            throw e;
        } finally {
            manager.close();
        }
    }

    public void delete(Long courseId) {
        EntityManager manager = entityManagerFactory.createEntityManager();
        EntityTransaction tx = manager.getTransaction();
        try {
            tx.begin();
            Course course = manager.find(Course.class, courseId);
            manager.remove(course);
            tx.commit();
        } catch (RuntimeException e) {
            tx.rollback();
            throw e;
        } finally {
            manager.close();
        }
    }

    public Course findById(Long courseId) {
        EntityManager manager = entityManagerFactory.createEntityManager();
        try {
            return manager.find(Course.class, courseId);
        } finally {
            manager.close();
        }
    }

    public List<Course> findAll() {
        EntityManager manager = entityManagerFactory.createEntityManager();
        try {
            Query query = manager.createQuery(
                "select course from Course course");
            return query.getResultList();
        } finally {
            manager.close();
        }
    }
}
```

The entity manager factory is built by the static method `createEntityManagerFactory()` of the `javax.persistence.Persistence` class. You have to pass in a persistence unit name defined in `persistence.xml` for an entity manager factory.

In the preceding DAO methods, you first create an entity manager from the entity manager factory. For any operation that involves database update, such as merge() and remove(), you must start a JPA transaction on the entity manager. For read-only operations such as find() and JPA queries, there's no need to start a transaction. Finally, you must close an entity manager to release the resources.

You can test this DAO with the similar Main class, but this time you instantiate the JPA DAO implementation instead.

```
package com.apress.springrecipes.course;
...
public class Main {

    public static void main(String[] args) {
        CourseDao courseDao = new JpaCourseDao();
        ...
    }
}
```

In the preceding DAO implementations for both Hibernate and JPA, there are only one or two lines that are different for each DAO method. The rest of the lines are boilerplate routine tasks that you have to repeat. Moreover, each ORM framework has its own API for local transaction management.

9-2. Configuring ORM Resource Factories in Spring

Problem

When using an ORM framework on its own, you have to configure its resource factory with its API. For Hibernate and JPA, you have to build a session factory and an entity manager factory from the native Hibernate API and JPA. In this way, you can only manage the session factory and entity manager factory by yourself. Besides, your application cannot utilize the data access facilities provided by Spring.

Solution

Spring provides several factory beans for you to create a Hibernate session factory or a JPA entity manager factory as a singleton bean in the IoC container. These factories can be shared between multiple beans via dependency injection. Moreover, this allows the session factory and the entity manager factory to integrate with other Spring data access facilities, such as data sources and transaction managers.

How It Works

Configuring a Hibernate Session Factory in Spring

First of all, let's modify HibernateCourseDao to accept a session factory via dependency injection, instead of creating it directly with the native Hibernate API in the constructor.

```
package com.apress.springrecipes.course.hibernate;
...
import org.hibernate.SessionFactory;

public class HibernateCourseDao implements CourseDao {

    private SessionFactory sessionFactory;

    public void setSessionFactory(SessionFactory sessionFactory) {
        this.sessionFactory = sessionFactory;
    }
    ...
}
```

Now let's see how to declare a session factory that uses XML mapping files in Spring. For this purpose, you have to enable the XML mapping file definition in `hibernate.cfg.xml` again.

```
<hibernate-configuration>
    <session-factory>
        ...
        <!-- For Hibernate XML mappings -->
        <mapping resource="com/apress/springrecipes/course/Course.hbm.xml" />
    </session-factory>
</hibernate-configuration>
```

Then you create a bean configuration file for using Hibernate as the ORM framework (e.g., `beans-hibernate.xml` in the classpath root). You can declare a session factory that uses XML mapping files with the factory bean `LocalSessionFactoryBean`. You can also declare a `HibernateCourseDao` instance under Spring's management.

```
<beans xmlns="http://www.springframework.org/schema/beans"
    xmlns:xsi="http://www.w3.org/2001/XMLSchema-instance"
    xsi:schemaLocation="http://www.springframework.org/schema/beans
        http://www.springframework.org/schema/beans/spring-beans-2.5.xsd">

    <bean id="sessionFactory"
        class="org.springframework.orm.hibernate3.LocalSessionFactoryBean">
        <property name="configLocation" value="classpath:hibernate.cfg.xml" />
    </bean>

    <bean id="courseDao"
        class="com.apress.springrecipes.course.hibernate.HibernateCourseDao">
        <property name="sessionFactory" ref="sessionFactory" />
    </bean>
</beans>
```

Note that you can specify the `configLocation` property for this factory bean to load the Hibernate configuration file. This property is of type `Resource`, but you can assign a string value to it. The built-in property editor `ResourceEditor` will convert it into a `Resource` object. The preceding factory bean loads the configuration file from the root of the classpath.

Now you can modify the Main class to retrieve the HibernateCourseDao instance from the Spring IoC container.

```
package com.apress.springrecipes.course;
...
import org.springframework.context.ApplicationContext;
import org.springframework.context.support.ClassPathXmlApplicationContext;

public class Main {

    public static void main(String[] args) {
        ApplicationContext context =
            new ClassPathXmlApplicationContext("beans-hibernate.xml");

        CourseDao courseDao = (CourseDao) context.getBean("courseDao");
        ...
    }
}
```

The preceding factory bean creates a session factory by loading the Hibernate configuration file, which includes the database settings (either JDBC connection properties or a data source's JNDI name). Now, suppose you have a data source defined in the Spring IoC container. If you want to use this data source for your session factory, you can inject it into the dataSource property of LocalSessionFactoryBean. The data source specified in this property will override the database settings in the Hibernate configuration file.

```
<beans ...>
    ...
    <bean id="dataSource"
        class="org.springframework.jdbc.datasource.DriverManagerDataSource">
        <property name="driverClassName"
            value="org.apache.derby.jdbc.ClientDriver" />
        <property name="url"
            value="jdbc:derby://localhost:1527/course;create=true" />
        <property name="username" value="app" />
        <property name="password" value="app" />
    </bean>

    <bean id="sessionFactory"
        class="org.springframework.orm.hibernate3.LocalSessionFactoryBean">
        <property name="dataSource" ref="dataSource" />
        <property name="configLocation" value="classpath:hibernate.cfg.xml" />
    </bean>
</beans>
```

Or, you may even ignore the Hibernate configuration file by merging all the configurations into LocalSessionFactoryBean. For example, you can specify the locations of the XML mapping files in the mappingResources property and other Hibernate properties such as the database dialect in the hibernateProperties property.

```
<bean id="sessionFactory"
    class="org.springframework.orm.hibernate3.LocalSessionFactoryBean">
    <property name="dataSource" ref="dataSource" />
    <property name="mappingResources">
        <list>
            <value>com/apress/springrecipes/course/Course.hbm.xml</value>
        </list>
    </property>
    <property name="hibernateProperties">
        <props>
            <prop key="hibernate.dialect">org.hibernate.dialect.DerbyDialect</prop>
            <prop key="hibernate.show_sql">true</prop>
            <prop key="hibernate.hbm2ddl.auto">update</prop>
        </props>
    </property>
</bean>
```

The mappingResources property's type is String[], so you can specify a set of mapping files in the classpath. LocalSessionFactoryBean also allows you take advantage of Spring's resource-loading support to load mapping files from various types of locations. You can specify the resource paths of the mapping files in the mappingLocations property, whose type is Resource[].

```
<bean id="sessionFactory"
    class="org.springframework.orm.hibernate3.LocalSessionFactoryBean">
    ...
    <property name="mappingLocations">
        <list>
            <value>classpath:com/apress/springrecipes/course/Course.hbm.xml</value>
        </list>
    </property>
    ...
</bean>
```

With Spring's resource-loading support, you can also use wildcards in a resource path to match multiple mapping files so that you don't need to configure their locations every time you add a new entity class. Spring's preregistered ResourceArrayPropertyEditor will convert this path into a Resource array.

```
<bean id="sessionFactory"
    class="org.springframework.orm.hibernate3.LocalSessionFactoryBean">
    ...
    <property name="mappingLocations"
        value="classpath:com/apress/springrecipes/course/*.hbm.xml" />
    ...
</bean>
```

If your mapping metadata is provided through JPA annotations, you have to make use of AnnotationSessionFactoryBean instead. You have to specify the persistent classes in the annotatedClasses property of AnnotationSessionFactoryBean.

```
<bean id="sessionFactory" class="org.springframework.orm.hibernate3.➥
    annotation.AnnotationSessionFactoryBean">
    <property name="dataSource" ref="dataSource" />
    <property name="annotatedClasses">
        <list>
            <value>com.apress.springrecipes.course.Course</value>
        </list>
    </property>
    <property name="hibernateProperties">
        <props>
            <prop key="hibernate.dialect">org.hibernate.dialect.DerbyDialect</prop>
            <prop key="hibernate.show_sql">true</prop>
            <prop key="hibernate.hbm2ddl.auto">update</prop>
        </props>
    </property>
</bean>
```

Now you can delete the Hibernate configuration file (i.e., hibernate.cfg.xml) because its configurations have been ported to Spring.

Configuring a JPA Entity Manager Factory in Spring

First of all, let's modify JpaCourseDao to accept an entity manager factory via dependency injection, instead of creating it directly in the constructor.

```
package com.apress.springrecipes.course.jpa;
...
import javax.persistence.EntityManagerFactory;

public class JpaCourseDao implements CourseDao {

    private EntityManagerFactory entityManagerFactory;

    public void setEntityManagerFactory(
            EntityManagerFactory entityManagerFactory) {
        this.entityManagerFactory = entityManagerFactory;
    }
    ...
}
```

The JPA specification defines how you should obtain an entity manager factory in Java SE and Java EE environments. In a Java SE environment, an entity manager factory is created manually by calling the createEntityManagerFactory() static method of the Persistence class.

Now let's create a bean configuration file for using JPA (e.g., beans-jpa.xml in the classpath root). Spring provides a factory bean, LocalEntityManagerFactoryBean, for you to create an entity manager factory in the IoC container. You must specify the persistence unit name defined in the JPA configuration file. You can also declare a JpaCourseDao instance under Spring's management.

```
<beans xmlns="http://www.springframework.org/schema/beans"
    xmlns:xsi="http://www.w3.org/2001/XMLSchema-instance"
    xsi:schemaLocation="http://www.springframework.org/schema/beans
        http://www.springframework.org/schema/beans/spring-beans-2.5.xsd">

    <bean id="entityManagerFactory"
        class="org.springframework.orm.jpa.LocalEntityManagerFactoryBean">
        <property name="persistenceUnitName" value="course" />
    </bean>

   <bean id="courseDao"
        class="com.apress.springrecipes.course.jpa.JpaCourseDao">
        <property name="entityManagerFactory" ref="entityManagerFactory" />
    </bean>
</beans>
```

Now you can test this JpaCourseDao instance with the Main class by retrieving it from the Spring IoC container.

```
package com.apress.springrecipes.course;
...
import org.springframework.context.ApplicationContext;
import org.springframework.context.support.ClassPathXmlApplicationContext;

public class Main {

    public static void main(String[] args) {
        ApplicationContext context =
            new ClassPathXmlApplicationContext("beans-jpa.xml");

        CourseDao courseDao = (CourseDao) context.getBean("courseDao");
        ...
    }
}
```

In a Java EE environment, you can look up an entity manager factory from a Java EE container with JNDI. In Spring 2.x, you can perform a JNDI lookup by using the <jee:jndi-lookup> element.

```
<jee:jndi-lookup id="entityManagerFactory" jndi-name="jpa/coursePU" />
```

LocalEntityManagerFactoryBean creates an entity manager factory by loading the JPA configuration file (i.e., persistence.xml). Spring supports a more flexible way to create an entity manager factory by another factory bean, LocalContainerEntityManagerFactoryBean. It allows you to override some of the configurations in the JPA configuration file, such as the data source and database dialect. So, you can take advantage of Spring's data access facilities to configure the entity manager factory.

```
<beans ...>
    ...
    <bean id="dataSource"
        class="org.springframework.jdbc.datasource.DriverManagerDataSource">
        <property name="driverClassName"
            value="org.apache.derby.jdbc.ClientDriver" />
        <property name="url"
            value="jdbc:derby://localhost:1527/course;create=true" />
        <property name="username" value="app" />
        <property name="password" value="app" />
    </bean>

    <bean id="entityManagerFactory" class="org.springframework.orm.jpa.➥
        LocalContainerEntityManagerFactoryBean">
        <property name="persistenceUnitName" value="course" />
        <property name="dataSource" ref="dataSource" />
        <property name="jpaVendorAdapter">
            <bean class="org.springframework.orm.jpa.vendor.➥
                HibernateJpaVendorAdapter">
                <property name="databasePlatform"
                    value="org.hibernate.dialect.DerbyDialect" />
                <property name="showSql" value="true" />
                <property name="generateDdl" value="true" />
            </bean>
        </property>
    </bean>
</beans>
```

In the preceding bean configurations, you inject a data source into this entity manager factory. It will override the database settings in the JPA configuration file. You can set a JPA vendor adapter to LocalContainerEntityManagerFactoryBean to specify JPA engine–specific properties. With Hibernate as the underlying JPA engine, you should choose HibernateJpaVendorAdapter. Other properties that are not supported by this adapter can be specified in the jpaProperties property.

Now your JPA configuration file (i.e., persistence.xml) can be simplified as follows because its configurations have been ported to Spring:

```
<persistence ...>
    <persistence-unit name="course" />
</persistence>
```

9-3. Persisting Objects with Spring's ORM Templates

Problem

When using an ORM framework on its own, you have to repeat certain routine tasks for each DAO operation. For example, in a DAO operation implemented with Hibernate or JPA, you have to open and close a session or an entity manager, and begin, commit, and roll back a transaction with the native API.

Solution

Spring's approach to simplifying an ORM framework's usage is the same as JDBC's—by defining template classes and DAO support classes. Also, Spring defines an abstract layer on top of different transaction management APIs. For different ORM frameworks, you only have to pick up a corresponding transaction manager implementation. Then you can manage transactions for them in a similar way.

In Spring's data access module, the support for different data access strategies is consistent. Table 9-2 compares the support classes for JDBC, Hibernate, and JPA.

Table 9-2. *Spring's Support Classes for Different Data Access Strategies*

Support Class	JDBC	Hibernate	JPA
Template class	`JdbcTemplate`	`HibernateTemplate`	`JpaTemplate`
DAO support class	`JdbcDaoSupport`	`HibernateDaoSupport`	`JpaDaoSupport`
Transaction manager	`DataSourceTransaction Manager`	`HibernateTransaction Manager`	`JpaTransactionManager`

Spring defines the `HibernateTemplate` and `JpaTemplate` classes to provide template methods for different types of Hibernate and JPA operations to minimize the effort involved in using them. The template methods in `HibernateTemplate` and `JpaTemplate` ensure that Hibernate sessions and JPA entity managers will be opened and closed properly. They will also have native Hibernate and JPA transactions participate in Spring-managed transactions. As a result, you will be able to manage transactions declaratively for your Hibernate and JPA DAOs without any boilerplate transaction code.

How It Works

Using a Hibernate Template and a JPA Template

First, the `HibernateCourseDao` class can be simplified as follows with the help of Spring's `HibernateTemplate`:

```
package com.apress.springrecipes.course.hibernate;
...
import org.springframework.orm.hibernate3.HibernateTemplate;
import org.springframework.transaction.annotation.Transactional;
```

```
public class HibernateCourseDao implements CourseDao {

    private HibernateTemplate hibernateTemplate;

    public void setHibernateTemplate(HibernateTemplate hibernateTemplate) {
        this.hibernateTemplate = hibernateTemplate;
    }

    @Transactional
    public void store(Course course) {
        hibernateTemplate.saveOrUpdate(course);
    }

    @Transactional
    public void delete(Long courseId) {
        Course course = (Course) hibernateTemplate.get(Course.class, courseId);
        hibernateTemplate.delete(course);
    }

    @Transactional(readOnly = true)
    public Course findById(Long courseId) {
        return (Course) hibernateTemplate.get(Course.class, courseId);
    }

    @Transactional(readOnly = true)
    public List<Course> findAll() {
        return hibernateTemplate.find("from Course");
    }
}
```

In this DAO implementation, you declare all the DAO methods to be transactional with the `@Transactional` annotation. Among these methods, `findById()` and `findAll()` are read-only. The template methods in `HibernateTemplate` are responsible for managing the sessions and transactions. If there are multiple Hibernate operations in a transactional DAO method, the template methods will ensure that they will run within the same session and transaction. As a result, you have no need to deal with the Hibernate API for session and transaction management.

The `HibernateTemplate` class is thread-safe, so you can declare a single instance of it in the bean configuration file for Hibernate (i.e., `beans-hibernate.xml`) and inject this instance into all Hibernate DAOs. A `HibernateTemplate` instance requires the `sessionFactory` property to be set. You can inject this property by either setter method or constructor argument.

```
<beans xmlns="http://www.springframework.org/schema/beans"
    xmlns:xsi="http://www.w3.org/2001/XMLSchema-instance"
    xmlns:tx="http://www.springframework.org/schema/tx"
    xsi:schemaLocation="http://www.springframework.org/schema/beans
        http://www.springframework.org/schema/beans/spring-beans-2.5.xsd
        http://www.springframework.org/schema/tx
```

```
        http://www.springframework.org/schema/tx/spring-tx-2.5.xsd">
    ...
    <tx:annotation-driven />

    <bean id="transactionManager"
        class="org.springframework.orm.hibernate3.HibernateTransactionManager">
        <property name="sessionFactory" ref="sessionFactory" />
    </bean>

    <bean id="hibernateTemplate"
        class="org.springframework.orm.hibernate3.HibernateTemplate">
        <property name="sessionFactory" ref="sessionFactory" />
    </bean>

    <bean name="courseDao"
        class="com.apress.springrecipes.course.hibernate.HibernateCourseDao">
        <property name="hibernateTemplate" ref="hibernateTemplate" />
    </bean>
</beans>
```

To enable declarative transaction management for the methods annotated with `@Transactional`, you have to enable the `<tx:annotation-driven>` element in your bean configuration file. By default, it will look for a transaction manager with the name `transactionManager`, so you have to declare a `HibernateTransactionManager` instance with that name. `HibernateTransactionManager` requires the session factory property to be set. It will manage transactions for sessions opened through this session factory.

Similarly, you can simplify the `JpaCourseDao` class as follows with the help of Spring's `JpaTemplate`. You also declare all the DAO methods to be transactional.

```
package com.apress.springrecipes.course.jpa;
...
import org.springframework.orm.jpa.JpaTemplate;
import org.springframework.transaction.annotation.Transactional;

public class JpaCourseDao implements CourseDao {

    private JpaTemplate jpaTemplate;

    public void setJpaTemplate(JpaTemplate jpaTemplate) {
        this.jpaTemplate = jpaTemplate;
    }

    @Transactional
    public void store(Course course) {
        jpaTemplate.merge(course);
    }
```

```
    @Transactional
    public void delete(Long courseId) {
        Course course = jpaTemplate.find(Course.class, courseId);
        jpaTemplate.remove(course);
    }

    @Transactional(readOnly = true)
    public Course findById(Long courseId) {
        return jpaTemplate.find(Course.class, courseId);
    }

    @Transactional(readOnly = true)
    public List<Course> findAll() {
        return jpaTemplate.find("from Course");
    }
}
```

In the bean configuration file for JPA (i.e., beans-jpa.xml), you can declare a JpaTemplate instance and inject it into all JPA DAOs. Also, you have to declare a JpaTransactionManager instance for managing JPA transactions.

```
<beans xmlns="http://www.springframework.org/schema/beans"
    xmlns:xsi="http://www.w3.org/2001/XMLSchema-instance"
    xmlns:tx="http://www.springframework.org/schema/tx"
    xsi:schemaLocation="http://www.springframework.org/schema/beans
        http://www.springframework.org/schema/beans/spring-beans-2.5.xsd
        http://www.springframework.org/schema/tx
        http://www.springframework.org/schema/tx/spring-tx-2.5.xsd">
    ...
    <tx:annotation-driven />

    <bean id="transactionManager"
        class="org.springframework.orm.jpa.JpaTransactionManager">
        <property name="entityManagerFactory" ref="entityManagerFactory" />
    </bean>

    <bean id="jpaTemplate"
        class="org.springframework.orm.jpa.JpaTemplate">
        <property name="entityManagerFactory" ref="entityManagerFactory" />
    </bean>

    <bean name="courseDao"
        class="com.apress.springrecipes.course.jpa.JpaCourseDao">
        <property name="jpaTemplate" ref="jpaTemplate" />
    </bean>
</beans>
```

Another advantage of HibernateTemplate and JpaTemplate is that they will translate native Hibernate and JPA exceptions into exceptions in Spring's DataAccessException hierarchy. This allows consistent exception handling for all the data access strategies in Spring. For instance, if a database constraint is violated when persisting an object, Hibernate will throw an org.hibernate.exception.ConstraintViolationException while JPA will throw a javax.persistence.EntityExistsException. These exceptions will be translated by HibernateTemplate and JpaTemplate into DataIntegrityViolationException, which is a subclass of Spring's DataAccessException.

If you want to get access to the underlying Hibernate session or JPA entity manager in HibernateTemplate or JpaTemplate in order to perform native Hibernate or JPA operations, you can implement the HibernateCallback or JpaCallback interface and pass its instance to the execute() method of the template.

```
hibernateTemplate.execute(new HibernateCallback() {
    public Object doInHibernate(Session session) throws HibernateException,
            SQLException {
        ...
    }
};

jpaTemplate.execute(new JpaCallback() {
    public Object doInJpa(EntityManager em) throws PersistenceException {
        ...
    }
};
```

Extending the Hibernate and JPA DAO Support Classes

Your Hibernate DAO can extend HibernateDaoSupport to have the setSessionFactory() and setHibernateTemplate() methods inherited. Then, in your DAO methods, you can simply call the getHibernateTemplate() method to retrieve the template instance.

```
package com.apress.springrecipes.course.hibernate;
...
import org.springframework.orm.hibernate3.support.HibernateDaoSupport;
import org.springframework.transaction.annotation.Transactional;

public class HibernateCourseDao extends HibernateDaoSupport implements
        CourseDao {

    @Transactional
    public void store(Course course) {
        getHibernateTemplate().saveOrUpdate(course);
    }

    @Transactional
    public void delete(Long courseId) {
        Course course = (Course) getHibernateTemplate().get(Course.class,
```

```
                courseId);
        getHibernateTemplate().delete(course);
    }

    @Transactional(readOnly = true)
    public Course findById(Long courseId) {
        return (Course) getHibernateTemplate().get(Course.class, courseId);
    }

    @Transactional(readOnly = true)
    public List<Course> findAll() {
        return getHibernateTemplate().find("from Course");
    }
}
```

As HibernateCourseDao inherits the setSessionFactory() and setHibernateTemplate() methods, you can inject either of them into your DAO so that you can retrieve the HibernateTemplate instance. If you inject a session factory, you will be able to delete the HibernateTemplate declaration.

```
<bean name="courseDao"
    class="com.apress.springrecipes.course.hibernate.HibernateCourseDao">
    <property name="sessionFactory" ref="sessionFactory" />
</bean>
```

Similarly, your JPA DAO can extend JpaDaoSupport to have setEntityManagerFactory() and setJpaTemplate() inherited. In your DAO methods, you can simply call the getJpaTemplate() method to retrieve the template instance.

```
package com.apress.springrecipes.course.jpa;
...
import org.springframework.orm.jpa.support.JpaDaoSupport;
import org.springframework.transaction.annotation.Transactional;

public class JpaCourseDao extends JpaDaoSupport implements CourseDao {

    @Transactional
    public void store(Course course) {
        getJpaTemplate().merge(course);
    }

    @Transactional
    public void delete(Long courseId) {
        Course course = getJpaTemplate().find(Course.class, courseId);
        getJpaTemplate().remove(course);
    }
```

```
    @Transactional(readOnly = true)
    public Course findById(Long courseId) {
        return getJpaTemplate().find(Course.class, courseId);
    }

    @Transactional(readOnly = true)
    public List<Course> findAll() {
        return getJpaTemplate().find("from Course");
    }
}
```

As `JpaCourseDao` inherits both `setEntityManagerFactory()` and `setJpaTemplate()`, you can inject either of them into your DAO. If you inject an entity manager factory, you will be able to delete the `JpaTemplate` declaration.

```
<bean name="courseDao"
    class="com.apress.springrecipes.course.jpa.JpaCourseDao">
    <property name="entityManagerFactory" ref="entityManagerFactory" />
</bean>
```

9-4. Persisting Objects with Hibernate's Contextual Sessions

Problem

Spring's `HibernateTemplate` can simplify your DAO implementation by managing sessions and transactions for you. However, using `HibernateTemplate` means your DAO has to depend on Spring's API.

Solution

An alternative to Spring's `HibernateTemplate` is to use Hibernate's contextual sessions. In Hibernate 3, a session factory is able to manage contextual sessions for you and allows you to retrieve them by the `getCurrentSession()` method. Within a single transaction, you will get the same session for each `getCurrentSession()` method call. This ensures that there will be only one Hibernate session per transaction, so it works nicely with Spring's transaction management support.

How It Works

To use the contextual session approach, your DAO methods require access to the session factory, which can be injected via a setter method or a constructor argument. Then, in each DAO method, you get the contextual session from the session factory and use it for object persistence.

```
package com.apress.springrecipes.course.hibernate;
...
import org.hibernate.Query;
import org.hibernate.SessionFactory;
import org.springframework.transaction.annotation.Transactional;
```

```
public class HibernateCourseDao implements CourseDao {

    private SessionFactory sessionFactory;

    public void setSessionFactory(SessionFactory sessionFactory) {
        this.sessionFactory = sessionFactory;
    }

    @Transactional
    public void store(Course course) {
        sessionFactory.getCurrentSession().saveOrUpdate(course);
    }

    @Transactional
    public void delete(Long courseId) {
        Course course = (Course) sessionFactory.getCurrentSession().get(
                Course.class, courseId);
        sessionFactory.getCurrentSession().delete(course);
    }

    @Transactional(readOnly = true)
    public Course findById(Long courseId) {
        return (Course) sessionFactory.getCurrentSession().get(
                Course.class, courseId);
    }

    @Transactional(readOnly = true)
    public List<Course> findAll() {
        Query query = sessionFactory.getCurrentSession().createQuery(
                "from Course");
        return query.list();
    }
}
```

Note that all your DAO methods must be made transactional. You can achieve this by annotating each method or the entire class with @Transactional. This ensures that the persistence operations within a DAO method will be executed in the same transaction and hence by the same session. Moreover, if a service layer component's method calls multiple DAO methods, and it propagates its own transaction to these methods, then all these DAO methods will run within the same session as well.

In the bean configuration file for Hibernate (i.e., beans-hibernate.xml), you have to declare a HibernateTransactionManager instance for this application and enable declarative transaction management via <tx:annotation-driven>.

```
<beans xmlns="http://www.springframework.org/schema/beans"
    xmlns:xsi="http://www.w3.org/2001/XMLSchema-instance"
    xmlns:tx="http://www.springframework.org/schema/tx"
    xsi:schemaLocation="http://www.springframework.org/schema/beans
```

```
        http://www.springframework.org/schema/beans/spring-beans-2.5.xsd
        http://www.springframework.org/schema/tx
        http://www.springframework.org/schema/tx/spring-tx-2.5.xsd">
    ...
    <tx:annotation-driven />

    <bean id="transactionManager"
        class="org.springframework.orm.hibernate3.HibernateTransactionManager">
        <property name="sessionFactory" ref="sessionFactory" />
    </bean>

    <bean name="courseDao"
        class="com.apress.springrecipes.course.hibernate.HibernateCourseDao">
        <property name="sessionFactory" ref="sessionFactory" />
    </bean>
</beans>
```

HibernateTemplate will translate the native Hibernate exceptions into exceptions in Spring's DataAccessException hierarchy. This allows consistent exception handling for different data access strategies in Spring. However, when calling the native methods on a Hibernate session, the exceptions thrown will be of native type HibernateException. If you want the Hibernate exceptions to be translated into Spring's DataAccessException for consistent exception handling, you have to apply the @Repository annotation to your DAO class that requires exception translation.

```
package com.apress.springrecipes.course.hibernate;
...
import org.springframework.stereotype.Repository;

@Repository
public class HibernateCourseDao implements CourseDao {
    ...
}
```

Then register a PersistenceExceptionTranslationPostProcessor instance to translate the native Hibernate exceptions into data access exceptions in Spring's DataAccessException hierarchy. This bean post processor will only translate exceptions for beans annotated with @Repository.

```
<beans ...>
    ...
    <bean class="org.springframework.dao.annotation.➥
        PersistenceExceptionTranslationPostProcessor" />
</beans>
```

In Spring 2.5, @Repository is a stereotype annotation. By annotating this, a component class can be auto-detected through component scanning. You can assign a component name in this annotation and have the session factory auto-wired by the Spring IoC container with @Autowired.

```
package com.apress.springrecipes.course.hibernate;
...
import org.hibernate.SessionFactory;
import org.springframework.beans.factory.annotation.Autowired;
import org.springframework.stereotype.Repository;

@Repository("courseDao")
public class HibernateCourseDao implements CourseDao {

    private SessionFactory sessionFactory;

    @Autowired
    public void setSessionFactory(SessionFactory sessionFactory) {
        this.sessionFactory = sessionFactory;
    }
    ...
}
```

Then, you can simply enable the `<context:component-scan>` element and delete the original `HibernateCourseDao` bean declaration.

```
<beans xmlns="http://www.springframework.org/schema/beans"
    xmlns:xsi="http://www.w3.org/2001/XMLSchema-instance"
    xmlns:context="http://www.springframework.org/schema/context"
    xmlns:tx="http://www.springframework.org/schema/tx"
    xsi:schemaLocation="http://www.springframework.org/schema/beans
        http://www.springframework.org/schema/beans/spring-beans-2.5.xsd
        http://www.springframework.org/schema/context
        http://www.springframework.org/schema/context/spring-context-2.5.xsd
        http://www.springframework.org/schema/tx
        http://www.springframework.org/schema/tx/spring-tx-2.5.xsd">

    <context:component-scan
        base-package="com.apress.springrecipes.course.hibernate" />
    ...
</beans>
```

9-5. Persisting Objects with JPA's Context Injection

Problem

In a Java EE environment, a Java EE container is able to manage entity managers for you and inject them into your EJB components directly. An EJB component can simply perform persistence operations on an injected entity manager without caring much about the entity manager creation and transaction management.

Similarly, Spring provides JpaTemplate to simplify your DAO implementation by managing entity managers and transactions for you. However, using Spring's JpaTemplate means your DAO is dependent on Spring's API.

Solution

An alternative to Spring's JpaTemplate is to use JPA's context injection. Originally, the @PersistenceContext annotation is used for entity manager injection in EJB components. Spring can also interpret this annotation by means of a bean post processor. It will inject an entity manager into a property with this annotation. Spring ensures that all your persistence operations within a single transaction will be handled by the same entity manager.

How It Works

To use the context injection approach, you can declare an entity manager field in your DAO and annotate it with the @PersistenceContext annotation. Spring will inject an entity manager into this field for you to persist your objects.

```
package com.apress.springrecipes.course.jpa;
...
import javax.persistence.EntityManager;
import javax.persistence.PersistenceContext;
import javax.persistence.Query;

import org.springframework.transaction.annotation.Transactional;

public class JpaCourseDao implements CourseDao {

    @PersistenceContext
    private EntityManager entityManager;

    @Transactional
    public void store(Course course) {
        entityManager.merge(course);
    }

    @Transactional
    public void delete(Long courseId) {
        Course course = entityManager.find(Course.class, courseId);
        entityManager.remove(course);
    }

    @Transactional(readOnly = true)
    public Course findById(Long courseId) {
        return entityManager.find(Course.class, courseId);
    }
```

```
    @Transactional(readOnly = true)
    public List<Course> findAll() {
        Query query = entityManager.createQuery("from Course");
        return query.getResultList();
    }
}
```

You can annotate each DAO method or the entire DAO class with @Transactional to make all of these methods transactional. This ensures that the persistence operations within a DAO method will by executed in the same transaction and hence by the same entity manager.

In the bean configuration file for JPA (i.e., beans-jpa.xml), you have to declare a JpaTransactionManager instance and enable declarative transaction management via <tx:annotation-driven>. You have to register a PersistenceAnnotationBeanPostProcessor instance to inject entity managers into properties annotated with @PersistenceContext.

```
<beans xmlns="http://www.springframework.org/schema/beans"
    xmlns:xsi="http://www.w3.org/2001/XMLSchema-instance"
    xmlns:tx="http://www.springframework.org/schema/tx"
    xsi:schemaLocation="http://www.springframework.org/schema/beans
        http://www.springframework.org/schema/beans/spring-beans-2.5.xsd
        http://www.springframework.org/schema/tx
        http://www.springframework.org/schema/tx/spring-tx-2.5.xsd">
    ...
    <tx:annotation-driven />

    <bean id="transactionManager"
        class="org.springframework.orm.jpa.JpaTransactionManager">
        <property name="entityManagerFactory" ref="entityManagerFactory" />
    </bean>

    <bean name="courseDao"
        class="com.apress.springrecipes.course.jpa.JpaCourseDao" />

    <bean class="org.springframework.orm.jpa.support.➥
        PersistenceAnnotationBeanPostProcessor" />
</beans>
```

In Spring 2.5, a PersistenceAnnotationBeanPostProcessor instance will be registered automatically once you enable the <context:annotation-config> element. So, you can delete its explicit bean declaration.

```
<beans xmlns="http://www.springframework.org/schema/beans"
    xmlns:xsi="http://www.w3.org/2001/XMLSchema-instance"
    xmlns:context="http://www.springframework.org/schema/context"
    xmlns:tx="http://www.springframework.org/schema/tx"
    xsi:schemaLocation="http://www.springframework.org/schema/beans
        http://www.springframework.org/schema/beans/spring-beans-2.5.xsd
        http://www.springframework.org/schema/context
        http://www.springframework.org/schema/context/spring-context-2.5.xsd
```

```
        http://www.springframework.org/schema/tx
        http://www.springframework.org/schema/tx/spring-tx-2.5.xsd">

    <context:annotation-config />
    ...
</beans>
```

This bean post processor can also inject the entity manager factory into a property with the @PersistenceUnit annotation. This allows you to create entity managers and manage transactions by yourself. It's no different from injecting the entity manager factory via a setter method.

```
package com.apress.springrecipes.course.jpa;
...
import javax.persistence.EntityManagerFactory;
import javax.persistence.PersistenceUnit;

public class JpaCourseDao implements CourseDao {

    @PersistenceUnit
    private EntityManagerFactory entityManagerFactory;
    ...
}
```

JpaTemplate will translate the native JPA exceptions into exceptions in Spring's DataAccessException hierarchy. However, when calling native methods on a JPA entity manager, the exceptions thrown will be of native type PersistenceException, or other Java SE exceptions like IllegalArgumentException and IllegalStateException. If you want JPA exceptions to be translated into Spring's DataAccessException, you have to apply the @Repository annotation to your DAO class.

```
package com.apress.springrecipes.course.jpa;
...
import org.springframework.stereotype.Repository;

@Repository("courseDao")
public class JpaCourseDao implements CourseDao {
    ...
}
```

Then register a PersistenceExceptionTranslationPostProcessor instance to translate the native JPA exceptions into exceptions in Spring's DataAccessException hierarchy. You can also enable <context:component-scan> and delete the original JpaCourseDao bean declaration, as @Repository is a stereotype annotation in Spring 2.5.

```
<beans ...>
    ...
    <context:component-scan
        base-package="com.apress.springrecipes.course.jpa" />
```

```
    <bean class="org.springframework.dao.annotation.➥
        PersistenceExceptionTranslationPostProcessor" />
</beans>
```

9-6. Summary

In this chapter, you have learned how to integrate two popular ORM frameworks—Hibernate and JPA—into your Spring applications. Spring's support for different ORM frameworks is consistent, so you can easily apply these techniques to other ORM frameworks as well.

When using an ORM framework, you have to configure its resource factory (e.g., a session factory in Hibernate and an entity manager factory in JPA) with its API. Spring provides several factory beans for you to create an ORM resource factory as a singleton bean in the IoC container, so it can be shared between multiple beans via dependency injection. This resource factory can also take advantage of Spring's data access facilities, such as data sources and transaction managers.

When using an ORM framework on its own, you have to repeat certain routine tasks for each DAO operation. Spring simplifies an ORM framework's usage by providing template classes, DAO support classes, and transaction manager implementations. You can use them in a similar way for different ORM frameworks, as well as for JDBC.

For Hibernate and JPA, you can also use their plain APIs to implement DAOs that can be integrated with Spring's ORM support. In this way, your DAOs don't need to depend on Spring's API, and they can achieve the same benefits as using template classes.

In the next chapter, you will learn how to build web-based applications with the Spring MVC framework.

CHAPTER 10

Spring MVC Framework

In this chapter, you will learn web-based application development using the Spring MVC framework. Spring MVC is one of the most important modules of the Spring framework. It builds on the powerful Spring IoC container and makes extensive use of the container features to simplify its configuration. Most Spring MVC configurations are written in bean configuration files.

Model-view-controller (MVC) is a common design pattern in UI design. It decouples business logic from UIs by separating the roles of model, view, and controller in an application. *Models* are responsible for encapsulating application data for views to present. *Views* should only present this data, without including any business logic. *Controllers* are responsible for receiving requests from users and invoking back-end services for business processing. After processing, back-end services may return some data for views to present. Controllers collect this data and prepare models for views to present. The core idea of the MVC pattern is to separate business logic from UIs to allow them to change independently without affecting each other.

In a Spring MVC application, models usually consist of domain objects that are processed by the service layer and persisted by the persistence layer. Views are usually JSP templates written with Java Standard Tag Library (JSTL). In Spring 2.0 and prior versions, controllers have to extend one of Spring's controller classes. In Spring 2.5, controllers can be arbitrary Java objects annotated with Spring's controller annotations. Controllers have to interact with service layer components for business processing, which often have transaction management enabled.

Upon finishing this chapter, you will be able to develop Java web applications using Spring MVC. You will also understand Spring MVC's common controller and view types, and under which circumstances they should be applied. Moreover, you will be able to develop web applications using the annotation-based approach introduced in Spring 2.5.

10-1. Developing a Simple Web Application with Spring MVC

Problem

You would like to develop a simple web application with Spring MVC to learn the basic concepts and configurations of this framework.

Solution

The central component of Spring MVC is DispatcherServlet. As its name indicates, it mainly dispatches requests to appropriate handlers for them to handle the requests. It is the only servlet you need to configure in the web deployment descriptor. DispatcherServlet implements one of Sun's core Java EE design patterns called *front controller*. It acts as the front controller of the Spring MVC framework, and every web request must go through it so that it can manage the entire request-handling process.

When a web request is sent to a Spring MVC application, DispatcherServlet will first receive the request. Then it will organize different components configured in Spring's web application context to handle this request. Figure 10-1 shows the primary flow of request handling in Spring MVC.

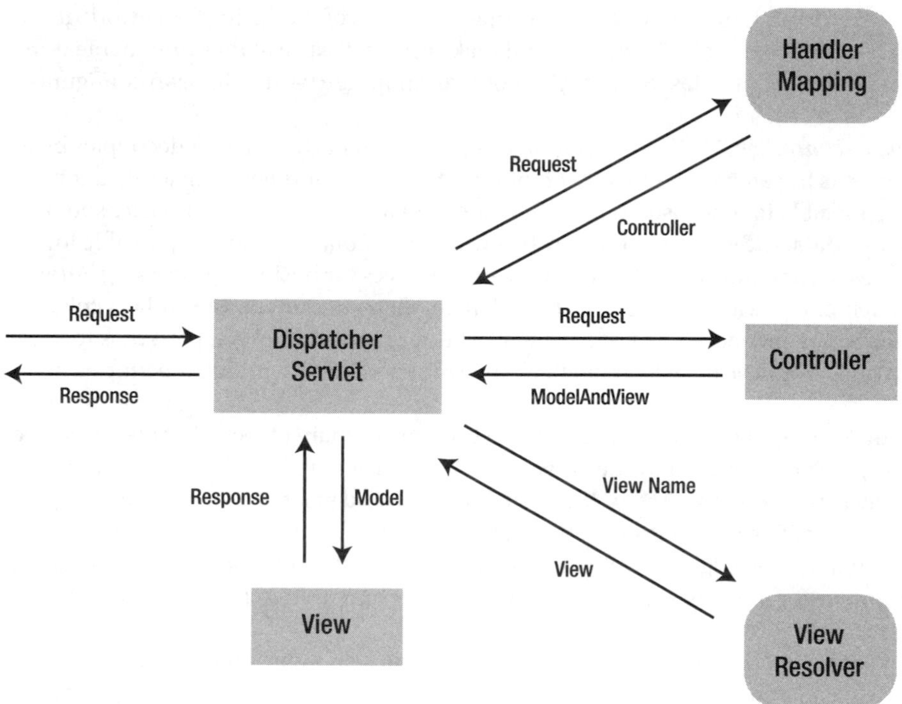

Figure 10-1. *Primary flow of request handling in Spring MVC*

When DispatcherServlet receives a request, it will first look for an appropriate handler to handle the request. DispatcherServlet maps each request to a handler by one or more handler mappings. A handler mapping is a bean configured in the web application context that implements the HandlerMapping interface. It is responsible for returning an appropriate handler for a request. Handler mappings usually map a request to a handler according to the request's URL.

Once DispatcherServlet has picked an appropriate handler, it will invoke this handler to handle the request. A handler is an arbitrary Java object that can handle web requests. The most typical handler used in Spring MVC for handling web requests is a *controller*. Usually, a controller has to invoke back-end services for request handling.

After a controller has finished handling the request, it returns a model and a view name, or sometimes a view object, to DispatcherServlet. The model contains the attributes that the controller wants to pass to the view for display. If a view name is returned, it will be resolved into a view object for rendering. The basic class that binds a model and a view is ModelAndView.

When DispatcherServlet receives a model and a view name, it will resolve the logical view name into a view object for rendering. DispatcherServlet resolves views from one or more view resolvers. A view resolver is a bean configured in the web application context that implements the ViewResolver interface. Its responsibility is to return a view object for a logical view name.

Once DispatcherServlet has resolved a view name into a view object, it will render the view object and pass in the model returned by the controller. The view's responsibility is to display the model attributes to the user.

How It Works

Suppose you are going to develop a court reservation system for a sports center. The UIs of this application are web-based so that users can make online reservations through the Internet. You will develop this application using Spring MVC. First of all, you create the following domain classes in the domain subpackage:

```
package com.apress.springrecipes.court.domain;
...
public class Reservation {

    private String courtName;
    private Date date;
    private int hour;
    private Player player;
    private SportType sportType;

    // Constructors, Getters and Setters
    ...
}

package com.apress.springrecipes.court.domain;

public class Player {

    private String name;
    private String phone;

    // Constructors, Getters and Setters
    ...
}

package com.apress.springrecipes.court.domain;

public class SportType {
```

```
    private int id;
    private String name;

    // Constructors, Getters and Setters
    ...
}
```

Then you define the following service interface in the service subpackage to provide reservation services to the presentation layer:

```
package com.apress.springrecipes.court.service;
...
public interface ReservationService {

    public List<Reservation> query(String courtName);
}
```

In a production application, you should implement this interface with database persistence. But for simplicity's sake, you can store the reservation records in a list and hard-code several reservations for testing purposes:

```
package com.apress.springrecipes.court.service;
...
public class ReservationServiceImpl implements ReservationService {

    public static final SportType TENNIS = new SportType(1, "Tennis");
    public static final SportType SOCCER = new SportType(2, "Soccer");

    private List<Reservation> reservations;

    public ReservationServiceImpl() {
        reservations = new ArrayList<Reservation>();
        reservations.add(new Reservation("Tennis #1",
                new GregorianCalendar(2008, 0, 14).getTime(), 16,
                new Player("Roger", "N/A"), TENNIS));
        reservations.add(new Reservation("Tennis #2",
                new GregorianCalendar(2008, 0, 14).getTime(), 20,
                new Player("James", "N/A"), TENNIS));
    }

    public List<Reservation> query(String courtName) {
        List<Reservation> result = new ArrayList<Reservation>();
        for (Reservation reservation : reservations) {
            if (reservation.getCourtName().equals(courtName)) {
                result.add(reservation);
            }
        }
        return result;
    }
}
```

Setting Up a Spring MVC Application

Before you start developing a web-based application using Spring MVC, you have to set it up properly. In general, a web application developed with Spring MVC is set up in the same way as a standard Java web application, except that you have to add a couple of configuration files and required libraries specific to Spring MVC.

The Java EE specification defines the valid directory structure of a Java web application. For example, you have to provide a web deployment descriptor (i.e., `web.xml`) in the `WEB-INF` root. The class files and JAR files for this web application should be put in the `WEB-INF/classes` and `WEB-INF/lib` directories, respectively.

For your court reservation system, you create the following directory structure. Note that the highlighted files are Spring-specific configuration files.

■ **Note** To develop a web application with Spring MVC, you have to copy `spring-webmvc.jar` (located in the `dist/modules` directory of the Spring installation) to the `WEB-INF/lib` directory. If you are going to use JSTL in your JSP files, you also have to copy `standard.jar` (located in `lib/jakarta-taglibs`) and `jstl.jar` (located in `lib/j2ee`).

```
court/
    css/
    images/
    WEB-INF/
        classes/
        lib/
            commons-logging.jar
            jstl.jar
            spring-webmvc.jar
            spring.jar
            standard.jar
        jsp/
            welcome.jsp
            reservationQuery.jsp
        court-service.xml
        court-servlet.xml
        web.xml
```

The files outside the `WEB-INF` directory are directly accessible to users via URLs, so the CSS files and image files should be put there. When using Spring MVC, the JSP files will act as templates only. They are read by the framework for generating dynamic content but not by users, so the JSP files should be put inside the `WEB-INF` directory to prevent direct access to them. However, some application servers don't allow the files inside `WEB-INF` to be read by a web application internally. In that case, you can only put them outside the `WEB-INF` directory.

Creating the Configuration Files

The web deployment descriptor `web.xml` is the essential configuration file for a Java web application. In this file, you define the servlets for your application and how web requests are mapped to them. For a Spring MVC application, you only have to define a single `DispatcherServlet` instance that acts as the front controller of Spring MVC, although you are allowed to define more than one.

```
<web-app version="2.4" xmlns="http://java.sun.com/xml/ns/j2ee"
    xmlns:xsi="http://www.w3.org/2001/XMLSchema-instance"
    xsi:schemaLocation="http://java.sun.com/xml/ns/j2ee
        http://java.sun.com/xml/ns/j2ee/web-app_2_4.xsd">

    <display-name>Court Reservation System</display-name>

    <servlet>
        <servlet-name>court</servlet-name>
        <servlet-class>
            org.springframework.web.servlet.DispatcherServlet
        </servlet-class>
        <load-on-startup>1</load-on-startup>
    </servlet>

    <servlet-mapping>
        <servlet-name>court</servlet-name>
        <url-pattern>*.htm</url-pattern>
    </servlet-mapping>
</web-app>
```

In this web deployment descriptor, you define a servlet of type `DispatcherServlet`. This is the core servlet class in Spring MVC that receives web requests and dispatches them to appropriate handlers. You set this servlet's name to `court` and map the URLs with `.htm` as the extension to it. Note that the URL extension is arbitrary, but in order to avoid revealing the implementation technology to the web application's users, it's generally preferred to pick `.htm`, `.html`, or something similar.

Another purpose of the servlet name is for `DispatcherServlet` to decide which file to load for Spring MVC configurations. By default, it will look for a file by joining the servlet name with `-servlet.xml` as the file name. You can explicitly specify a configuration file in the `contextConfigLocation` servlet parameter. With the preceding setting, the `court` servlet will load the Spring MVC configuration file `court-servlet.xml` by default. This file should be a standard Spring bean configuration file, as shown following:

```
<beans xmlns="http://www.springframework.org/schema/beans"
    xmlns:xsi="http://www.w3.org/2001/XMLSchema-instance"
    xsi:schemaLocation="http://www.springframework.org/schema/beans
        http://www.springframework.org/schema/beans/spring-beans-2.5.xsd">
    ...
</beans>
```

Later, you will configure Spring MVC with a series of Spring beans declared in this configuration file. You may also declare other application components such as data access objects and service objects in this file. However, it's not a good practice to mix beans of different layers in a single configuration file. Instead, you should declare one bean configuration file per layer (e.g., court-persistence.xml for the persistence layer and court-service.xml for the service layer). For example, court-service.xml should include the following service object:

```
<beans xmlns="http://www.springframework.org/schema/beans"
    xmlns:xsi="http://www.w3.org/2001/XMLSchema-instance"
    xsi:schemaLocation="http://www.springframework.org/schema/beans
        http://www.springframework.org/schema/beans/spring-beans-2.5.xsd">

    <bean id="reservationService"
        class="com.apress.springrecipes.court.service.ReservationServiceImpl" />
</beans>
```

In order for Spring to load your configuration files besides court-servlet.xml, you need to define the servlet listener ContextLoaderListener in web.xml. By default, it loads the bean configuration file /WEB-INF/applicationContext.xml, but you can specify your own in the context parameter contextConfigLocation. You can specify multiple configuration files by separating their locations with either commas or spaces.

```
<web-app ...>
    <context-param>
        <param-name>contextConfigLocation</param-name>
        <param-value>/WEB-INF/court-service.xml</param-value>
    </context-param>

    <listener>
        <listener-class>
            org.springframework.web.context.ContextLoaderListener
        </listener-class>
    </listener>
    ...
</web-app>
```

Note that ContextLoaderListener loads the specified bean configuration files into the root application context, while each DispatcherServlet instance loads its configuration file into its own application context and refers to the root application context as its parent. So, the context loaded by each DispatcherServlet instance can access and even override beans declared in the root application context (but not vice versa). However, the contexts loaded by the DispatcherServlet instances cannot access each other.

Creating Spring MVC Controllers

Spring MVC provides many types of controllers for different usage scenarios. Figure 10-2 shows the common controller types in Spring MVC.

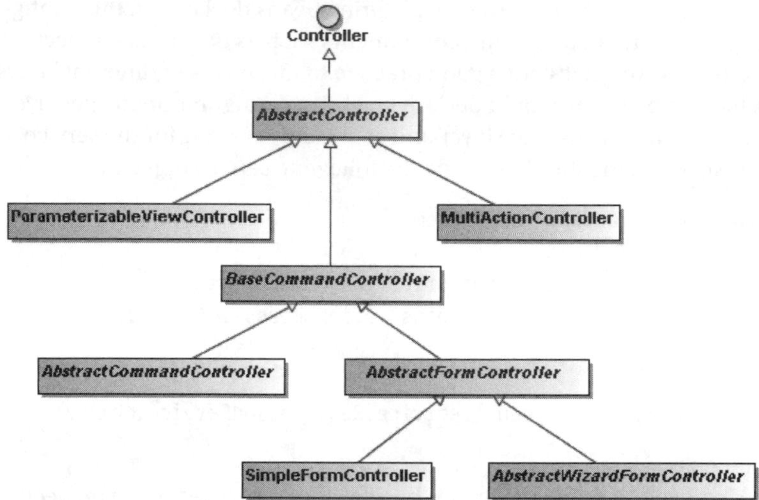

Figure 10-2. *Common controller types in Spring MVC*

The `Controller` interface is the base interface for all the controller classes in Spring MVC. You can create your own controller by implementing this interface. In the `handleRequest()` method, you are free to handle a web request just as you do in a servlet. Finally, you have to return a `ModelAndView` object that includes a view name or a view object, and some model attributes. For example, you can create a welcome controller for your court reservation system as follows.

■ **Note** To develop a web application that involves the Servlet API, you have to include `servlet-api.jar` (located in the `lib/j2ee` directory of the Spring installation) in your classpath.

```
package com.apress.springrecipes.court.web;
...
import javax.servlet.http.HttpServletRequest;
import javax.servlet.http.HttpServletResponse;

import org.springframework.web.servlet.ModelAndView;
import org.springframework.web.servlet.mvc.Controller;

public class WelcomeController implements Controller {

    public ModelAndView handleRequest(HttpServletRequest request,
            HttpServletResponse response) throws Exception {
        Date today = new Date();
        return new ModelAndView("welcome", "today", today);
    }
}
```

This controller simply creates a java.util.Date object to retrieve the current date, and then returns a ModelAndView object including the view name welcome and the current date as a model attribute for the target view to display.

After you create a controller class, you have to declare its instance in the web application context. As this is a presentation layer component, you should declare it in court-servlet.xml. By default, DispatcherServlet uses BeanNameUrlHandlerMapping as its default handler mapping if you don't configure one explicitly. This handler mapping maps requests to handlers according to the URL patterns specified in the bean names of the handlers. As a <bean> element's id attribute cannot contain the / character, you should use the name attribute instead.

```
<bean name="/welcome.htm"
    class="com.apress.springrecipes.court.web.WelcomeController" />
```

If you would like your controller to have some basic controller features like filtering the supported HTTP methods (GET, POST, and HEAD) and generating the cache-control header in HTTP responses, you can have it extend the AbstractController class, which implements the Controller interface. Note that the method you have to override in this controller class is handleRequestInternal().

```
package com.apress.springrecipes.court.web;
...
import org.springframework.web.servlet.mvc.AbstractController;

public class WelcomeController extends AbstractController {

    public ModelAndView handleRequestInternal(HttpServletRequest request,
            HttpServletResponse response) throws Exception {
        Date today = new Date();
        return new ModelAndView("welcome", "today", today);
    }
}
```

You can set several properties inherited from the AbstractController class to achieve the mentioned features:

```
<bean name="/welcome.htm"
    class="com.apress.springrecipes.court.web.WelcomeController">
    <property name="supportedMethods" value="GET" />
    <property name="cacheSeconds" value="60" />
</bean>
```

For example, you can set a controller's supported HTTP methods in the supportedMethods property, with commas as separators. If an HTTP request's method is not in this list, a ServletException will be thrown. You can also define the cache seconds for a controller so that it will be set in an HTTP response's header.

A typical controller may accept HTTP request parameters and invoke back-end services for business processing. For example, you can create a controller for querying reservations of a particular court as follows:

```
package com.apress.springrecipes.court.web;
...
import javax.servlet.http.HttpServletRequest;
import javax.servlet.http.HttpServletResponse;

import org.springframework.web.bind.ServletRequestUtils;
import org.springframework.web.servlet.ModelAndView;
import org.springframework.web.servlet.mvc.AbstractController;

public class ReservationQueryController extends AbstractController {

    private ReservationService reservationService;

    public void setReservationService(ReservationService reservationService) {
        this.reservationService = reservationService;
    }

    public ModelAndView handleRequestInternal(HttpServletRequest request,
            HttpServletResponse response) throws Exception {
        String courtName =
            ServletRequestUtils.getStringParameter(request, "courtName");

        Map<String, Object> model = new HashMap<String, Object>();
        if (courtName != null) {
            model.put("courtName", courtName);
            model.put("reservations", reservationService.query(courtName));
        }
        return new ModelAndView("reservationQuery", model);
    }
}
```

In this controller, you first retrieve the request parameter `courtName` from the request. You can make use of the standard Servlet API `HttpServletRequest.getParameter()` for this purpose, but Spring supplies more convenient static methods in the `ServletRequestUtils` class for you to retrieve request parameters of converted types and also required parameters. This can save you the trouble of performing conversion and checking. When you have more than one model attribute to pass to the view, you can store them in a map and pass this map to the constructor of `ModelAndView`.

Now you have to declare this controller in `court-servlet.xml`, referring to the reservation service bean declared in the service layer's configuration file (i.e., `court-service.xml`).

```
<bean name="/reservationQuery.htm"
    class="com.apress.springrecipes.court.web.ReservationQueryController">
    <property name="reservationService" ref="reservationService" />
</bean>
```

Creating JSP Views

Spring MVC supports many types of views for different presentation technologies. Figure 10-3 shows the common view types in Spring MVC.

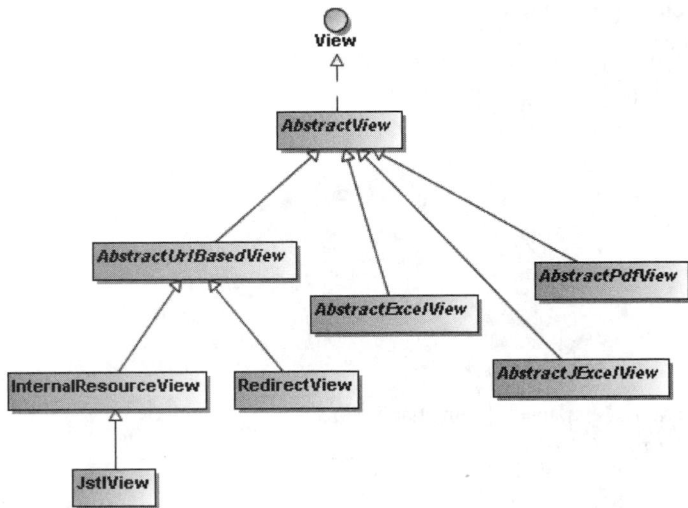

Figure 10-3. *Common view types in Spring MVC*

In a Spring MVC application, views are most commonly JSP templates written with JSTL. When `DispatcherServlet` receives a view name returned from a handler, it will resolve the logical view name into a view object for rendering. For example, you can configure an `InternalResourceViewResolver` bean in the web application context to resolve view names into JSP files in the `/WEB-INF/jsp/` directory:

```
<bean class="org.springframework.web.servlet.view.InternalResourceViewResolver">
    <property name="prefix" value="/WEB-INF/jsp/" />
    <property name="suffix" value=".jsp" />
</bean>
```

Then you can create the following JSP template for the welcome controller. You can name it `welcome.jsp` and put it in the `/WEB-INF/jsp/` directory:

```
<%@ taglib prefix="fmt" uri="http://java.sun.com/jsp/jstl/fmt" %>

<html>
<head>
<title>Welcome</title>
</head>

<body>
<h2>Welcome to Court Reservation System</h2>
Today is <fmt:formatDate value="${today}" pattern="yyyy-MM-dd" />.
</body>
</html>
```

In this JSP template, you make use of the fmt tag library in JSTL to format the today model attribute into the pattern yyyy-MM-dd. Don't forget to include the fmt tag library definition at the top of this JSP template.

Next, you can create another JSP template for the reservation query controller and name it reservationQuery.jsp to match the view name:

```
<%@ taglib prefix="c" uri="http://java.sun.com/jsp/jstl/core" %>
<%@ taglib prefix="fmt" uri="http://java.sun.com/jsp/jstl/fmt" %>

<html>
<head>
<title>Reservation Query</title>
</head>

<body>
<form method="POST">
Court Name
<input type="text" name="courtName" value="${courtName}" />
<input type="submit" value="Query" />
</form>

<table border="1">
  <tr>
    <th>Court Name</th>
    <th>Date</th>
    <th>Hour</th>
    <th>Player</th>
  </tr>
  <c:forEach items="${reservations}" var="reservation">
  <tr>
    <td>${reservation.courtName}</td>
    <td><fmt:formatDate value="${reservation.date}" pattern="yyyy-MM-dd" /></td>
    <td>${reservation.hour}</td>
    <td>${reservation.player.name}</td>
  </tr>
  </c:forEach>
</table>
</body>
</html>
```

In this JSP template, you include a form for users to input the court name they want to query, and then use the <c:forEach> tag to loop the reservations model attribute to generate the result table.

Deploying the Web Application

In a web application's development process, I strongly recommend installing a local Java EE application server that comes with a web container for testing and debugging purposes. For the sake of easy configuration and deployment, I have chosen Apache Tomcat 6.0 as my web container and created the context descriptor court.xml in its conf/Catalina/localhost directory, referring to my web application's root directory:

```
<Context docBase="c:/eclipse/workspace/Court/court" />
```

By default, Tomcat listens on port 8080 and uses the context descriptor's name (court in this case) as the context path, so the welcome controller and the reservation query controller can be accessed through the following URLs:

```
http://localhost:8080/court/welcome.htm
http://localhost:8080/court/reservationQuery.htm
```

10-2. Mapping Requests to Handlers

Problem

When DispatcherServlet receives a web request, it will simply dispatch the request to an appropriate handler for handling the request. You would like to define a strategy for DispatcherServlet to map requests to handlers.

Solution

In a Spring MVC application, web requests are mapped to handlers by one or more handler mapping beans declared in the web application context. These beans have to implement the HandlerMapping interface for DispatcherServlet to auto-detect them. Spring MVC comes with several HandlerMapping implementations for you to map requests using different strategies. By default, if you don't have a handler mapping configured explicitly, DispatcherServlet will use BeanNameUrlHandlerMapping as its default handler mapping, which maps requests to handlers according to the URL patterns specified in the bean names. So, if you are satisfied with this strategy, you don't need to define your own handler mappings.

Handler mappings match URLs according to their paths relative to the context path (i.e., the web application context's deployed path) and the servlet path (i.e., the path mapped to DispatcherServlet). So, for the URL http://localhost:8080/court/welcome.htm, the path to match is /welcome.htm, as the context path is /court and there's no servlet path.

How It Works

Mapping Requests by Bean Names

The simplest and default strategy to map requests to handlers is by the bean names of the handlers. For this strategy to work, you have to declare each handler's bean name as a form of URL pattern, which can accept wildcards for a handler to handle multiple URLs. If a handler's bean name matches a request's URL, DispatcherServlet will dispatch the request to this handler for it to handle the request.

```
<beans ...>
    ...
    <bean name="/welcome.htm"
        class="com.apress.springrecipes.court.web.WelcomeController">
```

```
    ...
    </bean>

    <bean name="/reservationQuery.htm"
        class="com.apress.springrecipes.court.web.ReservationQueryController">
        ...
    </bean>
</beans>
```

When using this mapping strategy, you have to set a handler's name via the name attribute, as the id attribute cannot contain the / character.

Mapping Requests by Controller Class Names

Another handler mapping provided by Spring is ControllerClassNameHandlerMapping, which generates handler mappings for handlers that implement the Controller interface. It generates mappings automatically according to the class names of the controllers declared in the web application context.

```
<beans ...>
    ...
    <bean class="org.springframework.web.servlet.mvc.support.➥
        ControllerClassNameHandlerMapping" />

    <bean class="com.apress.springrecipes.court.web.WelcomeController">
        ...
    </bean>

    <bean class="com.apress.springrecipes.court.web.ReservationQueryController">
        ...
    </bean>
</beans>
```

For these bean declarations, ControllerClassNameHandlerMapping will generate the handler mappings automatically by removing the Controller suffix in the class name and converting the remaining part to lowercase.

```
WelcomeController → /welcome*
ReservationQueryController → /reservationquery*
```

However, if you want your URL patterns to follow the variable-naming convention in Java (e.g., generating /reservationQuery* instead of /reservationquery*), you have to set the caseSensitive property to true. Besides, you can specify a prefix for the generated URL patterns in the pathPrefix property. You can also specify the base package in the basePackage property, and then the subpackage relative to it will be included in the mapping.

```
<bean class="org.springframework.web.servlet.mvc.support.➥
    ControllerClassNameHandlerMapping">
    <property name="caseSensitive" value="true" />
    <property name="pathPrefix" value="/reservation" />
```

```
    <property name="basePackage" value="com.apress.springrecipes.court" />
</bean>
```

This ControllerClassNameHandlerMapping definition will generate the following handler mappings:

```
WelcomeController → /reservation/web/welcome*
ReservationQueryController → /reservation/web/reservationQuery*
```

Mapping Requests with Custom Mapping Definitions

The most straightforward and flexible strategy for mapping requests to handlers is to specify the mapping definitions between URL patterns and handlers explicitly. You can achieve this with SimpleUrlHandlerMapping:

```
<beans ...>
    ...
    <bean class="org.springframework.web.servlet.handler.➥
        SimpleUrlHandlerMapping">
        <property name="mappings">
            <props>
                <prop key="/welcome.htm">welcomeController</prop>
                <prop key="/reservationQuery.htm">
                    reservationQueryController
                </prop>
            </props>
        </property>
    </bean>

    <bean id="welcomeController"
        class="com.apress.springrecipes.court.web.WelcomeController">
        ...
    </bean>

    <bean id="reservationQueryController"
        class="com.apress.springrecipes.court.web.ReservationQueryController">
        ...
    </bean>
</beans>
```

SimpleUrlHandlerMapping accepts the mapping definition as a Properties object. The property keys are the URL patterns while the property values are the handler IDs or names. The URL patterns can also accept wildcards for a handler to handle multiple URLs.

Mapping Requests by Multiple Strategies

In a web application with a large number of handlers, it is often insufficient to choose only one handler mapping strategy. Typically, ControllerClassNameHandlerMapping can satisfy most of the mappings. Usually, however, some of the mappings have to be mapped with

SimpleUrlHandlerMapping explicitly. In this case, you have to combine both strategies for handler mapping:

```
<beans ...>
    ...
    <bean class="org.springframework.web.servlet.handler.SimpleUrlHandlerMapping">
        <property name="mappings">
            <props>
                <prop key="/index.htm">welcomeController</prop>
                <prop key="/main.htm">welcomeController</prop>
            </props>
        </property>
        <property name="order" value="0" />
    </bean>

    <bean class="org.springframework.web.servlet.mvc.support.➥
        ControllerClassNameHandlerMapping">
        <property name="caseSensitive" value="true" />
        <property name="order" value="1" />
    </bean>
</beans>
```

When choosing more than one strategy at the same time, it's important to specify the mapping priority. You can set the order properties of the handler mapping beans for this purpose. The lower order value represents the higher priority. For these two handler mappings, web requests will be mapped to handlers as shown following:

```
/index.htm ➔ WelcomeController
/main.htm ➔ WelcomeController
/welcome* ➔ WelcomeController
/reservationQuery* ➔ ReservationQueryController
```

10-3. Intercepting Requests with Handler Interceptors

Problem

Servlet filters defined by the Servlet API can pre-handle and post-handle every web request before and after it's handled by a servlet. You would like to configure something with similar functions as filters in Spring's web application context to take advantage of the container features.

Moreover, sometimes you may want to pre-handle and post-handle only the web requests that will be handled by certain Spring MVC handlers, and manipulate the model attributes returned by these handlers before they are passed to the views.

Solution

Spring MVC allows you to intercept web requests for pre-handling and post-handling through *handler interceptors*. Handler interceptors are configured in Spring's web application context, so they can make use of any container features and refer to any beans declared in the container. A handler interceptor is registered for particular handler mappings, so it will only intercept requests mapped by these handler mappings.

Each handler interceptor must implement the HandlerInterceptor interface, which contains three callback methods for you to implement: preHandle(), postHandle(), and afterCompletion(). The first and second methods will be called before and after a request is handled by a handler. The second method also allows you to get access to the returned ModelAndView object, so you can manipulate the model attributes in it. The last method will be called after the completion of all request processing (i.e., after the view has been rendered).

How It Works

Suppose you are going to measure each web request's handling time by each request handler and allow the views to show this time to the user. You can create a custom handler interceptor for this purpose:

```
package com.apress.springrecipes.court.web;
...
import org.springframework.web.servlet.HandlerInterceptor;
import org.springframework.web.servlet.ModelAndView;

public class MeasurementInterceptor implements HandlerInterceptor {

    public boolean preHandle(HttpServletRequest request,
            HttpServletResponse response, Object handler) throws Exception {
        long startTime = System.currentTimeMillis();
        request.setAttribute("startTime", startTime);
        return true;
    }

    public void postHandle(HttpServletRequest request,
            HttpServletResponse response, Object handler,
            ModelAndView modelAndView) throws Exception {
        long startTime = (Long) request.getAttribute("startTime");
        request.removeAttribute("startTime");

        long endTime = System.currentTimeMillis();
        modelAndView.addObject("handlingTime", endTime - startTime);
    }

    public void afterCompletion(HttpServletRequest request,
            HttpServletResponse response, Object handler, Exception ex)
            throws Exception {
    }
}
```

In the preHandle() method of this interceptor, you record the start time and save it to a request attribute. This method should return true, allowing DispatcherServlet to proceed with request handling. Otherwise, DispatcherServlet assumes that this method has already handled the request, so DispatcherServlet will return the response to the user directly. Then, in the postHandle() method, you load the start time from the request attribute and compare it with the current time. You can calculate the total duration and then add this time to the model for passing to the view. Finally, as there is nothing for the afterCompletion() method to do, you can leave its body empty.

When implementing an interface, you must implement all the methods even though you may not have a need for all of them. A better way is to extend the interceptor adapter class instead. This class implements all the interceptor methods by default. You can override only the methods that you need.

```
package com.apress.springrecipes.court.web;
...
import org.springframework.web.servlet.ModelAndView;
import org.springframework.web.servlet.handler.HandlerInterceptorAdapter;

public class MeasurementInterceptor extends HandlerInterceptorAdapter {

    public boolean preHandle(HttpServletRequest request,
            HttpServletResponse response, Object handler) throws Exception {
        ...
    }

    public void postHandle(HttpServletRequest request,
            HttpServletResponse response, Object handler,
            ModelAndView modelAndView) throws Exception {
        ...
    }
}
```

A handler interceptor is registered to a handler mapping bean to intercept web requests mapped by this bean. You can specify multiple interceptors for a handler mapping in the interceptors property, whose type is an array. If you have more than one handler mapping configured in your web application context and you want to intercept all requests mapped by them, you must register this interceptor to each of them.

```
<beans ...>
    ...
    <bean id="measurementInterceptor"
        class="com.apress.springrecipes.court.web.MeasurementInterceptor" />

    <bean
        class="org.springframework.web.servlet.handler.SimpleUrlHandlerMapping">
        <property name="interceptors">
            <list>
                <ref bean="measurementInterceptor" />
            </list>
        </property>
```

```
        ...
    </bean>

    <bean class="org.springframework.web.servlet.mvc.support.➥
        ControllerClassNameHandlerMapping">
        <property name="interceptors">
            <list>
                <ref bean="measurementInterceptor" />
            </list>
        </property>
        ...
    </bean>
</beans>
```

Then you can show this time in `welcome.jsp` to verify this interceptor's functionality. As `WelcomeController` doesn't have much to do, you may likely see that the handling time is 0 milliseconds. If this is the case, you may add a `sleep` statement to this class to see a longer handling time.

```
<%@ taglib prefix="fmt" uri="http://java.sun.com/jsp/jstl/fmt" %>

<html>
<head>
<title>Welcome</title>
</head>

<body>
...
<hr />
Handling time : ${handlingTime} ms
</body>
</html>
```

10-4. Resolving User Locales

Problem

In order for your web application to support internationalization, you have to identify each user's preferred locale and display contents according to this locale.

Solution

In a Spring MVC application, a user's locale is identified by a locale resolver, which has to implement the `LocaleResolver` interface. Spring MVC comes with several `LocaleResolver` implementations for you to resolve locales by different criteria. Alternatively, you may create your own custom locale resolver by implementing this interface.

You can define a locale resolver simply by registering a bean of type `LocaleResolver` in the web application context. You must set the bean name of the locale resolver to `localeResolver` for DispatcherServlet to auto-detect. Note that you can register only one locale resolver per DispatcherServlet.

How It Works

Resolving Locales by an HTTP Request Header

The default locale resolver used by Spring is AcceptHeaderLocaleResolver. It resolves locales by inspecting the accept-language header of an HTTP request. This header is set by a user's web browser according to the locale setting of the underlying operating system. Note that this locale resolver cannot change a user's locale because it is unable to modify the locale setting of the user's operating system.

Resolving Locales by a Session Attribute

Another option of resolving locales is by SessionLocaleResolver. It resolves locales by inspecting a predefined attribute in a user's session. If the session attribute doesn't exist, this locale resolver will determine the default locale from the accept-language HTTP header.

```
<bean id="localeResolver"
    class="org.springframework.web.servlet.i18n.SessionLocaleResolver">
    <property name="defaultLocale" value="en" />
</bean>
```

You can set the defaultLocale property for this resolver in case the session attribute doesn't exist. Note that this locale resolver is able to change a user's locale by altering the session attribute that stores the locale.

Resolving Locales by a Cookie

You can also use CookieLocaleResolver to resolve locales by inspecting a cookie in a user's browser. If the cookie doesn't exist, this locale resolver will determine the default locale from the accept-language HTTP header.

```
<bean id="localeResolver"
    class="org.springframework.web.servlet.i18n.CookieLocaleResolver" />
```

The cookie used by this locale resolver can be customized by setting the cookieName and cookieMaxAge properties. The cookieMaxAge property indicates how many seconds this cookie should be persisted. The value -1 indicates that this cookie will be invalid after the browser is closed.

```
<bean id="localeResolver"
    class="org.springframework.web.servlet.i18n.CookieLocaleResolver">
    <property name="cookieName" value="language" />
    <property name="cookieMaxAge" value="3600" />
    <property name="defaultLocale" value="en" />
</bean>
```

You can also set the defaultLocale property for this resolver in case the cookie doesn't exist in a user's browser. This locale resolver is able to change a user's locale by altering the cookie that stores the locale.

Changing a User's Locale

In addition to changing a user's locale by calling LocaleResolver.setLocale() explicitly, you can also apply LocaleChangeInterceptor to your handler mappings. This interceptor will detect if a special parameter is present in the current HTTP request. The parameter name can be customized with the paramName property of this interceptor. If such a parameter is present in the current request, this interceptor will change the user's locale according to the parameter value.

```
<beans ...>
    ...
    <bean id="localeChangeInterceptor"
        class="org.springframework.web.servlet.i18n.LocaleChangeInterceptor">
        <property name="paramName" value="language" />
    </bean>

    <bean class="org.springframework.web.servlet.handler.SimpleUrlHandlerMapping">
        <property name="interceptors">
            <list>
                ...
                <ref bean="localeChangeInterceptor" />
            </list>
        </property>
        ...
    </bean>

    <bean class="org.springframework.web.servlet.mvc.support.➥
        ControllerClassNameHandlerMapping">
        <property name="interceptors">
            <list>
                ...
                <ref bean="localeChangeInterceptor" />
            </list>
        </property>
        ...
    </bean>
</beans>
```

LocaleChangeInterceptor can only detect the parameter for the handler mappings that enable it. So, if you have more than one handler mapping configured in your web application context, you have to register this interceptor to all of them to allow users to change their locales in any of the URLs.

Now a user's locale can be changed by any URLs with the language parameter. For example, the following two URLs change the user's locale to English for the United States, and to German, respectively:

```
http://localhost:8080/court/welcome.htm?language=en_US
http://localhost:8080/court/welcome.htm?language=de
```

Then you can show the HTTP response object's locale in `welcome.jsp` to verify the locale interceptor's configuration:

```
<%@ taglib prefix="fmt" uri="http://java.sun.com/jsp/jstl/fmt" %>

<html>
<head>
<title>Welcome</title>
</head>

<body>
...
<br />
Locale : ${pageContext.response.locale}
</body>
</html>
```

10-5. Externalizing Locale-Sensitive Text Messages

Problem

When developing an internationalized web application, you have to display your web pages in a user's preferred locale. You don't want to create different versions of the same page for different locales.

Solution

To avoid creating different versions of a page for different locales, you should make your web page independent of the locale by externalizing locale-sensitive text messages. Spring is able to resolve text messages for you by using a message source, which has to implement the `MessageSource` interface. Then your JSP files can use the `<spring:message>` tag, defined in Spring's tag library, to resolve a message given the code.

How It Works

You can define a message source simply by registering a bean of type `MessageSource` in the web application context. You must set the bean name of the message source to `messageSource` for `DispatcherServlet` to auto-detect. Note that you can register only one message source per `DispatcherServlet`.

The `ResourceBundleMessageSource` implementation resolves messages from different resource bundles for different locales. For example, you can register it in `court-servlet.xml` to load resource bundles whose base name is `messages`:

```
<bean id="messageSource"
    class="org.springframework.context.support.ResourceBundleMessageSource">
    <property name="basename" value="messages" />
</bean>
```

Then you create two resource bundles, messages.properties and messages_de.properties, to store messages for the default and German locales. These resource bundles should be put in the root of the classpath.

```
welcome.title=Welcome
welcome.message=Welcome to Court Reservation System
```

```
welcome.title=Willkommen
welcome.message=Willkommen zum Spielplatz-Reservierungssystem
```

Now, in a JSP file such as welcome.jsp, you can use the <spring:message> tag to resolve a message given the code. This tag will automatically resolve the message according to a user's current locale. Note that this tag is defined in Spring's tag library, so you have to declare it at the top of your JSP file.

```
<%@ taglib prefix="spring" uri="http://www.springframework.org/tags" %>

<html>
<head>
<title><spring:message code="welcome.title" text="Welcome" /></title>
</head>

<body>
<h2><spring:message code="welcome.message"
        text="Welcome to Court Reservation System" /></h2>
...
</body>
</html>
```

In <spring:message>, you can specify the default text to output when a message for the given code cannot be resolved.

10-6. Resolving Views by Names

Problem

After a handler has finished handling a request, it may return a view object or the logical name of this view object. In case it returns a view name, DispatcherServlet has to create the view object with this name and render it for the user. You would like to define a strategy for DispatcherServlet to resolve views by their names.

Solution

In a Spring MVC application, views are resolved by one or more view resolver beans declared in the web application context. These beans have to implement the ViewResolver interface for DispatcherServlet to auto-detect them. Spring MVC comes with several ViewResolver implementations for you to resolve views using different strategies.

How It Works

Resolving Views Based on URLs

The basic strategy of resolving views is to map them to URLs directly. The view resolver InternalResourceViewResolver maps each view name to a URL by adding a prefix and a suffix to it. To register InternalResourceViewResolver, you can declare a bean of this type in the web application context.

```
<bean class="org.springframework.web.servlet.view.InternalResourceViewResolver">
    <property name="viewClass"
        value="org.springframework.web.servlet.view.JstlView" />
    <property name="prefix" value="/WEB-INF/jsp/" />
    <property name="suffix" value=".jsp" />
</bean>
```

For example, InternalResourceViewResolver will resolve the view names welcome and reservationQuery in the following way:

```
welcome ➔ /WEB-INF/jsp/welcome.jsp
reservationQuery ➔ /WEB-INF/jsp/reservationQuery.jsp
```

The type of the resolved views can be specified by the viewClass property. By default, InternalResourceViewResolver resolves view names into view objects of type JstlView if the JSTL library (i.e., jstl.jar) is present in the classpath. So, you can simply omit the viewClass property if your views are JSP templates with JSTL tags.

InternalResourceViewResolver is simple, but it can only resolve internal resource views that can be forwarded by the Servlet API's RequestDispatcher (e.g., an internal JSP file or a servlet). As for other view types supported by Spring MVC, you have to resolve them using other strategies.

Resolving Views from an XML Configuration File

Another strategy for resolving views is to declare them as Spring beans and resolve them by their bean names. You can declare the view beans in the same configuration file as the web application context, but it would be better to isolate them in a separate configuration file. By default, XmlViewResolver loads view beans from /WEB-INF/views.xml, but this location can be overridden through the location property.

```
<bean class="org.springframework.web.servlet.view.XmlViewResolver">
    <property name="location">
        <value>/WEB-INF/court-views.xml</value>
    </property>
</bean>
```

In the court-views.xml configuration file, you can declare each view as a normal Spring bean by setting the class name and properties. In this way, you can declare any types of views (e.g., RedirectView and even custom view types).

```
<beans xmlns="http://www.springframework.org/schema/beans"
    xmlns:xsi="http://www.w3.org/2001/XMLSchema-instance"
    xsi:schemaLocation="http://www.springframework.org/schema/beans
        http://www.springframework.org/schema/beans/spring-beans-2.5.xsd">

    <bean id="welcome"
        class="org.springframework.web.servlet.view.JstlView">
        <property name="url" value="/WEB-INF/jsp/welcome.jsp" />
    </bean>

    <bean id="reservationQuery"
        class="org.springframework.web.servlet.view.JstlView">
        <property name="url" value="/WEB-INF/jsp/reservationQuery.jsp" />
    </bean>

    <bean id="welcomeRedirect"
        class="org.springframework.web.servlet.view.RedirectView">
        <property name="url" value="welcome.htm" />
    </bean>
</beans>
```

Resolving Views from a Resource Bundle

In addition to an XML configuration file, you can declare view beans in a resource bundle. ResourceBundleViewResolver loads view beans from a resource bundle in the classpath root. Note that ResourceBundleViewResolver can also take advantage of the resource bundle capability to load view beans from different resource bundles for different locales.

```
<bean class="org.springframework.web.servlet.view.ResourceBundleViewResolver">
    <property name="basename" value="views" />
</bean>
```

As you specify views as the base name of ResourceBundleViewResolver, the default resource bundle will be views.properties. In this resource bundle, you can declare view beans in the format of properties. This type of declaration is equivalent to the XML bean declaration, but it's less powerful.

```
welcome.(class)=org.springframework.web.servlet.view.JstlView
welcome.url=/WEB-INF/jsp/welcome.jsp

reservationQuery.(class)=org.springframework.web.servlet.view.JstlView
reservationQuery.url=/WEB-INF/jsp/reservationQuery.jsp

welcomeRedirect.(class)=org.springframework.web.servlet.view.RedirectView
welcomeRedirect.url=welcome.htm
```

Resolving Views with Multiple Resolvers

If you have a lot of views in your web application, it is often insufficient to choose only one view-resolving strategy. Typically, InternalResourceViewResolver can resolve most of the internal JSP views, but there are usually other types of views that have to be resolved by ResourceBundleViewResolver. In this case, you have to combine both strategies for view resolution.

```
<beans ...>
    ...
    <bean class="org.springframework.web.servlet.view.ResourceBundleViewResolver">
        <property name="basename" value="views" />
        <property name="order" value="0" />
    </bean>

    <bean
        class="org.springframework.web.servlet.view.InternalResourceViewResolver">
        <property name="prefix" value="/WEB-INF/jsp/" />
        <property name="suffix" value=".jsp" />
        <property name="order" value="1" />
    </bean>
</beans>
```

When choosing more than one strategy at the same time, it's important to specify the resolving priority. You can set the order properties of the view resolver beans for this purpose. The lower order value represents the higher priority. Note that you should assign the lowest priority to InternalResourceViewResolver because it will always resolve a view no matter whether it exists or not. So, other resolvers will have no chance to resolve a view if they have lower priorities.

Now the resource bundle views.properties should only contain the views that can't be resolved by InternalResourceViewResolver (e.g., the redirect views):

```
welcomeRedirect.(class)=org.springframework.web.servlet.view.RedirectView
welcomeRedirect.url=welcome.htm
```

The Redirect Prefix

If you have InternalResourceViewResolver configured in your web application context, it can resolve redirect views by using the redirect prefix in the view name. Then the rest of the view name will be treated as the redirect URL. For example, the view name redirect:welcome.htm will trigger a redirect to the relative URL welcome.htm. You may also specify an absolute URL in the view name.

10-7. Mapping Exceptions to Views

Problem

When an unknown exception occurs, your application server will usually display the evil exception stack trace to the user. Your users will have nothing to do with this stack trace and complain that your application is not user friendly. Moreover, it's also a potential security risk, as you may expose the internal method call hierarchy to users.

Solution

In a Spring MVC application, you can register one or more exception resolver beans in the web application context to resolve uncaught exceptions. These beans have to implement the `HandlerExceptionResolver` interface for `DispatcherServlet` to auto-detect them. Spring MVC comes with a simple exception resolver for you to map each category of exceptions to a view.

How It Works

Suppose your reservation service will throw the following exception due to a reservation not being available:

```
package com.apress.springrecipes.court.service;
...
public class ReservationNotAvailableException extends RuntimeException {

    private String courtName;
    private Date date;
    private int hour;

    // Constructors and Getters
    ...
}
```

To resolve uncaught exceptions, you can write your custom exception resolver by implementing the `HandlerExceptionResolver` interface. Usually, you'll want to map different categories of exceptions into different error pages. Spring MVC comes with the exception resolver `SimpleMappingExceptionResolver` for you to configure the exception mappings in the web application context. For example, you can register the following exception resolver in `court-servlet.xml`:

```
<bean class="org.springframework.web.servlet.handler.➥
    SimpleMappingExceptionResolver">
    <property name="exceptionMappings">
        <props>
            <prop key="com.apress.springrecipes.court.service.➥
                ReservationNotAvailableException">
                reservationNotAvailable
            </prop>
            <prop key="java.lang.Exception">error</prop>
        </props>
    </property>
</bean>
```

In this exception resolver, you define the logical view name `reservationNotAvailable` for `ReservationNotAvailableException`. If `InternalResourceViewResolver` is configured in your web application context, the following `reservationNotAvailable.jsp` page will be shown in case of a reservation not being available:

```
<%@ taglib prefix="fmt" uri="http://java.sun.com/jsp/jstl/fmt" %>

<html>
<head>
<title>Reservation Not Available</title>
</head>

<body>
Your reservation for ${exception.courtName} is not available on
<fmt:formatDate value="${exception.date}" pattern="yyyy-MM-dd" /> at
${exception.hour}:00.
</body>
</html>
```

In an error page, the exception instance can be accessed by the variable `${exception}`, so you can show the user more details on this exception.

It's a good practice to define a default error page for any unknown exceptions. You should map this page to the key `java.lang.Exception` as the last entry of the mapping, so it will be shown if no other entry has been matched before. Then create `error.jsp` as follows:

```
<html>
<head>
<title>Error</title>
</head>

<body>
An error has occurred. Please contact our administrator for details.
</body>
</html>
```

10-8. Constructing ModelAndView Objects

Problem

When a controller finishes handling a request, it usually returns a `ModelAndView` object that contains a view name or a view object, and some model attributes, to `DispatcherServlet`. Therefore, you often need to construct `ModelAndView` objects in controllers.

Solution

The `ModelAndView` class provides several overloaded constructors and convenient methods for you to construct a `ModelAndView` object in your favor. These constructors and methods support a view name and a view object in the similar way.

How It Works

When you have a single model attribute to return, you can simply construct a ModelAndView object by specifying the attribute in the constructor:

```
package com.apress.springrecipes.court.web;
...
import org.springframework.web.servlet.ModelAndView;
import org.springframework.web.servlet.mvc.AbstractController;

public class WelcomeController extends AbstractController {

    public ModelAndView handleRequestInternal(HttpServletRequest request,
            HttpServletResponse response) throws Exception {
        Date today = new Date();
        return new ModelAndView("welcome", "today", today);
    }
}
```

If there's more than one attribute to return, you can construct a ModelAndView object by passing in a map:

```
package com.apress.springrecipes.court.web;
...
import org.springframework.web.servlet.ModelAndView;
import org.springframework.web.servlet.mvc.AbstractController;

public class ReservationQueryController extends AbstractController {
    ...
    public ModelAndView handleRequestInternal(HttpServletRequest request,
            HttpServletResponse response) throws Exception {
        ...
        Map<String, Object> model = new HashMap<String, Object>();
        if (courtName != null) {
            model.put("courtName", courtName);
            model.put("reservations", reservationService.query(courtName));
        }
        return new ModelAndView("reservationQuery", model);
    }
}
```

Spring also provides ModelMap, a java.util.Map implementation that can automatically generate the names of model attributes according to their concrete types:

```
package com.apress.springrecipes.court.web;
...
import org.springframework.ui.ModelMap;
import org.springframework.web.servlet.ModelAndView;
import org.springframework.web.servlet.mvc.AbstractController;
```

```
public class ReservationQueryController extends AbstractController {
    ...
    public ModelAndView handleRequestInternal(HttpServletRequest request,
            HttpServletResponse response) throws Exception {
        ...
        ModelMap model = new ModelMap();
        if (courtName != null) {
            model.addAttribute("courtName", courtName);
            model.addAttribute("reservations",
                    reservationService.query(courtName));
        }
        return new ModelAndView("reservationQuery", model);
    }
}
```

As the types of these two model attributes are `String` and `List<Reservation>`, `ModelMap` will generate the default name `string` and `reservationList` for them. If you are not satisfied with these names, you can specify them explicitly.

After you construct a `ModelAndView` object, you can still add model attributes to it using the `addObject()` method. This method returns the `ModelAndView` object itself so that you can construct a `ModelAndView` object in one statement. Note that you can also omit the attribute name for the `addObject()` method. In this case, this method will generate the same attribute name as `ModelMap` will.

```
package com.apress.springrecipes.court.web;
...
import org.springframework.web.servlet.ModelAndView;
import org.springframework.web.servlet.mvc.AbstractController;

public class ReservationQueryController extends AbstractController {
    ...
    public ModelAndView handleRequestInternal(HttpServletRequest request,
            HttpServletResponse response) throws Exception {
        ...
        List<Reservation> reservations = null;
        if (courtName != null) {
            reservations = reservationService.query(courtName);
        }
        return new ModelAndView("reservationQuery", "courtName", courtName)
                .addObject("reservations", reservations);
    }
}
```

In fact, it is optional to return both a model and a view. In some cases, you may only return the view without any attributes in the model. Or you may return the model without the view and let Spring MVC determine it according to the request URL. Sometimes you may even return `null` if your controller handles the `HttpServletResponse` object directly, such as when streaming a binary file back to the user.

10-9. Creating a Controller with a Parameterized View

Problem

When creating a controller, you don't want to hard-code the view name in the controller class. Instead, you would like the view name to be parameterized so that you can specify it in the bean configuration file.

Solution

`ParameterizableViewController` is a subclass of `AbstractController` that defines a `viewName` property with both getter and setter methods. You can use this controller class directly for a controller that only renders a view to users without any processing logic, or you can extend this controller class to inherit the `viewName` property.

How It Works

For example, suppose you have a very simple controller whose purpose is only to render the about view. You can declare a controller of type `ParameterizableViewController` and specify the `viewName` property as `about`:

```
<bean id="aboutController"
    class="org.springframework.web.servlet.mvc.ParameterizableViewController">
    <property name="viewName" value="about" />
</bean>
```

Then you create `about.jsp` in `/WEB-INF/jsp/` as shown following:

```
<html>
<head>
<title>About</title>
</head>

<body>
<h2>Court Reservation System</h2>
<table>
  <tr>
    <td>Version:</td>
    <td>1.0</td>
  </tr>
</table>
</body>
</html>
```

If you would like to add some processing logic to your controller while preserving the parameterized view, your controller class can extend `ParameterizableViewController`. The following `AboutController` accepts an `email` property and includes it in the model:

```
package com.apress.springrecipes.court.web;
...
import org.springframework.web.servlet.ModelAndView;
import org.springframework.web.servlet.mvc.ParameterizableViewController;

public class AboutController extends ParameterizableViewController {

    private String email;

    public void setEmail(String email) {
        this.email = email;
    }

    protected ModelAndView handleRequestInternal(HttpServletRequest request,
            HttpServletResponse response) throws Exception {
        return new ModelAndView(getViewName(), "email", email);
    }
}
```

As AboutController extends ParameterizableViewController, it also has a viewName property that can be injected:

```
<bean id="aboutController"
    class="com.apress.springrecipes.court.web.AboutController">
    <property name="viewName" value="about" />
    <property name="email" value="reservation@court.com" />
</bean>
```

In about.jsp, you can show the email attribute taken from the model:

```
<html>
<head>
<title>About</title>
</head>

<body>
<h2>Court Reservation System</h2>
<table>
  ...
  <tr>
    <td>Email:</td>
    <td><a href="mailto:${email}">${email}</a></td>
  </tr>
</table>
</body>
</html>
```

As you have ControllerClassNameHandlerMapping configured in your web application context, you can access this controller through the following URL:

```
http://localhost:8080/court/about.htm
```

10-10. Handling Forms with Form Controllers

Problem

In a web application, you often have to deal with forms. A form controller has to show a form to a user and also handle the form submission. Form handling can be a very complex and variable task. You will get involved in too many form-handling details if you build your form controller from scratch.

Solution

The SimpleFormController class provided by Spring MVC defines the basic form-handling flow. It supports the concept of a command object and can bind form field values to a command object's properties of the same name. By extending the SimpleFormController class, your controller will inherit the ability to handle forms.

When SimpleFormController is asked to show a form by an HTTP GET request, it will render the form view to the user. Then when the form is submitted by an HTTP POST request, SimpleFormController will handle the form submission by binding the form field values to a command object and invoking the onSubmit() method. If the form is handled successfully, it will render the success view to the user. Otherwise, it will render the form view again with the errors.

To adapt to different form requirements, SimpleFormController allows you to customize the form-handling flow by overriding several life cycle methods.

How It Works

Suppose you would like to allow a user to make a court reservation by filling out a form. You first define a make() method in the ReservationService interface:

```
package com.apress.springrecipes.court.service;
...
public interface ReservationService {
    ...
    public void make(Reservation reservation)
            throws ReservationNotAvailableException;
}
```

Then you implement this make() method by adding a Reservation item to the list that stores the reservations. You throw a ReservationNotAvailableException in case of a duplicate reservation.

```
package com.apress.springrecipes.court.service;
...
public class ReservationServiceImpl implements ReservationService {
    ...
```

```
    public void make(Reservation reservation)
            throws ReservationNotAvailableException {
        for (Reservation made : reservations) {
            if (made.getCourtName().equals(reservation.getCourtName())
                    && made.getDate().equals(reservation.getDate())
                    && made.getHour() == reservation.getHour()) {
                throw new ReservationNotAvailableException(
                        reservation.getCourtName(), reservation.getDate(),
                        reservation.getHour());
            }
        }
        reservations.add(reservation);
    }
}
```

Creating a Form Controller

Now let's create a form controller to handle the court reservation form. By extending the `SimpleFormController` class, you can simply specify the command class (`Reservation` in this case) for this controller, and then the form field values will be bound to a command object's properties of the same name. You can also specify the name of the command object (`reservation` in this case) for the view to access, but this is optional, and the default name is `command`.

```
package com.apress.springrecipes.court.web;
...
import org.springframework.beans.propertyeditors.CustomDateEditor;
import org.springframework.web.bind.ServletRequestDataBinder;
import org.springframework.web.servlet.mvc.SimpleFormController;

public class ReservationFormController extends SimpleFormController {

    private ReservationService reservationService;

    public ReservationFormController() {
        setCommandClass(Reservation.class);
        setCommandName("reservation");
    }

    public void setReservationService(ReservationService reservationService) {
        this.reservationService = reservationService;
    }

    protected void initBinder(HttpServletRequest request,
            ServletRequestDataBinder binder) throws Exception {
        SimpleDateFormat dateFormat = new SimpleDateFormat("yyyy-MM-dd");
        dateFormat.setLenient(false);
```

```
        binder.registerCustomEditor(Date.class, new CustomDateEditor(
                dateFormat, true));
    }

    protected void doSubmitAction(Object command) throws Exception {
        Reservation reservation = (Reservation) command;
        reservationService.make(reservation);
    }
}
```

To bind form field values to a command object, a form controller may have to perform type conversions for the field values, as they are all submitted as strings. The type conversions are actually performed by property editors registered in this controller. Spring has preregistered several property editors to convert well-known data types such as numbers and Booleans. You have to register your custom editors for other data types such as `java.util.Date`. Custom property editors are registered to the `ServletRequestDataBinder` argument in the `initBinder()` method.

If there's anything wrong when binding the form field values, `SimpleFormController` will automatically render the form view again with the errors. Otherwise, it will call the `onSubmit()` method to handle the form submission. In the `onSubmit()` method, you can retrieve the created and bound command object through an argument. For this controller, it will be a `Reservation` object, as you have set the command class to `Reservation`. There are three variants of the `onSubmit()` method that you can override. You should override the simplest of them to get access to the method arguments that meet your needs.

```
protected ModelAndView onSubmit(Object command) throws Exception;

protected ModelAndView onSubmit(Object command, BindException errors)
    throws Exception;

protected ModelAndView onSubmit(HttpServletRequest request, HttpServletResponse
    response, Object command, BindException errors) throws Exception;
```

When overriding an `onSubmit()` method, you have to return a `ModelAndView` object. If you only need to perform an action on the command object and return the success view when this action completes, you can override the `doSubmitAction()` method instead, whose return type is `void`, and which will render the success view by default. In the preceding `doSubmitAction()` method, you pass the command object to `ReservationService` to make a reservation.

When you declare this controller, it requires a reference to the `reservationService` bean in the service layer to make reservations. In addition, you have to set the form view and success view for this form controller accordingly.

```
<bean id="reservationFormController"
    class="com.apress.springrecipes.court.web.ReservationFormController">
    <property name="reservationService" ref="reservationService" />
    <property name="formView" value="reservationForm" />
    <property name="successView" value="reservationSuccess" />
</bean>
```

Let's create the form view `reservationForm.jsp` first. It contains an HTML form with several form fields. In case of any binding or validation errors, `SimpleFormController` will redisplay the form view to the user and include the errors in the model for the view to access. You have to show the error messages and the original values entered by the user in your form view.

In Spring version 1.x, you had to use the `<spring:bind>` tag to bind each form field to a property of the command object, and then access the error message and original value using the expressions `${status.errorMessage}` and `${status.value}`. In Spring 2.x, you can use the powerful form tags defined in Spring's form tag library.

```
<%@ taglib prefix="form" uri="http://www.springframework.org/tags/form"%>

<html>
<head>
<title>Reservation Form</title>
<style>
.error {
  color: #ff0000;
  font-weight: bold;
}
</style>
</head>

<body>
<form:form method="POST" commandName="reservation">
<form:errors path="*" cssClass="error" />
<table>
  <tr>
    <td>Court Name</td>
    <td><form:input path="courtName" /></td>
    <td><form:errors path="courtName" cssClass="error" /></td>
  </tr>
  <tr>
    <td>Date</td>
    <td><form:input path="date" /></td>
    <td><form:errors path="date" cssClass="error" /></td>
  </tr>
  <tr>
    <td>Hour</td>
    <td><form:input path="hour" /></td>
    <td><form:errors path="hour" cssClass="error" /></td>
  </tr>
  <tr>
    <td colspan="3"><input type="submit" /></td>
  </tr>
</table>
</form:form>
</body>
</html>
```

The `<form:input>` and `<form:select>` tags can bind to a property path of the command object by specifying the `path` attribute. They will show the user the original value of the field, which is either the bound property value or the value rejected due to binding error. They must be used inside the `<form:form>` tag, which defines a form and binds to the command object by its name. If you don't specify the command object's name, then the default name `command` will be used. The `<form:error>` tag can show all the error messages for the specified property path. Putting an asterisk in the path indicates that all the errors will be shown.

Then you create the success view `reservationSuccess.jsp` to notify the user of a successful reservation:

```
<html>
<head>
<title>Reservation Success</title>
</head>

<body>
Your reservation has been made successfully.
</body>
</html>
```

In the form field–binding process, errors may occur due to invalid values. For example, if the date is not in a valid format as specified in `CustomDateEditor`, or an alphabetic character is presented for the hour, the preceding form controller won't be able to convert these fields. This controller will generate a list of selective error codes for each error. For an invalid value input in the `date` field, the following error codes will be generated:

```
typeMismatch.command.date
typeMismatch.date
typeMismatch.java.util.Date
typeMismatch
```

If you have `ResourceBundleMessageSource` defined, you can include the following error messages in your resource bundle for the appropriate locale (e.g., `messages.properties` for the default locale):

```
typeMismatch.date=Invalid date format
typeMismatch.hour=Invalid hour format
```

As you have `ControllerClassNameHandlerMapping` configured in your web application context, you can access this controller through the following URL:

```
http://localhost:8080/court/reservationForm.htm
```

When you enter this URL in your browser, it will send an HTTP `GET` request to your web application. This form controller will render the form view for this request. After you have filled in the form fields, you submit the form with an HTTP `POST` request. Then this form controller will handle your form submission. If the form is handled successfully, it will render the success view. Otherwise, it will render the form view again with the errors.

Applying the Post/Redirect/Get Design Pattern

However, when you refresh the web page in the form success view, the form you just submitted will be resubmitted again. This problem is known as *duplicate form submission*. To avoid this problem, you can apply the *post/redirect/get* design pattern, which recommends redirecting to another URL after a form submission is handled successfully, instead of returning an HTML page directly.

First, you use ParameterizableViewController to define a controller that only renders the reservationSuccess view, which is mapped to reservationSuccess.jsp.

```
<bean id="reservationSuccessController"
    class="org.springframework.web.servlet.mvc.ParameterizableViewController">
    <property name="viewName" value="reservationSuccess" />
</bean>
```

Then you define an explicit mapping for this controller in SimpleUrlHandlerMapping, as ControllerClassNameHandlerMapping won't generate a mapping for a built-in Spring MVC controller:

```
<bean class="org.springframework.web.servlet.handler.SimpleUrlHandlerMapping">
    ...
    <property name="mappings">
        <props>
            ...
            <prop key="/reservationSuccess.htm">reservationSuccessController</prop>
        </props>
    </property>
</bean>
```

As you have ResourceBundleViewResolver configured in your web application context, you can define the following redirect view in views.properties in the classpath root:

```
reservationSuccessRedirect.(class)=➥
    org.springframework.web.servlet.view.RedirectView
reservationSuccessRedirect.url=reservationSuccess.htm
```

Finally, you specify this redirect view for the success view of ReservationFormController. Now when the form submission is handled successfully, the user will be redirected to another URL. Even if the user refreshes this page, it won't cause the duplicate form submission problem.

```
<bean id="reservationFormController"
    class="com.apress.springrecipes.court.web.ReservationFormController">
    <property name="reservationService" ref="reservationService" />
    <property name="formView" value="reservationForm" />
    <property name="successView" value="reservationSuccessRedirect" />
</bean>
```

Initializing the Command Object

You can specify a command class for SimpleFormController, and it will be instantiated for binding form field values. However, in some cases you may have to initialize the command object by yourself. For example, let's consider a situation where you are going to bind a player's name and phone to a Reservation object's player property:

```
<html>
<head>
<title>Reservation Form</title>
</head>

<body>
<form method="POST">
<table>
  ...
  <tr>
    <td>Player Name</td>
    <td><form:input path="player.name" /></td>
    <td><form:errors path="player.name" cssClass="error" /></td>
  </tr>
  <tr>
    <td>Player Phone</td>
    <td><form:input path="player.phone" /></td>
    <td><form:errors path="player.phone" cssClass="error" /></td>
  </tr>
  <tr>
    <td colspan="3"><input type="submit" /></td>
  </tr>
</table>
</form>
</body>
</html>
```

However, when the command class Reservation has just been instantiated, the player property is null, so it will cause an exception when rendering this form.

To solve this problem, you have to initialize the command object by yourself. You can override the formBackingObject() method of SimpleFormController for this purpose. The default implementation of this method is just to instantiate the command class. When you override this method, the command class is not necessary, as SimpleFormController won't instantiate this class for you any more.

```
package com.apress.springrecipes.court.web;
...
public class ReservationFormController extends SimpleFormController {
    ...
    public ReservationFormController() {
        // Don't need to specify the command class
        // setCommandClass(Reservation.class);
```

```
        setCommandName("reservation");
    }

    protected Object formBackingObject(HttpServletRequest request)
            throws Exception {
        Reservation reservation = new Reservation();
        reservation.setPlayer(new Player());
        return reservation;
    }
}
```

Another typical use of this method is to get certain request parameters to initialize the command object (e.g., retrieving an entity from an ORM framework by its ID). As an example, you may get a username parameter from the request and initial the player with this name:

```
package com.apress.springrecipes.court.web;
...
import org.springframework.web.bind.ServletRequestUtils;

public class ReservationFormController extends SimpleFormController {
    ...
    protected Object formBackingObject(HttpServletRequest request)
            throws Exception {
        Reservation reservation = new Reservation();
        String username =
            ServletRequestUtils.getStringParameter(request, "username");
        reservation.setPlayer(new Player(username, null));
        return reservation;
    }
}
```

Now when the form is shown, the username parameter will be prefilled into the player name field. You can test this with the following URL:

```
http://localhost:8080/court/reservationForm.htm?username=Roger
```

There are two additional properties related to the command object that you can configure. First, the bindOnNewForm property sets whether the request parameters should be bound to the command object when creating a new form. The process is much like the way in which you bind the username parameter to the player name field. The only difference is that the request parameters are bound to the properties of the same name. For example, you can enable this property in the constructor:

```
package com.apress.springrecipes.court.web;
...
public class ReservationFormController extends SimpleFormController {
    ...
    public ReservationFormController() {
        ...
```

```
        setBindOnNewForm(true);
    }
}
```

Now when the form is shown, the request parameters will be bound to the properties of the same name. You can test this with the following URL:

```
http://localhost:8080/court/reservationForm.htm?date=2008-01-14
```

The second property, `sessionForm`, sets whether the command object should be stored in the session. By default, this is `false` so that a new command object will be created on each request, even when rendering the form again due to binding errors. If this property is set to `true`, the command object will be stored in the session for subsequent uses, until the form completes successfully. Then this command object will be cleared from the session. This is usually used when the command object is a persistent object that needs to be identical across different requests for tracking changes.

```
package com.apress.springrecipes.court.web;
...
public class ReservationFormController extends SimpleFormController {
    ...
    public ReservationFormController() {
        ...
        setSessionForm(true);
    }
}
```

Providing Form Reference Data

When a form controller is requested to render the form view, it may have some types of reference data to provide to the form (e.g., the items to display in an HTML selection). Now suppose you would like to allow a user to select the sport type when reserving a court. You first define the `getAllSportTypes()` method in the `ReservationService` interface for retrieving all available sport types:

```
package com.apress.springrecipes.court.service;
...
public interface ReservationService {
    ...
    public List<SportType> getAllSportTypes();
}
```

Then you can simply implement this method by returning a hard-coded list:

```
package com.apress.springrecipes.court.service;
...
public class ReservationServiceImpl implements ReservationService {
    ...
    public static final SportType TENNIS = new SportType(1, "Tennis");
    public static final SportType SOCCER = new SportType(2, "Soccer");
```

```
    public List<SportType> getAllSportTypes() {
        return Arrays.asList(new SportType[] { TENNIS, SOCCER });
    }
}
```

When ReservationFormController is requested to show the reservation form, you have to include all the available sport types in the model for this form to display them in an HTML selection. You can override the referenceData() method of SimpleFormController for this purpose. You should put the reference data in a map and return it for this method. This map will be added to the model and passed to the form view automatically. The default implementation of the referenceData() method returns null.

```
package com.apress.springrecipes.court.web;
...
public class ReservationFormController extends SimpleFormController {
    ...
    protected Map referenceData(HttpServletRequest request) throws Exception {
        Map referenceData = new HashMap();
        List<SportType> sportTypes = reservationService.getAllSportTypes();
        referenceData.put("sportTypes", sportTypes);
        return referenceData;
    }
}
```

Then, in the form view, you can use Spring's <form:select> tag to define this HTML selection. You just specify the item list, item value, and item label for this tag, and it will generate the select options automatically.

```
<%@ taglib prefix="c" uri="http://java.sun.com/jsp/jstl/core" %>

<html>
<head>
<title>Reservation Form</title>
</head>

<body>
<form method="POST">
<table>
  ...
  <tr>
    <td>Sport Type</td>
    <td>
      <form:select path="sportType" items="${sportTypes}"
        itemValue="id" itemLabel="name" />
    </td>
    <td><form:errors path="sportType" cssClass="error" /></td>
  </tr>
  <tr>
    <td colspan="3"><input type="submit" /></td>
```

```
  </tr>
</table>
</form>
</body>
</html>
```

Binding Properties of Custom Types

When a form is submitted, `SimpleFormController` can help you to bind the form field values to a command object's properties of the same name. However, for properties of custom types, `SimpleFormController` won't be able to convert them unless you specify the corresponding property editors for them. For example, the sport type selection field will only submit the selected sport type ID. You will have to convert this ID into a `SportType` object with a property editor. First of all, you require the `getSportType()` method in `ReservationService` to retrieve a `SportType` object by its ID:

```
package com.apress.springrecipes.court.service;
...
public interface ReservationService {
    ...
    public SportType getSportType(int sportTypeId);
}
```

For testing purposes, you can simply implement this method with a switch/case statement:

```
package com.apress.springrecipes.court.service;
...
public class ReservationServiceImpl implements ReservationService {
    ...
    public SportType getSportType(int sportTypeId) {
        switch (sportTypeId) {
        case 1:
            return TENNIS;
        case 2:
            return SOCCER;
        default:
            return null;
        }
    }
}
```

Then you create the `SportTypeEditor` class to convert a sport type ID into a `SportType` object. This property editor requires `ReservationService` to perform the lookup.

```
package com.apress.springrecipes.court.domain;
...
import java.beans.PropertyEditorSupport;

public class SportTypeEditor extends PropertyEditorSupport {
```

```
    private ReservationService reservationService;

    public SportTypeEditor(ReservationService reservationService) {
        this.reservationService = reservationService;
    }

    public void setAsText(String text) throws IllegalArgumentException {
        int sportTypeId = Integer.parseInt(text);
        SportType sportType = reservationService.getSportType(sportTypeId);
        setValue(sportType);
    }
}
```

The last step is to register this property editor to your controller. You should register it to the `ServletRequestDataBinder` object in the `initBinder()` method.

```
package com.apress.springrecipes.court.web;
...
public class ReservationFormController extends SimpleFormController {
    ...
    protected void initBinder(HttpServletRequest request,
            ServletRequestDataBinder binder) throws Exception {
        SimpleDateFormat dateFormat = new SimpleDateFormat("yyyy-MM-dd");
        dateFormat.setLenient(false);
        binder.registerCustomEditor(Date.class, new CustomDateEditor(
                dateFormat, true));
        binder.registerCustomEditor(SportType.class, new SportTypeEditor(
                reservationService));
    }
}
```

Validating Form Data

`SimpleFormController` can help you to validate the command object after it binds the form field values. The validation is done by a validator object that implements the `Validator` interface. You can write the following validator to check if the required form fields are filled, and if the reservation hour is valid on holidays and weekdays:

```
package com.apress.springrecipes.court.domain;
...
import org.springframework.validation.Errors;
import org.springframework.validation.ValidationUtils;
import org.springframework.validation.Validator;

public class ReservationValidator implements Validator {

    public boolean supports(Class clazz) {
        return Reservation.class.isAssignableFrom(clazz);
    }
```

```
    public void validate(Object target, Errors errors) {
        ValidationUtils.rejectIfEmptyOrWhitespace(errors, "courtName",
                "required.courtName", "Court name is required.");
        ValidationUtils.rejectIfEmpty(errors, "date",
                "required.date", "Date is required.");
        ValidationUtils.rejectIfEmpty(errors, "hour",
                "required.hour", "Hour is required.");
        ValidationUtils.rejectIfEmptyOrWhitespace(errors, "player.name",
                "required.playerName", "Player name is required.");
        ValidationUtils.rejectIfEmpty(errors, "sportType",
                "required.sportType", "Sport type is required.");

        Reservation reservation = (Reservation) target;
        Date date = reservation.getDate();
        int hour = reservation.getHour();
        if (date != null) {
            Calendar calendar = Calendar.getInstance();
            calendar.setTime(date);
            if (calendar.get(Calendar.DAY_OF_WEEK) == Calendar.SUNDAY) {
                if (hour < 8 || hour > 22) {
                    errors.reject("invalid.holidayHour", "Invalid holiday hour.");
                }
            } else {
                if (hour < 9 || hour > 21) {
                    errors.reject("invalid.weekdayHour", "Invalid weekday hour.");
                }
            }
        }
    }
}
```

In this validator, you use utility methods such as `rejectIfEmptyOrWhitespace()` and `rejectIfEmpty()` in the `ValidationUtils` class to validate the required form fields. If any of these form fields is empty, these methods will create a *field error* that will be bound to the field. The second argument of these methods is the property name, while the third and fourth are the error code and default error message.

You also check whether the reservation hour is valid on holidays and weekdays. In case of invalidity, you should use the `reject()` method to create an *object error* that will be bound to the reservation object, not to a field.

To apply this validator to your controller, you just configure an instance of it, either as an inner bean or via a bean reference, in the `validator` property. If you have multiple validators to apply for a controller, you can set them in the `validators` property instead, whose type is an array.

```
<bean id="reservationFormController"
    class="com.apress.springrecipes.court.web.ReservationFormController">
    ...
    <property name="validator">
```

```
        <bean class="com.apress.springrecipes.court.domain.➥
            ReservationValidator" />
    </property>
</bean>
```

As your validators may create errors during validation, you should define messages for the error codes for displaying to the user. If you have ResourceBundleMessageSource defined, you can include the following error messages in your resource bundle for the appropriate locale (e.g., messages.properties for the default locale):

```
required.courtName=Court name is required
required.date=Date is required
required.hour=Hour is required
required.playerName=Player name is required
required.sportType=Sport type is required
invalid.holidayHour=Invalid holiday hour
invalid.weekdayHour=Invalid weekday hour
```

10-11. Handling Multipage Forms with Wizard Form Controllers

Problem

In a web application, you sometimes have to deal with complex forms that span multiple pages. Forms like this are usually called *wizard forms*, as users have to fill them page by page—just like using a software wizard. Undoubtedly, you can create one or more form controllers by extending SimpleFormController to handle a wizard form. However, you will have much to do if you maintain the form status across multiple pages.

Solution

The AbstractWizardFormController class provided by Spring MVC defines the basic tasks for wizard form handling. It also supports the concept of a command object and can bind form fields in multiple pages to a single command object's properties of the same name. By extending the AbstractWizardFormController class, your form controller will inherit the ability to handle wizard forms.

As there are multiple form pages for a wizard form, you have to define multiple page views for a wizard form controller. This controller will then manage the form status across all these form pages. In a wizard form, there are multiple actions instead of a single submit action in SimpleFormController. AbstractWizardFormController will determine a user's action by a special request parameter, usually specified as the name of a submit button:

_finish: Finish the wizard form.

_cancel: Cancel the wizard form.

_target*x*: Step to the target page, where *x* is the zero-based page index.

The AbstractWizardFormController class supports most of the same life cycle methods as SimpleFormController for you to customize the form-handling flow. In fact, they both extend the AbstractFormController base class.

How It Works

Suppose you would like to provide a function that allows a user to reserve a court at fixed hours periodically. You first define the PeriodicReservation class in the domain subpackage:

```
package com.apress.springrecipes.court.domain;
...
public class PeriodicReservation {

    private String courtName;
    private Date fromDate;
    private Date toDate;
    private int period;
    private int hour;
    private Player player;

    // Getters and Setters
    ...
}
```

Then you add a makePeriodic() method to the ReservationService interface for making a periodic reservation:

```
package com.apress.springrecipes.court.service;
...
public interface ReservationService {
    ...
    public void makePeriodic(PeriodicReservation periodicReservation)
            throws ReservationNotAvailableException;
}
```

The implementation of this method involves generating a series of Reservation objects from PeriodicReservation and passing each reservation to the make() method. Obviously in this simple application, there's no transaction management support.

```
package com.apress.springrecipes.court.service;
...
public class ReservationServiceImpl implements ReservationService {
    ...
    public void makePeriodic(PeriodicReservation periodicReservation)
            throws ReservationNotAvailableException {
        Calendar fromCalendar = Calendar.getInstance();
        fromCalendar.setTime(periodicReservation.getFromDate());

        Calendar toCalendar = Calendar.getInstance();
        toCalendar.setTime(periodicReservation.getToDate());
```

```
        while (fromCalendar.before(toCalendar)) {
            Reservation reservation = new Reservation();
            reservation.setCourtName(periodicReservation.getCourtName());
            reservation.setDate(fromCalendar.getTime());
            reservation.setHour(periodicReservation.getHour());
            reservation.setPlayer(periodicReservation.getPlayer());
            make(reservation);

            fromCalendar.add(Calendar.DATE, periodicReservation.getPeriod());
        }
    }
}
```

Creating Wizard Form Pages

Suppose you want to show users the periodic reservation form split across three different pages. Each page has a portion of the form fields. The first page is reservationCourtForm.jsp, which contains only the court name field for the periodic reservation.

```
<%@ taglib prefix="form" uri="http://www.springframework.org/tags/form"%>

<html>
<head>
<title>Reservation Court Form</title>
<style>
.error {
  color: #ff0000;
  font-weight: bold;
}
</style>
</head>

<body>
<form:form method="POST" commandName="reservation">
<table>
  <tr>
    <td>Court Name</td>
    <td><form:input path="courtName" /></td>
    <td><form:errors path="courtName" cssClass="error" /></td>
  </tr>
  <tr>
    <td colspan="3">
      <input type="submit" value="Next" name="_target1" />
      <input type="submit" value="Cancel" name="_cancel" />
    </td>
  </tr>
</table>
</form:form>
```

```
</body>
</html>
```

The form and input fields in this page are defined with Spring's `<form:form>` and `<form:input>` tags. They are bound to the command object and its properties. There's also an error tag for displaying the field error message to the user. Note that there are two submit buttons in this page. The Next button's name must be `_target1`. It asks the wizard form controller to step forward to the second page, whose page index is `1` (zero-based). The Cancel button's name must be `_cancel`. It asks the controller to cancel this form.

The second page is `reservationTimeForm.jsp`. It contains the date and time fields for a periodic reservation:

```
<%@ taglib prefix="form" uri="http://www.springframework.org/tags/form"%>

<html>
<head>
<title>Reservation Time Form</title>
<style>
.error {
  color: #ff0000;
  font-weight: bold;
}
</style>
</head>

<body>
<form:form method="POST" commandName="reservation">
<table>
  <tr>
    <td>From Date</td>
    <td><form:input path="fromDate" /></td>
    <td><form:errors path="fromDate" cssClass="error" /></td>
  </tr>
  <tr>
    <td>To Date</td>
    <td><form:input path="toDate" /></td>
    <td><form:errors path="toDate" cssClass="error" /></td>
  </tr>
  <tr>
    <td>Period</td>
    <td><form:select path="period" items="${periods}" /></td>
    <td><form:errors path="period" cssClass="error" /></td>
  </tr>
  <tr>
    <td>Hour</td>
    <td><form:input path="hour" /></td>
    <td><form:errors path="hour" cssClass="error" /></td>
  </tr>
```

```
  <tr>
    <td colspan="3">
      <input type="submit" value="Previous" name="_target0" />
      <input type="submit" value="Next" name="_target2" />
      <input type="submit" value="Cancel" name="_cancel" />
    </td>
  </tr>
</table>
</form:form>
</body>
</html>
```

There are three submit buttons in this form. The names of the Previous and Next buttons must be `_target0` and `_target2`, respectively. They ask the wizard form controller to step to the first page and the third page. The Cancel button asks the controller to cancel this form.

The third page is `reservationPlayerForm.jsp`. It contains the player information fields for a periodic reservation:

```
<%@ taglib prefix="form" uri="http://www.springframework.org/tags/form"%>

<html>
<head>
<title>Reservation Player Form</title>
<style>
.error {
  color: #ff0000;
  font-weight: bold;
}
</style>
</head>

<body>
<form:form method="POST" commandName="reservation">
<table>
  <tr>
    <td>Player Name</td>
    <td><form:input path="player.name" /></td>
    <td><form:errors path="player.name" cssClass="error" /></td>
  </tr>
  <tr>
    <td>Player Phone</td>
    <td><form:input path="player.phone" /></td>
    <td><form:errors path="player.phone" cssClass="error" /></td>
  </tr>
  <tr>
    <td colspan="3">
      <input type="submit" value="Previous" name="_target1" />
      <input type="submit" value="Finish" name="_finish" />
```

```
      <input type="submit" value="Cancel" name="_cancel" />
    </td>
  </tr>
</table>
</form:form>
</body>
</html>
```

There are three submit buttons in this form. The Previous button asks the wizard form controller to step back to the second page. The Finish button's name must be _finish. It asks the controller to finish this form. The Cancel button asks the controller to cancel this form.

Creating a Wizard Form Controller

Now let's create a wizard form controller to handle this periodic reservation form. Like SimpleFormController, AbstractWizardFormController also supports the concept of a command object. You can either specify a command class for it to instantiate or initialize the command object by yourself in the formBackingObject() method. Then the form field values will be bound to the command object's properties of the same name. For a wizard form controller, all the form fields in different pages will be bound to a single command object, which is stored in the session across multiple requests.

```
package com.apress.springrecipes.court.web;
...
import org.springframework.beans.propertyeditors.CustomDateEditor;
import org.springframework.validation.BindException;
import org.springframework.web.bind.ServletRequestDataBinder;
import org.springframework.web.servlet.ModelAndView;
import org.springframework.web.servlet.mvc.AbstractWizardFormController;

public class PeriodicReservationController extends AbstractWizardFormController {

    private ReservationService reservationService;

    public PeriodicReservationController() {
        setCommandName("reservation");
    }

    public void setReservationService(ReservationService reservationService) {
        this.reservationService = reservationService;
    }

    protected Object formBackingObject(HttpServletRequest request)
            throws Exception {
        PeriodicReservation reservation = new PeriodicReservation();
        reservation.setPlayer(new Player());
        return reservation;
    }
```

```
    protected void initBinder(HttpServletRequest request,
            ServletRequestDataBinder binder) throws Exception {
        SimpleDateFormat dateFormat = new SimpleDateFormat("yyyy-MM-dd");
        dateFormat.setLenient(false);
        binder.registerCustomEditor(Date.class, new CustomDateEditor(
                dateFormat, true));
    }

    protected Map referenceData(HttpServletRequest request, int page)
            throws Exception {
        Map referenceData = new HashMap();
        if (page == 1) {
            Map<Integer, String> periods = new HashMap<Integer, String>();
            periods.put(1, "Daily");
            periods.put(7, "Weekly");
            referenceData.put("periods", periods);
        }
        return referenceData;
    }

    protected ModelAndView processFinish(HttpServletRequest request,
            HttpServletResponse response, Object command, BindException errors)
            throws Exception {
        PeriodicReservation reservation = (PeriodicReservation) command;
        reservationService.makePeriodic(reservation);
        return new ModelAndView("reservationSuccessRedirect");
    }

    protected ModelAndView processCancel(HttpServletRequest request,
            HttpServletResponse response, Object command, BindException errors)
            throws Exception {
        return new ModelAndView("welcomeRedirect");
    }
}
```

In order for a wizard form controller to convert form field values before binding, you may have to register your custom property editors to the `ServletRequestDataBinder` object in the `initBinder()` method.

Recall that you have to display the available periods in an HTML selection in the second page, `reservationTimeForm.jsp`. You can override the `referenceData()` method to create a map for the period options, and then put it into the model. Remember to check the rendering page's index before you create the period map. Actually, a wizard form controller will call the `referenceData()` method before rendering each page.

In the `processFinish()` and `processCancel()` methods, you can get access to the command object bound with all the form field values via a method argument. To finish the wizard, you pass this object to `ReservationService` to make a periodic reservation, and then redirect to the `reservationSuccess` page. If the user cancels this wizard, you simply redirect the user to the welcome page.

When you declare this controller, it requires a reference to the reservationService bean in the service layer to make periodic reservations. In addition, you have to set all the pages in correct order for this wizard form controller.

```
<bean id="periodicReservationController"
    class="com.apress.springrecipes.court.web.PeriodicReservationController">
    <property name="reservationService" ref="reservationService" />
    <property name="pages">
        <list>
            <value>reservationCourtForm</value>
            <value>reservationTimeForm</value>
            <value>reservationPlayerForm</value>
        </list>
    </property>
</bean>
```

As you have ControllerClassNameHandlerMapping configured in your web application context, you can access this controller through the following URL:

```
http://localhost:8080/court/periodicReservation.htm
```

Validating Wizard Form Data

In a simple form controller, you validate the entire command object in one shot when the form is submitted. However, as there are multiple form pages for a wizard form controller, you have to validate each page when it's submitted. For this reason, you create the following validator, which splits the validate() method into several fine-grained validate methods, each of which validates fields in a particular page:

```
package com.apress.springrecipes.court.domain;

import org.springframework.validation.Errors;
import org.springframework.validation.ValidationUtils;
import org.springframework.validation.Validator;

public class PeriodicReservationValidator implements Validator {

    public boolean supports(Class clazz) {
        return PeriodicReservation.class.isAssignableFrom(clazz);
    }

    public void validate(Object target, Errors errors) {
        validateCourt(target, errors);
        validateTime(target, errors);
        validatePlayer(target, errors);
    }

    public void validateCourt(Object target, Errors errors) {
        ValidationUtils.rejectIfEmptyOrWhitespace(errors, "courtName",
```

```
                "required.courtName", "Court name is required.");
    }

    public void validateTime(Object target, Errors errors) {
        ValidationUtils.rejectIfEmpty(errors, "fromDate",
                "required.fromDate", "From date is required.");
        ValidationUtils.rejectIfEmpty(errors, "toDate", "required.toDate",
                "To date is required.");
        ValidationUtils.rejectIfEmpty(errors, "period",
                "required.period", "Period is required.");
        ValidationUtils.rejectIfEmpty(errors, "hour", "required.hour",
                "Hour is required.");
    }

    public void validatePlayer(Object target, Errors errors) {
        ValidationUtils.rejectIfEmptyOrWhitespace(errors, "player.name",
                "required.playerName", "Player name is required.");
    }
}
```

In a simple form controller, validation is performed automatically by invoking your registered validators. But in a wizard form controller, the registered validators will not be invoked automatically. Instead, you have to perform validation by overriding `validatePage()`. In this method, you have to invoke the registered validators manually:

```
package com.apress.springrecipes.court.web;
...
import org.springframework.validation.Errors;
import org.springframework.validation.ValidationUtils;
import org.springframework.web.servlet.mvc.AbstractWizardFormController;

public class PeriodicReservationController extends AbstractWizardFormController {
    ...
    protected void validatePage(Object command, Errors errors, int page) {
        PeriodicReservationValidator validator =
            (PeriodicReservationValidator) getValidator();
        switch (page) {
        case 0:
            validator.validateCourt(command, errors);
            break;
        case 1:
            validator.validateTime(command, errors);
            break;
        case 2:
            validator.validatePlayer(command, errors);
            break;
        }
    }
}
```

This method will be called each time a page is submitted, so you should validate individual pages one at a time by looking at the page index. Using a switch statement would be a good way of matching the page index. Before this will work, however, you have to configure an instance of the preceding validator in the validator property:

```
<bean id="periodicReservationController"
    class="com.apress.springrecipes.court.web.PeriodicReservationController">
    ...
    <property name="validator">
        <bean class="com.apress.springrecipes.court.domain.➥
            PeriodicReservationValidator" />
    </property>
</bean>
```

If there are binding or validation errors in a form page, the wizard form controller will redisplay this page with the error messages.

10-12. Grouping Multiple Actions into a Controller

Problem

With the one-controller-per-action approach, adding an action to your application means you have to configure one more controller in the web application context. To make your configurations simpler, you would like to minimize the number of controllers in your Spring MVC application.

Solution

The MultiActionController class provided by Spring MVC allows you to group multiple related actions into a single controller. Your controller can extend MultiActionController and include multiple handler methods to handle multiple actions.

In a multi-action controller, you can define one or more handler methods of the following form:

```
public (ModelAndView | Map | String | void) actionName(
    HttpServletRequest, HttpServletResponse [,HttpSession] [,CommandObject]);
```

The return type of a handler method can be ModelAndView (a model, and a view name or a view object), Map (a model only), String (a view name only), or void (the method itself handles the HTTP response directly).

When a request is mapped to a multi-action controller by handler mappings, it has to be narrowed down to a particular handler method within the controller. MultiActionController allows you to configure method mappings with a MethodNameResolver object.

How It Works

Suppose you are asked to develop a function to maintain the member list of the sports center. First, you define the Member domain class and the MemberService interface for the administrators to add, remove, and list members:

```
package com.apress.springrecipes.court.domain;

public class Member {

    private String name;
    private String phone;
    private String email;

    // Getters and Setters
    ...
}
```

```
package com.apress.springrecipes.court.service;
...
public interface MemberService {

    public void add(Member member);
    public void remove(String memberName);
    public List<Member> list();
}
```

For demo purposes, you can implement this interface by storing the members in a map with the member names as the keys. In a production application, you should store them in a database.

```
package com.apress.springrecipes.court.service;
...
public class MemberServiceImpl implements MemberService {

    private Map<String, Member> members = new TreeMap<String, Member>();

    public void add(Member member) {
        members.put(member.getName(), member);
    }

    public void remove(String memberName) {
        members.remove(memberName);
    }

    public List<Member> list() {
        return new ArrayList<Member>(members.values());
    }
}
```

Then you declare a bean instance of this type in the service layer configuration file (i.e., `court-service.xml`):

```
<bean id="memberService"
    class="com.apress.springrecipes.court.service.MemberServiceImpl" />
```

Creating a Multi-Action Controller

Although you can write a simple controller to handle each action, that would require configuring three more controllers in your web application context. As these controllers are very simple and closely related indeed, you should consider grouping them into a single controller by extending the `MultiActionController` class. Then you can declare multiple handler methods within this controller:

```
package com.apress.springrecipes.court.web;
...
import org.springframework.web.bind.ServletRequestUtils;
import org.springframework.web.servlet.ModelAndView;
import org.springframework.web.servlet.mvc.multiaction.MultiActionController;

public class MemberController extends MultiActionController {

    private MemberService memberService;

    public void setMemberService(MemberService memberService) {
        this.memberService = memberService;
    }

    public ModelAndView add(HttpServletRequest request,
            HttpServletResponse response, Member member) throws Exception {
        memberService.add(member);
        return new ModelAndView("redirect:list.htm");
    }

    public ModelAndView remove(HttpServletRequest request,
            HttpServletResponse response) throws Exception {
        String memberName = ServletRequestUtils.getRequiredStringParameter(
                request, "memberName");
        memberService.remove(memberName);
        return new ModelAndView("redirect:list.htm");
    }

    public ModelAndView list(HttpServletRequest request,
            HttpServletResponse response) throws Exception {
        List<Member> members = memberService.list();
        return new ModelAndView("memberList", "members", members);
    }
}
```

For the `add()` handler method, you want the controller to bind the request parameters to a command object of type `Member`, so you declare the third method argument of this type. For the `remove()` and `list()` handler methods, you should only declare the request and response arguments. When either the `add()` or `remove()` methods complete, you redirect the user to the list page again to display the members.

When you declare this controller, it requires a reference to the memberService bean in the service layer to maintain the member list:

```
<bean id="memberController"
    class="com.apress.springrecipes.court.web.MemberController">
    <property name="memberService" ref="memberService" />
</bean>
```

As you have ControllerClassNameHandlerMapping configured in your web application context, it will notice that this controller's type is MultiActionController, and then generate the following mapping for it:

```
MemberController → /member/*
```

By default, MultiActionController maps URLs to handler methods by the method names. For this controller, the URLs will be mapped to the following methods:

```
/member/add.htm → add()
/member/remove.htm → remove()
/member/list.htm → list()
```

Now let's create the view page memberList.jsp for this controller. In this page, there's a form for adding a new member, followed by a list showing all the members. In the last column of the list, there's a link for removing a member.

```
<%@ taglib prefix="c" uri="http://java.sun.com/jsp/jstl/core" %>

<html>
<head>
<title>Member List</title>
</head>

<body>
<form action="add.htm">
  Name <input type="text" name="name" />
  Phone <input type="text" name="phone" />
  Email <input type="text" name="email" />
  <input type="submit" />
</form>
<table border="1">
  <tr>
    <th>Name</th>
    <th>Phone</th>
    <th>Email</th>
    <th></th>
  </tr>
  <c:forEach items="${members}" var="member">
  <tr>
    <td>${member.name}</td>
    <td>${member.phone}</td>
```

```
        <td>${member.email}</td>
        <td><a href="remove.htm?memberName=${member.name}">Remove</a></td>
    </tr>
    </c:forEach>
</table>
</body>
</html>
```

As the list action showing this page is accessed by /member/list.htm, the add member form should submit to the relative URL add.htm, which corresponds to /member/add.htm. For the same reason, the remove hyperlink should link to the relative URL remove.htm, which corresponds to /member/remove.htm.

Once the add action or remove action completes, you redirect the user's browser to the list action for it to display the member list again. Now you can list all the members through the following URL:

```
http://localhost:8080/court/member/list.htm
```

Mapping URLs to Handler Methods

By default, MultiActionController uses InternalPathMethodNameResolver to map URLs to handler methods by the method names. However, if you want to add a prefix or a suffix to the mapped method names, you have to configure this resolver explicitly:

```
<bean id="memberController"
    class="com.apress.springrecipes.court.web.MemberController">
    ...
    <property name="methodNameResolver">
        <bean class="org.springframework.web.servlet.mvc.multiaction.➥
            InternalPathMethodNameResolver">
            <property name="suffix" value="Member" />
        </bean>
    </property>
</bean>
```

Then the last path of a URL before the extension will be mapped to a handler method by adding Member as the suffix:

```
/member/add.htm → addMember()
/member/remove.htm → removeMember()
/member/list.htm → listMember()
```

You have to change the method names in MemberController to test this resolver:

```
package com.apress.springrecipes.court.web;
...
public class MemberController extends MultiActionController {
    ...
    public ModelAndView addMember(HttpServletRequest request,
            HttpServletResponse response, Member member) throws Exception {
```

```
        ...
    }

    public ModelAndView removeMember(HttpServletRequest request,
            HttpServletResponse response) throws Exception {
        ...
    }

    public ModelAndView listMember(HttpServletRequest request,
            HttpServletResponse response) throws Exception {
        ...
    }
}
```

Alternatively, you can configure PropertiesMethodNameResolver to map URLs to handler methods by specifying the mapping definition explicitly:

```
<bean id="memberController"
    class="com.apress.springrecipes.court.web.MemberController">
    ...
    <property name="methodNameResolver">
        <bean class="org.springframework.web.servlet.mvc.multiaction.➥
            PropertiesMethodNameResolver">
            <property name="mappings">
                <props>
                    <prop key="/member/add.htm">addMember</prop>
                    <prop key="/member/remove.htm">removeMember</prop>
                    <prop key="/member/list.htm">listMember</prop>
                </props>
            </property>
        </bean>
    </property>
</bean>
```

Then a URL will be mapped to a handler method whose name is specified in the mapping definition:

```
/member/add.htm → addMember()
/member/remove.htm → removeMember()
/member/list.htm → listMember()
```

Finally, you can configure ParameterMethodNameResolver to map URLs to handler methods according to a request parameter. The parameter name can be customized in this resolver with the paramName property. For example, if you set it to method, a URL will be mapped to a handler method whose name is the same as the value of the request parameter method. Note that the wildcards in the following URLs can match any strings.

```
/member/*.htm?method=addMember → addMember()
/member/*.htm?method=removeMember → removeMember()
/member/*.htm?method=listMember → listMember()
```

10-13. Creating Excel and PDF Views

Problem

Although HTML is the most common method of displaying web contents, sometimes your users may wish to export contents from your web application in Excel or PDF format. In Java, there are several libraries that can help generate Excel and PDF files. However, to use these libraries directly in a web application, you have to generate the files behind the scenes and return them to users as binary attachments. You have to deal with HTTP response headers and output streams for this purpose.

Solution

Spring integrates the generation of Excel and PDF files into its MVC framework. You can consider Excel and PDF files as special kinds of views, so you can consistently handle a web request in a controller and add data to a model for passing to Excel and PDF views. In this way, you have no need to deal with HTTP response headers and output streams.

Spring MVC supports generating Excel files using either the Apache POI library (`http://poi.apache.org/`) or the JExcelAPI library (`http://jexcelapi.sourceforge.net/`). The corresponding view classes are `AbstractExcelView` and `AbstractJExcelView`. PDF files are generated by the iText library (`http://www.lowagie.com/iText/`), and the corresponding view class is `AbstractPdfView`.

How It Works

Suppose your users wish to generate a report of the reservation summary for a particular day. They want this report to be generated in either the Excel or PDF format. For this report generation function, you need to declare a method in the service layer that returns all the reservations of a specified day:

```
package com.apress.springrecipes.court.service;
...
public interface ReservationService {
    ...
    public List<Reservation> findByDate(Date date);
}
```

Then you provide a simple implementation for this method by iterating over all the made reservations:

```
package com.apress.springrecipes.court.service;
...
public class ReservationServiceImpl implements ReservationService {
    ...
    public List<Reservation> findByDate(Date date) {
        List<Reservation> result = new ArrayList<Reservation>();
        for (Reservation reservation : reservations) {
            if (reservation.getDate().equals(date)) {
                result.add(reservation);
```

```
            }
        }
        return result;
    }
}
```

Now you can write a simple controller to get the date and format parameters from the URL. The date parameter will be formatted into a date object and passed to the service layer for querying reservations. The format parameter is used to indicate whether the report should be generated in the Excel or PDF format.

```
package com.apress.springrecipes.court.web;
...
import org.springframework.web.bind.ServletRequestUtils;
import org.springframework.web.servlet.ModelAndView;
import org.springframework.web.servlet.mvc.AbstractController;

public class ReservationSummaryController extends AbstractController {

    private ReservationService reservationService;

    public void setReservationService(ReservationService reservationService) {
        this.reservationService = reservationService;
    }

    protected ModelAndView handleRequestInternal(HttpServletRequest request,
            HttpServletResponse response) throws Exception {
        String date =
            ServletRequestUtils.getRequiredStringParameter(request, "date");
        String format =
            ServletRequestUtils.getRequiredStringParameter(request, "format");

        Date summaryDate = new SimpleDateFormat("yyyy-MM-dd").parse(date);
        List<Reservation> reservations =
            reservationService.findByDate(summaryDate);
        return new ModelAndView(format + "Summary", "reservations", reservations);
    }
}
```

This controller returns a view whose name will be excelSummary for the excel format parameter, or pdfSummary for the pdf format parameter.

When you declare this controller, it requires a reference to the reservationService bean in the service layer to query for reservations of a particular day:

```
<bean id="reservationSummaryController"
    class="com.apress.springrecipes.court.web.ReservationSummaryController">
    <property name="reservationService" ref="reservationService" />
</bean>
```

Creating Excel Views

An Excel view can be created by extending the AbstractExcelView class (for Apache POI) or the AbstractJExcelView class (for JExcelAPI). Here, AbstractExcelView will be introduced as an example. In the buildExcelDocument() method, you can access the model passed from the controller and also a precreated Excel workbook. Your task is simply to populate the workbook with the data in the model.

■ **Note** To generate Excel files with Apache POI in a web application, you must copy poi-2.5.1.jar (located in the lib/poi directory of the Spring installation) to the WEB-INF/lib directory.

```
package com.apress.springrecipes.court.web.view;
...
import org.apache.poi.hssf.usermodel.HSSFRow;
import org.apache.poi.hssf.usermodel.HSSFSheet;
import org.apache.poi.hssf.usermodel.HSSFWorkbook;

import org.springframework.web.servlet.view.document.AbstractExcelView;

public class ExcelReservationSummary extends AbstractExcelView {

    protected void buildExcelDocument(Map model, HSSFWorkbook workbook,
            HttpServletRequest request, HttpServletResponse response)
            throws Exception {
        List<Reservation> reservations = (List) model.get("reservations");
        DateFormat dateFormat = new SimpleDateFormat("yyyy-MM-dd");
        HSSFSheet sheet = workbook.createSheet();

        HSSFRow header = sheet.createRow(0);
        header.createCell((short) 0).setCellValue("Court Name");
        header.createCell((short) 1).setCellValue("Date");
        header.createCell((short) 2).setCellValue("Hour");
        header.createCell((short) 3).setCellValue("Player Name");
        header.createCell((short) 4).setCellValue("Player Phone");

        int rowNum = 1;
        for (Reservation reservation : reservations) {
            HSSFRow row = sheet.createRow(rowNum++);
            row.createCell((short) 0).setCellValue(reservation.getCourtName());
            row.createCell((short) 1).setCellValue(
                    dateFormat.format(reservation.getDate()));
            row.createCell((short) 2).setCellValue(reservation.getHour());
            row.createCell((short) 3).setCellValue(
                    reservation.getPlayer().getName());
            row.createCell((short) 4).setCellValue(
```

```
                    reservation.getPlayer().getPhone());
        }
    }
}
```

In the preceding Excel view, you first create a sheet in the workbook. In this sheet, you show the headers of this report in the first row. Then you iterate over the reservation list to create a row for each reservation.

As you have ResourceBundleViewResolver configured in your web application context, you can add the following entry to views.properties in the classpath root to define this view:

```
excelSummary.(class)=➥
    com.apress.springrecipes.court.web.view.ExcelReservationSummary
```

As you have ControllerClassNameHandlerMapping configured in your web application context, you can access this controller through the following URL. When calling this controller, you must specify the request parameters date and format.

```
http://localhost:8080/court/reservationSummary.htm?date=2008-01-14&format=excel
```

Creating PDF Views

A PDF view is created by extending the AbstractPdfView class. In the buildPdfDocument() method, you can access the model passed from the controller and also a precreated PDF document. Your task is simply to populate the document with the data in the model.

■ **Note** To generate PDF files with iText in a web application, you must copy itext-1.4.8.jar (located in the lib/itext directory of the Spring installation) to the WEB-INF/lib directory.

```
package com.apress.springrecipes.court.web.view;
...
import org.springframework.web.servlet.view.document.AbstractPdfView;

import com.lowagie.text.Document;
import com.lowagie.text.Table;
import com.lowagie.text.pdf.PdfWriter;

public class PdfReservationSummary extends AbstractPdfView {

    protected void buildPdfDocument(Map model, Document document,
            PdfWriter writer, HttpServletRequest request,
            HttpServletResponse response) throws Exception {
        List<Reservation> reservations = (List) model.get("reservations");
        DateFormat dateFormat = new SimpleDateFormat("yyyy-MM-dd");
        Table table = new Table(5);
```

```
        table.addCell("Court Name");
        table.addCell("Date");
        table.addCell("Hour");
        table.addCell("Player Name");
        table.addCell("Player Phone");

        for (Reservation reservation : reservations) {
            table.addCell(reservation.getCourtName());
            table.addCell(dateFormat.format(reservation.getDate()));
            table.addCell(Integer.toString(reservation.getHour()));
            table.addCell(reservation.getPlayer().getName());
            table.addCell(reservation.getPlayer().getPhone());
        }

        document.add(table);
    }
}
```

In the preceding PDF view, you create a PDF table and show the headers of this report in the first row. Then you iterate over the reservation list to create a row for each reservation. Finally, you add the table to the PDF document.

Then you can add the following entry to `views.properties` to define this view:

```
pdfSummary.(class)=com.apress.springrecipes.court.web.view.PdfReservationSummary
```

10-14. Developing Controllers with Annotations

Problem

In the traditional Spring MVC approach, you have to configure an instance and a request mapping for each controller class in the bean configuration file. You can decrease the amount of work needed for configuration if Spring MVC can auto-detect your controller classes and request mappings. Besides, it's also inflexible for each controller class to implement or extend a framework-specific interface or base class.

Solution

Spring 2.5 supports a new annotation-based approach for controller development. Spring can auto-detect your controller classes with the `@Controller` annotation, and also your request mappings in the `@RequestMapping` annotations. This saves you the trouble of configuring them in the bean configuration file. Moreover, if you use annotations, your controller classes and handler methods will be more flexible in accessing context resources (e.g., request parameters, model attributes, and session attributes).

The `@Controller` annotation marks an arbitrary class as a controller class. In contrast to traditional controllers, an annotated controller class needn't implement a framework-specific interface or extend a framework-specific base class. Within a controller class, there can be one or more handler methods annotated with the `@RequestMapping` annotation.

The signature of the handler methods is very flexible. You can specify an arbitrary name for a handler method and define any of the following types as its method arguments. Here, only the common argument types are mentioned. For a complete list of valid argument types, please refer to the Spring documentation on annotation-based controller configuration, or the javadoc for the @RequestMapping annotation.

- HttpServletRequest, HttpServletResponse, or HttpSession
- Request parameters of arbitrary type, annotated with @RequestParam
- Model attributes of arbitrary type, annotated with @ModelAttribute
- A command object of arbitrary type, for Spring to bind request parameters
- Map or ModelMap, for the handler method to add attributes to the model
- Errors or BindingResult, for the handler method to access the binding and validation result for the command object
- SessionStatus, for the handler method to notify its completion of session processing

The return type of a handler method can be ModelAndView (a model, and a view name or a view object), Map (a model only), String (a view name only), or void (the method itself handles the HTTP response directly).

How It Works

Before you create annotation-based controllers, you have to set up the web application context to process the annotations. First, for Spring to auto-detect your controllers with the @Controller annotation, you have to enable Spring's component scanning feature through the <context:component-scan> element.

Besides, Spring MVC is able to map requests to controller classes and handler methods according to the @RequestMapping annotations. To make this work, you have to register a DefaultAnnotationHandlerMapping instance and an AnnotationMethodHandlerAdapter instance in the web application context. They will process the @RequestMapping annotations at the class level and the method level, respectively.

To focus on the annotation-based controller approach, you may include only the necessary Spring MVC configurations in court-servlet.xml, as follows:

```
<beans xmlns="http://www.springframework.org/schema/beans"
    xmlns:xsi="http://www.w3.org/2001/XMLSchema-instance"
    xmlns:context="http://www.springframework.org/schema/context"
    xsi:schemaLocation="http://www.springframework.org/schema/beans
        http://www.springframework.org/schema/beans/spring-beans-2.5.xsd
        http://www.springframework.org/schema/context
        http://www.springframework.org/schema/context/spring-context-2.5.xsd">

    <context:component-scan
        base-package="com.apress.springrecipes.court.web" />
```

```
    <bean class="org.springframework.web.servlet.mvc.annotation.➥
        DefaultAnnotationHandlerMapping" />

    <bean class="org.springframework.web.servlet.mvc.annotation.➥
        AnnotationMethodHandlerAdapter" />

    <bean
        class="org.springframework.web.servlet.view.InternalResourceViewResolver">
        <property name="prefix" value="/WEB-INF/jsp/" />
        <property name="suffix" value=".jsp" />
    </bean>

    <bean id="messageSource"
        class="org.springframework.context.support.ResourceBundleMessageSource">
        <property name="basename" value="messages" />
    </bean>
</beans>
```

DefaultAnnotationHandlerMapping and AnnotationMethodHandlerAdapter are preregistered in the web application context by default. However, if you have other handler mappings or handler adapters registered explicitly, they won't be registered anymore. In this case, you must register them yourself.

Developing Single-Action and Multi-Action Controllers

An annotation-based controller class can be an arbitrary class that doesn't implement a particular interface or extend a particular base class. You can simply annotate it with the @Controller annotation. There can be one or more handler methods defined in a controller to handle single or multiple actions. The signature of the handler methods is flexible enough to accept a range of arguments.

The @RequestMapping annotation can be applied to the class level or the method level. The first mapping strategy is to map a particular URL pattern to a controller class, and then a particular HTTP method to each handler method:

```
package com.apress.springrecipes.court.web;
...
import org.springframework.stereotype.Controller;
import org.springframework.web.bind.annotation.RequestMapping;
import org.springframework.web.bind.annotation.RequestMethod;
import org.springframework.web.servlet.ModelAndView;

@Controller
@RequestMapping("/welcome.htm")
public class WelcomeController {

    @RequestMapping(method = RequestMethod.GET)
    public ModelAndView welcome() {
        Date today = new Date();
```

```
        return new ModelAndView("welcome", "today", today);
    }
}
```

The second strategy is to map a URL pattern to each handler method directly, without defining a mapping for the controller class:

```
package com.apress.springrecipes.court.web;
...
import org.springframework.beans.factory.annotation.Autowired;
import org.springframework.stereotype.Controller;
import org.springframework.web.bind.annotation.RequestMapping;
import org.springframework.web.bind.annotation.RequestParam;
import org.springframework.web.servlet.ModelAndView;

@Controller
public class MemberController {

    private MemberService memberService;

    @Autowired
    public MemberController(MemberService memberService) {
        this.memberService = memberService;
    }

    @RequestMapping("/member/add.htm")
    public String addMember(Member member) {
        memberService.add(member);
        return "redirect:list.htm";
    }

    @RequestMapping("/member/remove.htm")
    public String removeMember(
            @RequestParam("memberName") String memberName) {
        memberService.remove(memberName);
        return "redirect:list.htm";
    }

    @RequestMapping("/member/list.htm")
    public ModelAndView listMember() {
        List<Member> members = memberService.list();
        return new ModelAndView("memberList", "members", members);
    }
}
```

You can specify a range of arguments for a handler method. For example, in the `add()` method, you specify a command object of type `Member` as a method argument. Then request parameters will be bound to this object's properties of the same name. In the `remove()`

method, you specify a method argument that is bound to a request parameter by the @RequestParam() annotation. By default, request parameters bound with the @RequestParam() annotation are required. You can set the required attribute to false for optional request parameters.

Developing a Form Controller

In the traditional Spring MVC approach, you create a simple form controller by extending the SimpleFormController class. This defines the basic form-handling flow and allows you to customize the flow by overriding several life cycle methods. In Spring's annotation-based MVC approach, you can simulate the form-handling flow by using annotations.

Regarding the annotation-based approach, a basic controller class that is annotated with @Controller can also handle forms. The first thing you have to do is to map a URL pattern to this controller class through the @RequestMapping annotation. For a controller to handle forms, there are two important methods you must provide. One is for rendering the form in response to an HTTP GET request. Another is to handle the form submission for an HTTP POST request. These methods can have arbitrary names, but they must associate with an HTTP method using the @RequestMapping annotation.

```
package com.apress.springrecipes.court.web;
...
import org.springframework.beans.factory.annotation.Autowired;
import org.springframework.beans.propertyeditors.CustomDateEditor;
import org.springframework.stereotype.Controller;
import org.springframework.ui.ModelMap;
import org.springframework.validation.BindingResult;
import org.springframework.web.bind.WebDataBinder;
import org.springframework.web.bind.annotation.InitBinder;
import org.springframework.web.bind.annotation.ModelAttribute;
import org.springframework.web.bind.annotation.RequestMapping;
import org.springframework.web.bind.annotation.RequestMethod;
import org.springframework.web.bind.annotation.RequestParam;
import org.springframework.web.bind.annotation.SessionAttributes;
import org.springframework.web.bind.support.SessionStatus;

@Controller
@RequestMapping("/reservationForm.htm")
@SessionAttributes("reservation")
public class ReservationFormController {

    private ReservationService reservationService;
    private ReservationValidator validator;

    @Autowired
    public ReservationFormController(ReservationService reservationService,
            ReservationValidator validator) {
        this.reservationService = reservationService;
```

```
        this.validator = validator;
    }

    @InitBinder
    public void initBinder(WebDataBinder binder) {
        SimpleDateFormat dateFormat = new SimpleDateFormat("yyyy-MM-dd");
        dateFormat.setLenient(false);
        binder.registerCustomEditor(Date.class, new CustomDateEditor(
                dateFormat, true));
        binder.registerCustomEditor(SportType.class, new SportTypeEditor(
                reservationService));
    }

    @ModelAttribute("sportTypes")
    public List<SportType> populateSportTypes() {
        return reservationService.getAllSportTypes();
    }

    @RequestMapping(method = RequestMethod.GET)
    public String setupForm(
            @RequestParam(required = false, value = "username") String username,
            ModelMap model) {
        Reservation reservation = new Reservation();
        reservation.setPlayer(new Player(username, null));
        model.addAttribute("reservation", reservation);
        return "reservationForm";
    }

    @RequestMapping(method = RequestMethod.POST)
    public String processSubmit(
            @ModelAttribute("reservation") Reservation reservation,
            BindingResult result, SessionStatus status) {
        validator.validate(reservation, result);
        if (result.hasErrors()) {
            return "reservationForm";
        } else {
            reservationService.make(reservation);
            status.setComplete();
            return "redirect:reservationSuccess.htm";
        }
    }
}
```

The `setupForm()` method, associated with the HTTP `GET` method, corresponds to the `formBackingObject()` method of `SimpleFormController`, which initializes the command object for binding's needs. In this method, you can retrieve any request parameter for initializing the command object by using the `@RequestParam` annotation. Then you create the command object by yourself and store it into a model attribute. The model attribute name is actually the command object name you can access in JSP files. If you want to store the command object in the session, just as by enabling the sessionForm property of SimpleFormController, you can apply the @SessionAttributes annotation to the controller class and specify the name of the model attribute to store in the session.

The processSubmit() method, associated with the HTTP POST method, corresponds to the onSubmit() method of SimpleFormController, which handles the form submission. In this method, you can get the command object from the model by using the @ModelAttribute annotation. When applied to a method argument, the @ModelAttribute annotation is used for binding a model attribute to a method argument. Unlike the onSubmit() method of SimpleFormController, you have to perform form validation by yourself and decide whether to render the form view or the success view. After the form submission is handled successfully, you clear the command object from the session by calling the setComplete() method of SessionStatus.

When applied to a method like populateSportTypes(), the @ModelAttribute annotation is used for populating reference data to the model. This has the same effect as overriding the referenceData() method of SimpleFormController.

The initBinder() method annotated with the @InitBinder annotation registers your custom property editors to the binder object. It corresponds to the initBinder() method of SimpleFormController.

Note that the success view of this controller is a redirect view to the reservation success page. You can create another annotation-based controller for this view.

```
package com.apress.springrecipes.court.web;

import org.springframework.stereotype.Controller;
import org.springframework.web.bind.annotation.RequestMapping;

@Controller
public class ReservationSuccessController {

    @RequestMapping("/reservationSuccess.htm")
    public String reservationSuccess() {
        return "reservationSuccess";
    }
}
```

Finally, before this form controller will work, you have to define a validator instance for Spring to auto-wire it:

```
<bean id="reservationValidator"
    class="com.apress.springrecipes.court.domain.ReservationValidator" />
```

For reuse purposes, you can extract the binder initialization task from each controller class to form a binding initializer:

```
package com.apress.springrecipes.court.web;
...
import org.springframework.beans.factory.annotation.Autowired;
import org.springframework.beans.propertyeditors.CustomDateEditor;
```

```
import org.springframework.web.bind.WebDataBinder;
import org.springframework.web.bind.support.WebBindingInitializer;
import org.springframework.web.context.request.WebRequest;

public class ReservationBindingInitializer implements WebBindingInitializer {

    private ReservationService reservationService;

    @Autowired
    public ReservationBindingInitializer(ReservationService reservationService) {
        this.reservationService = reservationService;
    }

    public void initBinder(WebDataBinder binder, WebRequest request) {
        SimpleDateFormat dateFormat = new SimpleDateFormat("yyyy-MM-dd");
        dateFormat.setLenient(false);
        binder.registerCustomEditor(Date.class, new CustomDateEditor(
                dateFormat, true));
        binder.registerCustomEditor(SportType.class, new SportTypeEditor(
                reservationService));
    }
}
```

Then you can specify this binding initializer for `AnnotationMethodHandlerAdapter` so that all the handler methods can share the same property editors:

```
<bean class="org.springframework.web.servlet.mvc.annotation.➥
    AnnotationMethodHandlerAdapter">
    <property name="webBindingInitializer">
        <bean class="com.apress.springrecipes.court.web.➥
            ReservationBindingInitializer" />
    </property>
</bean>
```

Now you can delete the `initBinder()` method in `ReservationFormController`, as the binder will be shared between every annotation-based controller.

Comparison with the Traditional Controller Approach

As you can see, the annotation-based approach allows more flexibility in writing controller classes and handler methods because you have no need to implement a particular interface or extend a particular base class. However, in order for an annotation-based controller to handle forms, its handler methods have to perform some tasks that were originally handled by `SimpleFormController`, such as invoking the validator, stepping back to the form view in case of errors, and stepping forward to the success view if the handling succeeds. Thus, you have to drill deeper into the details of form handling.

10-15. Summary

In this chapter, you have learned how to develop a Java web application using the Spring MVC framework. The central component of Spring MVC is `DispatcherServlet`, which acts as a front controller that dispatches requests to appropriate handlers for them to handle requests. When `DispatcherServlet` receives a request, it first looks for a handler from one or more handler mappings. Once a handler is determined, `DispatcherServlet` invokes the handler to handle the request. The handler then returns a model, and a view name or a view object, after it completes the request handling. If a view name is returned, `DispatcherServlet` will ask view resolvers to resolve this view name into a view object, and then pass the model to this view object for rendering.

`DispatcherServlet` requires a set of facilities to help handle requests. These facilities include handler mappings, locale resolvers, view resolvers, a message source, and exception resolvers. You can easily configure and customize these facilities in the web application context.

Spring MVC provides several controller classes for you to extend in different usage scenarios, such as `AbstractController`, `ParameterizableViewController`, `SimpleFormController`, `AbstractWizardFormController`, and `MultiActionController`. They encapsulate most of the features so that your controllers can simply extend them to have those features inherited.

Spring MVC supports different types of views for different presentation technologies. For example, it considers Excel and PDF files special types of views so that you can consistently handle a web request in a controller and add data to a model for passing to Excel and PDF views.

Spring 2.5 supports annotation-based controller development. Your controllers have no need to extend the traditional controller classes—they can include the annotations only. By using annotations, Spring can auto-detect your controller classes and handler mappings so that you don't have to configure them manually.

In the next chapter, you will learn how to integrate Spring with several popular web application frameworks, including Struts, JSF, and DWR.

CHAPTER 11

Integrating Spring with Other Web Frameworks

In this chapter, you will learn how to integrate the Spring framework with several popular web application frameworks, including Struts, JSF, and DWR. Spring's powerful IoC container and enterprise support features make it very suitable for implementing the service and persistence layers of your Java EE applications. However, for the presentation layer, you have a choice between many different web frameworks. So, you often need to integrate Spring with whatever web application framework you are using. The integration mainly focuses on accessing beans declared in the Spring IoC container within these frameworks.

Apache Struts (`http://struts.apache.org/`) is a popular open source web application framework based on the MVC design pattern. Struts has been used in many web-based projects in the Java community and thus has a large user base. Note that Spring's Struts support features target Struts 1.x only. This is because after Struts joined with WebWork in Struts version 2, it's very easy to configure Struts actions in Spring by using the Spring IoC container as the object factory of Struts 2.

JSF (JavaServer Faces, `http://java.sun.com/javaee/javaserverfaces/`) is an excellent component-based and event-driven web application framework included as part of the Java EE specification. You can use the rich set of standard JSF components and also develop custom components for reuse. JSF can cleanly separate presentation logic from UIs by encapsulating it in one or more managed beans. Due to its component-based approach and popularity, JSF is supported by a wide range of IDEs for visual development.

DWR (Direct Web Remoting, `http://getahead.org/dwr`) is a library that brings Ajax (Asynchronous JavaScript and XML) features to your web applications. It allows you to invoke Java objects on the server side by using JavaScript in a web browser. You can also update parts of a web page dynamically, without refreshing the entire page.

Upon finishing this chapter, you will be able to integrate Spring into web applications implemented with Servlet/JSP and popular web application frameworks such as Struts, JSF, and DWR.

11-1. Accessing Spring in Generic Web Applications

Problem

You would like to access beans declared in the Spring IoC container in a web application, regardless of which framework it uses.

Solution

A web application can load Spring's application context by registering the servlet listener `ContextLoaderListener`. This listener stores the loaded application context into the web application's servlet context. Later, a servlet, or any object that can access the servlet context, can also access Spring's application context through a utility method.

How It Works

Suppose you are going to develop a web application for users to find the distance (measured in kilometers) between two cities. First, you define the following service interface:

```
package com.apress.springrecipes.city;

public interface CityService {

    public double findDistance(String srcCity, String destCity);
}
```

For simplicity's sake, let's implement this interface by using a Java map to store the distance data. This map's keys are source cities while its values are nested maps that contain destination cities and their distances from the source city.

```
package com.apress.springrecipes.city;
...
public class CityServiceImpl implements CityService {

    private Map<String, Map<String, Double>> distanceMap;

    public void setDistanceMap(Map<String, Map<String, Double>> distanceMap) {
        this.distanceMap = distanceMap;
    }

    public double findDistance(String srcCity, String destCity) {
        Map<String, Double> destinationMap = distanceMap.get(srcCity);
        if (destinationMap == null) {
            throw new IllegalArgumentException("Source city not found");
        }
        Double distance = destinationMap.get(destCity);
        if (distance == null) {
            throw new IllegalArgumentException("Destination city not found");
        }
        return distance;
    }
}
```

Next, you create the following directory structure for your web application. As this application requires access to the Spring IoC container, you have to put the two required Spring JAR files in the `WEB-INF/lib` directory.

```
city/
    WEB-INF/
        classes/
        lib/
            commons-logging.jar
            spring.jar
        jsp/
            distance.jsp
        applicationContext.xml
        web.xml
```

In Spring's bean configuration file, you can hard-code some distance data for several cities using the `<map>` element. You create this file with the name `applicationContext.xml` and put it in the root of `WEB-INF`.

```
<beans xmlns="http://www.springframework.org/schema/beans"
    xmlns:xsi="http://www.w3.org/2001/XMLSchema-instance"
    xsi:schemaLocation="http://www.springframework.org/schema/beans
        http://www.springframework.org/schema/beans/spring-beans-2.5.xsd">

    <bean id="cityService"
        class="com.apress.springrecipes.city.CityServiceImpl">
        <property name="distanceMap">
            <map>
                <entry key="New York">
                    <map>
                        <entry key="London" value="5574" />
                        <entry key="Beijing" value="10976" />
                    </map>
                </entry>
            </map>
        </property>
    </bean>
</beans>
```

In the web deployment descriptor (i.e., `web.xml`), you register the Spring-provided servlet listener `ContextLoaderListener` to load Spring's application context into the servlet context at startup. It will look for the context parameter `contextConfigLocation` for the location of the bean configuration file. You can specify multiple bean configuration files by separating them with either commas or spaces.

```
<web-app version="2.4" xmlns="http://java.sun.com/xml/ns/j2ee"
    xmlns:xsi="http://www.w3.org/2001/XMLSchema-instance"
    xsi:schemaLocation="http://java.sun.com/xml/ns/j2ee
        http://java.sun.com/xml/ns/j2ee/web-app_2_4.xsd">

    <context-param>
        <param-name>contextConfigLocation</param-name>
```

```
        <param-value>/WEB-INF/applicationContext.xml</param-value>
    </context-param>

    <listener>
        <listener-class>
            org.springframework.web.context.ContextLoaderListener
        </listener-class>
    </listener>
    ...
</web-app>
```

Actually, the default location where this listener will look for a bean configuration file is exactly what you specified (i.e., /WEB-INF/applicationContext.xml). So, you can simply omit this context parameter.

To allow users to query distances between cities, you have to create a JSP file that contains a form. You can name it distance.jsp and put it in the WEB-INF/jsp directory to prevent direct access to it. There are two text fields in this form for users to input the source and destination cities. There's also a table grid for showing the actual distance.

```
<html>
<head>
<title>City Distance</title>
</head>

<body>
<form method="POST">
<table>
  <tr>
    <td>Source City</td>
    <td><input type="text" name="srcCity" value="${param.srcCity}" /></td>
  </tr>
  <tr>
    <td>Destination City</td>
    <td><input type="text" name="destCity" value="${param.destCity}" /></td>
  </tr>
  <tr>
    <td>Distance</td>
    <td>${distance}</td>
  </tr>
  <tr>
    <td colspan="2"><input type="submit" value="Find" /></td>
  </tr>
</table>
</form>
</body>
</html>
```

You need a servlet to process the distance requests. When this servlet is accessed with the HTTP GET method, it simply displays the form. Later, when the form is submitted with the POST method, this servlet finds the distance between the two input cities and displays it in the form again.

■ **Note** To develop web applications that use the Servlet API, you have to include servlet-api.jar (located in the lib/j2ee directory of the Spring installation) in your classpath.

```
package com.apress.springrecipes.city.servlet;
...
import javax.servlet.RequestDispatcher;
import javax.servlet.ServletException;
import javax.servlet.http.HttpServlet;
import javax.servlet.http.HttpServletRequest;
import javax.servlet.http.HttpServletResponse;

import org.springframework.web.context.WebApplicationContext;
import org.springframework.web.context.support.WebApplicationContextUtils;

public class DistanceServlet extends HttpServlet {

    protected void doGet(HttpServletRequest request,
            HttpServletResponse response) throws ServletException, IOException {
        forward(request, response);
    }

    protected void doPost(HttpServletRequest request,
            HttpServletResponse response) throws ServletException, IOException {
        String srcCity = request.getParameter("srcCity");
        String destCity = request.getParameter("destCity");

        WebApplicationContext context =
            WebApplicationContextUtils.getRequiredWebApplicationContext(
                getServletContext());
        CityService cityService = (CityService) context.getBean("cityService");
        double distance = cityService.findDistance(srcCity, destCity);
        request.setAttribute("distance", distance);

        forward(request, response);
    }

    private void forward(HttpServletRequest request,
            HttpServletResponse response) throws ServletException, IOException {
        RequestDispatcher dispatcher =
            request.getRequestDispatcher("WEB-INF/jsp/distance.jsp");
```

```
        dispatcher.forward(request, response);
    }
}
```

This servlet needs to access the cityService bean declared in the Spring IoC container to find distances. As Spring's application context is stored in the servlet context, you can retrieve it through the WebApplicationContextUtils.getRequiredWebApplicationContext() method by passing in a servlet context.

Finally, you add this servlet declaration to web.xml and map it to the URL pattern /distance.

```
<web-app ...>
    ...
    <servlet>
        <servlet-name>distance</servlet-name>
        <servlet-class>
            com.apress.springrecipes.city.servlet.DistanceServlet
        </servlet-class>
    </servlet>

    <servlet-mapping>
        <servlet-name>distance</servlet-name>
        <url-pattern>/distance</url-pattern>
    </servlet-mapping>
</web-app>
```

Now you can deploy this web application to a web container (e.g., Apache Tomcat 6.0). By default, Tomcat listens on port 8080, so if you deploy your application to the city context path, you can access it with the following URL once it has been started up:

```
http://localhost:8080/city/distance
```

11-2. Integrating Spring with Struts 1.x

Problem

You would like to access beans declared in the Spring IoC container in a web application developed with Apache Struts 1.x.

Solution

A Struts application is able to load Spring's application context by registering the servlet listener ContextLoaderListener and access it from the servlet context just like in a generic web application. However, Spring offers better Struts-specific solutions for accessing its application context.

First, Spring allows you to load an application context by registering a Struts plug-in in the Struts configuration file. This application context will automatically refer to the application context loaded by the servlet listener as its parent so that it can refer to beans declared in its parent application context.

Second, Spring provides the ActionSupport class, a subclass of the Action base class that has a convenient getWebApplicationContext() method for you to access Spring's application context.

Finally, your Struts actions can have Spring beans injected via dependency injection. The prerequisite is to declare them in Spring's application context and ask Struts to look them up from Spring.

How It Works

Now let's implement your web application for finding city distances using Apache Struts. First, you create the following directory structure for your web application.

■Note For a web application developed with Struts 1.2, you have to copy struts.jar (located in the lib/struts directory of the Spring installation), commons-beanutils.jar, commons-digester.jar, and commons-logging.jar (located in lib/jakarta-commons) to the WEB-INF/lib directory. If you would like to use Spring's support for Struts, you will also have to copy spring-webmvc-struts.jar (located in dist/modules).

```
city/
    WEB-INF/
        classes/
        lib/
            commons-beanutils.jar
            commons-digester.jar
            commons-logging.jar
            spring.jar
            spring-webmvc-struts.jar
            struts.jar
        jsp/
            distance.jsp
        applicationContext.xml
        struts-config.xml
        web.xml
```

In the web deployment descriptor (i.e., web.xml) of a Struts application, you have to register the Struts servlet ActionServlet to handle web requests. You can map this servlet to the URL pattern *.do.

```
<web-app version="2.4" xmlns="http://java.sun.com/xml/ns/j2ee"
    xmlns:xsi="http://www.w3.org/2001/XMLSchema-instance"
    xsi:schemaLocation="http://java.sun.com/xml/ns/j2ee
        http://java.sun.com/xml/ns/j2ee/web-app_2_4.xsd">

    <servlet>
        <servlet-name>action</servlet-name>
        <servlet-class>
```

```
            org.apache.struts.action.ActionServlet
        </servlet-class>
    </servlet>

    <servlet-mapping>
        <servlet-name>action</servlet-name>
        <url-pattern>*.do</url-pattern>
    </servlet-mapping>
</web-app>
```

Loading Spring's Application Context into a Struts Application

There are two ways of loading Spring's application context into a Struts application. The first is to register the servlet listener `ContextLoaderListener` in `web.xml`. This listener loads `/WEB-INF/applicationContext.xml` as Spring's bean configuration file by default, so you don't need to specify its location explicitly.

```
<web-app ...>
    <listener>
        <listener-class>
            org.springframework.web.context.ContextLoaderListener
        </listener-class>
    </listener>
    ...
</web-app>
```

Another way is to register the Struts plug-in `ContextLoaderPlugin` in the Struts configuration file `struts-config.xml`. By default, this plug-in loads the bean configuration file using the name of the `ActionServlet` instance registered in `web.xml` with `-servlet.xml` as the suffix (`action-servlet.xml` in this case). If you would like to load another bean configuration file, you can specify its name in the `contextConfigLocation` property.

```
<!DOCTYPE struts-config PUBLIC
    "-//Apache Software Foundation//DTD Struts Configuration 1.1//EN"
    "http://jakarta.apache.org/struts/dtds/struts-config_1_1.dtd">

<struts-config>
    ...
    <plug-in className="org.springframework.web.struts.ContextLoaderPlugIn">
        <set-property property="contextConfigLocation"
            value="/WEB-INF/applicationContext.xml" />
    </plug-in>
</struts-config>
```

If both configurations exist at the same time, the Spring application context loaded by the Struts plug-in will automatically refer to the application context loaded by the servlet listener as its parent. Typically, business services should be declared in the application context loaded by the servlet listener, while web-related components should be separated in another application context loaded by the Struts plug-in. So let's omit the Struts plug-in setting for now.

Accessing Spring's Application Context in Struts Actions

Struts can help you to bind HTML form field values to a form bean's properties when a form is submitted. First, create a form class that extends ActionForm and includes two properties for a source city and a destination city.

```
package com.apress.springrecipes.city.struts;

import org.apache.struts.action.ActionForm;

public class DistanceForm extends ActionForm {

    private String srcCity;
    private String destCity;

    // Getters and Setters
    ...
}
```

Then you'll create a JSP file that has a form for users to input a source and a destination city. You should define this form and its fields using the tag library provided by Struts so that these fields can be bound to a form bean's properties automatically. You can name this JSP file distance.jsp and put it in the WEB-INF/jsp directory to prevent direct access to it.

```
<%@ taglib prefix="html" uri="http://struts.apache.org/tags-html" %>

<html>
<head>
<title>City Distance</title>
</head>

<body>
<html:form method="POST" action="/distance.do">
<table>
  <tr>
    <td>Source City</td>
    <td><html:text property="srcCity" /></td>
  </tr>
  <tr>
    <td>Destination City</td>
    <td><html:text property="destCity" /></td>
  </tr>
  <tr>
    <td>Distance</td>
    <td>${distance}</td>
  </tr>
  <tr>
    <td colspan="2"><input type="submit" value="Find" /></td>
  </tr>
```

```
</table>
</html:form>
</body>
</html>
```

In Struts, each web request is processed by an action that extends the Action class. Sometimes it's necessary for your Struts actions to access Spring beans. You can access the application context loaded by the servlet listener ContextLoaderListener through the static method WebApplicationContextUtils.getRequiredWebApplicationContext().

However, there's a better way to access Spring's application context in a Struts action: by extending the ActionSupport class. This class is a subclass of Action that provides a convenient method, getWebApplicationContext(), for you to access Spring's application context. This method first attempts to return the application context loaded by ContextLoaderPlugin. If it doesn't exist, this method attempts to return its parent (i.e., the application context loaded by ContextLoaderListener).

```
package com.apress.springrecipes.city.struts;
...
import javax.servlet.http.HttpServletRequest;
import javax.servlet.http.HttpServletResponse;

import org.apache.struts.action.ActionForm;
import org.apache.struts.action.ActionForward;
import org.apache.struts.action.ActionMapping;
import org.springframework.web.struts.ActionSupport;

public class DistanceAction extends ActionSupport {

    public ActionForward execute(ActionMapping mapping, ActionForm form,
            HttpServletRequest request, HttpServletResponse response) {
        if (request.getMethod().equals("POST")) {
            DistanceForm distanceForm = (DistanceForm) form;
            String srcCity = distanceForm.getSrcCity();
            String destCity = distanceForm.getDestCity();

            CityService cityService =
                (CityService) getWebApplicationContext().getBean("cityService");
            double distance = cityService.findDistance(srcCity, destCity);
            request.setAttribute("distance", distance);
        }
        return mapping.findForward("success");
    }
}
```

In the Struts configuration file struts-config.xml, you declare the form beans as well as the actions and their mappings for your application.

```
<struts-config>
    <form-beans>
        <form-bean name="distanceForm"
            type="com.apress.springrecipes.city.struts.DistanceForm" />
    </form-beans>

    <action-mappings>
        <action path="/distance"
            type="com.apress.springrecipes.city.struts.DistanceAction"
            name="distanceForm" validate="false">
            <forward name="success"
                path="/WEB-INF/jsp/distance.jsp" />
        </action>
    </action-mappings>
</struts-config>
```

Now you can deploy this application to your web container and access it through the URL `http://localhost:8080/city/distance.do`.

Declaring Struts Actions in Spring's Bean Configuration File

In addition to looking up Spring beans in a Struts action actively via Spring's application context, you can apply the dependency injection pattern to inject Spring beans into your Struts action. In this case, your Struts action no longer needs to extend the `ActionSupport` class, but simply extend the `Action` class.

```
package com.apress.springrecipes.city.struts;
...
import javax.servlet.http.HttpServletRequest;
import javax.servlet.http.HttpServletResponse;

import org.apache.struts.action.Action;
import org.apache.struts.action.ActionForm;
import org.apache.struts.action.ActionForward;
import org.apache.struts.action.ActionMapping;

public class DistanceAction extends Action {

    private CityService cityService;

    public void setCityService(CityService cityService) {
        this.cityService = cityService;
    }

    public ActionForward execute(ActionMapping mapping, ActionForm form,
            HttpServletRequest request, HttpServletResponse response) {
        if (request.getMethod().equals("POST")) {
            ...
            double distance = cityService.findDistance(srcCity, destCity);
```

```
            request.setAttribute("distance", distance);
        }
        return mapping.findForward("success");
    }
}
```

However, this action must be under Spring's management to have its dependencies injected. You can choose to declare it in either applicationContext.xml or another bean configuration file loaded by ContextLoaderPlugin. To better separate business services and web components, I recommend declaring it in action-servlet.xml in the root of WEB-INF, which will be loaded by ContextLoaderPlugin by default, as your ActionServlet instance has the name action.

```
<beans xmlns="http://www.springframework.org/schema/beans"
    xmlns:xsi="http://www.w3.org/2001/XMLSchema-instance"
    xsi:schemaLocation="http://www.springframework.org/schema/beans
        http://www.springframework.org/schema/beans/spring-beans-2.5.xsd">

    <bean name="/distance"
        class="com.apress.springrecipes.city.struts.DistanceAction">
        <property name="cityService" ref="cityService" />
    </bean>
</beans>
```

This action's bean name must be identical to its action path in struts-config.xml. As a <bean> element's id attribute cannot contain the / character, you should use the name attribute instead. In this configuration file, you can refer to beans declared in its parent application context, which is loaded by ContextLoaderListener.

In struts-config.xml, you have to register ContextLoaderPlugin to load the preceding bean configuration file.

```
<struts-config>
    ...
    <action-mappings>
        <action path="/distance"
            name="distanceForm" validate="false">
            <forward name="success"
                path="/WEB-INF/jsp/distance.jsp" />
        </action>
    </action-mappings>

    <controller processorClass="org.springframework.web.struts.➥
        DelegatingRequestProcessor" />

    <plug-in className="org.springframework.web.struts.ContextLoaderPlugIn" />
</struts-config>
```

Also, you have to register the Struts request processor DelegatingRequestProcessor to ask Struts to look up its actions from Spring's application context by matching the action path with the bean name. With this request processor registered, you no longer need to specify the type attribute for an action.

Sometimes you may already have another request processor registered so that you can't register DelegatingRequestProcessor. In this case, you can specify DelegatingActionProxy as your action's type to achieve the same effect.

```
<action path="/distance"
    type="org.springframework.web.struts.DelegatingActionProxy"
    name="distanceForm" validate="false">
    <forward name="success"
        path="/WEB-INF/jsp/distance.jsp" />
</action>
```

11-3. Integrating Spring with JSF

Problem

You would like to access beans declared in the Spring IoC container in a web application developed with JSF.

Solution

A JSF application is able to access Spring's application context just like a generic web application (i.e., by registering the servlet listener ContextLoaderListener and accessing it from the servlet context). However, due to the similarity between Spring's and JSF's bean models, it's very easy to integrate them by registering the Spring-provided JSF variable resolver DelegatingVariableResolver, which can resolve JSF variables into Spring beans. Furthermore, you can even declare JSF managed beans in Spring's bean configuration file to centralize them with your Spring beans.

How It Works

Suppose you are going to implement your web application for finding city distances using JSF. First, you create the following directory structure for your web application.

■ **Note** Before you start developing a web application using JSF, you need a JSF implementation library. You can download JSF Reference Implementation (JSF-RI) 1.2 from https://javaserverfaces.dev.java.net/. After downloading it, extract the ZIP file into a directory of your choice and then copy jsf-api.jar and jsf-impl.jar (located in the lib directory of the JSF-RI installation) to your WEB-INF/lib directory. JSF-RI depends on JSTL, so you also have to copy jstl.jar (located in the lib/j2ee directory of the Spring installation).

```
city/
    WEB-INF/
        classes/
        lib/
            commons-logging.jar
            jsf-api.jar
            jsf-impl.jar
            jstl.jar
            spring.jar
        applicationContext.xml
        faces-config.xml
        web.xml
    distance.jsp
```

In the web deployment descriptor (i.e., web.xml) of a JSF application, you have to register the JSF servlet FacesServlet to handle web requests. You can map this servlet to the URL pattern *.faces. To load Spring's application context at startup, you also have to register the servlet listener ContextLoaderListener.

```
<web-app version="2.4" xmlns="http://java.sun.com/xml/ns/j2ee"
    xmlns:xsi="http://www.w3.org/2001/XMLSchema-instance"
    xsi:schemaLocation="http://java.sun.com/xml/ns/j2ee
        http://java.sun.com/xml/ns/j2ee/web-app_2_4.xsd">

    <listener>
        <listener-class>
            org.springframework.web.context.ContextLoaderListener
        </listener-class>
    </listener>

    <servlet>
        <servlet-name>faces</servlet-name>
        <servlet-class>javax.faces.webapp.FacesServlet</servlet-class>
    </servlet>

    <servlet-mapping>
        <servlet-name>faces</servlet-name>
        <url-pattern>*.faces</url-pattern>
    </servlet-mapping>
</web-app>
```

The basic idea of JSF is to separate presentation logic from UIs by encapsulating it in one or more JSF managed beans. For your distance-finding function, you can create the following DistanceBean class for a JSF managed bean:

```
package com.apress.springrecipes.city.jsf;
...
public class DistanceBean {
```

```
    private String srcCity;
    private String destCity;
    private double distance;
    private CityService cityService;

    public String getSrcCity() {
        return srcCity;
    }

    public String getDestCity() {
        return destCity;
    }

    public double getDistance() {
        return distance;
    }

    public void setSrcCity(String srcCity) {
        this.srcCity = srcCity;
    }

    public void setDestCity(String destCity) {
        this.destCity = destCity;
    }

    public void setCityService(CityService cityService) {
        this.cityService = cityService;
    }

    public void find() {
        distance = cityService.findDistance(srcCity, destCity);
    }
}
```

There are four properties defined in this bean. As your page has to show the `srcCity`, `destCity`, and `distance` properties, you define a getter method for each of them. Users can only input the `srcCity` and `destCity` properties, so they require a setter method as well. The back-end `CityService` bean is injected via a setter method. When the `find()` method is called on this bean, it will invoke the back-end service to find the distance between these two cities, and then store it in the `distance` property for subsequent display.

Then you create `distance.jsp` in the root of your web application context. You have to put it here because when `FacesServlet` receives a request, it will map this request to a JSP file with the same name. For example, if you request the URL `/distance.faces`, then `FacesServlet` will load `/distance.jsp` accordingly.

```
<%@ taglib prefix="f" uri="http://java.sun.com/jsf/core" %>
<%@ taglib prefix="h" uri="http://java.sun.com/jsf/html" %>

<html>
<head>
<title>City Distance</title>
</head>

<body>
<f:view>
  <h:form>
    <h:panelGrid columns="2">
      <h:outputLabel for="srcCity">Source City</h:outputLabel>
      <h:inputText id="srcCity" value="#{distanceBean.srcCity}" />
      <h:outputLabel for="destCity">Destination City</h:outputLabel>
      <h:inputText id="destCity" value="#{distanceBean.destCity}" />
      <h:outputLabel>Distance</h:outputLabel>
      <h:outputText value="#{distanceBean.distance}" />
      <h:commandButton value="Find" action="#{distanceBean.find}" />
    </h:panelGrid>
  </h:form>
</f:view>
</body>
</html>
```

This JSP file contains an `<h:form>` component for users to input a source city and a destination city. These two fields are defined using two `<h:inputText>` components, whose values are bound to a JSF managed bean's properties. The distance result is defined using an `<h:outputText>` component because its value is read-only. Finally, you define an `<h:commandButton>` component whose action will be triggered on the server side when you click it.

Resolving Spring Beans in JSF

The JSF configuration file `faces-config.xml`, located in the root of `WEB-INF`, is where you configure your navigation rules and JSF managed beans. For this simple application with only one screen, there's no navigation rule to configure. You can simply configure the preceding `DistanceBean` here.

```
<faces-config xmlns="http://java.sun.com/xml/ns/javaee"
    xmlns:xsi="http://www.w3.org/2001/XMLSchema-instance"
    xsi:schemaLocation="http://java.sun.com/xml/ns/javaee
        http://java.sun.com/xml/ns/javaee/web-facesconfig_1_2.xsd"
    version="1.2">

    <application>
        <variable-resolver>
            org.springframework.web.jsf.DelegatingVariableResolver
```

```
        </variable-resolver>
    </application>

    <managed-bean>
        <managed-bean-name>distanceBean</managed-bean-name>
        <managed-bean-class>
            com.apress.springrecipes.city.jsf.DistanceBean
        </managed-bean-class>
        <managed-bean-scope>request</managed-bean-scope>
        <managed-property>
            <property-name>cityService</property-name>
            <value>#{cityService}</value>
        </managed-property>
    </managed-bean>
</faces-config>
```

The scope of DistanceBean is request, which means a new bean instance will be created on each request. Note that by registering the variable resolver DelegatingVariableResolver, you can easily refer to a bean declared in Spring's application context as a JSF variable in the form of #{beanName}. This variable resolver will first attempt to resolve variables from the original JSF variable resolver. If a variable cannot be resolved, this variable resolver will look up Spring's application context for a bean with the same name.

Now you can deploy this application to your web container and access it through the URL http://localhost:8080/city/distance.faces.

Declaring JSF Managed Beans in Spring's Bean Configuration File

By registering DelegatingVariableResolver, you can refer to beans declared in Spring from JSF managed beans. However, they are managed by two different containers: JSF's and Spring's. A better solution is to centralize them under the management of Spring's IoC container. Let's remove the managed bean declaration from the JSF configuration file and add the following Spring bean declaration in applicationContext.xml:

```
<bean id="distanceBean"
    class="com.apress.springrecipes.city.jsf.DistanceBean"
    scope="request">
    <property name="cityService" ref="cityService" />
</bean>
```

To enable the request bean scope in Spring's application context, you have to register RequestContextListener in the web deployment descriptor.

```
<web-app ...>
    <listener>
        <listener-class>
            org.springframework.web.context.ContextLoaderListener
        </listener-class>
    </listener>
```

```
    <listener>
        <listener-class>
            org.springframework.web.context.request.RequestContextListener
        </listener-class>
    </listener>
    ...
</web-app>
```

11-4. Integrating Spring with DWR

Problem

You would like to access beans declared in the Spring IoC container in a web application developed with DWR.

Solution

DWR supports Spring by allowing you to expose Spring beans for remote invocation via its `spring` creator. Moreover, DWR 2.0 offers an XML schema for Spring that enables you to configure DWR inside Spring's bean configuration file. You can simply configure which beans to expose for remote invocation by embedding the `<dwr:remote>` tag without involving the DWR configuration file.

How It Works

Suppose you are going to use DWR to implement your web application for finding city distances with Ajax enabled. First, you create the following directory structure for your web application.

Note To develop a web application using DWR, you have to download `dwr.jar` from `http://getahead.org/dwr/` and copy it to your `WEB-INF/lib` directory.

```
city/
    WEB-INF/
        classes/
        lib/
            commons-logging.jar
            dwr.jar
            spring.jar
        applicationContext.xml
        dwr.xml
        web.xml
    distance.html
```

In the web deployment descriptor (i.e., web.xml) of a DWR application, you have to register the DWR servlet DwrServlet to handle Ajax web requests. You can map this servlet to the URL pattern /dwr/*. To load Spring's application context at startup, you also have to register the servlet listener ContextLoaderListener.

```
<web-app version="2.4" xmlns="http://java.sun.com/xml/ns/j2ee"
    xmlns:xsi="http://www.w3.org/2001/XMLSchema-instance"
    xsi:schemaLocation="http://java.sun.com/xml/ns/j2ee
        http://java.sun.com/xml/ns/j2ee/web-app_2_4.xsd">

    <listener>
        <listener-class>
            org.springframework.web.context.ContextLoaderListener
        </listener-class>
    </listener>

    <servlet>
        <servlet-name>dwr</servlet-name>
        <servlet-class>
            org.directwebremoting.servlet.DwrServlet
        </servlet-class>
    </servlet>

    <servlet-mapping>
        <servlet-name>dwr</servlet-name>
        <url-pattern>/dwr/*</url-pattern>
    </servlet-mapping>
</web-app>
```

A DWR application requires a configuration file to define which objects to expose for remote invocation by JavaScript. By default, DwrServlet loads dwr.xml from the root of WEB-INF as its configuration file.

```
<!DOCTYPE dwr PUBLIC
    "-//GetAhead Limited//DTD Direct Web Remoting 2.0//EN"
    "http://getahead.org/dwr/dwr20.dtd">

<dwr>
    <allow>
        <create creator="new" javascript="CityService">
            <param name="class"
                value="com.apress.springrecipes.city.CityServiceImpl" />
            <include method="findDistance" />
        </create>
    </allow>
</dwr>
```

This DWR configuration file exposes the CityServiceImpl class for remote invocation by JavaScript. The source of this class will be generated dynamically in CityService.js. The new creator is the most common DWR creator that will create a new instance of this class each time it's invoked. You only allow the findDistance() method of this class to be invoked remotely.

Exposing Spring Beans for Remote Invocation

DWR's new creator creates a new object instance each time it's invoked. If you would like to expose a bean in Spring's application context for remote invocation, you can make use of the spring creator and specify the name of the bean to expose.

```
<dwr>
    <allow>
        <create creator="spring" javascript="CityService">
            <param name="beanName" value="cityService" />
            <include method="findDistance" />
        </create>
    </allow>
</dwr>
```

Now you can write a web page for users to find distances between cities. When using Ajax, your web page doesn't need to be refreshed like a traditional web page. So, you can simply create it as a static HTML page (e.g., distance.html, located in the root of your web application context).

```
<html>
<head>
<title>City Distance</title>
<script src='dwr/interface/CityService.js'></script>
<script src='dwr/engine.js'></script>
<script src='dwr/util.js'></script>
<script type="text/javascript">
function find() {
    var srcCity = dwr.util.getValue("srcCity");
    var destCity = dwr.util.getValue("destCity");
    CityService.findDistance(srcCity, destCity, function(data) {
        dwr.util.setValue("distance", data);
    });
}
</script>
</head>

<body>
<form>
<table>
  <tr>
    <td>Source City</td>
    <td><input type="text" id="srcCity" /></td>
  </tr>
```

```
  <tr>
    <td>Destination City</td>
    <td><input type="text" id="destCity" /></td>
  </tr>
  <tr>
    <td>Distance</td>
    <td><span id="distance" /></td>
  </tr>
  <tr>
    <td colspan="2"><input type="button" value="Find" onclick="find()" /></td>
  </tr>
</table>
</form>
</body>
</html>
```

When a user clicks the Find button, the JavaScript function `find()` will be called. It makes an Ajax request to the `CityService.findDistance()` method by passing the values in the source city and destination city fields. When the Ajax response arrives, it displays the distance result in the `distance` span. To make this function work, you have to include the JavaScript libraries generated dynamically by DWR.

Now you can deploy this application to your web container and access it through the URL `http://localhost:8080/city/distance.html`.

Configuring DWR in Spring's Bean Configuration File

DWR 2.0 supports configuring itself directly in Spring's bean configuration file. Before this is possible, however, you have to replace the previously registered `DwrServlet` with `DwrSpringServlet` in the web deployment descriptor.

```
<web-app ...>
    ...
    <servlet>
        <servlet-name>dwr</servlet-name>
        <servlet-class>
            org.directwebremoting.spring.DwrSpringServlet
        </servlet-class>
    </servlet>
</web-app>
```

In Spring's bean configuration file `applicationContext.xml`, you can configure DWR with the XML elements defined in the DWR schema. First, you have to declare the `<dwr:configuration>` element to enable DWR in Spring. Then, for each bean that you would like to expose for remote invocation, you embed a `<dwr:remote>` element with the configuration information equivalent to that in `dwr.xml`.

```
<beans xmlns="http://www.springframework.org/schema/beans"
    xmlns:xsi="http://www.w3.org/2001/XMLSchema-instance"
    xmlns:dwr="http://www.directwebremoting.org/schema/spring-dwr"
```

```
    xsi:schemaLocation="http://www.springframework.org/schema/beans
        http://www.springframework.org/schema/beans/spring-beans-2.5.xsd
        http://www.directwebremoting.org/schema/spring-dwr
        http://www.directwebremoting.org/schema/spring-dwr-2.0.xsd">

    <dwr:configuration />

    <bean id="cityService"
        class="com.apress.springrecipes.city.CityServiceImpl">
        <dwr:remote javascript="CityService">
            <dwr:include method="findDistance" />
        </dwr:remote>
        ...
    </bean>
</beans>
```

Now you can delete `dwr.xml` because all its configuration information has been ported to Spring's bean configuration file.

11-5. Summary

In this chapter, you have learned how to integrate Spring into web applications developed with Servlet/JSP and popular web application frameworks such as Struts, JSF, and DWR. The integration mainly focuses on accessing beans declared in the Spring IoC container within these frameworks.

In a generic web application, regardless of which framework it uses, you can register the Spring-provided servlet listener `ContextLoaderListener` to load Spring's application context into the servlet context of this web application. Later, a servlet or any object that can access the servlet context will also be able to access Spring's application context through a utility method.

In a web application developed with Struts, you can load Spring's application context by registering a Struts plug-in in addition to the servlet listener. This application context will automatically refer to the application context loaded by the servlet listener as its parent. Spring provides the `ActionSupport` class that has a convenient method for you to access Spring's application context. You can also declare Struts actions in Spring's application context to have Spring beans injected.

For JSF, you can register the variable resolver `DelegatingVariableResolver` to resolve JSF variables into Spring beans. Furthermore, you can even declare JSF managed beans in Spring's bean configuration file to centralize them with Spring beans.

DWR allows you to expose Spring beans for remote invocation by its `spring` creator. DWR 2.0 offers an XML schema for Spring that enables you to configure DWR inside Spring's bean configuration file.

In the next chapter, you will learn about the testing support features provided by Spring and how to test Spring-based applications.

CHAPTER 12

Spring Testing Support

In this chapter, you will learn about basic testing techniques you can apply in testing Java applications, and also the testing support features offered by the Spring framework. These features can make your testing tasks easier and lead you to better application design. In general, applications developed with the Spring framework and the dependency injection pattern are easy to test.

Testing is a key activity in software development for ensuring quality. There are many types of testing, including unit testing, integration testing, functional testing, system testing, performance testing, and acceptance testing. Spring's testing support focuses on unit and integration testing, but it can also help with other types of testing. Testing can be performed either manually or automatically. However, since automated tests can be run repeatedly and continuously at different phases of a development process, they are highly recommended, especially in agile development processes. The Spring framework is an agile framework that fits these kinds of processes.

There are many testing frameworks available on the Java platform. Currently, JUnit and TestNG are the most popular. JUnit has a long history and a large user group in the Java community. JUnit had major improvements from version 3.8 to 4.0, including support for annotations. TestNG is another popular Java testing framework that makes extensive use of annotations. Compared to JUnit, TestNG offers additional powerful features such as test grouping, dependent test methods, and data-driven tests.

In releases prior to 2.5, Spring offered testing support specific to JUnit 3.8, which is referred to as *JUnit 3.8 legacy support*. You can take advantage of this support by extending the base test classes it provides. Spring 2.5 upgrades its testing support features by offering the *Spring TestContext framework*, which requires Java 1.5 or higher. This framework abstracts the underlying testing framework with the following concepts:

Test context: This encapsulates the context of a test's execution, including the application context, test class, current test instance, current test method, and current test exception.

Test context manager: This manages a test context for a test and triggers test execution listeners at predefined test execution points, including when preparing a test instance, before executing a test method (before any framework-specific initialization methods), and after executing a test method (after any framework-specific cleanup methods).

Test execution listener: This defines a listener interface, by implementing which you can listen to test execution events. The TestContext framework provides several test execution listeners for common testing features, but you are free to create your own.

Spring 2.5 provides convenient TestContext support classes for JUnit 3.8, JUnit 4.4, and TestNG 5.5, with particular test execution listeners preregistered. You can simply extend these support classes to use the TestContext framework without having to know much about the framework details.

Upon finishing this chapter, you will understand the basic concepts and techniques of testing and the popular Java testing frameworks JUnit and TestNG. You will also be able to create unit tests and integration tests using both the JUnit 3.8 legacy support and the Spring TestContext framework.

12-1. Creating Tests with JUnit and TestNG

Problem

You would like to create automated tests for your Java application so that they can be run repeatedly to ensure the correctness of your application.

Solution

The most popular testing frameworks on the Java platform are JUnit and TestNG. JUnit 4 incorporates several major improvements over JUnit 3.8, which relies on the base class (i.e., `TestCase`) and the method signature (i.e., methods whose names begin with `test`) to identify test cases—an approach that lacks flexibility. JUnit 4 allows you to annotate your test methods with JUnit's `@Test` annotation, so an arbitrary public method can be run as a test case. TestNG is another powerful testing framework that makes use of annotations. It also provides a `@Test` annotation type for you to identify test cases.

How It Works

Suppose you are going to develop a system for a bank. To ensure the system's quality, you have to test every part of it. First, let's consider an interest calculator, whose interface is defined as follows:

```
package com.apress.springrecipes.bank;

public interface InterestCalculator {

    public void setRate(double rate);
    public double calculate(double amount, double year);
}
```

Each interest calculator requires a fixed interest rate to be set. Now you can implement this calculator with a simple interest formula:

```
package com.apress.springrecipes.bank;

public class SimpleInterestCalculator implements InterestCalculator {

    private double rate;
```

```
    public void setRate(double rate) {
        this.rate = rate;
    }

    public double calculate(double amount, double year) {
        if (amount < 0 || year < 0) {
            throw new IllegalArgumentException("Amount or year must be positive");
        }
        return amount * year * rate;
    }
}
```

Next, you will test this simple interest calculator with the popular testing frameworks JUnit (both versions 3.8 and 4) and TestNG (version 5).

Tip Usually, a test and its target class are located in the same package, but the source files of tests are stored in a separate directory (e.g., `test`) from the source files of other classes (e.g., `src`).

Testing with JUnit 3.8

In JUnit 3.8, a class that contains test cases must extend the framework class `TestCase`. Each test case must be a public method and its name must begin with `test`. Each test case should run in a fixed environment, which is made up of a particular set of objects called *test fixtures*. In JUnit 3.8, you can initialize test fixtures by overriding the `setUp()` method defined in `TestCase`. This method will be called by JUnit before each test case's execution. Accordingly, you can override the `tearDown()` method to perform cleanup tasks, such as releasing permanent resources. This method will be called by JUnit after each test case's execution. You can create the following JUnit 3.8 test cases to test your simple interest calculator.

Note To compile and run test cases created for JUnit 3.8, you have to include either `junit-3.8.2.jar` or `junit-4.4.jar` (located in the `lib/junit` directory of the Spring installation) in your classpath.

```
package com.apress.springrecipes.bank;

import junit.framework.TestCase;

public class SimpleInterestCalculatorJUnit38Tests extends TestCase {

    private InterestCalculator interestCalculator;

    protected void setUp() throws Exception {
        interestCalculator = new SimpleInterestCalculator();
```

```
        interestCalculator.setRate(0.05);
    }

    public void testCalculate() {
        double interest = interestCalculator.calculate(10000, 2);
        assertEquals(interest, 1000.0);
    }

    public void testIllegalCalculate() {
        try {
            interestCalculator.calculate(-10000, 2);
            fail("No exception on illegal argument");
        }
        catch (IllegalArgumentException e) {}
    }
}
```

In addition to normal cases, a typical test should include exceptional cases, which are usually expected to throw an exception. To test if a method throws an exception in JUnit 3.8, you can surround that method call with a try/catch block. Then, at the next line of the method call in the try block, the test should fail if there's no exception thrown.

Note Most Java IDEs, including Eclipse, provide JUnit test runners for you to run JUnit test cases. You will see a green bar if all your tests pass, and you will see a red bar if any of the tests fail. However, if you are not using an IDE that supports JUnit, you can still run JUnit tests at the command line. JUnit 3.8 provides both GUI-based and text-based test runners, but JUnit 4 doesn't come with a GUI-based test runner any more.

Testing with JUnit 4

In JUnit 4, a class that contains test cases no longer needs to extend the `TestCase` class. It can be an arbitrary class. A test case is simply a public method with the `@Test` annotation. Similarly, you no longer need to override the `setUp()` and `tearDown()` methods, but rather annotate a public method with the `@Before` or `@After` annotation. You can also annotate a public static method with `@BeforeClass` or `@AfterClass` to have it run once before or after all test cases in the class.

Since your class doesn't extend `TestCase`, it doesn't inherit the assert methods. So, you have to call the static assert methods declared in the `Assert` class directly. However, you can import all assert methods via a static import statement in Java 1.5. You can create the following JUnit 4 test cases to test your simple interest calculator.

Note To compile and run test cases created for JUnit 4.4, you have to include `junit-4.4.jar` (located in the `lib/junit` directory of the Spring installation) in your classpath.

```
package com.apress.springrecipes.bank;

import static org.junit.Assert.*;

import org.junit.Before;
import org.junit.Test;

public class SimpleInterestCalculatorJUnit4Tests {

    private InterestCalculator interestCalculator;

    @Before
    public void init() {
        interestCalculator = new SimpleInterestCalculator();
        interestCalculator.setRate(0.05);
    }

    @Test
    public void calculate() {
        double interest = interestCalculator.calculate(10000, 2);
        assertEquals(interest, 1000.0, 0);
    }

    @Test(expected = IllegalArgumentException.class)
    public void illegalCalculate() {
        interestCalculator.calculate(-10000, 2);
    }
}
```

JUnit 4 offers a powerful feature that allows you to expect an exception to be thrown in a test case. You can simply specify the exception type in the `expected` attribute of the `@Test` annotation.

Testing with TestNG

A TestNG test looks very similar to a JUnit 4 one, except that you have to use the classes and annotation types defined by the TestNG framework.

■ Note To compile and run test cases created for TestNG 5, you have to include `testng-5.5-jdk15.jar` (located in the `lib/testng` directory of the Spring installation) in your classpath.

```
package com.apress.springrecipes.bank;

import static org.testng.Assert.*;
```

```
import org.testng.annotations.BeforeMethod;
import org.testng.annotations.Test;

public class SimpleInterestCalculatorTestNG5Tests {

    private InterestCalculator interestCalculator;

    @BeforeMethod
    public void init() {
        interestCalculator = new SimpleInterestCalculator();
        interestCalculator.setRate(0.05);
    }

    @Test
    public void calculate() {
        double interest = interestCalculator.calculate(10000, 2);
        assertEquals(interest, 1000.0);
    }

    @Test(expectedExceptions = IllegalArgumentException.class)
    public void illegalCalculate() {
        interestCalculator.calculate(-10000, 2);
    }
}
```

■ **Note** If you are using Eclipse for development, you can download and install the TestNG Eclipse plug-in from `http://testng.org/doc/eclipse.html` to run TestNG tests in Eclipse. Again, you will see a green bar if all your tests pass, and a red bar otherwise.

One of the powerful features of TestNG is its built-in support for data-driven testing. TestNG cleanly separates test data from test logic so that you can run a test method multiple times for different data sets. In TestNG, test data sets are provided by data providers, which are methods with the `@DataProvider` annotation.

```
package com.apress.springrecipes.bank;

import static org.testng.Assert.*;

import org.testng.annotations.BeforeMethod;
import org.testng.annotations.DataProvider;
import org.testng.annotations.Test;

public class SimpleInterestCalculatorTestNG5Tests {

    private InterestCalculator interestCalculator;
```

```
    @BeforeMethod
    public void init() {
        interestCalculator = new SimpleInterestCalculator();
        interestCalculator.setRate(0.05);
    }

    @DataProvider(name = "legal")
    public Object[][] createLegalInterestParameters() {
        return new Object[][] { new Object[] { 10000, 2, 1000.0 } };
    }

    @DataProvider(name = "illegal")
    public Object[][] createIllegalInterestParameters() {
        return new Object[][] {new Object[] { -10000, 2 },
                new Object[] { 10000, -2 }, new Object[] { -10000, -2 }};
    }

    @Test(dataProvider = "legal")
    public void calculate(double amount, double year, double result) {
        double interest = interestCalculator.calculate(amount, year);
        assertEquals(interest, result);
    }

    @Test(
        dataProvider = "illegal",
        expectedExceptions = IllegalArgumentException.class)
    public void illegalCalculate(double amount, double year) {
        interestCalculator.calculate(amount, year);
    }
}
```

If you run the preceding test with TestNG, the `calculate()` method will be executed once, while the `illegalCalculate()` method will be executed three times, as there are three data sets returned by the `illegal` data provider.

12-2. Creating Unit Tests and Integration Tests

Problem

A common testing skill is to test each module of your application in isolation and then test them in combination. You would like to apply this skill in testing your Java applications.

Solution

Unit tests are used to test a single programming unit. In object-oriented languages, a unit is usually a class or a method. The scope of a unit test is a single unit, but in the real world, most units won't work in isolation. They often need to cooperate with others to complete their tasks. When testing a unit that depends on other units, a common technique you can apply is to simulate the unit's dependencies with stubs and mock objects, both of which can reduce complexity of your unit tests caused by dependencies.

A *stub* is an object that simulates a dependent object with the minimum number of methods required for a test. The methods are implemented in a predetermined way, usually with hard-coded data. A stub also exposes methods for a test to verify the stub's internal states. In contrast to a stub, a *mock object* usually knows how its methods are expected to be called in a test. The mock object then verifies the methods actually called against the expected ones. In Java, there are several libraries that can help create mock objects, including EasyMock and jMock. The main difference between a stub and a mock object is that a stub is usually used for *state verification*, while a mock object is used for *behavior verification*.

Integration tests, in contrast, are used to test several units in combination as a whole. They test if the integration and interaction between units are correct. Each of these units should already have been tested with unit tests, so integration testing is usually performed after unit testing.

Finally, note that applications developed using the principle of "separating interface from implementation" and the dependency injection pattern are easy to test, both for unit testing and integration testing. This is because that principle and pattern can reduce coupling between different units of your application.

How It Works

Creating Unit Tests for Isolated Classes

The core functions of your bank system should be designed around customer accounts. First of all, you create the following domain class, `Account`, with a custom `equals()` method:

```
package com.apress.springrecipes.bank;

public class Account {

    private String accountNo;
    private double balance;

    // Constructors, Getters and Setters
    ...

    public boolean equals(Object obj) {
        if (!(obj instanceof Account)) {
            return false;
        }
        Account account = (Account) obj;
        return account.accountNo.equals(accountNo) && account.balance == balance;
    }
}
```

Next, you define the following DAO interface for persisting account objects in your bank system's persistence layer:

```
package com.apress.springrecipes.bank;

public interface AccountDao {

    public void createAccount(Account account);
    public void updateAccount(Account account);
    public void removeAccount(Account account);
    public Account findAccount(String accountNo);
}
```

To demonstrate the unit testing concept, let's implement this interface by using a map to store account objects. The AccountNotFoundException and DuplicateAccountException classes are subclasses of RuntimeException that you should be able to create yourself.

```
package com.apress.springrecipes.bank;
...
public class InMemoryAccountDao implements AccountDao {

    private Map<String, Account> accounts;

    public InMemoryAccountDao() {
        accounts = Collections.synchronizedMap(new HashMap<String, Account>());
    }

    public boolean accountExists(String accountNo) {
        return accounts.containsKey(accountNo);
    }

    public void createAccount(Account account) {
        if (accountExists(account.getAccountNo())) {
            throw new DuplicateAccountException();
        }
        accounts.put(account.getAccountNo(), account);
    }

    public void updateAccount(Account account) {
        if (!accountExists(account.getAccountNo())) {
            throw new AccountNotFoundException();
        }
        accounts.put(account.getAccountNo(), account);
    }

    public void removeAccount(Account account) {
        if (!accountExists(account.getAccountNo())) {
            throw new AccountNotFoundException();
        }
        accounts.remove(account.getAccountNo());
    }
```

```
    public Account findAccount(String accountNo) {
        Account account = accounts.get(accountNo);
        if (account == null) {
            throw new AccountNotFoundException();
        }
        return account;
    }
}
```

Obviously, this simple DAO implementation doesn't support transactions. However, to make it thread-safe, you can wrap the map storing accounts with a synchronized map so that it will be accessed serially.

Now let's create unit tests for this DAO implementation with JUnit 4. As this class doesn't depend directly on other classes, it's easy to test. To ensure that this class works properly for exceptional cases as well as normal cases, you should also create exceptional test cases for it. Typically, exceptional test cases expect an exception to be thrown.

```
package com.apress.springrecipes.bank;

import static org.junit.Assert.*;

import org.junit.Before;
import org.junit.Test;

public class InMemoryAccountDaoTests {

    private static final String EXISTING_ACCOUNT_NO = "1234";
    private static final String NEW_ACCOUNT_NO = "5678";

    private Account existingAccount;
    private Account newAccount;
    private InMemoryAccountDao accountDao;

    @Before
    public void init() {
        existingAccount = new Account(EXISTING_ACCOUNT_NO, 100);
        newAccount = new Account(NEW_ACCOUNT_NO, 200);
        accountDao = new InMemoryAccountDao();
        accountDao.createAccount(existingAccount);
    }

    @Test
    public void accountExists() {
        assertTrue(accountDao.accountExists(EXISTING_ACCOUNT_NO));
        assertFalse(accountDao.accountExists(NEW_ACCOUNT_NO));
    }
```

```
    @Test
    public void createNewAccount() {
        accountDao.createAccount(newAccount);
        assertEquals(accountDao.findAccount(NEW_ACCOUNT_NO), newAccount);
    }

    @Test(expected = DuplicateAccountException.class)
    public void createDuplicateAccount() {
        accountDao.createAccount(existingAccount);
    }

    @Test
    public void updateExistedAccount() {
        existingAccount.setBalance(150);
        accountDao.updateAccount(existingAccount);
        assertEquals(accountDao.findAccount(EXISTING_ACCOUNT_NO), existingAccount);
    }

    @Test(expected = AccountNotFoundException.class)
    public void updateNotExistedAccount() {
        accountDao.updateAccount(newAccount);
    }

    @Test
    public void removeExistedAccount() {
        accountDao.removeAccount(existingAccount);
        assertFalse(accountDao.accountExists(EXISTING_ACCOUNT_NO));
    }

    @Test(expected = AccountNotFoundException.class)
    public void removeNotExistedAccount() {
        accountDao.removeAccount(newAccount);
    }

    @Test
    public void findExistedAccount() {
        Account account = accountDao.findAccount(EXISTING_ACCOUNT_NO);
        assertEquals(account, existingAccount);
    }

    @Test(expected = AccountNotFoundException.class)
    public void findNotExistedAccount() {
        accountDao.findAccount(NEW_ACCOUNT_NO);
    }
}
```

Creating Unit Tests for Dependent Classes Using Stubs and Mock Objects

Testing an independent class is easy because you needn't consider how its dependencies work and how to set them up properly. However, testing a class that depends on results of other classes or services (e.g., database services and network services) would be a little bit difficult. For example, let's consider the following AccountService interface in the service layer:

```
package com.apress.springrecipes.bank;

public interface AccountService {

    public void createAccount(String accountNo);
    public void removeAccount(String accountNo);
    public void deposit(String accountNo, double amount);
    public void withdraw(String accountNo, double amount);
    public double getBalance(String accountNo);
}
```

The implementation of this service interface has to depend on an AccountDao object in the persistence layer to persist account objects. The InsufficientBalanceException class is also a subclass of RuntimeException that you have to create.

```
package com.apress.springrecipes.bank;

public class AccountServiceImpl implements AccountService {

    private AccountDao accountDao;

    public AccountServiceImpl(AccountDao accountDao) {
        this.accountDao = accountDao;
    }

    public void createAccount(String accountNo) {
        accountDao.createAccount(new Account(accountNo, 0));
    }

    public void removeAccount(String accountNo) {
        Account account = accountDao.findAccount(accountNo);
        accountDao.removeAccount(account);
    }

    public void deposit(String accountNo, double amount) {
        Account account = accountDao.findAccount(accountNo);
        account.setBalance(account.getBalance() + amount);
        accountDao.updateAccount(account);
    }

    public void withdraw(String accountNo, double amount) {
        Account account = accountDao.findAccount(accountNo);
```

```
        if (account.getBalance() < amount) {
            throw new InsufficientBalanceException();
        }
        account.setBalance(account.getBalance() - amount);
        accountDao.updateAccount(account);
    }

    public double getBalance(String accountNo) {
        return accountDao.findAccount(accountNo).getBalance();
    }
}
```

A common technique used in unit testing to reduce complexity caused by dependencies is using stubs. A stub must implement the same interface as the target object so that it can substitute for the target object. For example, you can create a stub for AccountDao that stores a single customer account and implements only the findAccount() and updateAccount() methods, as they are required for deposit() and withdraw():

```
package com.apress.springrecipes.bank;

import static org.junit.Assert.*;

import org.junit.Before;
import org.junit.Test;

public class AccountServiceImplStubTests {

    private static final String TEST_ACCOUNT_NO = "1234";
    private AccountDaoStub accountDaoStub;
    private AccountService accountService;

    private class AccountDaoStub implements AccountDao {

        private String accountNo;
        private double balance;

        public void createAccount(Account account) {}
        public void removeAccount(Account account) {}

        public Account findAccount(String accountNo) {
            return new Account(this.accountNo, this.balance);
        }

        public void updateAccount(Account account) {
            this.accountNo = account.getAccountNo();
            this.balance = account.getBalance();
        }
    }
```

```
    @Before
    public void init() {
        accountDaoStub = new AccountDaoStub();
        accountDaoStub.accountNo = TEST_ACCOUNT_NO;
        accountDaoStub.balance = 100;
        accountService = new AccountServiceImpl(accountDaoStub);
    }

    @Test
    public void deposit() {
        accountService.deposit(TEST_ACCOUNT_NO, 50);
        assertEquals(accountDaoStub.accountNo, TEST_ACCOUNT_NO);
        assertEquals(accountDaoStub.balance, 150, 0);
    }

    @Test
    public void withdrawWithSufficientBalance() {
        accountService.withdraw(TEST_ACCOUNT_NO, 50);
        assertEquals(accountDaoStub.accountNo, TEST_ACCOUNT_NO);
        assertEquals(accountDaoStub.balance, 50, 0);
    }

    @Test(expected = InsufficientBalanceException.class)
    public void withdrawWithInsufficientBalance() {
        accountService.withdraw(TEST_ACCOUNT_NO, 150);
    }
}
```

However, writing stubs yourself requires a lot of coding. A more efficient technique is to use mock objects. The EasyMock library is able to dynamically create mock objects that work in a record/playback mechanism.

■ **Note** To use EasyMock for testing, you have to include `easymock.jar` (located in the `lib/easymock` directory of the Spring installation) in your classpath.

```
package com.apress.springrecipes.bank;

import org.easymock.MockControl;
import org.junit.Before;
import org.junit.Test;

public class AccountServiceImplMockTests {

    private static final String TEST_ACCOUNT_NO = "1234";
    private MockControl mockControl;
```

```
    private AccountDao accountDao;
    private AccountService accountService;

    @Before
    public void init() {
        mockControl = MockControl.createControl(AccountDao.class);
        accountDao = (AccountDao) mockControl.getMock();
        accountService = new AccountServiceImpl(accountDao);
    }

    @Test
    public void deposit() {
        Account account = new Account(TEST_ACCOUNT_NO, 100);
        accountDao.findAccount(TEST_ACCOUNT_NO);
        mockControl.setReturnValue(account);
        account.setBalance(150);
        accountDao.updateAccount(account);
        mockControl.replay();

        accountService.deposit(TEST_ACCOUNT_NO, 50);
        mockControl.verify();
    }

    @Test
    public void withdrawWithSufficientBalance() {
        Account account = new Account(TEST_ACCOUNT_NO, 100);
        accountDao.findAccount(TEST_ACCOUNT_NO);
        mockControl.setReturnValue(account);
        account.setBalance(50);
        accountDao.updateAccount(account);
        mockControl.replay();

        accountService.withdraw(TEST_ACCOUNT_NO, 50);
        mockControl.verify();
    }

    @Test(expected = InsufficientBalanceException.class)
    public void testWithdrawWithInsufficientBalance() {
        Account account = new Account(TEST_ACCOUNT_NO, 100);
        accountDao.findAccount(TEST_ACCOUNT_NO);
        mockControl.setReturnValue(account);
        mockControl.replay();

        accountService.withdraw(TEST_ACCOUNT_NO, 150);
        mockControl.verify();
    }
}
```

With EasyMock, you can create a mock object dynamically for an arbitrary interface or class. Once created by EasyMock, a mock object is in the *record* state. Any method calls made to it will be recorded for future verification. During recording, you can also specify the value that you want to return for a method. After calling the `replay()` method, a mock object will be in the *replay* state. Any method calls then made to it will be verified against the recorded ones. Finally, you can call the `verify()` method to check if all the recorded method calls have been made completely. Finally, you can call the `reset()` method to reset a mock object so that it can be reused again. But since you create a new mock object in the method with `@Before`, which will be called before each test method, you have no need to reuse a mock object.

Creating Integration Tests

Integration tests are used to test several units in combination to ensure that the units are properly integrated and can interact correctly. For example, you can create an integration test to test `AccountServiceImpl` using `InMemoryAccountDao` as the DAO implementation:

```
package com.apress.springrecipes.bank;

import static org.junit.Assert.*;

import org.junit.After;
import org.junit.Before;
import org.junit.Test;

public class AccountServiceTests {

    private static final String TEST_ACCOUNT_NO = "1234";
    private AccountService accountService;

    @Before
    public void init() {
        accountService = new AccountServiceImpl(new InMemoryAccountDao());
        accountService.createAccount(TEST_ACCOUNT_NO);
        accountService.deposit(TEST_ACCOUNT_NO, 100);
    }

    @Test
    public void deposit() {
        accountService.deposit(TEST_ACCOUNT_NO, 50);
        assertEquals(accountService.getBalance(TEST_ACCOUNT_NO), 150, 0);
    }

    @Test
    public void withDraw() {
        accountService.withdraw(TEST_ACCOUNT_NO, 50);
        assertEquals(accountService.getBalance(TEST_ACCOUNT_NO), 50, 0);
    }
```

```
    @After
    public void cleanup() {
        accountService.removeAccount(TEST_ACCOUNT_NO);
    }
}
```

12-3. Unit Testing Spring MVC Controllers

Problem

In a web application, you would like to test the web controllers developed with the Spring MVC framework.

Solution

A Spring MVC controller is invoked by `DispatcherServlet` with an HTTP request object and an HTTP response object. After processing a request, the controller creates a `ModelAndView` object and returns it to `DispatcherServlet` for rendering the view. The main challenge of unit testing Spring MVC controllers, as well as web controllers in other web application frameworks, is simulating HTTP request objects and response objects in a unit testing environment. Fortunately, Spring supports web controller testing by providing a set of mock objects for the Servlet API (including `MockHttpServletRequest`, `MockHttpServletResponse`, and `MockHttpSession`).

To test a Spring MVC controller's output, you need to check if the `ModelAndView` object returned to `DispatcherServlet` is correct. Spring also provides a set of assertion utilities for checking the contents of a `ModelAndView` object.

Spring 2.5 supports annotation-based controllers, which don't need to extend a Spring MVC controller base class or deal with HTTP requests and responses directly. Therefore, they can be tested just like simple Java classes.

How It Works

Unit Testing Classic Spring MVC Controllers

In your bank system, suppose you are going to develop a web interface with Spring MVC for bank staff to input the account number and amount of a deposit. You create a simple controller by extending Spring MVC's `AbstractController`.

■Note To develop a web controller using Spring MVC, you have to include `spring-webmvc.jar` (located in the `dist/modules` directory of the Spring installation) and `servlet-api.jar` (located in `lib/j2ee`) in your classpath.

```
package com.apress.springrecipes.bank;

import javax.servlet.http.HttpServletRequest;
import javax.servlet.http.HttpServletResponse;
```

```
import org.springframework.web.bind.ServletRequestUtils;
import org.springframework.web.servlet.ModelAndView;
import org.springframework.web.servlet.mvc.AbstractController;

public class DepositController extends AbstractController {

    private AccountService accountService;

    public DepositController(AccountService accountService) {
        this.accountService = accountService;
    }

    protected ModelAndView handleRequestInternal(HttpServletRequest request,
            HttpServletResponse response) throws Exception {
        String accountNo =
            ServletRequestUtils.getRequiredStringParameter(request, "accountNo");
        double amount =
            ServletRequestUtils.getRequiredDoubleParameter(request, "amount");

        accountService.deposit(accountNo, amount);

        double balance = accountService.getBalance(accountNo);
        return new ModelAndView("success", "accountNo", accountNo)
                .addObject("balance", balance);
    }
}
```

In the request-handling method of this controller, you simply retrieve the two required parameters, `accountNo` and `amount`, from the HTTP request object, and then pass them to the back-end `AccountService` object to make a deposit. After that, you query the current balance of this account and store it together with the account number in the `ModelAndView` object, whose view name is set to `success`.

With Spring's controller testing utilities, you can create a unit test for this controller as shown following. To ensure that the back-end `AccountService` object is invoked properly, you can make use of EasyMock.

■ Note To utilize Spring's testing utilities, you have to include `spring-test.jar` (located in the `dist/modules` directory of the Spring installation) in your classpath.

```
package com.apress.springrecipes.bank;

import static org.springframework.test.web.ModelAndViewAssert.*;

import javax.servlet.http.HttpServletResponse;
```

```
import org.easymock.MockControl;
import org.junit.Before;
import org.junit.Test;
import org.springframework.mock.web.MockHttpServletRequest;
import org.springframework.mock.web.MockHttpServletResponse;
import org.springframework.web.servlet.ModelAndView;

public class DepositControllerTests {

    private static final String TEST_ACCOUNT_NO = "1234";
    private static final double TEST_AMOUNT = 50;
    private MockControl mockControl;
    private AccountService accountService;
    private DepositController depositController;

    @Before
    public void init() {
        mockControl = MockControl.createControl(AccountService.class);
        accountService = (AccountService) mockControl.getMock();
        depositController = new DepositController(accountService);
    }

    @Test
    public void deposit() throws Exception {
        MockHttpServletRequest request = new MockHttpServletRequest();
        request.setMethod("POST");
        request.addParameter("accountNo", TEST_ACCOUNT_NO);
        request.addParameter("amount", String.valueOf(TEST_AMOUNT));
        HttpServletResponse response = new MockHttpServletResponse();

        accountService.deposit(TEST_ACCOUNT_NO, 50);
        accountService.getBalance(TEST_ACCOUNT_NO);
        mockControl.setReturnValue(150.0);
        mockControl.replay();

        ModelAndView modelAndView =
            depositController.handleRequest(request, response);
        mockControl.verify();

        assertViewName(modelAndView, "success");
        assertModelAttributeValue(modelAndView, "accountNo", TEST_ACCOUNT_NO);
        assertModelAttributeValue(modelAndView, "balance", 150.0);
    }
}
```

With MockHttpServletRequest, you can simulate an HTTP request's method (e.g., GET or POST), parameters, headers, cookies, and so on. To invoke a controller's handleRequest() method, you also have to create a MockHttpServletResponse object.

If DepositController works properly, it should call the back-end AccountService object with the account number and amount specified in the request parameters. You can use EasyMock to verify this behavior.

Finally, you have to check the contents of the returned ModelAndView object. For JUnit 3.8, your test class can extend the AbstractModelAndViewTests class to inherit the assertion method specific to ModelAndView. However, JUnit 4 doesn't require you to extend a base test class. You can use static import to import all static assertion methods of the ModelAndViewAssert class.

Unit Testing Annotation-Based Spring MVC Controllers

Now let's consider implementing DepositController with the annotation-based approach supported by Spring 2.5:

```
package com.apress.springrecipes.bank;

import org.springframework.beans.factory.annotation.Autowired;
import org.springframework.stereotype.Controller;
import org.springframework.ui.ModelMap;
import org.springframework.web.bind.annotation.RequestMapping;
import org.springframework.web.bind.annotation.RequestParam;

@Controller
public class DepositController {

    private AccountService accountService;

    @Autowired
    public DepositController(AccountService accountService) {
        this.accountService = accountService;
    }

    @RequestMapping("/deposit.do")
    protected String deposit(
            @RequestParam("accountNo") String accountNo,
            @RequestParam("amount") double amount,
            ModelMap model) {
        accountService.deposit(accountNo, amount);
        model.addAttribute("accountNo", accountNo);
        model.addAttribute("balance", accountService.getBalance(accountNo));
        return "success";
    }
}
```

Because this controller doesn't deal with the Servlet API directly and doesn't return a Spring-specific ModelAndView object, testing it is very easy. You can test it just like a simple Java class:

```
package com.apress.springrecipes.bank;

import static org.junit.Assert.*;

import org.easymock.MockControl;
import org.junit.Before;
import org.junit.Test;
import org.springframework.ui.ModelMap;

public class DepositControllerTests {

    private static final String TEST_ACCOUNT_NO = "1234";
    private static final double TEST_AMOUNT = 50;
    private MockControl mockControl;
    private AccountService accountService;
    private DepositController depositController;

    @Before
    public void init() {
        mockControl = MockControl.createControl(AccountService.class);
        accountService = (AccountService) mockControl.getMock();
        depositController = new DepositController(accountService);
    }

    @Test
    public void deposit() {
        accountService.deposit(TEST_ACCOUNT_NO, 50);
        accountService.getBalance(TEST_ACCOUNT_NO);
        mockControl.setReturnValue(150.0);
        mockControl.replay();

        ModelMap model = new ModelMap();
        String viewName =
            depositController.deposit(TEST_ACCOUNT_NO, TEST_AMOUNT, model);
        mockControl.verify();

        assertEquals(viewName, "success");
        assertEquals(model.get("accountNo"), TEST_ACCOUNT_NO);
        assertEquals(model.get("balance"), 150.0);
    }
}
```

12-4. Managing Application Contexts in Integration Tests

Problem

When creating integration tests for a Spring application, you have to access beans declared in the application context. Without Spring's testing support, you have to load the application context manually in an initialization method of your tests, such as `setUp()` in JUnit 3.8, or a method with `@Before` or `@BeforeClass` in JUnit 4. However, as an initialization method is called before each test method or test class, the same application context may be reloaded many times. In a large application with many beans, loading an application context may require a lot of time, which causes your tests to run slowly.

Solution

Spring's testing support facilities can help you manage the application context for your tests, including loading it from one or more bean configuration files and caching it across multiple test executions. An application context will be cached across all tests within a single JVM, using the configuration file locations as the key. As a result, your tests can run much faster without reloading the same application context many times.

With Spring's JUnit 3.8 legacy support in releases prior to 2.5, your test class can extend the `AbstractSingleSpringContextTests` base class to access the managed application context through the inherited `getApplicationContext()` method.

In Spring 2.5, the TestContext framework provides two test execution listeners related to context management. They will be registered with a test context manager by default if you don't specify your own explicitly.

`DependencyInjectionTestExecutionListener`: This injects dependencies, including the managed application context, into your tests.

`DirtiesContextTestExecutionListener`: This handles the `@DirtiesContext` annotation and reloads the application context when necessary.

To have the TestContext framework manage the application context, your test class has to integrate with a test context manager internally. For your convenience, the TestContext framework provides support classes that do this, as shown in Table 12-1. These classes integrate with a test context manager and implement the `ApplicationContextAware` interface, so they can provide access to the managed application context through the protected field `applicationContext`. Your test class can simply extend the corresponding TestContext support class for your testing framework.

Table 12-1. *TestContext Support Classes for Context Management*

Testing Framework	TestContext Support Class*
JUnit 3.8	`AbstractJUnit38SpringContextTests`
JUnit 4.4	`AbstractJUnit4SpringContextTests`
TestNG	`AbstractTestNGSpringContextTests`

* *These three TestContext support classes have only* `DependencyInjectionTestExecutionListener` *and* `DirtiesContextTestExecutionListener` *enabled.*

If you are using JUnit 4.4 or TestNG, you can integrate your test class with a test context manager by yourself and implement the ApplicationContextAware interface directly, without extending a TestContext support class. In this way, your test class doesn't bind to the TestContext framework class hierarchy, so you can extend your own base class. In JUnit 4.4, you can simply run your test with the test runner SpringJUnit4ClassRunner to have a test context manager integrated. However, in TestNG, you have to integrate with a test context manager manually.

How It Works

First, let's declare an AccountService instance and an AccountDao instance in the bean configuration file as follows. Later, you will create integration tests for them.

```
<beans xmlns="http://www.springframework.org/schema/beans"
    xmlns:xsi="http://www.w3.org/2001/XMLSchema-instance"
    xsi:schemaLocation="http://www.springframework.org/schema/beans
        http://www.springframework.org/schema/beans/spring-beans-2.5.xsd">

    <bean id="accountDao"
        class="com.apress.springrecipes.bank.InMemoryAccountDao" />

    <bean id="accountService"
        class="com.apress.springrecipes.bank.AccountServiceImpl">
        <constructor-arg ref="accountDao" />
    </bean>
</beans>
```

Accessing the Context with JUnit 3.8 Legacy Support

When using Spring's JUnit 3.8 legacy support to create tests, your test class can extend AbstractSingleSpringContextTests to access the managed application context:

```
package com.apress.springrecipes.bank;

import org.springframework.test.AbstractSingleSpringContextTests;

public class AccountServiceJUnit38LegacyTests extends
        AbstractSingleSpringContextTests {

    private static final String TEST_ACCOUNT_NO = "1234";
    private AccountService accountService;

    protected String[] getConfigLocations() {
        return new String[] { "beans.xml" };
    }

    protected void onSetUp() throws Exception {
        accountService =
```

```
            (AccountService) getApplicationContext().getBean("accountService");
        accountService.createAccount(TEST_ACCOUNT_NO);
        accountService.deposit(TEST_ACCOUNT_NO, 100);
    }

    public void testDeposit() {
        accountService.deposit(TEST_ACCOUNT_NO, 50);
        assertEquals(accountService.getBalance(TEST_ACCOUNT_NO), 150.0);
    }

    public void testWithDraw() {
        accountService.withdraw(TEST_ACCOUNT_NO, 50);
        assertEquals(accountService.getBalance(TEST_ACCOUNT_NO), 50.0);
    }

    protected void onTearDown() throws Exception {
        accountService.removeAccount(TEST_ACCOUNT_NO);
    }
}
```

In this class, you can override the `getConfigLocations()` method to return a list of bean configuration file locations, which are classpath locations relative to the root by default, but they support Spring's resource prefixes (e.g., `file` and `classpath`). Alternatively, you can override the `getConfigPath()` method or the `getConfigPaths()` method to return one or more bean configuration file paths, which can be absolute classpath locations starting with a slash, or paths relative to the package of the current test class.

By default, the application context will be cached and reused for each test method once loaded for the first time. However, in some cases, such as when you have modified the bean configurations or changed a bean's state in a test method, you have to reload the application context. You can call the `setDirty()` method to indicate that the application context is dirty so that it will be reloaded automatically for the next test method.

Finally, note that you cannot override the `setUp()` and `tearDown()` methods of the base class, since they are declared as final. To perform initialization and cleanup tasks, you have to override the `onSetUp()` and `onTearDown()` methods instead, which will be called by the parent's `setUp()` and `tearDown()` methods.

Accessing the Context with the TestContext Framework in JUnit 4.4

If you are using JUnit 4.4 to create tests with the TestContext framework, you will have two options to access the managed application context. The first option is by implementing the `ApplicationContextAware` interface. For this option, you have to explicitly specify a Spring-specific test runner for running your test: `SpringJUnit4ClassRunner`. You can specify this in the `@RunWith` annotation at the class level.

```
package com.apress.springrecipes.bank;

import static org.junit.Assert.*;
```

```
import org.junit.After;
import org.junit.Before;
import org.junit.Test;
import org.junit.runner.RunWith;
import org.springframework.context.ApplicationContext;
import org.springframework.context.ApplicationContextAware;
import org.springframework.test.context.ContextConfiguration;
import org.springframework.test.context.junit4.SpringJUnit4ClassRunner;

@RunWith(SpringJUnit4ClassRunner.class)
@ContextConfiguration(locations = "/beans.xml")
public class AccountServiceJUnit4ContextTests implements ApplicationContextAware {

    private static final String TEST_ACCOUNT_NO = "1234";
    private ApplicationContext applicationContext;
    private AccountService accountService;

    public void setApplicationContext(ApplicationContext applicationContext) {
        this.applicationContext = applicationContext;
    }

    @Before
    public void init() {
        accountService =
            (AccountService) applicationContext.getBean("accountService");
        accountService.createAccount(TEST_ACCOUNT_NO);
        accountService.deposit(TEST_ACCOUNT_NO, 100);
    }

    @Test
    public void deposit() {
        accountService.deposit(TEST_ACCOUNT_NO, 50);
        assertEquals(accountService.getBalance(TEST_ACCOUNT_NO), 150, 0);
    }

    @Test
    public void withDraw() {
        accountService.withdraw(TEST_ACCOUNT_NO, 50);
        assertEquals(accountService.getBalance(TEST_ACCOUNT_NO), 50, 0);
    }

    @After
    public void cleanup() {
        accountService.removeAccount(TEST_ACCOUNT_NO);
    }
}
```

You can specify the bean configuration file locations in the locations attribute of the @ContextConfiguration annotation at the class level. These locations are classpath locations relative to the test class by default, but they support Spring's resource prefixes. If you don't specify this attribute explicitly, the TestContext framework will load the file by joining the test class name with -context.xml as the suffix (i.e., AccountServiceJUnit4Tests-context.xml) from the same package as the test class.

By default, the application context will be cached and reused for each test method, but if you want it to be reloaded after a particular test method, you can annotate the test method with the @DirtiesContext annotation so that the application context will be reloaded for the next test method.

The second option to access the managed application context is by extending the TestContext support class specific to JUnit 4.4: AbstractJUnit4SpringContextTests. This class implements the ApplicationContextAware interface, so you can extend it to get access to the managed application context via the protected field applicationContext. However, you first have to delete the private field applicationContext and its setter method. Note that if you extend this support class, you don't need to specify SpringJUnit4ClassRunner in the @RunWith annotation, because this annotation is inherited from the parent.

```
package com.apress.springrecipes.bank;
...
import org.springframework.test.context.ContextConfiguration;
import org.springframework.test.context.junit4.AbstractJUnit4SpringContextTests;

@ContextConfiguration(locations = "/beans.xml")
public class AccountServiceJUnit4ContextTests extends
        AbstractJUnit4SpringContextTests {

    private static final String TEST_ACCOUNT_NO = "1234";
    private AccountService accountService;

    @Before
    public void init() {
        accountService =
            (AccountService) applicationContext.getBean("accountService");
        accountService.createAccount(TEST_ACCOUNT_NO);
        accountService.deposit(TEST_ACCOUNT_NO, 100);
    }
    ...
}
```

Accessing the Context with the TestContext Framework in JUnit 3.8

If you want to access the managed application context with the TestContext framework in JUnit 3.8, you must extend the TestContext support class AbstractJUnit38SpringContextTests. This class implements the ApplicationContextAware interface, so you can get access to the managed application context via the protected field applicationContext.

```
package com.apress.springrecipes.bank;

import org.springframework.test.context.ContextConfiguration;
import org.springframework.test.context.junit38.AbstractJUnit38SpringContextTests;

@ContextConfiguration(locations = "/beans.xml")
public class AccountServiceJUnit38ContextTests extends
        AbstractJUnit38SpringContextTests {

    private static final String TEST_ACCOUNT_NO = "1234";
    private AccountService accountService;

    protected void setUp() throws Exception {
        accountService =
            (AccountService) applicationContext.getBean("accountService");
        accountService.createAccount(TEST_ACCOUNT_NO);
        accountService.deposit(TEST_ACCOUNT_NO, 100);
    }

    public void testDeposit() {
        accountService.deposit(TEST_ACCOUNT_NO, 50);
        assertEquals(accountService.getBalance(TEST_ACCOUNT_NO), 150.0);
    }

    public void testWithDraw() {
        accountService.withdraw(TEST_ACCOUNT_NO, 50);
        assertEquals(accountService.getBalance(TEST_ACCOUNT_NO), 50.0);
    }

    protected void tearDown() throws Exception {
        accountService.removeAccount(TEST_ACCOUNT_NO);
    }
}
```

Accessing the Context with the TestContext Framework in TestNG

To access the managed application context with the TestContext framework in TestNG, you can extend the TestContext support class `AbstractTestNGSpringContextTests`. This class also implements the `ApplicationContextAware` interface.

```
package com.apress.springrecipes.bank;

import static org.testng.Assert.*;

import org.springframework.test.context.ContextConfiguration;
import org.springframework.test.context.testng.AbstractTestNGSpringContextTests;
import org.testng.annotations.AfterMethod;
```

```
import org.testng.annotations.BeforeMethod;
import org.testng.annotations.Test;

@ContextConfiguration(locations = "/beans.xml")
public class AccountServiceTestNGContextTests extends
        AbstractTestNGSpringContextTests {

    private static final String TEST_ACCOUNT_NO = "1234";
    private AccountService accountService;

    @BeforeMethod
    public void init() {
        accountService =
            (AccountService) applicationContext.getBean("accountService");
        accountService.createAccount(TEST_ACCOUNT_NO);
        accountService.deposit(TEST_ACCOUNT_NO, 100);
    }

    @Test
    public void deposit() {
        accountService.deposit(TEST_ACCOUNT_NO, 50);
        assertEquals(accountService.getBalance(TEST_ACCOUNT_NO), 150, 0);
    }

    @Test
    public void withDraw() {
        accountService.withdraw(TEST_ACCOUNT_NO, 50);
        assertEquals(accountService.getBalance(TEST_ACCOUNT_NO), 50, 0);
    }

    @AfterMethod
    public void cleanup() {
        accountService.removeAccount(TEST_ACCOUNT_NO);
    }
}
```

If you don't want your TestNG test class to extend a TestContext support class, you can implement the `ApplicationContextAware` interface just as you did for JUnit 4.4. However, you have to integrate with a test context manager by yourself. Please refer to the source code of `AbstractTestNGSpringContextTests` for details.

12-5. Injecting Test Fixtures into Integration Tests

Problem

The test fixtures of an integration test for a Spring application are mostly beans declared in the application context. You might wish to have the test fixtures automatically injected by Spring via dependency injection, which saves you the trouble of retrieving them from the application context manually.

Solution

Spring's testing support facilities can inject beans automatically from the managed application context into your tests as test fixtures.

When using Spring's JUnit 3.8 legacy support in releases prior to 2.5, your test class can extend the `AbstractDependencyInjectionSpringContextTests` base class, which is a subclass of `AbstractSingleSpringContextTests`, to have its test fixtures injected automatically. This class supports two ways of performing dependency injection. The first auto-wires beans by type via setter methods. The second auto-wires beans by name via protected fields.

In Spring 2.5's TestContext framework, `DependencyInjectionTestExecutionListener` can automatically inject dependencies into your tests. If you have this listener registered, you can simply annotate a setter method or field of your test with Spring's `@Autowired` annotation or JSR-250's `@Resource` annotation to have a fixture injected automatically. For `@Autowired`, the fixture will be injected by type, and for `@Resource`, it will be injected by name. This support is consistent with the annotation support in Spring 2.5.

How It Works

Injecting Test Fixtures with JUnit 3.8 Legacy Support

When using Spring's JUnit 3.8 legacy support to create tests, your test class can extend `AbstractDependencyInjectionSpringContextTests` to have its test fixtures injected from beans in the managed application context. You can define a setter method for the fixture you want to be injected.

```
package com.apress.springrecipes.bank;

import org.springframework.test.AbstractDependencyInjectionSpringContextTests;

public class AccountServiceJUnit38LegacyTests extends
        AbstractDependencyInjectionSpringContextTests {

    private AccountService accountService;

    public void setAccountService(AccountService accountService) {
        this.accountService = accountService;
    }

    protected void onSetUp() throws Exception {
        accountService.createAccount(TEST_ACCOUNT_NO);
        accountService.deposit(TEST_ACCOUNT_NO, 100);
    }
    ...
}
```

The AbstractDependencyInjectionSpringContextTests class you extend is a subclass of AbstractSingleSpringContextTests, so it also manages an application context loaded from your bean configuration files specified in the getConfigLocations() method. By default, this class uses auto-wiring by type to inject beans from the application context. However, if there's more than one bean of the target type in the application context, this auto-wiring will not work. In this case, you have to look up the bean explicitly from the application context retrieved from getApplicationContext() and remove the setter method that causes ambiguity.

Another method of injecting test fixtures using JUnit 3.8 legacy support is via protected fields. To make this work, you must enable the populateProtectedVariables property in a constructor. In this case, you needn't provide a setter method for each field that you want to be injected.

```
package com.apress.springrecipes.bank;

import org.springframework.test.AbstractDependencyInjectionSpringContextTests;

public class AccountServiceJUnit38LegacyTests extends
        AbstractDependencyInjectionSpringContextTests {

    protected AccountService accountService;

    public AccountServiceJUnit38LegacyTests() {
        setPopulateProtectedVariables(true);
    }
    ...
}
```

This protected field's name will be used to look up a bean with the same name from the managed application context.

Injecting Test Fixtures with the TestContext Framework in JUnit 4.4

When using the TestContext framework to create tests, you can have their test fixtures injected from the managed application context by annotating a field or setter method with the @Autowired or @Resource annotations. In JUnit 4.4, you can specify SpringJUnit4ClassRunner as your test runner without extending a support class.

```
package com.apress.springrecipes.bank;
...
import org.springframework.beans.factory.annotation.Autowired;
import org.springframework.test.context.ContextConfiguration;
import org.springframework.test.context.junit4.SpringJUnit4ClassRunner;

@RunWith(SpringJUnit4ClassRunner.class)
@ContextConfiguration(locations = "/beans.xml")
public class AccountServiceJUnit4ContextTests {

    private static final String TEST_ACCOUNT_NO = "1234";
```

```
    @Autowired
    private AccountService accountService;

    @Before
    public void init() {
        accountService.createAccount(TEST_ACCOUNT_NO);
        accountService.deposit(TEST_ACCOUNT_NO, 100);
    }
    ...
}
```

If you annotate a field or setter method of a test with `@Autowired`, it will be injected using auto-wiring by type. You can further specify a candidate bean for auto-wiring by providing its name in the `@Qualifier` annotation. However, if you want a field or setter method to be auto-wired by name, you can annotate it with `@Resource`.

By extending the TestContext support class `AbstractJUnit4SpringContextTests`, you can also have test fixtures injected from the managed application context. In this case, you don't need to specify `SpringJUnit4ClassRunner` for your test, as it is inherited from the parent.

```
package com.apress.springrecipes.bank;
...
import org.springframework.beans.factory.annotation.Autowired;
import org.springframework.test.context.ContextConfiguration;
import org.springframework.test.context.junit4.AbstractJUnit4SpringContextTests;

@ContextConfiguration(locations = "/beans.xml")
public class AccountServiceJUnit4ContextTests extends
        AbstractJUnit4SpringContextTests {

    private static final String TEST_ACCOUNT_NO = "1234";

    @Autowired
    private AccountService accountService;
    ...
}
```

Injecting Test Fixtures with the TestContext Framework in JUnit 3.8

In JUnit 3.8, you can also use the TestContext framework to create tests with the same test fixture–injection approach. However, your test class has to extend the TestContext support class `AbstractJUnit38SpringContextTests`.

```
package com.apress.springrecipes.bank;

import org.springframework.beans.factory.annotation.Autowired;
import org.springframework.test.context.ContextConfiguration;
import org.springframework.test.context.junit38.AbstractJUnit38SpringContextTests;
```

```
@ContextConfiguration(locations = "/beans.xml")
public class AccountServiceJUnit38ContextTests extends
        AbstractJUnit38SpringContextTests {

    private static final String TEST_ACCOUNT_NO = "1234";

    @Autowired
    private AccountService accountService;

    protected void setUp() throws Exception {
        accountService.createAccount(TEST_ACCOUNT_NO);
        accountService.deposit(TEST_ACCOUNT_NO, 100);
    }
    ...
}
```

Injecting Test Fixtures with the TestContext Framework in TestNG

In TestNG, you can extend the TestContext support class AbstractTestNGSpringContextTests to have test fixtures injected from the managed application context:

```
package com.apress.springrecipes.bank;
...
import org.springframework.beans.factory.annotation.Autowired;
import org.springframework.test.context.ContextConfiguration;
import org.springframework.test.context.testng.AbstractTestNGSpringContextTests;

@ContextConfiguration(locations = "/beans.xml")
public class AccountServiceTestNGContextTests extends
        AbstractTestNGSpringContextTests {

    private static final String TEST_ACCOUNT_NO = "1234";

    @Autowired
    private AccountService accountService;

    @BeforeMethod
    public void init() {
        accountService.createAccount(TEST_ACCOUNT_NO);
        accountService.deposit(TEST_ACCOUNT_NO, 100);
    }
    ...
}
```

12-6. Managing Transactions in Integration Tests

Problem

When creating integration tests for an application that accesses a database, you usually prepare the test data in the initialization method. After each test method runs, it may have modified the data in the database. So, you have to clean up the database to ensure that the next test method will run from a consistent state. As a result, you have to develop many database cleanup tasks.

Solution

Spring's testing support facilities can create and roll back a transaction for each test method, so the changes you make in a test method won't affect the next one. This can also save you the trouble of developing cleanup tasks to clean up the database.

When using Spring's JUnit 3.8 legacy support in releases prior to 2.5, your test class can extend the `AbstractTransactionalSpringContextTests` base class, which is a subclass of `AbstractDependencyInjectionSpringContextTests`, to create and roll back a transaction for each test method. This class requires a transaction manager to be configured properly in the bean configuration file.

In Spring 2.5, the TestContext framework provides a test execution listener related to transaction management. It will be registered with a test context manager by default if you don't specify your own explicitly.

`TransactionalTestExecutionListener`: This handles the `@Transactional` annotation at the class level or the method level, and has the methods run within transactions automatically.

Your test class can extend the corresponding TestContext support class for your testing framework, as shown in Table 12-2, to have its test methods run within transactions. These classes integrate with a test context manager and have `@Transactional` enabled at the class level. Note that a transaction manager is also required in the bean configuration file.

Table 12-2. *TestContext Support Classes for Transaction Management*

Testing Framework	TestContext Support Class*
JUnit 3.8	`AbstractTransactionalJUnit38SpringContextTests`
JUnit 4.4	`AbstractTransactionalJUnit4SpringContextTests`
TestNG	`AbstractTransactionalTestNGSpringContextTests`

* *These three TestContext support classes have* `TransactionalTestExecutionListener` *enabled in addition to* `DependencyInjectionTestExecutionListener` *and* `DirtiesContextTestExecutionListener`.

In JUnit 4.4 and TestNG, you can simply annotate `@Transactional` at the class level or the method level to have the test methods run within transactions, without extending a TestContext support class. However, to integrate with a test context manager, you have to run the JUnit 4.4 test with the test runner `SpringJUnit4ClassRunner`, and you have to do it manually for a TestNG test.

How It Works

Let's consider storing your bank system's accounts in a relational database. You can choose any JDBC-compliant database engine that supports transactions, and then execute the following SQL statement on it to create the ACCOUNT table. Here, I have chosen Apache Derby as my database engine and created the table in the bank instance.

```
CREATE TABLE ACCOUNT (
    ACCOUNT_NO    VARCHAR(10)    NOT NULL,
    BALANCE       DOUBLE         NOT NULL,
    PRIMARY KEY (ACCOUNT_NO)
);
```

Next, you create a new DAO implementation that uses JDBC to access the database. You can take advantage of SimpleJdbcTemplate to simplify your operations.

```
package com.apress.springrecipes.bank;

import org.springframework.jdbc.core.simple.SimpleJdbcDaoSupport;

public class JdbcAccountDao extends SimpleJdbcDaoSupport implements AccountDao {

    public void createAccount(Account account) {
        String sql = "INSERT INTO ACCOUNT (ACCOUNT_NO, BALANCE) VALUES (?, ?)";
        getSimpleJdbcTemplate().update(
                sql, account.getAccountNo(), account.getBalance());
    }

    public void updateAccount(Account account) {
        String sql = "UPDATE ACCOUNT SET BALANCE = ? WHERE ACCOUNT_NO = ?";
        getSimpleJdbcTemplate().update(
                sql, account.getBalance(), account.getAccountNo());
    }

    public void removeAccount(Account account) {
        String sql = "DELETE FROM ACCOUNT WHERE ACCOUNT_NO = ?";
        getSimpleJdbcTemplate().update(sql, account.getAccountNo());
    }

    public Account findAccount(String accountNo) {
        String sql = "SELECT BALANCE FROM ACCOUNT WHERE ACCOUNT_NO = ?";
        double balance = getSimpleJdbcTemplate().queryForObject(
                sql, Double.class, accountNo);
        return new Account(accountNo, balance);
    }
}
```

Before you create integration tests to test the AccountService instance that uses this DAO to persist account objects, you have to replace InMemoryAccountDao with this DAO in the bean configuration file, and configure the target data source as well.

Note To access a database running on the Derby server, you have to include derbyclient.jar (located in the lib directory of the Derby installation) in your classpath.

```
<beans ...>
    <bean id="dataSource"
        class="org.springframework.jdbc.datasource.DriverManagerDataSource">
        <property name="driverClassName"
            value="org.apache.derby.jdbc.ClientDriver" />
        <property name="url"
            value="jdbc:derby://localhost:1527/bank;create=true" />
        <property name="username" value="app" />
        <property name="password" value="app" />
    </bean>

    <bean id="accountDao"
        class="com.apress.springrecipes.bank.JdbcAccountDao">
        <property name="dataSource" ref="dataSource" />
    </bean>
    ...
</beans>
```

Managing Transactions with JUnit 3.8 Legacy Support

When using Spring's JUnit 3.8 legacy support to create tests, your test class can extend AbstractTransactionalSpringContextTests to have its test methods run within transactions:

```
package com.apress.springrecipes.bank;

import org.springframework.test.AbstractTransactionalSpringContextTests;

public class AccountServiceJUnit38LegacyTests extends
        AbstractTransactionalSpringContextTests {

    protected void onSetUpInTransaction() throws Exception {
        accountService.createAccount(TEST_ACCOUNT_NO);
        accountService.deposit(TEST_ACCOUNT_NO, 100);
    }

    // Don't need onTearDown() any more
    ...
}
```

By default, each test method will run within a transaction that will be rolled back at the end of this method. So, you needn't perform database cleanup tasks in the onTearDown() method, and therefore you can simply delete it. Note that the data preparation tasks must be performed in the onSetUpInTransaction() method—not onSetUp()—to have them run within the same transactions as test methods, which will be rolled back at the end.

However, if you would like a transaction to commit at the end of a test method, you can call the setComplete() method explicitly to cause it to commit instead of rolling back. Also, you can end a transaction during a test method by calling the endTransaction() method, which causes a transaction to roll back normally, or commit if you have called setComplete() before.

This class requires a transaction manager to be configured in the bean configuration file. By default, it looks for a bean whose type is PlatformTransactionManager, and uses this bean to manage transactions for your test methods.

```
<bean id="transactionManager"
    class="org.springframework.jdbc.datasource.DataSourceTransactionManager">
    <property name="dataSource" ref="dataSource" />
</bean>
```

Managing Transactions with the TestContext Framework in JUnit 4.4

When using the TestContext framework to create tests, you can have their test methods run within transactions by annotating @Transactional at the class level or the method level. In JUnit 4.4, you can specify SpringJUnit4ClassRunner for your test class so that it doesn't need to extend a support class.

```
package com.apress.springrecipes.bank;
...
import org.springframework.beans.factory.annotation.Autowired;
import org.springframework.test.context.ContextConfiguration;
import org.springframework.test.context.junit4.SpringJUnit4ClassRunner;
import org.springframework.transaction.annotation.Transactional;

@RunWith(SpringJUnit4ClassRunner.class)
@ContextConfiguration(locations = "/beans.xml")
@Transactional
public class AccountServiceJUnit4ContextTests {

    private static final String TEST_ACCOUNT_NO = "1234";

    @Autowired
    private AccountService accountService;

    @Before
    public void init() {
        accountService.createAccount(TEST_ACCOUNT_NO);
        accountService.deposit(TEST_ACCOUNT_NO, 100);
    }
```

```
    // Don't need cleanup() anymore
    ...
}
```

If you annotate a test class with @Transactional, all of its test methods will run within transactions. If you would like a particular method not to run within a transaction, you can annotate it with @NotTransactional. An alternative is to annotate individual methods with @Transactional, not the entire class.

By default, transactions for test methods will be rolled back at the end. You can alter this behavior by disabling the defaultRollback attribute of @TransactionConfiguration, which should be applied to the class level. Also, you can override this class-level rollback behavior at the method level with the @Rollback annotation, which requires a Boolean value.

Note that methods with the @Before or @After annotation will be executed within the same transactions as test methods. If you have methods that need to perform initialization or cleanup tasks before or after a transaction, you have to annotate them with @BeforeTransaction or @AfterTransaction. Notice that these methods will not be executed for test methods annotated with @NotTransactional.

Finally, you also need a transaction manager configured in the bean configuration file. By default, a bean whose type is PlatformTransactionManager will be used, but you can specify another one in the transactionManager attribute of the @TransactionConfiguration annotation by giving its name.

```
<bean id="transactionManager"
    class="org.springframework.jdbc.datasource.DataSourceTransactionManager">
    <property name="dataSource" ref="dataSource" />
</bean>
```

In JUnit 4.4, an alternative to managing transactions for test methods is to extend the transactional TestContext support class AbstractTransactionalJUnit4SpringContextTests, which has @Transactional enabled at the class level so that you don't need to enable it again. By extending this support class, you don't need to specify SpringJUnit4ClassRunner for your test, as it is inherited from the parent.

```
package com.apress.springrecipes.bank;
...
import org.springframework.test.context.ContextConfiguration;
import org.springframework.test.context.junit4.➥
        AbstractTransactionalJUnit4SpringContextTests;

@ContextConfiguration(locations = "/beans.xml")
public class AccountServiceJUnit4ContextTests extends
        AbstractTransactionalJUnit4SpringContextTests {
    ...
}
```

Managing Transactions with the TestContext Framework in JUnit 3.8

In JUnit 3.8, you can also use the TestContext framework to create tests that run within transactions. However, your test class has to extend the corresponding TestContext support class AbstractTransactionalJUnit38SpringContextTests.

```
package com.apress.springrecipes.bank;

import org.springframework.beans.factory.annotation.Autowired;
import org.springframework.test.context.ContextConfiguration;
import org.springframework.test.context.junit38.➥
        AbstractTransactionalJUnit38SpringContextTests;

@ContextConfiguration(locations = "/beans.xml")
public class AccountServiceJUnit38ContextTests extends
        AbstractTransactionalJUnit38SpringContextTests {

    private static final String TEST_ACCOUNT_NO = "1234";

    @Autowired
    private AccountService accountService;

    protected void setUp() throws Exception {
        accountService.createAccount(TEST_ACCOUNT_NO);
        accountService.deposit(TEST_ACCOUNT_NO, 100);
    }

    // Don't need tearDown() anymore
    ...
}
```

Managing Transactions with the TestContext Framework in TestNG

To create TestNG tests that run within transactions, your test class can extend the TestContext support class AbstractTransactionalTestNGSpringContextTests to have its methods run within transactions:

```
package com.apress.springrecipes.bank;
...
import org.springframework.beans.factory.annotation.Autowired;
import org.springframework.test.context.ContextConfiguration;
import org.springframework.test.context.testng.➥
        AbstractTransactionalTestNGSpringContextTests;

@ContextConfiguration(locations = "/beans.xml")
public class AccountServiceTestNGContextTests extends
        AbstractTransactionalTestNGSpringContextTests {
```

```
    private static final String TEST_ACCOUNT_NO = "1234";

    @Autowired
    private AccountService accountService;

    @BeforeMethod
    public void init() {
        accountService.createAccount(TEST_ACCOUNT_NO);
        accountService.deposit(TEST_ACCOUNT_NO, 100);
    }

    // Don't need cleanup() anymore
    ...
}
```

12-7. Accessing a Database in Integration Tests

Problem

When creating integration tests for an application that accesses a database, especially one developed with an ORM framework, you might wish to access the database directly to prepare test data and validate the data after a test method runs.

Solution

Spring's testing support facilities can create and provide a JDBC template for you to perform database-related tasks in your tests.

When using Spring's JUnit 3.8 legacy support in releases prior to 2.5, your test class can extend the `AbstractTransactionalDataSourceSpringContextTests` base class, which is a subclass of `AbstractTransactionalSpringContextTests`, to access the precreated `JdbcTemplate` instance via the `getJdbcTemplate()` method. This class requires a data source and a transaction manager to be configured properly in the bean configuration file.

In Spring 2.5's TestContext framework, your test class can extend one of the transactional TestContext support classes to access the precreated `SimpleJdbcTemplate` instance. These classes also require a data source and a transaction manager in the bean configuration file.

How It Works

Accessing a Database with JUnit 3.8 Legacy Support

When creating tests with Spring's JUnit 3.8 legacy support, your test class can extend `AbstractTransactionalDataSourceSpringContextTests` to use a `JdbcTemplate` instance through the `getJdbcTemplate()` method to prepare and validate test data:

```
package com.apress.springrecipes.bank;

import org.springframework.test.AbstractTransactionalDataSourceSpringContextTests;
```

```
public class AccountServiceJUnit38LegacyTests extends
        AbstractTransactionalDataSourceSpringContextTests {
    ...
    protected void onSetUpInTransaction() throws Exception {
        getJdbcTemplate().update(
                "INSERT INTO ACCOUNT (ACCOUNT_NO, BALANCE) VALUES (?, ?)",
                new Object[] { TEST_ACCOUNT_NO, 100 });
    }

    public void testDeposit() {
        accountService.deposit(TEST_ACCOUNT_NO, 50);
        double balance = (Double) getJdbcTemplate().queryForObject(
                "SELECT BALANCE FROM ACCOUNT WHERE ACCOUNT_NO = ?",
                new Object[] { TEST_ACCOUNT_NO }, Double.class);
        assertEquals(balance, 150.0);
    }

    public void testWithDraw() {
        accountService.withdraw(TEST_ACCOUNT_NO, 50);
        double balance = (Double) getJdbcTemplate().queryForObject(
                "SELECT BALANCE FROM ACCOUNT WHERE ACCOUNT_NO = ?",
                new Object[] { TEST_ACCOUNT_NO }, Double.class);
        assertEquals(balance, 50.0);
    }
}
```

In addition to the `getJdbcTemplate()` method, this class offers convenient methods for you to count the number of rows in a table, delete rows from a table, and execute a SQL script. Please refer to the javadoc of this class for details.

Accessing a Database with the TestContext Framework

When using the TestContext framework to create tests, you can extend the corresponding TestContext support class to use a `SimpleJdbcTemplate` instance via a protected field. For JUnit 4.4, this class is `AbstractTransactionalJUnit4SpringContextTests`, which provides similar convenient methods for you to count the number of rows in a table, delete rows from a table, and execute a SQL script:

```
package com.apress.springrecipes.bank;
...
import org.springframework.test.context.ContextConfiguration;
import org.springframework.test.context.junit4.➥
        AbstractTransactionalJUnit4SpringContextTests;

@ContextConfiguration(locations = "/beans.xml")
public class AccountServiceJUnit4ContextTests extends
        AbstractTransactionalJUnit4SpringContextTests {
    ...
    @Before
```

```
    public void init() {
        simpleJdbcTemplate.update(
                "INSERT INTO ACCOUNT (ACCOUNT_NO, BALANCE) VALUES (?, ?)",
                TEST_ACCOUNT_NO, 100);
    }

    @Test
    public void deposit() {
        accountService.deposit(TEST_ACCOUNT_NO, 50);
        double balance = simpleJdbcTemplate.queryForObject(
                "SELECT BALANCE FROM ACCOUNT WHERE ACCOUNT_NO = ?",
                Double.class, TEST_ACCOUNT_NO);
        assertEquals(balance, 150.0, 0);
    }

    @Test
    public void withDraw() {
        accountService.withdraw(TEST_ACCOUNT_NO, 50);
        double balance = simpleJdbcTemplate.queryForObject(
                "SELECT BALANCE FROM ACCOUNT WHERE ACCOUNT_NO = ?",
                Double.class, TEST_ACCOUNT_NO);
        assertEquals(balance, 50.0, 0);
    }
}
```

In JUnit 3.8, you can extend `AbstractTransactionalJUnit38SpringContextTests` to use a `SimpleJdbcTemplate` instance through a protected field:

```
package com.apress.springrecipes.bank;
...
import org.springframework.test.context.ContextConfiguration;
import org.springframework.test.context.junit38.➥
        AbstractTransactionalJUnit38SpringContextTests;

@ContextConfiguration(locations = "/beans.xml")
public class AccountServiceJUnit38ContextTests extends
        AbstractTransactionalJUnit38SpringContextTests {
    ...
    protected void setUp() throws Exception {
        simpleJdbcTemplate.update(
                "INSERT INTO ACCOUNT (ACCOUNT_NO, BALANCE) VALUES (?, ?)",
                TEST_ACCOUNT_NO, 100);
    }

    public void testDeposit() {
        accountService.deposit(TEST_ACCOUNT_NO, 50);
        double balance = simpleJdbcTemplate.queryForObject(
                "SELECT BALANCE FROM ACCOUNT WHERE ACCOUNT_NO = ?",
```

```
                Double.class, TEST_ACCOUNT_NO);
        assertEquals(balance, 150.0);
    }

    public void testWithDraw() {
        accountService.withdraw(TEST_ACCOUNT_NO, 50);
        double balance = simpleJdbcTemplate.queryForObject(
                "SELECT BALANCE FROM ACCOUNT WHERE ACCOUNT_NO = ?",
                Double.class, TEST_ACCOUNT_NO);
        assertEquals(balance, 50.0);
    }
}
```

In TestNG, you can extend `AbstractTransactionalTestNGSpringContextTests` to use a `SimpleJdbcTemplate` instance:

```
package com.apress.springrecipes.bank;
...
import org.springframework.beans.factory.annotation.Autowired;
import org.springframework.test.context.ContextConfiguration;
import org.springframework.test.context.testng.➥
        AbstractTransactionalTestNGSpringContextTests;

@ContextConfiguration(locations = "/beans.xml")
public class AccountServiceTestNGContextTests extends
        AbstractTransactionalTestNGSpringContextTests {
    ...
    @BeforeMethod
    public void init() {
        simpleJdbcTemplate.update(
                "INSERT INTO ACCOUNT (ACCOUNT_NO, BALANCE) VALUES (?, ?)",
                TEST_ACCOUNT_NO, 100);
    }

    @Test
    public void deposit() {
        accountService.deposit(TEST_ACCOUNT_NO, 50);
        double balance = simpleJdbcTemplate.queryForObject(
                "SELECT BALANCE FROM ACCOUNT WHERE ACCOUNT_NO = ?",
                Double.class, TEST_ACCOUNT_NO);
        assertEquals(balance, 150, 0);
    }

    @Test
    public void withDraw() {
        accountService.withdraw(TEST_ACCOUNT_NO, 50);
        double balance = simpleJdbcTemplate.queryForObject(
                "SELECT BALANCE FROM ACCOUNT WHERE ACCOUNT_NO = ?",
```

```
                Double.class, TEST_ACCOUNT_NO);
        assertEquals(balance, 50, 0);
    }
}
```

12-8. Using Spring's Common Testing Annotations

Problem

Because JUnit 3.8 doesn't provide built-in testing annotations as does JUnit 4, you often have to manually implement common testing tasks, such as expecting an exception to be thrown, repeating a test method multiple times, ensuring that a test method will complete in a particular time period, and so on.

Solution

Spring's testing support provides a common set of testing annotations to simplify your test creation. These annotations are Spring-specific but independent of the underlying testing framework. Of these, the following annotations are very useful for common testing tasks. However, they are only supported for use with JUnit (both 3.8 and 4.4):

`@Repeat`: This indicates that a test method has to run multiple times. The number of times it will run is specified as the annotation value.

`@Timed`: This indicates that a test method must complete in a specified time period (in milliseconds). Otherwise, the test fails. Note that the time period includes the repetitions of the test method and any initialization and cleanup methods.

`@IfProfileValue`: This indicates that a test method can only run in a specific testing environment. This test method will run only when the actual profile value matches the specified one. You can also specify multiple values so that the test method will run if any of the values is matched. By default, `SystemProfileValueSource` is used to retrieve system properties as profile values, but you can create your own `ProfileValueSource` implementation and specify it in the `@ProfileValueSourceConfiguration` annotation.

`@ExpectedException`: This has the same effect as JUnit 4 and TestNG's expected exception support. However, as JUnit 3.8 doesn't have similar support, this is a good complement for testing exceptions in JUnit 3.8.

When using Spring's JUnit 3.8 legacy support in releases prior to 2.5, your test class can extend the `AbstractAnnotationAwareTransactionalTests` base class, which is a subclass of `AbstractTransactionalDataSourceSpringContextTests`, to use Spring's common testing annotations.

In Spring 2.5's TestContext framework, you can use Spring's testing annotations by extending one of the TestContext support classes. If you don't extend a support class, but run your JUnit 4.4 test with the test runner `SpringJUnit4ClassRunner`, you can also use these annotations.

How It Works

Using Common Testing Annotations with JUnit 3.8 Legacy Support

When creating tests with Spring's JUnit 3.8 legacy support, your test class can extend `AbstractAnnotationAwareTransactionalTests` to use Spring's common testing annotations:

```
package com.apress.springrecipes.bank;

import org.springframework.test.annotation.➥
        AbstractAnnotationAwareTransactionalTests;
import org.springframework.test.annotation.Repeat;
import org.springframework.test.annotation.Timed;

public class AccountServiceJUnit38LegacyTests extends
        AbstractAnnotationAwareTransactionalTests {
    ...
    @Timed(millis = 1000)
    public void testDeposit() {
        ...
    }

    @Repeat(5)
    public void testWithDraw() {
        ...
    }
}
```

Using Common Testing Annotations with the TestContext Framework

When using the TestContext framework to create tests for JUnit 4.4, you can use Spring's testing annotations if you run your test with `SpringJUnit4ClassRunner` or extend a JUnit 4.4 TestContext support class:

```
package com.apress.springrecipes.bank;
...
import org.springframework.test.annotation.Repeat;
import org.springframework.test.annotation.Timed;
import org.springframework.test.context.ContextConfiguration;
import org.springframework.test.context.junit4.
        AbstractTransactionalJUnit4SpringContextTests;

@ContextConfiguration(locations = "/beans.xml")
public class AccountServiceJUnit4ContextTests extends
        AbstractTransactionalJUnit4SpringContextTests {
    ...
    @Test
    @Timed(millis = 1000)
    public void deposit() {
```

```
        ...
    }

    @Test
    @Repeat(5)
    public void withDraw() {
        ...
    }
}
```

When using the TestContext framework to create tests for JUnit 3.8, you must extend a TestContext support class to use Spring's testing annotations:

```
package com.apress.springrecipes.bank;
...
import org.springframework.test.annotation.Repeat;
import org.springframework.test.annotation.Timed;
import org.springframework.test.context.ContextConfiguration;
import org.springframework.test.context.junit38.➥
        AbstractTransactionalJUnit38SpringContextTests;

@ContextConfiguration(locations = "/beans.xml")
public class AccountServiceJUnit38ContextTests extends
        AbstractTransactionalJUnit38SpringContextTests {
    ...
    @Timed(millis = 1000)
    public void testDeposit() {
        ...
    }

    @Repeat(5)
    public void testWithDraw() {
        ...
    }
}
```

12-9. Summary

In this chapter, you have learned about the basic concepts and techniques used in testing Java applications. JUnit and TestNG are the most popular testing frameworks on the Java platform. JUnit 4 introduces several major improvements over JUnit 3.8. The most important of these is annotation support. TestNG is also a powerful annotation-based testing framework.

Unit tests are used for testing a single programming unit, which is usually a class or a method in object-oriented languages. When testing a unit that depends on other units, you can use stubs and mock objects to simulate its dependencies, thus making the tests simpler. In contrast, integration tests are used to test several units as a whole.

In the web layer, controllers are usually hard to test. Spring offers mock objects for the Servlet API so that you can easily simulate web request and response objects to test a web controller. Spring also offers a set of assertion utilities for you to check the `ModelAndView` object returned by a controller. In Spring 2.5, controllers do not have to depend on the Spring MVC API and the Servlet API, so they are easier to test.

Spring's testing support facilities can manage application contexts for your tests by loading them from bean configuration files and caching them across multiple test executions. In releases prior to 2.5, Spring offered testing support specific to JUnit 3.8. Spring 2.5 provides similar support through the TestContext framework.

You can access the managed application context in your tests, as well as have your test fixtures injected from the application context automatically. In addition, if your tests involve database updates, Spring can manage transactions for them so that changes made in one test method will be rolled back and thus won't affect the next test method. Spring can also create a JDBC template for you to prepare and validate your test data in the database.

Spring provides a common set of testing annotations to simplify your test creation. These annotations are Spring-specific but independent of the underlying testing framework. However, some of these are only supported for use with JUnit.

In the next chapter, you will learn how to create secure Spring applications using the Spring Security framework.

PART 3

Advanced

CHAPTER 13

■ ■ ■

Spring Security

In this chapter, you will learn how to secure applications using the Spring Security framework, a subproject of the Spring framework. Spring Security was formerly known as Acegi Security, but its name has been changed since joining with the Spring Portfolio projects. Spring Security can be used to secure any Java application, but it's mostly used for web-based applications. Web applications, especially those that can be accessed through the Internet, are vulnerable to hacker attacks if they are not secured properly.

Spring Security provides a set of servlet filters to perform various kinds of security services for web applications. In Spring Security 1.x, you had to configure these filters as Spring beans manually, so the configurations were very verbose and difficult to understand. Spring Security 2.0 significantly simplifies its configurations with an approach similar to that of the Spring framework 2.x: using XML schema-based and annotation-based configurations. This chapter will focus on Spring Security 2.0 only. *Note that Spring Security 2.0 requires the Spring framework 2.0.8 for the 2.0 release, and 2.5.2 for the 2.5 release.*

When talking about security, there are several terms and concepts that you must understand. *Authentication* is the process of verifying a principal's identity against what it claims to be. A *principal* can be a user, a device, or a system, but most typically it means a user. A principal has to provide evidence of its identity in order to be authenticated. This evidence is called a *credential*, which is usually a password when the target principal is a user.

Authorization is the process of granting *authorities* to an authenticated user so that this user is allowed to access particular resources of the target application. The authorization process must be performed after the authentication process. Typically, authorities are granted in terms of *roles*.

Access control means controlling access to an application's resources. It entails making a decision on whether a user is allowed to access a resource. This decision is called an *access control decision*, and it's made by comparing the resource's *access attributes* with the user's granted authorities or other characteristics.

Upon finishing this chapter, you will understand basic security concepts and know how to secure your web applications at the URL access level, the method invocation level, the view-rendering level, and the domain object level.

13-1. Securing URL Access

Problem

Many web applications have some particular URLs that are critically important and private. You must secure these URLs by preventing unauthorized access to them.

Solution

Spring Security enables you to secure a web application's URL access in a declarative way through simple configuration. It handles security by applying servlet filters to HTTP requests. You can configure these filters in Spring's bean configuration files using XML elements defined in the Spring Security schema. However, as servlet filters must be registered in the web deployment descriptor to take effect, you have to register a `DelegatingFilterProxy` instance in the web deployment descriptor, which is a servlet filter that delegates request filtering to a filter in Spring's application context.

Spring Security allows you to configure web application security through the `<http>` element. If your web application's security requirements are straightforward and typical, you can set this element's `auto-config` attribute to `true` so that Spring Security will automatically register and configure several basic security services, including the following:

Form-based login service: This provides a default page that contains a login form for users to log into this application.

Logout service: This provides a handler mapped with a URL for users to log out of this application.

HTTP Basic authentication: This can process the Basic authentication credentials presented in HTTP request headers. It can also be used for authenticating requests made with remoting protocols and web services.

Anonymous login: This assigns a principal and grants authorities to an anonymous user so that you can handle an anonymous user like a normal user.

Remember-me support: This can remember a user's identity across multiple browser sessions, usually by storing a cookie in the user's browser.

Servlet API integration: This allows you to access security information in your web application via standard Servlet APIs, such as `HttpServletRequest.isUserInRole()` and `HttpServletRequest.getUserPrincipal()`.

With these security services registered, you can specify the URL patterns that require particular authorities to access. Spring Security will perform security checks according to your configurations. A user must log into an application before accessing the secure URLs, unless these URLs are opened for anonymous access. Spring Security provides a set of authentication providers for you to choose from. An authentication provider authenticates a user and returns the authorities granted to this user.

How It Works

Suppose you are going to develop an online message board application for users to post their messages on. First, you create the domain class `Message` with three properties: `author`, `title`, and `body`:

```
package com.apress.springrecipes.board.domain;

public class Message {
```

```
    private Long id;
    private String author;
    private String title;
    private String body;

    // Getters and Setters
    ...
}
```

Next, you define the operations of your message board in a service interface, including listing all messages, posting a message, deleting a message, and finding a message by its ID:

```
package com.apress.springrecipes.board.service;
...
public interface MessageBoardService {

    public List<Message> listMessages();
    public void postMessage(Message message);
    public void deleteMessage(Message message);
    public Message findMessageById(Long messageId);
}
```

For testing purposes, let's implement this interface by using a list to store the posted messages. You can use the message posting time (in milliseconds) as a message's identifier. You also have to declare the `postMessage()` and `deleteMessage()` method as `synchronized` to make them thread-safe.

```
package com.apress.springrecipes.board.service;
...
public class MessageBoardServiceImpl implements MessageBoardService {

    private Map<Long, Message> messages = new LinkedHashMap<Long, Message>();

    public List<Message> listMessages() {
        return new ArrayList<Message>(messages.values());
    }

    public synchronized void postMessage(Message message) {
        message.setId(System.currentTimeMillis());
        messages.put(message.getId(), message);
    }

    public synchronized void deleteMessage(Message message) {
        messages.remove(message.getId());
    }

    public Message findMessageById(Long messageId) {
        return messages.get(messageId);
    }
}
```

Setting Up a Spring MVC Application That Uses Spring Security

To develop this application using Spring MVC as the web framework and Spring Security as the security framework, you first create the following directory structure for your web application.

Note Before using Spring Security, you have to download its distribution (e.g., v2.0.1) and extract it to a directory of your choice. To utilize the core Spring Security services, copy `spring-security-core-2.0.1.jar` (located in the `dist` directory of the Spring Security installation) to the `WEB-INF/lib` directory. Also, you have to copy `commons-codec.jar` (located in the `lib/jakarta-commons` directory of the Spring installation).

```
board/
    WEB-INF/
        classes/
        jsp/
        lib/
            commons-codec.jar
            commons-logging.jar
            jstl.jar
            spring-security-core-2.0.1.jar
            spring-webmvc.jar
            spring.jar
            standard.jar
        board-security.xml
        board-service.xml
        board-servlet.xml
        web.xml
```

The Spring configurations for this application are separated into three different files: `board-security.xml`, `board-service.xml`, and `board-servlet.xml`. Each of them configures a particular layer.

Creating the Configuration Files

In the web deployment descriptor (i.e., `web.xml`), you register `ContextLoaderListener` to load the root application context at startup, and also Spring MVC's `DispatcherServlet` for dispatching requests:

```
<web-app version="2.4" xmlns="http://java.sun.com/xml/ns/j2ee"
    xmlns:xsi="http://www.w3.org/2001/XMLSchema-instance"
    xsi:schemaLocation="http://java.sun.com/xml/ns/j2ee
        http://java.sun.com/xml/ns/j2ee/web-app_2_4.xsd">
```

```
    <context-param>
        <param-name>contextConfigLocation</param-name>
        <param-value>/WEB-INF/board-service.xml</param-value>
    </context-param>

    <listener>
        <listener-class>
            org.springframework.web.context.ContextLoaderListener
        </listener-class>
    </listener>

    <servlet>
        <servlet-name>board</servlet-name>
        <servlet-class>
            org.springframework.web.servlet.DispatcherServlet
        </servlet-class>
    </servlet>

    <servlet-mapping>
        <servlet-name>board</servlet-name>
        <url-pattern>*.htm</url-pattern>
    </servlet-mapping>
</web-app>
```

If the root application context's configuration file doesn't have the default name (i.e., applicationContext.xml), or if you configure it with multiple configuration files, you'll have to specify the file locations in the contextConfigLocation context parameter. Also note that you have mapped the URL pattern *.htm to DispatcherServlet.

In the web layer configuration file (i.e., board-servlet.xml), you define a view resolver to resolve view names into JSP files located in the /WEB-INF/jsp/ directory. Later, you will have to configure your controllers in this file.

```
<beans xmlns="http://www.springframework.org/schema/beans"
    xmlns:xsi="http://www.w3.org/2001/XMLSchema-instance"
    xsi:schemaLocation="http://www.springframework.org/schema/beans
        http://www.springframework.org/schema/beans/spring-beans-2.5.xsd">

    <bean class="org.springframework.web.servlet.view.➥
        InternalResourceViewResolver">
        <property name="prefix" value="/WEB-INF/jsp/" />
        <property name="suffix" value=".jsp" />
    </bean>
</beans>
```

In the service layer configuration file (i.e., board-service.xml), you only have to declare the message board service:

```
<beans xmlns="http://www.springframework.org/schema/beans"
    xmlns:xsi="http://www.w3.org/2001/XMLSchema-instance"
    xsi:schemaLocation="http://www.springframework.org/schema/beans
        http://www.springframework.org/schema/beans/spring-beans-2.5.xsd">

    <bean id="messageBoardService"
        class="com.apress.springrecipes.board.service.MessageBoardServiceImpl" />
</beans>
```

Creating the Controllers and Page Views

Suppose you have to implement a function for listing all messages posted on the message board. The first step is to create the following controller.

Note To develop web applications that involve the Servlet API, you have to include `servlet-api.jar` (located in the `lib/j2ee` directory of the Spring installation) in your classpath.

```
package com.apress.springrecipes.board.web;
...
import org.springframework.web.servlet.ModelAndView;
import org.springframework.web.servlet.mvc.AbstractController;

public class MessageListController extends AbstractController {

    private MessageBoardService messageBoardService;

    public void setMessageBoardService(MessageBoardService messageBoardService) {
        this.messageBoardService = messageBoardService;
    }

    protected ModelAndView handleRequestInternal(HttpServletRequest request,
            HttpServletResponse response) throws Exception {
        return new ModelAndView("messageList",
                "messages", messageBoardService.listMessages());
    }
}
```

Then you declare this controller in `board-servlet.xml`. As `BeanNameUrlHandlerMapping` is preconfigured for each Spring MVC application, you can specify the URL mapping in its bean name.

```
<bean name="/messageList.htm"
    class="com.apress.springrecipes.board.web.MessageListController">
    <property name="messageBoardService" ref="messageBoardService" />
</bean>
```

Finally, you create the view /WEB-INF/jsp/messageList.jsp showing all the messages passed from the controller:

```
<%@ taglib prefix="c" uri="http://java.sun.com/jsp/jstl/core" %>

<html>
<head>
<title>Message List</title>
</head>

<body>
<c:forEach items="${messages}" var="message">
<table>
  <tr>
    <td>Author</td>
    <td>${message.author}</td>
  </tr>
  <tr>
    <td>Title</td>
    <td>${message.title}</td>
  </tr>
  <tr>
    <td>Body</td>
    <td>${message.body}</td>
  </tr>
  <tr>
    <td colspan="2">
      <a href="messageDelete.htm?messageId=${message.id}">Delete</a>
    </td>
  </tr>
</table>
<hr />
</c:forEach>
<a href="messagePost.htm">Post</a>
</body>
</html>
```

Another function you have to implement is for users to post messages on the message board. You create the following form controller for this purpose:

```
package com.apress.springrecipes.board.web;
...
import org.springframework.validation.BindException;
import org.springframework.web.servlet.ModelAndView;
import org.springframework.web.servlet.mvc.SimpleFormController;

public class MessagePostController extends SimpleFormController {
```

```
    private MessageBoardService messageBoardService;

    public MessagePostController() {
        setCommandClass(Message.class);
    }

    public void setMessageBoardService(MessageBoardService messageBoardService) {
        this.messageBoardService = messageBoardService;
    }

    protected ModelAndView onSubmit(HttpServletRequest request,
            HttpServletResponse response, Object command, BindException errors)
            throws Exception {
        Message message = (Message) command;
        message.setAuthor(request.getRemoteUser());
        messageBoardService.postMessage(message);
        return new ModelAndView(getSuccessView());
    }
}
```

A user must have logged into the message board before posting a message. You can get a user's login name with the `getRemoteUser()` method defined in `HttpServletRequest`. This login name will be used as the message's author name. Then you declare this controller in `board-servlet.xml`.

```
<bean name="/messagePost.htm"
    class="com.apress.springrecipes.board.web.MessagePostController">
    <property name="messageBoardService" ref="messageBoardService" />
    <property name="formView" value="messagePost" />
    <property name="successView" value="redirect:messageList.htm" />
</bean>
```

You can create the form view `/WEB-INF/jsp/messagePost.jsp` with Spring's form tags for users to input message contents:

```
<%@ taglib prefix="form" uri="http://www.springframework.org/tags/form" %>

<html>
<head>
<title>Message Post</title>
</head>

<body>
<form:form method="POST">
<table>
  <tr>
    <td>Title</td>
    <td><form:input path="title" /></td>
  </tr>
```

```
  <tr>
    <td>Body</td>
    <td><form:textarea path="body" /></td>
  </tr>
  <tr>
    <td colspan="2"><input type="submit" value="Post" /></td>
  </tr>
</table>
</form:form>
</body>
</html>
```

The last function is to allow a user to delete a posted message by clicking the Delete link on the message list page. You create the following controller for this function:

```
package com.apress.springrecipes.board.web;
...
import org.springframework.web.bind.ServletRequestUtils;
import org.springframework.web.servlet.ModelAndView;
import org.springframework.web.servlet.mvc.AbstractController;

public class MessageDeleteController extends AbstractController {

    private MessageBoardService messageBoardService;

    public void setMessageBoardService(MessageBoardService messageBoardService) {
        this.messageBoardService = messageBoardService;
    }

    protected ModelAndView handleRequestInternal(HttpServletRequest request,
            HttpServletResponse response) throws Exception {
        Long messageId =
            ServletRequestUtils.getRequiredLongParameter(request, "messageId");
        Message message = messageBoardService.findMessageById(messageId);
        messageBoardService.deleteMessage(message);
        return new ModelAndView("redirect:messageList.htm");
    }
}
```

Also, you have to declare this controller in board-servlet.xml:

```
<bean name="/messageDelete.htm"
    class="com.apress.springrecipes.board.web.MessageDeleteController">
    <property name="messageBoardService" ref="messageBoardService" />
</bean>
```

Now you can deploy this application to a web container (e.g., Apache Tomcat 6.0). By default, Tomcat listens on port 8080, so if you deploy your application to the board context path, you can list all posted messages with the following URL:

```
http://localhost:8080/board/messageList.htm
```

Up to this time, you haven't configured any security service for this application, so you can access it directly without logging into it.

Securing URL Access

Now let's secure this web application's URL access with Spring Security. First, you have to configure a `DelegatingFilterProxy` instance in `web.xml` to delegate HTTP request filtering to a filter defined in Spring Security:

```
<web-app ...>
    <context-param>
        <param-name>contextConfigLocation</param-name>
        <param-value>
            /WEB-INF/board-service.xml
            /WEB-INF/board-security.xml
        </param-value>
    </context-param>
    ...
    <filter>
        <filter-name>springSecurityFilterChain</filter-name>
        <filter-class>
            org.springframework.web.filter.DelegatingFilterProxy
        </filter-class>
    </filter>

    <filter-mapping>
        <filter-name>springSecurityFilterChain</filter-name>
        <url-pattern>/*</url-pattern>
    </filter-mapping>
    ...
</web-app>
```

The responsibility of `DelegatingFilterProxy` is simply to delegate HTTP request filtering to a Spring bean that implements the `Filter` interface. By default, it delegates to a bean whose name is the same as its `<filter-name>` property, but you can override the bean name in its `targetBeanName` init parameter. As Spring Security will automatically configure a filter chain with the name `springSecurityFilterChain` when you enable web application security, you can simply use this name for your `DelegatingFilterProxy` instance.

Although you can configure Spring Security in the same configuration file as the web and service layers, it's better to separate the security configurations in an isolated file (e.g., `board-security.xml`). You have to add the file's location to the `contextConfigLocation` context parameter for `ContextLoaderListener` to load it at startup. Then you create it with the following content:

```
<beans:beans xmlns="http://www.springframework.org/schema/security"
    xmlns:beans="http://www.springframework.org/schema/beans"
    xmlns:xsi="http://www.w3.org/2001/XMLSchema-instance"
```

```
    xsi:schemaLocation="http://www.springframework.org/schema/beans
        http://www.springframework.org/schema/beans/spring-beans-2.5.xsd
        http://www.springframework.org/schema/security
        http://www.springframework.org/schema/security/spring-security-2.0.1.xsd">

    <http auto-config="true">
        <intercept-url pattern="/messageList.htm*"
            access="ROLE_USER,ROLE_ANONYMOUS" />
        <intercept-url pattern="/messagePost.htm*" access="ROLE_USER" />
        <intercept-url pattern="/messageDelete.htm*" access="ROLE_ADMIN" />
    </http>

    <authentication-provider>
        <user-service>
            <user name="admin" password="secret"
                authorities="ROLE_ADMIN,ROLE_USER" />
            <user name="user1" password="1111" authorities="ROLE_USER" />
        </user-service>
    </authentication-provider>
</beans:beans>
```

You may find that this file looks a bit different from a normal bean configuration file. Normally, the default namespace of a bean configuration file is beans, so you can use the <bean> and <property> elements without the beans prefix. However, if you use this style to declare the Spring Security services, all security elements must be appended with the security prefix. Because the elements in a security configuration file are mostly Spring Security's, you can define security as the default namespace instead, so you can use them without the security prefix. If you do it this way, however, when you declare normal Spring beans in this file, you have to include the beans prefix for the <bean> and <property> elements.

The <http auto-config="true"> element automatically configures the basic security services that a typical web application needs. You can fine-tune these services with the corresponding subelements inside it.

Inside the <http> configuration element, you can restrict access to particular URLs with one or more <intercept-url> elements. Each <intercept-url> element specifies a URL pattern and a set of access attributes required to access the URLs. Remember that you must always include a wildcard at the end of a URL pattern. Failing to do so will make the URL pattern unable to match a URL that has request parameters. As a result, hackers could easily skip the security check by appending an arbitrary request parameter.

Access attributes are compared with a user's authorities to decide if this user can access the URLs. In most cases, access attributes are defined in terms of roles. For example, users with the ROLE_USER role, or anonymous users, who have the ROLE_ANONYMOUS role by default, are able to access the URL /messageList.htm to list all messages. However, a user must have the ROLE_USER role to post a new message via the URL /messagePost.htm. Only an administrator who has the ROLE_ADMIN role can delete messages via /messageDelete.htm.

You can configure authentication services in the <authentication-provider> element. Spring Security supports several ways of authenticating users, including authenticating against a database or an LDAP repository. It also supports defining user details in

<user-service> directly for simple security requirements. You can specify a username, a password, and a set of authorities for each user.

Now you can redeploy this application to test its security configurations. You can enter the request path /messageList.htm to list all posted messages as usual, because it's open to anonymous users. But if you click the link to post a new message, you will be redirected to the default login page generated by Spring Security. You must log into this application with a correct username and password to post a message. Finally, to delete a message, you must log in as an administrator.

13-2. Logging In to Web Applications

Problem

A secure application requires its users to log in before they can access certain secure functions. This is especially important for web applications running on the open Internet because hackers can easily reach them. Most web applications have to provide a way for users to input their credentials to log in.

Solution

Spring Security supports multiple ways for users to log into a web application. It supports form-based login by providing a default web page that contains a login form. You can also provide a custom web page as the login page. In addition, Spring Security supports HTTP Basic authentication by processing the Basic authentication credentials presented in HTTP request headers. HTTP Basic authentication can also be used for authenticating requests made with remoting protocols and web services.

Some parts of your application may allow for anonymous access (e.g., access to the welcome page). Spring Security provides an anonymous login service that can assign a principal and grant authorities to an anonymous user so that you can handle an anonymous user like a normal user when defining security policies.

Spring Security also supports remember-me login, which is able to remember a user's identity across multiple browser sessions so that a user needn't log in again after logging in for the first time.

How It Works

To help you better understand the various login mechanisms in isolation, let's first disable HTTP auto-config by removing the auto-config attribute:

```
<http>
    <intercept-url pattern="/messageList.htm*" access="ROLE_USER,ROLE_ANONYMOUS" />
    <intercept-url pattern="/messagePost.htm*" access="ROLE_USER" />
    <intercept-url pattern="/messageDelete.htm*" access="ROLE_ADMIN" />
</http>
```

Note that the login services introduced next will be registered automatically if you enable HTTP auto-config. However, if you disable HTTP auto-config or you want to customize these services, you have to configure the corresponding XML elements explicitly.

HTTP Basic Authentication

The HTTP Basic authentication support can be configured via the <http-basic> element. When HTTP Basic authentication is required, a browser will typically display a login dialog or a specific login page for users to log in.

```
<http>
    ...
    <http-basic />
</http>
```

Note that when HTTP Basic authentication and form-based login are enabled at the same time, the latter will be used. So, if you want your web application users to log in with this authentication type, you should not enable form-based login.

Form-Based Login

The form-based login service will render a web page that contains a login form for users to input their login details, and also process the login form submission. It's configured via the <form-login> element:

```
<http>
    ...
    <form-login />
</http>
```

By default, Spring Security automatically creates a login page and maps it to the URL /spring_security_login. So, you can add a link to your application (e.g., in messageList.jsp) referring to this URL for login:

```
<a href="<c:url value="/spring_security_login" />">Login</a>
```

If you don't prefer the default login page, you can provide a custom login page of your own. For example, you can create the following login.jsp file in the root directory of the web application. Note that you shouldn't put this file inside WEB-INF, which would prevent users from accessing it directly.

```
<%@ taglib prefix="c" uri="http://java.sun.com/jsp/jstl/core" %>

<html>
<head>
<title>Login</title>
</head>

<body>
<form method="POST" action="<c:url value="/j_spring_security_check" />">
<table>
  <tr>
    <td align="right">Username</td>
    <td><input type="text" name="j_username" /></td>
  </tr>
```

```
    <tr>
      <td align="right">Password</td>
      <td><input type="password" name="j_password" /></td>
    </tr>
    <tr>
      <td align="right">Remember me</td>
      <td><input type="checkbox" name="_spring_security_remember_me" /></td>
    </tr>
    <tr>
      <td colspan="2" align="right">
        <input type="submit" value="Login" />
        <input type="reset" value="Reset" />
      </td>
    </tr>
  </table>
  </form>
  </body>
  </html>
```

Note that the form action URL and the input field names are Spring Security–specific. However, the action URL can be customized with the `login-url` attribute of `<form-login>`.

Now you have to change the previous login link to refer to this URL for login:

```
<a href="<c:url value="/login.jsp" />">Login</a>
```

In order for Spring Security to display your custom login page when a login is requested, you have to specify its URL in the `login-page` attribute:

```
<http>
    ...
    <form-login login-page="/login.jsp" />
</http>
```

If the login page is displayed by Spring Security when a user requests a secure URL, the user will be redirected to the target URL once the login succeeds. However, if the user requests the login page directly via its URL, by default the user will be redirected to the context path's root (i.e., `http://localhost:8080/board/`) after a successful login. If you have not defined a welcome page in your web deployment descriptor, you may wish to redirect the user to a default target URL when the login succeeds:

```
<http>
    ....
    <form-login login-page="/login.jsp" default-target-url="/messageList.htm" />
</http>
```

If you use the default login page created by Spring Security, then when a login fails, Spring Security will render the login page again with the error message. However, if you specify a custom login page, you will have to configure the `authentication-failure-url` attribute to specify which URL to redirect to on login error. For example, you can redirect to the custom login page again with the `error` request parameter:

```
<http>
    ....
    <form-login login-page="/login.jsp" default-target-url="/messageList.htm"
        authentication-failure-url="/login.jsp?error=true" />
</http>
```

Then your login page should test whether the error request parameter is present. If an error has occurred, you will have to display the error message by accessing the session scope attribute SPRING_SECURITY_LAST_EXCEPTION, which stores the last exception for the current user.

```
<%@ taglib prefix="c" uri="http://java.sun.com/jsp/jstl/core" %>

<html>
<head>
<title>Login</title>
</head>

<body>
<c:if test="${not empty param.error}">
  <font color="red">
  Login error. <br />
  Reason : ${sessionScope["SPRING_SECURITY_LAST_EXCEPTION"].message}
  </font>
</c:if>
...
</body>
</html>
```

The Logout Service

The logout service provides a handler to handle logout requests. It can be configured via the <logout> element:

```
<http>
    ...
    <logout />
</http>
```

By default, it's mapped to the URL /j_spring_security_logout, so you can add a link to a page referring to this URL for logout. Note that this URL can be customized with the logout-url attribute of <logout>.

```
<a href="<c:url value="/j_spring_security_logout" />">Logout</a>
```

By default, a user will be redirected to the context path's root when the logout succeeds. But sometimes you may wish to direct the user to another URL, which you can do as follows:

```
<http>
    ...
    <logout logout-success-url="/login.jsp" />
</http>
```

Anonymous Login

The anonymous login service can be configured via the <anonymous> element, where you can customize the username and authorities of an anonymous user, whose default values are anonymousUser and ROLE_ANONYMOUS:

```
<http>
    <intercept-url pattern="/messageList.htm*" access="ROLE_USER,ROLE_GUEST" />
    <intercept-url pattern="/messagePost.htm*" access="ROLE_USER" />
    <intercept-url pattern="/messageDelete.htm*" access="ROLE_ADMIN" />
    ...
    <anonymous username="guest" granted-authority="ROLE_GUEST" />
</http>
```

Remember-Me Support

Remember-me support can be configured via the <remember-me> element. By default, it encodes the username, password, remember-me expiration time, and a private key as a token, and stores it as a cookie in the user's browser. The next time the user accesses the same web application, this token will be detected so that the user can log in automatically.

```
<http>
    ...
    <remember-me />
</http>
```

However, static remember-me tokens can cause security issues because they may be captured by hackers. Spring Security supports rolling tokens for more advanced security needs, but this requires a database to persist the tokens. For details about rolling remember-me token deployment, please refer to the Spring Security reference documentation.

13-3. Authenticating Users

Problem

When a user attempts to log into your application to access its secure resources, you have to authenticate the user's principal and grant authorities to this user.

Solution

In Spring Security, authentication is performed by one or more *authentication providers*, connected as a chain. If any of these providers authenticates a user successfully, that user will be able to log into the application. If any provider reports that the user is disabled or locked or that the credential is incorrect, or if no provider can authenticate the user, then the user will be unable to log into this application.

Spring Security supports multiple ways of authenticating users and includes built-in provider implementations for them. You can easily configure these providers with the built-in XML elements. Most common authentication providers authenticate users against a user repository storing *user details* (e.g., in an application's memory, a relational database, or an LDAP repository).

When storing user details in a repository, you should avoid storing user passwords in clear text because they are vulnerable to hackers. Instead, you should always store encrypted passwords in your repository. A typical way of encrypting passwords is to use a one-way hash function to encode the passwords. When a user enters a password to log in, you apply the same hash function to this password and compare the result with the one stored in the repository. Spring Security supports several algorithms for encoding passwords (including MD5 and SHA), and provides built-in password encoders for these algorithms.

If you retrieve a user's details from a user repository every time a user attempts to log in, your application may incur a performance impact. This is because a user repository is usually stored remotely, and it has to perform some kinds of queries in response to a request. For this reason, Spring Security supports caching user details in local memory and storage to save you the overhead of performing remote queries.

How It Works

Authenticating Users with In-Memory Definitions

If you have only a few users in your application and you seldom modify their details, you can consider defining the user details in Spring Security's configuration file so that they will be loaded into your application's memory:

```
<authentication-provider>
    <user-service>
        <user name="admin" password="secret" authorities="ROLE_ADMIN,ROLE_USER" />
        <user name="user1" password="1111" authorities="ROLE_USER" />
        <user name="user2" password="2222" disabled="true"
            authorities="ROLE_USER" />
    </user-service>
</authentication-provider>
```

You can define user details in `<user-service>` with multiple `<user>` elements. For each user, you can specify a username, a password, a disabled status, and a set of granted authorities. A disabled user cannot log into an application.

Spring Security also allows you to externalize user details in a properties file, such as `/WEB-INF/users.properties`:

```
<authentication-provider>
    <user-service properties="/WEB-INF/users.properties" />
</authentication-provider>
```

Then you can create the specified properties file and define the user details in the form of properties:

```
admin=secret,ROLE_ADMIN,ROLE_USER
user1=1111,ROLE_USER
user2=2222,disabled,ROLE_USER
```

Each property in this file represents a user's details. The property key is the username, and the property value is divided into several parts separated by commas. The first part is the password and the second part is the enabled status, which is optional, and the default status is `enabled`. The following parts are the authorities granted to the user.

Authenticating Users Against a Database

More typically, user details should be stored in a database for easy maintenance. Spring Security has built-in support for querying user details from a database. By default, it queries user details, including authorities, with the following SQL statements:

```
SELECT username, password, enabled
FROM   users
WHERE  username = ?

SELECT username, authority
FROM   authorities
WHERE  username = ?
```

In order for Spring Security to query user details with these SQL statements, you have to create the corresponding tables in your database. For example, you can create them in the `board` schema of Apache Derby with the following SQL statements:

```
CREATE TABLE USERS (
    USERNAME    VARCHAR(10)    NOT NULL,
    PASSWORD    VARCHAR(32)    NOT NULL,
    ENABLED     SMALLINT,
    PRIMARY KEY (USERNAME)
);

CREATE TABLE AUTHORITIES (
    USERNAME    VARCHAR(10)    NOT NULL,
    AUTHORITY   VARCHAR(10)    NOT NULL,
    FOREIGN KEY (USERNAME) REFERENCES USERS
);
```

Then you can input some user details into these tables for testing purposes. The data for these two tables is shown in Tables 13-1 and 13-2.

Table 13-1. *Testing User Data for the USERS Table*

USERNAME	PASSWORD	ENABLED
admin	secret	1
user1	1111	1
user2	2222	0

Table 13-2. *Testing User Data for the AUTHORITIES Table*

USERNAME	AUTHORITY
admin	ROLE_ADMIN
admin	ROLE_USER
user1	ROLE_USER
user2	ROLE_USER

In order for Spring Security to access these tables, you have to declare a data source (e.g., in `board-service.xml`) for creating connections to this database.

■ Note To connect to a database in the Apache Derby server, you have to copy `derbyclient.jar` (located in the `lib` directory of the Derby installation) to the `WEB-INF/lib` directory.

```
<bean id="dataSource"
    class="org.springframework.jdbc.datasource.DriverManagerDataSource">
    <property name="driverClassName"
        value="org.apache.derby.jdbc.ClientDriver" />
    <property name="url"
        value="jdbc:derby://localhost:1527/board;create=true" />
    <property name="username" value="app" />
    <property name="password" value="app" />
</bean>
```

The final step is to configure an authentication provider that queries this database for user details. You can achieve this simply by using the `<jdbc-user-service>` element with a data source reference:

```
<authentication-provider>
    <jdbc-user-service data-source-ref="dataSource" />
</authentication-provider>
```

However, in some cases you may already have your own user repository defined in a legacy database. For example, suppose that the tables are created with the following SQL statements, and that all users in the `MEMBER` table have the enabled status:

```
CREATE TABLE MEMBER (
    ID          BIGINT          NOT NULL,
    USERNAME    VARCHAR(10)     NOT NULL,
    PASSWORD    VARCHAR(32)     NOT NULL,
    PRIMARY KEY (ID)
);
```

```
CREATE TABLE MEMBER_ROLE (
    MEMBER_ID    BIGINT         NOT NULL,
    ROLE         VARCHAR(10)    NOT NULL,
    FOREIGN KEY (MEMBER_ID) REFERENCES MEMBER
);
```

Suppose you have the legacy user data stored in these tables as shown in Tables 13-3 and 13-4.

Table 13-3. *Legacy User Data in the MEMBER Table*

ID	USERNAME	PASSWORD
1	admin	secret
2	user1	1111

Table 13-4. *Legacy User Data in the MEMBER_ROLE Table*

MEMBER_ID	ROLE
1	ROLE_ADMIN
1	ROLE_USER
2	ROLE_USER

Fortunately, Spring Security also supports using custom SQL statements to query a legacy database for user details. You can specify the statements for querying a user's information and authorities in the users-by-username-query and authorities-by-username-query attributes:

```
<jdbc-user-service data-source-ref="dataSource"
    users-by-username-query=
        "SELECT username, password, 'true' as enabled➥
         FROM   member➥
         WHERE  username = ?"
    authorities-by-username-query=
        "SELECT member.username, member_role.role as authorities➥
         FROM   member, member_role➥
         WHERE  member.username = ? AND member.id = member_role.member_id" />
```

Encrypting Passwords

Until now, you have been storing user details with clear-text passwords. But this approach is vulnerable to hacker attacks, so you should encrypt the passwords before storing them. Spring Security supports several algorithms for encrypting passwords. For example, you can choose MD5 (Message-Digest algorithm 5, a one-way hash algorithm) to encrypt your passwords.

■Note You may need a utility to calculate MD5 digests for your passwords. One such utility is Jacksum, which you can download from `http://sourceforge.net/projects/jacksum/` and extract to a directory of your choice. Then execute the following command to calculate a digest for a text:

```
java -jar jacksum.jar -a md5 -q "txt:secret"
```

Now you can store the encrypted passwords in your user repository. For example, if you are using in-memory user definitions, you can specify the encrypted passwords in the `password` attributes. Then you can configure a `<password-encoder>` element with a hashing algorithm specified in the `hash` attribute.

```
<authentication-provider>
    <password-encoder hash="md5" />
    <user-service>
        <user name="admin" password="5ebe2294ecd0e0f08eab7690d2a6ee69"
            authorities="ROLE_ADMIN, ROLE_USER" />
        <user name="user1" password="b59c67bf196a4758191e42f76670ceba"
            authorities="ROLE_USER" />
        <user name="user2" password="934b535800b1cba8f96a5d72f72f1611"
            disabled="true" authorities="ROLE_USER" />
    </user-service>
</authentication-provider>
```

A password encoder is also applicable to a user repository stored in a database:

```
<authentication-provider>
    <password-encoder hash="md5" />
    <jdbc-user-service data-source-ref="dataSource" />
</authentication-provider>
```

Of course, you have to store the encrypted passwords in the database tables, instead of the clear-text passwords, as shown in Table 13-5.

Table 13-5. *Testing User Data with Encrypted Passwords for the USERS Table*

USERNAME	PASSWORD	ENABLED
admin	5ebe2294ecd0e0f08eab7690d2a6ee69	1
user1	b59c67bf196a4758191e42f76670ceba	1
user2	934b535800b1cba8f96a5d72f72f1611	0

Authenticating Users Against an LDAP Repository

Spring Security also supports accessing an LDAP repository for authenticating users. First, you have to prepare some user data for populating the LDAP repository. Let's prepare the user data in the LDAP Data Interchange Format (LDIF), a standard plain-text data format for importing and exporting LDAP directory data. For example, create the `users.ldif` file containing the following contents:

```
dn: dc=springrecipes,dc=com
objectClass: top
objectClass: domain
dc: springrecipes

dn: ou=groups,dc=springrecipes,dc=com
objectclass: top
objectclass: organizationalUnit
ou: groups

dn: ou=people,dc=springrecipes,dc=com
objectclass: top
objectclass: organizationalUnit
ou: people

dn: uid=admin,ou=people,dc=springrecipes,dc=com
objectclass: top
objectclass: uidObject
objectclass: person
uid: admin
cn: admin
sn: admin
userPassword: secret

dn: uid=user1,ou=people,dc=springrecipes,dc=com
objectclass: top
objectclass: uidObject
objectclass: person
uid: user1
cn: user1
sn: user1
userPassword: 1111

dn: cn=admin,ou=groups,dc=springrecipes,dc=com
objectclass: top
objectclass: groupOfNames
cn: admin
member: uid=admin,ou=people,dc=springrecipes,dc=com

dn: cn=user,ou=groups,dc=springrecipes,dc=com
objectclass: top
objectclass: groupOfNames
cn: user
member: uid=admin,ou=people,dc=springrecipes,dc=com
member: uid=user1,ou=people,dc=springrecipes,dc=com
```

Don't worry if you don't understand this LDIF file very well. You probably won't need to use this file format to define LDAP data often, because most LDAP servers support GUI-based configuration. This `users.ldif` file includes the following contents:

- The default LDAP domain, `dc=springrecipes,dc=com`
- The `groups` and `people` organization units for storing groups and users
- The `admin` and `user1` users with the passwords `secret` and `1111`
- The `admin` group (including the `admin` user) and the `user` group (including the `admin` and `user1` users)

For testing purposes, you can install an LDAP server on your local machine to host this user repository. For the sake of easy installation and configuration, I would recommend installing OpenDS (`http://www.opends.org/`), a Java-based open source directory service engine that supports LDAP.

■ **Note** OpenDS supports two types of installation interfaces: command-line and GUI. This example uses the command-line interface, so you have to download the ZIP distribution and extract it to an arbitrary directory (e.g., `C:\OpenDS-1.0.0`), and then execute the `setup` script from the root of this directory.

```
C:\OpenDS-1.0.0>setup --cli

OpenDS Directory Server 1.0.0
Please wait while the setup program initializes...

What would you like to use as the initial root user DN for the Directory
Server? [cn=Directory Manager]:
Please provide the password to use for the initial root user: ldap
Please re-enter the password for confirmation: ldap

On which port would you like the Directory Server to accept connections from
LDAP clients? [389]:

What do you wish to use as the base DN for the directory data?
[dc=example,dc=com]:dc=springrecipes,dc=com
Options for populating the database:

    1)  Only create the base entry
    2)  Leave the database empty
    3)  Import data from an LDIF file
    4)  Load automatically-generated sample data

Enter choice [1]: 3
```

```
Please specify the path to the LDIF file containing the data to import: users.ldif

Do you want to enable SSL? (yes / no) [no]:

Do you want to enable Start TLS? (yes / no) [no]:

Enable OpenDS to run as a Windows Service? (yes / no) [no]:

Do you want to start the server when the configuration is completed? (yes /
no) [yes]:

Configuring Directory Server ..... Done.
Importing LDIF file users.ldif ....... Done.
Starting Directory Server ........ Done.
```

Note that the root user and password for this LDAP server are cn=Directory Manager and ldap, respectively. Later, you will have to use this user to connect to this server.

After the LDAP server has started up, you can configure Spring Security to authenticate users against its repository.

■ **Note** To authenticate users against an LDAP repository, you have to download the Spring LDAP project (e.g., v1.2.1) from http://www.springframework.org/ldap and extract it to a directory of your choice. Then copy spring-ldap-1.2.1.jar (located in the dist directory of the Spring LDAP installation) and commons-lang.jar (located in lib) to the WEB-INF/lib directory.

```
<beans:beans ...>
    ...
    <authentication-provider>
        <password-encoder hash="{sha}" />
        <ldap-user-service server-ref="ldapServer"
            user-search-filter="uid={0}" user-search-base="ou=people"
            group-search-filter="member={0}" group-search-base="ou=groups" />
    </authentication-provider>

    <ldap-server id="ldapServer"
        url="ldap://localhost:389/dc=springrecipes,dc=com"
        manager-dn="cn=Directory Manager" manager-password="ldap" />
</beans:beans>
```

You have to configure an <ldap-user-service> element to define how to search users from an LDAP repository. You can specify the search filters and search bases for searching users and groups via several attributes, whose values must be consistent with the repository's directory structure. With the preceding attribute values, Spring Security will search a user from the people organization unit with a particular user ID, and search a user's groups from the groups organization unit. Spring Security will automatically insert the ROLE_ prefix to each group as an authority.

As OpenDS uses SSHA (Salted Secure Hash Algorithm) to encode user passwords by default, you have to specify {sha} as the hash algorithm in <password-encoder>. Note that this value is different from sha, as it's specific to LDAP password encoding.

Finally, <ldap-user-service> has to refer to an LDAP server definition, which defines how to create connections to an LDAP server. You can specify the root user's username and password to connect to the LDAP server running on localhost.

Caching User Details

Both <jdbc-user-service> and <ldap-user-service> support caching user details. First of all, you have to choose a cache implementation that provides a caching service. As Spring and Spring Security have built-in support for Ehcache (http://ehcache.sourceforge.net/), you can choose it as your cache implementation and create a configuration file for it (e.g., ehcache.xml in the classpath root) with the following contents.

■ **Note** To use Ehcache to cache objects, you have to copy ehcache-1.3.0.jar (located in the lib/ehcache directory of the Spring installation) to the WEB-INF/lib directory.

```
<ehcache>
    <diskStore path="java.io.tmpdir"/>

    <defaultCache
        maxElementsInMemory="1000"
        eternal="false"
        timeToIdleSeconds="120"
        timeToLiveSeconds="120"
        overflowToDisk="true"
        />

    <cache name="userCache"
        maxElementsInMemory="100"
        eternal="false"
        timeToIdleSeconds="600"
        timeToLiveSeconds="3600"
        overflowToDisk="true"
        />
</ehcache>
```

This Ehcache configuration file defines two types of cache configurations. One is for the default while the other is for caching user details. If the user cache configuration is used, a cache instance will cache the details of at most 100 users in memory. The cached users will overflow to disk when this limit is exceeded. A cached user will expire if it has been idle for 10 minutes or live for 1 hour after its creation.

To enable caching user details in Spring Security, you can set the cache-ref attribute of either <jdbc-user-service> or <ldap-user-service> to refer to a UserCache object. For Ehcache, Spring Security comes with a UserCache implementation, EhCacheBasedUserCache, which has to refer to an Ehcache instance.

```
<beans:beans ...>
    ...
    <authentication-provider>
        ...
        <ldap-user-service server-ref="ldapServer"
            user-search-filter="uid={0}" user-search-base="ou=people"
            group-search-filter="member={0}" group-search-base="ou=groups"
            cache-ref="userCache" />
    </authentication-provider>

    <beans:bean id="userCache" class="org.springframework.security.providers.➥
        dao.cache.EhCacheBasedUserCache">
        <beans:property name="cache" ref="userEhCache" />
    </beans:bean>

    <beans:bean id="userEhCache"
        class="org.springframework.cache.ehcache.EhCacheFactoryBean">
        <beans:property name="cacheManager" ref="cacheManager" />
        <beans:property name="cacheName" value="userCache" />
    </beans:bean>
</beans:beans>
```

In Spring, an Ehcache instance can be created via EhCacheFactoryBean by providing a cache manager and a cache name. Spring also provides EhCacheManagerFactoryBean for you to create an Ehcache manager by loading a configuration file. By default, it loads ehcache.xml (located in the root of the classpath). As an Ehcache manager may be used by other service components, it should be defined in board-service.xml.

```
<bean id="cacheManager"
    class="org.springframework.cache.ehcache.EhCacheManagerFactoryBean" />
```

13-4. Making Access Control Decisions

Problem

In the authentication process, an application will grant a successfully authenticated user a set of authorities. When this user attempts to access a resource in the application, it has to make a decision on whether the resource is accessible with the granted authorities or other characteristics.

Solution

The decision on whether a user is allowed to access a resource in an application is called an access control decision. It is made based on the user's authentication status, and the resource's nature and access attributes. In Spring Security, access control decisions are made by *access decision managers*, which have to implement the `AccessDecisionManager` interface. You are free to create your own access decision managers by implementing this interface, but Spring Security comes with three convenient access decision managers based on the voting approach. They are shown in Table 13-6.

Table 13-6. *Access Decision Managers That Come with Spring Security*

Access Decision Manager	When to Grant Access
`AffirmativeBased`	At least one voter votes to grant access.
`ConsensusBased`	A consensus of voters votes to grant access.
`UnanimousBased`	All voters vote to abstain or grant access (no voter votes to deny access).

All these access decision managers require a group of *voters* to be configured for voting on access control decisions. Each voter has to implement the `AccessDecisionVoter` interface. A voter can vote to grant, abstain, or deny access to a resource. The voting results are represented by the `ACCESS_GRANTED`, `ACCESS_DENIED`, and `ACCESS_ABSTAIN` constant fields defined in the `AccessDecisionVoter` interface.

By default, if no access decision manager is specified explicitly, Spring Security will automatically configure an `AffirmativeBased` access decision manager with the following two voters configured:

`RoleVoter`: Votes for an access control decision based on a user's role. It will only process access attributes that start with the `ROLE_` prefix, but this prefix can be customized. It votes to grant access if the user has the same role as required to access the resource. It votes to deny access if the user lacks any role required to access the resource. If the resource does not have an access attribute starting with `ROLE_`, it will abstain from voting.

`AuthenticatedVoter`: Votes for an access control decision based on a user's authentication level. It will only process the access attributes `IS_AUTHENTICATED_FULLY`, `IS_AUTHENTICATED_REMEMBERED`, and `IS_AUTHENTICATED_ANONYMOUSLY`. It votes to grant access if the user's authentication level is higher than the required attribute. From highest to lowest, authentication levels are "fully authenticated," "authentication remembered," and "anonymously authenticated."

How It Works

By default, Spring Security will automatically configure an access decision manager if none is specified. This default access decision manager is equivalent to the one defined with the following bean configuration:

```
<bean id="_accessManager"
    class="org.springframework.security.vote.AffirmativeBased">
    <property name="decisionVoters">
        <list>
            <bean class="org.springframework.security.vote.RoleVoter" />
            <bean class="org.springframework.security.vote.AuthenticatedVoter" />
        </list>
    </property>
</bean>
```

This default access decision manager and its decision voters should satisfy most typical authorization requirements. However, if they don't satisfy yours, you can create your own. In most cases, you'll only need to create a custom voter. For example, you can create a voter to vote for a decision based on a user's IP address:

```
package com.apress.springrecipes.board.security;

import org.springframework.security.Authentication;
import org.springframework.security.ConfigAttribute;
import org.springframework.security.ConfigAttributeDefinition;
import org.springframework.security.ui.WebAuthenticationDetails;
import org.springframework.security.vote.AccessDecisionVoter;

public class IpAddressVoter implements AccessDecisionVoter {

    public static final String IP_PREFIX = "IP_";
    public static final String IP_LOCAL_HOST = "IP_LOCAL_HOST";

    public boolean supports(ConfigAttribute attribute) {
        return attribute.getAttribute() != null
                && attribute.getAttribute().startsWith(IP_PREFIX);
    }

    public boolean supports(Class clazz) {
        return true;
    }

    public int vote(Authentication authentication, Object object,
            ConfigAttributeDefinition config) {
        if (!(authentication.getDetails() instanceof WebAuthenticationDetails)) {
            return ACCESS_DENIED;
        }

        WebAuthenticationDetails details =
            (WebAuthenticationDetails) authentication.getDetails();
        String address = details.getRemoteAddress();
```

```
        int result = ACCESS_ABSTAIN;
        for (Object element : config.getConfigAttributes()) {
            ConfigAttribute attribute = (ConfigAttribute) element;

            if (this.supports(attribute)) {
                result = ACCESS_DENIED;
                if (IP_LOCAL_HOST.equals(attribute.getAttribute())) {
                    if (address.equals("127.0.0.1")) {
                        return ACCESS_GRANTED;
                    }
                }
            }
        }
        return result;
    }
}
```

Note that this voter will only process the access attributes that start with the IP_ prefix. At the moment, it only supports the IP_LOCAL_HOST access attribute. If the user is a web client whose IP address is equal to 127.0.0.1, this voter will vote to grant access. Otherwise, it will vote to deny access. If the resource does not have an access attribute starting with IP_, it will abstain from voting.

Next, you have to define a custom access decision manager that includes this voter. If you define this access decision manager in board-security.xml, you will have to include the beans prefix, because the default schema is security.

```
<beans:bean id="accessDecisionManager"
    class="org.springframework.security.vote.AffirmativeBased">
    <beans:property name="decisionVoters">
        <beans:list>
            <beans:bean
                class="org.springframework.security.vote.RoleVoter" />
            <beans:bean
                class="org.springframework.security.vote.AuthenticatedVoter" />
            <beans:bean
                class="com.apress.springrecipes.board.security.IpAddressVoter" />
        </beans:list>
    </beans:property>
</beans:bean>
```

Now suppose you would like to allow users of the machine running the web container (i.e., the server administrators) to delete messages without logging in. You have to refer to this access decision manager from the <http> configuration element and add the access attribute IP_LOCAL_HOST to the URL pattern /messageDelete.htm*:

```
<http access-decision-manager-ref="accessDecisionManager">
    <intercept-url pattern="/messageList.htm*" access="ROLE_USER,ROLE_GUEST" />
    <intercept-url pattern="/messagePost.htm*" access="ROLE_USER" />
    <intercept-url pattern="/messageDelete.htm*"
```

```
        access="ROLE_ADMIN,IP_LOCAL_HOST" />
    ...
</http>
```

Then if you access this message board application from localhost, you needn't log in as an administrator to delete a posted message.

13-5. Securing Method Invocations

Problem

As an alternative or a complement to securing URL access in the web layer, sometimes you may need to secure method invocations in the service layer. For example, in the case that a single controller has to invoke multiple methods in the service layer, you may wish to enforce fine-grained security controls on these methods.

Solution

Spring Security enables you to secure method invocations in a declarative way. First, you can embed a `<security:intercept-methods>` element in a bean definition to secure its methods. Alternatively, you can configure a global `<global-method-security>` element to secure multiple methods matched with AspectJ pointcut expressions. You can also annotate methods declared in a bean interface or an implementation class with the `@Secured` annotation, and then enable security for them in `<global-method-security>`.

How It Works

Securing Methods by Embedding a Security Interceptor

First, you can secure a bean's methods by embedding a `<security:intercept-methods>` element in the bean definition. For example, you can secure the methods of the `messageBoardService` bean defined in `board-service.xml`. As this element is defined in the `security` schema, you have to import it beforehand.

■ **Note** To match methods that are to be secured in Spring Security, you have to copy `aspectjrt.jar` and `aspectjweaver.jar` (located in the `lib/aspectj` directory of the Spring installation) to the `WEB-INF/lib` directory.

```
<beans xmlns="http://www.springframework.org/schema/beans"
    xmlns:xsi="http://www.w3.org/2001/XMLSchema-instance"
    xmlns:security="http://www.springframework.org/schema/security"
    xsi:schemaLocation="http://www.springframework.org/schema/beans
        http://www.springframework.org/schema/beans/spring-beans-2.5.xsd
        http://www.springframework.org/schema/security
        http://www.springframework.org/schema/security/spring-security-2.0.1.xsd">
```

```
    <bean id="messageBoardService"
        class="com.apress.springrecipes.board.service.MessageBoardServiceImpl">
        <security:intercept-methods
            access-decision-manager-ref="accessDecisionManager">
            <security:protect
                method="com.apress.springrecipes.board.service.➥
                    MessageBoardService.listMessages"
                access="ROLE_USER,ROLE_GUEST" />
            <security:protect
                method="com.apress.springrecipes.board.service.➥
                    MessageBoardService.postMessage"
                access="ROLE_USER" />
            <security:protect
                method="com.apress.springrecipes.board.service.➥
                    MessageBoardService.deleteMessage"
                access="ROLE_ADMIN,IP_LOCAL_HOST" />
            <security:protect
                method="com.apress.springrecipes.board.service.➥
                    MessageBoardService.findMessageById"
                access="ROLE_USER,ROLE_GUEST" />
        </security:intercept-methods>
    </bean>
    ...
</beans>
```

In a bean's `<security:intercept-methods>`, you can specify multiple `<security:protect>` elements to specify access attributes for this bean's methods. You can match multiple methods by specifying a method name pattern with wildcards. If you would like to use a custom access decision manager, you can specify it in the `access-decision-manager-ref` attribute.

Securing Methods with Pointcuts

Second, you can define global pointcuts in `<global-method-security>` to secure methods using AspectJ pointcut expressions, instead of embedding a security interceptor in each bean whose methods require security. You should configure the `<global-method-security>` element in `board-security.xml` for centralizing security configurations. As the default namespace of this configuration file is `security`, you needn't specify a prefix for this element explicitly. You can also specify a custom access decision manager in the `access-decision-manager-ref` attribute.

```
<global-method-security
    access-decision-manager-ref="accessDecisionManager">
    <protect-pointcut expression=
        "execution(* com.apress.springrecipes.board.service.*Service.list*(..))"
        access="ROLE_USER,ROLE_GUEST" />
    <protect-pointcut expression=
        "execution(* com.apress.springrecipes.board.service.*Service.post*(..))"
        access="ROLE_USER" />
    <protect-pointcut expression=
```

```
        "execution(* com.apress.springrecipes.board.service.*Service.delete*(..))"
        access="ROLE_ADMIN,IP_LOCAL_HOST" />
    <protect-pointcut expression=
        "execution(* com.apress.springrecipes.board.service.*Service.find*(..))"
        access="ROLE_USER,ROLE_GUEST" />
</global-method-security>
```

To test this approach, you have to delete the preceding `<security:intercept-methods>` element.

Securing Methods with Annotations

The third approach to securing methods is by annotating them with `@Secured`. For example, you can annotate the methods in `MessageBoardServiceImpl` with the `@Secured` annotation and specify the access attributes as its value, whose type is `String[]`.

Note To use Spring Security's annotation support, you have to copy `spring-security-core-tiger-2.0.1.jar` (located in the `dist` directory of the Spring Security installation) to the `WEB-INF/lib` directory.

```
package com.apress.springrecipes.board.service;
...
import org.springframework.security.annotation.Secured;

public class MessageBoardServiceImpl implements MessageBoardService {
    ...
    @Secured({"ROLE_USER", "ROLE_GUEST"})
    public List<Message> listMessages() {
        ...
    }

    @Secured("ROLE_USER")
    public synchronized void postMessage(Message message) {
        ...
    }

    @Secured({"ROLE_ADMIN", "IP_LOCAL_HOST"})
    public synchronized void deleteMessage(Message message) {
        ...
    }

    @Secured({"ROLE_USER", "ROLE_GUEST"})
    public Message findMessageById(Long messageId) {
        return messages.get(messageId);
    }
}
```

Then in <global-method-security>, you have to enable security for methods annotated with @Secured.

```
<global-method-security secured-annotations="enabled"
    access-decision-manager-ref="accessDecisionManager" />
```

13-6. Handling Security in Views

Problem

Sometimes you may wish to display a user's authentication information, such as the principal name and the granted authorities, in the views of your web application. In addition, you would like to render the view contents conditionally according to the user's authorities.

Solution

Although you can write JSP scriptlets in your JSP files to retrieve authentication and authorization information through the Spring Security API, it's not an efficient solution. Spring Security provides a JSP tag library for you to handle security in JSP views. It includes tags that can display a user's authentication information and render the view contents conditionally according to the user's authorities.

How It Works

Displaying Authentication Information

Suppose you would like to display a user's principal name and granted authorities in the header of the message listing page (i.e., messageList.jsp). First of all, you have to import Spring Security's tag library definition.

■ **Note** To use Spring Security's JSP tag library, you have to copy spring-security-taglibs-2.0.1.jar (located in the dist directory of the Spring Security installation) to the WEB-INF/lib directory.

```
<%@ taglib prefix="c" uri="http://java.sun.com/jsp/jstl/core" %>
<%@ taglib prefix="security" uri="http://www.springframework.org/security/tags" %>

<html>
<head>
<title>Message List</title>
</head>

<body>
<h2>Welcome! <security:authentication property="name" /></h2>
```

```
<security:authentication property="authorities" var="authorities" />
<ul>
<c:forEach items="${authorities}" var="authority">
  <li>${authority.authority}</li>
</c:forEach>
</ul>
<hr />
...
</body>
</html>
```

The <security:authentication> tag exposes the current user's Authentication object for you to render its properties. You can specify a property name or property path in its property attribute. For example, you can render a user's principal name through the name property.

In addition to rendering an authentication property directly, this tag supports storing the property in a JSP variable, whose name is specified in the var attribute. For example, you can store the authorities property, which contains the authorities granted to the user, in the JSP variable authorities, and render them one by one with a <c:forEach> tag. You can further specify the variable scope with the scope attribute.

Rendering View Contents Conditionally

If you would like to render view contents conditionally according to a user's authorities, you can use the <security:authorize> tag. For example, you can decide whether to render the message authors according to the user's authorities:

```
<%@ taglib prefix="c" uri="http://java.sun.com/jsp/jstl/core" %>
<%@ taglib prefix="security" uri="http://www.springframework.org/security/tags" %>

<html>
<head>
<title>Message List</title>
</head>

<body>
...
<c:forEach items="${messages}" var="message">
<table>
  <security:authorize ifAllGranted="ROLE_ADMIN,ROLE_USER">
  <tr>
    <td>Author</td>
    <td>${message.author}</td>
  </tr>
  </security:authorize>
  ...
</table>
<hr />
</c:forEach>
...
```

```
</body>
</html>
```

If you want the enclosing content to be rendered only when the user has been granted certain authorities at the same time, you have to specify them in the ifAllGranted attribute. Otherwise, if the enclosing content can be rendered with any of the authorities, you have to specify them in the ifAnyGranted attribute:

```
<security:authorize ifAnyGranted="ROLE_ADMIN,ROLE_USER">
<tr>
  <td>Author</td>
  <td>${message.author}</td>
</tr>
</security:authorize>
```

You can also render the enclosing content when a user has not been granted any of the authorities specified in the ifNotGranted attribute:

```
<security:authorize ifNotGranted="ROLE_GUEST">
<tr>
  <td>Author</td>
  <td>${message.author}</td>
</tr>
</security:authorize>
```

13-7. Handling Domain Object Security

Problem

Sometimes you may have complicated security requirements that require handling security at the domain object level. That means you have to allow each domain object to have different access attributes for different principals.

Solution

Spring Security provides a module named ACL that allows each domain object to have its own *access control list (ACL)*. An ACL contains a domain object's *object identity* to associate with the object, and also holds multiple *access control entries (ACEs)*, each of which contains the following two core parts:

Permissions: An ACE's permissions are represented by a particular bit mask, with each bit value for a particular type of permission. The BasePermission class predefines five basic permissions as constant values for you to use: READ (bit 0 or integer 1), WRITE (bit 1 or integer 2), CREATE (bit 2 or integer 4), DELETE (bit 3 or integer 8), and ADMINISTRATION (bit 4 or integer 16). You can also define your own using other unused bits.

Security Identity (SID): Each ACE contains permissions for a particular SID. An SID can be a principal (PrincipalSid) or an authority (GrantedAuthoritySid) to associate with permissions.

In addition to defining the ACL object model, Spring Security defines APIs for reading and maintaining the model, and provides high-performance JDBC implementations for these APIs. In order to simplify ACL's usages, Spring Security also provides facilities, such as access decision voters and JSP tags, for you to use ACL consistently with other security facilities in your application.

How It Works

Setting Up an ACL Service

Spring Security provides built-in support for storing ACL data in a relational database and accessing it with JDBC. First of all, you have to create the following tables in your database for storing ACL data:

```
CREATE TABLE ACL_SID(
    ID         BIGINT        NOT NULL GENERATED BY DEFAULT AS IDENTITY,
    SID        VARCHAR(100)  NOT NULL,
    PRINCIPAL  SMALLINT      NOT NULL,
    PRIMARY KEY (ID),
    UNIQUE (SID, PRINCIPAL)
);

CREATE TABLE ACL_CLASS(
    ID     BIGINT        NOT NULL GENERATED BY DEFAULT AS IDENTITY,
    CLASS  VARCHAR(100)  NOT NULL,
    PRIMARY KEY (ID),
    UNIQUE (CLASS)
);

CREATE TABLE ACL_OBJECT_IDENTITY(
    ID                  BIGINT    NOT NULL GENERATED BY DEFAULT AS IDENTITY,
    OBJECT_ID_CLASS     BIGINT    NOT NULL,
    OBJECT_ID_IDENTITY  BIGINT    NOT NULL,
    PARENT_OBJECT       BIGINT,
    OWNER_SID           BIGINT,
    ENTRIES_INHERITING  SMALLINT  NOT NULL,
    PRIMARY KEY (ID),
    UNIQUE (OBJECT_ID_CLASS, OBJECT_ID_IDENTITY),
    FOREIGN KEY (PARENT_OBJECT)   REFERENCES ACL_OBJECT_IDENTITY,
    FOREIGN KEY (OBJECT_ID_CLASS) REFERENCES ACL_CLASS,
    FOREIGN KEY (OWNER_SID)       REFERENCES ACL_SID
);

CREATE TABLE ACL_ENTRY(
    ID                  BIGINT    NOT NULL GENERATED BY DEFAULT AS IDENTITY,
    ACL_OBJECT_IDENTITY BIGINT    NOT NULL,
    ACE_ORDER           INT       NOT NULL,
    SID                 BIGINT    NOT NULL,
```

```
    MASK                 INTEGER   NOT NULL,
    GRANTING             SMALLINT  NOT NULL,
    AUDIT_SUCCESS        SMALLINT  NOT NULL,
    AUDIT_FAILURE        SMALLINT  NOT NULL,
    PRIMARY KEY (ID),
    UNIQUE (ACL_OBJECT_IDENTITY, ACE_ORDER),
    FOREIGN KEY (ACL_OBJECT_IDENTITY) REFERENCES ACL_OBJECT_IDENTITY,
    FOREIGN KEY (SID)                 REFERENCES ACL_SID
);
```

Spring Security defines APIs and provides high-performance JDBC implementations for you to access ACL data stored in these tables, so you'll seldom have a need to access ACL data from the database directly.

As each domain object can have its own ACL, there may be a large number of ACLs in your application. Fortunately, Spring Security supports caching ACL objects. You can continue to use Ehcache as your cache implementation and create a new configuration for ACL caching in `ehcache.xml` (located in the classpath root).

```
<ehcache>
    ...
    <cache name="aclCache"
        maxElementsInMemory="1000"
        eternal="false"
        timeToIdleSeconds="600"
        timeToLiveSeconds="3600"
        overflowToDisk="true"
        />
</ehcache>
```

Next, you have to set up an ACL service for your application. However, as Spring Security 2.0 doesn't support configuring the ACL module with XML schema-based configurations, you have to configure this module with a group of normal Spring beans. As the default namespace of `board-security.xml` is `security`, it's cumbersome to configure an ACL in this file using the standard XML elements in the `beans` namespace. For this reason, let's create a separate bean configuration file named `board-acl.xml`, which will store ACL-specific configurations, and add its location in the web deployment descriptor:

```
<web-app ...>
    ...
    <context-param>
        <param-name>contextConfigLocation</param-name>
        <param-value>
            /WEB-INF/board-service.xml
            /WEB-INF/board-security.xml
            /WEB-INF/board-acl.xml
        </param-value>
    </context-param>
</web-app>
```

In an ACL configuration file, the core bean is an ACL service. In Spring Security, there are two interfaces that define operations of an ACL service: `AclService` and `MutableAclService`. `AclService` defines operations for you to read ACLs. `MutableAclService` is a subinterface of `AclService` that defines operations for you to create, update, and delete ACLs. If your application only needs to read ACLs, you can simply choose an `AclService` implementation, such as `JdbcAclService`. Otherwise, you should choose a `MutableAclService` implementation, such as `JdbcMutableAclService`.

■ **Note** To use Spring Security's ACL module, you have to copy `spring-security-acl-2.0.1.jar` (located in the `dist` directory of the Spring Security installation) to the `WEB-INF/lib` directory.

```
<beans xmlns="http://www.springframework.org/schema/beans"
    xmlns:xsi="http://www.w3.org/2001/XMLSchema-instance"
    xsi:schemaLocation="http://www.springframework.org/schema/beans
        http://www.springframework.org/schema/beans/spring-beans-2.5.xsd">

    <bean id="aclCache"
        class="org.springframework.security.acls.jdbc.EhCacheBasedAclCache">
        <constructor-arg ref="aclEhCache" />
    </bean>

    <bean id="aclEhCache"
        class="org.springframework.cache.ehcache.EhCacheFactoryBean">
        <property name="cacheManager" ref="cacheManager" />
        <property name="cacheName" value="aclCache" />
    </bean>

    <bean id="lookupStrategy"
        class="org.springframework.security.acls.jdbc.BasicLookupStrategy">
        <constructor-arg ref="dataSource" />
        <constructor-arg ref="aclCache" />
        <constructor-arg>
            <bean class="org.springframework.security.acls.domain.➥
                AclAuthorizationStrategyImpl">
                <constructor-arg>
                    <list>
                        <ref local="adminRole" />
                        <ref local="adminRole" />
                        <ref local="adminRole" />
                    </list>
                </constructor-arg>
            </bean>
        </constructor-arg>
        <constructor-arg>
```

```
        <bean class="org.springframework.security.acls.domain.➥
            ConsoleAuditLogger" />
      </constructor-arg>
    </bean>

    <bean id="adminRole"
        class="org.springframework.security.GrantedAuthorityImpl">
        <constructor-arg value="ROLE_ADMIN" />
    </bean>

    <bean id="aclService"
        class="org.springframework.security.acls.jdbc.JdbcMutableAclService">
        <constructor-arg ref="dataSource" />
        <constructor-arg ref="lookupStrategy" />
        <constructor-arg ref="aclCache" />
        <property name="identityQuery" value="values identity_val_local()" />
    </bean>
</beans>
```

The core bean definition in this ACL configuration file is the ACL service, which is an instance of JdbcMutableAclService that allows you to maintain ACLs. This class requires three constructor arguments. The first is a data source for creating connections to a database that stores ACL data. You should have a data source defined in board-service.xml beforehand so that you can simply refer to it here (assuming that you have created the ACL tables in the same database). The third constructor argument is a cache instance to use with an ACL, which you can configure using Ehcache as the back-end cache implementation.

The second argument is a lookup strategy that performs lookup for an ACL service. The only implementation that comes with Spring Security is BasicLookupStrategy, which performs basic lookup using standard and compatible SQL statements. If you want to make use of advanced database features to increase lookup performance, you can create your own lookup strategy by implementing the LookupStrategy interface. A BasicLookupStrategy instance also requires a data source and a cache instance. Besides, it requires a constructor argument whose type is AclAuthorizationStrategy. This object determines whether a principal is authorized to change certain properties of an ACL, usually by specifying a required authority for each category of properties. For the preceding configurations, only a user who has the ROLE_ADMIN role can change an ACL's ownership, an ACE's auditing details, or other ACL and ACE details, respectively.

Finally, JdbcMutableAclService embeds standard SQL statements for maintaining ACL data in a relational database. However, those SQL statements may not be compatible with all database products. For example, you have to customize the identity query statement for Apache Derby.

Maintaining ACLs for Domain Objects

In your back-end services and DAOs, you can maintain ACLs for domain objects with the previously defined ACL service via dependency injection. For your message board, you have to create an ACL for a message when it is posted and delete the ACL when this message is deleted:

```
package com.apress.springrecipes.board.service;
...
import org.springframework.security.acls.MutableAcl;
import org.springframework.security.acls.MutableAclService;
import org.springframework.security.acls.domain.BasePermission;
import org.springframework.security.acls.objectidentity.ObjectIdentity;
import org.springframework.security.acls.objectidentity.ObjectIdentityImpl;
import org.springframework.security.acls.sid.GrantedAuthoritySid;
import org.springframework.security.acls.sid.PrincipalSid;
import org.springframework.security.annotation.Secured;
import org.springframework.transaction.annotation.Transactional;

public class MessageBoardServiceImpl implements MessageBoardService {
    ...
    private MutableAclService mutableAclService;

    public void setMutableAclService(MutableAclService mutableAclService) {
        this.mutableAclService = mutableAclService;
    }

    @Transactional
    @Secured("ROLE_USER")
    public synchronized void postMessage(Message message) {
        ...
        ObjectIdentity oid =
            new ObjectIdentityImpl(Message.class, message.getId());
        MutableAcl acl = mutableAclService.createAcl(oid);
        acl.insertAce(0, BasePermission.ADMINISTRATION,
                new PrincipalSid(message.getAuthor()), true);
        acl.insertAce(1, BasePermission.DELETE,
                new GrantedAuthoritySid("ROLE_ADMIN"), true);
        acl.insertAce(2, BasePermission.READ,
                new GrantedAuthoritySid("ROLE_USER"), true);
        mutableAclService.updateAcl(acl);
    }

    @Transactional
    @Secured({"ROLE_ADMIN", "IP_LOCAL_HOST"})
    public synchronized void deleteMessage(Message message) {
        ...
        ObjectIdentity oid =
            new ObjectIdentityImpl(Message.class, message.getId());
        mutableAclService.deleteAcl(oid, false);
    }
}
```

When a user posts a message, you create a new ACL for this message at the same time, using the message ID as the ACL's object identity. When a user deletes a message, you delete the corresponding ACL as well. For a new message, you insert the following three ACEs into its ACL:

- The message author is permitted to administrate this message.
- A user who has the ROLE_ADMIN role is permitted to delete this message.
- A user who has the ROLE_USER role is permitted to read this message.

JdbcMutableAclService requires that the calling methods have transactions enabled so that its SQL statements can run within transactions. So, you annotate the two methods involving ACL maintenance with the @Transactional annotation, and then define a transaction manager and <tx:annotation-driven> in board-service.xml. Also, don't forget to inject the ACL service into the message board service for it to maintain ACLs.

```
<beans xmlns="http://www.springframework.org/schema/beans"
    xmlns:xsi="http://www.w3.org/2001/XMLSchema-instance"
    xmlns:tx="http://www.springframework.org/schema/tx"
    xsi:schemaLocation="http://www.springframework.org/schema/beans
        http://www.springframework.org/schema/beans/spring-beans-2.5.xsd
        http://www.springframework.org/schema/tx
        http://www.springframework.org/schema/tx/spring-tx-2.5.xsd">
    ...
    <tx:annotation-driven />

    <bean id="transactionManager"
        class="org.springframework.jdbc.datasource.DataSourceTransactionManager">
        <property name="dataSource" ref="dataSource" />
    </bean>

    <bean id="messageBoardService"
        class="com.apress.springrecipes.board.service.MessageBoardServiceImpl">
        <property name="mutableAclService" ref="aclService" />
    </bean>
</beans>
```

Making Access Control Decisions Based on ACLs

With an ACL for each domain object, you can use an object's ACL to make access control decisions on methods that involve this object. For example, when a user attempts to delete a posted message, you can consult this message's ACL about whether the user is permitted to delete this message.

Spring Security comes with the AclEntryVoter class, which allows you to define a decision voter that votes for decisions based on ACLs. The following ACL voter in board-acl.xml votes for an access control decision if a method has the ACL_MESSAGE_DELETE access attribute and a method argument whose type is Message. If the current user has the ADMINISTRATION or DELETE permissions in the message domain object's ACL, then that user will be permitted to delete this message.

```
<beans xmlns="http://www.springframework.org/schema/beans"
    xmlns:xsi="http://www.w3.org/2001/XMLSchema-instance"
    xmlns:util="http://www.springframework.org/schema/util"
    xsi:schemaLocation="http://www.springframework.org/schema/beans
        http://www.springframework.org/schema/beans/spring-beans-2.5.xsd
        http://www.springframework.org/schema/util
        http://www.springframework.org/schema/util/spring-util-2.5.xsd">
    ...
    <bean id="aclMessageDeleteVoter"
        class="org.springframework.security.vote.AclEntryVoter">
        <constructor-arg ref="aclService" />
        <constructor-arg value="ACL_MESSAGE_DELETE" />
        <constructor-arg>
            <list>
                <util:constant static-field="org.springframework.security.➥
                    acls.domain.BasePermission.ADMINISTRATION" />
                <util:constant static-field="org.springframework.security.➥
                    acls.domain.BasePermission.DELETE" />
            </list>
        </constructor-arg>
        <property name="processDomainObjectClass"
            value="com.apress.springrecipes.board.domain.Message" />
    </bean>

    <bean id="aclAccessDecisionManager"
        class="org.springframework.security.vote.AffirmativeBased">
        <property name="decisionVoters">
            <list>
                <bean class="org.springframework.security.vote.RoleVoter" />
                <ref local="aclMessageDeleteVoter" />
            </list>
        </property>
    </bean>
</beans>
```

After configuring a voter, you have to include it in an access decision manager for it to vote for decisions. Because an ACL voter cannot vote for HTTP-based access decisions, you can't include it in the global access decision manager, as this manager is used for the <http> element. Instead, you should configure another access decision manager that is specific for method invocations (aclAccessDecisionManager in this case) and include the ACL voter in this manager. In board-security.xml, you have to modify the <global-method-security> element to use this access decision manager for method invocation security:

```
<global-method-security secured-annotations="enabled"
    access-decision-manager-ref="aclAccessDecisionManager" />
```

With the voter and access decision manager set up, the last step is to specify the access attribute ACL_MESSAGE_DELETE for the deleteMessage() method:

```
package com.apress.springrecipes.board.service;
...
import org.springframework.security.annotation.Secured;

public class MessageBoardServiceImpl implements MessageBoardService {
    ...
    @Transactional
    @Secured("ACL_MESSAGE_DELETE")
    public synchronized void deleteMessage(Message message) {
        ...
    }
}
```

With this attribute, only a user who has the ADMINISTRATION permission (by default, the message author) or the DELETE permission (by default, an administrator who has the ROLE_ADMIN role) on the message argument can delete a message.

If you want to hide a message's Delete link if the current user isn't permitted to delete the message, you can wrap the link with the <security:accesscontrollist> tag, whose function is to render its body conditionally according to a domain object's ACL:

```
<%@ taglib prefix="c" uri="http://java.sun.com/jsp/jstl/core" %>
<%@ taglib prefix="security" uri="http://www.springframework.org/security/tags" %>

<html>
<head>
<title>Message List</title>
</head>

<body>
...
<c:forEach items="${messages}" var="message">
<table>
  ...
  <security:accesscontrollist domainObject="${message}" hasPermission="8,16">
  <tr>
    <td colspan="2">
      <a href="messageDelete.htm?messageId=${message.id}">Delete</a>
    </td>
  </tr>
  </security:accesscontrollist>
</table>
<hr />
</c:forEach>
...
</body>
</html>
```

The <security:accesscontrollist> tag consults the specified domain object's ACL to check whether the current user has the specified permissions. This tag will only render its body if the user has one of the required permissions. Note that in this tag, permissions are defined as integers translated from their bit mask values. The values 8 and 16 represent the DELETE and ADMINISTRATION permissions, respectively.

Handling Domain Objects Returned from Methods

Spring Security can use *after invocation providers* to handle domain objects returned from methods according to the ACLs of these objects. For methods that return a single domain object, you can register an AclEntryAfterInvocationProvider instance to check whether the current user has specified permissions to access the returned domain object. If the user is not permitted to access the object, this provider will throw an exception to prevent the object from being returned.

On the other hand, for methods that return a collection of domain objects, you can register an AclEntryAfterInvocationCollectionFilteringProvider instance to filter the returned collection according to the ACLs of this collection's domain object elements. The domain objects that the current user doesn't have specified permissions on will be removed from the collection before it's returned to the calling method.

```
<beans xmlns="http://www.springframework.org/schema/beans"
    xmlns:xsi="http://www.w3.org/2001/XMLSchema-instance"
    xmlns:util="http://www.springframework.org/schema/util"
    xmlns:security="http://www.springframework.org/schema/security"
    xsi:schemaLocation="http://www.springframework.org/schema/beans
        http://www.springframework.org/schema/beans/spring-beans-2.5.xsd
        http://www.springframework.org/schema/util
        http://www.springframework.org/schema/util/spring-util-2.5.xsd
        http://www.springframework.org/schema/security
        http://www.springframework.org/schema/security/spring-security-2.0.1.xsd">
    ...
    <bean id="afterAclRead" class="org.springframework.security.➥
        afterinvocation.AclEntryAfterInvocationProvider">
        <security:custom-after-invocation-provider />
        <constructor-arg ref="aclService" />
        <constructor-arg>
            <list>
                <util:constant static-field="org.springframework.security.➥
                    acls.domain.BasePermission.ADMINISTRATION" />
                <util:constant static-field="org.springframework.security.➥
                    acls.domain.BasePermission.READ" />
            </list>
        </constructor-arg>
    </bean>

    <bean id="afterAclCollectionRead" class="org.springframework.security.➥
        afterinvocation.AclEntryAfterInvocationCollectionFilteringProvider">
        <security:custom-after-invocation-provider />
```

```
        <constructor-arg ref="aclService" />
        <constructor-arg>
            <list>
                <util:constant static-field="org.springframework.security.➥
                    acls.domain.BasePermission.ADMINISTRATION" />
                <util:constant static-field="org.springframework.security.➥
                    acls.domain.BasePermission.READ" />
            </list>
        </constructor-arg>
    </bean>
</beans>
```

To register a custom after invocation provider to Spring Security, you can simply embed a <custom-after-invocation-provider> element in the bean definition. This element is defined in the security schema, so you have to import it beforehand.

Now you can specify the access attributes AFTER_ACL_COLLECTION_READ and AFTER_ACL_READ, which will be handled by the preceding after invocation providers, for the listMessages() and findMessageById() methods.

```
package com.apress.springrecipes.board.service;
...
import org.springframework.security.annotation.Secured;

public class MessageBoardServiceImpl implements MessageBoardService {
    ...
    @Secured({"ROLE_USER", "ROLE_GUEST", "AFTER_ACL_COLLECTION_READ"})
    public List<Message> listMessages() {
        ...
    }

    @Secured({"ROLE_USER", "ROLE_GUEST", "AFTER_ACL_READ"})
    public Message findMessageById(Long messageId) {
        ...
    }
}
```

13-8. Summary

In this chapter, you have learned how to secure applications using Spring Security 2.0. It can be used to secure any Java application, but it's mostly used for web applications. The concepts of authentication, authorization, and access control are essential in the security area, so you should have a clear understanding of them.

You often have to secure critical URLs by preventing unauthorized access to them. Spring Security can help you to achieve this in a declarative way. It handles security by applying servlet filters, which can be configured with simple XML elements. If your web application's security requirements are simple and typical, you can enable the HTTP auto-config feature so that Spring Security will automatically configure the basic security services for you.

Spring Security supports multiple ways for users to log into a web application, such as form-based login and HTTP Basic authentication. It also provides an anonymous login service that allows you to handle an anonymous user just like a normal user. Remember-me support allows an application to remember a user's identity across multiple browser sessions.

Spring Security supports multiple ways of authenticating users and has built-in provider implementations for them. For example, it supports authenticating users against in-memory definitions, a relational database, and an LDAP repository. You should always store encrypted passwords in your user repository, because clear-text passwords are vulnerable to hacker attacks. Spring Security also supports caching user details locally to save you the overhead of performing remote queries.

Decisions on whether a user is allowed to access a given resource are made by access decision managers. Spring Security comes with three access decision managers that are based on the voting approach. All of them require a group of voters to be configured for voting on access control decisions.

Spring Security enables you to secure method invocations in a declarative way, either by embedding a security interceptor in a bean definition, or matching multiple methods with AspectJ pointcut expressions or annotations. Spring Security also allows you to display a user's authentication information in JSP views and render view contents conditionally according to a user's authorities.

Spring Security provides an ACL module that allows each domain object to have an ACL for controlling access. You can read and maintain an ACL for each domain object with Spring Security's high-performance APIs, which are implemented with JDBC. Spring Security also provides facilities such as access decision voters and JSP tags for you to use ACLs consistently with other security facilities.

In the next chapter, you will learn how to develop portlet applications using the Spring Portlet MVC framework.

CHAPTER 14

Spring Portlet MVC Framework

In this chapter, you will learn about portlet development using the Spring Portlet MVC framework, which is very similar to the Spring Web MVC framework because most of it is ported from Web MVC. You can often find their classes and interfaces with the same names but in different packages. Due to their similarity, I am not going to cover Spring Portlet MVC feature by feature, but rather focus on those of its portlet-specific features that are different from Web MVC. Before reading this chapter, please be sure that you have gone through Chapter 10, or have a basic understanding of Spring Web MVC.

A *portal* is a web site that collects information from different sources and presents it to users in a unified, centralized, and personalized way. This gives users a single access point to various information sources, such as applications and systems. In Java, a portal can use portlets to generate its contents. A *portlet* is a servlet-like web component technology that can process requests and generate responses dynamically. The content generated by a portlet is usually an HTML fragment that is aggregated into a portal page. Portlets need to be managed by a portlet container. The Java Portlet specification defines the contract between a portlet and a portlet container to ensure interoperability between different portal servers. In Spring 2.5, the Portlet MVC framework supports version 1.0 of this specification: JSR-168.

Upon finishing this chapter, you will be able to develop portlet applications using the Spring Portlet MVC framework and understand the differences between portlet and servlet development.

14-1. Developing a Simple Portlet with Spring Portlet MVC

Problem

You would like to develop a simple portlet with Spring Portlet MVC to learn the basic concepts and configurations of this framework.

Solution

The central component of Spring Portlet MVC is `DispatcherPortlet`. It mainly dispatches portlet requests to appropriate handlers that handle the requests. It acts as the front controller of Spring Portlet MVC, and every portlet request must go through it so that it can manage the entire request-handling process. When `DispatcherPortlet` receives a portlet request, it will organize different components configured in the portlet application context to handle this request. Figure 14-1 shows the primary flow of request handling in Spring Portlet MVC.

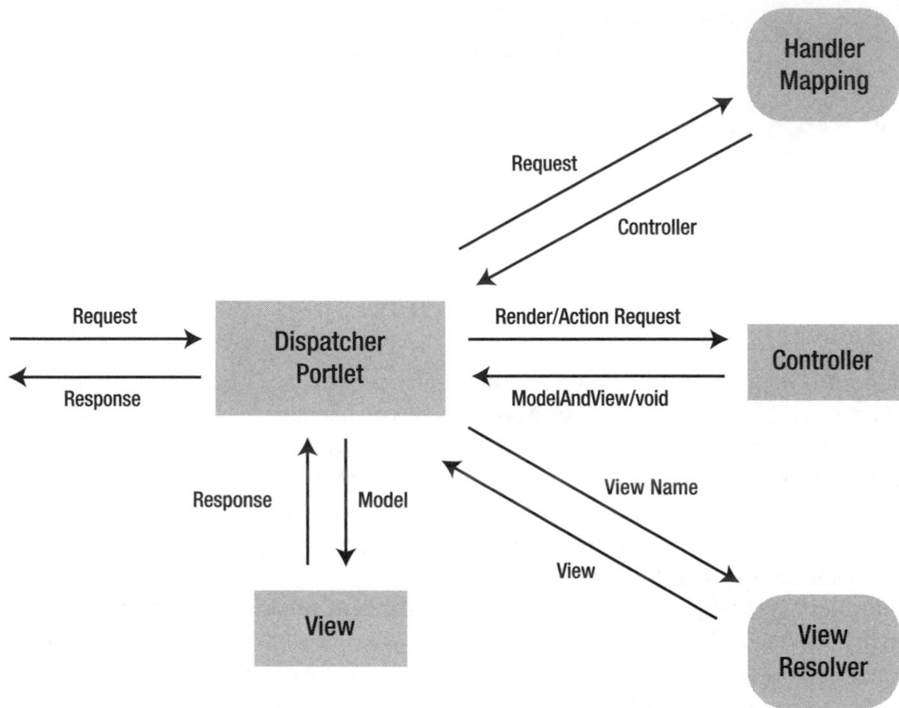

Figure 14-1. *Primary flow of request handling in Spring Portlet MVC*

When DispatcherPortlet receives a portlet request, it first looks for an appropriate handler to handle the request. DispatcherPortlet maps each request to a handler through one or more handler mapping beans. Once it has picked an appropriate handler, it will invoke this handler to handle the request. The most typical handler used in Spring Portlet MVC is a controller.

In portlets, there are two types of URLs: *render URLs* and *action URLs*. In most cases, there will be multiple portlets displaying in a page. When a user triggers a render URL, the portlet container will ask all the portlets in the same page to handle a *render request* to render its view, unless the view's content has been cached. A controller should return a ModelAndView object in response to a render request. However, when a user triggers an action URL in a portlet, the portlet container will first ask the target portlet to handle an *action request*. A controller needn't return anything for an action request. When the action request finishes, the portlet container will ask all the portlets in the same page, including the target portlet, to handle a render request to render its view.

After a controller has finished handling a render request, it returns a model and a view name, or sometimes a view object, to DispatcherPortlet. If a view name is returned, it will be resolved into a view object for rendering. DispatcherPortlet resolves a view name from one or more view resolver beans. Finally, DispatcherPortlet renders the view and passes in the model returned by the controller. Note that an action request doesn't need to render a view.

How It Works

Suppose you are going to develop a travel portal for a travel agency. In this portal, there's a portlet displaying weather information such as the temperatures of major cities. First of all, you design the service interface as follows:

```
package com.apress.springrecipes.travel.weather;
...
public interface WeatherService {

    public Map<String, Double> getMajorCityTemperatures();
}
```

For testing purposes, you can return some hard-coded data for the implementation of this service interface.

```
package com.apress.springrecipes.travel.weather;
...
public class WeatherServiceImpl implements WeatherService {

    public Map<String, Double> getMajorCityTemperatures() {
        Map<String, Double> temperatures = new HashMap<String, Double>();
        temperatures.put("New York", 6.0);
        temperatures.put("London", 10.0);
        temperatures.put("Beijing", 5.0);
        return temperatures;
    }
}
```

Setting Up a Portlet Application

The Java Portlet specification defines the valid structure of a portlet application, which is very similar to that of a web application, but with the addition of a portlet deployment descriptor (i.e., `portlet.xml`). Now let's create the following directory structure for your travel portlet application.

■ **Note** To develop a portlet application with Spring Portlet MVC, you have to copy `spring-webmvc.jar` and `spring-webmvc-portlet.jar` (located in the `dist/modules` directory of the Spring installation) to the `WEB-INF/lib` directory. If you are going to use JSTL in your JSPs, you also have to copy `standard.jar` (located in `lib/jakarta-taglibs`) and `jstl.jar` (located in `lib/j2ee`).

```
travel/
    WEB-INF/
        classes/
        lib/
            commons-logging.jar
```

```
            jstl.jar
            spring-webmvc-portlet.jar
            spring-webmvc.jar
            spring.jar
            standard.jar
        jsp/
            weather/
                weatherView.jsp
        applicationContext.xml
        portlet.xml
        weather-portlet.xml
        web.xml
```

Creating the Configuration Files

Next, you define the weather service in the root application context's bean configuration file (i.e., applicationContext.xml). Beans in this context are accessible to the contexts of all portlets within this application.

```
<beans xmlns="http://www.springframework.org/schema/beans"
    xmlns:xsi="http://www.w3.org/2001/XMLSchema-instance"
    xsi:schemaLocation="http://www.springframework.org/schema/beans
        http://www.springframework.org/schema/beans/spring-beans-2.5.xsd">

    <bean id="weatherService"
        class="com.apress.springrecipes.travel.weather.WeatherServiceImpl" />
</beans>
```

In the web deployment descriptor (i.e., web.xml), you have to register the servlet listener ContextLoaderListener to load the root application context at startup. By default, it loads applicationContext.xml from the root of WEB-INF, but you can override this location with the context parameter contextConfigLocation.

```
<web-app version="2.4" xmlns="http://java.sun.com/xml/ns/j2ee"
    xmlns:xsi="http://www.w3.org/2001/XMLSchema-instance"
    xsi:schemaLocation="http://java.sun.com/xml/ns/j2ee
        http://java.sun.com/xml/ns/j2ee/web-app_2_4.xsd">

    <display-name>Travel Portal</display-name>

    <listener>
        <listener-class>
            org.springframework.web.context.ContextLoaderListener
        </listener-class>
    </listener>

    <servlet>
        <servlet-name>view</servlet-name>
```

```
        <servlet-class>
            org.springframework.web.servlet.ViewRendererServlet
        </servlet-class>
    </servlet>

    <servlet-mapping>
        <servlet-name>view</servlet-name>
        <url-pattern>/WEB-INF/servlet/view</url-pattern>
    </servlet-mapping>
</web-app>
```

In order for Spring Portlet MVC to reuse the view technologies of Spring Web MVC, you have to configure the bridge servlet `ViewRendererServlet` in the portlet application's web deployment descriptor. This servlet converts portlet requests and responses into servlet requests and responses so that you can render Spring Web MVC's servlet-based views for portlets. By default, `DispatcherPortlet` will request the relative URL `/WEB-INF/servlet/view` for view rendering.

In the portlet development descriptor (i.e., `portlet.xml`), you declare a weather portlet for displaying weather information.

```
<portlet-app version="1.0"
    xmlns="http://java.sun.com/xml/ns/portlet/portlet-app_1_0.xsd"
    xmlns:xsi="http://www.w3.org/2001/XMLSchema-instance"
    xsi:schemaLocation="http://java.sun.com/xml/ns/portlet/portlet-app_1_0.xsd
        http://java.sun.com/xml/ns/portlet/portlet-app_1_0.xsd">

    <portlet>
        <portlet-name>weather</portlet-name>
        <portlet-class>
            org.springframework.web.portlet.DispatcherPortlet
        </portlet-class>
        <supports>
            <mime-type>text/html</mime-type>
            <portlet-mode>view</portlet-mode>
        </supports>
        <portlet-info>
            <title>Weather</title>
        </portlet-info>
    </portlet>
</portlet-app>
```

For a portlet developed with Spring Portlet MVC, you specify `DispatcherPortlet` as its portlet class. It acts as the front controller of Spring Portlet MVC, dispatching requests to appropriate controllers. It's the central component of Spring Portlet MVC, just as `DispatcherServlet` is for Spring Web MVC. Each `DispatcherPortlet` instance also has its own Spring application context that is able to access and even override beans declared in the root application context (but not vice versa).

By default, DispatcherPortlet loads its configuration file from the root of WEB-INF by joining the portlet name with -portlet.xml as the file name (e.g., weather-portlet.xml). You can override its location with the contextConfigLocation parameter.

The JSR-168 specification defines three standard portlet modes: *view*, *edit*, and *help*. The view mode usually displays information to users and handles user inputs. Typically, portlets in the edit mode allow users to update their preferences. Finally, help information should be displayed in the help mode. You can specify which modes your portlet supports in the portlet deployment descriptor. For example, your weather portlet only supports the view mode.

Creating Portlet Controllers

The controllers in Spring Portlet MVC are very similar to those in Spring Web MVC, so it is very easy to port controller code from Web MVC to Portlet MVC. However, as there are two types of portlet requests—render requests and action requests—the Controller interface in Spring Portlet MVC defines two methods for a portlet controller to implement: handleActionRequest() and handleRenderRequest(). You don't need to return a result for handleActionRequest(), but you have to return a ModelAndView object for handleRenderRequest(). Your portlet controller can implement the Controller interface directly or extend the AbstractController base class, which provides some basic controller features such as content caching.

Note To compile your portlet controllers, you have to include portlet-api.jar (located in the lib/portlet directory of the Spring installation) in your classpath.

```
package com.apress.springrecipes.travel.weather;

import javax.portlet.RenderRequest;
import javax.portlet.RenderResponse;

import org.springframework.web.portlet.ModelAndView;
import org.springframework.web.portlet.mvc.AbstractController;

public class WeatherController extends AbstractController {

    private WeatherService weatherService;

    public void setWeatherService(WeatherService weatherService) {
        this.weatherService = weatherService;
    }

    public ModelAndView handleRenderRequestInternal(
            RenderRequest request, RenderResponse response) throws Exception {
        return new ModelAndView("weatherView",
                "temperatures", weatherService.getMajorCityTemperatures());
    }
}
```

The AbstractController class provides a default implementation for both methods of the Controller interface. When extending AbstractController, you can implement either the handleActionRequestInternal() or handleRenderRequestInternal() method as appropriate. You can implement both of them if your portlet needs to handle both types of requests. The preceding WeatherController only handles render requests.

Then you declare this controller in the configuration file weather-portlet.xml. This controller has to refer to the weather service declared in the root application context.

```
<beans xmlns="http://www.springframework.org/schema/beans"
    xmlns:xsi="http://www.w3.org/2001/XMLSchema-instance"
    xsi:schemaLocation="http://www.springframework.org/schema/beans
        http://www.springframework.org/schema/beans/spring-beans-2.5.xsd">

    <bean id="weatherController"
        class="com.apress.springrecipes.travel.weather.WeatherController">
        <property name="weatherService" ref="weatherService" />
    </bean>
</beans>
```

Mapping Portlet Requests to Handlers

When DispatcherPortlet receives a portlet request, it will first look for an appropriate handler to handle the request. In Spring Web MVC, handler mappings are typically based on URLs. However, unlike in web applications, you don't deal with URLs in portlets, and a portlet usually contains fewer pages than a web application. There are several handler mappings built into Spring Portlet MVC. The simplest is for mapping handlers by portlet modes. For example, you can declare the following handler mapping in weather-portlet.xml:

```
<bean class="org.springframework.web.portlet.handler.PortletModeHandlerMapping">
    <property name="portletModeMap">
        <map>
            <entry key="view" value-ref="weatherController" />
        </map>
    </property>
</bean>
```

By declaring a PortletModeHandlerMapping bean, you can assign a controller for each portlet mode in the portletModeMap property.

Resolving View Names into Views

When DispatcherPortlet receives a view name returned from a handler, it will resolve the logical view name into a view object for rendering. Spring Portlet MVC reuses all the view technologies from Spring Web MVC so that you can use the same view resolvers in a portlet. For example, you can declare an InternalResourceViewResolver bean to resolve view names into JSP files inside the WEB-INF directory. Putting the JSP files here can prevent direct access to them for security reasons.

```
<bean class="org.springframework.web.servlet.view.InternalResourceViewResolver">
    <property name="viewClass"
        value="org.springframework.web.servlet.view.JstlView" />
    <property name="prefix" value="/WEB-INF/jsp/weather/" />
    <property name="suffix" value=".jsp" />
</bean>
```

Creating Portlet Views

Although Spring Portlet MVC reuses the view technologies from Spring Web MVC, portlets don't support HTTP redirect, so you can't use `RedirectView` and the `redirect` prefix. Typically, a portlet view should be an HTML fragment, not a complete HTML page. Let's create the weather portlet view in `/WEB-INF/jsp/weather/weatherView.jsp` to show weather information.

```
<%@ taglib prefix="c" uri="http://java.sun.com/jsp/jstl/core" %>

<table border="1">
  <tr>
    <th>City</th>
    <th>Temperature</th>
  </tr>
  <c:forEach items="${temperatures}" var="temperature">
  <tr>
    <td>${temperature.key}</td>
    <td>${temperature.value}</td>
  </tr>
  </c:forEach>
</table>
```

Deploying the Portlet Application

Now your portlet application is ready and you can deploy it to a Java portal server that supports JSR-168. For the sake of easy installation and configuration, I recommend installing Apache Pluto (`http://portals.apache.org/pluto/`), a subproject of the Apache Portals project. Pluto is the reference implementation of the Java Portlet specification. Pluto 1.x supports JSR-168, version 1.0 of this specification.

■ Note You can download the Apache Pluto distribution bundled with Tomcat (`pluto-current-bundle.zip`) from the Apache Pluto web site and extract it to a directory of your choice to complete the installation.

Typically, a portal server or a portlet container is deployed in a servlet container as a web application, and your portlet applications are deployed as other web applications in the same servlet container. The portlet container will make cross-context calls to your portlet applications. For this to work, you have to register one or more vendor-specific servlets in your portlet applications to handle the calls from the portlet container.

Pluto follows this practice for portlet deployment. To deploy your portlet application, you have to add a context descriptor, such as travel.xml, in its conf/Catalina/localhost directory, pointing to your portlet application context's root directory. You also have to turn on the crossContext attribute to enable cross-context calls.

```
<Context docBase="c:/eclipse/workspace/Travel/travel" crossContext="true" />
```

Pluto requires registering one org.apache.pluto.core.PortletServlet for each portlet of a portlet application. For your weather portlet, you register this servlet in your web.xml and map it to the /PlutoInvoker/weather URL pattern.

```
<web-app ...>
    ...
    <servlet>
        <servlet-name>weather</servlet-name>
        <servlet-class>
            org.apache.pluto.core.PortletServlet
        </servlet-class>
        <init-param>
            <param-name>portlet-name</param-name>
            <param-value>weather</param-value>
        </init-param>
    </servlet>
    ...
    <servlet-mapping>
        <servlet-name>weather</servlet-name>
        <url-pattern>/PlutoInvoker/weather</url-pattern>
    </servlet-mapping>
</web-app>
```

■ **Note** To start up Pluto, just execute its startup script for your platform (located in the bin directory).

After Pluto has started up, you can open the URL http://localhost:8080/pluto/ in your browser and log in with the default username pluto and password pluto. From the Pluto Admin page, you can then add your weather portlet to a portal page.

14-2. Mapping Portlet Requests to Handlers

Problem

When DispatcherPortlet receives a portlet request, it will dispatch this request to an appropriate handler. You have to define how DispatcherPortlet should map portlet requests to handlers.

Solution

In a portlet application developed with Spring Portlet MVC, portlet requests are mapped to handlers by one or more handler mapping beans configured in the portlet application context. You can chain multiple handler mapping beans as required. The handler mapping beans have to implement the `org.springframework.web.portlet.HandlerMapping` interface. Spring Portlet MVC comes with several `HandlerMapping` implementations for you to map portlet requests by different strategies.

Unlike in a web application, you can't control URLs directly in a portlet. So the main strategies offered by Spring Portlet MVC for mapping portlet requests are based on the portlet mode and a request parameter. Of course, you can combine them together or even develop your own custom strategies.

How It Works

Suppose you are going to develop another portlet in your travel portal for showing flight information. First of all, you define the `Flight` domain class.

```
package com.apress.springrecipes.travel.flight;
...
public class Flight {

    private String number;
    private String origin;
    private String destination;
    private Date departureTime;

    // Constructors, Getters and Setters
    ...
}
```

Next, you define the service interface for querying all flights departing today, and also a particular flight by its flight number.

```
package com.apress.springrecipes.travel.flight;
...
public interface FlightService {

    public List<Flight> findTodayFlights();
    public Flight findFlight(String flightNo);
}
```

For testing purposes, you can store the flights in a map and hard-code some flights for the service implementation.

```
package com.apress.springrecipes.travel.flight;
...
public class FlightServiceImpl implements FlightService {

    private Map<String, Flight> flights;
```

```
    public FlightServiceImpl() {
        flights = new HashMap<String, Flight>();
        flights.put("CX888", new Flight("CX888", "HKG", "YVR", new Date()));
        flights.put("CX889", new Flight("CX889", "HKG", "JFK", new Date()));
    }

    public List<Flight> findTodayFlights() {
        return new ArrayList<Flight>(flights.values());
    }

    public Flight findFlight(String flightNo) {
        return flights.get(flightNo);
    }
}
```

Then you define the flight service in the root application context's bean configuration file (i.e., applicationContext.xml) so that it can be accessed by all portlet contexts.

```
<bean id="flightService"
    class="com.apress.springrecipes.travel.flight.FlightServiceImpl" />
```

To add a new portlet to your portlet application, you create a <portlet> entry in the portlet deployment descriptor portlet.xml

```
<portlet-app ...>
    ...
    <portlet>
        <portlet-name>flight</portlet-name>
        <portlet-class>
            org.springframework.web.portlet.DispatcherPortlet
        </portlet-class>
        <supports>
            <mime-type>text/html</mime-type>
            <portlet-mode>view</portlet-mode>
            <portlet-mode>edit</portlet-mode>
            <portlet-mode>help</portlet-mode>
        </supports>
        <portlet-info>
            <title>Flight</title>
        </portlet-info>
        <portlet-preferences>
            <preference>
                <name>timeZone</name>
                <value>GMT-08:00</value>
            </preference>
        </portlet-preferences>
    </portlet>
</portlet-app>
```

This portlet supports all the standard portlet modes: view, edit, and help. In addition, you set the default time zone for this portlet as a custom preference attribute. It will be used by JSTL to format departure dates. Please refer to the javadoc of `java.util.TimeZone` for its valid formats.

Mapping Requests by the Portlet Mode

The simplest strategy to map portlet requests is by the portlet mode. As this flight portlet supports all three standard portlet modes, let's create a portlet controller for each of these modes. First, you create a controller for displaying all flights departing today. It will be used for the view mode.

```
package com.apress.springrecipes.travel.flight;
...
import javax.portlet.PortletPreferences;
import javax.portlet.RenderRequest;
import javax.portlet.RenderResponse;

import org.springframework.web.portlet.ModelAndView;
import org.springframework.web.portlet.mvc.AbstractController;

public class FlightListController extends AbstractController {

    private FlightService flightService;

    public void setFlightService(FlightService flightService) {
        this.flightService = flightService;
    }

    public ModelAndView handleRenderRequestInternal(
            RenderRequest request, RenderResponse response) throws Exception {
        List<Flight> flights = flightService.findTodayFlights();
        PortletPreferences preferences = request.getPreferences();
        String timeZone = preferences.getValue("timeZone", null);
        return new ModelAndView("flightList", "flights", flights)
                .addObject("timeZone", timeZone);
    }
}
```

In this controller, you find all today's flights from the back-end service and pass them to the view. Also, you pass the time zone preference attribute to the view for it to format the departure times. Then you create the JSP file `/WEB-INF/jsp/flight/flightList.jsp` to list all flights returned by this controller.

```
<%@ taglib prefix="c" uri="http://java.sun.com/jsp/jstl/core" %>
<%@ taglib prefix="fmt" uri="http://java.sun.com/jsp/jstl/fmt" %>

<table border="1">
  <tr>
```

```
    <th>Flight Number</th>
    <th>Origin</th>
    <th>Destination</th>
    <th>Departure Time</th>
  </tr>
  <c:forEach items="${flights}" var="flight">
  <tr>
    <td>${flight.number}</td>
    <td>${flight.origin}</td>
    <td>${flight.destination}</td>
    <td><fmt:formatDate value="${flight.departureTime}"
            pattern="yyyy-MM-dd HH:mm" timeZone="${timeZone}" /></td>
  </tr>
  </c:forEach>
</table>
```

In this JSP, you use the `<fmt:formatDate>` tag to format each flight's departure time, using the time zone attribute passed from the controller.

Most portlets allow users to set their preferences in the edit mode. For example, your flight portlet may allow users to edit their preferred time zone. You create the following controller for this purpose:

```
package com.apress.springrecipes.travel.flight;

import javax.portlet.ActionRequest;
import javax.portlet.ActionResponse;
import javax.portlet.PortletPreferences;
import javax.portlet.RenderRequest;
import javax.portlet.RenderResponse;

import org.springframework.web.portlet.ModelAndView;
import org.springframework.web.portlet.bind.PortletRequestUtils;
import org.springframework.web.portlet.mvc.AbstractController;

public class FlightPreferencesController extends AbstractController {

    protected ModelAndView handleRenderRequestInternal(RenderRequest request,
            RenderResponse response) throws Exception {
        PortletPreferences preferences = request.getPreferences();
        String timeZone = preferences.getValue("timeZone", null);
        return new ModelAndView("flightPreferences", "timeZone", timeZone);
    }

    protected void handleActionRequestInternal(ActionRequest request,
            ActionResponse response) throws Exception {
        String timeZone = PortletRequestUtils.getRequiredStringParameter(
                request, "timeZone");
        PortletPreferences preferences = request.getPreferences();
```

```
            preferences.setValue("timeZone", timeZone);
            preferences.store();
        }
    }
```

The preceding controller handles two types of portlet requests: render requests and action requests. When handling a render request, it gets the time zone attribute from the portlet preferences and passes it to the view for editing. When handling an action request, it gets the time zone parameter from the portlet request and stores it in the portlet preferences as an attribute, which will override the existing one.

The view for this controller is as simple as an HTML form. Let's create it in the JSP file `/WEB-INF/jsp/flight/flightPreferences.jsp`.

```
<%@ taglib prefix="portlet" uri="http://java.sun.com/portlet" %>

<form method="post" action="<portlet:actionURL />">
  Time Zone
  <input type="text" name="timeZone" value="${timeZone}" />
  <input type="submit" value="Modify" />
</form>
```

The submission URL of this form should be a portlet action URL that will trigger an action request to the current portlet. In portlets, you have to construct an action URL with the `<portlet:actionURL>` tag defined in the portlet tag library.

In the help mode, a portlet usually displays some help information about itself. You can simply use the built-in `ParameterizableViewController` to render a fixed view. Let's create this view in the JSP file `/WEB-INF/jsp/flight/flightHelp.jsp`.

```
This portlet lists flights departing today.
```

Finally, you create the Spring configuration file for this portlet. As its `DispatcherPortlet` instance has the name `flight` in `portlet.xml`, you create the following `flight-portlet.xml` in the `WEB-INF` root, which will be loaded by default:

```
<beans xmlns="http://www.springframework.org/schema/beans"
    xmlns:xsi="http://www.w3.org/2001/XMLSchema-instance"
    xsi:schemaLocation="http://www.springframework.org/schema/beans
        http://www.springframework.org/schema/beans/spring-beans-2.5.xsd">

    <bean class="org.springframework.web.servlet.view.➥
        InternalResourceViewResolver">
        <property name="viewClass"
            value="org.springframework.web.servlet.view.JstlView" />
        <property name="prefix" value="/WEB-INF/jsp/flight/" />
        <property name="suffix" value=".jsp" />
    </bean>

    <bean class="org.springframework.web.portlet.handler.➥
        PortletModeHandlerMapping">
        <property name="portletModeMap">
```

```
            <map>
                <entry key="view" value-ref="flightListController" />
                <entry key="edit" value-ref="flightPreferencesController" />
                <entry key="help" value-ref="flightHelpController" />
            </map>
        </property>
    </bean>

    <bean id="flightListController"
        class="com.apress.springrecipes.travel.flight.FlightListController">
        <property name="flightService" ref="flightService" />
    </bean>

    <bean id="flightPreferencesController" class="com.apress.springrecipes.➥
        travel.flight.FlightPreferencesController" />

    <bean id="flightHelpController" class="org.springframework.web.portlet.➥
        mvc.ParameterizableViewController">
        <property name="viewName" value="flightHelp"/>
    </bean>
</beans>
```

In this configuration file, you simply configure an `InternalResourceViewResolver` bean to map view names to JSP files under the `/WEB-INF/jsp/flight/` directory. You also declare an instance for each of the preceding controllers and map them to the portlet modes with a `PortletModeHandlerMapping` bean.

To deploy this portlet in Pluto, you add a `PortletServlet` instance for this portlet in `web.xml` and map it to the corresponding URL pattern.

```
<web-app ...>
    ...
    <servlet>
        <servlet-name>flight</servlet-name>
        <servlet-class>
            org.apache.pluto.core.PortletServlet
        </servlet-class>
        <init-param>
            <param-name>portlet-name</param-name>
            <param-value>flight</param-value>
        </init-param>
    </servlet>
    ...
    <servlet-mapping>
        <servlet-name>flight</servlet-name>
        <url-pattern>/PlutoInvoker/flight</url-pattern>
    </servlet-mapping>
</web-app>
```

After starting up and logging into Pluto, you can add your flight portlet to a portal page from the Pluto Admin page. You can switch the mode of this portlet using the icons in its upper-right corner.

Mapping Requests by a Parameter

Another strategy for mapping portlet requests is by a particular request parameter. To illustrate how this is done, let's make each of the flight numbers in the flight list view a hyperlink that will show the flight's details when clicked.

```
<%@ taglib prefix="portlet" uri="http://java.sun.com/portlet" %>
...
<table border="1">
  ...
  <c:forEach items="${flights}" var="flight">
  <tr>
    <td>
      <portlet:renderURL var="detailUrl">
        <portlet:param name="action" value="flightDetail" />
        <portlet:param name="flightNo" value="${flight.number}" />
      </portlet:renderURL>
      <a href="${detailUrl}">${flight.number}</a>
    </td>
    ...
  </tr>
  </c:forEach>
</table>
```

A portlet render URL has to be constructed by the `<portlet:renderURL>` tag defined in the portlet tag library. You can specify parameters for this URL with the `<portlet:param>` element. Note that you have set the `action` parameter value to `flightDetail`, which will be mapped to the controller showing flight details later. Finally, you can store the generated URL in a JSP variable such as `detailUrl` and use it for the flight number hyperlink.

To show flight details, you need another portlet controller to query for a flight by the flight number specified in the request parameter. You also have to pass the time zone preference attribute for its view to format the departure time.

```
package com.apress.springrecipes.travel.flight;

import javax.portlet.PortletPreferences;
import javax.portlet.RenderRequest;
import javax.portlet.RenderResponse;

import org.springframework.web.portlet.ModelAndView;
import org.springframework.web.portlet.bind.PortletRequestUtils;
import org.springframework.web.portlet.mvc.AbstractController;

public class FlightDetailController extends AbstractController {
```

```
    private FlightService flightService;

    public void setFlightService(FlightService flightService) {
        this.flightService = flightService;
    }

    public ModelAndView handleRenderRequestInternal(
            RenderRequest request, RenderResponse response) throws Exception {
        String flightNo = PortletRequestUtils.getRequiredStringParameter(
                request, "flightNo");
        Flight flight = flightService.findFlight(flightNo);
        PortletPreferences preferences = request.getPreferences();
        String timeZone = preferences.getValue("timeZone", null);
        return new ModelAndView("flightDetail", "flight", flight)
                .addObject("timeZone", timeZone);
    }
}
```

Then you create the detail view in the JSP file `/WEB-INF/jsp/flight/flightDetail.jsp` to show the details of a selected flight.

```
<%@ taglib prefix="fmt" uri="http://java.sun.com/jsp/jstl/fmt" %>
<%@ taglib prefix="portlet" uri="http://java.sun.com/portlet" %>

<table>
  <tr>
    <td>Flight Number</td>
    <td>${flight.number}</td>
  </tr>
  <tr>
    <td>Origin</td>
    <td>${flight.origin}</td>
  </tr>
  <tr>
    <td>Destination</td>
    <td>${flight.destination}</td>
  </tr>
  <tr>
    <td>Departure Time</td>
    <td><fmt:formatDate value="${flight.departureTime}"
            pattern="yyyy-MM-dd HH:mm" timeZone="${timeZone}" /></td>
  </tr>
  <tr>
    <td colspan="2">
      <a href="<portlet:renderURL portletMode="view" />">Return</a>
    </td>
  </tr>
</table>
```

In this JSP, you provide a link for users to return to the flight list page. The URL for this link should be a render URL constructed by the <portlet:renderURL> tag. You set its portlet mode to view, which has already been mapped to the controller listing all flights departing today.

Finally, you declare FlightDetailController in flight-portlet.xml and configure a ParameterHandlerMapping bean for mapping handlers by a particular parameter whose default name is action, but you can override it with the parameterName property. For this mapping to work with the PortletModeHandlerMapping bean defined previously, you have to chain them by setting their order property. You should make the ParameterHandlerMapping bean precede the PortletModeHandlerMapping bean by giving the former a lower order value.

```
<beans ...>
    ...
    <bean
        class="org.springframework.web.portlet.handler.ParameterHandlerMapping">
        <property name="parameterMap">
            <map>
                <entry key="flightDetail" value-ref="flightDetailController" />
            </map>
        </property>
        <property name="order" value="0" />
    </bean>

    <bean class="org.springframework.web.portlet.handler.➥
        PortletModeHandlerMapping">
        <property name="portletModeMap">
            <map>
                <entry key="view" value-ref="flightListController" />
                <entry key="edit" value-ref="flightPreferencesController" />
                <entry key="help" value-ref="flightHelpController" />
            </map>
        </property>
        <property name="order" value="1" />
    </bean>

    <bean id="flightDetailController"
        class="com.apress.springrecipes.travel.flight.FlightDetailController">
        <property name="flightService" ref="flightService" />
    </bean>
</beans>
```

Mapping Requests by Both the Portlet Mode and Parameter

Lastly, the most advanced strategy for mapping portlet requests is by both the portlet mode and a request parameter via PortletModeParameterHandlerMapping, which has a two-level map property to configure. The first level is for the portlet modes and the second is for the parameter values. For example, you can refine the flightDetail parameter mapping to the view mode only.

```
<bean class="org.springframework.web.portlet.handler.➥
    PortletModeParameterHandlerMapping">
    <property name="portletModeParameterMap">
        <map>
            <entry key="view">
                <map>
                    <entry key="flightDetail"
                        value-ref="flightDetailController" />
                </map>
            </entry>
        </map>
    </property>
    <property name="order" value="0" />
</bean>
```

14-3. Handling Portlet Forms with Simple Form Controllers

Problem

In portlet applications, you sometimes have to deal with forms. In order for a controller to handle forms, it has to render the form view to a user and also handle the form submission. You will get involved in too many form-handling details if you build your form controller from scratch.

Solution

Spring Portlet MVC offers a `SimpleFormController` class that is very similar to that in Spring Web MVC. It also supports command objects and is able to bind form field values to a command object's properties of the same names. By extending `SimpleFormController`, your controller will inherit the ability to handle forms.

When `SimpleFormController` is asked to show a form by a portlet render request, it will render the form view to the user. Later, when the form is submitted by a portlet action request, `SimpleFormController` will bind the form field values to a command object and then validate this object with its validators. If no error occurs, it will invoke the `onSubmitAction()` method. After the action request completes, `SimpleFormController` will be asked to handle a render request. If the form has been handled successfully, it will render the success view to the user. Otherwise, it will render the form view again with the errors.

How It Works

Suppose you are going to create a portlet for users to book tours through your travel portal. First of all, you define the following `BookingForm` domain class, whose instances will be used as form command objects. As command objects may be persisted in sessions, this class should implement the `Serializable` interface.

```
package com.apress.springrecipes.travel.tour;
...
public class BookingForm implements Serializable {

    private String tourist;
    private String phone;
    private String origin;
    private String destination;
    private Date departureDate;
    private Date returnDate;

    // Getters and Setters
    ...
}
```

Then you define the interface for the back-end tour service as follows. In addition to the `processBooking()` method, there's also a `getLocations()` method for returning all available tour locations.

```
package com.apress.springrecipes.travel.tour;
...
public interface TourService {

    public List<String> getLocations();
    public void processBooking(BookingForm form);
}
```

For simplicity's sake, let's implement this interface by storing the completed booking forms in a list and providing a setter method for the location list.

```
package com.apress.springrecipes.travel.tour;
...
public class TourServiceImpl implements TourService {

    private List<BookingForm> forms = new ArrayList<BookingForm>();
    private List<String> locations;

    public List<String> getLocations() {
        return locations;
    }

    public void setLocations(List<String> locations) {
        this.locations = locations;
    }

    public void processBooking(BookingForm form) {
        forms.add(form);
    }
}
```

Now you define the tour service in the root application context's bean configuration file (i.e., applicationContext.xml) so that it can be accessed by all portlet contexts. You can also hard-code some locations for testing purposes.

```
<bean id="tourService"
    class="com.apress.springrecipes.travel.tour.TourServiceImpl">
    <property name="locations">
        <list>
            <value>France</value>
            <value>Switzerland</value>
            <value>New Zealand</value>
        </list>
    </property>
</bean>
```

To add a new portlet to your portlet application, you create a <portlet> entry in the portlet deployment descriptor portlet.xml. Note that this portlet supports the view mode only.

```
<portlet-app ...>
    ...
    <portlet>
        <portlet-name>tour</portlet-name>
        <portlet-class>
            org.springframework.web.portlet.DispatcherPortlet
        </portlet-class>
        <supports>
            <mime-type>text/html</mime-type>
            <portlet-mode>view</portlet-mode>
        </supports>
        <portlet-info>
            <title>Tour</title>
        </portlet-info>
    </portlet>
</portlet-app>
```

Creating Form Controllers

Now let's create a controller to handle the tour booking forms. The SimpleFormController class provided by Spring Portlet MVC can also bind form field values to its command object's properties of the same names. It supports most of the same life cycle callback methods as its Web MVC counterpart. For instance, you can register custom property editors in initBinder(), and provide reference data for this form in referenceData().

```
package com.apress.springrecipes.travel.tour;
...
import javax.portlet.PortletRequest;
```

```
import org.springframework.beans.propertyeditors.CustomDateEditor;
import org.springframework.web.portlet.bind.PortletRequestDataBinder;
import org.springframework.web.portlet.mvc.SimpleFormController;

public class BookingFormController extends SimpleFormController {

    private TourService tourService;

    public BookingFormController() {
        setCommandClass(BookingForm.class);
        setCommandName("bookingForm");
    }

    public void setTourService(TourService tourService) {
        this.tourService = tourService;
    }

    protected void initBinder(PortletRequest request,
            PortletRequestDataBinder binder) {
        SimpleDateFormat dateFormat = new SimpleDateFormat("yyyy-MM-dd");
        dateFormat.setLenient(false);
        binder.registerCustomEditor(Date.class, new CustomDateEditor(
                dateFormat, true));
    }

    protected Map referenceData(PortletRequest request) {
        Map referenceData = new HashMap();
        referenceData.put("locations", tourService.getLocations());
        return referenceData;
    }

    protected void onSubmitAction(Object command) {
        BookingForm form = (BookingForm) command;
        tourService.processBooking(form);
    }
}
```

The SimpleFormController class in Portlet MVC differs from its Web MVC counterpart in that it has to handle both types of portlet requests: render requests and action requests. When a form is submitted by an action request mapped to a form controller without errors, its onSubmitAction() method will be called to handle the form submission. In this method, you have to process the form data, for instance by storing it in a database. However, you don't need to return a ModelAndView object for this method because an action request doesn't expect a view to be rendered. After the action request finishes, the portlet container will ask each portlet in the same page to handle a render request. The onSubmitRender() method of the form controller will be called if no error occurs in form handling. By default, it simply renders the form success view, so you don't need to override it in most cases.

You can create the form view for this controller using the Spring 2.0 form tag library. Let's create it in the JSP file /WEB-INF/jsp/tour/bookingForm.jsp. Note that this form will be submitted to the action URL.

```
<%@ taglib prefix="portlet" uri="http://java.sun.com/portlet" %>
<%@ taglib prefix="form" uri="http://www.springframework.org/tags/form" %>

<portlet:actionURL var="formAction" />

<form:form method="POST" action="${formAction}" commandName="bookingForm">
<table>
  <tr>
    <td>Tourist</td>
    <td><form:input path="tourist" /></td>
    <td><form:errors path="tourist" cssClass="portlet-msg-error" /></td>
  </tr>
  <tr>
    <td>Phone</td>
    <td><form:input path="phone" /></td>
    <td><form:errors path="phone" cssClass="portlet-msg-error" /></td>
  </tr>
  <tr>
    <td>Origin</td>
    <td><form:select path="origin" items="${locations}" /></td>
    <td><form:errors path="origin" cssClass="portlet-msg-error" /></td>
  </tr>
  <tr>
    <td>Destination</td>
    <td><form:select path="destination" items="${locations}" /></td>
    <td><form:errors path="destination" cssClass="portlet-msg-error" /></td>
  </tr>
  <tr>
    <td>Departure Date</td>
    <td><form:input path="departureDate" /></td>
    <td><form:errors path="departureDate" cssClass="portlet-msg-error" /></td>
  </tr>
  <tr>
    <td>Return Date</td>
    <td><form:input path="returnDate" /></td>
    <td><form:errors path="returnDate" cssClass="portlet-msg-error" /></td>
  </tr>
  <tr>
    <td colspan="3"><input type="submit" /></td>
  </tr>
</table>
</form:form>
```

Note that you will output the error messages with the CSS class portlet-msg-error, which is defined by the Java Portlet specification for you to display error messages.

The success view for this form controller is very simple. Let's create it in the JSP file /WEB-INF/jsp/tour/bookingSuccess.jsp. From this view, users can return to the form view by a render URL, which will trigger all the portlets in the same page to handle a new render request. Then the form controller will render its form view in response.

```
<%@ taglib prefix="portlet" uri="http://java.sun.com/portlet" %>

Your booking has been made successfully.
<br />
<a href="<portlet:renderURL />">Return</a>
```

Finally, you create the Spring configuration file for this portlet. As its DispatcherPortlet instance has the name tour in portlet.xml, you create the following tour-portlet.xml in the WEB-INF root, which will be loaded by default:

```
<beans xmlns="http://www.springframework.org/schema/beans"
    xmlns:xsi="http://www.w3.org/2001/XMLSchema-instance"
    xsi:schemaLocation="http://www.springframework.org/schema/beans
        http://www.springframework.org/schema/beans/spring-beans-2.5.xsd">

    <bean class="org.springframework.web.servlet.view.➥
        InternalResourceViewResolver">
        <property name="viewClass"
            value="org.springframework.web.servlet.view.JstlView" />
        <property name="prefix" value="/WEB-INF/jsp/tour/" />
        <property name="suffix" value=".jsp" />
    </bean>

    <bean class="org.springframework.web.portlet.handler.➥
        PortletModeHandlerMapping">
        <property name="portletModeMap">
            <map>
                <entry key="view" value-ref="bookingFormController" />
            </map>
        </property>
    </bean>

    <bean id="bookingFormController"
        class="com.apress.springrecipes.travel.tour.BookingFormController">
        <property name="tourService" ref="tourService" />
        <property name="formView" value="bookingForm" />
        <property name="successView" value="bookingSuccess" />
    </bean>
</beans>
```

In this configuration file, you simply configure an InternalResourceViewResolver bean to map view names to JSP files under the /WEB-INF/jsp/tour/ directory. You also declare a form controller instance. As this is the only controller in this portlet at this moment, you can map it to the view mode with PortletModeHandlerMapping. Later, if you have more controllers, you can consider distinguishing them with a request parameter.

To deploy this portlet in Pluto, you add a PortletServlet instance for this portlet in web.xml and map it to the corresponding URL pattern.

```
<web-app ...>
    ...
    <servlet>
        <servlet-name>tour</servlet-name>
        <servlet-class>
            org.apache.pluto.core.PortletServlet
        </servlet-class>
        <init-param>
            <param-name>portlet-name</param-name>
            <param-value>tour</param-value>
        </init-param>
    </servlet>
    ...
    <servlet-mapping>
        <servlet-name>tour</servlet-name>
        <url-pattern>/PlutoInvoker/tour</url-pattern>
    </servlet-mapping>
</web-app>
```

After starting up and logging into Pluto, you can add your tour portlet to a portal page from the Pluto Admin page.

Validating Form Data

Validation in Portlet MVC is performed in the same way as in Web MVC. By registering a validator that implements the Validator interface, SimpleFormController can help you to validate the command object after it binds the form field values. For example, you can create the following validator to validate a booking form:

```
package com.apress.springrecipes.travel.tour;

import org.springframework.validation.Errors;
import org.springframework.validation.ValidationUtils;
import org.springframework.validation.Validator;

public class BookingFormValidator implements Validator {

    public boolean supports(Class clazz) {
        return BookingForm.class.isAssignableFrom(clazz);
    }
```

```
    public void validate(Object target, Errors errors) {
        ValidationUtils.rejectIfEmptyOrWhitespace(errors, "tourist",
                "required.tourist");
        ValidationUtils.rejectIfEmptyOrWhitespace(errors, "phone",
                "required.phone");
        ValidationUtils.rejectIfEmpty(errors, "origin",
                "required.origin");
        ValidationUtils.rejectIfEmpty(errors, "destination",
                "required.destination");
        ValidationUtils.rejectIfEmpty(errors, "departureDate",
                "required.departureDate");
        ValidationUtils.rejectIfEmpty(errors, "returnDate",
                "required.returnDate");

        BookingForm form = (BookingForm) target;
        if (form.getOrigin().equals(form.getDestination())) {
            errors.rejectValue("destination", "invalid.destination");
        }
        if (form.getDepartureDate() != null && form.getReturnDate() != null
                && !form.getDepartureDate().before(form.getReturnDate())) {
            errors.rejectValue("returnDate", "invalid.returnDate");
        }
    }
}
```

To apply this validator to your form controller, you just create an instance of it for the `validator` property, either as an inner bean or via a bean reference. If you have multiple validators to apply to a form controller, you can configure them in the `validators` property of the array type instead.

```
<bean id="bookingFormController"
    class="com.apress.springrecipes.travel.tour.BookingFormController">
    ...
    <property name="validator">
        <bean class="com.apress.springrecipes.travel.tour.➥
            BookingFormValidator" />
    </property>
</bean>
```

In order to display user-friendly messages in case of binding or validation errors, you have to define the error messages in resource bundles of appropriate locales in the root of the classpath (e.g., `messages.properties` for the default locale).

```
typeMismatch.java.util.Date=Invalid date format.
required.tourist=Tourist is required.
required.phone=Phone is required.
required.origin=Origin is required.
required.destination=Destination is required.
required.departureDate=Departure date is required.
```

```
required.returnDate=Return date is required.
invalid.destination=Destination cannot be the same as origin.
invalid.returnDate=Return date must be later than departure date.
```

Finally, you declare a ResourceBundleMessageSource bean in the Spring configuration file for this portlet, whose bean name must be messageSource.

```
<bean id="messageSource"
    class="org.springframework.context.support.ResourceBundleMessageSource">
    <property name="basename" value="messages" />
</bean>
```

14-4. Developing Portlet Controllers with Annotations

Problem

In the traditional Portlet MVC approach, you have to configure an instance and a request mapping for each controller class, which must implement or extend a framework-specific interface or base class. You would like Spring to auto-detect your controller classes and request mappings without explicit configuration.

Solution

Spring 2.5 supports a new annotation-based approach for controller development, both for web controllers and portlet controllers. Spring can auto-detect your controller classes with the @Controller annotation, and they needn't implement or extend a framework-specific interface or class. Also, Spring can auto-detect your request mappings in the @RequestMapping annotation to save you the trouble of configuring them in the portlet configuration file. Moreover, controller classes and handler methods using annotations are more flexible in accessing context resources such as request parameters, model attributes, and session attributes.

How It Works

Developing Multi-Action Controllers

In the annotation-based Portlet MVC approach, a controller class can be an arbitrary class with the @Controller annotation or a custom annotation type that is itself annotated with @Controller. One or more handler methods can be defined in a controller to handle single or multiple actions.

The @RequestMapping annotation can be applied at the class level or the method level. The common mapping strategy for portlets is to map a portlet mode to a controller class and map a request parameter to each handler method. For example, you can combine the controllers for listing flights and showing flight details in a multi-action controller.

```
package com.apress.springrecipes.travel.flight;

import javax.portlet.PortletPreferences;
```

```
import org.springframework.beans.factory.annotation.Autowired;
import org.springframework.stereotype.Controller;
import org.springframework.ui.ModelMap;
import org.springframework.web.bind.annotation.ModelAttribute;
import org.springframework.web.bind.annotation.RequestMapping;
import org.springframework.web.bind.annotation.RequestParam;

@Controller
@RequestMapping("VIEW")
public class FlightViewController {

    private FlightService flightService;

    @Autowired
    public FlightViewController(FlightService flightService) {
        this.flightService = flightService;
    }

    @ModelAttribute("timeZone")
    public String getTimeZone(PortletPreferences preferences) {
        return preferences.getValue("timeZone", null);
    }

    @RequestMapping
    public String flightList(ModelMap model) {
        model.addAttribute("flights", flightService.findTodayFlights());
        return "flightList";
    }

    @RequestMapping(params = "action=flightDetail")
    public String flightDetail(
            @RequestParam("flightNo") String flightNo, ModelMap model) {
        model.addAttribute("flight", flightService.findFlight(flightNo));
        return "flightDetail";
    }
}
```

This controller is mapped to the view mode at the class level, so its handler methods will only handle view mode requests. The `flightList()` method is annotated with `@RequestMapping`, which has no value or attribute, so it will handle default view mode requests. The `flightDetail()` method will handle view mode requests with an `action` parameter whose value is `flightDetail`.

A controller can also be configured to handle both render requests and action requests. For example, you can reimplement the controller for changing portlet preferences in the flight portlet.

```
package com.apress.springrecipes.travel.flight;

import javax.portlet.PortletPreferences;

import org.springframework.stereotype.Controller;
import org.springframework.ui.ModelMap;
import org.springframework.web.bind.annotation.RequestMapping;
import org.springframework.web.bind.annotation.RequestParam;

@Controller
@RequestMapping("EDIT")
public class FlightPreferencesController {

    @RequestMapping
    public String showPreferences(PortletPreferences preferences, ModelMap model) {
        model.addAttribute("timeZone", preferences.getValue("timeZone", null));
        return "flightPreferences";
    }

    @RequestMapping
    public void changePreference(PortletPreferences preferences,
            @RequestParam("timeZone") String timeZone) throws Exception {
        preferences.setValue("timeZone", timeZone);
        preferences.store();
    }
}
```

This controller is mapped to the edit mode, so its methods will only handle edit mode requests. Both `showPreferences()` and `changePreference()` are annotated with `@RequestMapping`, which has no value or attribute. In this case, the method whose return type is `void` will handle action requests. Otherwise, it will handle render requests.

Finally, you can reimplement the controller for displaying help information in your flight portlet also.

```
package com.apress.springrecipes.travel.flight;

import org.springframework.stereotype.Controller;
import org.springframework.web.bind.annotation.RequestMapping;

@Controller
@RequestMapping("HELP")
public class FlightHelpController {

    @RequestMapping
    public String showHelp() {
        return "flightHelp";
    }
}
```

In order for Spring to auto-detect your controllers and handler mappings, you have to enable Spring's component scan feature through the `<component-scan>` element defined in the `context` schema. You can now delete the handler mapping bean as well as the controller instances from `flight-portlet.xml`.

```
<beans xmlns="http://www.springframework.org/schema/beans"
    xmlns:xsi="http://www.w3.org/2001/XMLSchema-instance"
    xmlns:context="http://www.springframework.org/schema/context"
    xsi:schemaLocation="http://www.springframework.org/schema/beans
        http://www.springframework.org/schema/beans/spring-beans-2.5.xsd
        http://www.springframework.org/schema/context
        http://www.springframework.org/schema/context/spring-context-2.5.xsd">

    <context:component-scan
        base-package="com.apress.springrecipes.travel.flight" />

    <bean class="org.springframework.web.servlet.view.➥
        InternalResourceViewResolver">
        <property name="viewClass"
            value="org.springframework.web.servlet.view.JstlView" />
        <property name="prefix" value="/WEB-INF/jsp/flight/" />
        <property name="suffix" value=".jsp" />
    </bean>
</beans>
```

Developing Form Controllers

In the traditional Portlet MVC approach, you create a simple form controller by extending the `SimpleFormController` class, which has basic form-handling flow defined and allows you to customize it. In the new annotation-based approach, you can simulate this flow by using annotations.

An annotation-based portlet form controller has to provide two handler methods, one for handling render requests and another for handling action requests. For example, you can reimplement the booking form controller in the tour portlet with annotations.

```
package com.apress.springrecipes.travel.tour;
...
import javax.portlet.ActionResponse;

import org.springframework.beans.factory.annotation.Autowired;
import org.springframework.beans.propertyeditors.CustomDateEditor;
import org.springframework.stereotype.Controller;
import org.springframework.ui.ModelMap;
import org.springframework.validation.BindingResult;
import org.springframework.web.bind.WebDataBinder;
import org.springframework.web.bind.annotation.InitBinder;
import org.springframework.web.bind.annotation.ModelAttribute;
import org.springframework.web.bind.annotation.RequestMapping;
```

```
import org.springframework.web.bind.annotation.RequestParam;
import org.springframework.web.bind.annotation.SessionAttributes;
import org.springframework.web.bind.support.SessionStatus;

@Controller
@RequestMapping("VIEW")
@SessionAttributes("bookingForm")
public class BookingFormController {

    private TourService tourService;
    private BookingFormValidator validator;

    @Autowired
    public BookingFormController(TourService tourService,
            BookingFormValidator validator) {
        this.tourService = tourService;
        this.validator = validator;
    }

    @InitBinder
    public void initBinder(WebDataBinder binder) {
        SimpleDateFormat dateFormat = new SimpleDateFormat("yyyy-MM-dd");
        dateFormat.setLenient(false);
        binder.registerCustomEditor(Date.class, new CustomDateEditor(
                dateFormat, true));
    }

    @ModelAttribute("locations")
    protected List<String> getLocations() {
        return tourService.getLocations();
    }

    @RequestMapping
    public String showForm(
            @RequestParam(required = false, value = "form-submit")
            Boolean isFormSubmission, ModelMap model) {
        if (isFormSubmission == null) {
            BookingForm bookingForm = new BookingForm();
            model.addAttribute("bookingForm", bookingForm);
            return "bookingForm";
        }
        return "bookingSuccess";
    }

    @RequestMapping
    public void processSubmit(
            @ModelAttribute("bookingForm") BookingForm form,
```

```
            BindingResult result, SessionStatus status,
            ActionResponse response) {
        validator.validate(form, result);
        if (!result.hasErrors()) {
            tourService.processBooking(form);
            status.setComplete();
            response.setRenderParameter("form-submit", "true");
        }
    }
}
```

In portlet form controllers, you have to use a request parameter, such as `form-submit`, to distinguish whether a render request is made before or after a form submission. When this form controller is asked to show the form by a portlet render request, the `showForm()` method will be called since its return type is not `void`, and it will handle a render request. In this case, the `form-submit` parameter is `null`, so you simply render the form view to the user with an initialized command object.

When the form is submitted by a portlet action request, the `processSubmit()` method will be called since its return type is `void`, and it will handle an action request. If the form is handled successfully, you will call the `setRenderParameter()` method on the response to set the `form-submit` request parameter for the next render request. After the action request finishes, the portlet container will ask this controller to handle a new render request. This time, the request should contain the `form-submit` parameter, so the `showForm()` method will render the success view.

You have to enable the component scan feature through the `<context:component-scan>` element for Spring to auto-detect your controllers and handler mappings. You can now delete the handler mapping bean as well as the controller instance from `tour-portlet.xml`, but you must retain the validator bean for auto-wiring.

```
<beans xmlns="http://www.springframework.org/schema/beans"
    xmlns:xsi="http://www.w3.org/2001/XMLSchema-instance"
    xmlns:context="http://www.springframework.org/schema/context"
    xsi:schemaLocation="http://www.springframework.org/schema/beans
        http://www.springframework.org/schema/beans/spring-beans-2.5.xsd
        http://www.springframework.org/schema/context
        http://www.springframework.org/schema/context/spring-context-2.5.xsd">

    <context:component-scan
        base-package="com.apress.springrecipes.travel.tour" />

    <bean class="org.springframework.web.servlet.view.➥
        InternalResourceViewResolver">
        <property name="viewClass"
            value="org.springframework.web.servlet.view.JstlView" />
        <property name="prefix" value="/WEB-INF/jsp/tour/" />
        <property name="suffix" value=".jsp" />
    </bean>
```

```
    <bean id="messageSource"
        class="org.springframework.context.support.ResourceBundleMessageSource">
        <property name="basename" value="messages" />
    </bean>

    <bean id="bookingFormValidator"
        class="com.apress.springrecipes.travel.tour.BookingFormValidator" />
</beans>
```

14-5. Summary

In this chapter, you have learned how to develop a portlet application using Spring Portlet MVC, which is very similar to Spring Web MVC because most of it is ported from Web MVC. The main difference between portlets and servlets is that there are two types of URLs in portlets: render URLs and action URLs. When a user triggers a render URL, the portlet container will ask all the portlets in the same page to handle a render request to render its view. However, when a user triggers an action URL, the portlet container will first ask the target portlet to handle an action request. When the action request finishes, the portlet container will ask all the portlets in the same page, including the target portlet, to handle a render request to render its view.

Unlike in a web application, you can't control URLs directly in a portlet. So the main strategies for mapping portlet requests in Spring Portlet MVC are based on the portlet mode and a request parameter, or both combined. You can also chain multiple handler mappings to meet your needs.

Spring Portlet MVC provides a form controller that is very similar to that in Spring Web MVC. However, as there are two types of portlet requests, the form-handling flow is a bit different from the form controller in Spring Web MVC.

Spring 2.5 supports annotation-based controller development both for Web MVC and Portlet MVC. Your controllers have no need to extend the traditional controller classes, but only to include the annotations. Spring can auto-detect your controllers and handler mappings, so you needn't configure them manually.

In the next chapter, you will learn how to manage complex web application page flows with Spring WebFlow.

CHAPTER 15

Spring Web Flow

In this chapter, you will learn how to use Spring Web Flow, a subproject of the Spring framework, to model and manage your web application's UI flows. Spring Web Flow's usage has changed significantly from version 1.0 to 2.0. Spring Web Flow 2.0 is simpler than 1.0 and makes a lot of convention-over-configuration improvements. This chapter will focus on Spring Web Flow 2.0 only. *Note that Spring Web Flow 2.0 requires the Spring framework 2.5.4 or higher.*

In traditional web application development, developers often manage their UI flows programmatically, so these flows are hard to maintain and reuse. Spring Web Flow offers a flow definition language that can help separate UI flows from presentation logic in a highly configurable way, so the flows can be easily changed and reused. Spring Web Flow supports not just Spring Web MVC, but also Spring Portlet MVC and other web application frameworks such as Struts and JSF.

Upon finishing this chapter, you will be able to develop basic Spring MVC–based and JSF-based web applications that use Spring Web Flow to manage their UI flows. This chapter only touches on the basic features and configurations of Spring Web Flow, so please consult the Spring Web Flow reference guide for further details.

15-1. Managing a Simple UI Flow with Spring Web Flow

Problem

You would like to manage a simple UI flow in a Spring MVC application using Spring Web Flow.

Solution

Spring Web Flow allows you to model UI activities as *flows*. It supports defining a flow either by Java or by XML. XML-based flow definitions are widely used due to the power and popularity of XML. You can also easily modify your XML-based flow definitions without recompiling your code. Moreover, Spring IDE supports Spring Web Flow by offering a visual editor for you to edit XML-based flow definitions.

A flow definition consists of one or more *states*, each of which corresponds to a step in the flow. Spring Web Flow builds in several state types, including view state, action state, decision state, subflow state, and end state. Once a state has completed its tasks, it fires an *event*. An event contains a source and an event ID, and perhaps some attributes. Each state may contain zero or more *transitions*, each of which maps a returned event ID to the next state.

When a user triggers a new flow, Spring Web Flow can auto-detect the start state of that flow (i.e., the state without transitions from other states), so you don't need to specify the start state explicitly. A flow can terminate at one of its defined end states. This marks the flow as ended and releases resources held by the flow.

How It Works

Suppose you are going to develop an online system for a library. The first page of this system is a welcome page. There are two links on this page. When a user clicks on the Next link, the system will show the library introduction page. There's another Next link on this introduction page, clicking which will show the menu page. If a user clicks the Skip link on the welcome page, the system will skip the introduction page and show the menu page directly. This welcome UI flow is illustrated in Figure 15-1. This example will show you how to develop this application with Spring MVC and use Spring Web Flow to manage the flow.

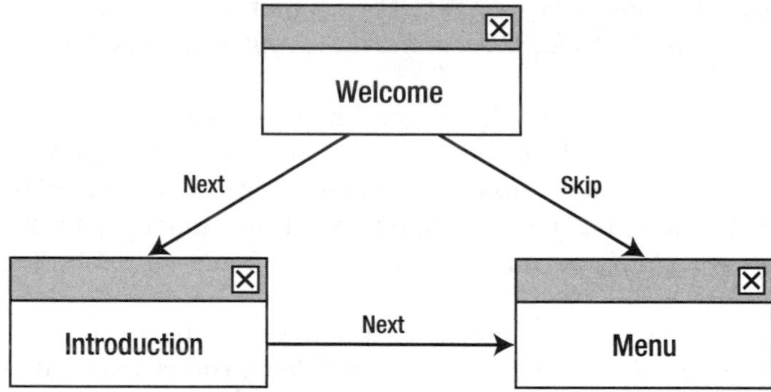

Figure 15-1. *The welcome UI flow*

In the library introduction page, you would like to show the public holidays on which this library will close. They are queried from a back-end service whose interface is defined as shown following:

```
package com.apress.springrecipes.library.service;
...
public interface LibraryService {

    public List<Date> getHolidays();
}
```

For testing purposes, you can hard-code several holidays for this service implementation as follows:

```
package com.apress.springrecipes.library.service;
...
public class LibraryServiceImpl implements LibraryService {

    public List<Date> getHolidays() {
        List<Date> holidays = new ArrayList<Date>();
```

```
        holidays.add(new GregorianCalendar(2007, 11, 25).getTime());
        holidays.add(new GregorianCalendar(2008, 0, 1).getTime());
        return holidays;
    }
}
```

Setting Up a Spring MVC Application That Uses Spring Web Flow

To develop the library system using Spring MVC and Spring Web Flow, you first create the following directory structure for this web application.

Note To manage your web UI flows with Spring Web Flow, download the Spring Web Flow distribution (e.g., v2.0.0) and extract it to a directory of your choice. Then copy `spring-webflow-2.0.0.jar`, `spring-binding-2.0.0.jar`, and `spring-js-2.0.0.jar` (located in the `dist` directory of the Spring Web Flow installation) to the `WEB-INF/lib` directory.

```
library/
    WEB-INF/
        classes/
        flows/
            welcome/
                introduction.jsp
                menu.jsp
                welcome.jsp
                welcome.xml
        lib/
            commons-logging.jar
            jstl.jar
            spring-binding-2.0.0.jar
            spring-js-2.0.0.jar
            spring-webflow-2.0.0.jar
            spring-webmvc.jar
            spring.jar
            standard.jar
        library-service.xml
        library-servlet.xml
        library-webflow.xml
        web.xml
```

Spring Web Flow supports using an expression language in flow definitions to access its data model and invoke back-end services. Spring Web Flow 2.0 supports using Unified EL (used in JSF 1.2 and JSP 2.1) and OGNL (Object-Graph Navigation Language) as its expression language. These two languages have a very similar syntax. For basic expressions such as property access and method invocations, the syntax is identical. The expressions used in this chapter are valid for both Unified EL and OGNL, so you are free to choose either of them as your expression language. Unified EL is recommended in a JSF environment because it allows you to use the same expression language in flow definitions as in JSF views. However, developers using Spring Web Flow 1.0 may prefer OGNL because it is the only supported expression language for the 1.0 version.

Spring Web Flow is able to detect the libraries of JBoss EL (as the default Unified EL implementation) and OGNL from the classpath. You can enable either of them (but not both) by including the corresponding JAR file in your classpath.

■ **Note** If you are going to use Unified EL as your Web Flow expression language, you can download JBoss EL (e.g., v2.0.0 GA) from `http://repository.jboss.org/maven2/org/jboss/seam/jboss-el/` and copy the downloaded `jboss-el-2.0.0.GA.jar` file to the `WEB-INF/lib` directory. If you choose OGNL, you can download `ognl-2.6.9.jar` from `http://www.ognl.org/` and copy it to the `WEB-INF/lib` directory.

Creating the Configuration Files

In the web deployment descriptor (i.e., `web.xml`), you register `ContextLoaderListener` to load the root application context at startup, and also Spring MVC's `DispatcherServlet` for dispatching requests. You can map the URL pattern `/flow/*` to this servlet so that all requests under the request path `flow` will be handled by it.

```
<web-app version="2.4" xmlns="http://java.sun.com/xml/ns/j2ee"
    xmlns:xsi="http://www.w3.org/2001/XMLSchema-instance"
    xsi:schemaLocation="http://java.sun.com/xml/ns/j2ee
        http://java.sun.com/xml/ns/j2ee/web-app_2_4.xsd">

    <context-param>
        <param-name>contextConfigLocation</param-name>
        <param-value>/WEB-INF/library-service.xml</param-value>
    </context-param>

    <listener>
        <listener-class>
            org.springframework.web.context.ContextLoaderListener
        </listener-class>
    </listener>

    <servlet>
        <servlet-name>library</servlet-name>
        <servlet-class>
            org.springframework.web.servlet.DispatcherServlet
        </servlet-class>
    </servlet>
```

```
    <servlet-mapping>
        <servlet-name>library</servlet-name>
        <url-pattern>/flow/*</url-pattern>
    </servlet-mapping>
</web-app>
```

ContextLoaderListener will load the root application context from the configuration file you specify in the contextConfigLocation context parameter (library-service.xml in this case). This configuration file declares beans in the service layer. For the welcome flow, you can declare the library service in this file for returning public holidays when queried.

```
<beans xmlns="http://www.springframework.org/schema/beans"
    xmlns:xsi="http://www.w3.org/2001/XMLSchema-instance"
    xsi:schemaLocation="http://www.springframework.org/schema/beans
        http://www.springframework.org/schema/beans/spring-beans-2.5.xsd">

    <bean name="libraryService"
        class="com.apress.springrecipes.library.service.LibraryServiceImpl" />
</beans>
```

As the DispatcherServlet instance in the web deployment descriptor has the name library, you create library-servlet.xml in the root of WEB-INF with the following content:

```
<beans xmlns="http://www.springframework.org/schema/beans"
    xmlns:xsi="http://www.w3.org/2001/XMLSchema-instance"
    xsi:schemaLocation="http://www.springframework.org/schema/beans
        http://www.springframework.org/schema/beans/spring-beans-2.5.xsd">

    <import resource="library-webflow.xml" />
</beans>
```

In order to separate the configurations of Spring MVC and Spring Web Flow, you can centralize Spring Web Flow's configurations in another file (e.g., library-webflow.xml) and import it into library-servlet.xml. Then create this file with the following contents:

```
<beans xmlns="http://www.springframework.org/schema/beans"
    xmlns:xsi="http://www.w3.org/2001/XMLSchema-instance"
    xmlns:webflow="http://www.springframework.org/schema/webflow-config"
    xsi:schemaLocation="http://www.springframework.org/schema/beans
        http://www.springframework.org/schema/beans/spring-beans-2.5.xsd
        http://www.springframework.org/schema/webflow-config
        http://www.springframework.org/schema/webflow-config/➥
            spring-webflow-config-2.0.xsd">

    <bean name="/*" class="org.springframework.webflow.mvc.servlet.FlowController">
        <property name="flowExecutor" ref="flowExecutor" />
    </bean>

    <webflow:flow-executor id="flowExecutor" />
```

```
    <webflow:flow-registry id="flowRegistry">
        <webflow:flow-location path="/WEB-INF/flows/welcome/welcome.xml" />
    </webflow:flow-registry>
</beans>
```

As BeanNameUrlHandlerMapping is preconfigured for each Spring MVC application, you can map all URLs to FlowController by specifying the URL pattern /* as its bean name. If you have other controllers in addition to FlowController, you have to refine your URL mappings. FlowController is a Spring MVC controller provided by Spring Web Flow that delegates request handling to a flow executor. The flow executor is the central entry point to Spring Web Flow. It drives the execution of web flows registered in a flow registry. By default, it looks up a flow registry with the ID flowRegistry.

Then you have to register your flow definitions in a flow registry by specifying their locations. The file name of a flow definition (e.g., welcome.xml) will be used as the flow ID by default (e.g., welcome), but you can specify a custom ID with the id attribute.

Creating Web Flow Definitions

Spring Web Flow offers an XML-based flow definition language that can be validated by Spring Web Flow's XSD and supported by Spring IDE. Please refer to Spring IDE's online documentation (at http://springide.org/) on its support for Spring Web Flow. Now you can define your welcome flow in the definition file /WEB-INF/flows/welcome/welcome.xml:

```
<flow xmlns="http://www.springframework.org/schema/webflow"
    xmlns:xsi="http://www.w3.org/2001/XMLSchema-instance"
    xsi:schemaLocation="http://www.springframework.org/schema/webflow
        http://www.springframework.org/schema/webflow/spring-webflow-2.0.xsd">

    <view-state id="welcome">
        <transition on="next" to="introduction" />
        <transition on="skip" to="menu" />
    </view-state>

    <view-state id="introduction">
        <on-render>
            <evaluate expression="libraryService.getHolidays()"
                result="requestScope.holidays" />
        </on-render>
        <transition on="next" to="menu" />
    </view-state>

    <view-state id="menu" />
</flow>
```

In this welcome flow, you have defined three view states: welcome, introduction, and menu. As its name indicates, a view state will render a view to a user. Typically, in Spring MVC, a view is a JSP file. By default, a view state will render a JSP file with the state ID as the file name and .jsp as the file extension, located in the same path as this flow definition. If you want to render another view, you can specify its logical view name in the view attribute and define a corresponding Spring MVC view resolver to resolve it.

You can use the <on-render> element to trigger an action for a view state before its view renders. Spring Web Flow supports using an expression of Unified EL or OGNL to invoke a method. For more about Unified EL and OGNL, please refer to the article "Unified Expression Language," at http://java.sun.com/products/jsp/reference/techart/unifiedEL.html, and the OGNL language guide, at http://www.ognl.org/. The preceding expression is valid for both Unified EL and OGNL. It invokes the getHolidays() method on the libraryService bean and stores the result in the holidays variable in the request scope.

The flow diagram for this welcome flow is illustrated in Figure 15-2.

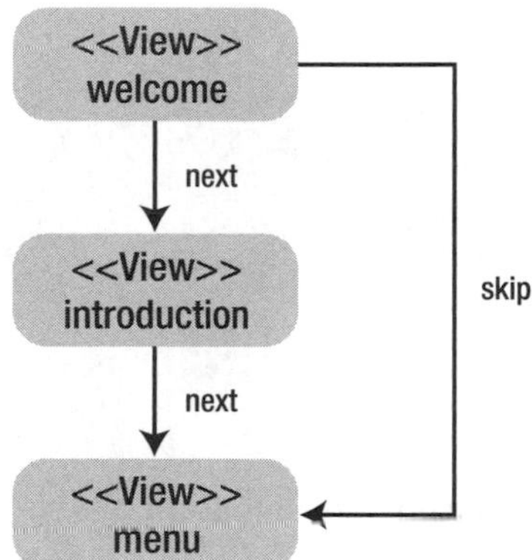

Figure 15-2. *The flow diagram for the welcome flow*

Creating the Page Views

Now you have to create the JSP files for the preceding three view states. You can create them at the same location as the flow definition and with the same name as the view states so that they can be loaded by default. First, you create welcome.jsp:

```
<html>
<head>
<title>Welcome</title>
</head>

<body>
<h2>Welcome!</h2>
<a href="${flowExecutionUrl}&_eventId=next">Next</a>
<a href="${flowExecutionUrl}&_eventId=skip">Skip</a>
</body>
</html>
```

In this JSP file, there are two links to fire events, with next and skip as the event IDs. In Spring Web Flow, an event ID can be specified either as the _eventId request parameter's value (e.g., _eventId=next), or in a request parameter's name, with _eventId_ as the prefix (e.g., _eventId_next), no matter what the parameter value is. Also, you have to start the URLs with the variable ${flowExecutionUrl} to trigger a flow execution. This variable will be evaluated by Spring Web Flow at runtime.

Next, you create introduction.jsp to display the library holidays, which are loaded by the action specified in <on-render> before this view renders:

```
<%@ taglib prefix="c" uri="http://java.sun.com/jsp/jstl/core" %>
<%@ taglib prefix="fmt" uri="http://java.sun.com/jsp/jstl/fmt" %>

<html>
<head>
<title>Introduction</title>
</head>

<body>
<h2>Library Holidays</h2>
<c:forEach items="${holidays}" var="holiday">
  <fmt:formatDate value="${holiday}" pattern="yyyy-MM-dd" /><br />
</c:forEach>
<a href="${flowExecutionUrl}&_eventId=next">Next</a>
</body>
</html>
```

Finally, you create menu.jsp. This view is very simple, as there's no transition from this state to others.

```
<html>
<head>
<title>Menu</title>
</head>

<body>
<h2>Menu</h2>
</body>
</html>
```

Now you can deploy this web flow application to a web container (e.g., Apache Tomcat 6.0). By default, Tomcat listens on port 8080, so if you deploy your application to the library context path, you can access this welcome web flow with the following URL, since the URLs under the flow request path will be mapped to DispatcherServlet:

```
http://localhost:8080/library/flow/welcome
```

15-2. Modeling Web Flows with Different State Types

Problem

You would like to model various types of UI activities as web flows to execute in Spring Web Flow.

Solution

In Spring Web Flow, each step of a flow is denoted by a state. A state may contain zero or more transitions to the next states according to an event ID. Spring Web Flow provides several built-in state types for you to model web flows. It also allows you to define custom state types. Table 15-1 shows the built-in state types in Spring Web Flow.

Table 15-1. *Built-In State Types in Spring Web Flow*

State Type	Description
View	Renders a view for a user to participate in the flow (e.g., by displaying information and gathering user input). The flow's execution pauses until an event is triggered to resume the flow (e.g., by a hyperlink click or a form submission).
Action	Executes actions for the flow, such as updating a database and gathering information for displaying.
Decision	Evaluates a Boolean expression to decide which state to transition to next.
Subflow	Launches another flow as a subflow of the current flow. The subflow will return to the launching flow when it ends.
End	Terminates the flow, after which all flow scope variables become invalid.

How It Works

Suppose you are going to build a web flow for library users to search books. First, a user has to enter the book criteria in the criteria page. If there's more than one book matching the criteria, they will be displayed in the list page. In this page, the user can select a book to browse its details in the details page. However, if there's exactly one book matching the criteria, its details will be shown directly in the details page, without going through the list page. This book search UI flow is illustrated in Figure 15-3.

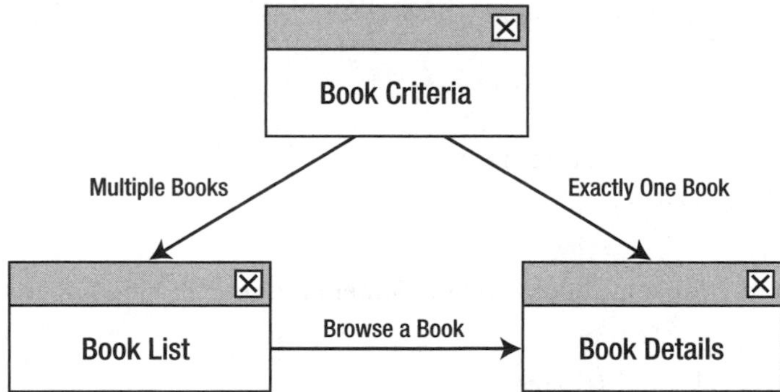

Figure 15-3. *The book search UI flow*

First of all, let's create the domain class `Book`. It should implement the `Serializable` interface, as its instances may need to be persisted in sessions.

```
package com.apress.springrecipes.library.domain;
...
public class Book implements Serializable {

    private String isbn;
    private String name;
    private String author;
    private Date publishDate;

    // Constructors, Getters and Setters
    ...
}
```

Next, you create the BookCriteria class, whose instances will act as form command objects for binding form fields. It should also implement the Serializable interface for the same reason.

```
package com.apress.springrecipes.library.domain;
...
public class BookCriteria implements Serializable {

    private String keyword;
    private String author;

    // Getters and Setters
    ...
}
```

In the service layer, you design a service interface for providing book search services to the presentation layer:

```
package com.apress.springrecipes.library.service;
...
public interface BookService {

    public List<Book> search(BookCriteria criteria);
    public Book findByIsbn(String isbn);
}
```

For testing purposes, let's hard-code some books and implement the search() method by matching the books one by one:

```
package com.apress.springrecipes.library.service;
...
public class BookServiceImpl implements BookService {

    private Map<String, Book> books;
```

```
    public BookServiceImpl() {
        books = new HashMap<String, Book>();
        books.put("0001", new Book("0001", "Spring Framework", "Ray",
                new GregorianCalendar(2007, 0, 1).getTime()));
        books.put("0002", new Book("0002", "Spring Web MVC", "Paul",
                new GregorianCalendar(2007, 3, 1).getTime()));
        books.put("0003", new Book("0003", "Spring Web Flow", "Ray",
                new GregorianCalendar(2007, 6, 1).getTime()));
    }

    public List<Book> search(BookCriteria criteria) {
        List<Book> results = new ArrayList<Book>();
        for (Book book : books.values()) {
            String keyword = criteria.getKeyword().trim();
            String author = criteria.getAuthor().trim();
            boolean keywordMatches = keyword.length() > 0
                    && book.getName().contains(keyword);
            boolean authorMatches = book.getAuthor().equals(author);
            if (keywordMatches || authorMatches) {
                results.add(book);
            }
        }
        return results;
    }

    public Book findByIsbn(String isbn) {
        return books.get(isbn);
    }
}
```

To make this book service accessible to all the library web flows, you declare it in the service layer configuration file (i.e., `library-service.xml`), which will be loaded for the root application context:

```
<bean name="bookService"
    class="com.apress.springrecipes.library.service.BookServiceImpl" />
```

Now you can start with your book search flow development. First, you add the flow definition's location to the flow registry in `library-webflow.xml` and create the flow definition XML file as well:

```
<webflow:flow-registry id="flowRegistry">
    ...
    <webflow:flow-location path="/WEB-INF/flows/bookSearch/bookSearch.xml" />
</webflow:flow-registry>
```

Next, let's build this web flow incrementally with different types of states offered by Spring Web Flow.

Defining View States

According to the requirement of the book search flow, you first need a view state to show a form so that a user can enter the book criteria. In Spring Web Flow, you can create an action corresponding to a controller in Spring MVC to handle flow requests. Spring Web Flow provides a FormAction class to assist you in handling forms. For complicated form processing, you can extend this class and add your own processing logic. But for a simple form's needs, you can use this class directly by populating its properties (e.g., the form object class, property editors, and validators). Now you can define a form action with this class to handle the book criteria form in library-webflow.xml:

```
<bean id="bookCriteriaAction"
    class="org.springframework.webflow.action.FormAction">
    <property name="formObjectClass"
        value="com.apress.springrecipes.library.domain.BookCriteria" />
    <property name="propertyEditorRegistrar">
        <bean class="com.apress.springrecipes.library.web.PropertyEditors" />
    </property>
</bean>
```

A form action can bind form fields to a form object's properties of the same name. But you first have to specify the form object class in the formObjectClass property for this action to instantiate form objects. In order to convert form field values into proper data types, you have to register custom property editors to this form action. You can create a property editor registrar to register your own editors, and specify it in the propertyEditorRegistrar property:

```
package com.apress.springrecipes.library.web;
...
import org.springframework.beans.PropertyEditorRegistrar;
import org.springframework.beans.PropertyEditorRegistry;
import org.springframework.beans.propertyeditors.CustomDateEditor;

public class PropertyEditors implements PropertyEditorRegistrar {

    public void registerCustomEditors(PropertyEditorRegistry registry) {
        SimpleDateFormat dateFormat = new SimpleDateFormat("yyyy-MM-dd");
        dateFormat.setLenient(false);
        registry.registerCustomEditor(Date.class, new CustomDateEditor(
                dateFormat, true));
    }
}
```

With the form action ready, you can define the first view state for handling the book criteria form. In order to test your flow as soon as possible, you can directly display the search results in the list page, without considering the size of the results. You define the book search flow in the definition file /WEB-INF/flows/bookSearch/bookSearch.xml.

```
<flow xmlns="http://www.springframework.org/schema/webflow"
    xmlns:xsi="http://www.w3.org/2001/XMLSchema-instance"
    xsi:schemaLocation="http://www.springframework.org/schema/webflow
        http://www.springframework.org/schema/webflow/spring-webflow-2.0.xsd">

    <view-state id="bookCriteria">
        <on-render>
            <evaluate expression="bookCriteriaAction.setupForm" />
        </on-render>
        <transition on="search" to="bookList">
            <evaluate expression="bookCriteriaAction.bindAndValidate" />
            <evaluate expression="bookService.search(bookCriteria)"
                result="flowScope.books" />
        </transition>
    </view-state>
</flow>
```

Before this view state renders its view, it invokes the `setupForm()` method of the form action `bookCriteriaAction` defined previously. This method prepares the form object for this form by instantiating the form object class you specified. After a user submits the form with the event ID `search`, this state will transition to the `bookList` state, displaying all the search results.

Before the transition takes place, you have to invoke the `bindAndValidate()` method of the form action to bind the form field values to the form object's properties, and then validate this object with the validators, if registered. Then you call the back-end service to search books for the bound criteria object and store the results in the flow scope variable `books` so that it can be accessed by other states. Flow scope variables are stored in the session, so they must implement `Serializable`.

Then you create the view for this view state in the JSP file with the same name as the view state and in the same location (i.e., `/WEB-INF/flows/bookSearch/bookCriteria.jsp`) so that it can be loaded by default.

```
<%@ taglib prefix="form" uri="http://www.springframework.org/tags/form" %>

<html>
<head>
<title>Book Criteria</title>
</head>

<body>
<form:form commandName="bookCriteria">
<table>
  <tr>
    <td>Keyword</td>
    <td><form:input path="keyword" /></td>
  </tr>
  <tr>
    <td>Author</td>
```

```
    <td><form:input path="author" /></td>
  </tr>
  <tr>
    <td colspan="2">
      <input type="submit" name="_eventId_search" value="Search" />
    </td>
  </tr>
</table>
</form:form>
</body>
</html>
```

This JSP file contains a form defined with Spring's form tags. It's bound to the form object with the name bookCriteria, which is generated automatically according to the form object's class name, BookCriteria. There's a submit button in this form, clicking which will trigger an event with search as the ID.

The second view state in this book search flow is for displaying the search results. It will render a view listing all results in a table, with links for showing book details. When the user clicks one of these links, it will trigger a select event that will cause a transition to the bookDetails state showing the book's details.

```
<view-state id="bookList">
    <transition on="select" to="bookDetails">
        <evaluate expression="bookService.findByIsbn(requestParameters.isbn)"
            result="flowScope.book" />
    </transition>
</view-state>
```

The link should pass the book ISBN as a request parameter, so you can find the book from the back-end service and store it in the flow scope variable book.

The view for this state should be created in /WEB-INF/flows/bookSearch/bookList.jsp so that it will be loaded by default.

```
<%@ taglib prefix="c" uri="http://java.sun.com/jsp/jstl/core" %>
<%@ taglib prefix="fmt" uri="http://java.sun.com/jsp/jstl/fmt" %>

<html>
<head>
<title>Book List</title>
</head>

<body>
<table border="1">
  <tr>
    <th>ISBN</th>
    <th>Book Name</th>
    <th>Author</th>
    <th>Publish Date</th>
  </tr>
```

```
  <c:forEach items="${books}" var="book">
  <tr>
    <td>
      <a href="${flowExecutionUrl}&_eventId=select&isbn=${book.isbn}">
        ${book.isbn}
      </a>
    </td>
    <td>${book.name}</td>
    <td>${book.author}</td>
    <td><fmt:formatDate value="${book.publishDate}" pattern="yyyy-MM-dd" /></td>
  </tr>
  </c:forEach>
</table>
</body>
</html>
```

The ISBN column of each table row is a link that will trigger a `select` event with the book ISBN as a request parameter.

The last view state in this book search flow shows a selected book's details. It has no transition to other states at this moment.

```
<view-state id="bookDetails" />
```

You create the view for this state in `/WEB-INF/flows/bookSearch/bookDetails.jsp` so that it will be loaded by default.

```
<%@ taglib prefix="c" uri="http://java.sun.com/jsp/jstl/core" %>
<%@ taglib prefix="fmt" uri="http://java.sun.com/jsp/jstl/fmt" %>

<html>
<head>
<title>Book Details</title>
</head>

<body>
<table border="1">
  <tr>
    <td>ISBN</td>
    <td>${book.isbn}</td>
  </tr>
  <tr>
    <td>Book Name</td>
    <td>${book.name}</td>
  </tr>
  <tr>
    <td>Author</td>
    <td>${book.author}</td>
  </tr>
  <tr>
```

```
    <td>Publish Date</td>
    <td><fmt:formatDate value="${book.publishDate}" pattern="yyyy-MM-dd" /></td>
  </tr>
</table>
</body>
</html>
```

Now you can deploy this application and test this simplified book search flow with the URL `http://localhost:8080/library/flow/bookSearch`. The current flow diagram for this book search flow is illustrated in Figure 15-4.

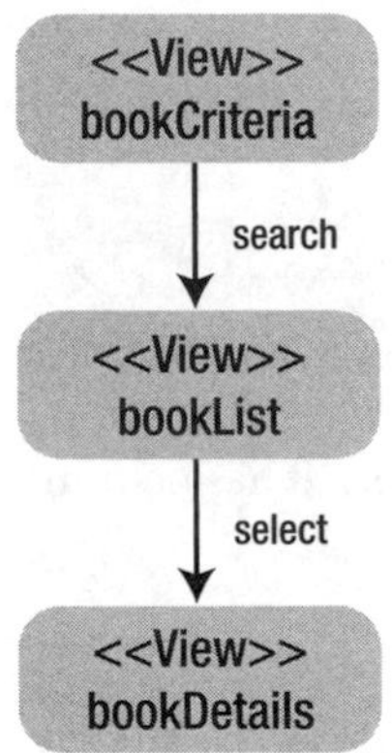

Figure 15-4. *The flow diagram for the book search flow with view states only*

Defining Action States

Although you can include the search action in the `bookCriteria` view state, this action cannot be reused for other states that require book searching. The best practice is to extract reusable actions into stand-alone action states. An action state simply defines one or more actions to perform in a flow, and these actions will be performed in the declared order. If an action returns an `Event` object containing an ID that matches a transition, the transition will take place immediately without performing the subsequent actions. But if all of the actions have been performed without a matching transition, the `success` transition will take place.

For the purposes of reuse, you can extract the book search action in a `searchBook` state. Then modify the transition of the `bookCriteria` state to go through this state.

```
<flow ...>
    <view-state id="bookCriteria">
        <on-render>
            <evaluate expression="bookCriteriaAction.setupForm" />
        </on-render>
        <transition on="search" to="searchBook">
            <evaluate expression="bookCriteriaAction.bindAndValidate" />
        </transition>
    </view-state>
```

```
    <action-state id="searchBook">
        <evaluate expression="bookService.search(bookCriteria)"
            result="flowScope.books" />
        <transition on="success" to="bookList" />
    </action-state>
    ...
</flow>
```

The current flow diagram for this book search flow is illustrated in Figure 15-5.

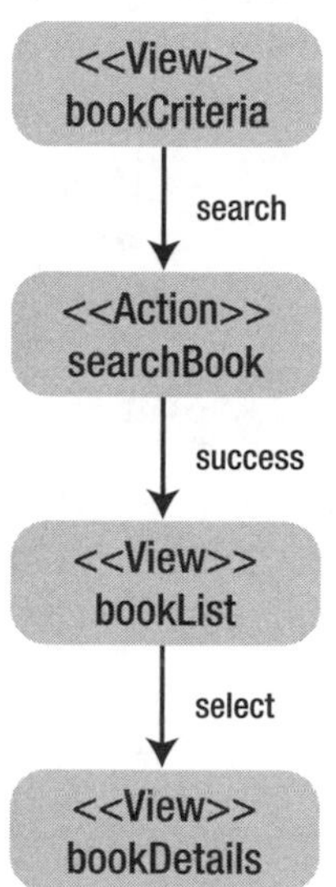

Figure 15-5. *The flow diagram for the book search flow with an action state*

Defining Decision States

Now you are going to satisfy the book search flow's requirement: if there's more than one search result, display them in the list page; otherwise, show its details directly in the details page without going through the list page. For this purpose, you need a decision state that can evaluate a Boolean expression to determine the transition:

```
<flow ...>
    ...
    <action-state id="searchBook">
        <evaluate expression="bookService.search(bookCriteria)"
            result="flowScope.books" />
        <transition on="success" to="checkResultSize" />
    </action-state>

    <decision-state id="checkResultSize">
        <if test="books.size() == 1" then="extractResult" else="bookList" />
    </decision-state>
```

```
    <action-state id="extractResult">
        <set name="flowScope.book" value="books.get(0)" />
        <transition on="success" to="bookDetails" />
    </action-state>
    ...
</flow>
```

The success transition of the searchBook state has been changed to checkResultSize, a decision state that checks if there's exactly one search result. If true, it will transition to the extractResult action state to extract the first and only result into the flow scope variable book. Otherwise, it will transition to the bookList state to display all search results in the list page. The current flow diagram is illustrated in Figure 15-6.

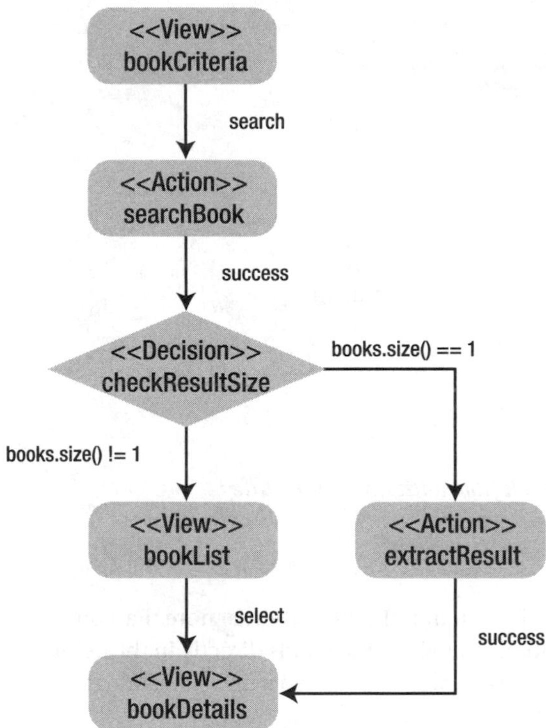

Figure 15-6. *The flow diagram for the book search flow with a decision state*

Defining End States

The basic requirement of the book search flow has been finished. However, you might be asked to provide a New Search link in both the book list page and the book details page for starting a new search. You can simply add the following link to both pages:

```
<a href="${flowExecutionUrl}&_eventId=newSearch">New Search</a>
```

As you can see, this link will trigger a newSearch event. Instead of transitioning to the first view state, bookCriteria, it's better to define an end state that restarts this flow. An end state will invalidate all flow scope variables to release their resources.

```
<flow ...>
    ...
    <view-state id="bookList">
        <transition on="select" to="bookDetails">
            <evaluate expression="bookService.findByIsbn(requestParameters.isbn)"
                result="flowScope.book" />
        </transition>
        <transition on="newSearch" to="newSearch" />
    </view-state>

    <view-state id="bookDetails">
        <transition on="newSearch" to="newSearch" />
    </view-state>

    <end-state id="newSearch" />
</flow>
```

By default, an end state restarts the current flow to the start state, but you can redirect to another flow by specifying the flow name with flowRedirect as the prefix in the end state's view attribute. The current flow diagram is illustrated in Figure 15-7.

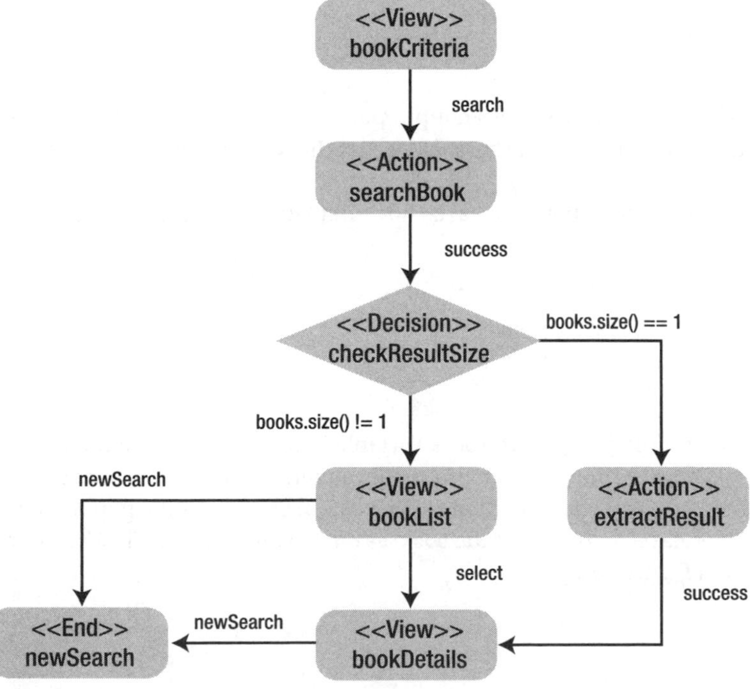

Figure 15-7. *The flow diagram for the book search flow with an end state*

Defining Subflow States

Suppose you have another web flow that also requires showing a book's details. For reuse purposes, you extract the bookDetails state into a new web flow that can be called by other flows as a subflow. First of all, you have to add the flow definition's location to the flow registry in library-webflow.xml and create the flow definition XML file as well:

```
<webflow:flow-registry id="flowRegistry">
    ...
    <webflow:flow-location path="/WEB-INF/flows/bookDetails/bookDetails.xml" />
</webflow:flow-registry>
```

Then you move the bookDetails view state to this flow and bookDetails.jsp to this directory. As the bookDetails state has a transition to the newSearch state, you also define it in this flow as an end state.

```
<flow xmlns="http://www.springframework.org/schema/webflow"
    xmlns:xsi="http://www.w3.org/2001/XMLSchema-instance"
    xsi:schemaLocation="http://www.springframework.org/schema/webflow
        http://www.springframework.org/schema/webflow/spring-webflow-2.0.xsd">

    <input name="book" value="flowScope.book" />

    <view-state id="bookDetails">
        <transition on="newSearch" to="newSearch" />
    </view-state>

    <end-state id="newSearch" />
</flow>
```

The book instance to be shown is passed as an input parameter to this flow with the name book, and it is stored in the flow scope variable book. Note that the flow scope is only visible to the current flow.

Then you define a subflow state in the bookSearch flow that launches the bookDetails flow to show a book's details:

```
<subflow-state id="bookDetails" subflow="bookDetails">
    <input name="book" value="flowScope.book" />
    <transition on="newSearch" to="newSearch" />
</subflow-state>
```

In this subflow state definition, you pass the book variable in the flow scope of the bookSearch flow to the bookDetails subflow as an input parameter. When the bookDetails subflow ends in its newSearch state, it will transition to the newSearch state of the parent flow, which happens to be the newSearch end state of the bookSearch flow in this case. The current flow diagram is illustrated in Figure 15-8.

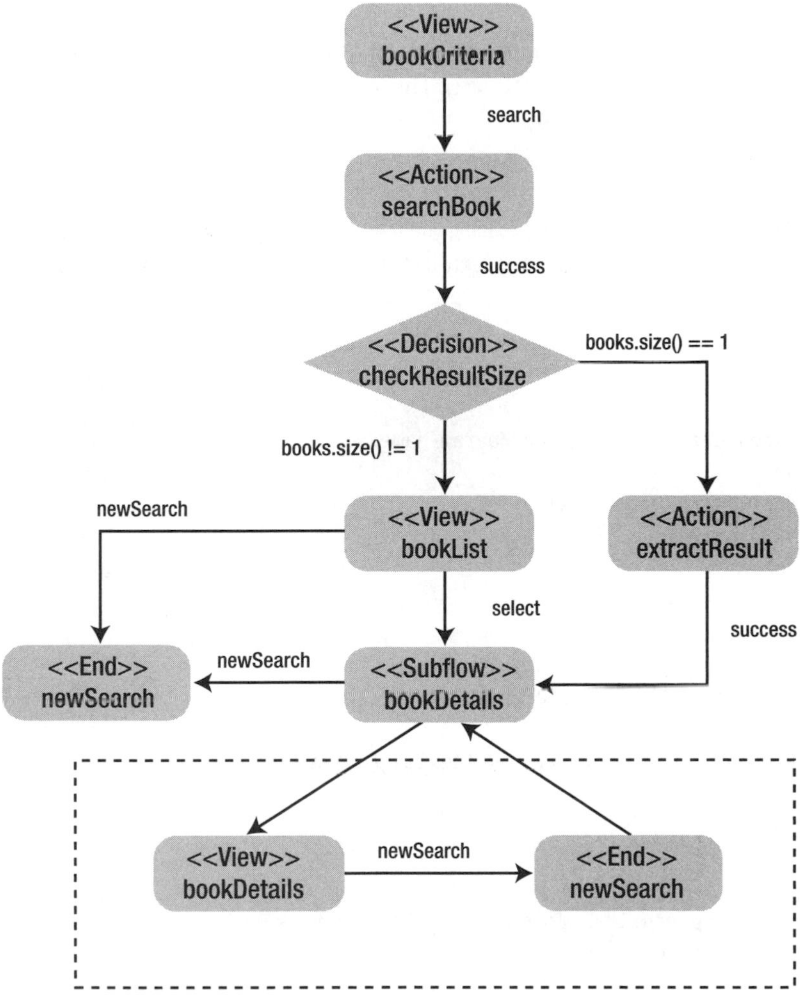

Figure 15-8. *The flow diagram for the book search flow with a subflow*

15-3. Securing Web Flows

Problem

You would like to secure certain web flows in your application by allowing only authorized users access.

Solution

Spring Web Flow offers integration for Spring Security so that you can easily secure your web flows with Spring Security. With Spring Security configured properly, you can simply secure a flow, a state, or a transition by embedding the `<secured>` element with required access attributes specified.

How It Works

To secure web flows with Spring Security, you first have to configure a `DelegatingFilterProxy` filter in the web deployment descriptor (i.e., `web.xml`). This filter will delegate HTTP request filtering to a filter defined in Spring Security.

Note To use Spring Security in your web flow application, you have to copy `spring-security-core-2.0.1.jar` (located in the `dist` directory of the Spring Security installation) to the `WEB-INF/lib` directory.

```
<web-app ...>
    <context-param>
        <param-name>contextConfigLocation</param-name>
        <param-value>
            /WEB-INF/library-service.xml
            /WEB-INF/library-security.xml
        </param-value>
    </context-param>
    ...
    <filter>
        <filter-name>springSecurityFilterChain</filter-name>
        <filter-class>
            org.springframework.web.filter.DelegatingFilterProxy
        </filter-class>
    </filter>

    <filter-mapping>
        <filter-name>springSecurityFilterChain</filter-name>
        <url-pattern>/*</url-pattern>
    </filter-mapping>
    ...
</web-app>
```

As security configurations should be applied to the entire application, you centralize them in `/WEB-INF/library-security.xml` and load this file into the root application context. Then you create this file with the following contents:

```
<beans:beans xmlns="http://www.springframework.org/schema/security"
    xmlns:beans="http://www.springframework.org/schema/beans"
    xmlns:xsi="http://www.w3.org/2001/XMLSchema-instance"
    xsi:schemaLocation="http://www.springframework.org/schema/beans
        http://www.springframework.org/schema/beans/spring-beans-2.5.xsd
        http://www.springframework.org/schema/security
        http://www.springframework.org/schema/security/spring-security-2.0.xsd">

    <http auto-config="true" />
```

```
    <authentication-provider>
        <user-service>
            <user name="user1" password="1111" authorities="ROLE_USER" />
            <user name="user2" password="2222" authorities="ROLE_USER" />
        </user-service>
    </authentication-provider>
</beans:beans>
```

In the preceding security configurations, you enable Spring Security's HTTP auto-config, which provides a default form-based login service, an anonymous login service, and so on. You also define two user accounts for testing purposes.

In the web flow configuration file (i.e., `library-webflow.xml`), you have to register the flow execution listener `SecurityFlowExecutionListener` in the flow executor to enable Spring Security for web flows:

```
<beans ...>
    ...
    <webflow:flow-executor id="flowExecutor">
        <webflow:flow-execution-listeners>
            <webflow:listener ref="securityFlowExecutionListener" />
        </webflow:flow-execution-listeners>
    </webflow:flow-executor>

    <bean id="securityFlowExecutionListener" class="org.springframework.➥
        webflow.security.SecurityFlowExecutionListener" />
</beans>
```

Now Spring Security has been configured for your web flow application. You can simply secure a web flow by embedding a `<secured>` element in a flow definition. For example, let's secure the `bookSearch` flow defined in `/WEB-INF/flows/bookSearch/bookSearch.xml`.

```
<flow xmlns="http://www.springframework.org/schema/webflow"
    xmlns:xsi="http://www.w3.org/2001/XMLSchema-instance"
    xsi:schemaLocation="http://www.springframework.org/schema/webflow
        http://www.springframework.org/schema/webflow/spring-webflow-2.0.xsd">

    <secured attributes="ROLE_USER" />
    ...
</flow>
```

You can specify multiple access attributes required for accessing this web flow in the `attributes` attribute, separated by commas. By default, a user who has any of the attributes can access this web flow, but you can allow access only to users with all the attributes by setting the `match` attribute of `<secured>` to `all`.

Now if you deploy this application and test the book search flow, you will have to log into the application before you can access this flow. Similarly, you can finely secure a particular state or transaction by embedding a `<secured>` element.

15-4. Persisting Objects in Web Flows

Problem

In many cases, you may have to create and update persistent objects in different states of a web flow. According to the nature of a web flow, the changes made to these persistent objects should not be flushed to the database until the final state of this web flow, which either commits all these changes in a transaction or ignores them if the flow fails or is cancelled. You can maintain a persistence context across different web flow states, but it's hardly an efficient way.

Solution

Spring Web Flow is able to manage a persistence context across different states of a web flow without your involvement. You can simply access the managed persistence context with a flow scope variable exposed by Spring Web Flow. Spring Web Flow 2.0 comes with support for JPA and Hibernate.

To have Spring Web Flow manage the persistence contexts for your web flows, you have to register a flow execution listener (e.g., `JpaFlowExecutionListener` for JPA and `HibernateFlowExecutionListener` for Hibernate) in the flow executor. When a new flow starts, this listener creates a new persistence context (e.g., a JPA entity manager or a Hibernate session) and binds it to the flow scope. Then you can persist your objects with this persistence context in different web flow states. Finally, you can define an end state that either commits the changes or ignores them.

How It Works

Suppose you are going to build a web flow for readers to borrow books from the library. You would like to store the borrowing records in a database managed by a database engine such as Apache Derby. You consider using JPA to persist the records, with Hibernate as the underlying PA engine. First of all, you define the `BorrowingRecord` entity class with JPA annotations.

■Note To use Hibernate as the JPA engine, you have to copy `persistence.jar` (located in the `lib/j2ee` directory of the Spring installation), `hibernate3.jar`, `hibernate-annotations.jar`, `hibernate-commons-annotations.jar`, `hibernate-entitymanager.jar` (located in `lib/hibernate`), `antlr-2.7.6.jar` (located in `lib/antlr`), `asm-2.2.3.jar` (located in `lib/asm`), `cglib-nodep-2.1_3.jar` (located in `lib/cglib`), `dom4j-1.6.1.jar` (located in `lib/dom4j`), `ehcache-1.2.4.jar` (located in `lib/ehcache`), `jta.jar` (located in `lib/j2ee`), `commons-collections.jar`, `commons-logging.jar` (located in `lib/jakarta-commons`), and `log4j-1.2.14.jar` (located in `lib/log4j`) to the `WEB-INF/lib` directory. As Hibernate EntityManager depends on Javassist, you have to include `javassist.jar` in your classpath. To use Apache Derby as the database engine, you also have to copy `derbyclient.jar` (located in the `lib` directory of the Derby installation).

```
package com.apress.springrecipes.library.domain;
...
import javax.persistence.Entity;
import javax.persistence.GeneratedValue;
import javax.persistence.GenerationType;
import javax.persistence.Id;

@Entity
public class BorrowingRecord implements Serializable {

    @Id
    @GeneratedValue(strategy = GenerationType.IDENTITY)
    private Long id;

    private String isbn;
    private Date borrowDate;
    private Date returnDate;
    private String reader;

    // Getters and Setters
    ...
}
```

Next, you create the JPA configuration file `persistence.xml` in the `META-INF` directory of the classpath root:

```
<persistence xmlns="http://java.sun.com/xml/ns/persistence"
    xmlns:xsi="http://www.w3.org/2001/XMLSchema-instance"
    xsi:schemaLocation="http://java.sun.com/xml/ns/persistence
        http://java.sun.com/xml/ns/persistence/persistence_1_0.xsd"
    version="1.0">

    <persistence-unit name="library" />
</persistence>
```

In this configuration file, you only define the persistence unit `library`. The JPA provider information will be configured in Spring's application context.

Configuring JPA in Spring's Application Context

In the service layer configuration file (i.e., `library-service.xml`), you can configure a JPA entity manager factory by providing a data source and a JPA vendor adaptor, where you can configure JPA vendor–specific information. In addition, you have to configure a JPA transaction manager for managing JPA transactions. For details about configuring JPA in Spring, please refer to Chapter 9.

```
<beans ...>
    ...
    <bean id="dataSource"
```

```
        class="org.springframework.jdbc.datasource.DriverManagerDataSource">
        <property name="driverClassName"
            value="org.apache.derby.jdbc.ClientDriver" />
        <property name="url"
            value="jdbc:derby://localhost:1527/library;create=true" />
        <property name="username" value="app" />
        <property name="password" value="app" />
    </bean>

    <bean id="entityManagerFactory" class="org.springframework.orm.jpa.➥
        LocalContainerEntityManagerFactoryBean">
        <property name="dataSource" ref="dataSource" />
        <property name="jpaVendorAdapter">
            <bean class="org.springframework.orm.jpa.vendor.➥
                HibernateJpaVendorAdapter">
                <property name="databasePlatform"
                    value="org.hibernate.dialect.DerbyDialect" />
                <property name="showSql" value="true" />
                <property name="generateDdl" value="true" />
            </bean>
        </property>
    </bean>

    <bean id="transactionManager"
        class="org.springframework.orm.jpa.JpaTransactionManager">
        <property name="entityManagerFactory" ref="entityManagerFactory" />
    </bean>
</beans>
```

Setting Up JPA for Spring Web Flow

To have Spring Web Flow manage the persistence contexts for your web flows, you have to register a flow execution listener in the flow executor. As you are using JPA, you have to register `JpaFlowExecutionListener`.

```
<beans ...>
    ...
    <webflow:flow-executor id="flowExecutor">
        <webflow:flow-execution-listeners>
            ...
            <webflow:listener ref="jpaFlowExecutionListener" />
        </webflow:flow-execution-listeners>
    </webflow:flow-executor>

    <bean id="jpaFlowExecutionListener"
        class="org.springframework.webflow.persistence.JpaFlowExecutionListener">
        <constructor-arg ref="entityManagerFactory" />
```

```
        <constructor-arg ref="transactionManager" />
    </bean>
</beans>
```

`JpaFlowExecutionListener` requires a JPA entity manager factory and a transaction manager as its constructor arguments, which you have configured in the service layer. You can filter the names of the flows to listen for in the `criteria` attribute, with commas as separators or an asterisk for all flows, which is the default value.

Using JPA in Web Flows

Now let's define the flow for borrowing books from the library. First, you register a new flow definition in the flow registry:

```
<webflow:flow-registry id="flowRegistry">
    ...
    <webflow:flow-location path="/WEB-INF/flows/borrowBook/borrowBook.xml" />
</webflow:flow-registry>
```

This flow's first state will show a form for library users to input the borrowing details, which will be bound to a form object of type `BorrowingRecord`. You can define a form action in `library-webflow.xml` to handle this borrowing form.

```
<bean id="borrowBookAction"
    class="org.springframework.webflow.action.FormAction">
    <property name="formObjectClass"
        value="com.apress.springrecipes.library.domain.BorrowingRecord" />
    <property name="propertyEditorRegistrar">
        <bean class="com.apress.springrecipes.library.web.PropertyEditors" />
    </property>
</bean>
```

In the flow definition file `/WEB-INF/flows/borrowBook/borrowBook.xml`, you have to define a `<persistence-context>` element to ask Spring Web Flow to manage a persistence context for each flow instance:

```
<flow xmlns="http://www.springframework.org/schema/webflow"
    xmlns:xsi="http://www.w3.org/2001/XMLSchema-instance"
    xsi:schemaLocation="http://www.springframework.org/schema/webflow
        http://www.springframework.org/schema/webflow/spring-webflow-2.0.xsd">

    <persistence-context />

    <view-state id="borrowForm">
        <on-render>
            <evaluate expression="borrowBookAction.setupForm" />
        </on-render>
        <transition on="proceed" to="borrowReview">
            <evaluate expression="borrowBookAction.bindAndValidate" />
        </transition>
```

```
        <transition on="cancel" to="cancel" />
    </view-state>

    <view-state id="borrowReview">
        <on-render>
            <evaluate expression="borrowBookAction.setupForm" />
        </on-render>
        <transition on="confirm" to="confirm">
            <evaluate expression="persistenceContext.persist(borrowingRecord)" />
        </transition>
        <transition on="revise" to="borrowForm" />
        <transition on="cancel" to="cancel" />
    </view-state>

    <end-state id="confirm" commit="true" />

    <end-state id="cancel" />
</flow>
```

This flow includes two view states and two end states. The borrowForm state shows a form for a user to input the borrowing details, which will be bound to a flow scope object with the name borrowingRecord, derived from the form object's class name BorrowingRecord. If the user proceeds with the borrowing form, this state will transition to the borrowReview state, which shows the borrowing details for confirmation. If the user confirms the borrowing details, the form object in the flow scope will be persisted with the managed persistence context, and this state will transition to the end state confirm. As this state has its commit attribute set to true, it will commit the changes to the database. However, in either view state, the user can choose to cancel the borrowing form that will cause a transition to the end state cancel, which ignores the changes. The flow diagram for this book-borrowing flow is illustrated in Figure 15-9.

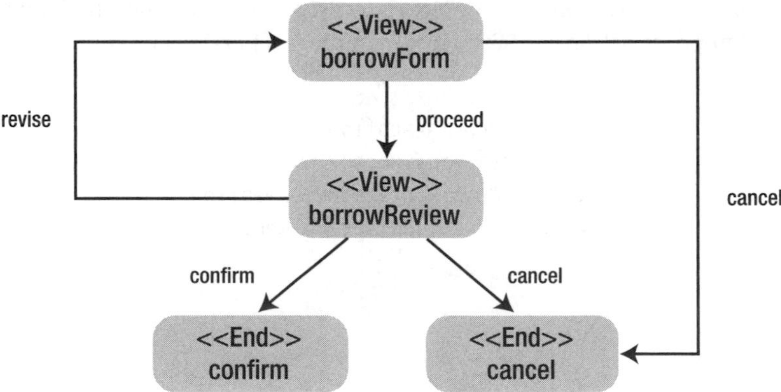

Figure 15-9. *The flow diagram for the book-borrowing flow*

The final step is to create the views for the two view states. For the borrowForm state, you create borrowForm.jsp in /WEB-INF/flows/borrowBook/ so that it will be loaded by default:

```
<%@ taglib prefix="form" uri="http://www.springframework.org/tags/form" %>

<html>
<head>
<title>Borrow Form</title>
</head>

<body>
<form:form commandName="borrowingRecord">
<table>
  <tr>
    <td>ISBN</td>
    <td><form:input path="isbn" /></td>
  </tr>
  <tr>
    <td>Borrow Date</td>
    <td><form:input path="borrowDate" /></td>
  </tr>
  <tr>
    <td>Return Date</td>
    <td><form:input path="returnDate" /></td>
  </tr>
  <tr>
    <td>Reader</td>
    <td><form:input path="reader" /></td>
  </tr>
  <tr>
    <td colspan="2">
      <input type="submit" name="_eventId_proceed" value="Proceed" />
      <input type="submit" name="_eventId_cancel" value="Cancel" />
    </td>
  </tr>
</table>
</form:form>
</body>
</html>
```

For the borrowReview state, you create borrowReview.jsp in the same location for confirming the borrowing details:

```
<%@ taglib prefix="fmt" uri="http://java.sun.com/jsp/jstl/fmt" %>

<html>
<head>
<title>Borrow Review</title>
</head>
```

```
<body>
<form method="POST">
<table>
  <tr>
    <td>ISBN</td>
    <td>${borrowingRecord.isbn}</td>
  </tr>
  <tr>
    <td>Borrow Date</td>
    <td>
      <fmt:formatDate value="${borrowingRecord.borrowDate}" pattern="yyyy-MM-dd" />
    </td>
  </tr>
  <tr>
    <td>Return Date</td>
    <td>
      <fmt:formatDate value="${borrowingRecord.returnDate}" pattern="yyyy-MM-dd" />
    </td>
  </tr>
  <tr>
    <td>Reader</td>
    <td>${borrowingRecord.reader}</td>
  </tr>
  <tr>
    <td colspan="2">
      <input type="submit" name="_eventId_confirm" value="Confirm" />
      <input type="submit" name="_eventId_revise" value="Revise" />
      <input type="submit" name="_eventId_cancel" value="Cancel" />
    </td>
  </tr>
</table>
</form>
</body>
</html>
```

Now you can deploy the application and test this book-borrowing flow with the URL `http://localhost:8080/library/flow/borrowBook`.

15-5. Integrating Spring Web Flow with JSF

Problem

By default, Spring Web Flow relies on Spring MVC's view technologies (e.g., JSP and Tiles) to render its views. However, you might wish to use JSF's rich set of UI components in your web flow's views or manage the UI flows of your existing JSF applications with Spring Web Flow. In either case, you have to integrate Spring Web Flow with JSF.

Solution

Spring Web Flow provides two submodules, Spring Faces and Spring JavaScript, to simplify using JSF and JavaScript in Spring. Spring Faces integrates Spring with JSF 1.2 or higher by allowing you to use JSF's UI components with Spring MVC and Spring Web Flow. Spring Faces supports rendering JSF views in Spring Web Flow and offers a number of JSF integration features for Spring Web Flow.

Spring JavaScript is a JavaScript abstraction framework that integrates the Dojo JavaScript toolkit (`http://dojotoolkit.org/`) as the underlying UI toolkit. Spring Faces provides a set of client-side validation components for standard JSF input components, building on top of Spring JavaScript. These components are provided as Facelets tags, so you have to use Facelets as your JSF view technology in order to use them.

How It Works

Rendering JSF Views for Spring Web Flow

Now let's consider reimplementing the book-borrowing flow's views with JSF. In order to use the JSF validation components provided by Spring Faces, you have to use Facelets to create your JSF views. First, configure JSF's `FacesServlet` in `web.xml`.

■ **Note** To integrate JSF and Facelets with Spring Web Flow, you have to copy `spring-faces-2.0.0.jar` (located in the `dist` directory of the Spring Web Flow installation) to the `WEB-INF/lib` directory. If you choose Sun's JSF Reference Implementation (JSF-RI) as your JSF implementation library, you have to copy `jsf-api.jar` and `jsf-impl.jar` (located in the `lib` directory of the JSF-RI installation). To use Facelets, you have to download its distribution (e.g., `facelets-1.1.14.zip`) from `https://facelets.dev.java.net/`, and then copy `jsf-facelets.jar` (located in the root of the Facelets installation). Finally, Facelets uses Unified EL as its expression language, so you should also use this language in flow definitions for consistency. If you are using OGNL as your expression language, you can remove the OGNL library from `WEB-INF/lib` and copy the JBoss EL library to this directory.

```
<web-app ...>
    ...
    <servlet>
        <servlet-name>faces</servlet-name>
        <servlet-class>javax.faces.webapp.FacesServlet</servlet-class>
    </servlet>
</web-app>
```

Note that this servlet is only registered for initializing a web application that uses JSF. It won't be used to handle web flow requests, so you needn't specify a `<servlet-mapping>` definition for it. However, if you are going to use the legacy JSF request handling at the same time, you will have to specify that.

In the JSF configuration file (i.e., faces-config.xml in the root of WEB-INF), you have to configure FaceletViewHandler as the JSF view handler to enable Facelets:

```
<faces-config xmlns="http://java.sun.com/xml/ns/javaee"
    xmlns:xsi="http://www.w3.org/2001/XMLSchema-instance"
    xsi:schemaLocation="http://java.sun.com/xml/ns/javaee
        http://java.sun.com/xml/ns/javaee/web-facesconfig_1_2.xsd"
    version="1.2">

    <application>
        <view-handler>com.sun.facelets.FaceletViewHandler</view-handler>
    </application>
</faces-config>
```

In library-webflow.xml, you have to specify the JSF flow builder services for your flow registry, instead of the default Spring MVC flow builder services in use. This way, the JSF flow builder services can render JSF views for web flows.

```
<beans xmlns="http://www.springframework.org/schema/beans"
    xmlns:xsi="http://www.w3.org/2001/XMLSchema-instance"
    xmlns:webflow="http://www.springframework.org/schema/webflow-config"
    xmlns:faces="http://www.springframework.org/schema/faces"
    xsi:schemaLocation="http://www.springframework.org/schema/beans
        http://www.springframework.org/schema/beans/spring-beans-2.5.xsd
        http://www.springframework.org/schema/webflow-config
        http://www.springframework.org/schema/webflow-config/➥
            spring-webflow-config-2.0.xsd
        http://www.springframework.org/schema/faces
        http://www.springframework.org/schema/faces/spring-faces-2.0.xsd">
    ...
    <webflow:flow-registry id="flowRegistry"
        flow-builder-services="facesFlowBuilderServices">
        ...
    </webflow:flow-registry>

    <faces:flow-builder-services id="facesFlowBuilderServices" />
</beans>
```

The JSF flow builder services internally use a JSF view factory, which will by default load a Facelets page using a view state's name and .xhtml as the file extension. Before you create the Facelets pages for the borrowForm and borrowReview states, you can define a page template to unify your web application's layout (e.g., in /WEB-INF/template.xhtml):

```
<!DOCTYPE html PUBLIC "-//W3C//DTD XHTML 1.0 Transitional//EN"
    "http://www.w3.org/TR/xhtml1/DTD/xhtml1-transitional.dtd">

<html xmlns="http://www.w3.org/1999/xhtml"
      xmlns:ui="http://java.sun.com/jsf/facelets">
<head>
```

```
<title><ui:insert name="title">Library</ui:insert></title>
</head>

<body>
<ui:insert name="content" />
</body>
</html>
```

The preceding template defines two areas, with the names `title` and `content`. The pages that use this template will insert their own contents into these two areas.

Now let's create `/WEB-INF/flows/borrowBook/borrowForm.xhtml` for the `borrowForm` state so that it will be loaded by default:

```
<!DOCTYPE html PUBLIC "-//W3C//DTD XHTML 1.0 Transitional//EN"
    "http://www.w3.org/TR/xhtml1/DTD/xhtml1-transitional.dtd">

<ui:composition xmlns="http://www.w3.org/1999/xhtml"
                xmlns:f="http://java.sun.com/jsf/core"
                xmlns:h="http://java.sun.com/jsf/html"
                xmlns:ui="http://java.sun.com/jsf/facelets"
                template="/WEB-INF/template.xhtml">

  <ui:define name="title">Borrow Form</ui:define>

  <ui:define name="content">
    <h:form>
      <h:panelGrid columns="2">
        <h:outputLabel for="isbn">ISBN</h:outputLabel>
        <h:inputText id="isbn" value="#{borrowingRecord.isbn}" />

        <h:outputLabel for="borrowDate">Borrow Date</h:outputLabel>
        <h:inputText id="borrowDate" value="#{borrowingRecord.borrowDate}">
          <f:convertDateTime pattern="yyyy-MM-dd" />
        </h:inputText>

        <h:outputLabel for="returnDate">Return Date</h:outputLabel>
        <h:inputText id="returnDate" value="#{borrowingRecord.returnDate}">
          <f:convertDateTime pattern="yyyy-MM-dd" />
        </h:inputText>

        <h:outputLabel for="reader">Reader</h:outputLabel>
        <h:inputText id="reader" value="#{borrowingRecord.reader}" />
      </h:panelGrid>

      <h:commandButton value="Proceed" action="proceed" />
      <h:commandButton value="Cancel" action="cancel" />
    </h:form>
  </ui:define>
</ui:composition>
```

In this page, you use standard JSF components like form, outputLabel, inputText, and commandButton to create a form that binds the field values to a form object. The action triggered by a command button will be mapped to a Spring Web Flow event ID that will cause a transition.

Next, create /WEB-INF/flows/borrowBook/borrowReview.xhtml for the borrowReview state:

```
<!DOCTYPE html PUBLIC "-//W3C//DTD XHTML 1.0 Transitional//EN"
    "http://www.w3.org/TR/xhtml1/DTD/xhtml1-transitional.dtd">

<ui:composition xmlns="http://www.w3.org/1999/xhtml"
                xmlns:f="http://java.sun.com/jsf/core"
                xmlns:h="http://java.sun.com/jsf/html"
                xmlns:ui="http://java.sun.com/jsf/facelets"
                template="/WEB-INF/template.xhtml">

  <ui:define name="title">Borrow Review</ui:define>

  <ui:define name="content">
    <h:form>
      <h:panelGrid columns="2">
        <h:outputLabel for="isbn">ISBN</h:outputLabel>
        <h:outputText id="isbn" value="#{borrowingRecord.isbn}" />

        <h:outputLabel for="borrowDate">Borrow Date</h:outputLabel>
        <h:outputText id="borrowDate" value="#{borrowingRecord.borrowDate}">
          <f:convertDateTime pattern="yyyy-MM-dd" />
        </h:outputText>

        <h:outputLabel for="returnDate">Return Date</h:outputLabel>
        <h:outputText id="returnDate" value="#{borrowingRecord.returnDate}">
          <f:convertDateTime pattern="yyyy-MM-dd" />
        </h:outputText>

        <h:outputLabel for="reader">Reader</h:outputLabel>
        <h:outputText id="reader" value="#{borrowingRecord.reader}" />
      </h:panelGrid>

      <h:commandButton value="Confirm" action="confirm" />
      <h:commandButton value="Revise" action="revise" />
      <h:commandButton value="Cancel" action="cancel" />
    </h:form>
  </ui:define>
</ui:composition>
```

Using the JSF Components of Spring Faces

Before you can use the Spring Faces components, you have to register ResourceServlet, which is provided by Spring JavaScript for accessing static resources in JAR files, in the web deployment descriptor. These components will retrieve static JavaScript and CSS resources from Spring JavaScript through this servlet.

```
<web-app ...>
    ...
    <servlet>
        <servlet-name>resources</servlet-name>
        <servlet-class>
            org.springframework.js.resource.ResourceServlet
        </servlet-class>
    </servlet>

    <servlet-mapping>
        <servlet-name>resources</servlet-name>
        <url-pattern>/resources/*</url-pattern>
    </servlet-mapping>
</web-app>
```

Spring Faces provides a set of validation components to perform client-side validation for standard JSF input components. These components are provided as Facelets tags defined in the Spring Faces tag library, so you have to include this tag library in the root element beforehand. For example, you can enable client-side validation for the borrow form components in /WEB-INF/flows/borrowBook/borrowForm.xhtml:

```
<ui:composition xmlns="http://www.w3.org/1999/xhtml"
                xmlns:f="http://java.sun.com/jsf/core"
                xmlns:h="http://java.sun.com/jsf/html"
                xmlns:ui="http://java.sun.com/jsf/facelets"
                xmlns:sf="http://www.springframework.org/tags/faces"
                template="/WEB-INF/template.xhtml">

  <ui:define name="title">Borrow Form</ui:define>

  <ui:define name="content">
    <h:form>
      <h:panelGrid columns="2">
        <h:outputLabel for="isbn">ISBN</h:outputLabel>
        <sf:clientTextValidator required="true" regExp="[0-9]{10}">
          <h:inputText id="isbn" value="#{borrowingRecord.isbn}" />
        </sf:clientTextValidator>

        <h:outputLabel for="borrowDate">Borrow Date</h:outputLabel>
        <sf:clientDateValidator required="true">
          <h:inputText id="borrowDate" value="#{borrowingRecord.borrowDate}">
            <f:convertDateTime pattern="yyyy-MM-dd" />
          </h:inputText>
        </sf:clientDateValidator>
```

```
        <h:outputLabel for="returnDate">Return Date</h:outputLabel>
        <sf:clientDateValidator required="true">
          <h:inputText id="returnDate" value="#{borrowingRecord.returnDate}">
            <f:convertDateTime pattern="yyyy-MM-dd" />
          </h:inputText>
        </sf:clientDateValidator>

        <h:outputLabel for="reader">Reader</h:outputLabel>
        <sf:clientTextValidator required="true">
          <h:inputText id="reader" value="#{borrowingRecord.reader}" />
        </sf:clientTextValidator>
      </h:panelGrid>

      <sf:validateAllOnClick>
        <h:commandButton value="Proceed" action="proceed" />
      </sf:validateAllOnClick>

      <h:commandButton value="Cancel" action="cancel" />
    </h:form>
  </ui:define>
</ui:composition>
```

The validation components enable client-side validation for the `inputText` components. You will see that the `clientDateValidator` component additionally provides a pop-up date picker control for its enclosed input field. Finally, when a command button enclosed by a `validateAllInClick` component is clicked, it will trigger all validators in the same page to validate their fields.

Finally, you have to choose a Dojo theme for rendering these components. For example, you can specify using the `tundra` theme in the `<body>` element of the page template:

```
<html xmlns="http://www.w3.org/1999/xhtml"
      xmlns:ui="http://java.sun.com/jsf/facelets">
<head>
<title><ui:insert name="title">Library</ui:insert></title>
</head>

<body class="tundra">
<ui:insert name="content"/>
</body>
</html>
```

15-6. Summary

In this chapter, you have learned how to model and manage your web application's UI flows with Spring Web Flow 2.0. Spring Web Flow offers a flow definition language for modeling web flows. A flow definition consists of one or more states, each of which corresponds to a step in the flow. Once a state has completed its tasks, it triggers an event that contains an event ID. Each state may contain zero or more transitions, each of which maps a returned event ID to the next state. Spring Web Flow has several built-in state types for modeling flows, including view, action, decision, subflow, and end.

Spring Web Flow offers integration for Spring Security so that you can easily secure your web flows with Spring Security. Additionally, Spring Web Flow can manage a persistence context across different states of a web flow. You can access the managed persistence context with a flow scope variable exposed by Spring Web Flow. You can persist your objects with this persistence context in different web flow states, and then define an end state that either commits the changes or ignores them automatically. Spring Web Flow 2.0 comes with support for JPA and Hibernate.

Spring Web Flow provides two submodules, Spring Faces and Spring JavaScript, for integrating Spring with JSF and the Dojo JavaScript toolkit. Spring Faces supports rendering JSF views for Spring Web Flow and provides a set of JSF validation components to perform client-side validation on standard JSF input components. These components are built on top of Spring JavaScript.

In the next chapter, you will learn about Spring's support for various remoting technologies and how to develop web services with both the contract-first and contract-last approaches.

CHAPTER 16

Spring Remoting and Web Services

In this chapter, you will learn about Spring's support for various remoting technologies, such as RMI, Hessian, Burlap, HTTP Invoker, and Web Services. Remoting is a key technology in developing distributed applications, especially multitier enterprise applications. It allows different applications or components, running in different JVMs or on different machines, to communicate with each other using a specific protocol.

Spring's remoting support is consistent across different remoting technologies. On the server side, Spring allows you to expose an arbitrary bean as a remote service through a service exporter. On the client side, Spring provides various proxy factory beans for you to create a local proxy for a remote service so that you can use the remote service as if it were a local bean. Figure 16-1 shows the architecture of Spring's remoting support.

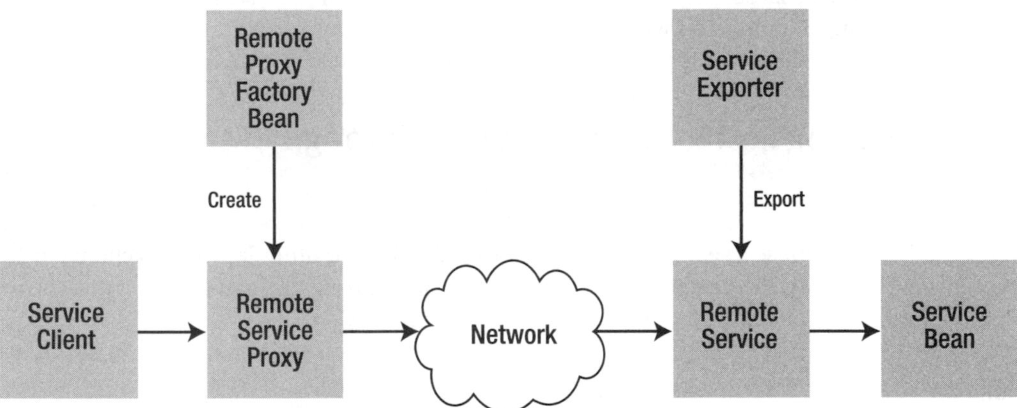

Figure 16-1. *The architecture of Spring's remoting support*

Nowadays, there are two main approaches to developing web services: *contract-first* and *contract-last*. Automatically exposing a bean from the IoC container as a web service means that the service is contract-last because the service contract is generated from an existing bean. The Spring team has created a subproject called Spring Web Services (Spring-WS), which focuses on the development of contract-first web services. In this approach, a service contract is defined first, and code is then written to fulfill this contract. Figure 16-2 shows the architecture of a Spring-WS application.

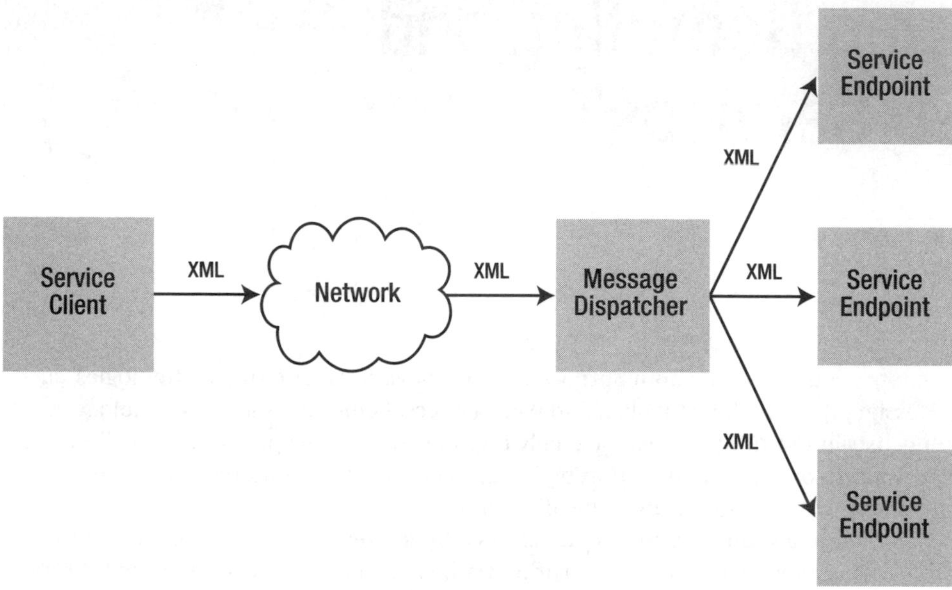

Figure 16-2. *The architecture of a Spring-WS application*

Upon finishing this chapter, you will be able to expose and invoke remote services using different remoting technologies with Spring's remoting support. In addition, you will be able to develop contract-first web services using Spring-WS and different XML technologies.

16-1. Exposing and Invoking Services Through RMI

Problem

You would like to expose a service from your Java application for other Java-based clients to invoke remotely. As both parties are running on the Java platform, you can choose a pure Java-based solution without considering cross-platform portability.

Solution

Remote Method Invocation (RMI) is a Java-based remoting technology that allows two Java applications running in different JVMs to communicate with each other. With RMI, an object can invoke the methods of a remote object. RMI relies on object serialization to marshal and unmarshal method arguments and return values.

Considering the typical RMI usage scenario, to expose a service through RMI, you have to create the service interface that extends `java.rmi.Remote` and whose methods declare throwing `java.rmi.RemoteException`. Then you create the service implementation for this interface. After that, you start an RMI registry and register your service to it. As you can see, there are quite a lot of steps required for exposing a simple service.

To invoke a service through RMI, you first look up the remote service reference in an RMI registry, and then you can call the methods on it. However, to call the methods on a remote service, you must handle `java.rmi.RemoteException` in case of any exception thrown by the remote service.

Fortunately, Spring's remoting facilities can significantly simplify the RMI usage on both the server and client sides. On the server side, you can use `RmiServiceExporter` to export a Spring bean as an RMI service, whose methods can be invoked remotely. It's just several lines of bean configuration without any programming. On the client side, you can simply use `RmiProxyFactoryBean` to create a proxy for the remote service. It allows you to use the remote service as if it were a local bean. Again, it requires no additional programming at all.

How It Works

Suppose you are going to build a weather web service for clients running on different platforms to invoke. This service includes an operation for querying a city's temperatures on multiple dates. First, you create the `TemperatureInfo` class representing the minimum, maximum, and average temperatures of a particular city and date.

```
package com.apress.springrecipes.weather;
...
public class TemperatureInfo implements Serializable {

    private String city;
    private Date date;
    private double min;
    private double max;
    private double average;

    // Constructors, Getters and Setters
    ...
}
```

Next, you define the service interface that includes the `getTemperatures()` operation, which returns a city's temperatures on multiple dates as requested.

```
package com.apress.springrecipes.weather;
...
public interface WeatherService {

    public List<TemperatureInfo> getTemperatures(String city, List<Date> dates);
}
```

You have to provide an implementation for this interface. In a production application, you would likely implement this service interface by querying the database. Here, you may hard-code the temperatures for testing purposes.

```
package com.apress.springrecipes.weather;
...
public class WeatherServiceImpl implements WeatherService {
```

```
    public List<TemperatureInfo> getTemperatures(String city, List<Date> dates) {
        List<TemperatureInfo> temperatures = new ArrayList<TemperatureInfo>();
        for (Date date : dates) {
            temperatures.add(new TemperatureInfo(city, date, 5.0, 10.0, 8.0));
        }
        return temperatures;
    }
}
```

Exposing an RMI Service

Suppose you would like to expose the weather service as an RMI service. To use Spring's remoting facilities for this purpose, create a bean configuration file such as rmi-server.xml in the classpath root to define the service. In this file, you declare a bean for the weather service implementation and export it as an RMI service by using RmiServiceExporter.

```
<beans xmlns="http://www.springframework.org/schema/beans"
    xmlns:xsi="http://www.w3.org/2001/XMLSchema-instance"
    xsi:schemaLocation="http://www.springframework.org/schema/beans
        http://www.springframework.org/schema/beans/spring-beans-2.5.xsd">

    <bean id="weatherService"
        class="com.apress.springrecipes.weather.WeatherServiceImpl" />

    <bean class="org.springframework.remoting.rmi.RmiServiceExporter">
        <property name="serviceName" value="WeatherService" />
        <property name="serviceInterface"
            value="com.apress.springrecipes.weather.WeatherService" />
        <property name="service" ref="weatherService" />
    </bean>
</beans>
```

There are several properties you must configure for an RmiServiceExporter instance, including the service name, the service interface, and the service object to export. You can export any bean configured in the IoC container as an RMI service. RmiServiceExporter will create an RMI proxy to wrap this bean and bind it to the RMI registry. When the proxy receives an invocation request from the RMI registry, it will invoke the corresponding method on the bean.

By default, RmiServiceExporter attempts to look up an RMI registry at localhost port 1099. If it can't find the RMI registry, it will start a new one. However, if you would like to bind your service to another running RMI registry, you can specify the host and port of that registry in the registryHost and registryPort properties. Note that once you specify the registry host, RmiServiceExporter will not start a new registry, even if the specified registry doesn't exist.

To start a server that provides the RMI weather service, run the following class to create an application context for the preceding bean configuration file:

```
package com.apress.springrecipes.weather;

import org.springframework.context.support.ClassPathXmlApplicationContext;

public class RmiServer {

    public static void main(String[] args) {
        new ClassPathXmlApplicationContext("rmi-server.xml");
    }
}
```

Invoking an RMI Service

By using Spring's remoting facilities, you can invoke a remote service just like a local bean. For example, you can create a client that refers to the weather service by its interface.

```
package com.apress.springrecipes.weather;
...
public class WeatherServiceClient {

    private WeatherService weatherService;

    public void setWeatherService(WeatherService weatherService) {
        this.weatherService = weatherService;
    }

    public TemperatureInfo getTodayTemperature(String city) {
        List<Date> dates = Arrays.asList(new Date[] { new Date() });
        List<TemperatureInfo> temperatures =
            weatherService.getTemperatures(city, dates);
        return temperatures.get(0);
    }
}
```

In a client bean configuration file, such as `client.xml` located in the classpath root, you can use `RmiProxyFactoryBean` to create a proxy for the remote service. Then you can use this service as if it were a local bean (e.g., inject it into the weather service client).

```
<beans xmlns="http://www.springframework.org/schema/beans"
    xmlns:xsi="http://www.w3.org/2001/XMLSchema-instance"
    xsi:schemaLocation="http://www.springframework.org/schema/beans
        http://www.springframework.org/schema/beans/spring-beans-2.5.xsd">

    <bean id="client"
        class="com.apress.springrecipes.weather.WeatherServiceClient">
        <property name="weatherService" ref="weatherService" />
    </bean>
```

```
    <bean id="weatherService"
        class="org.springframework.remoting.rmi.RmiProxyFactoryBean">
        <property name="serviceUrl"
            value="rmi://localhost:1099/WeatherService" />
        <property name="serviceInterface"
            value="com.apress.springrecipes.weather.WeatherService" />
    </bean>
</beans>
```

There are two properties you must configure for an `RmiProxyFactoryBean` instance. The service URL property specifies the host and port of the RMI registry, as well as the service name. The service interface allows this factory bean to create a proxy for the remote service. The proxy will transfer the invocation requests to the remote service transparently. You can test this service with the following `Client` main class:

```
package com.apress.springrecipes.weather;

import org.springframework.context.ApplicationContext;
import org.springframework.context.support.ClassPathXmlApplicationContext;

public class Client {

    public static void main(String[] args) {
        ApplicationContext context =
            new ClassPathXmlApplicationContext("client.xml");
        WeatherServiceClient client =
            (WeatherServiceClient) context.getBean("client");

        TemperatureInfo temperature = client.getTodayTemperature("Houston");
        System.out.println("Min temperature : " + temperature.getMin());
        System.out.println("Max temperature : " + temperature.getMax());
        System.out.println("Average temperature : " + temperature.getAverage());
    }
}
```

16-2. Exposing and Invoking Services Through HTTP

Problem

As RMI communicates over its own protocol, which may not be able to pass through firewalls, you would like to expose a service from your Java application for clients to invoke over HTTP, which is allowed to pass through most firewalls.

Solution

Hessian and *Burlap* are two simple lightweight remoting technologies developed by Caucho Technology (`http://www.caucho.com/`). They both communicate using proprietary messages over HTTP and have their own serialization mechanism, but they are much simpler than web services. The only difference between them is that Hessian communicates using binary messages while Burlap communicates using XML messages. The message formats of both Hessian and Burlap are also supported on other platforms besides Java, such as PHP, Python, C#, and Ruby. This allows your Java applications to communicate with applications running on the other platforms.

In addition to the preceding two technologies, the Spring framework itself also offers a remoting technology called *HTTP Invoker*. It also communicates over HTTP, but uses Java's object serialization mechanism to serialize objects. Unlike Hessian and Burlap, HTTP Invoker requires both sides of a service to be running on the Java platform and using the Spring framework. However, it can serialize all kinds of Java objects, some of which may not be serialized by Hessian/Burlap's proprietary mechanism.

Spring's remoting facilities are consistent in exposing and invoking remote services with these technologies. On the server side, you can create a service exporter such as `HessianServiceExporter`, `BurlapServiceExporter`, or `HttpInvokerServiceExporter` to export a Spring bean as a remote service whose methods can be invoked remotely. It's just several lines of bean configurations without any programming. On the client side, you can simply configure a proxy factory bean such as `HessianProxyFactoryBean`, `BurlapProxyFactoryBean`, or `HttpInvokerProxyFactoryBean` to create a proxy for a remote service. It allows you to use the remote service as if it were a local bean. Again, it requires no additional programming at all.

How It Works

Exposing a Hessian Service

To expose a Hessian service with Spring, you have to create a web application using Spring MVC. First, you create the following directory structure for your web application context.

■ **Note** To expose a Hessian or Burlap service, you have to copy `hessian-3.0.20.jar` (located in the `lib/caucho` directory of the Spring installation) to the `WEB-INF/lib` directory.

```
weather/
    WEB-INF/
        classes/
        lib/
            commons-logging.jar
            hessian-3.0.20.jar
            spring-webmvc.jar
            spring.jar
        weather-servlet.xml
        web.xml
```

In the web deployment descriptor (i.e., `web.xml`), you have to configure Spring MVC's `DispatcherServlet`.

```
<web-app version="2.4" xmlns="http://java.sun.com/xml/ns/j2ee"
    xmlns:xsi="http://www.w3.org/2001/XMLSchema-instance"
    xsi:schemaLocation="http://java.sun.com/xml/ns/j2ee
        http://java.sun.com/xml/ns/j2ee/web-app_2_4.xsd">

    <servlet>
        <servlet-name>weather</servlet-name>
        <servlet-class>
            org.springframework.web.servlet.DispatcherServlet
        </servlet-class>
        <load-on-startup>1</load-on-startup>
    </servlet>

    <servlet-mapping>
        <servlet-name>weather</servlet-name>
        <url-pattern>/services/*</url-pattern>
    </servlet-mapping>
</web-app>
```

In the preceding servlet mapping definition, you map all URLs under the `services` path to `DispatcherServlet`. As the name of this servlet is `weather`, you create the following Spring MVC configuration file, `weather-servlet.xml`, in the root of `WEB-INF`. In this file, you declare a bean for the weather service implementation and export it as a Hessian service using `HessianServiceExporter`.

```
<beans xmlns="http://www.springframework.org/schema/beans"
    xmlns:xsi="http://www.w3.org/2001/XMLSchema-instance"
    xsi:schemaLocation="http://www.springframework.org/schema/beans
        http://www.springframework.org/schema/beans/spring-beans-2.5.xsd">

    <bean id="weatherService"
        class="com.apress.springrecipes.weather.WeatherServiceImpl" />

    <bean name="/WeatherService"
        class="org.springframework.remoting.caucho.HessianServiceExporter">
        <property name="service" ref="weatherService" />
        <property name="serviceInterface"
            value="com.apress.springrecipes.weather.WeatherService" />
    </bean>
</beans>
```

For a `HessianServiceExporter` instance, you have to configure a service object to export and its service interface. You can export any bean configured in the IoC container as a Hessian service, and then `HessianServiceExporter` will create a proxy to wrap this bean. When the proxy receives an invocation request, it will invoke the corresponding method on that bean. By default, `BeanNameUrlHandlerMapping` is preconfigured for a Spring MVC application. It maps requests to handlers according to the URL patterns specified as bean names. The preceding configuration maps the URL pattern `/WeatherService` to this exporter.

Now you can deploy this web application to a web container (e.g., Apache Tomcat 6.0). By default, Tomcat listens on port 8080, so if you deploy your application to the `weather` context path, you can access this service with the following URL:

```
http://localhost:8080/weather/services/WeatherService
```

Invoking a Hessian Service

By using Spring's remoting facilities, you can invoke a remote service just like a local bean. In the client bean configuration file `client.xml`, you can use `HessianProxyFactoryBean` to create a proxy for the remote Hessian service. Then you can use this service as if it were a local bean.

■ **Note** To invoke a Hessian or Burlap service, you have to include `hessian-3.0.20.jar` (located in the `lib/caucho` directory of the Spring installation) in your classpath.

```
<bean id="weatherService"
    class="org.springframework.remoting.caucho.HessianProxyFactoryBean">
    <property name="serviceUrl"
        value="http://localhost:8080/weather/services/WeatherService" />
    <property name="serviceInterface"
        value="com.apress.springrecipes.weather.WeatherService" />
</bean>
```

There are two properties you have to configure for a `HessianProxyFactoryBean` instance. The service URL property specifies the URL for the target service. The service interface property is for this factory bean to create a local proxy for the remote service. The proxy will send the invocation requests to the remote service transparently.

Exposing a Burlap Service

The configuration for exposing a Burlap service is similar to that for Hessian, except you should use `BurlapServiceExporter` instead.

```
<bean name="/WeatherService"
    class="org.springframework.remoting.caucho.BurlapServiceExporter">
    <property name="service" ref="weatherService" />
    <property name="serviceInterface"
        value="com.apress.springrecipes.weather.WeatherService" />
</bean>
```

Invoking a Burlap Service

Invoking a Burlap service is very similar to Hessian. The only difference is that you should use `BurlapProxyFactoryBean`.

```
<bean id="weatherService"
    class="org.springframework.remoting.caucho.BurlapProxyFactoryBean">
    <property name="serviceUrl"
        value="http://localhost:8080/weather/services/WeatherService" />
    <property name="serviceInterface"
        value="com.apress.springrecipes.weather.WeatherService" />
</bean>
```

Exposing an HTTP Invoker Service

Again, the configuration for exposing a service using HTTP Invoker is similar to that for Hessian and Burlap, except you have to use `HttpInvokerServiceExporter` instead.

```
<bean name="/WeatherService"
    class="org.springframework.remoting.httpinvoker.HttpInvokerServiceExporter">
    <property name="service" ref="weatherService" />
    <property name="serviceInterface"
        value="com.apress.springrecipes.weather.WeatherService" />
</bean>
```

Invoking an HTTP Invoker Service

Invoking a service exposed by HTTP Invoker is also similar to Hessian and Burlap. This time you have to use `HttpInvokerProxyFactoryBean`.

```
<bean id="weatherService"
    class="org.springframework.remoting.httpinvoker.HttpInvokerProxyFactoryBean">
    <property name="serviceUrl"
        value="http://localhost:8080/weather/services/WeatherService" />
    <property name="serviceInterface"
        value="com.apress.springrecipes.weather.WeatherService" />
</bean>
```

16-3. Choosing a Web Service Development Approach

Problem

When you are asked to develop a web service, you first have to consider which web service development approach you are going to use.

Solution

There are two approaches to developing a web service, depending on whether you define the contract first or last. A web service contract is described using *Web Services Description Language (WSDL)*. In contract-last, you expose an existing service interface as a web service whose service contract is generated automatically. In contract-first, you design the service contract in terms of XML and then write code to fulfill it.

How It Works

Contract-Last Web Services

In contract-last web service development, you expose an existing service interface as a web service. There are many tools and libraries that can help expose a Java class/interface as a web service. They can generate the WSDL file for the class/interface by applying rules, such as turning the class/interface into a port type, turning the methods into operations, and generating the request/response message formats according to the method arguments and return value. All in all, everything is generated from a service interface like the following:

```
package com.apress.springrecipes.weather;
...
public interface WeatherService {

    public List<TemperatureInfo> getTemperatures(String city, List<Date> dates);
}
```

This approach is called contract-last since you define the contract for this web service as the last step in the development process by generating it from Java code. In other words, you are designing the service with Java, not with WSDL or XML.

Contract-First Web Services

In contrast, the contract-first approach encourages you to think of the service contract first, in terms of XML including XSD and WSDL. In this approach, you design the request and response messages for your service first. The messages are designed with XML, which is very good at representing complex data structures in a platform- and language-independent way. The next step is to implement this contract in a particular platform and programming language.

For example, the request message of your weather service contains a `city` element and multiple `date` elements. Note that you should specify the namespace for your messages to avoid naming conflicts with other XML documents.

```
<GetTemperaturesRequest
    xmlns="http://springrecipes.apress.com/weather/schemas">
    <city>Houston</city>
    <date>2007-12-01</date>
    <date>2007-12-08</date>
    <date>2007-12-15</date>
</GetTemperaturesRequest>
```

Then the response message would contain multiple `Temperature` elements in response to the requested city and dates.

```
<GetTemperaturesResponse
    xmlns="http://springrecipes.apress.com/weather/schemas">
    <TemperatureInfo city="Houston" date="2007-12-01">
        <min>5.0</min>
        <max>10.0</max>
        <average>8.0</average>
```

```
    </TemperatureInfo>
    <TemperatureInfo city="Houston" date="2007-12-08">
        <min>4.0</min>
        <max>13.0</max>
        <average>7.0</average>
    </TemperatureInfo>
    <TemperatureInfo city="Houston" date="2007-12-15">
        <min>10.0</min>
        <max>18.0</max>
        <average>15.0</average>
    </TemperatureInfo>
</GetTemperaturesResponse>
```

After designing the sample request and response messages, you can start creating the contract for this web service using XSD and WSDL. There are many tools and IDEs that can help generate the default XSD and WSDL files for an XML document. You only need to carry out a few optimizations to have it fit your requirements.

Comparison

When developing a contract-last web service, you are actually exposing the internal API of your application to clients. But this API is likely to be changed—and once it's changed, you will also have to change the contract of your web service, which may involve changing all the clients. However, if you design the contract first, it reflects the external API that you would like to expose. It's not as likely to need changing as the internal API.

Although many tools and libraries can expose a Java class/interface as a web service, the fact is that the contract generated from Java is not always portable to other platforms. For example, a Java map may not be portable to other programming languages without a similar data structure. Sometimes you have to change the method signature in order to make a service contract portable. In some cases, it's also hard to map an object to XML (e.g., an object graph with cyclic references), because there's actually an *impedance mismatch* between an object model and an XML model, just like that between an object model and a relational model.

XML is good at representing complex data structures in a platform- and language-independent way. A service contract defined with XML is 100 percent portable to any platform. In addition, you can define constraints in the XSD file for your messages so that they can be validated automatically. For these reasons, it's more efficient to design a service contract with XML and implement it with a programming language such as Java. There are many libraries in Java for processing XML efficiently.

From performance's view point, generating a service contract from Java code may lead to an inefficient design. This is because you might not consider the message granularity carefully, as it's derived from the method signature directly. In contrast, defining the service contract first is more likely to lead to an efficient design.

Finally, the biggest reason for choosing the contract-last approach is its simplicity. Exposing a Java class/interface as a web service doesn't require you to know much about XML, WSDL, SOAP, and so on. You can expose a web service very quickly.

16-4. Exposing and Invoking Web Services Using XFire

Problem

As Web Services is a standard and cross-platform application communication technology, you would like to expose a web service from your Java application for clients on different platforms to invoke.

Solution

Spring comes with several service exporters that can export a bean as a remote service based on the RMI, Hessian, Burlap, or HTTP Invoker remoting technologies, but Spring doesn't come with a service exporter that can export a bean as a web service. However, there's an external library called *XFire* (`http://xfire.codehaus.org/`) that supplies one. XFire is an open source Java SOAP framework that can export a simple Java object as a web service. XFire supports Spring by providing facilities such as a service exporter and a client proxy factory bean, whose usage is consistent with those provided by Spring for other remoting technologies.

How It Works

Exposing a Web Service Using XFire

To expose a web service using XFire in Spring, you first create the following directory structure for your web application context.

■ Note To expose a web service using XFire, you have to download and install XFire (e.g., v1.2.6). Then copy `xfire-all-1.2.6.jar` (located in the root of the XFire installation), `activation-1.1.jar`, `jdom-1.0.jar`, `stax-api-1.0.1.jar`, `wsdl4j-1.6.1.jar`, and `wstx-asl-3.2.0.jar` (all located in the `lib` directory) to the `WEB-INF/lib` directory.

```
weather/
    WEB-INF/
        classes/
        lib/
            activation-1.1.jar
            commons-logging.jar
            jdom-1.0.jar
            spring-webmvc.jar
            spring.jar
            stax-api-1.0.1.jar
            wsdl4j-1.6.1.jar
            wstx-asl-3.2.0.jar
            xfire-all-1.2.6.jar
        weather-servlet.xml
        web.xml
```

In `web.xml`, you configure Spring MVC's `DispatcherServlet` and map all the URLs under the `services` path to it.

```
<web-app version="2.4" xmlns="http://java.sun.com/xml/ns/j2ee"
    xmlns:xsi="http://www.w3.org/2001/XMLSchema-instance"
    xsi:schemaLocation="http://java.sun.com/xml/ns/j2ee
        http://java.sun.com/xml/ns/j2ee/web-app_2_4.xsd">

    <servlet>
        <servlet-name>weather</servlet-name>
        <servlet-class>
            org.springframework.web.servlet.DispatcherServlet
        </servlet-class>
        <load-on-startup>1</load-on-startup>
    </servlet>

    <servlet-mapping>
        <servlet-name>weather</servlet-name>
        <url-pattern>/services/*</url-pattern>
    </servlet-mapping>
</web-app>
```

In the Spring MVC configuration file, `weather-servlet.xml`, you declare a bean for the weather service implementation and export it as a web service by using `XFireExporter`.

```
<beans xmlns="http://www.springframework.org/schema/beans"
    xmlns:xsi="http://www.w3.org/2001/XMLSchema-instance"
    xsi:schemaLocation="http://www.springframework.org/schema/beans
        http://www.springframework.org/schema/beans/spring-beans-2.5.xsd">

    <bean id="weatherService"
        class="com.apress.springrecipes.weather.WeatherServiceImpl" />

    <bean name="/WeatherService"
        class="org.codehaus.xfire.spring.remoting.XFireExporter">
        <property name="xfire" ref="xfire" />
        <property name="serviceBean" ref="weatherService" />
        <property name="serviceInterface"
            value="com.apress.springrecipes.weather.WeatherService" />
    </bean>
</beans>
```

For an `XFireExporter` instance, you have to configure a service object to export and its service interface. Note that this exporter requires a reference to the core `xfire` bean for actual web service processing. The `xfire` bean is defined in the bean configuration file bundled with the XFire library. You only have to configure `ContextLoaderListener` in your `web.xml` to load this file from the classpath.

```
<web-app ...>
    <context-param>
        <param-name>contextConfigLocation</param-name>
        <param-value>
            classpath:org/codehaus/xfire/spring/xfire.xml
        </param-value>
    </context-param>

    <listener>
        <listener-class>
            org.springframework.web.context.ContextLoaderListener
        </listener-class>
    </listener>
    ...
</web-app>
```

Now you can deploy your web application to a web container such as Apache Tomcat 6.0. Then you can access this web service with the following URL:

```
http://localhost:8080/weather/services/WeatherService
```

Inspecting the Generated WSDL File

Each web service requires a WSDL file for describing the service contract. XFire is able to generate the WSDL file for your service dynamically. For the weather service, you can access the WSDL file through the following URL:

```
http://localhost:8080/weather/services/WeatherService?wsdl
```

The generated WSDL file for your weather service is shown following. For simplicity, the less important parts are omitted.

```
<?xml version="1.0" encoding="UTF-8" ?>
<wsdl:definitions targetNamespace="http://weather.springrecipes.apress.com"
    xmlns:tns="http://weather.springrecipes.apress.com"
    ...>
    <wsdl:types>
        <xsd:schema xmlns:xsd="http://www.w3.org/2001/XMLSchema"
            attributeFormDefault="qualified" elementFormDefault="qualified"
            targetNamespace="http://weather.springrecipes.apress.com">
            <xsd:complexType name="ArrayOfDateTime">
                <xsd:sequence>
                    <xsd:element maxOccurs="unbounded" minOccurs="0"
                        name="dateTime" type="xsd:dateTime" />
                </xsd:sequence>
            </xsd:complexType>
            <xsd:element name="getTemperatures">
                <xsd:complexType>
                    <xsd:sequence>
```

```
                <xsd:element maxOccurs="1" minOccurs="1" name="in0"
                    nillable="true" type="xsd:string" />
                <xsd:element maxOccurs="1" minOccurs="1" name="in1"
                    nillable="true" type="tns:ArrayOfDateTime" />
            </xsd:sequence>
        </xsd:complexType>
    </xsd:element>
    <xsd:complexType name="ArrayOfTemperatureInfo">
        <xsd:sequence>
            <xsd:element maxOccurs="unbounded" minOccurs="0"
                name="TemperatureInfo" nillable="true"
                type="tns:TemperatureInfo" />
        </xsd:sequence>
    </xsd:complexType>
    <xsd:complexType name="TemperatureInfo">
        <xsd:sequence>
            <xsd:element minOccurs="0" name="average" type="xsd:double" />
            <xsd:element minOccurs="0" name="city"
                nillable="true" type="xsd:string" />
            <xsd:element minOccurs="0" name="date" type="xsd:dateTime" />
            <xsd:element minOccurs="0" name="max" type="xsd:double" />
            <xsd:element minOccurs="0" name="min" type="xsd:double" />
        </xsd:sequence>
    </xsd:complexType>
    <xsd:element name="getTemperaturesResponse">
        <xsd:complexType>
            <xsd:sequence>
                <xsd:element maxOccurs="1" minOccurs="1" name="out"
                    nillable="true" type="tns:ArrayOfTemperatureInfo" />
            </xsd:sequence>
        </xsd:complexType>
    </xsd:element>
</xsd:schema>
</wsdl:types>
<wsdl:message name="getTemperaturesRequest">
    <wsdl:part name="parameters" element="tns:getTemperatures" />
</wsdl:message>
<wsdl:message name="getTemperaturesResponse">
    <wsdl:part name="parameters" element="tns:getTemperaturesResponse" />
</wsdl:message>
<wsdl:portType name="WeatherServicePortType">
    <wsdl:operation name="getTemperatures">
        <wsdl:input name="getTemperaturesRequest"
            message="tns:getTemperaturesRequest" />
        <wsdl:output name="getTemperaturesResponse"
            message="tns:getTemperaturesResponse" />
    </wsdl:operation>
</wsdl:portType>
```

```
    ...
    <wsdl:service name="WeatherService">
        <wsdl:port name="WeatherServiceHttpPort"
            binding="tns:WeatherServiceHttpBinding">
            <wsdlsoap:address location=
                "http://localhost:8080/weather/services/WeatherService" />
        </wsdl:port>
    </wsdl:service>
</wsdl:definitions>
```

From the preceding WSDL file, you can see that XFire generates this file by making the following conversions:

- The package `com.apress.springrecipes.weather` is turned into the target namespace `http://weather.springrecipes.apress.com`.
- The class `WeatherService` is turned into the port type `WeatherServicePortType`.
- The method `getTemperatures()` is turned into the operation `getTemperatures`.
- The method arguments are turned into the `getTemperatures` element, including two subelements, `in0` and `in1`, whose types are `string` and the `ArrayOfDateTime` complex type.
- The return value is turned into the `getTemperaturesResponse` element, including the subelement `out`, whose type is the `ArrayOfTemperatureInfo` complex type. It's an array of another complex type, `TemperatureInfo`, which has five elements: `average`, `city`, `date`, `max`, and `min`.

Invoking a Web Service Using XFire

By using XFire's client factory bean, you can invoke a web service just like a local bean. In the client bean configuration file, `client.xml`, you can use `XFireClientFactoryBean` to create a proxy for the web service. Then you can use this service as if it were a local bean.

Note To invoke a web service using XFire, you have to include `xfire-all-1.2.6.jar` (located in the root of the XFire installation), `activation-1.1.jar`, `jdom-1.0.jar`, `stax-api-1.0.1.jar`, `wsdl4j-1.6.1.jar`, `wstx-asl-3.2.0.jar`, `XmlSchema-1.1.jar`, `commons-codec-1.3.jar`, and `commons-httpclient-3.0.jar` (all located in the `lib` directory) in your classpath.

```
<bean id="weatherService"
    class="org.codehaus.xfire.spring.remoting.XFireClientFactoryBean">
    <property name="wsdlDocumentUrl"
        value="http://localhost:8080/weather/services/WeatherService?wsdl" />
    <property name="serviceInterface"
        value="com.apress.springrecipes.weather.WeatherService" />
</bean>
```

There are two properties you must configure for an XFireClientFactoryBean instance. The WSDL URL property specifies the URL for the WSDL file. The service interface property is for this factory bean to create a proxy for the web service. The proxy will transfer the invocation requests to the web service transparently.

Exposing an Annotation-Based Web Service Using XFire

XFire also supports the web service annotations defined by JSR-181: Web Services Metadata for the Java Platform. It can automatically export your beans annotated with the web service annotations without manual configuration. First of all, you have to annotate your web service implementation class with these annotations.

Note To use the JSR-181 web service annotations, you have to copy xfire-jsr181-api-1.0-M1.jar (located in the lib directory of the XFire installation) to the WEB-INF/lib directory.

```
package com.apress.springrecipes.weather;
...
import javax.jws.WebMethod;
import javax.jws.WebService;

@WebService(serviceName = "WeatherService")
public class WeatherServiceImpl implements WeatherService {

    @WebMethod(operationName = "getTemperatures")
    public List<TemperatureInfo> getTemperatures(String city, List<Date> dates) {
        ...
    }
}
```

Then you can simply define a Jsr181HandlerMapping bean to map the web service requests to appropriate service beans according to the JSR-181 annotations. To make the mappings consistent with before, you should set the urlPrefix property to / so that it will be added in front of the service names specified in the annotation. Remember that you also have to inject the core xfire bean into this handler mapping.

```
<beans ...>
    <bean id="weatherService"
        class="com.apress.springrecipes.weather.WeatherServiceImpl" />

    <bean class="org.codehaus.xfire.spring.remoting.Jsr181HandlerMapping">
        <property name="xfire" ref="xfire" />
        <property name="webAnnotations">
            <bean class="org.codehaus.xfire.annotations.jsr181.➥
                Jsr181WebAnnotations" />
        </property>
```

```
        <property name="urlPrefix" value="/" />
    </bean>
</beans>
```

16-5. Defining the Contract of Web Services

Problem

According to the contract-first web service approach, the first step of developing a web service is to define the service contract.

Solution

A web service's contract consists of two parts: the data contract and the service contract. They are both defined with the XML technology in a platform- and language-independent way.

Data contract: Describes the complex data types and request and response messages of this web service. A data contract is defined with XSD.

Service contract: Describes the operations of this web service. A web service may have multiple operations. A service contract is defined with WSDL.

When using a comprehensive web service development framework like Spring-WS, the service contract can usually be generated automatically. But you must create the data contract yourself.

To create the data contract for your web service, you can start by creating the XSD file. As there are many powerful XML tools available in the community, this won't be too hard. However, most developers prefer to start by creating some sample XML messages, and then generate the XSD file from them. Of course, you need to optimize the generated XSD file yourself, as it may not fit your requirements entirely, and sometimes you may wish to add more constraints to it.

How It Works

Creating Sample XML Messages

For your weather service, you can represent the temperature of a particular city and date as in the following XML message:

```
<TemperatureInfo city="Houston" date="2007-12-01">
    <min>5.0</min>
    <max>10.0</max>
    <average>8.0</average>
</TemperatureInfo>
```

Then, you can define the data contract for your weather service. Suppose you want to define an operation that allows clients to query the temperatures of a particular city for multiple dates. Each request consists of a `city` element and multiple `date` elements. You should also specify the namespace for this request to avoid naming conflicts with other XML documents. Let's save this XML message to `request.xml`.

```
<GetTemperaturesRequest
    xmlns="http://springrecipes.apress.com/weather/schemas">
    <city>Houston</city>
    <date>2007-12-01</date>
    <date>2007-12-08</date>
    <date>2007-12-15</date>
</GetTemperaturesRequest>
```

The response consists of multiple `TemperatureInfo` elements, each of which represents the temperature of a particular city and date, in accordance with the requested dates. Let's save this XML message to `response.xml`.

```
<GetTemperaturesResponse
    xmlns="http://springrecipes.apress.com/weather/schemas">
    <TemperatureInfo city="Houston" date="2007-12-01">
        <min>5.0</min>
        <max>10.0</max>
        <average>8.0</average>
    </TemperatureInfo>
    <TemperatureInfo city="Houston" date="2007-12-08">
        <min>4.0</min>
        <max>13.0</max>
        <average>7.0</average>
    </TemperatureInfo>
    <TemperatureInfo city="Houston" date="2007-12-15">
        <min>10.0</min>
        <max>18.0</max>
        <average>15.0</average>
    </TemperatureInfo>
</GetTemperaturesResponse>
```

Generating an XSD File from Sample XML Messages

Now you can generate the XSD file from the preceding sample XML messages. Most popular XML tools and enterprise Java IDEs can generate an XSD file from a couple of XML files. Here, I have chosen Apache XMLBeans (`http://xmlbeans.apache.org/`) to generate my XSD file.

■ **Note** You can download Apache XMLBeans (e.g., v2.3.0) from the Apache XMLBeans web site and extract it to a directory of your choice to complete the installation.

Apache XMLBeans provides a tool called `inst2xsd` for generating XSD files from XML instance files. It supports several design types for generating XSD files. The simplest is called *Russian doll design*, which generates local elements and local types for the target XSD file. As there's no enumeration type used in your XML messages, you should also disable the enumeration generation feature. You can execute the following command to generate the XSD file for your data contract:

```
inst2xsd -design rd -enumerations never request.xml response.xml
```

The generated XSD file will have the default name schema0.xsd, located in the same directory. Let's rename it to temperature.xsd.

```
<?xml version="1.0" encoding="UTF-8"?>
<xs:schema attributeFormDefault="unqualified"
    elementFormDefault="qualified"
    targetNamespace="http://springrecipes.apress.com/weather/schemas"
    xmlns:xs="http://www.w3.org/2001/XMLSchema">

    <xs:element name="GetTemperaturesRequest">
        <xs:complexType>
            <xs:sequence>
                <xs:element type="xs:string" name="city" />
                <xs:element type="xs:date" name="date"
                    maxOccurs="unbounded" minOccurs="0" />
            </xs:sequence>
        </xs:complexType>
    </xs:element>

    <xs:element name="GetTemperaturesResponse">
        <xs:complexType>
            <xs:sequence>
                <xs:element name="TemperatureInfo"
                    maxOccurs="unbounded" minOccurs="0">
                    <xs:complexType>
                        <xs:sequence>
                            <xs:element type="xs:float" name="min" />
                            <xs:element type="xs:float" name="max" />
                            <xs:element type="xs:float" name="average" />
                        </xs:sequence>
                        <xs:attribute type="xs:string" name="city"
                            use="optional" />
                        <xs:attribute type="xs:date" name="date"
                            use="optional" />
                    </xs:complexType>
                </xs:element>
            </xs:sequence>
        </xs:complexType>
    </xs:element>
</xs:schema>
```

Optimizing the Generated XSD File

As you can see, the generated XSD file allows clients to query temperatures of unlimited dates. If you would like to add a constraint on the maximum and minimum query dates, you can modify the maxOccurs and minOccurs attributes.

```
<?xml version="1.0" encoding="UTF-8"?>
<xs:schema attributeFormDefault="unqualified"
    elementFormDefault="qualified"
    targetNamespace="http://springrecipes.apress.com/weather/schemas"
    xmlns:xs="http://www.w3.org/2001/XMLSchema">

    <xs:element name="GetTemperaturesRequest">
        <xs:complexType>
            <xs:sequence>
                <xs:element type="xs:string" name="city" />
                <xs:element type="xs:date" name="date"
                    maxOccurs="5" minOccurs="1" />
            </xs:sequence>
        </xs:complexType>
    </xs:element>

    <xs:element name="GetTemperaturesResponse">
        <xs:complexType>
            <xs:sequence>
                <xs:element name="TemperatureInfo"
                    maxOccurs="5" minOccurs="1">
                    ...
                </xs:element>
            </xs:sequence>
        </xs:complexType>
    </xs:element>
</xs:schema>
```

Previewing the Generated WSDL File

As you will learn later, Spring-WS can automatically generate the service contract for you, based on the data contract and some conventions that you can override. Here, you can preview the generated WSDL file to better understand the service contract. For simplicity's sake, the less important parts are omitted.

```
<?xml version="1.0" encoding="UTF-8" ?>
<wsdl:definitions ...
    targetNamespace="http://springrecipes.apress.com/weather/schemas">
    <wsdl:types>
        <!-- Copied from the XSD file -->
        ...
    </wsdl:types>
    <wsdl:message name="GetTemperaturesResponse">
```

```
        <wsdl:part element="schema:GetTemperaturesResponse"
            name="GetTemperaturesResponse">
        </wsdl:part>
    </wsdl:message>
    <wsdl:message name="GetTemperaturesRequest">
        <wsdl:part element="schema:GetTemperaturesRequest"
            name="GetTemperaturesRequest">
        </wsdl:part>
    </wsdl:message>
    <wsdl:portType name="Weather">
        <wsdl:operation name="GetTemperatures">
            <wsdl:input message="schema:GetTemperaturesRequest"
                name="GetTemperaturesRequest">
            </wsdl:input>
            <wsdl:output message="schema:GetTemperaturesResponse"
                name="GetTemperaturesResponse">
            </wsdl:output>
        </wsdl:operation>
    </wsdl:portType>
    ...
    <wsdl:service name="WeatherService">
        <wsdl:port binding="schema:WeatherBinding" name="WeatherPort">
            <soap:address
                location="http://localhost:8080/weather/services" />
        </wsdl:port>
    </wsdl:service>
</wsdl:definitions>
```

In the Weather port type, a GetTemperatures operation is defined, whose name is derived from the prefix of the input and output messages (i.e., <GetTemperaturesRequest> and <GetTemperaturesResponse>). The definitions of these two elements are included in the <wsdl:types> part, as defined in the data contract.

16-6. Implementing Web Services Using Spring-WS

Problem

Once you have defined the contract for your web service, you can start implementing the service itself according to this contract. You would like to use Spring-WS to implement this service.

Solution

Spring-WS provides a set of facilities for you to develop contract-first web services. The essential tasks for building a Spring-WS web service include the following:

- Setting up and configuring a Spring MVC application for Spring-WS
- Mapping web service requests to endpoints

- Creating service endpoints to handle the request messages and return the response messages
- Publishing the WSDL file for this web service

The concept of an *endpoint* in web services is much like that of a controller in web applications. The difference is that a web controller deals with HTTP requests and HTTP responses, while a service endpoint deals with XML request messages and XML response messages. They both need to invoke other back-end services to handle the requests.

Spring-WS provides various abstract endpoint classes for you to process the request and response XML messages using different XML processing technologies/APIs. These classes are all located in the `org.springframework.ws.server.endpoint` package. You can simply extend one of them to process the XML messages with a particular technology/API. Table 16-1 lists these endpoint classes.

Table 16-1. *Endpoint Classes for Different XML Processing Technologies/APIs*

Technology/API	Endpoint Class
DOM	`AbstractDomPayloadEndpoint`
JDOM	`AbstractJDomPayloadEndpoint`
dom4j	`AbstractDom4jPayloadEndpoint`
XOM	`AbstractXomPayloadEndpoint`
SAX	`AbstractSaxPayloadEndpoint`
Event-based StAX	`AbstractStaxEventPayloadEndpoint`
Streaming StAX	`AbstractStaxStreamPayloadEndpoint`
XML marshalling	`AbstractMarshallingPayloadEndpoint`

Note that the preceding endpoint classes are all for creating payload endpoints. That means you can only access the payloads of the request and response messages (i.e., the contents in the SOAP body, but not other parts of the messages like the SOAP headers). If you need to get access to the entire SOAP message, you should write an endpoint class by implementing the `org.springframework.ws.server.endpoint.MessageEndpoint` interface.

How It Works

Setting Up a Spring-WS Application

To implement a web service using Spring-WS, you first create the following directory structure for your web application context.

■ Note To create a Spring MVC application for Spring-WS, you have to download and install Spring-WS (e.g., v1.5). Then copy `spring-ws-1.5.0.jar` (located in the `dist` directory of the Spring-WS installation), `stax-api-1.0.1.jar` (located in `lib/stax`), `activation-1.1.1.jar` and `saaj-api-1.3.jar` (located in `lib/java-ee`), `saaj-impl-1.3.jar` (located in `lib/saaj`), and `wsdl4j-1.6.1.jar` (located in `lib/wsdl4j`) to the `WEB-INF/lib` directory.

```
weather/
    WEB-INF/
        classes/
        lib/
            activation-1.1.1.jar
            commons-logging.jar
            saaj-api-1.3.jar
            saaj-impl-1.3.jar
            spring-webmvc.jar
            spring-ws-1.5.0.jar
            spring.jar
            stax-api-1.0.1.jar
            wsdl4j-1.6.1.jar
        temperature.xsd
        weather-servlet.xml
        web.xml
```

In web.xml, you have to configure the MessageDispatcherServlet servlet of Spring-WS, which is different from DispatcherServlet for a typical Spring MVC application. This servlet specializes in dispatching web service messages to appropriate endpoints and detecting the framework facilities of Spring-WS.

```
<web-app version="2.4" xmlns="http://java.sun.com/xml/ns/j2ee"
    xmlns:xsi="http://www.w3.org/2001/XMLSchema-instance"
    xsi:schemaLocation="http://java.sun.com/xml/ns/j2ee
        http://java.sun.com/xml/ns/j2ee/web-app_2_4.xsd">

    <servlet>
        <servlet-name>weather</servlet-name>
        <servlet-class>
            org.springframework.ws.transport.http.MessageDispatcherServlet
        </servlet-class>
        <load-on-startup>1</load-on-startup>
    </servlet>

    <servlet-mapping>
        <servlet-name>weather</servlet-name>
        <url-pattern>/services/*</url-pattern>
    </servlet-mapping>
</web-app>
```

In the Spring MVC configuration file, weather-servlet.xml, you first declare a bean for the weather service implementation. Later, you will define endpoints and mappings to handle the web service requests.

```
<beans xmlns="http://www.springframework.org/schema/beans"
    xmlns:xsi="http://www.w3.org/2001/XMLSchema-instance"
    xsi:schemaLocation="http://www.springframework.org/schema/beans
        http://www.springframework.org/schema/beans/spring-beans-2.5.xsd">
```

```
    <bean id="weatherService"
        class="com.apress.springrecipes.weather.WeatherServiceImpl" />
</beans>
```

Mapping Web Service Requests to Endpoints

In a Spring MVC application, you use handler mapping to map web requests to handlers. But in a Spring-WS application, you should use endpoint mapping to map web service requests to endpoints.

The most common endpoint mapping is PayloadRootQNameEndpointMapping. It maps web service requests to endpoints according to the name of the request payload's root element. The name used by this endpoint mapping is the qualified name (i.e., including the namespace). So you must include the namespace in the mapping keys, which is presented inside a brace.

```
<bean class="org.springframework.ws.server.endpoint.mapping.➥
    PayloadRootQNameEndpointMapping">
    <property name="mappings">
        <props>
            <prop key="{http://springrecipes.apress.com/weather/schemas}➥
                GetTemperaturesRequest">
                temperatureEndpoint
            </prop>
        </props>
    </property>
</bean>
```

Creating Service Endpoints

Spring-WS supports various XML parsing APIs, including DOM, JDOM, dom4j, SAX, StAX, and XOM. As an example, I will use dom4j (http://www.dom4j.org) to create a service endpoint. Creating an endpoint using other XML parsing APIs is very similar.

You can create a dom4j endpoint by extending the AbstractDom4jPayloadEndpoint class. The core method defined in this class that you must override is invokeInternal(). In this method, you can access the request XML element, whose type is org.dom4j.Element, and the response document, whose type is org.dom4j.Document, as method arguments. The purpose of the response document is for you to create the response element from it. Now all you have to do in this method is handle the request message and return the response message.

■ **Note** To create a service endpoint using dom4j with XPath, you have to copy dom4j-1.6.1.jar (located in the lib/dom4j directory of the Spring-WS installation) and jaxen-1.1.1.jar (located in lib/jaxen) to the WEB-INF/lib directory.

```
package com.apress.springrecipes.weather;
...
import org.dom4j.Document;
import org.dom4j.Element;
import org.dom4j.XPath;
import org.dom4j.xpath.DefaultXPath;
import org.springframework.ws.server.endpoint.AbstractDom4jPayloadEndpoint;

public class TemperatureDom4jEndpoint extends AbstractDom4jPayloadEndpoint {

    private static final String namespaceUri =
        "http://springrecipes.apress.com/weather/schemas";

    private XPath cityPath;
    private XPath datePath;
    private DateFormat dateFormat;
    private WeatherService weatherService;

    public TemperatureDom4jEndpoint() {

        // Create the XPath objects, including the namespace
        Map<String, String> namespaceUris = new HashMap<String, String>();
        namespaceUris.put("weather", namespaceUri);
        cityPath = new DefaultXPath(
            "/weather:GetTemperaturesRequest/weather:city");
        cityPath.setNamespaceURIs(namespaceUris);
        datePath = new DefaultXPath(
            "/weather:GetTemperaturesRequest/weather:date");
        datePath.setNamespaceURIs(namespaceUris);

        dateFormat = new SimpleDateFormat("yyyy-MM-dd");
    }

    public void setWeatherService(WeatherService weatherService) {
        this.weatherService = weatherService;
    }

    protected Element invokeInternal(Element requestElement,
            Document responseDocument) throws Exception {

        // Extract the service parameters from the request message
        String city = cityPath.valueOf(requestElement);
        List<Date> dates = new ArrayList<Date>();
        for (Object node : datePath.selectNodes(requestElement)) {
            Element element = (Element) node;
            dates.add(dateFormat.parse(element.getText()));
        }
```

```
        // Invoke the back-end service to handle the request
        List<TemperatureInfo> temperatures =
            weatherService.getTemperatures(city, dates);

        // Build the response message from the result of back-end service
        Element responseElement = responseDocument.addElement(
                "GetTemperaturesResponse", namespaceUri);
        for (TemperatureInfo temperature : temperatures) {
            Element temperatureElement = responseElement.addElement(
                    "TemperatureInfo");
            temperatureElement.addAttribute("city", temperature.getCity());
            temperatureElement.addAttribute(
                    "date", dateFormat.format(temperature.getDate()));
            temperatureElement.addElement("min").setText(
                    Double.toString(temperature.getMin()));
            temperatureElement.addElement("max").setText(
                    Double.toString(temperature.getMax()));
            temperatureElement.addElement("average").setText(
                    Double.toString(temperature.getAverage()));
        }
        return responseElement;
    }
}
```

In the preceding `invokeInternal()` method, you first extract the service parameters from the request message. Here, you use XPath to help locate the elements. The XPath objects are created in the constructor so that they can be reused for subsequent request handling. Note that you must also include the namespace in the XPath expressions, or else they will not be able to locate the elements correctly.

After extracting the service parameters, you invoke the back-end service to handle the request. As this endpoint is configured in the Spring IoC container, it can easily refer to other beans through dependency injection.

Finally, you build the response message from the back-end service's result. The dom4j library provides a rich set of APIs for you to build an XML message. Remember that you must include the default namespace in your response element.

With the service endpoint written, you can declare it in `weather-servlet.xml`. As this endpoint needs the weather service bean's help to query temperatures, you have to make a reference to it.

```
<bean id="temperatureEndpoint"
    class="com.apress.springrecipes.weather.TemperatureDom4jEndpoint">
    <property name="weatherService" ref="weatherService" />
</bean>
```

Publishing the WSDL File

The last step to complete your web service is to publish the WSDL file. In Spring-WS, it's not necessary for you to write the WSDL file manually, although you may still supply a manually written WSDL file. You only declare a DynamicWsdl11Definition bean in the web application context, and then it can generate the WSDL file dynamically. MessageDispatcherServlet can also detect this bean by the WsdlDefinition interface.

```
<bean id="temperature"
    class="org.springframework.ws.wsdl.wsdl11.DynamicWsdl11Definition">
    <property name="builder">
        <bean class="org.springframework.ws.wsdl.wsdl11.builder.➥
            XsdBasedSoap11Wsdl4jDefinitionBuilder">
            <property name="schema" value="/WEB-INF/temperature.xsd" />
            <property name="portTypeName" value="Weather" />
            <property name="locationUri"
                value="http://localhost:8080/weather/services" />
        </bean>
    </property>
</bean>
```

The only property you must configure for this WSDL definition bean is a builder that builds the WSDL file from your XSD file. XsdBasedSoap11Wsdl4jDefinitionBuilder builds the WSDL file using the WSDL4J library. Suppose that you have put your XSD file in the WEB-INF directory—you specify this location in the schema property. This builder scans the XSD file for elements that end with the Request or Response suffix. Then it generates WSDL operations using these elements as input and output messages, inside a WSDL port type specified by the portTypeName property.

As you have defined <GetTemperaturesRequest> and <GetTemperaturseResponse> in your XSD file, and you have specified the port type name as Weather, the WSDL builder will generate the following WSDL port type and operation for you. The following snippet is taken from the generated WSDL file:

```
<wsdl:portType name="Weather">
    <wsdl:operation name="GetTemperatures">
        <wsdl:input message="schema:GetTemperaturesRequest"
            name="GetTemperaturesRequest" />
        <wsdl:output message="schema:GetTemperaturesResponse"
            name="GetTemperaturesResponse" />
    </wsdl:operation>
</wsdl:portType>
```

The last property, locationUri, is for you to include this web service's deployed location in the WSDL file. To allow an easy switch to a production URI, you should externalize this URI in a properties file and use Spring's PropertyPlaceholderConfigurer to read the properties from it.

Finally, you can access this WSDL file by joining its definition's bean name and the .wsdl suffix. Supposing that your service is deployed in http://localhost:8080/weather/services, this WSDL file's URL would be http://localhost:8080/weather/services/temperature.wsdl, given that the bean name of the WSDL definition is temperature.

16-7. Invoking Web Services Using Spring-WS

Problem

Given the contract of a web service, you can start creating a service client to invoke this service according to the contract. You would like to use Spring-WS to create the service client.

Solution

When using Spring-WS on the client side, web services can be invoked through the core template class `org.springframework.ws.client.core.WebServiceTemplate`. It's very like the `JdbcTemplate` class and other data access templates in that it defines template methods for sending and receiving request and response messages.

How It Works

Now let's create a Spring-WS client to invoke the weather service according to the contract it publishes. You can create a Spring-WS client by parsing the request and response XML messages. As an example, I will use dom4j to implement it. You are free to choose other XML parsing APIs for it, however.

To shield the client from the low-level invocation details, you can create a local proxy for the remote web service. This proxy also implements the `WeatherService` interface, and it will translate local method calls into remote web service calls.

■ **Note** To invoke a web service using Spring-WS, you have to include `spring-ws-1.5.0.jar` (located in the `dist` directory of the Spring-WS installation), `stax-api-1.0.1.jar` (located in `lib/stax`), `activation-1.1.1.jar` and `saaj-api-1.3.jar` (located in `lib/java-ee`), and `saaj-impl-1.3.jar` (located in `lib/saaj`) in your classpath. To use dom4j, you also have to include `dom4j-1.6.1.jar` (located in `lib/dom4j`).

```
package com.apress.springrecipes.weather;
...
import org.dom4j.Document;
import org.dom4j.DocumentHelper;
import org.dom4j.Element;
import org.dom4j.io.DocumentResult;
import org.dom4j.io.DocumentSource;
import org.springframework.ws.client.core.WebServiceTemplate;

public class WeatherServiceProxy implements WeatherService {

    private static final String namespaceUri =
        "http://springrecipes.apress.com/weather/schemas";
```

```
    private DateFormat dateFormat;
    private WebServiceTemplate webServiceTemplate;

    public WeatherServiceProxy() throws Exception {
        dateFormat = new SimpleDateFormat("yyyy-MM-dd");
    }

    public void setWebServiceTemplate(WebServiceTemplate webServiceTemplate) {
        this.webServiceTemplate = webServiceTemplate;
    }

    public List<TemperatureInfo> getTemperatures(String city, List<Date> dates) {

        // Build the request document from the method arguments
        Document requestDocument = DocumentHelper.createDocument();
        Element requestElement = requestDocument.addElement(
                "GetTemperaturesRequest", namespaceUri);
        requestElement.addElement("city").setText(city);
        for (Date date : dates) {
            requestElement.addElement("date").setText(dateFormat.format(date));
        }

        // Invoke the remote web service
        DocumentSource source = new DocumentSource(requestDocument);
        DocumentResult result = new DocumentResult();
        webServiceTemplate.sendSourceAndReceiveToResult(source, result);

        // Extract the result from the response document
        Document responsetDocument = result.getDocument();
        Element responseElement = responsetDocument.getRootElement();
        List<TemperatureInfo> temperatures = new ArrayList<TemperatureInfo>();
        for (Object node : responseElement.elements("TemperatureInfo")) {
            Element element = (Element) node;
            try {
                Date date = dateFormat.parse(element.attributeValue("date"));
                double min = Double.parseDouble(element.elementText("min"));
                double max = Double.parseDouble(element.elementText("max"));
                double average = Double.parseDouble(
                        element.elementText("average"));
                temperatures.add(
                        new TemperatureInfo(city, date, min, max, average));
            } catch (ParseException e) {
                throw new RuntimeException(e);
            }
        }
        return temperatures;
    }
}
```

In the getTemperatures() method, you first build the request message using the dom4j API. WebServiceTemplate provides a sendSourceAndReceiveToResult() method that accepts a java.xml.transform.Source and a java.xml.transform.Result object as arguments. You have to build a dom4j DocumentSource object to wrap your request document, and create a new dom4j DocumentResult object for the method to write the response document to it. Finally, you get the response message and extract the results from it.

With the service proxy written, you can declare it in a client bean configuration file such as client.xml. As this proxy requires an instance of WebServiceTemplate for sending and receiving the messages, you have to instantiate it and inject this instance into the proxy. Also, you specify the default service URI for the template so that all the requests will be sent to this URI by default.

```
<beans xmlns="http://www.springframework.org/schema/beans"
    xmlns:xsi="http://www.w3.org/2001/XMLSchema-instance"
    xsi:schemaLocation="http://www.springframework.org/schema/beans
        http://www.springframework.org/schema/beans/spring-beans-2.5.xsd">

    <bean id="client"
        class="com.apress.springrecipes.weather.WeatherServiceClient">
        <property name="weatherService" ref="weatherServiceProxy" />
    </bean>

    <bean id="weatherServiceProxy"
        class="com.apress.springrecipes.weather.WeatherServiceProxy">
        <property name="webServiceTemplate" ref="webServiceTemplate" />
    </bean>

    <bean id="webServiceTemplate"
        class="org.springframework.ws.client.core.WebServiceTemplate">
        <property name="defaultUri"
            value="http://localhost:8080/weather/services" />
    </bean>
</beans>
```

Now you can inject this manually written proxy into WeatherServiceClient and run it with the Client main class.

As your DAO class can extend JdbcDaoSupport to get a precreated JdbcTemplate instance, your web service client can similarly extend the WebServiceGatewaySupport class to retrieve a WebServiceTemplate instance without explicit injection.

```
package com.apress.springrecipes.weather;
...
import org.springframework.ws.client.core.support.WebServiceGatewaySupport;

public class WeatherServiceProxy extends WebServiceGatewaySupport
        implements WeatherService {
```

```
    public List<TemperatureInfo> getTemperatures(String city, List<Date> dates) {
        ...
        // Invoke the remote web service
        DocumentSource source = new DocumentSource(requestDocument);
        DocumentResult result = new DocumentResult();
        getWebServiceTemplate().sendSourceAndReceiveToResult(source, result);
        ...
    }
}
```

However, without a `WebServiceTemplate` bean declared explicitly, you have to inject the default URI to the proxy directly. The setter method for this property is inherited from the `WebServiceGatewaySupport` class.

```
<beans ...>
    ...
    <bean id="weatherServiceProxy"
        class="com.apress.springrecipes.weather.WeatherServiceProxy">
        <property name="defaultUri"
            value="http://localhost:8080/weather/services" />
    </bean>
</beans>
```

16-8. Developing Web Services with XML Marshalling

Problem

To develop web services with the contract-first approach, you have to process request and response XML messages. If you parse the XML messages with XML parsing APIs directly, you'll have to deal with the XML elements one by one with low-level APIs, which is a cumbersome and inefficient task.

Solution

Spring-WS supports using XML marshalling technology to marshal/unmarshal objects to/from XML documents. In this way, you can deal with object properties instead of XML elements. This technology is also known as *object/XML mapping (OXM)*, since you are actually mapping objects to and from XML documents.

To implement endpoints with an XML marshalling technology, you have to extend the `AbstractMarshallingPayloadEndpoint` class and configure an XML marshaller for it. Table 16-2 lists the marshallers provided by Spring-WS for different XML marshalling APIs.

Table 16-2. *Marshallers for Different XML Marshalling APIs*

API	Marshaller
JAXB 1.0	org.springframework.oxm.jaxb.Jaxb1Marshaller
JAXB 2.0	org.springframework.oxm.jaxb.Jaxb2Marshaller
Castor	org.springframework.oxm.castor.CastorMarshaller
XMLBeans	org.springframework.oxm.xmlbeans.XmlBeansMarshaller
JiBX	org.springframework.oxm.jibx.JibxMarshaller
XStream	org.springframework.oxm.xstream.XStreamMarshaller

To invoke a web service, WebServiceTemplate also allows you to choose an XML marshalling technology to process the request and response XML messages.

How It Works

Creating Service Endpoints with XML Marshalling

Spring-WS supports various XML marshalling APIs, including JAXB 1.0, JAXB 2.0, Castor, XMLBeans, JiBX, and XStream. As an example, I will create a service endpoint using Castor (http://www.castor.org/) as the marshaller. Using other XML marshalling APIs is very similar.

The first step in using XML marshalling is creating the object model according to the XML message formats. This model can usually be generated by the marshalling API. For some marshalling APIs, the object model must be generated by them so that they can insert marshalling-specific information. As Castor supports marshalling between XML messages and arbitrary Java objects, you can start creating the following classes by yourself.

```
package com.apress.springrecipes.weather;
...
public class GetTemperaturesRequest {

    private String city;
    private List<Date> dates;

    // Constructors, Getters and Setters
    ...
}
```

```
package com.apress.springrecipes.weather;
...
public class GetTemperaturesResponse {

    private List<TemperatureInfo> temperatures;

    // Constructors, Getters and Setters
    ...
}
```

With the object model created, you can write a marshalling endpoint by extending the AbstractMarshallingPayloadEndpoint class. The core method defined in this class that you must override is invokeInternal(). In this method, you can access the request object, which is unmarshalled from the request message, as the method argument. Now all you have to do in this method is handle the request object and return the response object. Then it will be marshalled to the response XML message.

Note To create a service endpoint using Castor, you have to copy castor-1.1.2.jar (located in the lib/castor directory of the Spring-WS installation) and xercesImpl-2.8.1.jar (located in lib/xerces) to the WEB-INF/lib directory.

```
package com.apress.springrecipes.weather;
...
import org.springframework.ws.server.endpoint.AbstractMarshallingPayloadEndpoint;

public class TemperatureMarshallingEndpoint extends
        AbstractMarshallingPayloadEndpoint {

    private WeatherService weatherService;

    public void setWeatherService(WeatherService weatherService) {
        this.weatherService = weatherService;
    }

    protected Object invokeInternal(Object requestObject) throws Exception {
        GetTemperaturesRequest request = (GetTemperaturesRequest) requestObject;

        List<TemperatureInfo> temperatures =
            weatherService.getTemperatures(request.getCity(), request.getDates());

        return new GetTemperaturesResponse(temperatures);
    }
}
```

A marshalling endpoint requires both the marshaller and unmarshaller properties to be set. Usually, you can specify a single marshaller for both properties. For Castor, you declare a CastorMarshaller bean as the marshaller.

```
<beans ...>
    ...
    <bean id="temperatureEndpoint"
        class="com.apress.springrecipes.weather.TemperatureMarshallingEndpoint">
        <property name="marshaller" ref="marshaller" />
        <property name="unmarshaller" ref="marshaller" />
        <property name="weatherService" ref="weatherService" />
    </bean>
```

```
    <bean id="marshaller"
        class="org.springframework.oxm.castor.CastorMarshaller">
        <property name="mappingLocation" value="classpath:mapping.xml" />
    </bean>
</beans>
```

Note that Castor requires a mapping configuration file to know how to map objects to and from XML documents. You can create this file in the classpath root and specify it in the mappingLocation property (e.g., mapping.xml). The following Castor mapping file defines the mappings for the GetTemperaturesRequest, GetTemperaturesResponse, and TemperatureInfo classes:

```
<!DOCTYPE mapping PUBLIC "-//EXOLAB/Castor Mapping DTD Version 1.0//EN"
    "http://castor.org/mapping.dtd">

<mapping>
    <class name="com.apress.springrecipes.weather.GetTemperaturesRequest">
        <map-to xml="GetTemperaturesRequest"
            ns-uri="http://springrecipes.apress.com/weather/schemas" />
        <field name="city" type="string">
            <bind-xml name="city" node="element" />
        </field>
        <field name="dates" collection="arraylist" type="string"
            handler="com.apress.springrecipes.weather.DateFieldHandler">
            <bind-xml name="date" node="element" />
        </field>
    </class>

    <class name="com.apress.springrecipes.weather.GetTemperaturesResponse">
        <map-to xml="GetTemperaturesResponse"
            ns-uri="http://springrecipes.apress.com/weather/schemas" />
        <field name="temperatures" collection="arraylist"
            type="com.apress.springrecipes.weather.TemperatureInfo">
            <bind-xml name="TemperatureInfo" node="element" />
        </field>
    </class>

    <class name="com.apress.springrecipes.weather.TemperatureInfo">
        <map-to xml="TemperatureInfo"
            ns-uri="http://springrecipes.apress.com/weather/schemas" />
        <field name="city" type="string">
            <bind-xml name="city" node="attribute" />
        </field>
        <field name="date" type="string"
            handler="com.apress.springrecipes.weather.DateFieldHandler">
            <bind-xml name="date" node="attribute" />
        </field>
        <field name="min" type="double">
```

```
            <bind-xml name="min" node="element" />
        </field>
        <field name="max" type="double">
            <bind-xml name="max" node="element" />
        </field>
        <field name="average" type="double">
            <bind-xml name="average" node="element" />
        </field>
    </class>
</mapping>
```

Remember that for each class mapping, you must specify the namespace URI for the element. Besides, for all the date fields, you have to specify a handler to convert the dates with a particular date format. The handler is implemented as shown following:

```
package com.apress.springrecipes.weather;
...
import org.exolab.castor.mapping.GeneralizedFieldHandler;

public class DateFieldHandler extends GeneralizedFieldHandler {

    private DateFormat format = new SimpleDateFormat("yyyy-MM-dd");

    public Object convertUponGet(Object value) {
        return format.format((Date) value);
    }

    public Object convertUponSet(Object value) {
        try {
            return format.parse((String) value);
        } catch (ParseException e) {
            throw new RuntimeException(e);
        }
    }

    public Class getFieldType() {
        return Date.class;
    }
}
```

Invoking Web Services with XML Marshalling

A Spring-WS client can also marshal/unmarshal the request and response objects to/from XML messages. As an example, I will create a client using Castor as the marshaller so that you can reuse the object models `GetTemperaturesRequest`, `GetTemperaturesResponse`, and `TemperatureInfo`, and also the mapping configuration file, `mapping.xml`, from the service endpoint.

Let's implement the service proxy with XML marshalling. `WebServiceTemplate` provides a `marshalSendAndReceive()` method that accepts a request object as the method argument, which will be marshalled to the request message. This method has to return a response object that will be unmarshalled from the response message.

Note To create a service client using Castor, you have to include `castor-1.1.2.jar` (located in the `lib/castor` directory of the Spring-WS installation) and `xercesImpl-2.8.1.jar` (located in `lib/xerces`) in your classpath.

```
package com.apress.springrecipes.weather;
...
import org.springframework.ws.client.core.support.WebServiceGatewaySupport;

public class WeatherServiceProxy extends WebServiceGatewaySupport
        implements WeatherService {

    public List<TemperatureInfo> getTemperatures(String city, List<Date> dates) {
        GetTemperaturesRequest request = new GetTemperaturesRequest(city, dates);
        GetTemperaturesResponse response = (GetTemperaturesResponse)
            getWebServiceTemplate().marshalSendAndReceive(request);
        return response.getTemperatures();
    }
}
```

When using XML marshalling, `WebServiceTemplate` requires both the `marshaller` and `unmarshaller` properties to be set. You can also set them to `WebServiceGatewaySupport` if you extend this class to have `WebServiceTemplate` auto-created. Usually, you can specify a single marshaller for both properties. For Castor, you declare a `CastorMarshaller` bean as the marshaller.

```
<beans ...>
    <bean id="client"
        class="com.apress.springrecipes.weather.WeatherServiceClient">
        <property name="weatherService" ref="weatherServiceProxy" />
    </bean>

    <bean id="weatherServiceProxy"
        class="com.apress.springrecipes.weather.WeatherServiceProxy">
        <property name="defaultUri"
            value="http://localhost:8080/weather/services" />
        <property name="marshaller" ref="marshaller" />
        <property name="unmarshaller" ref="marshaller" />
    </bean>
```

```
    <bean id="marshaller"
        class="org.springframework.oxm.castor.CastorMarshaller">
        <property name="mappingLocation" value="classpath:mapping.xml" />
    </bean>
</beans>
```

16-9. Creating Service Endpoints with Annotations

Problem

By extending a Spring-WS base endpoint class, your endpoint class will be bound to the Spring-WS class hierarchy, and each endpoint class will only be able to handle one type of web service request.

Solution

Spring-WS supports annotating an arbitrary class as a service endpoint by the @Endpoint annotation, without extending a framework-specific class. You can also group multiple handler methods in an endpoint class so that it can handle multiple types of web service requests.

How It Works

For example, you can annotate your temperature endpoint with the @Endpoint annotation so that it doesn't need to extend a Spring-WS base endpoint class. The signature of the handler methods can also be more flexible.

```
package com.apress.springrecipes.weather;
...
import org.springframework.ws.server.endpoint.annotation.Endpoint;
import org.springframework.ws.server.endpoint.annotation.PayloadRoot;

@Endpoint
public class TemperatureMarshallingEndpoint {

    private static final String namespaceUri =
        "http://springrecipes.apress.com/weather/schemas";

    private WeatherService weatherService;

    public void setWeatherService(WeatherService weatherService) {
        this.weatherService = weatherService;
    }

    @PayloadRoot(
            localPart = "GetTemperaturesRequest",
            namespace = namespaceUri)
    public GetTemperaturesResponse getTemperature(GetTemperaturesRequest request) {
        List<TemperatureInfo> temperatures =
```

```
            weatherService.getTemperatures(request.getCity(), request.getDates());
        return new GetTemperaturesResponse(temperatures);
    }
}
```

Besides the @Endpoint annotation, you have to annotate each handler method with the @PayloadRoot annotation for mapping a service request. In this annotation, you specify the local name and namespace of the payload root element to be handled. Then you just declare a PayloadRootAnnotationMethodEndpointMapping bean, and it will be able to detect the mapping from the @PayloadRoot annotation automatically.

```
<beans ...>
    ...
    <bean class="org.springframework.ws.server.endpoint.mapping.➥
        PayloadRootAnnotationMethodEndpointMapping" />

    <bean id="temperatureEndpoint"
        class="com.apress.springrecipes.weather.TemperatureMarshallingEndpoint">
        <property name="weatherService" ref="weatherService" />
    </bean>

    <bean class="org.springframework.ws.server.endpoint.adapter.➥
        GenericMarshallingMethodEndpointAdapter">
        <property name="marshaller" ref="marshaller" />
        <property name="unmarshaller" ref="marshaller" />
    </bean>

    <bean id="marshaller"
        class="org.springframework.oxm.castor.CastorMarshaller">
        <property name="mappingLocation" value="classpath:mapping.xml" />
    </bean>
</beans>
```

As your endpoint class no longer extends a base endpoint class, it doesn't inherit the capabilities of marshalling and unmarshalling XML messages. You have to configure a GenericMarshallingMethodEndpointAdapter to do so.

16-10. Summary

In this chapter, you have learned how to expose and invoke remote services with Spring's remoting support. Spring builds in support for many remoting technologies, such as RMI, Hessian, Burlap, and HTTP Invoker. Although Spring doesn't come with similar support for web services, there's an external library called XFire that does.

Spring's remoting support is consistent across different remoting technologies. On the server side, Spring allows you to expose an arbitrary bean as a remote service through a service exporter. On the client side, Spring provides various proxy factory beans for you to create a local proxy for a remote service, so that you can use the remote service as if it were a local bean.

You have also learned the benefits of contract-first web services and how to develop them with Spring-WS. The first step is to define the service contract, which consists of two parts: the data contract and the service contract. The data contract is defined with XSD while the service contract is defined with WSDL. You have to define the XSD file by yourself, and then the WSDL file can be generated from it.

Once you have defined the contract for your web service, you can start implementing the service itself according to this contract. Service requests are handled by endpoints, which are similar to controllers in a web application. You can implement an endpoint by using an XML parsing or XML marshalling technology.

According to the contract of a web service, you can create a service client to invoke this service. You can also implement a service client using an XML parsing or an XML marshalling technology.

In the next chapter, you will learn about Spring's support for two key Java EE technologies: EJB and JMS.

CHAPTER 17

Spring Support for EJB and JMS

In this chapter, you will learn about Spring's support for two key Java EE technologies: *EJB (Enterprise JavaBeans)* and *JMS (Java Message Service)*.

EJB is the core technology of the Java EE platform, which allows you to create components that leverage the enterprise services provided by an EJB container. However, before the announcement of EJB 3.0, many developers preferred to develop their applications with POJOs due to the complexity of EJB 2.x. Spring integrates both the EJB and POJO approaches by using its POJO-based IoC container to simplify the implementation of EJB 2.x components.

Although you may not like EJB 2.x very much, it's possible for you to access EJB 2.x components developed by someone else. Accessing EJB 2.x components is a cumbersome task since you need to deal with home interface lookup and handle several exceptions. Spring is able to simplify EJB 2.x access by applying a proxy-based approach. In EJB 3.0, EJB access is simpler, but you can still leverage Spring's JNDI utilities to make it even simpler.

JMS defines a set of standard APIs for message-oriented communication in the Java EE platform. With JMS, different applications can communicate in a loosely coupled way compared to other remoting technologies such as RMI. However, when using the JMS API to send and receive messages, you have to manage the JMS resources yourself and handle the JMS API's exceptions, which results in many lines of JMS-specific code. Spring simplifies JMS's usage with a template-based approach just as it does for JDBC. Moreover, Spring enables beans declared in its IoC container to listen for JMS messages and react to them.

Upon finishing this chapter, you will be able to create and access EJB components with Spring's support. You will also know how to use Spring's JMS support to simplify sending, receiving, and listening for JMS messages.

17-1. Creating EJB 2.x Components with Spring

Problem

In EJB 2.x, each EJB component requires a remote/local interface, a remote/local home interface, and a bean implementation class, in which you must implement all EJB life cycle callback methods even if you don't need them. In that case, you have to provide an empty implementation for them.

Solution

Spring comes with a set of EJB support classes to simplify your implementation of different types of EJB. These classes provide empty implementation for all EJB life cycle callback methods. Your EJB classes can extend these classes to inherit the methods. Table 17-1 shows Spring's EJB support classes for different types of EJB.

Table 17-1. *Spring's EJB Support Classes for Different Types of EJB*

EJB Support Class	EJB Type
`AbstractStatelessSessionBean`	Stateless session bean
`AbstractStatefulSessionBean`	Stateful session bean
`AbstractMessageDrivenBean`	General message-driven bean that may not use JMS
`AbstractJmsMessageDrivenBean`	Message-driven bean that uses JMS

Moreover, the EJB support classes provide access to the Spring IoC container for you to implement your business logic in POJOs and wrap them with EJB components. Since POJOs are easier to develop and test, implementing business logic in POJOs can accelerate your EJB development.

How It Works

Suppose you are going to develop a system for a post office. You are asked to develop a stateless session bean for calculating postage based on the destination country and the weight. The target runtime environment is an application server that supports EJB 2.x only, so you have to develop the EJB component that will work with this version.

Compared to lightweight POJOs, EJB 2.x components are more difficult to build, deploy, and test. A good practice for developing EJB 2.x components is to implement business logic in POJOs and then wrap them with EJB components. First, you define the following business interface for postage calculation:

```
package com.apress.springrecipes.post;

public interface PostageService {

    public double calculatePostage(String country, double weight);
}
```

Then you have to implement this interface. Typically, it should query the database for the postage and perform some calculation. Here, you may hard-code the result for testing purposes.

```
package com.apress.springrecipes.post;

public class PostageServiceImpl implements PostageService {

    public double calculatePostage(String country, double weight) {
        return 1.0;
```

```
    }
}
```

Before you start creating your EJB component, you might like to have a simple EJB container for testing purposes. For simplicity's sake, I have chosen Apache OpenEJB (http://openejb.apache.org/) as my EJB container, which is very easy to install, configure, and deploy. OpenEJB is an open source EJB container designed for the Apache Geronimo server runtime project (http://geronimo.apache.org/).

■ **Note** You can download OpenEJB Standlone Server (e.g., v3.0 beta 1) from the OpenEJB web site and extract it to a directory of your choice to complete the installation.

Creating EJB 2.x Components Without Spring's Support

First, let's create the EJB component without Spring's support. To allow remote access to this EJB component, you expose the following remote interface to clients.

■ **Note** To compile and build your EJB component, you have to include the library that contains standard EJB classes and interfaces in your classpath. For OpenEJB 3.0 beta 1, it's geronimo-ejb_3.0_spec-1.0.jar (located in the lib directory of the OpenEJB installation).

```
package com.apress.springrecipes.post;

import java.rmi.RemoteException;

import javax.ejb.EJBObject;

public interface PostageServiceRemote extends EJBObject {

    public double calculatePostage(String country, double weight)
        throws RemoteException;
}
```

This calculatePostage() method has a signature similar to that in the business interface, except it declares throwing RemoteException.

Also, you need a remote home interface for clients to retrieve a remote reference to this EJB component, whose methods must declare throwing RemoteException and CreateException.

```
package com.apress.springrecipes.post;

import java.rmi.RemoteException;
```

```
import javax.ejb.CreateException;
import javax.ejb.EJBHome;

public interface PostageServiceHome extends EJBHome {

    public PostageServiceRemote create() throws RemoteException, CreateException;
}
```

If you would like to expose this EJB component for local access within an enterprise application, the preceding two interfaces should extend `EJBLocalObject` and `EJBLocalHome` instead, whose methods don't need to throw `RemoteException`. For simplicity's sake, I'm omitting the local and local home interfaces here.

Note that the following EJB implementation class also implements the `PostageService` business interface so that you can delegate requests to the POJO service implementation.

```
package com.apress.springrecipes.post;

import javax.ejb.SessionBean;
import javax.ejb.SessionContext;

public class PostageServiceBean implements SessionBean, PostageService {

    private PostageService postageService;
    private SessionContext sessionContext;

    public void ejbCreate() {
        postageService = new PostageServiceImpl();
    }

    public void ejbActivate() {}
    public void ejbPassivate() {}
    public void ejbRemove() {}

    public void setSessionContext(SessionContext sessionContext) {
        this.sessionContext = sessionContext;
    }

    public double calculatePostage(String country, double weight) {
        return postageService.calculatePostage(country, weight);
    }
}
```

In the `ejbCreate()` life cycle method, you instantiate the POJO service implementation class. It's up to this object to perform the actual postage calculation. The EJB component just delegates requests to this object.

Finally, you require an EJB deployment descriptor for your EJB component. You create the file `ejb-jar.xml` in the `META-INF` directory of your classpath and add the following contents to describe your EJB component:

```
<ejb-jar>
    <enterprise-beans>
        <session>
            <display-name>PostageService</display-name>
            <ejb-name>PostageService</ejb-name>
            <home>com.apress.springrecipes.post.PostageServiceHome</home>
            <remote>com.apress.springrecipes.post.PostageServiceRemote</remote>
            <ejb-class>
                com.apress.springrecipes.post.PostageServiceBean
            </ejb-class>
            <session-type>Stateless</session-type>
            <transaction-type>Bean</transaction-type>
        </session>
    </enterprise-beans>
</ejb-jar>
```

Now your EJB component is finished, and you should pack your interfaces, classes, and deployment descriptors in a JAR file. Then start up your EJB container and deploy this EJB component to it.

■ Note To start the OpenEJB container, you first set the OPENEJB_HOME environment variable to point to your OpenEJB installation directory. Then execute the OpenEJB startup script (located in the `bin` directory) with the parameter `start`. To deploy an EJB component, you also execute the OpenEJB startup script, but this time you pass `deploy` and the location of your EJB JAR file as parameters.

For OpenEJB, the default JNDI name for a remote home interface of an EJB 2.x component is the EJB name with `RemoteHome` as its suffix (`PostageServiceRemoteHome` in this case). If the deployment is successful, you should see the following output:

```
C:\openejb-3.0\bin>openejb deploy c:\PostageService.jar
Application deployed successfully at "c:\PostageService.jar"
App(id=c:\PostageService.jar)
    EjbJar(id=PostageService.jar, path=c:\PostageService.jar)
        Ejb(ejb-name=PostageService, id=PostageService)
            Jndi(name=PostageServiceRemoteHome)
            Jndi(name=PostageServiceLocal)
```

Creating EJB 2.x Components with Spring's Support

As you can see, your EJB implementation class needs to implement all EJB life cycle methods even if you don't need them. Actually, it can extend Spring's EJB support class to get the life cycle methods implemented by default. The support class for stateless session beans is `AbstractStatelessSessionBean`.

Note To use Spring's EJB support for your EJB implementation classes, you have to include `spring.jar` (located in the `dist` directory of the Spring installation) and `commons-logging.jar` (located in `lib/jakarta-commons`) in the classpath of your EJB container. For OpenEJB, you can copy these JAR files to the `lib` directory of the OpenEJB home. If your OpenEJB container is running, you will have to restart it.

```
package com.apress.springrecipes.post;

import javax.ejb.CreateException;

import org.springframework.ejb.support.AbstractStatelessSessionBean;

public class PostageServiceBean extends AbstractStatelessSessionBean
        implements PostageService {

    private PostageService postageService;

    protected void onEjbCreate() throws CreateException {
        postageService = (PostageService)
                getBeanFactory().getBean("postageService");
    }

    public double calculatePostage(String country, double weight) {
        return postageService.calculatePostage(country, weight);
    }
}
```

When you extend the `AbstractStatelessSessionBean` class, your EJB class no longer needs to implement any EJB life cycle methods, but you can still override them if necessary. Note that this class has an `onEjbCreate()` method that you must implement to perform initialization tasks. Here, you just retrieve the `postageService` bean from the Spring IoC container for this EJB component to use. Of course, you must define it in a bean configuration file. This file can have an arbitrary name, but must be located in the classpath. For example, you can create it as `beans-ejb.xml` in the root of the classpath.

```
<beans xmlns="http://www.springframework.org/schema/beans"
    xmlns:xsi="http://www.w3.org/2001/XMLSchema-instance"
    xsi:schemaLocation="http://www.springframework.org/schema/beans
        http://www.springframework.org/schema/beans/spring-beans-2.5.xsd">

    <bean id="postageService"
        class="com.apress.springrecipes.post.PostageServiceImpl" />
</beans>
```

The final step is to tell the EJB support class where your bean configuration is. By default, it looks at the JNDI environment variable `java:comp/env/ejb/BeanFactoryPath` for the file location. So, you add an environment entry to your EJB deployment descriptor for this location.

```
<ejb-jar>
    <enterprise-beans>
        <session>
            <display-name>PostageService</display-name>
            <ejb-name>PostageService</ejb-name>
            <home>com.apress.springrecipes.post.PostageServiceHome</home>
            <remote>com.apress.springrecipes.post.PostageServiceRemote</remote>
            <ejb-class>
                com.apress.springrecipes.post.PostageServiceBean
            </ejb-class>
            <session-type>Stateless</session-type>
            <transaction-type>Bean</transaction-type>
            <env-entry>
                <env-entry-name>ejb/BeanFactoryPath</env-entry-name>
                <env-entry-type>java.lang.String</env-entry-type>
                <env-entry-value>beans-ejb.xml</env-entry-value>
            </env-entry>
        </session>
    </enterprise-beans>
</ejb-jar>
```

The EJB support classes instantiate the Spring IoC container using `BeanFactoryLocator`. The default `BeanFactoryLocator` they use is `ContextJndiBeanFactoryLocator`, which instantiates the IoC container using a bean configuration file specified by the JNDI environment variable `java:comp/env/ejb/BeanFactoryPath`. You can override this variable name by calling the `setBeanFactoryLocatorKey()` method in a constructor or in the `setSessionContext()` method.

Now you can repack your EJB JAR file to include the preceding bean configuration file and redeploy it to your EJB container.

17-2. Accessing EJB 2.x Components in Spring

Problem

In EJB 2.x, you have to perform the following tasks to invoke a method on a remote EJB component. Invoking a method on a local EJB component is very similar, except that you have no need to handle `RemoteException`.

- Initialize the JNDI lookup context, which may throw a `NamingException`.
- Look up the home interface from JNDI, which may throw a `NamingException`.
- Retrieve a remote EJB reference from the home interface, which may throw a `CreateException` or a `RemoteException`.
- Invoke the method on the remote interface, which may throw a `RemoteException`.

As you can see, it requires a lot of coding to invoke a method on an EJB component. The exceptions NamingException, CreateException, and RemoteException are all checked exceptions that you must handle. Moreover, your client is bound to EJB and would require a lot of changes if you ever switched the service implementation from EJB to another technology.

Solution

Spring offers two factory beans, SimpleRemoteStatelessSessionProxyFactoryBean and LocalStatelessSessionProxyFactoryBean, for creating a proxy for a remote/local stateless session bean. They allow EJB clients to invoke an EJB component by the business interface as if it were a simple local object. The proxy handles the JNDI context initialization, home interface lookup, and invocation of local/remote EJB methods behind the scenes.

The EJB proxy also converts exceptions like NamingException, CreateException, and RemoteException into runtime exceptions, so the client code is not required to handle them. For example, if a RemoteException is thrown when accessing a remote EJB component, the EJB proxy will convert it into Spring's runtime exception RemoteAccessException.

How It Works

Suppose there's a front desk subsystem in your post office system that requires postage calculation. First, let's define the FrontDesk interface as follows:

```
package com.apress.springrecipes.post;

public interface FrontDesk {

    public double calculatePostage(String country, double weight);
}
```

As there's an EJB 2.x remote stateless session bean for calculating postage, you only have to access it in your front desk subsystem. You are given the following remote interface and home interface for this EJB component:

```
package com.apress.springrecipes.post;

import java.rmi.RemoteException;

import javax.ejb.EJBObject;

public interface PostageServiceRemote extends EJBObject {

    public double calculatePostage(String country, double weight)
        throws RemoteException;
}
```

```
package com.apress.springrecipes.post;

import java.rmi.RemoteException;
```

```
import javax.ejb.CreateException;
import javax.ejb.EJBHome;

public interface PostageServiceHome extends EJBHome {

    public PostageServiceRemote create() throws RemoteException, CreateException;
}
```

Suppose this EJB component has already been deployed in an EJB container (e.g., an OpenEJB container started up on localhost). The JNDI name of this EJB component is `PostageServiceRemoteHome`.

Note To access an EJB component deployed in an EJB container, you have to include the EJB container's client library in your classpath. For OpenEJB 3.0 beta 1, it's `openejb-client-3.0-beta-1.jar` (located in the `lib` directory of the OpenEJB installation).

Accessing EJB 2.x Components Without Spring's Support

Now you are going to implement the `FrontDesk` interface by accessing the remote stateless session bean for postage calculation.

```
package com.apress.springrecipes.post;

import java.rmi.RemoteException;
import java.util.Hashtable;

import javax.ejb.CreateException;
import javax.naming.Context;
import javax.naming.InitialContext;
import javax.naming.NamingException;

public class FrontDeskImpl implements FrontDesk {

    public double calculatePostage(String country, double weight) {
        try {
            Hashtable env = new Hashtable();
            env.put(Context.INITIAL_CONTEXT_FACTORY,
                    "org.apache.openejb.client.RemoteInitialContextFactory");
            env.put(Context.PROVIDER_URL, "ejbd://localhost:4201");
            Context ctx = new InitialContext(env);

            PostageServiceHome home =
                (PostageServiceHome) ctx.lookup("PostageServiceRemoteHome");
            PostageServiceRemote postageService = home.create();
```

```
            return postageService.calculatePostage(country, weight);
        } catch (NamingException e) {
            ...
        } catch (RemoteException e) {
            ...
        } catch (CreateException e) {
            ...
        }
    }
}
```

In this method, you first initialize the JNDI lookup context by providing a context factory class and a provider URL. These parameters are EJB container–specific, and the preceding values are defaults for OpenEJB. Then you look up the remote home interface from the JNDI context and retrieve a remote EJB reference from it. Up to now, you can invoke the method on the remote EJB component. In the entire process, you also have to handle NamingException, CreateException, and RemoteException. As a result, you need many lines of code to invoke a single method on the EJB component.

Now you should declare this bean in the front desk subsystem's bean configuration file (such as beans-front.xml in the classpath root).

```
<beans xmlns="http://www.springframework.org/schema/beans"
    xmlns:xsi="http://www.w3.org/2001/XMLSchema-instance"
    xsi:schemaLocation="http://www.springframework.org/schema/beans
        http://www.springframework.org/schema/beans/spring-beans-2.5.xsd">

    <bean id="frontDesk"
        class="com.apress.springrecipes.post.FrontDeskImpl" />
</beans>
```

Then you can test the postage calculation function with the following FrontDeskMain class for the front desk subsystem:

```
package com.apress.springrecipes.post;

import org.springframework.context.ApplicationContext;
import org.springframework.context.support.ClassPathXmlApplicationContext;

public class FrontDeskMain {

    public static void main(String[] args) {
        ApplicationContext context =
            new ClassPathXmlApplicationContext("beans-front.xml");

        FrontDesk frontDesk = (FrontDesk) context.getBean("frontDesk");
        double postage = frontDesk.calculatePostage("US", 1.5);
        System.out.println(postage);
    }
}
```

Accessing EJB 2.x Components with Spring's Support

With Spring's support, accessing an EJB component can be significantly simplified. You can access an EJB component by its business interface. A business interface differs from an EJB remote interface in that it doesn't extend EJBObject, and its method declarations don't throw RemoteException, which means that the client doesn't have to handle this type of exception, and it doesn't know that the service is implemented by an EJB component. The business interface for postage calculation is shown following:

```
package com.apress.springrecipes.post;

public interface PostageService {

    public double calculatePostage(String country, double weight);
}
```

Now, in FrontDeskImpl, you can define a setter method for the PostageService business interface to let Spring inject the service implementation so that your FrontDeskImpl will no longer be EJB specific. Later, if you reimplement the PostageService interface with another technology, you won't need to modify a single line of code.

```
package com.apress.springrecipes.post;

public class FrontDeskImpl implements FrontDesk {

    private PostageService postageService;

    public void setPostageService(PostageService postageService) {
        this.postageService = postageService;
    }

    public double calculatePostage(String country, double weight) {
        return postageService.calculatePostage(country, weight);
    }
}
```

Spring offers the proxy factory bean SimpleRemoteStatelessSessionProxyFactoryBean to create a local proxy for a remote stateless session bean.

```
<beans xmlns="http://www.springframework.org/schema/beans"
    xmlns:xsi="http://www.w3.org/2001/XMLSchema-instance"
    xsi:schemaLocation="http://www.springframework.org/schema/beans
        http://www.springframework.org/schema/beans/spring-beans-2.5.xsd">

    <bean id="postageService" class="org.springframework.ejb.access.➥
        SimpleRemoteStatelessSessionProxyFactoryBean">
        <property name="jndiEnvironment">
            <props>
                <prop key="java.naming.factory.initial">
                    org.apache.openejb.client.RemoteInitialContextFactory
```

```
                </prop>
                <prop key="java.naming.provider.url">
                    ejbd://localhost:4201
                </prop>
            </props>
        </property>
        <property name="jndiName" value="PostageServiceRemoteHome" />
        <property name="businessInterface"
            value="com.apress.springrecipes.post.PostageService" />
    </bean>

    <bean id="frontDesk"
        class="com.apress.springrecipes.post.FrontDeskImpl">
        <property name="postageService" ref="postageService" />
    </bean>
</beans>
```

You have to configure the JNDI details for this EJB proxy in the jndiEnvironment and jndiName properties. The most important is to specify the business interface for this proxy to implement. The calls to methods declared in this interface will be translated into remote method calls to the remote EJB component. You can inject this proxy into FrontDeskImpl in the same way as a normal bean.

In Spring 2.x, EJB proxies can also be defined using the <jee:remote-slsb> and <jee:local-slsb> elements in the jee schema. You must add the jee schema definition to the <beans> root element beforehand.

```
<beans xmlns="http://www.springframework.org/schema/beans"
    xmlns:xsi="http://www.w3.org/2001/XMLSchema-instance"
    xmlns:jee="http://www.springframework.org/schema/jee"
    xsi:schemaLocation="http://www.springframework.org/schema/beans
        http://www.springframework.org/schema/beans/spring-beans-2.5.xsd
        http://www.springframework.org/schema/jee
        http://www.springframework.org/schema/jee/spring-jee-2.5.xsd">

    <jee:remote-slsb id="postageService"
        jndi-name="PostageServiceRemoteHome"
        business-interface="com.apress.springrecipes.post.PostageService">
        <jee:environment>
            java.naming.factory.initial=➥
                org.apache.openejb.client.RemoteInitialContextFactory
            java.naming.provider.url=ejbd://localhost:4201
        </jee:environment>
    </jee:remote-slsb>
    ...
</bean>
```

17-3. Accessing EJB 3.0 Components in Spring

Problem

EJB 3.0 offers certain improvements on EJB 2.x. First, the EJB interface is a simple Java interface whose methods don't throw RemoteException, while the implementation class is a simple Java class annotated with EJB annotations. Moreover, the concept of home interface has been eliminated in order to simplify the EJB lookup process. You can look up an EJB reference from JNDI directly in EJB 3.0. However, the JNDI lookup code is still complex, and you also have to handle NamingException.

Solution

By using Spring's JndiObjectFactoryBean, you can easily declare a JNDI object reference in the Spring IoC container. You can use this factory bean to declare a reference to an EJB 3.0 component.

How It Works

Let's create the stateless session bean for calculating postage using EJB 3.0. This EJB component's interface can simply be a business interface.

```
package com.apress.springrecipes.post;

public interface PostageService {

    public double calculatePostage(String country, double weight);
}
```

The bean implementation class can be a simple Java class that implements this interface and is annotated with the EJB annotations. A remote stateless session bean requires the @Stateless and @Remote annotations. In the @Remote annotation, you have to specify the remote interface for this EJB component.

```
package com.apress.springrecipes.post;

import javax.ejb.Remote;
import javax.ejb.Stateless;

@Stateless
@Remote( { PostageService.class })
public class PostageServiceBean implements PostageService {

    public double calculatePostage(String country, double weight) {
        return 1.0;
    }
}
```

Now your EJB component is finished, and you should pack your EJB interface and implementation class in a JAR file. Then start up your EJB container and deploy this EJB component to it. If you have chosen OpenEJB as your EJB container, the default JNDI name for a remote EJB 3.0 component is the EJB class name with `Remote` as its suffix (`PostageServiceBeanRemote` in this case).

Accessing EJB 3.0 Components Without Spring's Support

Accessing EJB 3.0 components is simpler than EJB 2.x. You can look up an EJB reference from JNDI directly without looking up its home interface first so that you don't need to handle `CreateException`. Moreover, the EJB interface is a business interface that doesn't throw a `RemoteException`.

```
package com.apress.springrecipes.post;

import java.util.Hashtable;

import javax.naming.Context;
import javax.naming.InitialContext;
import javax.naming.NamingException;

public class FrontDeskImpl implements FrontDesk {

    public double calculatePostage(String country, double weight) {
        try {
            Hashtable env = new Hashtable();
            env.put(Context.INITIAL_CONTEXT_FACTORY,
                    "org.apache.openejb.client.RemoteInitialContextFactory");
            env.put(Context.PROVIDER_URL, "ejbd://localhost:4201");
            Context ctx = new InitialContext(env);

            PostageService postageService =
                (PostageService) ctx.lookup("PostageServiceBeanRemote");

            return postageService.calculatePostage(country, weight);
        } catch (NamingException e) {
            ...
        }
    }
}
```

Accessing EJB 3.0 Components with Spring's Support

Although accessing EJB 3.0 components is simpler than EJB 2.x, the JNDI lookup code is still too complex, and you have to handle `NamingException`. With Spring's support, your `FrontDeskImpl` class can define a setter method for this EJB component's business interface for Spring to inject the EJB reference that is looked up from JNDI.

```
package com.apress.springrecipes.post;

public class FrontDeskImpl implements FrontDesk {

    private PostageService postageService;

    public void setPostageService(PostageService postageService) {
        this.postageService = postageService;
    }

    public double calculatePostage(String country, double weight) {
        return postageService.calculatePostage(country, weight);
    }
}
```

Spring offers the factory bean `JndiObjectFactoryBean` to declare a JNDI object reference in its IoC container. You declare this bean in the front desk system's bean configuration file.

```
<beans xmlns="http://www.springframework.org/schema/beans"
    xmlns:xsi="http://www.w3.org/2001/XMLSchema-instance"
    xsi:schemaLocation="http://www.springframework.org/schema/beans
        http://www.springframework.org/schema/beans/spring-beans-2.5.xsd">

    <bean id="postageService"
        class="org.springframework.jndi.JndiObjectFactoryBean">
        <property name="jndiEnvironment">
            <props>
                <prop key="java.naming.factory.initial">
                    org.apache.openejb.client.RemoteInitialContextFactory
                </prop>
                <prop key="java.naming.provider.url">
                    ejbd://localhost:4201
                </prop>
            </props>
        </property>
        <property name="jndiName" value="PostageServiceBeanRemote" />
    </bean>

    <bean id="frontDesk"
        class="com.apress.springrecipes.post.FrontDeskImpl">
        <property name="postageService" ref="postageService" />
    </bean>
</beans>
```

You can configure the JNDI details for this factory bean in the `jndiEnvironment` and `jndiName` properties. Then you can inject this proxy into `FrontDeskImpl` in the same way as a normal bean.

In Spring 2.x, JNDI objects can also be defined using the `<jee:jndi-lookup>` element in the `jee` schema.

```
<beans xmlns="http://www.springframework.org/schema/beans"
    xmlns:xsi="http://www.w3.org/2001/XMLSchema-instance"
    xmlns:jee="http://www.springframework.org/schema/jee"
    xsi:schemaLocation="http://www.springframework.org/schema/beans
        http://www.springframework.org/schema/beans/spring-beans-2.5.xsd
        http://www.springframework.org/schema/jee
        http://www.springframework.org/schema/jee/spring-jee-2.5.xsd">

    <jee:jndi-lookup id="postageService"
        jndi-name="PostageServiceBeanRemote">
        <jee:environment>
            java.naming.factory.initial=➥
                org.apache.openejb.client.RemoteInitialContextFactory
            java.naming.provider.url=ejbd://localhost:4201
        </jee:environment>
    </jee:jndi-lookup>
    ...
</beans>
```

17-4. Sending and Receiving JMS Messages with Spring

Problem

In the Java EE platform, applications often need to communicate using JMS. However, to send or receive a JMS message, you have to perform the following tasks:

- Create a JMS connection factory on a message broker.
- Create a JMS destination, which can be either a queue or a topic.
- Open a JMS connection from the connection factory.
- Obtain a JMS session from the connection.
- Send/receive the JMS message with a message producer/consumer.
- Handle `JMSException`, which is a checked exception that must be handled.
- Close the JMS session and connection.

As you can see, it requires a lot of coding to send or receive a simple JMS message. In fact, most of these tasks are boilerplate and require you to repeat them each time when dealing with JMS.

Solution

Spring offers a template-based solution for simplifying your JMS code. With a JMS template, you can send and receive JMS messages with much less code. The template handles the boilerplate tasks for you and also converts the JMS API's `JMSException` hierarchy into Spring's runtime exception `org.springframework.jms.JmsException` hierarchy.

In JMS 1.0.2, topics and queues are known as domains and are handled with a totally different API. However, JMS 1.1 provides a domain-independent API, treating topic and queue as alternative message destinations. To address different JMS APIs, Spring provides two JMS template classes, `JmsTemplate` and `JmsTemplate102`, for these two versions of JMS. In this chapter, I will focus on JMS 1.1, which is available for Java EE 1.4 and higher versions.

How It Works

Suppose you are developing a post office system that includes two subsystems: the front desk subsystem and the back office subsystem. When the front desk receives mail from a citizen, it passes the mail to the back office for categorizing and delivering. At the same time, the front desk subsystem sends a JMS message to the back office subsystem notifying it of new mail. The mail information is represented by the following class:

```
package com.apress.springrecipes.post;

public class Mail {

    private String mailId;
    private String country;
    private double weight;

    // Constructors, Getters and Setters
    ...
}
```

The methods for sending and receiving mail information are defined in the `FrontDesk` and `BackOffice` interfaces as follows:

```
package com.apress.springrecipes.post;

public interface FrontDesk {

    public void sendMail(Mail mail);
}
```

```
package com.apress.springrecipes.post;

public interface BackOffice {

    public Mail receiveMail();
}
```

Before you can send and receive JMS messages, you need to install a JMS message broker. For simplicity's sake, I have chosen Apache ActiveMQ (`http://activemq.apache.org/`) as my message broker, which is very easy to install and configure. ActiveMQ is an open source message broker that fully supports JMS 1.1.

Note You can download ActiveMQ (e.g., v5.0.0) from the ActiveMQ web site and extract it to a directory of your choice to complete the installation.

Sending and Receiving Messages Without Spring's Support

First, let's see how to send and receive JMS messages without Spring's support. The following `FrontDeskImpl` class sends JMS messages with the JMS API directly.

Note To send/receive JMS messages to/from a JMS message broker, you have to include the library of the message broker in your classpath. For ActiveMQ 5.0.0, it's `activemq-all-5.0.0.jar` (located in the root of the ActiveMQ installation).

```
package com.apress.springrecipes.post;

import javax.jms.Connection;
import javax.jms.ConnectionFactory;
import javax.jms.Destination;
import javax.jms.JMSException;
import javax.jms.MapMessage;
import javax.jms.MessageProducer;
import javax.jms.Session;

import org.apache.activemq.ActiveMQConnectionFactory;
import org.apache.activemq.command.ActiveMQQueue;

public class FrontDeskImpl implements FrontDesk {

    public void sendMail(Mail mail) {
        ConnectionFactory cf =
            new ActiveMQConnectionFactory("tcp://localhost:61616");
        Destination destination = new ActiveMQQueue("mail.queue");

        Connection conn = null;
        try {
            conn = cf.createConnection();
            Session session =
                conn.createSession(false, Session.AUTO_ACKNOWLEDGE);
            MessageProducer producer = session.createProducer(destination);

            MapMessage message = session.createMapMessage();
            message.setString("mailId", mail.getMailId());
            message.setString("country", mail.getCountry());
```

```
            message.setDouble("weight", mail.getWeight());
            producer.send(message);

            session.close();
        } catch (JMSException e) {
            throw new RuntimeException(e);
        } finally {
            if (conn != null) {
                try {
                    conn.close();
                } catch (JMSException e) {
                }
            }
        }
    }
}
```

In the preceding `sendMail()` method, you first create JMS-specific `ConnectionFactory` and `Destination` objects with the classes provided by ActiveMQ. The message broker URL is the default for ActiveMQ if you run it on localhost. In JMS, there are two types of destination: queue and topic. *Queue* is for the point-to-point communication model, while *topic* is for the publish-subscribe communication model. As you are sending JMS messages point to point from front desk to back office, you should use a message queue. You can easily create a topic as a destination using the `ActiveMQTopic` class.

Next, you have to create a connection, session, and message producer before you can send your message. There are several types of messages defined in the JMS API, including `TextMessage`, `MapMessage`, `BytesMessage`, `ObjectMessage`, and `StreamMessage`. `MapMessage` contains message content in key/value pairs like a map. In the meantime, you have to handle `JMSException`, which may be thrown by the JMS API. Finally, you must remember to close the session and connection to release system resources. Every time a JMS connection is closed, all its opened sessions will be closed automatically. So, you only have to ensure that the JMS connection is closed properly in the `finally` block.

On the other hand, the following `BackOfficeImpl` class receives JMS messages with the JMS API directly:

```
package com.apress.springrecipes.post;

import javax.jms.Connection;
import javax.jms.ConnectionFactory;
import javax.jms.Destination;
import javax.jms.JMSException;
import javax.jms.MapMessage;
import javax.jms.MessageConsumer;
import javax.jms.Session;

import org.apache.activemq.ActiveMQConnectionFactory;
import org.apache.activemq.command.ActiveMQQueue;
```

```
public class BackOfficeImpl implements BackOffice {

    public Mail receiveMail() {
        ConnectionFactory cf =
            new ActiveMQConnectionFactory("tcp://localhost:61616");
        Destination destination = new ActiveMQQueue("mail.queue");

        Connection conn = null;
        try {
            conn = cf.createConnection();
            Session session =
                conn.createSession(false, Session.AUTO_ACKNOWLEDGE);
            MessageConsumer consumer = session.createConsumer(destination);

            conn.start();
            MapMessage message = (MapMessage) consumer.receive();
            Mail mail = new Mail();
            mail.setMailId(message.getString("mailId"));
            mail.setCountry(message.getString("country"));
            mail.setWeight(message.getDouble("weight"));

            session.close();
            return mail;
        } catch (JMSException e) {
            throw new RuntimeException(e);
        } finally {
            if (conn != null) {
                try {
                    conn.close();
                } catch (JMSException e) {
                }
            }
        }
    }
}
```

Most of the code in this method is similar to that for sending JMS messages, except that you create a message consumer and receive a JMS message from it.

Finally, you create two bean configuration files—one for the front desk subsystem (e.g., `beans-front.xml`), and one for the back office subsystem (e.g., `beans-back.xml`)—in the root of the classpath.

```
<beans xmlns="http://www.springframework.org/schema/beans"
    xmlns:xsi="http://www.w3.org/2001/XMLSchema-instance"
    xsi:schemaLocation="http://www.springframework.org/schema/beans
        http://www.springframework.org/schema/beans/spring-beans-2.5.xsd">
```

```
    <bean id="frontDesk"
        class="com.apress.springrecipes.post.FrontDeskImpl" />
</beans>

<beans xmlns="http://www.springframework.org/schema/beans"
    xmlns:xsi="http://www.w3.org/2001/XMLSchema-instance"
    xsi:schemaLocation="http://www.springframework.org/schema/beans
        http://www.springframework.org/schema/beans/spring-beans-2.5.xsd">

    <bean id="backOffice"
        class="com.apress.springrecipes.post.BackOfficeImpl" />
</beans>
```

Now your front desk and back office subsystems are ready to send and receive JMS messages. You must start up your message broker before sending and receiving messages with the following main classes.

■Note To start ActiveMQ, you just execute one of the ActiveMQ startup scripts (located in the `bin` directory) for your operating system.

```
package com.apress.springrecipes.post;

import org.springframework.context.ApplicationContext;
import org.springframework.context.support.ClassPathXmlApplicationContext;

public class FrontDeskMain {

    public static void main(String[] args) {
        ApplicationContext context =
            new ClassPathXmlApplicationContext("beans-front.xml");

        FrontDesk frontDesk = (FrontDesk) context.getBean("frontDesk");
        frontDesk.sendMail(new Mail("1234", "US", 1.5));
    }
}

package com.apress.springrecipes.post;

import org.springframework.context.ApplicationContext;
import org.springframework.context.support.ClassPathXmlApplicationContext;

public class BackOfficeMain {
```

```
    public static void main(String[] args) {
        ApplicationContext context =
            new ClassPathXmlApplicationContext("beans-back.xml");

        BackOffice backOffice = (BackOffice) context.getBean("backOffice");
        Mail mail = backOffice.receiveMail();
        System.out.println("Mail #" + mail.getMailId() + " received");
    }
}
```

Sending and Receiving Messages with Spring's JMS Template

Spring offers a JMS template that can significantly simplify your JMS code. To send a JMS message with this template, you simply call the `send()` method and provide a message destination, as well as a `MessageCreator` object, which creates the JMS message you are going to send. The `MessageCreator` object is usually implemented as an anonymous inner class.

```
package com.apress.springrecipes.post;

import javax.jms.Destination;
import javax.jms.JMSException;
import javax.jms.MapMessage;
import javax.jms.Message;
import javax.jms.Session;

import org.springframework.jms.core.JmsTemplate;
import org.springframework.jms.core.MessageCreator;

public class FrontDeskImpl implements FrontDesk {

    private JmsTemplate jmsTemplate;
    private Destination destination;

    public void setJmsTemplate(JmsTemplate jmsTemplate) {
        this.jmsTemplate = jmsTemplate;
    }

    public void setDestination(Destination destination) {
        this.destination = destination;
    }

    public void sendMail(final Mail mail) {
        jmsTemplate.send(destination, new MessageCreator() {
            public Message createMessage(Session session) throws JMSException {
                MapMessage message = session.createMapMessage();
                message.setString("mailId", mail.getMailId());
```

```
                message.setString("country", mail.getCountry());
                message.setDouble("weight", mail.getWeight());
                return message;
            }
        });
    }
}
```

Note that an inner class can only access arguments or variables of the enclosing method that are declared as final. The `MessageCreator` interface declares only a `createMessage()` method for you to implement. In this method, you create and return your JMS message with the JMS session provided.

A JMS template helps you to obtain and release the JMS connection and session, and sends the JMS message created by your `MessageCreator` object. Moreover, it converts the JMS API's `JMSException` hierarchy into Spring's JMS runtime exception hierarchy, whose base exception class is `org.springframework.jms.JmsException`.

In the front desk subsystem's bean configuration file, you declare a JMS template that refers to the JMS connection factory for opening connections. Then you inject this template as well as the message destination into your front desk bean.

```
<beans ...>
    <bean id="connectionFactory"
        class="org.apache.activemq.ActiveMQConnectionFactory">
        <property name="brokerURL" value="tcp://localhost:61616" />
    </bean>

    <bean id="mailDestination"
        class="org.apache.activemq.command.ActiveMQQueue">
        <constructor-arg value="mail.queue" />
    </bean>

    <bean id="jmsTemplate"
        class="org.springframework.jms.core.JmsTemplate">
        <property name="connectionFactory" ref="connectionFactory" />
    </bean>

    <bean id="frontDesk"
        class="com.apress.springrecipes.post.FrontDeskImpl">
        <property name="destination" ref="mailDestination" />
        <property name="jmsTemplate" ref="jmsTemplate" />
    </bean>
</beans>
```

To receive a JMS message with a JMS template, you call the `receive()` method by providing a message destination. This method returns a JMS message whose type is the base JMS message type `java.jms.Message`, so you have to cast it into proper type before further processing.

```
package com.apress.springrecipes.post;

import javax.jms.Destination;
import javax.jms.JMSException;
import javax.jms.MapMessage;

import org.springframework.jms.core.JmsTemplate;
import org.springframework.jms.support.JmsUtils;

public class BackOfficeImpl implements BackOffice {

    private JmsTemplate jmsTemplate;
    private Destination destination;

    public void setJmsTemplate(JmsTemplate jmsTemplate) {
        this.jmsTemplate = jmsTemplate;
    }

    public void setDestination(Destination destination) {
        this.destination = destination;
    }

    public Mail receiveMail() {
        MapMessage message = (MapMessage) jmsTemplate.receive(destination);
        try {
            if (message == null) {
                return null;
            }
            Mail mail = new Mail();
            mail.setMailId(message.getString("mailId"));
            mail.setCountry(message.getString("country"));
            mail.setWeight(message.getDouble("weight"));
            return mail;
        } catch (JMSException e) {
            throw JmsUtils.convertJmsAccessException(e);
        }
    }
}
```

However, when extracting information from the received `MapMessage` object, you still have to handle the JMS API's `JMSException`. To make the type of the exception thrown by this method consistent, you have to make a call to `JmsUtils.convertJmsAccessException()` to convert the JMS API's `JMSException` into Spring's `JmsException`.

In the back office subsystem's bean configuration file, you declare a JMS template and inject it together with the message destination into your back office bean.

```
<beans ...>
    <bean id="connectionFactory"
        class="org.apache.activemq.ActiveMQConnectionFactory">
        <property name="brokerURL" value="tcp://localhost:61616" />
    </bean>

    <bean id="mailDestination"
        class="org.apache.activemq.command.ActiveMQQueue">
        <constructor-arg value="mail.queue" />
    </bean>

    <bean id="jmsTemplate"
        class="org.springframework.jms.core.JmsTemplate">
        <property name="connectionFactory" ref="connectionFactory" />
        <property name="receiveTimeout" value="10000" />
    </bean>

    <bean id="backOffice"
        class="com.apress.springrecipes.post.BackOfficeImpl">
        <property name="destination" ref="mailDestination" />
        <property name="jmsTemplate" ref="jmsTemplate" />
    </bean>
</beans>
```

Pay special attention to the `receiveTimout` property of the JMS template. By default, this template will wait for a JMS message at the destination forever, and the calling thread is blocked in the meantime. To avoid waiting for a message so long, you should specify a receive timeout for this template. If there's no message available at the destination in the duration, the JMS template's `receive()` method will return a null message.

Sending and Receiving Messages to and from a Default Destination

Instead of specifying a message destination for each JMS template's `send()` and `receive()` method call, you can specify a default destination for a JMS template. Then you will no longer need to inject it into your message sender and receiver beans again.

```
<beans ...>
    ...
    <bean id="jmsTemplate"
        class="org.springframework.jms.core.JmsTemplate">
        ...
        <property name="defaultDestination" ref="mailDestination" />
    </bean>

    <bean id="frontDesk"
        class="com.apress.springrecipes.post.FrontDeskImpl">
        <property name="jmsTemplate" ref="jmsTemplate" />
    </bean>
</beans>
```

```
<beans ...>
    ...
    <bean id="jmsTemplate"
        class="org.springframework.jms.core.JmsTemplate">
        ...
        <property name="defaultDestination" ref="mailDestination" />
    </bean>

    <bean id="backOffice"
        class="com.apress.springrecipes.post.BackOfficeImpl">
        <property name="jmsTemplate" ref="jmsTemplate" />
    </bean>
</beans>
```

With the default destination specified for a JMS template, you can delete the setter method for a message destination from your message sender and receiver classes. Now when you call the send() and receive() methods, you no longer need to specify a message destination.

```
package com.apress.springrecipes.post;
...
import org.springframework.jms.core.MessageCreator;

public class FrontDeskImpl implements FrontDesk {
    ...
    public void sendMail(final Mail mail) {
        jmsTemplate.send(new MessageCreator() {
            ...
        });
    }
}
```

```
package com.apress.springrecipes.post;
...
import javax.jms.MapMessage;

public class BackOfficeImpl implements BackOffice {
    ...
    public Mail receiveMail() {
        MapMessage message = (MapMessage) jmsTemplate.receive();
        ...
    }
}
```

Instead of specifying a Destination object for a JMS template, you can specify the destination name to let the JMS template resolve it for you, so you can delete the Destination object's declaration from both bean configuration files.

```
<bean id="jmsTemplate"
    class="org.springframework.jms.core.JmsTemplate">
    ...
    <property name="defaultDestinationName" value="mail.queue" />
</bean>
```

Extending the JmsGatewaySupport Class

Just like your DAO class can extend `JdbcDaoSupport` to retrieve a JDBC template, your JMS sender and receiver classes can also extend `JmsGatewaySupport` to retrieve a JMS template. You have the following two options for classes that extend `JmsGatewaySupport` to create their JMS template:

- Inject a JMS connection factory for `JmsGatewaySupport` to create a JMS template on it automatically. However, if you do it this way, you won't be able to configure the details of the JMS template.
- Inject a JMS template that is created and configured by you.

Of them, the second approach is more suitable if you have to configure the JMS template yourself. You can delete the private field `jmsTemplate` and its setter method from both your sender and receiver classes. When you need access to the JMS template, you just make a call to `getJmsTemplate()`.

```
package com.apress.springrecipes.post;

import org.springframework.jms.core.support.JmsGatewaySupport;

public class FrontDeskImpl extends JmsGatewaySupport implements FrontDesk {
    ...
    public void sendMail(final Mail mail) {
        getJmsTemplate().send(new MessageCreator() {
            ...
        });
    }
}
```

```
package com.apress.springrecipes.post;

import org.springframework.jms.core.support.JmsGatewaySupport;

public class BackOfficeImpl extends JmsGatewaySupport implements BackOffice {
    ...
    public Mail receiveMail() {
        MapMessage message = (MapMessage) getJmsTemplate().receive();
        ...
    }
}
```

Converting JMS Messages

So far, you have been handling the raw JMS messages by yourself. Actually, Spring's JMS template can help you convert JMS messages to and from Java objects using a message converter. By default, the JMS template uses `SimpleMessageConverter` for converting `TextMessage` to/from a string, `BytesMessage` to/from a byte array, `MapMessage` to/from a map, and `ObjectMessage` to/from a serializable object. For your front desk and back office classes, you can send and receive a map using the `convertAndSend()` and `receiveAndConvert()` methods, and the map will be converted to/from `MapMessage`.

```
package com.apress.springrecipes.post;
...
public class FrontDeskImpl extends JmsGatewaySupport implements FrontDesk {
    ...
    public void sendMail(Mail mail) {
        Map<String, Object> map = new HashMap<String, Object>();
        map.put("mailId", mail.getMailId());
        map.put("country", mail.getCountry());
        map.put("weight", mail.getWeight());
        getJmsTemplate().convertAndSend(map);
    }
}

package com.apress.springrecipes.post;
...
public class BackOfficeImpl extends JmsGatewaySupport implements BackOffice {
    ...
    public Mail receiveMail() {
        Map map = (Map) getJmsTemplate().receiveAndConvert();
        Mail mail = new Mail();
        mail.setMailId((String) map.get("mailId"));
        mail.setCountry((String) map.get("country"));
        mail.setWeight((Double) map.get("weight"));
        return mail;
    }
}
```

You can also create a custom message converter by implementing the `MessageConverter` interface for converting mail objects.

```
package com.apress.springrecipes.post;

import javax.jms.JMSException;
import javax.jms.MapMessage;
import javax.jms.Message;
import javax.jms.Session;

import org.springframework.jms.support.converter.MessageConversionException;
import org.springframework.jms.support.converter.MessageConverter;
```

```
public class MailMessageConverter implements MessageConverter {

    public Object fromMessage(Message message) throws JMSException,
            MessageConversionException {
        MapMessage mapMessage = (MapMessage) message;
        Mail mail = new Mail();
        mail.setMailId(mapMessage.getString("mailId"));
        mail.setCountry(mapMessage.getString("country"));
        mail.setWeight(mapMessage.getDouble("weight"));
        return mail;
    }

    public Message toMessage(Object object, Session session) throws JMSException,
            MessageConversionException {
        Mail mail = (Mail) object;
        MapMessage message = session.createMapMessage();
        message.setString("mailId", mail.getMailId());
        message.setString("country", mail.getCountry());
        message.setDouble("weight", mail.getWeight());
        return message;
    }
}
```

To apply this message converter, you have to declare it in both bean configuration files and inject it into the JMS template.

```
<beans ...>
    ...
    <bean id="mailMessageConverter"
        class="com.apress.springrecipes.post.MailMessageConverter" />

    <bean id="jmsTemplate"
        class="org.springframework.jms.core.JmsTemplate">
        ...
        <property name="messageConverter" ref="mailMessageConverter" />
    </bean>
</beans>
```

When you set a message converter for a JMS template explicitly, it will override the default `SimpleMessageConverter`. Now you can call the JMS template's `convertAndSend()` and `receiveAndConvert()` methods to send and receive mail objects.

```
package com.apress.springrecipes.post;
...
public class FrontDeskImpl extends JmsGatewaySupport implements FrontDesk {
    ...
    public void sendMail(Mail mail) {
        getJmsTemplate().convertAndSend(mail);
```

```
    }
}

package com.apress.springrecipes.post;
...
public class BackOfficeImpl extends JmsGatewaySupport implements BackOffice {
    ...
    public Mail receiveMail() {
        return (Mail) getJmsTemplate().receiveAndConvert();
    }
}
```

Managing JMS Transactions

When producing or consuming multiple JMS messages in a single method, if an error occurs in the middle, the JMS messages produced or consumed at the destination may be left in an inconsistent state. You have to surround the method with a transaction to avoid this problem.

In Spring, JMS transaction management is consistent with other data access strategies. For example, you can annotate the methods that require transaction management with the `@Transactional` annotation.

```
package com.apress.springrecipes.post;

import org.springframework.jms.core.support.JmsGatewaySupport;
import org.springframework.transaction.annotation.Transactional;

public class FrontDeskImpl extends JmsGatewaySupport implements FrontDesk {

    @Transactional
    public void sendMail(Mail mail) {
        ...
    }
}

package com.apress.springrecipes.post;

import org.springframework.jms.core.support.JmsGatewaySupport;
import org.springframework.transaction.annotation.Transactional;

public class BackOfficeImpl extends JmsGatewaySupport implements BackOffice {

    @Transactional
    public Mail receiveMail() {
        ...
    }
}
```

Then, in both bean configuration files, you add the `<tx:annotation-driven />` element and declare a transaction manager. The corresponding transaction manager for local JMS transactions is `JmsTransactionManager`, which requires a reference to the JMS connection factory.

```
<beans xmlns="http://www.springframework.org/schema/beans"
    xmlns:xsi="http://www.w3.org/2001/XMLSchema-instance"
    xmlns:tx="http://www.springframework.org/schema/tx"
    xsi:schemaLocation="http://www.springframework.org/schema/beans
        http://www.springframework.org/schema/beans/spring-beans-2.5.xsd
        http://www.springframework.org/schema/tx
        http://www.springframework.org/schema/tx/spring-tx-2.5.xsd">
    ...
    <tx:annotation-driven />

    <bean id="transactionManager"
        class="org.springframework.jms.connection.JmsTransactionManager">
        <property name="connectionFactory">
            <ref bean="connectionFactory" />
        </property>
    </bean>
</beans>
```

If you require transaction management across multiple resources, such as a data source and an ORM resource factory, or if you need distributed transaction management, you have to configure JTA transaction in your application server and use `JtaTransactionManager`. Of course, your JMS connection factory must be XA compliant (i.e., supporting distributed transactions).

17-5. Creating Message-Driven POJOs in Spring

Problem

When you call the `receive()` method on a JMS message consumer to receive a message, the calling thread is blocked until a message is available. During the duration, the thread can do nothing but wait. This type of message reception is called *synchronous reception,* as your application must wait for the message to arrive before it can finish its work.

Starting with EJB 2.0, a new kind of EJB component called an *MDB (message-driven bean)* has been introduced for *asynchronous reception* of JMS messages. An EJB container can listen for JMS messages at a message destination and trigger MDBs to react to these messages so that your application no longer has to wait for messages. In EJB 2.x, an MDB must implement both the `javax.ejb.MessageDrivenBean` and `javax.jms.MessageListener` interfaces and override all EJB life cycle methods. In EJB 3.0, an MDB can be a POJO that implements the `MessageListener` interface and is annotated with the `@MessageDriven` annotation.

Although MDBs are able to listen for JMS messages, they must be deployed in an EJB container to run. You may prefer to add the same capability to POJOs so that they can listen for JMS messages without an EJB container.

Solution

Spring allows beans declared in its IoC container to listen for JMS messages in the same way as MDBs. As Spring adds message-listening capabilities to POJOs, they are called *message-driven POJOs (MDPs).*

How It Works

Suppose you would like to add an electronic board to the post office's back office to display mail information in real time as it arrives from the front desk. As the front desk sends a JMS message along with mail, the back office subsystem can listen for these messages and display them on the electronic board. For better system performance, you should apply the asynchronous JMS reception approach to avoid blocking the thread that receives these JMS messages.

Listening for JMS Messages with Message Listeners

First, you create a message listener to listen for JMS messages. For example, the following `MailListener` listens for JMS messages that contain mail information:

```
package com.apress.springrecipes.post;

import javax.jms.JMSException;
import javax.jms.MapMessage;
import javax.jms.Message;
import javax.jms.MessageListener;

import org.springframework.jms.support.JmsUtils;

public class MailListener implements MessageListener {

    public void onMessage(Message message) {
        MapMessage mapMessage = (MapMessage) message;
        try {
            Mail mail = new Mail();
            mail.setMailId(mapMessage.getString("mailId"));
            mail.setCountry(mapMessage.getString("country"));
            mail.setWeight(mapMessage.getDouble("weight"));
            displayMail(mail);
        } catch (JMSException e) {
            throw JmsUtils.convertJmsAccessException(e);
        }
    }

    private void displayMail(Mail mail) {
        System.out.println("Mail #" + mail.getMailId() + " received");
    }
}
```

A message listener must implement the `javax.jms.MessageListener` interface. When a JMS message arrives, the `onMessage()` method will be called with the message as the method argument. In this sample, you simply display the mail information to the console. Note that when extracting message information from a MapMessage object, you need to handle the JMS API's JMSException. You can make a call to JmsUtils.convertJmsAccessException() to convert it into Spring's runtime exception JmsException.

Next, you have to configure this listener in the back office's bean configuration file. Declaring this listener alone is not enough to listen for JMS messages. You need a message listener container to monitor JMS messages at a message destination and trigger your message listener on message arrival.

```
<beans xmlns="http://www.springframework.org/schema/beans"
    xmlns:xsi="http://www.w3.org/2001/XMLSchema-instance"
    xsi:schemaLocation="http://www.springframework.org/schema/beans
        http://www.springframework.org/schema/beans/spring-beans-2.5.xsd">

    <bean id="connectionFactory"
        class="org.apache.activemq.ActiveMQConnectionFactory">
        <property name="brokerURL" value="tcp://localhost:61616" />
    </bean>

    <bean id="mailListener"
        class="com.apress.springrecipes.post.MailListener" />

    <bean
        class="org.springframework.jms.listener.SimpleMessageListenerContainer">
        <property name="connectionFactory" ref="connectionFactory" />
        <property name="destinationName" value="mail.queue" />
        <property name="messageListener" ref="mailListener" />
    </bean>
</beans>
```

Spring provides several types of message listener containers for you to choose from, of which SimpleMessageListenerContainer and DefaultMessageListenerContainer are the most commonly used. SimpleMessageListenerContainer is the simplest one that doesn't support transaction. If you have a transaction requirement in receiving messages, you have to use DefaultMessageListenerContainer.

Now you can start your message listener with the following main class, which starts the Spring IoC container only:

```
package com.apress.springrecipes.post;

import org.springframework.context.support.ClassPathXmlApplicationContext;

public class BackOfficeMain {

    public static void main(String[] args) {
        new ClassPathXmlApplicationContext("beans-back.xml");
    }
}
```

Listening for JMS Messages with POJOs

While a listener that implements the `MessageListener` interface can listen for messages, so can an arbitrary bean declared in the Spring IoC container. For a method of this bean to be triggered on message arrival, it must accept one of the following types as its sole method argument:

Raw JMS message type: For `TextMessage`, `MapMessage`, `BytesMessage`, and `ObjectMessage`

String: For `TextMessage` only

Map: For `MapMessage` only

byte[]: For `BytesMessage` only

Serializable: For `ObjectMessage` only

For example, to listen for `MapMessage`, you declare a method that accepts a map as its argument. This listener no longer needs to implement the `MessageListener` interface.

```
package com.apress.springrecipes.post;
...
public class MailListener {

    public void displayMail(Map map) {
        Mail mail = new Mail();
        mail.setMailId((String) map.get("mailId"));
        mail.setCountry((String) map.get("country"));
        mail.setWeight((Double) map.get("weight"));
        System.out.println("Mail #" + mail.getMailId() + " received");
    }
}
```

A POJO is registered to a listener container through a `MessageListenerAdapter` instance. This adapter implements the `MessageListener` interface and will delegate message handling to the target bean's method via reflection.

```
<beans ...>
    ...
    <bean id="mailListener"
        class="com.apress.springrecipes.post.MailListener" />

    <bean id="mailListenerAdapter"
        class="org.springframework.jms.listener.adapter.MessageListenerAdapter">
        <property name="delegate" ref="mailListener" />
        <property name="defaultListenerMethod" value="displayMail" />
    </bean>

    <bean
        class="org.springframework.jms.listener.SimpleMessageListenerContainer">
        <property name="connectionFactory" ref="connectionFactory" />
        <property name="destinationName" value="mail.queue" />
```

```
        <property name="messageListener" ref="mailListenerAdapter" />
    </bean>
</beans>
```

You have to set the delegate property of MessageListenerAdapter to your target bean. By default, this adapter will call the method whose name is handleMessage on that bean. If you would like to call another method, you can specify it in the defaultListenerMethod property. Finally, notice that you have to register the listener adapter, not the target bean, with the listener container.

Converting JMS Messages

You can also create a message converter for converting mail objects from JMS messages that contain mail information. As message listeners receive messages only, the method toMessage() will not be called, so you can simply return null for it. However, if you use this message converter for sending messages too, you have to implement this method.

```
package com.apress.springrecipes.post;

import javax.jms.JMSException;
import javax.jms.MapMessage;
import javax.jms.Message;
import javax.jms.Session;

import org.springframework.jms.support.converter.MessageConversionException;
import org.springframework.jms.support.converter.MessageConverter;

public class MailMessageConverter implements MessageConverter {

    public Object fromMessage(Message message) throws JMSException,
            MessageConversionException {
        MapMessage mapMessage = (MapMessage) message;
        Mail mail = new Mail();
        mail.setMailId(mapMessage.getString("mailId"));
        mail.setCountry(mapMessage.getString("country"));
        mail.setWeight(mapMessage.getDouble("weight"));
        return mail;
    }

    public Message toMessage(Object object, Session session) throws JMSException,
            MessageConversionException {
        ...
    }
}
```

A message converter should be applied to a listener adapter for it to convert messages into objects before calling your POJO's methods.

```
<beans ...>
    ...
    <bean id="mailMessageConverter"
        class="com.apress.springrecipes.post.MailMessageConverter" />

    <bean id="mailListenerAdapter"
        class="org.springframework.jms.listener.adapter.MessageListenerAdapter">
        <property name="delegate" ref="mailListener" />
        <property name="defaultListenerMethod" value="displayMail" />
        <property name="messageConverter" ref="mailMessageConverter" />
    </bean>
</beans>
```

With this message converter, the listener method of your POJO is able to accept a mail object as the method argument.

```
package com.apress.springrecipes.post;

public class MailListener {

    public void displayMail(Mail mail) {
        System.out.println("Mail #" + mail.getMailId() + " received");
    }
}
```

Managing JMS Transactions

As mentioned before, `SimpleMessageListenerContainer` doesn't support transactions. So, if you need transaction management for your message listener method, you have to use `DefaultMessageListenerContainer` instead. For local JMS transactions, you can simply enable its `sessionTransacted` property, and your listener method will run within a local JMS transaction.

```
<bean
    class="org.springframework.jms.listener.DefaultMessageListenerContainer">
    <property name="connectionFactory" ref="connectionFactory" />
    <property name="destinationName" value="mail.queue" />
    <property name="messageListener" ref="mailListenerAdapter" />
    <property name="sessionTransacted" value="true" />
</bean>
```

However, if you want your listener to participate in a JTA transaction, you need to declare a `JtaTransactionManager` instance and inject it into your listener container.

Using Spring's JMS Schema

Spring 2.5 offers a new JMS schema to simplify your JMS listener and listener container configuration. You must add the `jms` schema definition to the `<beans>` root element beforehand.

```
<beans xmlns="http://www.springframework.org/schema/beans"
    xmlns:xsi="http://www.w3.org/2001/XMLSchema-instance"
    xmlns:jms="http://www.springframework.org/schema/jms"
    xsi:schemaLocation="http://www.springframework.org/schema/beans
        http://www.springframework.org/schema/beans/spring-beans-2.5.xsd
        http://www.springframework.org/schema/jms
        http://www.springframework.org/schema/jms/spring-jms-2.5.xsd">

    <bean id="connectionFactory"
        class="org.apache.activemq.ActiveMQConnectionFactory">
        <property name="brokerURL" value="tcp://localhost:61616" />
    </bean>

    <bean id="transactionManager"
        class="org.springframework.jms.connection.JmsTransactionManager">
        <property name="connectionFactory">
            <ref bean="connectionFactory" />
        </property>
    </bean>

    <bean id="mailMessageConverter"
        class="com.apress.springrecipes.post.MailMessageConverter" />

    <bean id="mailListener"
        class="com.apress.springrecipes.post.MailListener" />

    <jms:listener-container
        connection-factory="connectionFactory"
        transaction-manager="transactionManager"
        message-converter="mailMessageConverter">
        <jms:listener
            destination="mail.queue"
            ref="mailListener" method="displayMail" />
    </jms:listener-container>
</beans>
```

Actually, you don't need to specify the connection-factory attribute for a listener container explicitly if your JMS connection factory's name is connectionFactory, which can be located by default.

17-6. Summary

In this chapter, you have learned how Spring can simplify your EJB 2.x development with its EJB support classes. These classes provide empty implementations for all EJB life cycle callback methods so that your EJB classes can extend them to inherit the methods. They also provide access to the Spring IoC container so that you can implement your business logic in POJOs and wrap them with EJB components.

On the client side, Spring provides proxy factory beans to create proxies for remote/local stateless session EJB 2.x components, which allow EJB clients to invoke an EJB component through a business interface as if it were a simple local object. The EJB proxy handles the necessary tasks and exception conversion behind the scenes. Spring also provides a factory bean for creating JNDI object references in its IoC container. You can use this factory bean to declare a reference to an EJB 3.0 component.

Spring offers a template-based solution for simplifying the sending and receiving of JMS messages. This template handles the boilerplate tasks for you and also converts the JMS API's exceptions into Spring's JMS runtime exceptions.

In response to MDBs defined by EJB, Spring allows beans declared in its IoC container to listen for JMS messages in a similar way. As Spring adds message-listening capability to POJOs, they are called message-driven POJOs. They are triggered to react to JMS messages at a particular destination.

In the next chapter, you will learn about Spring's support for other common technologies: JMX, e-mail, and scheduling.

CHAPTER 18

Spring Support for JMX, E-mail, and Scheduling

In this chapter, you will learn about Spring's support for three common technologies on the Java SE/Java EE platform: *JMX (Java Management Extensions)*, sending e-mail, and scheduling tasks.

JMX is a technology for managing and monitoring system resources such as devices, applications, and objects. These resources are represented by *MBeans (managed beans)*. Originally, JMX was distributed separately, but it has been part of Java SE since version 5.0. Spring supports JMX by allowing you to export any Spring beans as *model MBeans* (a kind of *dynamic MBean*), without programming against the JMX API. In addition, Spring enables you to access remote MBeans easily.

JavaMail is the standard API and implementation for sending e-mail in Java. Spring further provides an abstract layer for you to send e-mail in an implementation-independent fashion. Spring 2.0 supplies implementations based on JavaMail and Jason Hunter's COS (com.oreilly.servlet). But Spring 2.5 removes the support for COS, so you can only use JavaMail as the underlying implementation.

There are two main options for scheduling tasks on the Java platform: JDK Timer and Quartz Scheduler (`http://www.opensymphony.com/quartz/`). JDK Timer offers simple task scheduling features that you can use conveniently, because the features are bundled with JDK. Compared to JDK Timer, Quartz offers more powerful job scheduling features. For both options, Spring supplies utility classes for you to configure scheduling tasks in the bean configuration file, without programming against their APIs.

Upon finishing this chapter, you will be able to export and access MBeans in a Spring application. You will also be able to utilize Spring's supporting features to simplify sending e-mail and scheduling tasks.

18-1. Exporting Spring Beans As JMX MBeans

Problem

You would like to register an object from your Java application as a JMX MBean to allow management and monitoring. However, if you call the JMX API for this purpose, a lot of coding will be required, and you'll have to deal with JMX's complexity.

Solution

Spring supports JMX by allowing you to export any beans in its IoC container as model MBeans. This can be done simply by declaring an `MBeanExporter` instance. With Spring's JMX support, you no longer need to deal with the JMX API directly, so you can write code that is not JMX specific. In addition, Spring enables you to declare JSR-160 (Java Management Extensions Remote API) connectors to expose your MBeans for remote access over a specific protocol, by using a factory bean.

Spring's JMX support comes with several MBean assemblers for you to assemble an MBean's management interface based on different information, such as method names, interfaces, and annotations. Spring can also detect and export your MBeans automatically from beans declared in the IoC container and annotated with particular JMX annotations defined by Spring.

How It Works

Suppose you are going to develop a utility for replicating files from a source directory to a destination directory. Let's design the interface for this utility as follows:

```
package com.apress.springrecipes.replicator;
...
public interface FileReplicator {

    public String getSrcDir();
    public void setSrcDir(String srcDir);

    public String getDestDir();
    public void setDestDir(String destDir);

    public void replicate() throws IOException;
}
```

The source and destination directories are designed as properties of a replicator object, not method arguments. That means each file replicator instance only replicates files for a particular source and destination directory. You can create multiple replicator instances in your application.

Before you implement this replicator, you need another class that copies a file from one directory to another, given its name.

```
package com.apress.springrecipes.replicator;
...
public interface FileCopier {

    public void copyFile(String srcDir, String destDir, String filename)
            throws IOException;
}
```

There are many strategies for implementing this file copier. For instance, you can make use of the FileCopyUtils class provided by Spring.

```
package com.apress.springrecipes.replicator;
...
import org.springframework.util.FileCopyUtils;

public class FileCopierImpl implements FileCopier {

    public void copyFile(String srcDir, String destDir, String filename)
            throws IOException {
        File srcFile = new File(srcDir, filename);
        File destFile = new File(destDir, filename);
        FileCopyUtils.copy(srcFile, destFile);
    }
}
```

With the help of a file copier, you can implement your file replicator as shown following. Each time you call the replicate() method, all files in the source directory will be replicated to the destination directory. To avoid unexpected problems caused by concurrent replication, you declare this method as synchronized.

```
package com.apress.springrecipes.replicator;
...
public class FileReplicatorImpl implements FileReplicator {

    private String srcDir;
    private String destDir;
    private FileCopier fileCopier;

    // Getters and Setters for srcDir and destDir
    ...

    // Setter for fileCopier
    ...

    public synchronized void replicate() throws IOException {
        File[] files = new File(srcDir).listFiles();
        for (File file : files) {
            if (file.isFile()) {
                fileCopier.copyFile(srcDir, destDir, file.getName());
            }
        }
    }
}
```

Now you can configure one or more file replicator instances in the bean configuration file for your needs.

```
<beans xmlns="http://www.springframework.org/schema/beans"
    xmlns:xsi="http://www.w3.org/2001/XMLSchema-instance"
    xsi:schemaLocation="http://www.springframework.org/schema/beans
        http://www.springframework.org/schema/beans/spring-beans-2.5.xsd">

    <bean id="fileCopier"
        class="com.apress.springrecipes.replicator.FileCopierImpl" />

    <bean id="documentReplicator"
        class="com.apress.springrecipes.replicator.FileReplicatorImpl">
        <property name="srcDir" value="c:/documents" />
        <property name="destDir" value="d:/documents" />
        <property name="fileCopier" ref="fileCopier" />
    </bean>
</beans>
```

Registering MBeans Without Spring's Support

First, let's see how to register a model MBean using the JMX API directly. In the following `Main` class, you get the `documentReplicator` bean from the IoC container and register it as an MBean for management and monitoring. All properties and methods are included in the MBean's management interface.

```
package com.apress.springrecipes.replicator;
...
import java.lang.management.ManagementFactory;

import javax.management.Descriptor;
import javax.management.JMException;
import javax.management.MBeanServer;
import javax.management.ObjectName;
import javax.management.modelmbean.DescriptorSupport;
import javax.management.modelmbean.InvalidTargetObjectTypeException;
import javax.management.modelmbean.ModelMBeanAttributeInfo;
import javax.management.modelmbean.ModelMBeanInfo;
import javax.management.modelmbean.ModelMBeanInfoSupport;
import javax.management.modelmbean.ModelMBeanOperationInfo;
import javax.management.modelmbean.RequiredModelMBean;

import org.springframework.context.ApplicationContext;
import org.springframework.context.support.ClassPathXmlApplicationContext;

public class Main {
```

```
public static void main(String[] args) throws IOException {
    ApplicationContext context =
        new ClassPathXmlApplicationContext("beans.xml");

    FileReplicator documentReplicator =
        (FileReplicator) context.getBean("documentReplicator");

    try {
        MBeanServer mbeanServer = ManagementFactory.getPlatformMBeanServer();
        ObjectName objectName = new ObjectName("bean:name=documentReplicator");

        RequiredModelMBean mbean = new RequiredModelMBean();
        mbean.setManagedResource(documentReplicator, "objectReference");

        Descriptor srcDirDescriptor = new DescriptorSupport(new String[] {
                "name=SrcDir", "descriptorType=attribute",
                "getMethod=getSrcDir", "setMethod=setSrcDir" });
        ModelMBeanAttributeInfo srcDirInfo = new ModelMBeanAttributeInfo(
                "SrcDir", "java.lang.String", "Source directory",
                true, true, false, srcDirDescriptor);

        Descriptor destDirDescriptor = new DescriptorSupport(new String[] {
                "name=DestDir", "descriptorType=attribute",
                "getMethod=getDestDir", "setMethod=setDestDir" });
        ModelMBeanAttributeInfo destDirInfo = new ModelMBeanAttributeInfo(
                "DestDir", "java.lang.String", "Destination directory",
                true, true, false, destDirDescriptor);

        ModelMBeanOperationInfo getSrcDirInfo = new ModelMBeanOperationInfo(
                "Get source directory",
                FileReplicator.class.getMethod("getSrcDir"));
        ModelMBeanOperationInfo setSrcDirInfo = new ModelMBeanOperationInfo(
                "Set source directory",
                FileReplicator.class.getMethod("setSrcDir", String.class));
        ModelMBeanOperationInfo getDestDirInfo = new ModelMBeanOperationInfo(
                "Get destination directory",
                FileReplicator.class.getMethod("getDestDir"));
        ModelMBeanOperationInfo setDestDirInfo = new ModelMBeanOperationInfo(
                "Set destination directory",
                FileReplicator.class.getMethod("setDestDir", String.class));
        ModelMBeanOperationInfo replicateInfo = new ModelMBeanOperationInfo(
                "Replicate files",
                FileReplicator.class.getMethod("replicate"));

        ModelMBeanInfo mbeanInfo = new ModelMBeanInfoSupport(
                "FileReplicator", "File replicator",
                new ModelMBeanAttributeInfo[] { srcDirInfo, destDirInfo },
```

```
                null,
                new ModelMBeanOperationInfo[] { getSrcDirInfo, setSrcDirInfo,
                        getDestDirInfo, setDestDirInfo, replicateInfo },
                null);
            mbean.setModelMBeanInfo(mbeanInfo);

            mbeanServer.registerMBean(mbean, objectName);
        } catch (JMException e) {
            ...
        } catch (InvalidTargetObjectTypeException e) {
            ...
        } catch (NoSuchMethodException e) {
            ...
        }

        System.in.read();
    }
}
```

To register an MBean, you need an MBeanServer instance. In JDK 1.5, you can call the static method ManagementFactory.getPlatformMBeanServer() to locate a platform MBean server. It will create an MBean server if none exists, and then register this server instance for future use. Each MBean requires an MBean *object name* that includes a domain. The preceding MBean is registered under the domain bean with the name documentReplicator.

From the preceding code, you can see that for each MBean attribute and MBean operation, you need to create a ModelMBeanAttributeInfo object and a ModelMBeanOperationInfo object for describing it. After those, you have to create a ModelMBeanInfo object for describing the MBean's management interface by assembling the preceding information. For details about using these classes, you can consult their javadocs.

Moreover, you have to handle the JMX-specific exceptions when calling the JMX API. These exceptions are checked exceptions that you must handle.

Note that you must prevent your application from terminating before you look inside it with a JMX client tool. Requesting a key from the console using System.in.read() would be a good choice.

Finally, you have to add the VM argument -Dcom.sun.management.jmxremote to enable local monitoring of this application.

```
java -Dcom.sun.management.jmxremote com.apress.springrecipes.replicator.Main
```

Now you can use any JMX client tools to monitor your MBeans locally. The simplest one may be JConsole, which comes with JDK 1.5.

Note To start JConsole, just execute the jconsole executable file (located in the bin directory of the JDK installation).

When JConsole starts, you can see a list of JMX-enabled applications on the Local tab of the connection window. After connecting to the replicator application, you can see your `documentReplicator` MBean under the `bean` domain.

Exporting Spring Beans As MBeans

To export beans configured in the Spring IoC container as MBeans, you simply declare an `MBeanExporter` instance and specify the beans to export, with their MBean object names as the keys.

```
<bean id="mbeanExporter"
    class="org.springframework.jmx.export.MBeanExporter">
    <property name="beans">
        <map>
            <entry key="bean:name=documentReplicator"
                value-ref="documentReplicator" />
        </map>
    </property>
</bean>
```

The preceding configuration exports the `documentReplicator` bean as an MBean, under the domain `bean` and with the name `documentReplicator`. By default, all public properties and all public methods are included in the MBean's management interface.

`MBeanExporter` attempts to locate an MBean server instance and register your MBeans with it. If your application is running in an environment that provides an MBean server (e.g., most Java EE application servers), `MBeanExporter` will be able to locate this MBean server instance. However, in an environment with no MBean server available, you have to create one explicitly using Spring's `MBeanServerFactoryBean`. To make your application portable to different runtime environments, you should enable the `locateExistingServerIfPossible` property so that this factory bean will only create an MBean server if there is none available.

■ Note JDK 1.5 will create an MBean server for the first time when you locate it. So, if you're using JDK 1.5 or above, you needn't create an MBean server explicitly.

```
<beans ...>
    ...
    <bean id="mbeanServer"
        class="org.springframework.jmx.support.MBeanServerFactoryBean">
        <property name="locateExistingServerIfPossible" value="true" />
    </bean>

    <bean id="mbeanExporter"
        class="org.springframework.jmx.export.MBeanExporter">
        ...
```

```
        <property name="server" ref="mbeanServer" />
    </bean>
</beans>
```

You can also specify an MBean server for MBeanExporter explicitly for it to export your MBeans to. In this case, MBeanExporter will not locate an MBean server, but will use the specified MBean server instance. This property is for you to specify a particular MBean server when there's more than one available.

The Main class for exporting an MBean can be simplified as shown following. You have to retain the key-requesting statement to prevent your application from terminating.

```
package com.apress.springrecipes.replicator;
...
import org.springframework.context.support.ClassPathXmlApplicationContext;

public class Main {

    public static void main(String[] args) throws IOException {
        new ClassPathXmlApplicationContext("beans.xml");
        System.in.read();
    }
}
```

Exposing MBeans for Remote Access

If you want your MBeans to be accessed remotely, you need to enable a remoting protocol for JMX. JSR-160 defines a standard for JMX remoting through a JMX connector. Spring allows you to create a JMX connector server through ConnectorServerFactoryBean.

By default, ConnectorServerFactoryBean creates and starts a JMX connector server bound to the service URL service:jmx:jmxmp://localhost:9875, which exposes the JMX connector through the JMX Messaging Protocol (JMXMP). However, most JMX implementations, including JDK 1.5's, don't support JMXMP. Therefore, you should choose a widely supported remoting protocol for your JMX connector, such as RMI. To expose your JMX connector through a specific protocol, you just provide the service URL for it.

```
<beans ...>
    ...
    <bean id="rmiRegistry"
        class="org.springframework.remoting.rmi.RmiRegistryFactoryBean" />

    <bean id="connectorServer"
        class="org.springframework.jmx.support.ConnectorServerFactoryBean"
        depends-on="rmiRegistry">
        <property name="serviceUrl" value=
            "service:jmx:rmi://localhost/jndi/rmi://localhost:1099/replicator" />
    </bean>
</beans>
```

You specify the preceding URL to bind your JMX connector to an RMI registry listening on port 1099 of localhost. If no RMI registry has been created externally, you should create one by using RmiRegistryFactoryBean. The default port for this registry is 1099, but you can specify another one in its port property. Note that ConnectorServerFactoryBean must create the connector server after the RMI registry is created and ready. You can set the depends-on attribute for this purpose.

Now your MBeans can be accessed remotely via RMI. When JConsole starts, you can enter the following service URL on the Advanced tab of the connection window.

```
service:jmx:rmi://localhost/jndi/rmi://localhost:1099/replicator
```

Assembling the Management Interface of MBeans

Recall that by default, Spring exports all public properties of a bean as MBean attributes and all public methods as MBean operations. In fact, you can assemble the management interface of your MBeans using an MBean assembler. The simplest MBean assembler in Spring is MethodNameBasedMBeanInfoAssembler, which allows you to specify the names of the methods to export.

```
<beans ...>
    ...
    <bean id="mbeanExporter"
        class="org.springframework.jmx.export.MBeanExporter">
        ...
        <property name="assembler" ref="assembler" />
    </bean>

    <bean id="assembler" class="org.springframework.jmx.export.assembler.➥
        MethodNameBasedMBeanInfoAssembler">
        <property name="managedMethods">
            <list>
                <value>getSrcDir</value>
                <value>setSrcDir</value>
                <value>getDestDir</value>
                <value>setDestDir</value>
                <value>replicate</value>
            </list>
        </property>
    </bean>
</beans>
```

Another MBean assembler is InterfaceBasedMBeanInfoAssembler, which exports all methods defined in the interfaces you specified.

```
<bean id="assembler" class="org.springframework.jmx.export.assembler.➥
    InterfaceBasedMBeanInfoAssembler">
    <property name="managedInterfaces">
        <list>
```

```
            <value>com.apress.springrecipes.replicator.FileReplicator</value>
        </list>
    </property>
</bean>
```

Spring also provides MetadataMBeanInfoAssembler to assemble an MBean's management interface based on the metadata in the bean class. It supports two types of metadata: JDK annotations and Apache Commons Attributes. For a bean class annotated with JDK annotations, you specify an AnnotationJmxAttributeSource instance as the attribute source of MetadataMBeanInfoAssembler.

```
<bean id="assembler" class="org.springframework.jmx.export.assembler.➥
    MetadataMBeanInfoAssembler">
    <property name="attributeSource">
        <bean class="org.springframework.jmx.export.annotation.➥
            AnnotationJmxAttributeSource" />
    </property>
</bean>
```

Then you annotate your bean class and methods with the annotations @ManagedResource, @ManagedAttribute, and @ManagedOperation for MetadataMBeanInfoAssembler to assemble the management interface for this bean.

```
package com.apress.springrecipes.replicator;
...
import org.springframework.jmx.export.annotation.ManagedAttribute;
import org.springframework.jmx.export.annotation.ManagedOperation;
import org.springframework.jmx.export.annotation.ManagedResource;

@ManagedResource(description = "File replicator")
public class FileReplicatorImpl implements FileReplicator {
    ...
    @ManagedAttribute(description = "Get source directory")
    public String getSrcDir() {
        ...
    }

    @ManagedAttribute(description = "Set source directory")
    public void setSrcDir(String srcDir) {
        ...
    }

    @ManagedAttribute(description = "Get destination directory")
    public String getDestDir() {
        ...
    }
```

```
    @ManagedAttribute(description = "Set destination directory")
    public void setDestDir(String destDir) {
        ...
    }

    @ManagedOperation(description = "Replicate files")
    public synchronized void replicate() throws IOException {
        ...
    }
}
```

Auto-Detecting MBeans by Annotations

In addition to exporting a bean explicitly with `MBeanExporter`, you can simply configure its subclass `AnnotationMBeanExporter` to auto-detect MBeans from beans declared in the IoC container. You needn't configure an MBean assembler for this exporter, because it uses `MetadataMBeanInfoAssembler` with `AnnotationJmxAttributeSource` by default. You can delete the previous `beans` and `assembler` properties for this exporter.

```
<bean id="mbeanExporter"
    class="org.springframework.jmx.export.annotation.AnnotationMBeanExporter">
    ...
</bean>
```

`AnnotationMBeanExporter` detects any beans configured in the IoC container with the `@ManagedResource` annotation and exports them as MBeans. By default, this exporter exports a bean to the domain whose name is the same as its package name. Also, it uses the bean's name in the IoC container as its MBean name, and the bean's short class name as its type. So your `documentReplicator` bean will be exported under the following MBean object name:

```
com.apress.springrecipes.replicator:➥
    name=documentReplicator,type=FileReplicatorImpl
```

If you don't want to use the package name as the domain name, you can set the default domain for this exporter.

```
<bean id="mbeanExporter"
    class="org.springframework.jmx.export.annotation.AnnotationMBeanExporter">
    ...
    <property name="defaultDomain" value="bean" />
</bean>
```

After setting the default domain to `bean`, the `documentReplicator` bean will be exported under the following MBean object name:

```
bean:name=documentReplicator,type=FileReplicatorImpl
```

Moreover, you can specify a bean's MBean object name in the `objectName` attribute of the `@ManagedResource` annotation. For example, you can export your file copier as an MBean by annotating it with the following annotations:

```
package com.apress.springrecipes.replicator;
...
import org.springframework.jmx.export.annotation.ManagedOperation;
import org.springframework.jmx.export.annotation.ManagedOperationParameter;
import org.springframework.jmx.export.annotation.ManagedOperationParameters;
import org.springframework.jmx.export.annotation.ManagedResource;

@ManagedResource(
    objectName = "bean:name=fileCopier,type=FileCopierImpl",
    description = "File Copier")
public class FileCopierImpl implements FileCopier {

    @ManagedOperation(
        description = "Copy file from source directory to destination directory")
    @ManagedOperationParameters( {
        @ManagedOperationParameter(
            name = "srcDir", description = "Source directory"),
        @ManagedOperationParameter(
            name = "destDir", description = "Destination directory"),
        @ManagedOperationParameter(
            name = "filename", description = "File to copy") })
    public void copyFile(String srcDir, String destDir, String filename)
            throws IOException {
        ...
    }
}
```

However, specifying the object name in this way works only for classes that you're going to create a single instance of in the IoC container (e.g., file copier), not for classes that you may create multiple instances of (e.g., file replicator). This is because you can only specify a single object name for a class.

In Spring 2.5, you can simply declare a <context:mbean-export> element in your bean configuration file, instead of the AnnotationMBeanExporter declaration.

```
<beans xmlns="http://www.springframework.org/schema/beans"
    xmlns:xsi="http://www.w3.org/2001/XMLSchema-instance"
    xmlns:context="http://www.springframework.org/schema/context"
    xsi:schemaLocation="http://www.springframework.org/schema/beans
        http://www.springframework.org/schema/beans/spring-beans-2.5.xsd
        http://www.springframework.org/schema/context
        http://www.springframework.org/schema/context/spring-context-2.5.xsd">

    <context:mbean-export server="mbeanServer" default-domain="bean" />
    ...
</beans>
```

You can specify an MBean server and a default domain name for this element through the server and default-domain attributes. However, you won't be able to set other MBean exporter properties such as notification listener mappings. Whenever you have to set these properties, you need to declare an `AnnotationMBeanExporter` instance explicitly.

18-2. Publishing and Listening to JMX Notifications

Problem

You would like to publish JMX notifications from your MBeans and listen to them with JMX notification listeners.

Solution

Spring allows your beans to publish JMX notifications through `NotificationPublisher`. You can also register standard JMX notification listeners in the IoC container to listen to JMX notifications.

How It Works

Publishing JMX Notifications

The Spring IoC container supports the beans that are going to be exported as MBeans to publish JMX notifications. These beans must implement the `NotificationPublisherAware` interface to get access to `NotificationPublisher` so that they can publish notifications.

```
package com.apress.springrecipes.replicator;
...
import javax.management.Notification;

import org.springframework.jmx.export.notification.NotificationPublisher;
import org.springframework.jmx.export.notification.NotificationPublisherAware;

public class FileReplicatorImpl implements FileReplicator,
        NotificationPublisherAware {
    ...
    private int sequenceNumber;
    private NotificationPublisher notificationPublisher;

    public void setNotificationPublisher(
            NotificationPublisher notificationPublisher) {
        this.notificationPublisher = notificationPublisher;
    }

    public void replicate() throws IOException {
        notificationPublisher.sendNotification(
                new Notification("replication.start", this, sequenceNumber));
        ...
        notificationPublisher.sendNotification(
                new Notification("replication.complete", this, sequenceNumber));
```

```
        sequenceNumber++;
    }
}
```

In this file replicator, you send a JMX notification whenever a replication starts or completes. The first argument in the `Notification` constructor is the notification type, while the second is the notification source. Each notification requires a sequence number. You can use the same sequence for a notification pair to keep track of them.

Listening to JMX Notifications

Now let's create a notification listener to listen to JMX notifications. As a listener will be notified of many different types of notifications, such as `AttributeChangeNotification` when an MBean's attribute has changed, you have to filter those notifications that you are interested in handling.

```
package com.apress.springrecipes.replicator;

import javax.management.Notification;
import javax.management.NotificationListener;

public class ReplicationNotificationListener implements NotificationListener {

    public void handleNotification(Notification notification, Object handback) {
        if (notification.getType().startsWith("replication")) {
            System.out.println(
                    notification.getSource() + " " +
                    notification.getType() + " #" +
                    notification.getSequenceNumber());
        }
    }
}
```

Then you can register this notification listener with your MBean exporter to listen to notifications emitted from certain MBeans.

```
<bean id="mbeanExporter"
    class="org.springframework.jmx.export.annotation.AnnotationMBeanExporter">
    <property name="defaultDomain" value="bean" />
    <property name="notificationListenerMappings">
        <map>
            <entry key="bean:name=documentReplicator,type=FileReplicatorImpl">
                <bean class="com.apress.springrecipes.replicator.➥
                    ReplicationNotificationListener" />
            </entry>
        </map>
    </property>
</bean>
```

18-3. Accessing Remote JMX MBeans in Spring

Problem

You would like to access JMX MBeans running on a remote MBean server exposed by a JMX connector. When accessing remote MBeans directly with the JMX API, you have to write complex JMX-specific code.

Solution

Spring offers two approaches to simplify your remote MBean access. First, it provides a factory bean for you to create an MBean server connection declaratively. With this server connection, you can query and update an MBean's attributes, as well as invoke its operations. Second, Spring provides another factory bean that allows you to create a proxy for a remote MBean. With this proxy, you can operate a remote MBean as if it were a local bean.

How It Works

Accessing Remote MBeans Through an MBean Server Connection

A JMX client requires an MBean server connection to access MBeans running on a remote MBean server. Spring provides `MBeanServerConnectionFactoryBean` for you to create a connection to a remote MBean server declaratively. You only have to provide the service URL for it to locate the MBean server. Now let's declare this factory bean in your client bean configuration file (e.g., `beans-client.xml`).

```
<beans xmlns="http://www.springframework.org/schema/beans"
    xmlns:xsi="http://www.w3.org/2001/XMLSchema-instance"
    xsi:schemaLocation="http://www.springframework.org/schema/beans
        http://www.springframework.org/schema/beans/spring-beans-2.5.xsd">

    <bean id="mbeanServerConnection"
        class="org.springframework.jmx.support.MBeanServerConnectionFactoryBean">
        <property name="serviceUrl" value=
            "service:jmx:rmi://localhost/jndi/rmi://localhost:1099/replicator" />
    </bean>
</beans>
```

With the MBean server connection created by this factory bean, you can access and operate the MBeans running on this server. For example, you can query and update an MBean's attributes through the `getAttribute()` and `setAttribute()` methods, giving the MBean's object name and attribute name. You can also invoke an MBean's operations using the `invoke()` method.

```
package com.apress.springrecipes.replicator;

import javax.management.Attribute;
import javax.management.MBeanServerConnection;
import javax.management.ObjectName;
```

```
import org.springframework.context.ApplicationContext;
import org.springframework.context.support.ClassPathXmlApplicationContext;

public class Client {

    public static void main(String[] args) throws Exception {
        ApplicationContext context =
            new ClassPathXmlApplicationContext("beans-client.xml");

        MBeanServerConnection mbeanServerConnection =
            (MBeanServerConnection) context.getBean("mbeanServerConnection");

        ObjectName mbeanName = new ObjectName(
                "bean:name=documentReplicator,type=FileReplicatorImpl");

        String srcDir = (String) mbeanServerConnection.getAttribute(
                mbeanName, "SrcDir");

        mbeanServerConnection.setAttribute(
                mbeanName, new Attribute("DestDir", srcDir + "_1"));

        mbeanServerConnection.invoke(
                mbeanName, "replicate", new Object[] {}, new String[] {});
    }
}
```

Suppose you've created the following JMX notification listener, which listens to file replication notifications.

```
package com.apress.springrecipes.replicator;

import javax.management.Notification;
import javax.management.NotificationListener;

public class ReplicationNotificationListener implements NotificationListener {

    public void handleNotification(Notification notification, Object handback) {
        if (notification.getType().startsWith("replication")) {
            System.out.println(
                    notification.getSource() + " " +
                    notification.getType() + " #" +
                    notification.getSequenceNumber());
        }
    }
}
```

You can register this notification listener to the MBean server connection to listen to notifications emitted from this MBean server.

```
package com.apress.springrecipes.replicator;
...
import javax.management.MBeanServerConnection;
import javax.management.ObjectName;

public class Client {

    public static void main(String[] args) throws Exception {
        ...
        MBeanServerConnection mbeanServerConnection =
            (MBeanServerConnection) context.getBean("mbeanServerConnection");

        ObjectName mbeanName = new ObjectName(
                "bean:name=documentReplicator,type=FileReplicatorImpl");

        mbeanServerConnection.addNotificationListener(
                mbeanName, new ReplicationNotificationListener(), null, null);
        ...
    }
}
```

Accessing Remote MBeans Through an MBean Proxy

Another approach Spring offers for remote MBean access is through `MBeanProxy`, which can be created by `MBeanProxyFactoryBean`.

```
<beans ...>
    <bean id="mbeanServerConnection"
        class="org.springframework.jmx.support.MBeanServerConnectionFactoryBean">
        <property name="serviceUrl" value=
            "service:jmx:rmi://localhost/jndi/rmi://localhost:1099/replicator" />
    </bean>

    <bean id="fileReplicatorProxy"
        class="org.springframework.jmx.access.MBeanProxyFactoryBean">
        <property name="server" ref="mbeanServerConnection" />
        <property name="objectName"
            value="bean:name=documentReplicator,type=FileReplicatorImpl" />
        <property name="proxyInterface"
            value="com.apress.springrecipes.replicator.FileReplicator" />
    </bean>
</beans>
```

You need to specify the object name and the server connection for the MBean you are going to proxy. The most important is the proxy interface, whose local method calls will be translated into remote MBean calls behind the scenes.

Now you can operate the remote MBean through this proxy as if it were a local bean. The preceding MBean operations invoked on the MBean server connection directly can be simplified as follows:

```
package com.apress.springrecipes.replicator;
...
public class Client {

    public static void main(String[] args) throws Exception {
        ...
        FileReplicator fileReplicatorProxy =
            (FileReplicator) context.getBean("fileReplicatorProxy");

        String srcDir = fileReplicatorProxy.getSrcDir();
        fileReplicatorProxy.setDestDir(srcDir + "_1");
        fileReplicatorProxy.replicate();
    }
}
```

18-4. Sending E-mail with Spring's E-mail Support

Problem

Many applications need to send e-mail. In a Java application, you can send e-mail with the JavaMail API. However, when using JavaMail, you have to handle the JavaMail-specific mail sessions and exceptions. As a result, your application becomes JavaMail dependent and hard to switch to another e-mail API.

Solution

Spring's e-mail support makes it easier to send e-mail by providing an abstract and implementation-independent API for sending e-mail. The core interface of Spring's e-mail support is `MailSender`.

The `JavaMailSender` interface is a subinterface of `MailSender` that includes specialized JavaMail features such as *MIME (Multipurpose Internet Mail Extensions)* message support. To send an e-mail message with HTML content, inline images, or attachments, you have to send it as a MIME message.

How It Works

Suppose you would like your file replicator application to notify the administrator of any error. First, you create the following `ErrorNotifier` interface, which includes a method for notifying of a file copy error:

```
package com.apress.springrecipes.replicator;

public interface ErrorNotifier {
```

```
    public void notifyCopyError(String srcDir, String destDir, String filename);
}
```

Note Invoking this notifier in case of error is left for you to accomplish. As you can consider error handling a crosscutting concern, AOP would be an ideal solution to this problem. You can write an after throwing advice to invoke this notifier.

Next, you can implement this interface to send a notification in a way of your choice. The most common way is to send e-mail. Before you implement the interface in this way, you may need a local e-mail server that supports SMTP for testing purposes. I recommend installing Apache James Server (`http://james.apache.org/server/index.html`), which is very easy to install and configure.

Note You can download Apache James Server (e.g., v2.3.1) from the Apache James web site and extract it to a directory of your choice to complete the installation. To start it, just execute the `run` script (located in the `bin` directory).

Let's create two user accounts for sending and receiving e-mail with this server. By default, the remote manager service of James listens on port 4555. You can telnet to this port and run the following commands (displayed in bold) to add the users `system` and `admin`, whose passwords are `12345`:

```
JAMES Remote Administration Tool 2.3.1
Please enter your login and password
Login id:
root
Password:
root
Welcome root. HELP for a list of commands
adduser system 12345
User system added
adduser admin 12345
User admin added
listusers
Existing accounts 2
user: admin
user: system
quit
Bye
```

Sending E-mail Using the JavaMail API

Now let's take a look at how to send e-mail using the JavaMail API. You can implement the `ErrorNotifier` interface to send e-mail notifications in case of errors.

■ **Note** To use JavaMail in your application, you have to include `mail.jar` and `activation.jar` (located in the `lib/j2ee` directory of the Spring installation) in your classpath.

```
package com.apress.springrecipes.replicator;

import java.util.Properties;

import javax.mail.Message;
import javax.mail.MessagingException;
import javax.mail.Session;
import javax.mail.Transport;
import javax.mail.internet.InternetAddress;
import javax.mail.internet.MimeMessage;

public class EmailErrorNotifier implements ErrorNotifier {

    public void notifyCopyError(String srcDir, String destDir, String filename) {
        Properties props = new Properties();
        props.put("mail.smtp.host", "localhost");
        props.put("mail.smtp.port", "25");
        props.put("mail.smtp.username", "system");
        props.put("mail.smtp.password", "12345");
        Session session = Session.getDefaultInstance(props, null);
        try {
            Message message = new MimeMessage(session);
            message.setFrom(new InternetAddress("system@localhost"));
            message.setRecipients(Message.RecipientType.TO,
                    InternetAddress.parse("admin@localhost"));
            message.setSubject("File Copy Error");
            message.setText(
                "Dear Administrator,\n\n" +
                "An error occurred when copying the following file :\n" +
                "Source directory : " + srcDir + "\n" +
                "Destination directory : " + destDir + "\n" +
                "Filename : " + filename);
            Transport.send(message);
        } catch (MessagingException e) {
            throw new RuntimeException(e);
```

```
        }
    }
}
```

You first open a mail session connecting to an SMTP server by defining the properties. Then you create a message from this session for constructing your e-mail. After that, you send the e-mail by making a call to `Transport.send()`. When dealing with the JavaMail API, you have to handle the checked exception `MessagingException`. Note that all these classes, interfaces, and exceptions are defined by JavaMail.

Next, you declare an instance of `EmailErrorNotifier` in the Spring IoC container for sending e-mail notifications in case of file replication errors.

```
<bean id="errorNotifier"
    class="com.apress.springrecipes.replicator.EmailErrorNotifier" />
```

You can write the following `Main` class to test `EmailErrorNotifier`. After running it, you can configure your e-mail application to receive the e-mail from your James Server via POP3.

```
package com.apress.springrecipes.replicator;

import org.springframework.context.ApplicationContext;
import org.springframework.context.support.ClassPathXmlApplicationContext;

public class Main {

    public static void main(String[] args) {
        ApplicationContext context =
            new ClassPathXmlApplicationContext("beans.xml");

        ErrorNotifier errorNotifier =
            (ErrorNotifier) context.getBean("errorNotifier");
        errorNotifier.notifyCopyError(
            "c:/documents", "d:/documents", "spring.doc");
    }
}
```

Sending E-mail with Spring's MailSender

Now let's see how to send e-mail with the help of Spring's `MailSender` interface, which is able to send `SimpleMailMessage` in its `send()` method. With this interface, your code is no longer JavaMail specific, and now it's simpler and easier to test.

```
package com.apress.springrecipes.replicator;

import org.springframework.mail.MailSender;
import org.springframework.mail.SimpleMailMessage;

public class EmailErrorNotifier implements ErrorNotifier {
```

```
    private MailSender mailSender;

    public void setMailSender(MailSender mailSender) {
        this.mailSender = mailSender;
    }

    public void notifyCopyError(String srcDir, String destDir, String filename) {
        SimpleMailMessage message = new SimpleMailMessage();
        message.setFrom("system@localhost");
        message.setTo("admin@localhost");
        message.setSubject("File Copy Error");
        message.setText(
                "Dear Administrator,\n\n" +
                "An error occurred when copying the following file :\n" +
                "Source directory : " + srcDir + "\n" +
                "Destination directory : " + destDir + "\n" +
                "Filename : " + filename);
        mailSender.send(message);
    }
}
```

Next, you have to configure a `MailSender` implementation in the bean configuration file and inject it into `EmailErrorNotifier`. In Spring 2.5, the unique implementation of this interface is `JavaMailSenderImpl`, which uses JavaMail to send e-mail.

```
<beans ...>
    ...
    <bean id="mailSender"
        class="org.springframework.mail.javamail.JavaMailSenderImpl">
        <property name="host" value="localhost" />
        <property name="port" value="25" />
        <property name="username" value="system" />
        <property name="password" value="12345" />
    </bean>

    <bean id="errorNotifier"
        class="com.apress.springrecipes.replicator.EmailErrorNotifier">
        <property name="mailSender" ref="mailSender" />
    </bean>
</beans>
```

The default port used by `JavaMailSenderImpl` is the standard SMTP port 25, so if your e-mail server listens on this port for SMTP, you can simply omit this property. Also, if your SMTP server doesn't require user authentication, you needn't set the username and password.

If you have a JavaMail session configured in your Java EE application server, you can first look it up with the help of `JndiObjectFactoryBean`.

```
<bean id="mailSession"
    class="org.springframework.jndi.JndiObjectFactoryBean">
    <property name="jndiName" value="mail/Session" />
</bean>
```

Or you can look up a JavaMail session through the `<jee:jndi-lookup>` element if you are using Spring 2.x.

```
<jee:jndi-lookup id="mailSession" jndi-name="mail/Session" />
```

You can inject the JavaMail session into `JavaMailSenderImpl` for its use. In this case, you no longer need to set the host, port, username, or password.

```
<bean id="mailSender"
    class="org.springframework.mail.javamail.JavaMailSenderImpl">
    <property name="session" ref="mailSession" />
</bean>
```

Defining an E-mail Template

Constructing an e-mail message from scratch in the method body is not efficient since you have to hard-code the e-mail properties. Also, you may have difficulty in writing the e-mail text in terms of Java strings. You can consider defining an e-mail message template in the bean configuration file and construct a new e-mail message from it.

```
<beans ...>
    ...
    <bean id="copyErrorMailMessage"
        class="org.springframework.mail.SimpleMailMessage">
        <property name="from" value="system@localhost" />
        <property name="to" value="admin@localhost" />
        <property name="subject" value="File Copy Error" />
        <property name="text">
            <value>
<![CDATA[
Dear Administrator,

An error occurred when copying the following file :
Source directory : %s
Destination directory : %s
Filename : %s
]]>
            </value>
        </property>
    </bean>

    <bean id="errorNotifier"
        class="com.apress.springrecipes.replicator.EmailErrorNotifier">
        ...
```

```
        <property name="copyErrorMailMessage" ref="copyErrorMailMessage" />
    </bean>
</beans>
```

Note that in the preceding message text, you include the placeholders %s, which will be replaced by message parameters through String.format(). Of course, you can also use a powerful templating language such as Velocity or FreeMarker to generate the message text according to a template. It's also a good practice to separate mail message templates from bean configuration files.

Each time you send e-mail, you can construct a new SimpleMailMessage instance from this injected template. Then you can generate the message text using String.format() to replace the %s placeholders with your message parameters.

```
package com.apress.springrecipes.replicator;
...
import org.springframework.mail.SimpleMailMessage;

public class EmailErrorNotifier implements ErrorNotifier {
    ...
    private SimpleMailMessage copyErrorMailMessage;

    public void setCopyErrorMailMessage(SimpleMailMessage copyErrorMailMessage) {
        this.copyErrorMailMessage = copyErrorMailMessage;
    }

    public void notifyCopyError(String srcDir, String destDir, String filename) {
        SimpleMailMessage message = new SimpleMailMessage(copyErrorMailMessage);
        message.setText(String.format(
                copyErrorMailMessage.getText(), srcDir, destDir, filename));
        mailSender.send(message);
    }
}
```

Sending MIME Messages

So far, the SimpleMailMessage class you used can only send a simple plain text e-mail message. To send e-mail that contains HTML content, inline images, or attachments, you have to construct and send a MIME message instead. MIME is supported by JavaMail through the MimeMessage class.

First of all, you have to use the JavaMailSender interface instead of its parent interface MailSender. The JavaMailSenderImpl instance you injected does implement this interface, so you needn't modify your bean configurations. The following notifier sends Spring's bean configuration file as an e-mail attachment to the administrator:

```
package com.apress.springrecipes.replicator;

import javax.mail.MessagingException;
import javax.mail.internet.MimeMessage;
```

```
import org.springframework.core.io.ClassPathResource;
import org.springframework.mail.MailParseException;
import org.springframework.mail.SimpleMailMessage;
import org.springframework.mail.javamail.JavaMailSender;
import org.springframework.mail.javamail.MimeMessageHelper;

public class EmailErrorNotifier implements ErrorNotifier {

    private JavaMailSender mailSender;
    private SimpleMailMessage copyErrorMailMessage;

    public void setMailSender(JavaMailSender mailSender) {
        this.mailSender = mailSender;
    }

    public void setCopyErrorMailMessage(SimpleMailMessage copyErrorMailMessage) {
        this.copyErrorMailMessage = copyErrorMailMessage;
    }

    public void notifyCopyError(String srcDir, String destDir, String filename) {
        MimeMessage message = mailSender.createMimeMessage();
        try {
            MimeMessageHelper helper = new MimeMessageHelper(message, true);
            helper.setFrom(copyErrorMailMessage.getFrom());
            helper.setTo(copyErrorMailMessage.getTo());
            helper.setSubject(copyErrorMailMessage.getSubject());
            helper.setText(String.format(
                    copyErrorMailMessage.getText(), srcDir, destDir, filename));

            ClassPathResource config = new ClassPathResource("beans.xml");
            helper.addAttachment("beans.xml", config);
        } catch (MessagingException e) {
            throw new MailParseException(e);
        }
        mailSender.send(message);
    }
}
```

Unlike `SimpleMailMessage`, the `MimeMessage` class is defined by JavaMail, so you can only instantiate it by calling `JavaMailSender.createMimeMessage()`. Spring provides the helper class `MimeMessageHelper` to simplify the operations of `MimeMessage`. It allows you to add an attachment from a Spring `Resource` object. However, the operations of this helper class still throw JavaMail's `MessagingException`. You have to convert this exception into Spring's mail runtime exception for consistency.

Spring offers another method for you to construct a MIME message, which is through implementing the `MimeMessagePreparator` interface.

```
package com.apress.springrecipes.replicator;
...
import javax.mail.internet.MimeMessage;

import org.springframework.mail.javamail.MimeMessagePreparator;

public class EmailErrorNotifier implements ErrorNotifier {
    ...
    public void notifyCopyError(
            final String srcDir, final String destDir, final String filename) {
        MimeMessagePreparator preparator = new MimeMessagePreparator() {

            public void prepare(MimeMessage mimeMessage) throws Exception {
                MimeMessageHelper helper =
                    new MimeMessageHelper(mimeMessage, true);
                helper.setFrom(copyErrorMailMessage.getFrom());
                helper.setTo(copyErrorMailMessage.getTo());
                helper.setSubject(copyErrorMailMessage.getSubject());
                helper.setText(String.format(
                    copyErrorMailMessage.getText(), srcDir, destDir, filename));

                ClassPathResource config = new ClassPathResource("beans.xml");
                helper.addAttachment("beans.xml", config);
            }
        };
        mailSender.send(preparator);
    }
}
```

In the `prepare()` method, you can prepare the `MimeMessage` object, which is precreated by `JavaMailSender`. If there's any exception thrown, it will be converted into Spring's mail runtime exception automatically.

18-5. Scheduling with Spring's JDK Timer Support

Problem

Your application has a basic scheduling requirement that you would like to fulfill using JDK Timer. Moreover, you want to configure your scheduling tasks in a declarative way.

Solution

Spring provides utility classes for JDK Timer to enable you to configure scheduling tasks in the bean configuration file, without programming against the JDK Timer API.

How It Works

Creating a Timer Task

To use JDK Timer for scheduling, first create your task by extending the abstract class `TimerTask`. For example, the following timer task executes the `replicate()` method of a file replicator:

```
package com.apress.springrecipes.replicator;
...
import java.util.TimerTask;

public class FileReplicationTask extends TimerTask {

    private FileReplicator fileReplicator;

    public void setFileReplicator(FileReplicator fileReplicator) {
        this.fileReplicator = fileReplicator;
    }

    public void run() {
        try {
            fileReplicator.replicate();
        } catch (IOException e) {
            throw new RuntimeException(e);
        }
    }
}
```

Then you define this task in the bean configuration file referring to the file replicator `documentReplicator`.

```
<bean id="documentReplicationTask"
    class="com.apress.springrecipes.replicator.FileReplicationTask">
    <property name="fileReplicator" ref="documentReplicator" />
</bean>
```

Using JDK Timer Without Spring's Support

After creating a timer task, you can schedule it by calling one of the overloaded `schedule()` methods of `Timer`. For example, the following timer runs the file replication task every 60 seconds with a 5-second delay for the first time of execution.

```
package com.apress.springrecipes.replicator;

import java.util.Timer;
import java.util.TimerTask;
```

```
import org.springframework.context.ApplicationContext;
import org.springframework.context.support.ClassPathXmlApplicationContext;

public class Main {

    public static void main(String[] args) throws Exception {
        ApplicationContext context =
            new ClassPathXmlApplicationContext("beans.xml");

        TimerTask documentReplicationTask =
            (TimerTask) context.getBean("documentReplicationTask");

        Timer timer = new Timer();
        timer.schedule(documentReplicationTask, 5000, 60000);
    }
}
```

Using JDK Timer with Spring's Support

First, Spring offers `MethodInvokingTimerTaskFactoryBean` for you to define a timer task that executes a single method of a particular object. This saves you the trouble of extending `TimerTask`. You can use the following task definition to replace the previous:

```
<bean id="documentReplicationTask" class="org.springframework.scheduling.➥
    timer.MethodInvokingTimerTaskFactoryBean">
    <property name="targetObject" ref="documentReplicator" />
    <property name="targetMethod" value="replicate" />
</bean>
```

Next, Spring allows you to configure the scheduling details of your task in the bean configuration file, through a `ScheduledTimerTask` instance that wraps a `TimerTask` instance.

```
<bean id="scheduledDocumentReplicationTask"
    class="org.springframework.scheduling.timer.ScheduledTimerTask">
    <property name="timerTask" ref="documentReplicationTask" />
    <property name="delay" value="5000" />
    <property name="period" value="60000" />
</bean>
```

Finally, you can configure a `TimerFactoryBean` instance to create and set up a timer to run your `ScheduledTimerTask` instance. You can specify multiple tasks in this factory bean.

```
<bean class="org.springframework.scheduling.timer.TimerFactoryBean">
    <property name="scheduledTimerTasks">
        <list>
            <ref local="scheduledDocumentReplicationTask" />
        </list>
    </property>
</bean>
```

Now you can simply start your timer with the following `Main` class. In this way, you don't require a single line of code for scheduling tasks.

```
package com.apress.springrecipes.replicator;

import org.springframework.context.support.ClassPathXmlApplicationContext;

public class Main {

    public static void main(String[] args) throws Exception {
        new ClassPathXmlApplicationContext("beans.xml");
    }
}
```

18-6. Scheduling with Spring's Quartz Support

Problem

Your application has an advanced scheduling requirement that you would like to fulfill using Quartz Scheduler. Moreover, you want to configure your scheduling jobs in a declarative way.

Solution

Spring provides utility classes for Quartz to enable you to configure scheduling jobs in the bean configuration file, without programming against the Quartz API.

How It Works

Using Quartz Without Spring's Support

To use Quartz for scheduling, first create your job by implementing the `Job` interface. For example, the following job executes the `replicate()` method of a file replicator, retrieved from the job data map through the `JobExecutionContext` object that's passed in.

■ **Note** To use Quartz in your application, you must include `quartz-all-1.6.0.jar` (located in the `lib/quartz` directory of the Spring installation), `commons-collections.jar` (located in `lib/jakarta-commons`), and `jta.jar` (located in `lib/j2ee`) in your classpath.

```
package com.apress.springrecipes.replicator;
...
import org.quartz.Job;
import org.quartz.JobExecutionContext;
import org.quartz.JobExecutionException;

public class FileReplicationJob implements Job {
```

```
    public void execute(JobExecutionContext context)
            throws JobExecutionException {
        Map dataMap = context.getJobDetail().getJobDataMap();
        FileReplicator fileReplicator =
            (FileReplicator) dataMap.get("fileReplicator");
        try {
            fileReplicator.replicate();
        } catch (IOException e) {
            throw new JobExecutionException(e);
        }
    }
}
```

After creating the job, you configure and schedule it with the Quartz API. For instance, the following scheduler runs your file replication job every 60 seconds with a 5-second delay for the first time of execution:

```
package com.apress.springrecipes.replicator;
...
import org.quartz.JobDetail;
import org.quartz.Scheduler;
import org.quartz.SimpleTrigger;
import org.quartz.impl.StdSchedulerFactory;
import org.springframework.context.ApplicationContext;
import org.springframework.context.support.ClassPathXmlApplicationContext;

public class Main {

    public static void main(String[] args) throws Exception {
        ApplicationContext context =
            new ClassPathXmlApplicationContext("beans.xml");

        FileReplicator documentReplicator =
            (FileReplicator) context.getBean("documentReplicator");

        JobDetail job = new JobDetail();
        job.setName("documentReplicationJob");
        job.setJobClass(FileReplicationJob.class);
        Map dataMap = job.getJobDataMap();
        dataMap.put("fileReplicator", documentReplicator);

        SimpleTrigger trigger = new SimpleTrigger();
        trigger.setName("documentReplicationJob");
        trigger.setStartTime(new Date(System.currentTimeMillis() + 5000));
        trigger.setRepeatCount(SimpleTrigger.REPEAT_INDEFINITELY);
        trigger.setRepeatInterval(60000);
```

```
        Scheduler scheduler = new StdSchedulerFactory().getScheduler();
        scheduler.start();
        scheduler.scheduleJob(job, trigger);
    }
}
```

In the `Main` class, you first configure the job details for your file replication job in a `JobDetail` object and prepare job data in its `jobDataMap` property. Next, you create a `SimpleTrigger` object to configure the scheduling properties. Finally, you create a scheduler to run your job using this trigger.

Quartz supports two types of triggers: `SimpleTrigger` and `CronTrigger`. `SimpleTrigger` allows you to set trigger properties such as start time, end time, repeat interval, and repeat count. `CronTrigger` accepts a Unix *cron* expression for you to specify the times to run your job. For example, you can replace the preceding `SimpleTrigger` with the following `CronTrigger` to run your job at 17:30 every day:

```
CronTrigger trigger = new CronTrigger();
trigger.setName("documentReplicationJob");
trigger.setCronExpression("0 30 17 * * ?");
```

A cron expression is made up of seven fields (the last field is optional), separated by spaces. Table 18-1 shows the field description for a cron expression.

Table 18-1. *Field Description for a Cron Expression*

Position	Field Name	Range
1	Second	0–59
2	Minute	0–59
3	Hour	0–23
4	Day of month	1–31
5	Month	1–12 or JAN–DEC
6	Day of week	1–7 or SUN–SAT
7	Year (optional)	1970–2099

Each part of a cron expression can be assigned a specific value (e.g., 3), a range (e.g., 1–5), a list (e.g., 1,3,5), a wildcard (*; matches all values), or a question mark (?; used in either of the "Day of month" and "Day of week" fields for matching one of these fields but not both). For more information on the cron expressions supported by `CronTrigger`, refer to its javadoc (`http://quartz.sourceforge.net/javadoc/org/quartz/CronTrigger.html`).

Using Quartz with Spring's Support

When using Quartz, you can create a job by implementing the `Job` interface and retrieve job data from the job data map through `JobExecutionContext`. To decouple your job class from the Quartz API, Spring provides `QuartzJobBean`, which you can extend to retrieve job data through setter methods. `QuartzJobBean` converts the job data map into properties and injects them via the setter methods.

```
package com.apress.springrecipes.replicator;
...
import org.quartz.JobExecutionContext;
import org.quartz.JobExecutionException;
import org.springframework.scheduling.quartz.QuartzJobBean;

public class FileReplicationJob extends QuartzJobBean {

    private FileReplicator fileReplicator;

    public void setFileReplicator(FileReplicator fileReplicator) {
        this.fileReplicator = fileReplicator;
    }

    protected void executeInternal(JobExecutionContext context)
            throws JobExecutionException {
        try {
            fileReplicator.replicate();
        } catch (IOException e) {
            throw new JobExecutionException(e);
        }
    }
}
```

Then you can configure a Quartz `JobDetail` object in Spring's bean configuration file through `JobDetailBean`. By default, Spring uses this bean's name as the job name. You can modify it by setting the `name` property.

```
<bean name="documentReplicationJob"
    class="org.springframework.scheduling.quartz.JobDetailBean">
    <property name="jobClass"
        value="com.apress.springrecipes.replicator.FileReplicationJob" />
    <property name="jobDataAsMap">
        <map>
            <entry key="fileReplicator" value-ref="documentReplicator" />
        </map>
    </property>
</bean>
```

Spring also offers `MethodInvokingJobDetailFactoryBean` for you to define a job that executes a single method of a particular object. This saves you the trouble of creating a job class. You can use the following job detail to replace the previous:

```
<bean id="documentReplicationJob" class="org.springframework.➥
    scheduling.quartz.MethodInvokingJobDetailFactoryBean">
    <property name="targetObject" ref="documentReplicator" />
    <property name="targetMethod" value="replicate" />
</bean>
```

You can configure a Quartz SimpleTrigger object in Spring's bean configuration file through SimpleTriggerBean, which requires a reference to a JobDetail object. This bean provides common default values for certain trigger properties, such as using the bean name as the job name, setting indefinite repeat count, and so on.

```
<bean id="documentReplicationTrigger"
    class="org.springframework.scheduling.quartz.SimpleTriggerBean">
    <property name="jobDetail" ref="documentReplicationJob" />
    <property name="repeatInterval" value="60000" />
    <property name="startDelay" value="5000" />
</bean>
```

You can also configure a Quartz CronTrigger object in the bean configuration file through CronTriggerBean.

```
<bean id="documentReplicationTrigger"
    class="org.springframework.scheduling.quartz.CronTriggerBean">
    <property name="jobDetail" ref="documentReplicationJob" />
    <property name="cronExpression" value="0 30 17 * * ?" />
</bean>
```

Finally, you can configure a SchedulerFactoryBean instance to create a Scheduler object for running your trigger. You can specify multiple triggers in this factory bean.

```
<bean class="org.springframework.scheduling.quartz.SchedulerFactoryBean">
    <property name="triggers">
        <list>
            <ref bean="documentReplicationTrigger" />
        </list>
    </property>
</bean>
```

Now you can simply start your scheduler with the following Main class. In this way, you don't require a single line of code for scheduling jobs.

```
package com.apress.springrecipes.replicator;

import org.springframework.context.support.ClassPathXmlApplicationContext;

public class Main {

    public static void main(String[] args) throws Exception {
        new ClassPathXmlApplicationContext("beans.xml");
    }
}
```

18-7. Summary

In this chapter, you have learned how to export Spring beans as JMX MBeans by using `MBeanExporter`. Spring also allows you to define JSR-160 connectors in the IoC container to expose your MBeans for remote access over a specific protocol. Spring comes with several MBean assemblers for you to assemble an MBean's management interface. By annotating your beans with Spring's JMX annotations, Spring can detect and export them as MBeans automatically.

Spring allows your beans that are going to be exported as MBeans to publish JMX notifications through a notification publisher. You can register standard JMX notification listeners in the IoC container to listen to JMX notifications.

Spring supports two approaches for remote MBean access. First, it provides a factory bean for creating an MBean server connection, which allows you to operate an MBean using the JMX API. Second, it provides another factory bean for creating an MBean proxy, which allows you to operate a remote MBean as if it's a local bean.

Spring's e-mail support simplifies the task of sending e-mail by providing an abstract and implementation-independent API for sending e-mail. In Spring 2.5, the e-mail support offers only a JavaMail-based implementation.

Spring comes with utility classes for both JDK Timer and Quartz for you to configure scheduling tasks in the bean configuration file, without programming against the JDK Timer and Quartz APIs.

In the next chapter, you will learn about Spring's support for three common scripting languages: JRuby, Groovy, and BeanShell.

CHAPTER 19

Scripting in Spring

In this chapter, you will learn how to use scripting languages in Spring applications. Spring 2.5 supports three different scripting languages: JRuby, Groovy, and BeanShell. They are the most popular scripting languages in the Java community, and most Java developers find these languages easy to learn.

JRuby (`http://jruby.codehaus.org/`) is an open source Java-based implementation of the popular Ruby programming language (`http://www.ruby-lang.org/`). JRuby supports two-way access between Java and Ruby, which means that you can call a Ruby script directly from a Java program and also access Java classes in a Ruby script.

Groovy (`http://groovy.codehaus.org/`) is a dynamic language for the Java platform that integrates the features of other excellent programming languages. It can be compiled directly into Java bytecode or used as a dynamic scripting language. The syntax of Groovy is very similar to Java, so Java developers can learn Groovy quickly. Moreover, you can access all Java classes and libraries in Groovy.

BeanShell (`http://www.beanshell.org/`) is a lightweight Java scripting language that can dynamically execute Java code fragments while supporting scripting features like those of other scripting languages. With BeanShell, you can simply script a dynamic module of your Java application without having to learn a new language.

Upon finishing this chapter, you will be able to script parts of your Spring application using these scripting languages.

19-1. Implementing Beans with Scripting Languages

Problem

Sometimes your application may have certain modules that require frequent and dynamic changes. If implementing these modules with Java, you have to recompile, repackage, and redeploy your application each time after the change. You may not be allowed to perform these actions at any time you want, especially for a 24/7 application.

Solution

You can consider implementing any modules that require frequent and dynamic changes with scripting languages. The advantage of scripting languages is that they don't need to be recompiled after changes, so you can simply deploy the new script for the change to take effect.

Spring allows you to implement a bean with one of its supported scripting languages. You can configure a scripted bean in the IoC container just like a normal bean implemented with Java.

How It Works

Suppose you are going to develop an application that requires interest calculation. First of all, you define the following InterestCalculator interface:

```
package com.apress.springrecipes.interest;

public interface InterestCalculator {

    public void setRate(double rate);
    public double calculate(double amount, double year);
}
```

Implementing this interface is not difficult at all. However, as there are many interest calculation strategies, the users may need to change the implementation very frequently and dynamically. You don't want to recompile, repackage, and redeploy your application every time this happens. So, you consider implementing this interface with one of the supported scripting languages in Spring.

In Spring's bean configuration file, you have to include the lang schema definition in the <beans> root element to make use of the scripting language support.

```
<beans xmlns="http://www.springframework.org/schema/beans"
    xmlns:xsi="http://www.w3.org/2001/XMLSchema-instance"
    xmlns:lang="http://www.springframework.org/schema/lang"
    xsi:schemaLocation="http://www.springframework.org/schema/beans
        http://www.springframework.org/schema/beans/spring-beans-2.5.xsd
        http://www.springframework.org/schema/lang
        http://www.springframework.org/schema/lang/spring-lang-2.5.xsd">
    ...
</beans>
```

Spring 2.5 supports three scripting languages: JRuby, Groovy, and BeanShell. Next, you will implement the InterestCalculator interface with these languages one by one. For simplicity's sake, let's consider the following simple interest formula for interest calculation:

```
Interest = Amount x Rate x Year
```

Scripting Beans with JRuby

First, let's implement the InterestCalculator interface with JRuby by creating the JRuby script, SimpleInterestCalculator.rb, in the com.apress.springrecipes.interest package of your classpath.

```
class SimpleInterestCalculator

    def setRate(rate)
        @rate = rate
    end

    def calculate(amount, year)
        amount * year * @rate
    end
end

SimpleInterestCalculator.new
```

The preceding JRuby script declares a `SimpleInterestCalculator` class with a setter method for the `rate` property, and also a `calculate()` method. In Ruby, an instance variable begins with the `@` sign. Note that in the last line, you return a new instance of your target JRuby class. Failure to return this instance may result in Spring performing a lookup for an appropriate Ruby class to instantiate. As there can be multiple classes defined in a single JRuby script file, Spring will throw an exception if it cannot find an appropriate one that implements the methods declared in the interface.

In the bean configuration file, you can declare a bean implemented with JRuby by using the `<lang:jruby>` element and specifying the script's location in the `script-source` attribute. You can specify any resource path with a resource prefix supported by Spring, such as `file` or `classpath`.

■ **Note** To use JRuby in your Spring application, you have to include `jruby.jar` (located in the `lib/jruby` directory of the Spring installation), `asm-2.2.3.jar` (located in `lib/asm`), `backport-util-concurrent.jar` (located in `lib/concurrent`), and `cglib-nodep-2.1_3.jar` (located in `lib/cglib`) in your classpath.

```
<lang:jruby id="interestCalculator"
    script-source="classpath:com/apress/springrecipes/interest/➥
        SimpleInterestCalculator.rb"
    script-interfaces="com.apress.springrecipes.interest.InterestCalculator">
    <lang:property name="rate" value="0.05" />
</lang:jruby>
```

You also have to specify one or more interfaces in the `script-interfaces` attribute for a JRuby bean. It's up to Spring to create a dynamic proxy for this bean and convert the Java method calls into JRuby method calls. Finally, you can specify the property values for a scripting bean in the `<lang:property>` elements.

Now you can get the `interestCalculator` bean from the IoC container to use, and inject it into other bean properties as well. The following `Main` class will help you verify whether your scripted bean works properly:

```
package com.apress.springrecipes.interest;

import org.springframework.context.ApplicationContext;
import org.springframework.context.support.ClassPathXmlApplicationContext;

public class Main {

    public static void main(String[] args) throws Exception {
        ApplicationContext context =
            new ClassPathXmlApplicationContext("beans.xml");

        InterestCalculator calculator =
            (InterestCalculator) context.getBean("interestCalculator");
        System.out.println(calculator.calculate(100000, 1));
    }
}
```

Scripting Beans with Groovy

Next, let's implement the `InterestCalculator` interface with Groovy by creating the Groovy script, `SimpleInterestCalculator.groovy`, in the `com.apress.springrecipes.interest` package of your classpath.

```
import com.apress.springrecipes.interest.InterestCalculator;

class SimpleInterestCalculator implements InterestCalculator {

    double rate

    double calculate(double amount, double year) {
        return amount * year * rate
    }
}
```

The preceding Groovy script declares a `SimpleInterestCalculator` class that implements the `InterestCalculator` interface. In Groovy, you can simply declare a property with no access modifier, and then it will generate a private field with a public getter and setter automatically.

In the bean configuration file, you can declare a bean implemented with Groovy by using the `<lang:groovy>` element and specifying the script's location in the `script-source` attribute. You can specify the property values for a scripting bean in the `<lang:property>` elements.

■Note To use Groovy in your Spring application, you have to include `groovy.jar` (located in the `lib/groovy` directory of the Spring installation), `antlr-2.7.6.jar` (located in `lib/antlr`), and `asm-2.2.3.jar` (located in `lib/asm`) in your classpath.

```
<lang:groovy id="interestCalculator"
    script-source="classpath:com/apress/springrecipes/interest/➥
        SimpleInterestCalculator.groovy">
    <lang:property name="rate" value="0.05" />
</lang:groovy>
```

Notice that it's unnecessary to specify the `script-interfaces` attribute for a Groovy bean, as the Groovy class has declared which interfaces it implements.

Scripting Beans with BeanShell

Last, let's implement the `InterestCalculator` interface with BeanShell by creating the BeanShell script, `SimpleInterestCalculator.bsh`, in the `com.apress.springrecipes.interest` package of your classpath.

```
double rate;

void setRate(double aRate) {
    rate = aRate;
}

double calculate(double amount, double year) {
    return amount * year * rate;
}
```

In BeanShell, you cannot declare classes explicitly, but you can declare variables and methods. So, you implement your `InterestCalculator` interface by providing all the methods required by this interface.

In the bean configuration file, you can declare a bean implemented with BeanShell by using the `<lang:bsh>` element and specifying the script's location in the `script-source` attribute. You can specify the property values for a scripting bean in the `<lang:property>` elements.

■ **Note** To use BeanShell in your Spring application, you have to include `bsh-2.0b4.jar` (located in the `lib/bsh` directory of the Spring installation) and `cglib-nodep-2.1_3.jar` (located in `lib/cglib`) in your classpath.

```
<lang:bsh id="interestCalculator"
    script-source="classpath:com/apress/springrecipes/interest/➥
        SimpleInterestCalculator.bsh"
    script-interfaces="com.apress.springrecipes.interest.InterestCalculator">
    <lang:property name="rate" value="0.05" />
</lang:bsh>
```

You also have to specify one or more interfaces in the `script-interfaces` attribute for a bean implemented with BeanShell. It's up to Spring to create a dynamic proxy for this bean and convert the Java method calls into BeanShell calls.

19-2. Injecting Spring Beans into Scripts

Problem

Sometimes your scripts may need the help of certain Java objects to complete their tasks. In Spring, you have to allow your scripts to access beans declared in the IoC container.

Solution

You can inject beans declared in the Spring IoC container into scripts in the same way as properties of simple data types.

How It Works

Suppose you would like the interest rate to be calculated dynamically. First, you define the following interface to allow implementations to return the annual, monthly, and daily interest rates:

```
package com.apress.springrecipes.interest;

public interface RateCalculator {

    public double getAnnualRate();
    public double getMonthlyRate();
    public double getDailyRate();
}
```

For this example, you simply implement this interface by calculating these rates from a fixed annual interest rate, which can be injected through a setter method.

```
package com.apress.springrecipes.interest;

public class FixedRateCalculator implements RateCalculator {

    private double rate;

    public void setRate(double rate) {
        this.rate = rate;
    }

    public double getAnnualRate() {
        return rate;
    }

    public double getMonthlyRate() {
        return rate / 12;
    }
```

```
    public double getDailyRate() {
        return rate / 365;
    }
}
```

Then declare this rate calculator in the IoC container by supplying an annual interest rate.

```
<bean id="rateCalculator"
    class="com.apress.springrecipes.interest.FixedRateCalculator">
    <property name="rate" value="0.05" />
</bean>
```

Last, your interest calculator should use a RateCalculator object rather than a fixed rate value.

```
package com.apress.springrecipes.interest;

public interface InterestCalculator {

    public void setRateCalculator(RateCalculator rateCalculator);
    public double calculate(double amount, double year);
}
```

Injecting Spring Beans into JRuby

In the JRuby script, you can store the injected RateCalculator object in an instance variable and use it for rate calculation.

```
class SimpleInterestCalculator

    def setRateCalculator(rateCalculator)
        @rateCalculator = rateCalculator
    end

    def calculate(amount, year)
        amount * year * @rateCalculator.getAnnualRate
    end
end

SimpleInterestCalculator.new
```

In the bean declaration, you can inject another bean into a scripted bean's property by specifying the bean name in the ref attribute.

```
<lang:jruby id="interestCalculator"
    script-source="classpath:com/apress/springrecipes/interest/➥
        SimpleInterestCalculator.rb"
    script-interfaces="com.apress.springrecipes.interest.InterestCalculator">
    <lang:property name="rateCalculator" ref="rateCalculator" />
</lang:jruby>
```

Injecting Spring Beans into Groovy

In the Groovy script, you just declare a property of type RateCalculator, and it will generate a public getter and setter automatically.

```
import com.apress.springrecipes.interest.InterestCalculator;
import com.apress.springrecipes.interest.RateCalculator;

class SimpleInterestCalculator implements InterestCalculator {

    RateCalculator rateCalculator

    double calculate(double amount, double year) {
        return amount * year * rateCalculator.getAnnualRate()
    }
}
```

Again, you can inject another bean into a scripted bean's property by specifying the bean name in the ref attribute.

```
<lang:groovy id="interestCalculator"
    script-source="classpath:com/apress/springrecipes/interest/➥
        SimpleInterestCalculator.groovy">
    <lang:property name="rateCalculator" ref="rateCalculator" />
</lang:groovy>
```

Injecting Spring Beans into BeanShell

In the BeanShell script, you need a global variable of type RateCalculator and a setter method for it.

```
import com.apress.springrecipes.interest.RateCalculator;

RateCalculator rateCalculator;

void setRateCalculator(RateCalculator aRateCalculator) {
    rateCalculator = aRateCalculator;
}

double calculate(double amount, double year) {
    return amount * year * rateCalculator.getAnnualRate();
}
```

Also, you can inject another bean into a scripted bean's property by specifying the bean name in the ref attribute.

```
<lang:bsh id="interestCalculator"
    script-source="classpath:com/apress/springrecipes/interest/➥
        SimpleInterestCalculator.bsh"
```

```
    script-interfaces="com.apress.springrecipes.interest.InterestCalculator">
    <lang:property name="rateCalculator" ref="rateCalculator" />
</lang:bsh>
```

19-3. Refreshing Beans from Scripts

Problem

As the modules implemented with scripting languages may have to be changed frequently and dynamically, you would like the Spring IoC container to be able to detect and refresh changes automatically from the script sources.

Solution

Spring is able to refresh a scripted bean definition from its source once you have specified the checking interval in the `refresh-check-delay` attribute. When a method is called on that bean, Spring will check the script source if the specified checking interval has elapsed. Then Spring will refresh the bean definition from the script source if it has been changed.

How It Works

By default, the `refresh-check-delay` attribute is negative, so the refresh checking feature is disabled. You can assign the milliseconds for refresh checking in this attribute to enable this feature. For example, you can specify 5 seconds for the refresh checking interval of your JRuby bean.

```
<lang:jruby id="interestCalculator"
    script-source="classpath:com/apress/springrecipes/interest/➥
        SimpleInterestCalculator.rb"
    script-interfaces="com.apress.springrecipes.interest.InterestCalculator"
    refresh-check-delay="5000">
    ...
</lang:jruby>
```

Of course, the `refresh-check-delay` attribute also works for a bean implemented with Groovy or BeanShell.

```
<lang:groovy id="interestCalculator"
    script-source="classpath:com/apress/springrecipes/interest/➥
        SimpleInterestCalculator.groovy"
    refresh-check-delay="5000">
    ...
</lang:groovy>

<lang:bsh id="interestCalculator"
    script-source="classpath:com/apress/springrecipes/interest/➥
        SimpleInterestCalculator.bsh"
    script-interfaces="com.apress.springrecipes.interest.InterestCalculator"
```

```
    refresh-check-delay="5000">
    ...
</lang:bsh>
```

19-4. Defining Script Sources Inline

Problem

You would like to define the script sources, which are less likely to be changed, in the bean configuration file directly, rather than in external script source files.

Solution

You can define an inline script source in the `<lang:inline-script>` element of a scripted bean to replace a reference to an external script source file by the `script-source` attribute. Note that the refresh checking feature is not applicable for an inline script source, because the Spring IoC container only loads the bean configuration once, at startup.

How It Works

For example, you can define the JRuby script inline using the `<lang:inline-script>` element. To prevent the characters in your script from conflicting with the reserved XML characters, you should surround your script source with the `<![CDATA[...]]>` tag. You no longer have to specify the reference to the external script source file in the `script-source` attribute.

```
<lang:jruby id="interestCalculator"
    script-interfaces="com.apress.springrecipes.interest.InterestCalculator">
    <lang:inline-script>
    <![CDATA[
    class SimpleInterestCalculator

        def setRateCalculator(rateCalculator)
            @rateCalculator = rateCalculator
        end

        def calculate(amount, year)
            amount * year * @rateCalculator.getAnnualRate
        end
    end

    SimpleInterestCalculator.new
    ]]>
    </lang:inline-script>
    <lang:property name="rateCalculator" ref="rateCalculator" />
</lang:jruby>
```

Of course, you can also define the Groovy and BeanShell script sources inline using the `<lang:inline-script>` element.

```
<lang:groovy id="interestCalculator">
    <lang:inline-script>
    <![CDATA[
    import com.apress.springrecipes.interest.InterestCalculator;
    import com.apress.springrecipes.interest.RateCalculator;

    class SimpleInterestCalculator implements InterestCalculator {

        RateCalculator rateCalculator

        double calculate(double amount, double year) {
            return amount * year * rateCalculator.getAnnualRate()
        }
    }
    ]]>
    </lang:inline-script>
    <lang:property name="rateCalculator" ref="rateCalculator" />
</lang:groovy>

<lang:bsh id="interestCalculator"
    script-interfaces="com.apress.springrecipes.interest.InterestCalculator">
    <lang:inline-script>
    <![CDATA[
    import com.apress.springrecipes.interest.RateCalculator;

    RateCalculator rateCalculator;

    void setRateCalculator(RateCalculator aRateCalculator) {
        rateCalculator = aRateCalculator;
    }

    double calculate(double amount, double year) {
        return amount * year * rateCalculator.getAnnualRate();
    }
    ]]>
    </lang:inline-script>
    <lang:property name="rateCalculator" ref="rateCalculator" />
</lang:bsh>
```

19-5. Summary

In this chapter, you have learned how to use the scripting languages supported by Spring to implement your beans and how to declare them in the Spring IoC container. Spring 2.5 supports three scripting languages: JRuby, Groovy, and BeanShell. You can specify the location for an external script source file or define an inline script source in the bean configuration file. As the script sources may require frequent and dynamic changes, Spring can detect and refresh changes from the script source files automatically. Finally, you can inject property values as well as bean references into your scripts.

This is the last chapter of the book. Congratulations on having learned so much about the Spring framework, and I hope you enjoy using it!

Index

B

E

F

G

H

N

O

P

Q

R

S

T

U

V

W

X